Representative
Modern
Plays
Ibsen to
Tennessee
Williams

ROBERT WARNOCK
UNIVERSITY OF CONNECTICUT

SCOTT, FORESMAN AND COMPANY
CHICAGO ATLANTA DALLAS PALO ALTO FAIR LAWN, N.J.

- **KEY EDITIONS**

JOHN GERBER GENERAL EDITOR

L. C. #64–16005

Copyright © 1964 by Scott, Foresman and Company

Printed in the United States of America

acknowledgments

Desire Under the Elms by Eugene O'Neill: Copyright 1924 and renewed 1952 by Eugene O'Neill. Reprinted from *Nine Plays by Eugene O'Neill* by permission of Random House, Inc.

The Glass Menagerie by Tennessee Williams: Copyright 1945 by Tennessee Williams and Edwina D. Williams. Reprinted from *Six Modern American Plays* by permission of Random House, Inc.

Biography by S. N. Behrman: Copyright 1932, 1933, and renewed 1960 by S. N. Behrman. Reprinted from *Sixteen Famous American Plays* by permission of Random House, Inc.

Miss Julie by August Strindberg: From *Plays of Strindberg,* Vol. translated by Edith and Warner Oland. Reprinted by permission Bruce Humphries, Publishers.

The Master Builder by Henrik Ibsen: Copyright 1907 by Cha Scribner's Sons; renewal copyright 1935 by William Archer. printed with the permission of Charles Scribner's Sons from *The lected Works of Henrik Ibsen,* Vol. X, translated by William A and Edmund Gosse.

Riders to the Sea by John Millington Synge: Reprinted by ̣ sion of Bruce Humphries, Publishers.

54628

CONTENTS

reading a play

Reading a play is unlike reading any other type of literature, because a drama script is not conceived by its author as a literary end in itself, like a novel or a poem, but only as one means to the end of an experience in the theater. Though it may be the core of the dramatic performance, the bare dialogue of the writer is vitalized on the stage by a battery of other artists—the actors, the director, the designers of scenery and costumes, to say nothing of the stage managers, stagehands, electricians, musicians, and humbler assistants behind the scenes. Bringing the play to life as the author visualized it is a group project which can never be duplicated in the library.

Any type of narrative literature makes demands upon a reader's imagination, but a play, which assumes at the start the assistance of so many other artists, gives the reader far fewer clues to work with. In the theater a play may become the most direct form of narrative art, because all of the settings and characters and dialogue take on an unmistakable definiteness which allows little leeway to the spectator's imagination. But the bare text of the play is certainly the most indirect, because the author has denied himself almost completely the opportunity to comment on his people and their actions and to tell us what to think about them.

Hence, as has been said so often, to read a play with pleasure one must somehow stage it in the theater of his mind. In realizing the intention of the dramatist, one must himself take the roles of the designer, the actors, and most of all the director, who welds the various forces into a single dramatic experience. Readers differ widely in their ability to do this and hence in their capacity to enjoy the printed text of a play. In part this is a matter of experience with the theater itself. One who has seen many dramas on the stage will readily focus that background on a new script. A producer in deciding whether to take a chance on a new work must have an unusual skill in picturing it in his mind as the audience will finally see and hear it. An experienced playgoer can do the same, for the very legend "Act One" brings him to 8:45 and a seat in the tenth row center as the audience settle in their seats and the house lights dim. He supplies the conventions of the theater as he moves down the printed page.

In part, reading a play is a matter of the reader's experience with the kind of life and people that the author is presenting. An American who has lived on the fringe of the South will probably bring greater understanding to the faded, genteel, unrealistic Southern ladies of *The Glass Menagerie* than an Englishman or even a New Yorker who has grown up in a brash, big-city environment. A student of psychiatry or psychoanalysis should fathom the tormented personality of Miss Julia more profoundly than will a layman. An Irishman who knows the Dublin slums will relish (or deplore) national traits in the characters of *Juno and the Paycock* as no outsider can. The point of view of Constance in *The Constant Wife* may seem puzzling or even shocking to a reader reared in a conservative household remote from the elegant cynicism of Maugham's cosmopolitan world. In a superficial way the movies and television have familiarized us with many kinds of life in America and elsewhere that may be remote from our actual experience. Whether accurate or not, this background will rise in our minds, to provide setting and atmosphere for the play. But the world of *The Seagull* is gone forever, so that a well-read American may understand it today better than a Soviet Russian.

But ultimately it is not so much the reader's background as his imagination that determines what he can get from a printed play. Some students consider drama the easiest kind of literature to read, just as many consider it the hardest. Your enjoyment here will depend upon your power of visualizing, of cooperating with the playwright to bring to life the picture in his mind. With fewer guides than in the novel, you can have the fun of re-creating these images very much as you choose. This is to some extent a matter of training, and the more plays you read, the easier the process will become.

At the start you may find some preparation for your reading helpful. Begin with the setting. If a photograph of the original set is given in your text, study it carefully. But usually you must build the set yourself. In that case, take a few minutes to draw a ground plan according to the author's instructions, so as to picture where the doors and other entrances are, what relation the chairs and other pieces of furniture have to each other, where the characters are when they use them. Refer to your plan occasionally as the stage directions indicate the movements of the actors.

Constructing character is a different matter. A good playwright will no more give away all the facts about his people at the start than will a good novelist. But at least you should pay attention to his first description of their physical appearance, because this will be one clue to what we are to find beneath. When O'Casey says that Mrs. Boyle's "face has now assumed that look which ultimately settles down upon the faces of the women of the working-class: a look of listless monotony and harassed anxiety. . . . Were circumstances favorable, she would probably be a handsome, active and clever woman," you can have little doubt of where his sympathies lie.

Next, you should pause at the end of each act, as the author intended you to, for that ten-minute stretch and discussion of the play with yourself in the lobby of your mind. Consider how much you know of each major character by this time. Remember that in drama, characters are revealed exclusively by what they say and do and by what others may say about them. Now that the aside and the soliloquy have been banished almost entirely from our stages, the playwright cannot go far in telling you what they think.

At the end of the play you will consider each of the major characters as a whole. Has each been consistently projected so that the motivation of his decisions and actions has been clear and plausible? Is each sufficiently complex to seem a human being, or do you end with the uncomfortable feeling that you have been following the conflict of two-dimensional heroes and villains, pasteboard figures simplified out of all resemblance to real people? Of course you must be reasonable, because, unlike a novelist, a playwright has only two hours in which to project his characters and tell his story, and he is depending upon the help of actors who may be more skillful than you.

Then there is the action to be thought through, and

here the problems of reading a play loom even larger. In the theater the physical activity of the players brings action to life with a vividness found in no other form of narrative; in the library the reverse is true. With only the most perfunctory assistance from the author, you must visualize people eating and dancing, and fighting and making love.

But in another sense, action means plot, the story that the drama sets out to tell, and here the two-hour limitation restricts the playwright most severely. Although dramatists have seldom heeded the exact laws for play construction worked out by dogmatic critics, it is true that the peculiar demands of their medium have led them to standardize their approach to plot much more than the novelists. Although Shakespeare might develop four plots all at once in *A Midsummer-Night's Dream,* and a modern drama like *Juno and the Paycock* may tell simultaneously the life stories of a good many people, most playwrights find it wise to follow the advice of Aristotle, more or less, and concentrate on one central plot, which should be enough for two hours. By the end of the first act you ought to have a clear idea of the direction in which the playwright is taking you.

It was the French critic Brunetière who crystallized the idea that the plot usually evolves from a dramatic conflict within one or more of the characters. After you have finished your play, you should consider whether this was true of it and if so, just where the conflict lay. Was it between two individuals, as between the father and son in *Desire Under the Elms;* or between an individual and a group, as in Ibsen's *Enemy of the People;* or between two groups, as in Hauptmann's *The Weavers;* or between an individual or a group and the forces of fate or nature or social change, as in Synge's *Riders to the Sea;* or between an individual and himself, as in Strindberg's *Miss Julia;* or between two ideas, as in Pirandello's *Six Characters in Search of an Author?* Not all plots submit readily to such analysis. Comedies, in particular, may take a very light view of plot conflict, though in *The Doctor's Dilemma* and *A Phoenix Too Frequent* the opposing forces are clearly drawn. And there have been dissenters from Brunetière's neat definition, especially in recent years, when plays have grown increasingly free in style and conception.

In the same way the old arrangement of the stages of action has been very liberally interpreted away from the nineteenth-century ideal of "the well-made play." Nevertheless, you will find that most plays illustrate after a fashion the traditional cycle of action: (1) *Exposition* of the background of the plot and characters, providing what we must know to develop an interest in the proceedings. In a serious play this will probably involve a statement in indirect terms of the basic problem. (2) *Development* of this situation with the addition of complications, often leading to a *minor climax,* or high point of interest, at the end of the first act of a three-act play. (3) *Development,* or involution, continued up to the highest point of suspense, the *major climax,* which often appears at the end of the second act, but sometimes later. In tragedy the hero may reach the zenith of his hopes in this scene, in a comedy the nadir of his difficulties, for in any case the plot has found its turning point. (4) The *resolution,* or untangling of the plot strands, as we see with increasing clarity in the last act the hopelessness of the tragic hero's plight or the way out of the comic hero's troubles. (5) The *solution,* or denouement, in which the hero's fate is finally settled. If the play has posed a problem of some kind, the author will probably settle it here. Beyond that the final curtain cannot be long delayed, because the dramatic suspense is now at an end.

When you have finished the play, test your understanding of it—and the clarity of the author's presentation —by phrasing a generalized statement of the theme. This will incorporate the original problem and his answer to it in a sentence or two. It may range from so simple a theme as "Crime does not pay" for a melodrama up to a very subtle and complex idea. If the author has tried to persuade you to his way of thinking, as Shaw does in *The Doctor's Dilemma,* evaluate also the cogency of his argument.

If you must be your own director in reading a play, you must also be your own audience. The performance of a play is a group experience in which the audience collaborates with all that happens on the stage. People who have paid good money to be entertained are usually in a mood to be. It is true that a coughing child or a snoring grandfather may disrupt the proceedings, and the slightest noise may blot out an important line. But in general the participation of the audience serves the objective of the playwright extremely well. He has them where he wants them, anchored to their seats and required to listen through the act without the accompaniment of the radio or other distractions. It is this concentration of a group of people who are of a common mind for the evening that makes the electric quality of the theater experience when the play itself is right. A comic line that would produce a smile in the library inspires a roar of infectious laughter in the theater. And the intense stillness during an emotional scene heightens the excitement of everyone in the auditorium.

There is no real substitute for this, of course, in reading a play. The best you can do is to approximate the concentrated conditions of the theater. Try to read in a quiet room by yourself, without the interference of other people doing other things. Only under such conditions can you lend the playwright the full power of your imagination to do what he originally expected others would do for him—and you. Then you will discover that a play, even in the library, makes an ideal evening's entertainment.

HENRIK IBSEN (1828–1906)

Although Ibsen's name is indissolubly linked with the realistic prose play of social problems that officially launched the modern drama, this was only one aspect of his long and restless career. Twenty years of writing and stage production preceded *The League of Youth* (1869), his first play of this kind; and his only unmistakable specimens of it were four highly inflammatory dramas concentrated in the years surrounding 1880. He had begun as a romanticist and nationalist, a democratic revolutionary in the spirit of 1848, a poetic playwright in the tradition of Schiller and Hugo. The last fifteen years of his creative life were to take him into his own brand of symbolism and critical examination of the very social movements that he had helped to initiate. Nevertheless, his most striking contributions do belong to the middle period of *A Doll's House* (1879) and *Ghosts* (1881), when his name became a rallying symbol to social liberals and dramatic rebels everywhere, and anathema to the vested interests who saw ruin in his revolutionary ideas.

The dour, bewhiskered, bespectacled old titan in the stovepipe hat and black frock coat began as a poor boy in Skien, a remote town in southeastern Norway, where his family had once been wealthy and influential but had fallen on evil days. Personal hardships and lack of sympathy from his elders increased his natural reticence, and he became a silent, resentful youth. Eager to leave home, he dreamed of a prosperous career in medicine, but his poverty and inadequate education made him accept a post as druggist's assistant in another provincial town. A local library gave him a chance to explore literary classics, and he now began to dream of a career in poetry. Encouraged by sympathetic friends, he published some verses in newspapers, romantic poems of nature and Norwegian nationalism inspired by the Continental revolutions of 1848 and the growing threat of Prussia to neighboring Denmark. Norway was at this time ruled by the Swedish king, but a movement for independence was underway.

This political climate inspired Ibsen's first play, *Catilina* (1850), a romantic re-creation of history that represented the Roman foe of Cicero as a heroic spirit in revolt against a degenerate society and a corrupt, self-seeking government. It was his first projection of himself in one of his heroes. The play was published but not produced, and Ibsen was emboldened to strike out for the larger world of Christiania (Oslo), the Norwegian capital. As he was cramming for the entrance examinations to the university, his second play was accepted for production at the state theater, and this promise of success led him to abandon all plans for a medical career.

Full of youthful swagger, he joined a group of literary and political rebels, but when their activities received unfavorable attention from the police, he hastily accepted an invitation to serve as director and writer for a new national theater in Bergen, the second largest city in Norway. Here during six years of hard work in producing over a hundred plays, he mastered the craft of the stage, and when he returned to Christiania in 1857, it was as artistic director of the Norwegian Theatre, a new playhouse established to protest the tyranny of Danish drama in the national theater. The failure of this enterprise five years later led him into a period of depression and dissipation, from which he eventually rallied to resume writing after five fallow years.

He was now happily married and the father of a son, but he was living on borrowed money with debts mounting on all sides. Only the assistance of literary friends, notably Björnstjerne Björnson, his chief rival among Norwegian writers of the time, got him through these difficult years. The success of his fine historical drama, *The Pretenders,* in 1863 fired him with new ambition, but the failure of Norway to help Denmark in her war with Prussia and Austria in 1864 led Ibsen to leave his native land in disgust, not to return permanently for twenty-seven years. A further reason for this self-imposed exile was his anger at not receiving a pension from the government such as had recently been granted to Björnson.

To this long period of voluntary exile belong his mature works. He lived in various European capitals—Rome, Dresden, Munich—but remained a provincial Norwegian at heart, little touched by the cosmopolitanism of the Continent. With methodical regularity he sent back to Christiania a new play nearly every two years, and the growing success of his works plus a belated pension freed him at last from concern for his livelihood. Despite the indignation that his social dramas aroused, his prestige grew until he came to be recognized as the patriarch of modern drama. Enthusiastic champions fought the Ibsen battle in foreign lands—Antoine in France, the Duke of Saxe-Meiningen and others in Germany, Shaw, William Archer, and Edmund Gosse in England. Eventually a pride in their world-famous countryman rose among Norwegians. When at last he returned to Christiania in 1891 to live out the remaining fifteen years of his life, he was greeted with reverence. Björnson had remained at home to become the national poet of Norway and to work for her independence (which was finally achieved in 1905). But there was now no friction between them. Ibsen's son married one of Björnson's daughters, and today the two Norwegian masters lie side by side in a cemetery in Oslo.

The romantic plays in verse that Ibsen wrote before leaving Norway are now unread outside that country. But he ended his first period with two fine poetic dramas about Norwegian life, written abroad, which are classics of the modern stage. *Brand* (1866) tells of an idealistic clergyman in a lonely fjord village who preaches uncompromising austerity to his simple congregation. When they reject him and drive him out into the snow, he climbs bleeding up the side of the fjord, where an insane girl mistakes him for the thorn-crowned Jesus. At last he is engulfed in a sudden avalanche. As in his later studies of uncompromising reformers, Ibsen has mixed feelings about this puritanical hero. Though true to his principles, Pastor Brand is an intolerable fanatic in dealing with his wife and child, and we are led to question the validity of fire-breathing saintliness in the modern world.

If *Brand* was a sardonic study of Norwegian character as it is in theory, *Peer Gynt* (1867) is a much more critical study of the romantic Norwegian character as Ibsen thought it really was. Peer, the problem child, is a pretentious fraud, a lying braggart and shiftless opportunist who swaggers through a series of shady adventures that take him from his native village to an American town, an African oasis, and a madhouse in Cairo and back home to Norway. As he faces death at the end, he is told that he is not sinner enough for hell but must be melted down and recast. He is not even a hero of evil, but merely the selfish, ambitious mediocrity of our time.

After ten years of transition Ibsen launched a second phase of his dramatic career with *The Pillars of Society* (1877), which ominously indicted the respectable leaders of society with a failure to provide moral leadership in their communities. It was his second prose drama of modern life and the first to show the capacity of the realistic play to project social issues with rousing conviction. The suspicions awakened in conservatives by this play were amply justified two years later by *A Doll's House,* the first of Ibsen's dramas of "the new woman." When Nora innocently compromises herself in a well-intentioned effort to help her husband, she suddenly realizes that he has kept her as a doll in his house, an ornament rather than a true helpmate. When he refuses to let her share his life completely, she defiantly slams the door on him and their children. This daring conclusion (for 1879) brought a storm of condemnation upon Ibsen's head, but he merely set his jaw still firmer and went on to a more shocking sequel.

With a tendency to write his plays in pairs, he now offered a drama about a wife who accepted the dictates of society and continued to live with a worthless husband who was deceiving her with her own housemaid. In *Ghosts* (1881) we find her twenty years later, left with a son who has been blighted by the venereal disease of his father, and the illegitimate daughter of her husband serving now as housemaid in her mother's stead. When Mrs. Alving overhears her son flirting with his own half-sister, a horrible ghost of the past seems to rise again. But the horror reaches its height when her son suffers a degeneration of the brain because of his disease and she debates whether to resort to a mercy killing, as he had asked. The combination of so many forbidden subjects in this daring tragedy kept *Ghosts* under a ban of censorship for years, but in our century it has been frequently staged with success.

Ibsen's indignation at the attack of the conservatives upon his fearless exposés of rottenness in society led him to produce *An Enemy of the People* (1883), a militant defense of himself as a heroic idealist who is cynically defeated by the mercenary majority. But two years later he seemed to reverse his position with a companion piece, *The Wild Duck,* which presented a meddling idealist who foolishly destroyed the happiness of others through unmasking their working compromise with truth.

Because his plays were contributing to the emancipation of women in his time and to the establishment of a single sex standard, he began with *Rosmersholm* (1886) a study of the much-discussed "new woman" that did not always redound to her credit. The best-known play in this series, *Hedda Gabler* (1890), offers a brilliant picture of a reckless, idle wife, selfish and good-for-nothing, who "lives dangerously" without direction and brings death and tragedy to others before she finally commits suicide. These dramas, though still within the style of prose realism, go beyond the objective of social reform that had absorbed Ibsen earlier, and lead us into the final period of his dramatic writing, in which he is concerned with moral and psychological problems of the individual, especially of a complex hero into whom he must have put a good deal of himself.

The Master Builder (1892) and *John Gabriel Borkman* (1896) are the finest of this series and among the most enduring of all his works, because they get beyond topical issues to timeless human questions. Since symbolism plays an important part in them, we find here the more imaginative approach to realism characteristic of our best drama today. Indeed, both of these plays show a curious affinity with Arthur Miller's *Death of a Salesman* (1949) in their studies of men made and destroyed by ambition in business, which they have used as a mechanism of self-respect. Like Miller's hero they have sacrificed honesty to the pursuit of success and have lost their souls in the process. It is not surprising that Miller has been drawn to Ibsen and has taken time out from his own playwriting to adapt one of Ibsen's works to the modern stage.

Ibsen is an authentic titan of literature, who showed to the end a great capacity for growth. He identified himself with many causes in his day, but in the long run remained aloof from them all. His philosophy was probably best expressed in *An Enemy of the People,* where he argued for individualism in sweeping terms. Convinced that society is always conservative and dishonest and exerts stifling pressures upon the high-minded and able individual, he campaigned for personal freedom and the rights of the well-endowed. The best service that organized society can perform is not to impede the self-fulfillment of the gifted and worthy ones in its midst, and its best course is to accept the leadership of the enlightened.

If he did not find this climate for self-expression in a democratic state, he was certainly opposed even more to dictatorship. Although he had an almost aristocratic faith in the superior individual, this did not lead him to anything like fascism. Indeed, he seems to have had no political convictions as such in his later years, and it is hard to fit him into the war of political creeds in our day. His interest was rather in social reform, which he did not think could be achieved by political means but by sweeping changes in social attitudes and relief from social pressures. The vast revolution in the mores of modern society during the past half century owes an incalculable debt to his influence.

HENRIK IBSEN

THE MASTER BUILDER[1]

A Play in Three Acts

PERSONS

Halvard Solness, the Master Builder
Aline Solness, his wife
Doctor Herdal, physician
Knut Brovik, formerly an architect, now in Solness's employment
Ragnar Brovik, his son, draughtsman
Kaia Fosli, his niece, book-keeper
Miss Hilda Wangel
Some Ladies
A Crowd in the street

The action passes in and about the house of Solness.

act 1

A plainly-furnished work-room in the house of HALVARD
SOLNESS. *Folding doors on the left lead out to the hall. On*

[1] *Translated from the Norwegian by Edmund Gosse and William Archer.*

the right is the door leading to the inner rooms of the house. At the back is an open door into the draughtsmen's office. In front, on the left, a desk with books, papers, and writing materials. Further back than the folding door, a stove. In the right-hand corner, a sofa, a table, and one or two chairs. On the table a water-bottle and glass. A smaller table, with a rocking-chair and arm-chair, in front on the right. Lighted lamps with shades on the table in the draughtsmen's office, on the table in the corner, and on the desk.

In the draughtsmen's office sit KNUT BROVIK *and his son* RAGNAR, *occupied with plans and calculations. At the desk in the outer office stands* KAIA FOSLI, *writing in the ledger.* KNUT BROVIK *is a spare old man with white hair and beard. He wears a rather threadbare but well-brushed black coat, spectacles, and a somewhat discolored white neckcloth.* RAGNAR BROVIK *is a well-dressed, light-haired man of about thirty, who stoops a little.* KAIA FOSLI *is a slightly-built girl, a little over twenty, carefully dressed, and delicate-looking. She has a green shade over her eyes.—All three go on working for some time in silence.*

KNUT BROVIK [*rises suddenly, as if in distress, from the table; breathes heavily and laboriously as he comes forward into the doorway*]. No, I can't bear it much longer!

KAIA [*going up to him*]. You're feeling very ill this evening, aren't you, Uncle?

BROVIK. Oh, I seem to get worse every day.

RAGNAR [*has risen and advances*]. You ought to go home, father. Try to get a little sleep——

BROVIK [*impatiently*]. Go to bed, I suppose? Would you have me stifled outright?

KAIA. Then take a little walk.

RAGNAR. Yes, do. I will come with you.

BROVIK [*with warmth*]. I'll not go till he comes! I'm determined to have it out this evening with—[*in a tone of suppressed bitterness*] —with him—with the chief.

KAIA [*anxiously*]. Oh no, uncle,—do wait awhile before doing *that!*

RAGNAR. Yes, better wait, father!

BROVIK [*draws his breath laboriously*]. Ha—ha—! *I* haven't much time for waiting.

KAIA [*listening*]. Hush! I hear him on the stairs.

[*All three go back to their work. A short silence.*]

[HALVARD SOLNESS *comes in through the hall-door. He is a man of mature age, healthy and vigorous, with close-cut curly hair, dark mustache and dark thick eyebrows. He wears a grayish-green buttoned jacket with an upstanding collar and broad lapels. On his head he wears a soft gray felt hat, and he has one or two light portfolios under his arm.*]

SOLNESS [*near the door, points towards the draughtsmen's office, and asks in a whisper*]. Are they gone?

KAIA [*softly, shaking her head*]. No.

[*She takes the shade off her eyes.* SOLNESS *crosses the room, throws his hat on a chair, places the portfolios on the table by the sofa, and approaches the desk again.* KAIA *goes on writing without intermission, but seems nervous and uneasy.*]

SOLNESS [*aloud*]. What is that you're entering, Miss Fosli?

KAIA [*starts*]. Oh, it's only something that——

SOLNESS. Let me look at it, Miss Fosli. [*Bends over her, pretends to be looking into the ledger, and whispers:*] Kaia?

KAIA [*softly, still writing*]. Well?

SOLNESS. Why do you always take that shade off when I come?

KAIA [*as before*]. I look so ugly with it on.

SOLNESS [*smiling*]. Then you don't like to look ugly, Kaia?

KAIA [*half glancing up at him*]. Not for all the world. Not in your eyes.

SOLNESS [*strokes her hair gently*]. Poor, poor little Kaia——

KAIA [*bending her head*]. Hush, they can hear you!

[SOLNESS *strolls across the room to the right, turns and pauses at the door of the draughtsmen's office.*]

SOLNESS. Has any one been here for me?

RAGNAR [*rising*]. Yes, the young couple who want a villa built out at Lövstrand.

SOLNESS [*growling*]. Oh, those two! They must wait. I'm not quite clear about the plans yet.

RAGNAR [*advancing, with some hesitation*]. They were very anxious to have the drawings at once.

SOLNESS [*as before*]. Yes, of course—so they all are.

BROVIK [*looks up*]. They say they're longing so to get into a house of their own.

SOLNESS. Yes, yes—we know all that! And so they're content to take whatever's offered them. They get a—a roof over their heads—an address—but nothing to call a home. No thank you! In that case, let them apply to somebody else. Tell them *that,* the next time they call.

BROVIK [*pushes his glasses up on to his forehead and looks in astonishment at him*]. To somebody else? Are you prepared to give up the commission?

SOLNESS [*impatiently*]. Yes, yes, yes, devil take it! If that's to be the way of it. ——Rather that, than build away at random. [*Vehemently*] Besides, I know very little about these people as yet.

BROVIK. The people are safe enough. Ragnar knows them. He's a friend of the family. Perfectly safe people.

SOLNESS. Oh, safe—safe enough! That's not at all what I mean. Good lord—don't *you* understand me either? [*Angrily*] I won't have anything to do with these strangers. They may apply to whom they please, so far as I'm concerned.

BROVIK [*rising*]. Do you really mean it?

SOLNESS [*sulkily*]. Yes I do.—For once in a way. [*He comes forward.*]

[BROVIK *exchanges a glance with* RAGNAR, *who makes a warning gesture. Then* BROVIK *comes into the front room.*]

BROVIK. May I have a few words with you?

SOLNESS. Certainly.

BROVIK [*to* KAIA]. Just go in there for a moment, Kaia.

KAIA [*uneasily*]. Oh, but Uncle——

BROVIK. Do as I say, child. And shut the door after you.

[KAIA *goes reluctantly into the draughtsmen's office, glances anxiously and entreatingly at* SOLNESS, *and shuts the door.*]

BROVIK [*lowering his voice a little*]. I don't want the poor children to know how ill I am.

SOLNESS. Yes, you've been looking very poorly of late.

BROVIK. It will soon be all over with me. My strength is ebbing from day to day.

SOLNESS. Won't you sit down?

BROVIK. Thanks—may I?

SOLNESS [*placing the arm-chair more conveniently*]. Here—take this chair.—And now?

BROVIK [*has seated himself with difficulty*]. Well, you see, it's about Ragnar. That's what weighs most upon me. What is to become of him?

SOLNESS. Of course your son will stay with me as long as ever he likes.

BROVIK. But that's just what he doesn't like. He feels that he can't stay any longer.

SOLNESS. Why, I should say he was very well off here. But if he wants a raise, I shouldn't object to——

BROVIK. No, no! It's not *that*. [*Impatiently*] But sooner or later he, too, must have a chance of doing something on his own account.

SOLNESS [*without looking at him*]. Do you think that Ragnar has quite talent enough to stand alone?

BROVIK. No, that's just the heart-breaking part of it—I've begun to have my doubts about the boy. For you've never said so much as— as one encouraging word about him. And yet I can't help thinking there must be something in him—he can't possibly be without talent.

SOLNESS. Well, but he has learnt nothing—nothing thoroughly, I mean. Except, of course, to draw.

BROVIK [*looks at him with covert hatred, and says hoarsely*]. You had learned little enough of the business when you were in my employment. But that didn't prevent you from setting to work—[*breathing with difficulty*]—and pushing your way up, and taking the wind out of my sails—mine, and other people's.

SOLNESS. Yes, you see—circumstances favored me.

BROVIK. You're right there. Everything favored you. But then how can you have the heart to let me go to my grave—without having seen what Ragnar is fit for? And of course I'm anxious to see them married, too—before I go.

SOLNESS [*sharply*]. Is it she who wishes it?

BROVIK. Not Kaia so much as Ragnar—he talks about it every day. [*Appealingly*] You must—you *must* help him to get some independent work now! I *must* see something that the lad has done. Do you hear?

SOLNESS [*peevishly*]. You can't expect me to drag commissions down from the moon for him!

BROVIK. He has the chance of a capital commission at this very moment. A big bit of work.

SOLNESS [*uneasily, startled*]. Has he?

BROVIK. If *you* would give your consent.

SOLNESS. What sort of work do you mean?

BROVIK [*with some hesitation*]. He can have the building of that villa out at Lövstrand.

SOLNESS. That! Why, I'm going to build that myself!

BROVIK. Oh, you don't much care about doing it.

SOLNESS [*flaring up*]. Don't care! I! Who dares to say that?

BROVIK. You said so yourself just now.

SOLNESS. Oh, never mind what I *say*.—Would they give Ragnar the building of that villa?

BROVIK. Yes. You see, he knows the family. And then—just for the fun of the thing—he's made drawings and estimates and so forth——

SOLNESS. Are they pleased with the drawings? The people who've got to live in the house?

BROVIK. Yes. If you would only look through them and approve of them——

SOLNESS. Then they would let Ragnar build their home for them?

BROVIK. They were immensely pleased with his idea. They thought it exceedingly original, they said.

SOLNESS. Oho! Original! Not the old-fashioned stuff that *I'm* in the habit of turning out.

BROVIK. It seemed to them *different*.

SOLNESS [*with suppressed irritation*]. So it was to see Ragnar that they came here—whilst I was out!

BROVIK. They came to call upon you—and at the same time to ask whether you would mind retiring——

SOLNESS [*angrily*]. Retire? I?

BROVIK. In case you thought that Ragnar's drawings——

SOLNESS. I? Retire in favor of your son?

BROVIK. Retire from the agreement, they meant.

SOLNESS. Oh, it comes to the same thing. [*Laughs angrily*] So that's it, is it? Halvard Solness is to see about retiring now! To make room for younger men! For the very youngest, perhaps! He's got to make room! Room! Room!

BROVIK. Why, good heavens! there's surely room for more than one single man——

SOLNESS. Oh, there's not so very much room to spare either. But be that as it may—I will never retire! I will never give way to anybody! Never of my own free will. Never in this world will I do *that!*

BROVIK [*rises with difficulty*]. Then I am to pass out of life without any certainty? Without a gleam of happiness? Without any faith or trust in Ragnar? Without having seen a single piece of work of his doing? Is that to be the way of it?

SOLNESS [*turns half aside, and mutters*]. H'm—don't ask more just now.

BROVIK. But answer me this one thing. Am I to pass out of life in such utter poverty?

SOLNESS [*seems to struggle with himself; finally he says in a low but firm voice*]. You must pass out of life as best you can.

BROVIK. Then bè it so. [*He goes up the room.*]

SOLNESS [*following him, half in desperation*]. Don't you understand that I *cannot* help it? I am what I am, and I can't change my nature!

BROVIK. No, no; you evidently can't. [*Reels and supports himself against the sofa-table*] May I have a glass of water?

SOLNESS. By all means. [*Fills a glass and hands it to him.*]

BROVIK. Thanks. [*Drinks and puts the glass down again.*]

[SOLNESS *goes up and opens the door of the draughtsmen's office.*]

SOLNESS. Ragnar—you must come and take your father home.

[RAGNAR *rises quickly. He and* KAIA *come into the work-room.*]

RAGNAR. What's the matter, father?

BROVIK. Give me your arm. Now let us go.

RAGNAR. All right. You'd better put your things on, too, Kaia.

SOLNESS. Miss Fosli must stay—just a moment. There's a letter I want written.

BROVIK [*looks at* SOLNESS]. Good-night. Sleep well—if you can.

SOLNESS. Good-night.

[BROVIK *and* RAGNAR *go out through the hall-door.* KAIA *goes to the desk.* SOLNESS *stands with bent head, to the right, by the arm-chair.*]

KAIA [*dubiously*]. Is there any letter——?

SOLNESS [*curtly*]. No, of course not. [*Looks sternly at her*] Kaia!

KAIA [*anxiously, in a low voice*]. Yes?

SOLNESS [*points imperatively to a spot on the floor*]. Come here! At once!

KAIA [*hesitatingly*]. Yes.

SOLNESS [*as before*]. Nearer!

KAIA [*obeying*]. What do you want with me?

SOLNESS [*looks at her for a while*]. Is it you I have to thank for all this?

KAIA. No, no, don't think that!

SOLNESS. But confess now—you want to get married!

KAIA [*softly*]. Ragnar and I have been engaged for four or five years, and so——

SOLNESS. And so you think it's time there were an end of it. Isn't that so?

KAIA. Ragnar and Uncle say I *must*. So I suppose I'll have to give in.

SOLNESS [*more gently*]. Kaia, don't you really care a little bit for Ragnar, too?

KAIA. I cared very much for Ragnar once—before I came here to you.

SOLNESS. But you don't now? Not in the least?

KAIA [*passionately, clasping her hands and holding them out towards him*]. Oh, you know very well that there's only *one* person I care for now! One, and one only, in all the world. I shall never care for any one else again!

SOLNESS. Yes, you say that. And yet you go away from me—leave me alone here with everything on my hands.

KAIA. But couldn't I stay with you, even if Ragnar——?

SOLNESS [*repudiating the idea*]. No, no, that's quite impossible. If Ragnar leaves me and starts work on his own account, then of course he'll need you himself.

KAIA [*wringing her hands*]. Oh, I feel as if I *couldn't* be separated from you! It's quite, quite impossible!

SOLNESS. Then be sure you get those foolish notions out of Ragnar's mind. Marry him as much as you please—[*Alters his tone*] I mean—don't let him throw up his good situation with me. For then I can keep *you* too, my dear Kaia.

KAIA. Oh yes, how lovely that would be, if it could only be managed.

SOLNESS [*clasps her head with his two hands and whispers*]. For I *can't* get on without you, you see. I must have you with me every single day.

KAIA [*in nervous exaltation*]. My God! My God!

SOLNESS [*kisses her hair*]. Kaia—Kaia!

KAIA [*sinks down before him*]. Oh, how good you are to me! How unspeakably good you are!

SOLNESS [*vehemently*]. Get up! For goodness' sake get up! I think I hear some one!

[*He helps her to rise. She staggers over to the desk.* MRS. SOLNESS *enters by the door on the right. She looks thin and wasted with grief, but shows traces of bygone beauty. Blonde ringlets. Dressed with good taste, wholly in black. Speaks somewhat slowly and in a plaintive voice.*]

MRS. SOLNESS [*in the doorway*]. Halvard!

SOLNESS [*turns*]. Oh, are you there, dear——?

MRS. SOLNESS [*with a glance at* KAIA]. I'm afraid I'm disturbing you.

SOLNESS. Not in the least. Miss Fosli has only a short letter to write.

MRS. SOLNESS. Yes, so I see.

SOLNESS. What do you want with me, Aline?

MRS. SOLNESS. I merely wanted to tell you that Dr. Herdal is in the drawing-room. Won't you come and see him, Halvard?

SOLNESS [*looks suspiciously at her*]. H'm—is the doctor so very anxious to talk to me?

MRS. SOLNESS. Well, not exactly anxious. He really came to see me; but he would like to say how-do-you-do to you at the same time.

SOLNESS [*laughs to himself*]. Yes, I dare say. Well, you must ask him to wait a little.

MRS. SOLNESS. Then you'll come in later on?

SOLNESS. Perhaps I will. Later on, later on, dear. Presently.

MRS. SOLNESS [*glancing again at* KAIA]. Well now, don't forget, Halvard. [*Withdraws and closes the door behind her.*]

KAIA [*softly*]. Oh dear, oh dear—I'm sure Mrs. Solness thinks ill of me in some way!

SOLNESS. Oh, not in the least. Not more than usual at any rate. But you'd better go now, all the same, Kaia.

KAIA. Yes, yes, now I must go.

SOLNESS [*severely*]. And mind you get that matter settled for me. Do you hear?

KAIA. Oh, if it only depended on *me*——

SOLNESS. I *will* have it settled, I say! And to-morrow too—not a day later!

KAIA [*terrified*]. If there's nothing else for it, I'm quite willing to break off the engagement.

SOLNESS [*angrily*]. Break it off! Are you mad? Would you think of breaking it off?

KAIA [*distracted*]. Yes, if necessary. For I *must*—I *must* stay here with you! I can't leave you! That's utterly—utterly impossible!

SOLNESS [*with a sudden outburst*]. But deuce take it—how about Ragnar then! It's Ragnar that I——

KAIA [*looks at him with terrified eyes*]. It is chiefly on Ragnar's account, that—that you——?

SOLNESS [*collecting himself*]. No, no, of course not! You don't understand me either. [*Gently and softly*] Of course it's *you* I want to keep—you above everything, Kaia. But for that very reason you must prevent Ragnar too from throwing up his situation. There, there,—now go home.

KAIA. Yes, yes—good-night, then.

SOLNESS. Good-night. [*As she is going*] Oh! stop a moment! Are Ragnar's drawings in there?

KAIA. I didn't see him take them with him.

SOLNESS. Then just go in and find them for me. I might perhaps glance over them.

KAIA [*happy*]. Oh yes, please do!

SOLNESS. For your sake, Kaia dear. Now, let me have them at once, please.

> [KAIA *hurries into the draughtsmen's office, searches anxiously in the table-drawer, finds a portfolio and brings it with her.*]

KAIA. Here are all the drawings.

SOLNESS. Good. Put them down there on the table.

KAIA [*putting down the portfolio*]. Good-night, then. [*Beseechingly*] And think kindly of me.

SOLNESS. Oh, that I always do. Good-night, my dear little Kaia. [*Glances to the right*] Go, go now!

> [MRS. SOLNESS *and* DR. HERDAL *enter by the door on the right. He is a stoutish, elderly man, with a round, good-humored face, clean shaven, with thin, light hair, and gold spectacles.*]

MRS. SOLNESS [*still in the doorway*]. Halvard, I cannot keep the doctor any longer.

SOLNESS. Well then, come in here.

MRS. SOLNESS [*to* KAIA, *who is turning down the desk-lamp*]. Have you finished the letter already, Miss Fosli.

KAIA [*in confusion*]. The letter——?

SOLNESS. Yes, it was quite a short one.

MRS. SOLNESS. It must have been very short.

SOLNESS. You may go now, Miss Fosli. And please come in good time to-morrow morning.

KAIA. I will be sure to. Good-night, Mrs. Solness.

> [*She goes out by the hall-door.*]

MRS. SOLNESS. She must be quite an acquisition to you, Halvard, this Miss Fosli.

SOLNESS. Yes, indeed. She's useful in all sorts of ways.

MRS. SOLNESS. So it seems.

DR. HERDAL. Is she good at book-keeping, too?

SOLNESS. Well—of course she's had a good deal of practice during these two years. And then she's so nice and obliging in every possible way.

MRS. SOLNESS. Yes, that must be very delightful.

SOLNESS. It *is*. Especially when one doesn't get too much of that sort of thing.

MRS. SOLNESS [*in a tone of general remonstrance*]. Can *you* say that, Halvard?

SOLNESS. Oh, no, no, my dear Aline; I beg your pardon.

MRS. SOLNESS. There's no occasion. Well, then, doctor, you'll come back later on and have a cup of tea with us?

DR. HERDAL. I've only a professional visit to pay, and then I'll come back.

MRS. SOLNESS. Thank you. [*She goes out by the door on the right.*]

SOLNESS. Are you in a hurry, doctor?

DR. HERDAL. No, not at all.

SOLNESS. May I have a little chat with you?

DR. HERDAL. With the greatest of pleasure.

SOLNESS. Then let us sit down.

[*He motions the doctor to take the rocking-chair and sits down himself in the arm-chair.*]

SOLNESS [*looks searchingly at him*]. Tell me, did you notice anything odd about Aline?

DR. HERDAL. Do you mean just now when she was here?

SOLNESS. Yes, in her manner to me. Did you notice anything?

DR. HERDAL [*smiling*]. Well, I admit—one couldn't well avoid noticing that your wife—h'm——

SOLNESS. Well?

DR. HERDAL. —that your wife isn't particularly fond of this Miss Fosli.

SOLNESS. Is that all? I've noticed that myself.

DR. HERDAL. And I must say it doesn't surprise me.

SOLNESS. What doesn't?

DR. HERDAL. That she shouldn't exactly approve of you seeing so much of another woman, all day and every day.

SOLNESS. No, no, I suppose you're right there—and Aline too. But it's impossible to make any change.

DR. HERDAL. Could you not engage a clerk?

SOLNESS. The first man that came to hand? No, thanks—that would never do for me.

DR. HERDAL. But now, if your wife——? Suppose, with her delicate health, all this tries her too much?

SOLNESS. Well then there's no help for it—I could almost say. I *must* keep Kaia Fosli. No one else could fill her place.

DR. HERDAL. No one else?

SOLNESS [*curtly*]. No, no one.

DR. HERDAL [*drawing his chair closer*]. Now listen to me, my dear Mr. Solness. May I ask you a question, quite between ourselves?

SOLNESS. By all means.

DR. HERDAL. Women, you see—in certain matters, they have a deucedly keen intuition——

SOLNESS. They have indeed. There's not the least doubt of that. But——?

DR. HERDAL. Well, tell me now—if your wife can't endure this Kaia Fosli——?

SOLNESS. Well, what then?

DR. HERDAL. —hasn't she got just—just the least little bit of reason for this involuntary dislike?

SOLNESS [*looks at him and rises*]. Oho!

DR. HERDAL. Now don't be offended—but *hasn't* she?

SOLNESS [*with curt decision*]. No.

DR. HERDAL. No reason of any sort?

SOLNESS. No other reason than her own suspicious nature.

DR. HERDAL. I know you've known a good many women in your time.

SOLNESS. Yes, I have.

DR. HERDAL. And have been a good deal taken with some of them, too?

SOLNESS. Oh yes, I don't deny it.

DR. HERDAL. But as regards Miss Fosli, then—there's nothing of that sort in the case?

SOLNESS. No; nothing at all—on *my* side.

DR. HERDAL. But on her side?

SOLNESS. I don't think you have any right to ask that question, doctor.

DR. HERDAL. Well, you know, we were discussing your wife's intuition.

SOLNESS. So we were. And for that matter—[*lowers his voice*]— Aline's intuition, as you call it—in a certain sense, it's not been so far out.

DR. HERDAL. Ah! there we have it!

SOLNESS [*sits down*]. Doctor Herdal—I'm going to tell you a strange story—if you care to listen to it.

DR. HERDAL. I like listening to strange stories.

SOLNESS. Very well then. I daresay you recollect that I took Knut Brovik and his son into my service—after the old man's business had gone to the dogs.

DR. HERDAL. Yes, so I've understood.

SOLNESS. You see, they really are clever fellows, these two. Each of them has talent in his way. But then the son took it into his head to get engaged; and the next thing, of course, was that he wanted to get married—and begin to build on his own account. That's the way with all these young people.

DR. HERDAL [*laughing*]. Yes, they've a bad habit of wanting to marry.

SOLNESS. Just so. But of course that didn't suit *my* plans; for I needed Ragnar myself—and the old man, too. He's exceedingly good at calculating bearing-strains[1] and cubic contents—and all that sort of devilry, you know.

DR. HERDAL. Oh yes, no doubt that's very important.

SOLNESS. Yes, it is. But Ragnar was absolutely bent on setting to work for himself. He wouldn't hear of anything else.

DR. HERDAL. But he has stayed with you all the same.

SOLNESS. Yes, I'll tell you how that came about. One day this girl, Kaia Fosli, came to see them on some errand or other. She had never been here before. And when I saw how utterly infatuated they were with each other, the thought occurred to me: If only I could get her into the office here, then perhaps Ragnar too would stay where she is.

DR. HERDAL. That was not at all a bad idea.

SOLNESS. Yes, but at the time I didn't breathe a word of what was in my mind. I merely stood and looked at her, and kept wishing intently that I could have her here. Then I talked to her a little, in a friendly way—about one thing and another. And then she went away.

DR. HERDAL. Well?

SOLNESS. Well then, next day, pretty late in the evening, when old Brovik and Ragnar had gone home, she came here again, and behaved as if I had made an arrangement with her.

DR. HERDAL. An arrangement? What about?

SOLNESS. About the very thing my mind had been fixed on. But I hadn't said one single word about it.

---

[1] *bearing-strains, the amount of stress that can be borne by a beam resting on a masonry wall or footing.*

DR. HERDAL. That was most extraordinary.

SOLNESS. Yes, wasn't it? And now she wanted to know what she was to do here, whether she could begin the very next morning, and so forth.

DR. HERDAL. Don't you think she did it in order to be with her sweetheart?

SOLNESS. That was what occurred to me at first. But no, that wasn't it. She seemed to drift quite away from *him*—when once she had come here to me.

DR. HERDAL. She drifted over to you, then?

SOLNESS. Yes, entirely. If I happen to look at her when her back is turned, I can tell that she feels it. She quivers and trembles the moment I come near her. What do you think of that?

DR. HERDAL. H'm—that's not very hard to explain.

SOLNESS. Well, but what about the other thing? That she believed I had said to her what I had only wished and willed—silently—inwardly—to myself? What do you say to that? Can you explain that, Dr. Herdal?

DR. HERDAL. No, I won't undertake to do that.

SOLNESS. I felt sure you wouldn't; and so I've never cared to talk about it till now. But it's a cursed nuisance to me in the long run, you understand. Here have I got to go on day after day pretending—. And it's a shame to treat her so, too, poor girl. [*Vehemently*] But I *can't* do anything else. For if *she* runs away from me—then Ragnar will be off too.

DR. HERDAL. And you haven't told your wife the rights of the story?

SOLNESS. No.

DR. HERDAL. Then why on earth don't you?

SOLNESS [*looks fixedly at him and says in a low voice*]. Because I seem to find a sort of—of salutary self-torture in allowing Aline to do me an injustice.

DR. HERDAL [*shakes his head*]. I don't in the least understand what you mean.

SOLNESS. Well, you see, it's like paying off a little bit of a huge, immeasurable debt——

DR. HERDAL. To your wife?

SOLNESS. Yes; and that always helps to relieve one's mind a little. One can breathe more freely for a while, you see.

DR. HERDAL. No, goodness knows, I don't see at all——

SOLNESS [*breaking off, rises again*]. Well, well, well—then we won't talk any more about it. [*He saunters across the room, returns, and stops beside the table. Looks at the doctor with a sly smile.*] I suppose you think you've drawn me out nicely now, doctor?

DR. HERDAL [*with some irritation*]. Drawn you out? Again I haven't the faintest notion what you mean, Mr. Solness.

SOLNESS. Oh come, out with it; for I've seen it quite clearly, you know.

DR. HERDAL. *What* have you seen?

SOLNESS [*in a low voice, slowly*]. That you've been quietly keeping an eye upon me.

DR. HERDAL. That *I* have! And why in all the world should I *do that?*

SOLNESS. Because you think that I——[*Passionately*] Well, devil take it—you think the same of me as Aline does.

DR. HERDAL. And what does *she* think about you?

SOLNESS [*having recovered his self-control*]. She has begun to think that I'm—that I'm—ill.

DR. HERDAL. Ill! *You!* She has never hinted such a thing to me. Why, what can she think is the matter with you?

SOLNESS [*leans over the back of the chair and whispers*]. Aline has made up her mind that I am mad. *That's* what she thinks.

DR. HERDAL [*rising*]. Why, my dear, good fellow——!

SOLNESS. Yes, on my soul she does! I tell you it's so! And she has got you to think the same. Oh, I can assure you, doctor, I see it in your face as clearly as possible. You don't take me in so easily, I can tell you.

DR. HERDAL [*looks at him in amazement*]. Never, Mr. Solness— never has such a thought entered my mind.

SOLNESS [*with an incredulous smile*]. Really? Has it not?

DR. HERDAL. No, never! Nor your wife's mind either, I'm convinced. I could almost swear to that.

SOLNESS. Well, I wouldn't advise you to. For, in a certain sense, you see, perhaps—perhaps she's not so far wrong in thinking something of the kind.

DR. HERDAL. Come now, I really must say——

SOLNESS [*interrupting with a sweep of his hand*]. Well, well, my dear doctor—don't let us discuss this any further. We had better agree to differ. [*Changes to a tone of quiet merriment*] But look here now, doctor—hm—

DR. HERDAL. Well?

SOLNESS. Since you don't believe that I am—ill—and crazy—and mad, and so forth——

DR. HERDAL. What then?

SOLNESS. Then I daresay you fancy that I'm an extremely happy man?

DR. HERDAL. Is *that* mere fancy?

SOLNESS [*laughs*]. No, no—of course not! Heaven forbid! Only think—to be Solness the master builder! Halvard Solness! What could be more delightful?

DR. HERDAL. Yes, I must say it seems to me you've had the luck on your side to an astounding degree.

SOLNESS [*suppresses a gloomy smile*]. So I have. I can't complain on *that* score.

DR. HERDAL. First of all that grim old robber's-castle was burnt down for you. And that was certainly a great piece of luck.

SOLNESS [*seriously*]. It was the home of Aline's family. Remember that.

DR. HERDAL. Yes, it must have been a great grief to *her*.

SOLNESS. She hasn't got over it to this day—not in all these twelve or thirteen years.

DR. HERDAL. Ah, but what followed must have been the worst blow for her.

SOLNESS. The one thing with the other.

DR. HERDAL. But you—yourself—*you* rose upon the ruins. You began as a poor boy from a country village—and now you're at the head of your profession. Ah, yes, Mr. Solness, you've undoubtedly had the luck on your side.

SOLNESS [*looks doubtfully across at him*]. Yes, but that's just what makes me so horribly afraid.

DR. HERDAL. Afraid? Because you have the luck on your side!

SOLNESS. It terrifies me—terrifies me every hour of the day. For sooner or later the luck must turn, you see.

DR. HERDAL. Oh, nonsense! What should make the luck turn?

SOLNESS [*with firm assurance*]. The younger generation.

DR. HERDAL. Pooh! The younger generation! You're not laid on the shelf yet, I should hope. Oh no—your position here is probably firmer now than it has ever been.

SOLNESS. The luck *will* turn. I know it—I feel the day approaching. Some one or other will take it into his head to say: Give *me* a chance! And then all the rest will come clamoring after him, and shake their fists at me and shout: Make room—make room—make room! Yes, just you see, doctor—presently the younger generation will come knocking at my door——

DR. HERDAL [*laughing*]. Well, and what if they do?

SOLNESS. What if they do? Then there's an end of Halvard Solness.

[*There is a knock at the door on the left.*]

SOLNESS [*starts*]. What's that? Didn't you hear something?

DR. HERDAL. Some one is knocking at the door.

SOLNESS [*loudly*]. Come in.

[*HILDA WANGEL enters through the hall door. She is of middle height, supple, and delicately built. Somewhat sunburnt. Dressed in a tourist costume, with skirt caught up for walking, a sailor's collar open at the throat, and a small sailor hat on her head. Knapsack on back, plaid shawl in strap, and alpenstock.[1]*]

HILDA [*goes straight up to* SOLNESS, *her eyes sparkling with happiness*]. Good-evening!

SOLNESS [*looks doubtfully at her*]. Good-evening——

HILDA [*laughs*]. I almost believe you don't recognize me!

SOLNESS. No—I must admit that—just for the moment——

DR. HERDAL [*approaching*]. But *I* recognize you, my dear young lady——

HILDA [*pleased*]. Oh, is it you that——

DR. HERDAL. Of course it is. [*To* SOLNESS] We met at one of the mountain stations this summer. [*To* HILDA] What became of the other ladies?

HILDA. Oh, they went westward.

DR. HERDAL. They didn't much like all the fun we used to have in the evenings.

HILDA. No, I believe they didn't.

DR. HERDAL [*holds up his finger at her*]. And I'm afraid it can't be denied that you flirted a little with us.

HILDA. Well, that was better fun than to sit there knitting stockings with all those old women.

DR. HERDAL [*laughs*]. There I entirely agree with you!

SOLNESS. Have you come to town this evening?

HILDA. Yes, I've just arrived.

DR. HERDAL. Quite alone, Miss Wangel?

[1] *alpenstock, a long, iron-pointed staff used in mountain-climbing, especially in the Alps.*

HILDA. Oh yes!

SOLNESS. Wangel? Is your name Wangel?

HILDA [*looks in amused surprise at him*]. Yes, of course it is.

SOLNESS. Then you must be the daughter of the district doctor up at Lysanger?

HILDA [*as before*]. Yes, who else's daughter should I be?

SOLNESS. Oh, then I suppose we met up there, that summer when I was building a tower on the old church.

HILDA [*more seriously*]. Yes, of course it was then we met.

SOLNESS. Well, that's a long time ago.

HILDA [*looks hard at him*]. It's just ten years.

SOLNESS. You must have been a mere child then, I should think.

HILDA [*carelessly*]. Well, I was twelve or thirteen.

DR. HERDAL. Is this the first time you've ever been up to town, Miss Wangel?

HILDA. Yes, it is indeed.

SOLNESS. And don't you know any one here?

HILDA. Nobody but you. And of course, your wife.

SOLNESS. So you know *her* too?

HILDA. Only a little. We spent a few days together at the sanatorium.

SOLNESS. Ah, up there?

HILDA. She said I might come and pay her a visit if ever I came up to town. [*Smiles*] Not that that was necessary.

SOLNESS. Odd that she should never have mentioned it.

[HILDA *puts her stick down by the stove, takes off the knapsack and lays it and the plaid on the sofa.* DR. HERDAL *offers to help her.* SOLNESS *stands and gazes at her.*]

HILDA [*going towards him*]. Well, now I must ask you to let me spend the night here.

SOLNESS. I'm sure we can manage that.

HILDA. For I've no other clothes than those I stand in, except a change of linen in my knapsack. And that has to go to the wash, for it's very dirty.

SOLNESS. Oh yes, we'll see to that. Now I'll just let my wife know——

DR. HERDAL. Meanwhile, I'll visit my patient.

SOLNESS. Yes, do; and come again later on.

DR. HERDAL [*playfully, with a glance at* HILDA]. Oh that I will, you may be very certain! [*Laughs*] So your prediction has come true, Mr. Solness!

SOLNESS. How so?

DR. HERDAL. The younger generation *did* come knocking at your door.[1]

SOLNESS [*cheerfully*]. Yes, but in a very different way from what I meant.

DR. HERDAL. Very different, yes. That's undeniable.

[*He goes out by the hall-door.* SOLNESS *opens the door on the right and speaks into the side room.*]

SOLNESS. Aline! Will you come in here, please. Here's a friend of yours—Miss Wangel.

MRS. SOLNESS [*appears in the door-way*]. Who do you say it is? [*Sees* HILDA] Oh, is it you, Miss Wangel? [*Goes up to her and offers her hand*] So you've come to town after all.

SOLNESS. Miss Wangel has this moment arrived; and she would like to stay the night here.

MRS. SOLNESS. Here with us? Oh yes, with pleasure.

SOLNESS. So as to get her things a little in order, you see.

MRS. SOLNESS. I will do the best I can for you. It's no more than my duty. I suppose your trunk is coming on later?

HILDA. I *have* no trunk.

MRS. SOLNESS. Well, it will be all right, I daresay. In the meantime, you must excuse my leaving you here with my husband until I can get a room made a little comfortable for you.

SOLNESS. Can't we give her one of the nurseries? *They* are all ready as it is.

MRS. SOLNESS. Oh yes. There we have room and to spare. [*To* HILDA] Sit down now and rest a little.

[*She goes out to the right.* HILDA, *with her hands behind her back, strolls about the room and looks at various objects.* SOLNESS *stands in front, beside the table, also with his hands behind his back, and follows her with his eyes.*]

HILDA [*stops and looks at him*]. Have you several nurseries?

SOLNESS. There are three nurseries in the house.

HILDA. That's a lot. Then I suppose you have a great many children?

SOLNESS. No. We have no child. But now *you* can be the child here, for the time being.

HILDA. For to-night, yes. I sha'n't cry. I mean to sleep as sound as a stone.

SOLNESS. Yes, you must be very tired, I should think.

[1] *The younger generation, etc.,* the fateful fulfillment characteristic of Ibsen's pattern of symbols.

HILDA. Oh no! But all the same——It's so delicious to lie and dream.

SOLNESS. Do you dream much of nights?

HILDA. Oh yes! Almost always.

SOLNESS. What do you dream about most?

HILDA. I sha'n't tell you to-night. Another time, perhaps.

[*She again strolls about the room, stops at the desk and turns over the books and papers a little.*]

SOLNESS [*approaching*]. Are you searching for anything?

HILDA. No, I'm merely looking at all these things. [*Turns*] Perhaps I mustn't?

SOLNESS. Oh, by all means.

HILDA. Is it you that writes in this great ledger?

SOLNESS. No, it's my book-keeper.

HILDA. Is it a woman?

SOLNESS [*smiles*]. Yes.

HILDA. One you employ here, in your office?

SOLNESS. Yes.

HILDA. Is she married?

SOLNESS. No, she's single.

HILDA. Ah!

SOLNESS. But I believe she's soon going to be married.

HILDA. That's a good thing for *her*.

SOLNESS. But not such a good thing for *me*. For then I shall have nobody to help me.

HILDA. Can't you get hold of some one else who'll do just as well?

SOLNESS. Perhaps *you* would stop here and—and write in the ledger?

HILDA [*measures him with a glance*]. Yes, I daresay! No, thanks—nothing of that sort for *me*—[*She again strolls across the room, and sits down in the rocking-chair.* SOLNESS *too goes to the table.* HILDA *continues:*]—for there must surely be other things than *that* to be done here. [*Looks smilingly at him*] Don't you think so too?

SOLNESS. Of course. First and foremost, I suppose you want to make a round of the shops, and get yourself up in the height of fashion.

HILDA [*amused*]. No, I think I shall let *that* alone.

SOLNESS. Indeed!

HILDA. For you must know I've run through all my money.

SOLNESS [*laughs*]. Neither trunk nor money, then!

HILDA. Neither one nor the other. But never mind—it doesn't matter now.

SOLNESS. Come now, I like you for *that*.

HILDA. Only for *that*?

SOLNESS. For that among other things. [*Sits in the arm-chair*] Is your father alive still?

HILDA. Yes, father's alive.

SOLNESS. Perhaps you're thinking of studying here?

HILDA. No, that hadn't occurred to me.

SOLNESS. But I suppose you'll be stopping for some time.

HILDA. That must depend upon circumstances.

[*She sits awhile rocking herself and looking at him, half seriously, half with a suppressed smile. Then she takes off her hat and puts it on the table in front of her.*]

HILDA. Mr. Solness!

SOLNESS. Well?

HILDA. Have you a very bad memory?

SOLNESS. A bad memory? No, not that I'm aware of.

HILDA. Then haven't you anything to say to me about what happened up there?

SOLNESS [*in momentary surprise*]. Up at Lysanger? [*Indifferently*] Why, it was nothing much to talk about, it seems to me.

HILDA [*looks reproachfully at him*]. How can you sit there and say such things?

SOLNESS. Well, then, *you* talk to *me* about it.

HILDA. When the tower was finished, we had grand doings in the town.

SOLNESS. Yes, I sha'n't easily forget that day.

HILDA [*smiles*]. Won't you? That's good of you!

SOLNESS. Good?

HILDA. There was music in the churchyard—and many, many hundreds of people. We school-girls were dressed in white; and we all carried flags.

SOLNESS. Ah yes, those flags—I can tell you I remember them!

HILDA. Then you climbed up over the scaffolding, straight to the very top; and you had a great wreath with you; and you hung that wreath right away up on the weathercock.

SOLNESS [*curtly interrupting*]. I always did that in those days. It's an old custom.

HILDA. It was so wonderfully thrilling to stand below and look up at you. Fancy, if he should fall over! He—the master builder himself!

SOLNESS [*as if to lead her away from the subject*]. Yes, yes, yes, that might very well have happened, too. For one of those white-frocked little devils,—she went on in such a way, and screamed up at me so——

HILDA [*sparkling with pleasure*]. "Hurra for Mr. Solness!" Yes!

SOLNESS. —and waved and flourished with her flag so that I—so that it almost made me giddy to look at it.

HILDA [*in a lower voice, seriously*]. That little devil—that was *I*.

SOLNESS [*fixes his eyes steadily upon her*]. I'm sure of that now. It *must* have been you.

HILDA [*lively again*]. Oh, it was so gloriously thrilling! I couldn't have believed there was a builder in the whole world that could have built such a tremendously high tower. And then, that you yourself should stand at the very top of it, as large as life! And that you shouldn't be the least bit dizzy! It was that above everything that made one—made one dizzy to think of.

SOLNESS. How could you be so certain that I wasn't——?

HILDA [*scouting the idea*]. No indeed! Oh no! I knew that instinctively. For if you had been you could never have stood up there and sung.

SOLNESS [*looks at her in astonishment*]. Sung? Did I sing?

HILDA. Yes, I should think you did.

SOLNESS [*shakes his head*]. I've never sung a note in my life.

HILDA. Yes, you sang then. It sounded like harps in the air.

SOLNESS [*thoughtfully*]. This is very strange—all this.

HILDA [*is silent awhile, looks at him and says in a low voice*]. But then,—it was after that—that the *real* thing happened.

SOLNESS. The real thing?

HILDA [*sparkling with vivacity*]. Yes, I surely don't need to remind you of *that*?

SOLNESS. Oh yes, do remind me a little of *that,* too.

HILDA. Don't you remember that a great dinner was given in your honor at the Club?

SOLNESS. Yes, to be sure. It must have been the same afternoon, for I left the place next morning.

HILDA. And from the Club you were invited to come round to our house to supper.

SOLNESS. Quite right, Miss Wangel. It's wonderful how all these trifles have impressed themselves on your mind.

HILDA. Trifles! I like that! Perhaps it was a trifle, too, that I was *alone* in the room when you came in?

SOLNESS. *Were* you alone?

HILDA [*without answering him*]. You didn't call me a little devil *then*.

SOLNESS. No, I probably didn't.

HILDA. You said I was lovely in my white dress, and that I looked like a little princess.

SOLNESS. I've no doubt you did, Miss Wangel.—And besides—I was feeling so buoyant and free that day——

HILDA. And then you said that when I grew up I should be *your* princess.

SOLNESS [*laughing a little*]. Dear, dear—did I say *that* too?

HILDA. Yes, you did. And when I asked how long I should have to wait, you said that you would come again in ten years—like a troll[1] —and carry me off—to Spain or some such place. And you promised you would buy me a kingdom there.

SOLNESS [*as before*]. Yes, after a good dinner one doesn't haggle about the halfpence. But did I really *say* all that?

HILDA [*laughs to herself*]. Yes. And you told me, too, what the kingdom was to be called.

SOLNESS. Well, what was it?

HILDA. It was to be called the kingdom of Orangia,[2] you said.

SOLNESS. Well, that was an appetizing name.

HILDA. No, I didn't like it a bit; for it seemed as though you wanted to make game of me.

SOLNESS. I'm sure *that* can't have been my intention.

HILDA. No, I should hope not—considering what you did next——

SOLNESS. What in the world did I do next?

HILDA. Well, that's the finishing touch, if you've forgotten *that* too. I should have thought one couldn't help remembering such a thing as that.

SOLNESS. Yes, yes, just give me a hint, and then perhaps—Well?

HILDA [*looks fixedly at him*]. You came and kissed me, Mr. Solness.

SOLNESS [*open-mouthed, rising from his chair*]. *I* did!

HILDA. Yes, indeed you did. You took me in both your arms, and bent my head back, and kissed me—many times.

SOLNESS. Now, really, my dear Miss Wangel——!

HILDA [*rises*]. You surely don't mean to deny it?

SOLNESS. Yes, I do. I deny it altogether!

---

[1] *troll. In Scandinavian folklore the troll is pictured as either a giant or an imp with sinister supernatural powers, living in a cave or subterranean dwelling.*
[2] *In the original "Appelsinia," "appelsin" meaning "orange"*—**Translators' note.**

HILDA [*looks scornfully at him*]. Oh, indeed!

[*She turns and goes slowly close up to the stove, where she remains standing motionless, her face averted from him, her hands behind her back. Short pause.*]

SOLNESS [*goes cautiously up behind her*]. Miss Wangel!——

HILDA [*is silent and does not move*].

SOLNESS. Don't stand there like a statue. You must have dreamt all this. [*Lays his hand on her arm*] Now just listen——

HILDA [*makes an impatient movement with her arm*].

SOLNESS [*as a thought flashes upon him*]. Or——! Wait a moment! There is something under all this, you may depend!

HILDA [*does not move*].

SOLNESS [*in a low voice, but with emphasis*]. I must have *thought* all that. I must have *wished* it—have *willed* it—have *longed* to do it. And then——. May not that be the explanation?

HILDA [*is still silent*].

SOLNESS [*impatiently*]. Oh very well, deuce take it all—then I *did* do it, I suppose!

HILDA [*turns her head a little, but without looking at him*]. Then you admit it now?

SOLNESS. Yes—whatever you like.

HILDA. You came and put your arms round me?

SOLNESS. Oh yes.

HILDA. And bent my head back?

SOLNESS. Very far back.

HILDA. And kissed me?

SOLNESS. Yes, I did.

HILDA. Many times?

SOLNESS. As many as ever you like.

HILDA [*turns quickly towards him and has once more the sparkling expression of gladness in her eyes*]. Well, you see, I got it out of you at last!

SOLNESS [*with a slight smile*]. Yes—just think of my forgetting such a thing as that.

HILDA [*again a little sulky, retreats from him*]. Oh, you've kissed so many people in your time, I suppose.

SOLNESS. No, you mustn't think *that* of me.

[HILDA *seats herself in the arm-chair.* SOLNESS *stands and leans against the rocking-chair.*]

SOLNESS [*looks observantly at her*]. Miss Wangel?

HILDA. Yes?

SOLNESS. How *was* it now? What came of all this—between us two?

HILDA. Why, nothing more came of it. You know that quite well. For then the other guests came in, and then—bah!

SOLNESS. Quite so! The others came in. To think of my forgetting *that* too!

HILDA. Oh, you haven't really forgotten anything: you're only a little ashamed of it all. I'm sure one doesn't forget things of that kind.

SOLNESS. No, one would suppose not.

HILDA [*lively again, looks at him*]. Perhaps you've even forgotten what day it was?

SOLNESS. What day?

HILDA. Yes, on what day did you hang the wreath on the tower? well? Tell me at once!

SOLNESS. H'm—I confess I've forgotten the particular day. I only know it was ten years ago. Some time in the autumn.

HILDA [*nods her head slowly several times*]. It was ten years ago— on the 19th of September.

SOLNESS. Yes, it must have been about that time. Fancy your re- membering that too! [*Stops*] But wait a moment—! Yes—it's the 19th of September to-day.

HILDA. Yes, it is; and the ten years are gone. And you didn't come— as you had promised me.

SOLNESS. Promised you? Threatened, I suppose you mean?

HILDA. I don't think there was any sort of threat in *that*.

SOLNESS. Well then, a little bit of a hoax.

HILDA. Was that all you wanted to do? To hoax me?

SOLNESS. Well, or to have a little joke with you! Upon my soul I don't recollect. But it must have been something of that kind; for you were a mere child then.

HILDA. Oh, perhaps I wasn't quite such a child either. Not such a mere chit as you imagine.

SOLNESS [*looks searchingly at her*]. Did you really and seriously expect me to come again?

HILDA [*conceals a half-teasing smile*]. Yes, indeed! I did expect *that* of you.

SOLNESS. That I should come back to your home, and take you away with me?

HILDA. Just like a troll—yes.

SOLNESS. And make a princess of you?

HILDA. That's what you promised.

SOLNESS. And give you a kingdom as well?

HILDA [*looks up at the ceiling*]. Why not? Of course it needn't have been an actual, every-day sort of a kingdom.

SOLNESS. But something else just as good?

HILDA. Yes, at least as good. [*Looks at him a moment*] I thought if you could build the highest church-towers in the world, you could surely manage to raise a kingdom of one sort or another as well.

SOLNESS [*shakes his head*]. I can't quite make you out, Miss Wangel.

HILDA. Can't you? To me it seems all so simple.

SOLNESS. No, I can't make up my mind whether you mean all you say, or are simply having a joke with me.

HILDA [*smiles*]. Hoaxing you, perhaps? I, too?

SOLNESS. Yes, exactly. Hoaxing—both of us. [*Looks at her*] Is it long since you found out that I was married?

HILDA. I've known it all along. Why do you ask me *that*?

SOLNESS [*lightly*]. Oh, well, it just occurred to me. [*Looks earnestly at her, and says in a low voice:*] What have you come for?

HILDA. I want my kingdom. The time is up.

SOLNESS [*laughs involuntarily*]. What a girl you are!

HILDA [*gayly*]. Out with my kingdom, Mr. Solness! [*Raps with her fingers*] The kingdom on the table!

SOLNESS [*pushing the rocking-chair nearer and sitting down*]. Now, seriously speaking—what have you come for? What do you really want to do here?

HILDA. Oh, first of all, I want to go round and look at all the things that you've built.

SOLNESS. That will give you plenty of exercise.

HILDA. Yes, I know you've built a tremendous lot.

SOLNESS. I have indeed—especially of late years.

HILDA. Many church-towers among the rest? Immensely high ones?

SOLNESS. No. I build no more church-towers now. Nor churches either.

HILDA. What *do* you build then?

SOLNESS. Homes for human beings.

HILDA [*reflectively*]. Couldn't you build a little—a little bit of a church-tower over these homes as well?

SOLNESS [*starting*]. What do you mean by *that*?

HILDA. I mean—something that points—points up into the free air. With the vane at a dizzy height.

SOLNESS [*pondering a little*]. Strange that you should say *that*—for that's just what I'm most anxious to do.

HILDA [*impatiently*]. Then why don't you do it?

SOLNESS [*shakes his head*]. No, the people won't have it.

HILDA. Fancy their not wanting it!

SOLNESS [*more lightly*]. But now I'm building a new home for my-self—just opposite here.

HILDA. For yourself?

SOLNESS. Yes. It's almost finished. And on that there's a tower.

HILDA. A high tower?

SOLNESS. Yes.

HILDA. Very high?

SOLNESS. No doubt people will say that it's too high—too high for a dwelling-house.

HILDA. I'll go out and look at that tower the first thing to-morrow morning.

SOLNESS [*sits with his hand under his cheek and gazes at her*]. Tell me, Miss Wangel—what is your name? Your Christian name, I mean?

HILDA. Why, Hilda, of course.

SOLNESS [*as before*]. Hilda? Ah?

HILDA. Don't you remember *that*? You called me Hilda yourself—that day when you misbehaved.

SOLNESS. Did I really?

HILDA. But then you said *"little* Hilda"; and I didn't like that.

SOLNESS. Oh, you didn't like that, Miss Hilda?

HILDA. No, not at such a time as that. But—"Princess Hilda"—that will sound very well, I think.

SOLNESS. Very well indeed. Princess Hilda of—of—what was to be the name of the kingdom?

HILDA. Pooh! I won't have anything to do with *that* stupid kingdom. I've set my heart upon quite a different one!

SOLNESS [*has leaned back in the chair, still gazing at her*]. Isn't it strange——? The more I think of it now, the more it seems to me as though I had gone about all these years torturing myself with—h'm——

HILDA. With what?

SOLNESS. With the effort to recover something—some experience, which I seemed to have forgotten. But I never had the least inkling of what it would be.

HILDA. You should have tied a knot in your pocket-handkerchief, Mr. Solness.

SOLNESS. In that case, I should simply have had to go racking my brains to discover what the knot could mean.

HILDA. Oh yes, I suppose there are trolls of *that* kind in the world, too.

SOLNESS [*rises slowly*]. What a good thing it is that *you* have come to me now.

HILDA [*looks deeply into his eyes*]. *Is* it a good thing?

SOLNESS. For I've been so lonely here. I've been gazing so helplessly at it all. [*In a lower voice*] I must tell you—I've begun to be so afraid —so terribly afraid of the younger generation.

HILDA [*with a little snort of contempt*]. Pooh—is the younger generation a thing to be afraid of?

SOLNESS. It is indeed. And that's why I've locked and barred myself in. [*Mysteriously*] I tell you the younger generation will one day come and thunder at my door! They'll break in upon me!

HILDA. Then I should say you ought to go out and open the door to the younger generation.

SOLNESS. Open the door?

HILDA. Yes. Let them come in to you on friendly terms, as it were.

SOLNESS. No, no, no! The younger generation—it means retribution, you see. It comes, as if under a new banner, heralding the turn of fortune.

HILDA [*rises, looks at him, and says with a quivering twitch of her lips*]. Can *I* be of any use to you, Mr. Solness?

SOLNESS. Yes, you can indeed! For you, too, come—under a new banner, it seems to me. Youth marshalled against youth——!

[DR. HERDAL *comes in by the hall-door.*]

DR. HERDAL. What—you and Miss Wangel here still?

SOLNESS. Yes. We've had no end of things to talk about.

HILDA. Both old and new.

DR. HERDAL. Have you really?

HILDA. Oh, it has been the greatest fun. For Mr. Solness—he has such a miraculous memory. All the least little details he remembers instantly.

[MRS. SOLNESS *enters by the door on the right.*]

MRS. SOLNESS. Well, Miss Wangel, your room is quite ready for you now.

HILDA. Oh, how kind you are to me!

SOLNESS [*to* MRS. SOLNESS]. The nursery?

MRS. SOLNESS. Yes, the middle one. But first let us go in to supper.

SOLNESS [*nods to* HILDA]. Hilda shall sleep in the nursery.

MRS. SOLNESS [*looks at him*]. Hilda?

SOLNESS. Yes, Miss Wangel's name is Hilda. I knew her when she was a child.

MRS. SOLNESS. Did you really, Halvard? Well, shall we go? Supper is on the table.

[*She takes* DR. HERDAL's *arm and goes out with him to the right.* HILDA *has meanwhile been collecting her travelling things.*]

HILDA [*softly and rapidly to* SOLNESS]. Is it true, what you said? *Can* I be of use to you?

SOLNESS [*takes the things from her*]. You *are* the very one I have most needed.

HILDA [*looks at him with happy, wondering eyes and clasps her hands*]. Oh heavens, how lovely——!

SOLNESS [*eagerly*]. What——?

HILDA. Then I *have* my kingdom!

SOLNESS [*involuntarily*]. Hilda——!

HILDA [*again with the quivering twitch of her lips*]. Almost—I was going to say.

[*She goes out to the right.* SOLNESS *follows her.*]

act 2

A prettily furnished small drawing-room in the house of SOLNESS. *In the back, a glass-door leading out to the veranda and garden. The right-hand corner is cut off transversely by a large bay-window, in which are flower-stands. The left-hand corner is similarly cut off by a transverse wall, in which is a small door papered like the wall. On each side, an ordinary door. In front, on the right, a console table with a large mirror over it. Well-filled stands of plants and flowers. In front, on the left, a sofa with a table and chairs. Further back, a bookcase. Well forward in the room, before the bay-window, a small table and some chairs. It is early in the day.*

SOLNESS *sits by the little table with* RAGNAR BROVIK's *portfolio open in front of him. He is turning the drawings over and closely examining some of them.* MRS. SOLNESS *walks about noiselessly with a small watering-pot, attending to her flowers. She is dressed in black as before. Her hat, cloak*

*and parasol lie on a chair near the mirror. Unobserved by
her,* SOLNESS *now and again follows her with his eyes.
Neither of them speaks.*

KAIA FOSLI *enters quietly by the door on the left.*

SOLNESS [*turns his head and says in an off-hand tone of indifference*].
Well, is that you?

KAIA. I merely wished to let you know I've come.

SOLNESS. Yes, yes, that's all right. Hasn't Ragnar come too?

KAIA. No, not yet. He had to wait a little while to see the doctor.
But he's coming presently to hear——

SOLNESS. How is the old man to-day?

KAIA. Not well. He begs you to excuse him, for he must keep his
bed to-day.

SOLNESS. Quite so; by all means let him rest. But now, get to your
work.

KAIA. Yes. [*Pauses at the door*] Do you wish to speak to Ragnar
when he comes?

SOLNESS. No—I don't know that I've anything special to say to him.

[KAIA *goes out again to the left.* SOLNESS *remains seated, turning
over the drawings.*]

MRS. SOLNESS [*over beside the plants*]. I wonder if *he* isn't going to
die now, as well?

SOLNESS [*looks up at her*]. As well as who?

MRS. SOLNESS [*without answering*]. Yes, yes—depend upon it,
Halvard, old Brovik's going to die too. You'll see that he will.

SOLNESS. My dear Aline, oughtn't you to go out for a little walk?

MRS. SOLNESS. Yes, I suppose I ought to. [*She continues to attend to
the flowers.*]

SOLNESS [*bending over the drawings*]. Is she still asleep?

MRS. SOLNESS [*looking at him*]. Is it Miss Wangel you're sitting
there thinking about?

SOLNESS [*indifferently*]. I just happened to recollect her.

MRS. SOLNESS. Miss Wangel was up long ago.

SOLNESS. Oh, was she?

MRS. SOLNESS. When I went in to see her, she was busy putting
her things in order.

[*She goes in front of the mirror and slowly begins to put on her
hat.*]

SOLNESS [*after a short pause*]. So we've found a use for one of our
nurseries after all, Aline.

MRS. SOLNESS. Yes, we have.

SOLNESS. That seems to me better than to have them all standing empty.

MRS. SOLNESS. That emptiness is dreadful; you're right there.

SOLNESS [*closes the portfolio, rises and approaches her*]. You'll find that we shall get on far better after this, Aline. Things will be more comfortable. Life will be easier—especially for *you*.

MRS. SOLNESS [*looks at him*]. After this?

SOLNESS. Yes, believe me, Aline——

MRS. SOLNESS. Do you mean—because *she* has come here?

SOLNESS [*checking himself*]. I mean, of course—when once we've moved into the new house.

MRS. SOLNESS [*takes her cloak*]. Ah, do you think so, Halvard? Will it be better then?

SOLNESS. I can't think otherwise. And surely you think so too?

MRS. SOLNESS. I think nothing at all about the new house.

SOLNESS [*cast down*]. It's hard for me to hear you say that; for you know it's mainly for your sake that I've built it.

[*He offers to help her on with her cloak.*]

MRS. SOLNESS [*evades him*]. The fact is, you do far too much for my sake.

SOLNESS [*with a certain vehemence*]. No, no, you really mustn't say that, Aline. I can't bear to hear you say such things.

MRS. SOLNESS. Very well, then I won't say it, Halvard.

SOLNESS. But I stick to what *I* said. You'll see that things'll be easier for you in the new place.

MRS. SOLNESS. Oh heavens—easier for me—!

SOLNESS [*eagerly*]. Yes, indeed they will! You may be quite sure of that! For you see—there'll be so very, very much there that'll remind you of your own home——

MRS. SOLNESS. The home that used to be father's and mother's— and that was burnt to the ground——

SOLNESS [*in a low voice*]. Yes, yes, my poor Aline. That was a terrible blow for you.

MRS. SOLNESS [*breaking out in lamentation*]. You may build as much as ever you like, Halvard—you can never build up again a real home for *me*!

SOLNESS [*crosses the room*]. Well, in Heaven's name, let us talk no more about it then.

MRS. SOLNESS. We're not in the habit of talking about it. For you always put the thought away from you——

SOLNESS [*stops suddenly and looks at her*]. Do I? And why should I do *that*? Put the thought away from me?

MRS. SOLNESS. Oh yes, Halvard, I understand very well. You're so anxious to spare me—and to find excuses for me too—as much as ever you can.

SOLNESS [*with astonishment in his eyes*]. You! Is it *you*—yourself, that you're talking about, Aline?

MRS. SOLNESS. Yes, who else should it be but myself?

SOLNESS [*involuntarily, to himself*]. *That* too!

MRS. SOLNESS. As for the old house, I wouldn't mind so much about that. When once misfortune was in the air—why——

SOLNESS. Ah, you're right there. Misfortune will have its way—as the saying goes.

MRS. SOLNESS. But it's what came of the fire—the dreadful thing that followed—! *That* is the thing! That, that, that!

SOLNESS [*vehemently*]. Don't think about *that,* Aline.

MRS. SOLNESS. Ah, that's exactly what I can't help thinking about. And now, at last, I must speak about it, too; for I don't seem able to bear it any longer. And then never to be able to forgive myself——

SOLNESS [*vehemently*]. Yourself?

MRS. SOLNESS. Yes, for I had duties on both sides—both towards you and towards the little ones. I ought to have hardened myself—not to have let the horror take such hold upon me, nor the grief for the burning for my home. [*Wrings her hands*] Oh, Halvard, if I'd only had the strength!

SOLNESS [*softly, much moved, comes closer*]. Aline—you must promise me never to think these thoughts any more. Promise me that, dear!

MRS. SOLNESS. Oh, promise, promise! One can promise anything.

SOLNESS [*clenches his hands and crosses the room*]. Oh, but this is hopeless, hopeless! Never a ray of sunlight! Not so much as a gleam of brightness to light up our home!

MRS. SOLNESS. This is no home, Halvard.

SOLNESS. Oh no, you may well say that. [*Gloomily*] And God knows whether you're not right in saying that it will be no better for us in the new house, either.

MRS. SOLNESS. It will never be any better. Just as empty—just as desolate—there as here.

SOLNESS [*vehemently*]. Why in all the world have we built it then? Can you tell me that?

MRS. SOLNESS. No; you must answer that question for yourself.

SOLNESS [*glances suspiciously at her*]. What do you mean by *that,* Aline?

MRS. SOLNESS. What do I mean?

SOLNESS. Yes, in the devil's name! You said it so strangely—as if you had some hidden meaning in it.

MRS. SOLNESS. No, indeed, I assure you——

SOLNESS [*comes closer*]. Oh, come now—I know what I know. I've both my eyes and my ears about me, Aline—you may depend upon that!

MRS. SOLNESS. Why, what are you talking about? What is it?

SOLNESS [*places himself in front of her*]. Do you mean to say you don't find a kind of lurking, hidden meaning in the most innocent word I happen to say?

MRS. SOLNESS. *I,* do say? I do that?

SOLNESS [*laughs*]. Ho-ho-ho! It's natural enough, Aline! When you've a sick man on your hands——

MRS. SOLNESS [*anxiously*]. Sick? Are you ill, Halvard?

SOLNESS [*violently*]. A half-mad man, then! A crazy man! Call me what you will.

MRS. SOLNESS [*feels gropingly for a chair and sits down*]. Halvard—for God's sake——

SOLNESS. But you're wrong, both you and the doctor. That's not what's the matter with me.

[*He walks up and down the room.* MRS. SOLNESS *follows him anxiously with her eyes. Finally he goes up to her.*]

SOLNESS [*calmly*]. In reality there's nothing whatever wrong with me.

MRS. SOLNESS. No, there isn't, is there? But then what is it that troubles you so?

SOLNESS. Why this, that I often feel ready to sink under this terrible burden of debt——

MRS. SOLNESS. Debt, do you say? But you owe no one anything, Halvard!

SOLNESS [*softly, with emotion*]. I owe a boundless debt to you—to you—to you, Aline.

MRS. SOLNESS [*rises slowly*]. What is behind all this? You may just as well tell me at once.

SOLNESS. But there *is* nothing behind it. I've never done you any wrong—not wittingly and wilfully, at any rate. And yet—and yet it seems as though a crushing debt rested upon me and weighed me down.

MRS. SOLNESS. A debt to me?

SOLNESS. Chiefly to you.

MRS. SOLNESS. Then you are—ill after all, Halvard.

SOLNESS [*gloomily*]. I suppose I must be—or not far from it. [*Looks towards the door to the right, which is opened at this moment*] Ah! now it grows lighter.

[HILDA WANGEL *comes in. She has made some alterations in her dress, and let down her skirt.*]

HILDA. Good-morning, Mr. Solness!

SOLNESS [*nods*]. Slept well?

HILDA. Quite deliciously! As if in a cradle. Oh—I lay and stretched myself like—like a princess!

SOLNESS [*smiles a little*]. You were thoroughly comfortable then?

HILDA. I should think so.

SOLNESS. And no doubt you dreamed, too.

HILDA. Yes, I did. But *that* was horrid.

SOLNESS. Indeed?

HILDA. Yes, for I dreamed I was falling over a frightfully high, sheer precipice. Do you never have that kind of dream?

SOLNESS. Oh yes—now and then——

HILDA. It's tremendously thrilling—when you fall and fall——

SOLNESS. It seems to make one's blood run cold.

HILDA. Do you draw your legs up under you while you're falling?

SOLNESS. Yes, as high as ever I can.

HILDA. So do I.

MRS. SOLNESS [*takes her parasol*]. I must go into town now, Halvard. [*To* HILDA] And I'll try to get one or two things that may be of use to you.

HILDA [*making a motion to throw her arms round her neck*]. Oh, you dear, sweet Mrs. Solness! You're really much too kind to me! Frightfully kind——

MRS. SOLNESS [*deprecatingly, freeing herself*]. Oh, far from it. It's only my duty, so I'm very glad to do it.

HILDA [*offended, pouts*]. But really, I think I'm quite fit to be seen in the streets—now that I've put my dress to rights. Or do you think I'm not?

MRS. SOLNESS. To tell you the truth, I think people would stare at you a little.

HILDA [*contemptuously*]. Pooh! Is that all? That only amuses me.

SOLNESS [*with suppressed ill-humor*]. Yes, but people might take it into their heads that *you* were mad too, you see.

HILDA. Mad? Are there so many mad people here in town, then?

SOLNESS [*points to his own forehead*]. Here you see *one* at all events.

HILDA. You—Mr. Solness!

MRS. SOLNESS. Oh, don't talk like that, my dear Halvard!

SOLNESS. Haven't you noticed that yet?

HILDA. No, I certainly haven't. [*Reflects and laughs a little*] And yet—perhaps in one single thing.

SOLNESS. Ah, do you hear *that* Aline?

MRS. SOLNESS. What is that one single thing, Miss Wangel?

HILDA. No, I won't say.

SOLNESS. Oh yes, do!

HILDA. No thanks—I'm not so mad as all that.

MRS. SOLNESS. When you and Miss Wangel are alone, I daresay she'll tell you, Halvard.

SOLNESS. Ah—you think she will?

MRS. SOLNESS. Oh yes, certainly. For you've known her so well in the past. Ever since she was a child—you tell me.

[*She goes out by the door on the left.*]

HILDA [*after a little while*]. Does your wife dislike me very much?

SOLNESS. Did you think you noticed anything of the kind?

HILDA. Didn't you notice it yourself?

SOLNESS [*evasively*]. Aline has become exceedingly shy with strangers of late years.

HILDA. Has she really?

SOLNESS. But if only you could get to know her thoroughly—Ah, she's so nice—and so kind—and so good at heart.

HILDA [*impatiently*]. But if she's all that—what made her say that about her duty?

SOLNESS. Her duty?

HILDA. She said that she would go out and buy something for me, because it was her *duty*. Oh I can't bear that ugly, horrid word!

SOLNESS. Why not?

HILDA. It sounds so cold, and sharp, and stinging. Duty—duty—duty. Don't *you* think so, too? Doesn't it seem to sting you?

SOLNESS. H'm—haven't thought much about it.

HILDA. Yes, it does. And if she's so nice—as you say she is—why should she talk in that way?

SOLNESS. But, good Lord, what would you have had her say, then?

HILDA. She might have said she would do it because she had taken a tremendous fancy to me. She might have said something like that—

something really warm and cordial, you understand.

SOLNESS [*looks at her*]. Is that how you'd like to have it?

HILDA. Yes, precisely.

[*She wanders about the room, stops at the bookcase and looks at the books.*]

HILDA. What a lot of books you have!

SOLNESS. Yes, I've got together a good many.

HILDA. Do you read them all, too?

SOLNESS. I used to try to. Do you read much?

HILDA. No, never! I've given it up. For it all seems so irrelevant.

SOLNESS. That's just my feeling.

[HILDA *wanders about a little, stops at the small table, opens the portfolio and turns over the contents.*]

HILDA. Are all these drawings yours?

SOLNESS. No, they're drawn by a young man whom I employ to help me.

HILDA. Some one you've taught?

SOLNESS. Oh yes, no doubt he's learnt something from me, too.

HILDA [*sits down*]. Then I suppose he's very clever. [*Looks at a drawing*] Isn't he?

SOLNESS. Oh, he's not bad. For *my* purpose——

HILDA. Oh yes—I'm sure he's frightfully clever.

SOLNESS. Do you think you can see that in the drawings?

HILDA. Pooh—these scrawlings! But if he's been learning from *you*——

SOLNESS. Oh, as far as that goes—there are plenty of people here that have learnt from *me*, and have come to little enough for all that.

HILDA [*looks at him and shakes her head*]. No, I can't for the life of me understand how you can be so stupid.

SOLNESS. Stupid? Do you think I'm so very stupid?

HILDA. Yes, I do indeed. If you're content to go about here teaching all these people——

SOLNESS [*with a slight start*]. Well, and why not?

HILDA [*rises, half-serious, half-laughing*]. No indeed, Mr. Solness! What can be the good of that? No one but yourself should be allowed to build. You should stand quite alone—do it all yourself. Now you know it.

SOLNESS [*involuntarily*]. Hilda——!

HILDA. Well!

SOLNESS. How in the world did that come into your head?

HILDA. Do you think I'm so very far wrong then?

SOLNESS. No, that's not what I mean. But now I'll tell you something.

HILDA. Well?

SOLNESS. I keep on—incessantly—in silence and alone—brooding on that very thought.

HILDA. Yes, that seems to me perfectly natural.

SOLNESS [*looks somewhat searchingly at her*]. Perhaps you've already noticed it?

HILDA. No, indeed I haven't.

SOLNESS. But just now—when you said you thought I was—off my balance? In one thing you said——

HILDA. Oh, I was thinking of something quite different.

SOLNESS. What was it?

HILDA. I'm not going to tell you.

SOLNESS [*crosses the room*]. Well, well—as you please. [*Stops at the bow-window*] Come here and I'll show you something.

HILDA [*approaching*]. What is it?

SOLNESS. Do you see—over there in the garden——?

HILDA. Yes?

SOLNESS [*points*]. Right above the great quarry——?

HILDA. That new house, you mean?

SOLNESS. The one that's being built, yes. Almost finished.

HILDA. It seems to have a very high tower.

SOLNESS. The scaffolding is still up.

HILDA. Is that your new house?

SOLNESS. Yes.

HILDA. The house you're soon going to move into?

SOLNESS. Yes.

HILDA [*looks at him*]. Are there nurseries in *that* house, too?

SOLNESS. Three, as there are here.

HILDA. And no child.

SOLNESS. And there never will be one.

HILDA [*with a half-smile*]. Well, isn't it just as I said——

SOLNESS. That——?

HILDA. That you *are* a little—a little mad after all.

SOLNESS. Was that what you were thinking of?

HILDA. Yes, of all the empty nurseries I slept in.

SOLNESS [*lowers his voice*]. We *have* had children—Aline and I.

HILDA [*looks eagerly at him*]. Have you——?

SOLNESS. Two little boys. They were of the same age.

HILDA. Twins, then.

SOLNESS. Yes, twins. It's eleven or twelve years ago now.

HILDA [*cautiously*]. And so both of them——? You have lost both the twins, then?

SOLNESS [*with quiet emotion*]. We only kept them about three weeks. Or scarcely so much. [*Bursts forth*] Oh, Hilda, I can't tell you what a good thing it is for me that you have come! For now at last I have some one I can talk to!

HILDA. Can't you talk to—to *her,* too?

SOLNESS. Not about this. Not as I want to talk and must talk. [*Gloomily*] And not about so many other things, too.

HILDA [*in a subdued voice*]. Was that all you meant when you said you needed me?

SOLNESS. That was mainly what I meant—at all events, yesterday. For to-day I'm not so sure. [*Breaking off*] Come here and let us sit down, Hilda. Sit there on the sofa—so that you can look into the garden. [HILDA *seats herself in the corner of the sofa.* SOLNESS *brings a chair closer.*] Would you like to hear about it?

HILDA. Yes, I shall love to sit and listen to you.

SOLNESS [*sits down*]. Then I'll tell you all about it.

HILDA. Now I can see both the garden and you, Mr. Solness. So now, tell away! Go on!

SOLNESS [*points towards the bow-window*]. Out there on the rising ground—where you see the new house——

HILDA. Yes?

SOLNESS. Aline and I lived there in the first years of our married life. There was an old house up there that had belonged to her mother; and we inherited it, and the whole of the great garden with it.

HILDA. Was there a tower on *that* house, too?

SOLNESS. No, nothing of the kind. From the outside it looked like a great, dark, ugly wooden box; but, all the same, it was snug and comfortable enough inside.

HILDA. Then did you pull down the ramshackle old place?

SOLNESS. No, it was burnt down.

HILDA. The whole of it?

SOLNESS. Yes.

HILDA. Was that a great misfortune for you?

SOLNESS. That depends on how you look at it. As a builder, the fire was the making of me——

HILDA. Well, but——?

SOLNESS. It was just after the birth of the two little boys.

HILDA. The poor little twins, yes.

SOLNESS. They came healthy and bonny into the world. And they were growing too—you could see the difference from day to day.

HILDA. Little children do grow quickly at first.

SOLNESS. It was the prettiest sight in the world to see Aline lying with the two of them in her arms. But then came the night of the fire——

HILDA [*excitedly*]. What happened? Do tell me! Was any one burnt?

SOLNESS. No, not that. Every one got safe and sound out of the house——

HILDA. Well, and what then?

SOLNESS. The fright had shaken Aline terribly. The alarm—the escape—the break-neck hurry—and then the ice-cold night air—for they had to be carried out just as they lay—both she and the little ones——

HILDA. Was it too much for them?

SOLNESS. Oh no, *they* stood it well enough. But Aline fell into a fever, and it affected her milk. She would insist on nursing them herself; because it was her duty, she said. And both our little boys, they—[*clenching his hands*]—they—oh!

HILDA. They didn't get over *that*?

SOLNESS. No, *that* they didn't get over. That was how we lost them.

HILDA. It must have been terribly hard for you.

SOLNESS. Hard enough for me; but ten times harder for Aline. [*Clenching his hands in suppressed fury*] Oh, that such things should be allowed to happen here on earth! [*Shortly and firmly*] From the day I lost them, I had no heart for building churches.

HILDA. Didn't you like building the church-tower in our town?

SOLNESS. I didn't like it. I know how free and happy I felt when that tower was finished.

HILDA. *I* know that, too.

SOLNESS. And now I shall never—never build anything of that sort again! Neither churches nor church-towers.

HILDA [*nods slowly*]. Nothing but houses for people to live in.

SOLNESS. Homes for human beings, Hilda.

HILDA. But homes with high towers and pinnacles upon them.

SOLNESS. If possible. [*Adopts a lighter tone*] Well, you see, as I said, that fire was the making of me—as a builder, I mean.

HILDA. Why don't you call yourself an architect, like the others?

SOLNESS. I haven't been systematically enough taught for that. Most of what I know, I've found out for myself.

HILDA. But you succeeded all the same.

SOLNESS. Yes, thanks to the fire. I laid out almost the whole of the garden in villa-lots; and *there* I was able to build entirely after my own heart. So I came to the front with a rush.

HILDA [*looks keenly at him*]. You must surely be a very happy man—situated as you are.

SOLNESS [*gloomily*]. Happy? Do *you* say that, too—like all the rest of them?

HILDA. Yes, I should say you must be. If you could only get the two little children out of your head——

SOLNESS [*slowly*]. The two little children—they're not so easy to forget, Hilda.

HILDA [*somewhat uncertainly*]. Do you still feel their loss so much —after all these years?

SOLNESS [*looks fixedly at her, without replying*]. A happy man, you said——

HILDA. Well now, *are* you not happy—in other respects?

SOLNESS [*continues to look at her*]. When I told you all this about the fire—h'm——

HILDA. Well?

SOLNESS. Was there not one special thought that you—that you seized upon?

HILDA [*reflects in vain*]. No. What thought should that be?

SOLNESS [*with subdued emphasis*]. It was simply and solely by that fire that I was enabled to build homes for human beings. Cosy, comfortable, bright homes, where father and mother and the whole troop of children can live in safety and gladness, feeling what a happy thing it is to be alive in the world—and most of all to belong to each other —in great things and in small.

HILDA [*ardently*]. Well, and isn't it a great happiness for you to be able to build such beautiful homes?

SOLNESS. The price, Hilda! The terrible price I had to pay for it!

HILDA. But can you *never* get over that?

SOLNESS. No. That I might build homes for others, I had to forego— to forego for all time—the home that might have been my own. I mean a home for a troop of children—and for father and mother, too.

HILDA [*cautiously*]. But need you have done that? For all time, you say?

SOLNESS [*nods slowly*]. *That* was the price of this happiness that people talk about. [*Breathes heavily*] This happiness—h'm—this happiness was not to be bought any cheaper, Hilda.

HILDA [*as before*]. But may it not come right even yet?

SOLNESS. Never in this world—never. That is another consequence of the fire—and of Aline's illness afterwards.

HILDA [*looks at him with an indefinable expression*]. And yet you build all these nurseries?

SOLNESS [*seriously*]. Have you never noticed, Hilda, how the impossible—how it seems to beckon and cry aloud to one?

HILDA [*reflecting*]. The impossible? [*With animation*] Yes, indeed! Is that how *you* feel too?

SOLNESS. Yes, I do.

HILDA. Then there must be—a little of the troll in you too?

SOLNESS. Why of the troll?

HILDA. What would *you* call it, then?

SOLNESS [*rises*]. Well, well, perhaps you're right. [*Vehemently*] But how can I help turning into a troll, when this is how it always goes with me in everything—in everything!

HILDA. How do you mean?

SOLNESS [*speaking low, with inward emotion*]. Mark what I say to you, Hilda. All that I have succeeded in doing, building, creating—all the beauty, security, cheerful comfort—ay, and magnificence too— [*clenches his hands*]—oh, isn't it terrible even to think of——!

HILDA. *What* is so terrible?

SOLNESS. That all this I have to make up for, to pay for—not in money, but in human happiness. And not with my own happiness only, but with other people's too. Yes, yes, do you see that, Hilda? That is the price which my position as an artist has cost me—and others. And every single day I have to look on while the price is paid for me anew. Over again, and over again—and over again forever.

HILDA [*rises and looks steadily at him*]. Now I can see you're thinking of—of *her*.

SOLNESS. Yes, mainly of Aline. For Aline—she, too, had her vocation in life, just as much as I had mine. [*His voice quivers.*] But her vocation has had to be stunted, and crushed, and shattered—in order that mine might force its way to—to a sort of great victory. For you must know that Aline—she, too, had a turn for building.

HILDA. She? For building?

SOLNESS [*shakes his head*]. Not houses, and towers, and spires—not such things as I work away at——

HILDA. Well, but *what*, then?

SOLNESS [*softly, with emotion*]. For building up the souls of little children, Hilda. For building up children's souls in perfect balance, and in noble and beautiful forms. For enabling them to soar up into erect and full-grown human souls. That was Aline's talent. And there it all lies now—unused and unusable forever—of no earthly service to any one—just like the ruins left by a fire.

HILDA. Yes, but even if this were so——

SOLNESS. It *is* so! It *is* so! I know it.

HILDA. Well, but in any case it's not *your* fault.

SOLNESS [*fixes his eyes on her, and nods slowly*]. Ah, *that* is the great, the terrible question. *That* is the doubt that's gnawing me—night and day.

HILDA. That?

SOLNESS. Yes. Suppose the fault *was* mine—in a certain sense.

HILDA. Your fault! the fire!

SOLNESS. All of it; the whole thing. And yet, perhaps—I mayn't have had anything to do with it.

HILDA [*looks at him with a troubled expression*]. Oh, Mr. Solness, if you can talk like that, I'm afraid you must be—ill, after all.

SOLNESS. H'm—I don't think I shall ever be of quite sound mind on that point.

[RAGNAR BROVIK *cautiously opens the little door in the left-hand corner.* HILDA *comes forward.*]

RAGNAR [*when he sees* HILDA]. Oh—I beg pardon, Mr. Solness—— [*He makes a movement to withdraw.*]

SOLNESS. No, no, don't go. Let's get it over.

RAGNAR. Oh, yes—if only we could.

SOLNESS. I hear your father is no better?

RAGNAR. Father is fast growing weaker—and therefore I beg and implore you to write a few kind words for me on one of the plans! Something for father to read before he——

SOLNESS [*vehemently*]. I won't hear anything more about those drawings of yours!

RAGNAR. Have you looked at them?

SOLNESS. Yes, I have.

RAGNAR. And they're good for nothing? And *I* am good for nothing, too?

SOLNESS [*evasively*]. Stay here with me, Ragnar. You shall have everything your own way. And then you can marry Kaia, and live at your ease—and—and happily too, who knows? Only don't think of building on your own account.

RAGNAR. Well, well, then I must go home and tell father what you say—I promised I would. *Is* this what I am to tell father—before he dies?

SOLNESS [*with a groan*]. Oh tell him—tell him what you will for me. Best to say nothing at all to him! [*With a sudden outburst*] I *cannot* do anything else, Ragnar!

RAGNAR. May I have the drawings to take with me?

SOLNESS. Yes, take them—take them by all means! They're lying there on the table.

RAGNAR [*goes to the table*]. Thanks.

HILDA [*puts her hand on the portfolio*]. No, no; leave them here.

SOLNESS. Why?

HILDA. Because I want to look at them too.

SOLNESS. But you *have* been——[*To* RAGNAR] Well, leave them here, then.

RAGNAR. Very well.

SOLNESS. And go home at once to your father.

RAGNAR. Yes, I suppose I must.

SOLNESS [*as if in desperation*]. Ragnar—you *must* not ask me to do what's beyond my power! Do you hear, Ragnar? You *must* not!

RAGNAR. No, no. I beg your pardon——

[*He bows, and goes out by the corner door.* HILDA *goes over and sits down on a chair near the mirror.*]

HILDA [*looks angrily at* SOLNESS]. That was a very ugly thing to do.

SOLNESS. Do *you* think so, too?

HILDA. Yes, it was horribly ugly—and hard and bad and cruel as well.

SOLNESS. Oh, you don't understand my position.

HILDA. All the same——. No, you oughtn't to be like that.

SOLNESS. You said yourself, only just now, that no one but *I* ought to be allowed to build.

HILDA. *I* may say such things—but *you* mayn't.

SOLNESS. I most of all, surely, who have paid so dear for my position.

HILDA. Oh, yes—with what you call domestic comfort—and that sort of thing.

SOLNESS. And with my peace of soul into the bargain.

HILDA [*rising*]. Peace of soul! [*With feeling*] Yes, yes, you're right in that! Poor Mr. Solness—you fancy that——

SOLNESS [*with a quiet, chuckling laugh*]. Just sit down again, Hilda, and I'll tell you something funny.

HILDA [*sits down; with intent interest*]. Well?

SOLNESS. It sounds such a ludicrous little thing; for, you see, the whole story turns upon nothing but a crack in a chimney.

HILDA. No more than that?

SOLNESS. No, not to begin with.

[*He moves a chair nearer to* HILDA *and sits down.*]

HILDA [*impatiently, taps on her knee*]. Well, now for the crack in the chimney!

SOLNESS. I had noticed the split in the flue long, long before the fire. Every time I went up into the attic, I looked to see if it was still there.

HILDA. And it was?

SOLNESS. Yes; for no one else knew about it.

HILDA. And you said nothing?

SOLNESS. Nothing.

HILDA. And didn't think of repairing the flue either.

SOLNESS. Oh yes, I thought about it—but never got any further. Every time I intended to set to work, it seemed just as if a hand held me back. Not to-day, I thought—to-morrow; and nothing ever came of it.

HILDA. But why did you keep putting it off like that?

SOLNESS. Because I was revolving something in my mind. [*Slowly, and in a low voice*] Through that little black crack in the chimney I might, perhaps, force my way upwards—as a builder.

HILDA [*looking straight in front of her*]. That must have been thrilling.

SOLNESS. Almost irresistible—quite irresistible. For at that time it appeared to me a perfectly simple and straightforward matter. I would have had it happen in the winter time—a little before midday. I was to be out driving Aline in the sleigh. The servants at home would have made a huge fire in the stove.

HILDA. For, of course, it was to be bitterly cold that day?

SOLNESS. Rather biting, yes—and they would want Aline to find it thoroughly snug and warm when she came home.

HILDA. I suppose she's very chilly by nature?

SOLNESS. She *is*. And as we drove home, we were to see the smoke.

HILDA. Only the smoke?

SOLNESS. The smoke first. But when we came up to the garden gate, the whole of the old timber-box was to be a rolling mass of flames.— That's how I wanted it to be, you see.

HILDA. Oh, why, *why* couldn't it have happened so!

SOLNESS. You may well say that, Hilda.

HILDA. Well, but now listen, Mr. Solness. Are you perfectly certain that the fire was caused by that little crack in the chimney?

SOLNESS. No, on the contrary—I'm perfectly certain that the crack in the chimney had nothing whatever to do with the fire.

HILDA. What!

SOLNESS. It has been clearly ascertained that the fire broke out in a clothes-cupboard—in a totally different part of the house.

HILDA. Then what's all this nonsense you're talking about the crack in the chimney?

SOLNESS. May I go on talking to you a little, Hilda?

HILDA. Yes, if you'll only talk sensibly,——

SOLNESS. I'll try to. [*He moves his chair nearer.*]

HILDA. Out with it, then, Mr. Solness.

SOLNESS [*confidentially*]. Don't you agree with me, Hilda, that there exist special, chosen people who have been endowed with the power and faculty of *desiring* a thing, *craving* for a thing, willing a thing—so persistently and so—so inexorably—that at last it *has* to happen? Don't you believe that?

HILDA [*with an indefinable expression in her eyes*]. If that is so, we shall see one of these days—whether *I* am one of the chosen.

SOLNESS. It's not one's self alone that can do such great things. Oh, no—the helpers and the servers—they must do their part too, if it's to be of any good. But they never come of themselves. One has to call upon them very persistently—inwardly, you understand.

HILDA. What are these helpers and servers?

SOLNESS. Oh, we can talk about that some other time. For the present, let us keep to this business of the fire.

HILDA. Don't you think the fire would have happened all the same— even if you hadn't wished for it?

SOLNESS. If the house had been old Knut Brovik's, it would never have burnt down so conveniently for *him*. I'm sure of that; for he doesn't know how to call for the helpers—no, nor for the servers, either. [*Rises in agitation*] So you see, Hilda—it's my fault, after all, that the lives of the two little boys had to be sacrificed. And do you think it isn't my fault, too, that Aline has never been the woman she should and might have been—and that she most longed to be?

HILDA. Yes, but if it's all the work of those helpers and servers—?

SOLNESS. *Who* called for the helpers and servers? It was *I*! And they came and obeyed my will. [*In increasing excitement*] That's what good people call having the luck on your side; but I must tell you what this sort of luck feels like! It feels like a great raw place here on my breast. And the helpers and servers keep on flaying pieces of skin off

other people in order to close my sore. But still the sore is not healed—
never, never! Oh, if you knew how it can sometimes gnaw and burn.

HILDA [*looks attentively at him*]. You *are* ill, Mr. Solness. Very ill,
I almost think.

SOLNESS. Say *mad;* for that's what you mean.

HILDA. No, I don't think there's much amiss with your intellect.

SOLNESS. With *what*, then? Out with it!

HILDA. I wonder whether you weren't sent into the world with a
sickly conscience.

SOLNESS. A sickly conscience? What devilry is that?

HILDA. I mean that your conscience is feeble—too delicately built,
as it were—hasn't strength to take a grip of things—to lift and bear
what's heavy.

SOLNESS [*growls*]. H'm! May I ask, then, what sort of a conscience
one ought to have?

HILDA. I should like *your* conscience to be thoroughly robust.

SOLNESS. Indeed? Robust, eh? Is your own conscience robust?

HILDA. Yes, I think it is. I've never noticed that it wasn't.

SOLNESS. It hasn't been put very severely to the test, I should think.

HILDA [*with a quivering of the lips*]. Oh, it wasn't such a simple
matter to leave father—I'm so awfully fond of him.

SOLNESS. Dear me! for a month or two——

HILDA. I don't think I shall ever go home again.

SOLNESS. Never? Then why did you leave him?

HILDA [*half-seriously, half-banteringly*]. Have you forgotten again
that the ten years are up?

SOLNESS. Oh, nonsense. Was anything wrong at home? Eh?

HILDA [*quite seriously*]. It *was* this something within me that drove
and spurred me here—and allured and attracted me, too.

SOLNESS [*eagerly*]. There we have it! There we have it, Hilda!
There's a troll in you too, as in me. For it's the troll in one, you see—
it's *that* that calls to the powers outside us. And then you *must* give
in—whether you will or no.

HILDA. I almost think you're right, Mr. Solness.

SOLNESS [*walks about the room*]. Oh, there are devils innumerable
abroad in the world, Hilda, that one never *sees!*

HILDA. Devils, too?

SOLNESS [*stops*]. Good devils and bad devils; light-haired devils and
black-haired devils. If only you could always tell whether it's the light
or the dark ones that have got hold of you! [*Paces about*] Ho, ho!
Then it would be simple enough!

HILDA [*follows him with her eyes*]. Or if one had a really vigorous, radiantly healthy conscience—so that one *dared* to do what one *would*.

SOLNESS [*stops beside the console table*]. I believe, now, that most people are just as puny creatures as I am in this respect.

HILDA. I shouldn't wonder.

SOLNESS [*leaning against the table*]. In the sagas[1]——Have you read any of the old sagas?

HILDA. Oh yes! When I used to read books, I——

SOLNESS. In the sagas you read about vikings, who sailed to foreign lands, and plundered and burned and killed men——

HILDA. And carried off women——

SOLNESS. ——and kept them in captivity——

HILDA. ——took them home in their ships——

SOLNESS. ——and behaved to them like—like the very worst of trolls.

HILDA [*looks straight before her with a half-veiled look*]. I think *that* must have been thrilling.

SOLNESS [*with a short, deep laugh*]. To carry off women, eh?

HILDA. To *be* carried off.

SOLNESS [*looks at her a moment*]. Oh, indeed.

HILDA [*as if breaking the thread of conversation*]. But what made you speak of these vikings, Mr. Solness?

SOLNESS. Because *those* fellows must have had robust consciences, if you like! When they got home again they could eat and drink, and be as happy as children. And the women, too! They often wouldn't leave them on any account. Can you understand that, Hilda?

HILDA. Those women I can understand exceedingly well.

SOLNESS. Oho! Perhaps you could do the same yourself?

HILDA. Why not?

SOLNESS. Live—of your own free will—with a ruffian like that?

HILDA. If it was a ruffian I had come to love——

SOLNESS. *Could* you come to love a man like that?

HILDA. Good heavens, you know very well one can't choose whom one's going to love.

SOLNESS [*looks meditatively at her*]. Oh no, I suppose it's the troll within one that's responsible for that.

HILDA [*half laughing*]. And all those blessed devils, that *you* know so well—both the light-haired and the dark-haired ones.

SOLNESS [*quietly and warmly*]. Then I hope with all my heart that

---

[1] *saga, a Viking hero-tale.*

the devils will choose carefully for you, Hilda.

HILDA. For me they *have* chosen already—once and for all.

SOLNESS [*looks earnestly at her*]. Hilda, you are like a wild bird of the woods.

HILDA. Far from it. I don't hide myself away under the bushes.

SOLNESS. No, no. There's rather something of the bird of prey in you.

HILDA. That's nearer it—perhaps. [*Very vehemently*] And why not a bird of prey? Why shouldn't *I* go a-hunting—I, as well as the rest? Carry off the prey I want—if I can only get my claws into it, and have my own way with it.

SOLNESS. Hilda,—do you know what you are?

HILDA. Yes, I suppose I'm a strange sort of bird.

SOLNESS. No. You are like a dawning day. When I look at you, I seem to be looking towards the sunrise.

HILDA. Tell me, Mr. Solness—are you certain that you've never called me to you?—Inwardly, you know?

SOLNESS [*softly and slowly*]. I almost think I must have.

HILDA. What did you want with me?

SOLNESS. You are the younger generation, Hilda.

HILDA [*smiles*]. That younger generation that you're so afraid of.

SOLNESS [*nods slowly*]. And which, in my heart, I yearn towards so deeply.

[HILDA *rises, goes to the little table, and fetches* RAGNAR BROVIK's *portfolio.*]

HILDA [*holds out the portfolio to him*]. We were talking of these drawings——

SOLNESS [*shortly, waving them away*]. Put those things away! I've seen enough of them.

HILDA. Yes, but you have to write your approval on them.

SOLNESS. Write my approval on them? Never!

HILDA. But the poor old man is lying at death's door! Can't you give him and his son this pleasure before they're parted? And perhaps he might get the commission to carry them out, too.

SOLNESS. Yes, that's just what he would get. He's made sure of that —has my fine gentleman!

HILDA. Then good heavens—if that's so—can't you tell the least little bit of a lie for once?

SOLNESS. A lie? [*Raging*] Hilda—take those devil's drawings out of my sight!

HILDA [*draws the portfolio a little nearer to herself*]. Well, well,

well—don't bite me.—You talk of trolls—but I think you go on like a troll yourself. [*Looks round*] Where do you keep your pen and ink?

SOLNESS. There's nothing of the sort in here.

HILDA [*goes towards the door*]. But in the office where that young lady is——

SOLNESS. Stay where you are, Hilda!—I ought to tell a lie, you say. Oh yes, for the sake of his old father I might well do that—for in my time I've crushed him, trodden him under foot——

HILDA. Him, too?

SOLNESS. I needed room for myself. But this Ragnar—he must on no account be allowed to come to the front.

HILDA. Poor fellow, there's surely no fear of that. If he has nothing in him——

SOLNESS [*comes closer, looks at her, and whispers*]. If Ragnar Brovik comes to the front he will strike *me* to the earth. Crush me—as I crushed his father.

HILDA. Crush you? Has he the ability for that?

SOLNESS. Yes, you may depend upon it *he* has the ability! He is the younger generation that stands ready to knock at my door—to make an end of Halvard Solness.

HILDA [*looks at him with quiet reproach*]. And yet you would bar him out. Fie, Mr. Solness!

SOLNESS. The fight I have been fighting has cost heart's blood enough.—And I'm afraid, too, that the helpers and servers won't obey me any longer.

HILDA. Then you must go ahead without them. There's nothing else for it.

SOLNESS. It's hopeless, Hilda. The luck is bound to turn. A little sooner or a little later. Retribution is inexorable.

HILDA [*in distress putting her hands over her ears*]. Don't talk like that! Do you want to kill me? To take from me what is more than my life?

SOLNESS. And what is that?

HILDA. The longing to see you great. To see you, with a wreath in your hand, high, high up upon a church-tower. [*Calm again*] Come, out with your pencil now. You must have a pencil about you!

SOLNESS [*takes out his pocket-book*]. I have one here.

HILDA [*puts the portfolio on the sofa-table*]. Very well. Now let us two sit down here, Mr. Solness.

[SOLNESS *seats himself at the table.*]

HILDA [*behind him leaning over the back of the chair*]. And now we'll write on the drawings. We must write very, very nicely and cordially—for this horrid Ruar—or whatever his name is.

SOLNESS [*writes a few words, turns his head and looks at her*]. Tell me one thing, Hilda.

HILDA. Yes?

SOLNESS. If you've been waiting for me all these ten years——

HILDA. What then?

SOLNESS. Why have you never written to me? Then I could have answered you.

HILDA [*hastily*]. No, no, no! That was just what I didn't want.

SOLNESS. Why not?

HILDA. I was afraid the whole thing might fall to pieces.—But we were going to write on the drawings, Mr. Solness.

SOLNESS. So we were.

HILDA [*bends forward and looks over his shoulder while he writes*]. Mind now! kindly and cordially! Oh how I hate—how I hate this Ruald——

SOLNESS [*writing*]. Have you never really cared for anyone, Hilda?

HILDA [*harshly*]. What do you say?

SOLNESS. Have you never cared for any one?

HILDA. For any one else, I suppose you mean?

SOLNESS [*looks up at her*]. For any one else, yes. Have you never? In all these ten years? Never?

HILDA. Oh yes, now and then. When I was perfectly furious with you for not coming.

SOLNESS. Then you did take an interest in other people, too?

HILDA. A little bit—for a week or so. Good heavens, Mr. Solness, you surely know how such things come about.

SOLNESS. Hilda—what is it you've come for?

HILDA. Don't waste time in talking. The poor old man might go and die in the meantime.

SOLNESS. Answer me, Hilda. What do you want of me?

HILDA. I want my kingdom.

SOLNESS. H'm——

[*He gives a rapid glance towards the door on the left, and then goes on writing on the drawings. At the same moment* MRS. SOLNESS *enters; she has some packages in her hand.*]

MRS. SOLNESS. Here are a few things I've got for you, Miss Wangel. The large parcels will be sent later on.

HILDA. Oh, how very, very kind of you!

MRS. SOLNESS. Only my simple duty. Nothing more than that.

SOLNESS [*reading over what he has written*]. Aline!

MRS. SOLNESS. Yes?

SOLNESS. Did you notice whether the—the book-keeper was out there?

MRS. SOLNESS. Yes, of course, *she* was there.

SOLNESS [*puts the drawings in the portfolio*]. H'm——

MRS. SOLNESS. She was standing at the desk, as she always is—when *I* go through the room.

SOLNESS [*rises*]. Then I'll give this to her, and tell her that——

HILDA [*takes the portfolio from him*]. Oh, no, let me have the pleasure of doing that! [*Goes to the door, but turns*] What's her name?

SOLNESS. Her name is Miss Fosli.

HILDA. Pooh, that sounds so cold. Her Christian name, I mean?

SOLNESS. Kaia—I believe.

HILDA [*opens the door and calls out*]. Kaia, come in here! Make haste! Mr. Solness wants to speak to you.

[KAIA FOSLI *appears at the door.*]

KAIA [*looking at him in alarm*]. Here I am.

HILDA [*handing her the portfolio*]. See here, Kaia? You can take these home; Mr. Solness has written on them now.

KAIA. Oh, at last!

SOLNESS. Give them to the old man as soon as you can.

KAIA. I will go straight home with them.

SOLNESS. Yes, do. Now Ragnar will have a chance of building for himself.

KAIA. Oh, may he come and thank you for all——

SOLNESS [*harshly*]. I won't have any thanks. Tell him *that* from me.

KAIA. Yes, I will——

SOLNESS. And tell him at the same time that henceforward I don't require his services—nor yours either.

KAIA [*softly and quiveringly*]. Not mine either?

SOLNESS. You will have other things to think of now, and to attend to; and that's a very good thing for you. Well, go home with the drawings now, Miss Fosli. Quickly! Do you hear?

KAIA [*as before*]. Yes, Mr. Solness. [*She goes out.*]

MRS. SOLNESS. Heavens! what deceitful eyes she has.

SOLNESS. She? That poor little creature?

MRS. SOLNESS. Oh—I can see what I can see, Halvard.——Are you really dismissing them?

SOLNESS. Yes.

MRS. SOLNESS. Her as well?

SOLNESS. Wasn't that what you wished?

MRS. SOLNESS. But how can you get on without *her*——? Oh well, no doubt you have some one else in reserve, Halvard.

HILDA [*playfully*]. Well, *I* for one am not the person to stand at that desk.

SOLNESS. Never mind, never mind—it'll be all right, Aline. Now all you have to do is to think about moving into our new home—as quickly as you can. This evening we'll hang up the wreath—[*turns to* HILDA]—right on the very pinnacle of the tower. What do you say to that, Miss Hilda?

HILDA [*looks at him with sparkling eyes*]. It'll be splendid to see you so high up once more.

SOLNESS. Me!

MRS. SOLNESS. For Heaven's sake, Miss Wangel, don't imagine such a thing! My husband!—when he always gets so dizzy!

HILDA. *He* get *dizzy!* No, I know quite well he doesn't.

MRS. SOLNESS. Oh, yes, indeed he does.

HILDA. But I've seen him with my own eyes right up at the top of a high church-tower.

MRS. SOLNESS. Yes, I hear people talk of that; but it's utterly impossible——

SOLNESS [*vehemently*]. Impossible—impossible, yes! But there I stood all the same!

MRS. SOLNESS. Oh, how can you say so, Halvard? Why, you can't even bear to go out on the second-story balcony here. You've always been like that.

SOLNESS. You may perhaps see something different this evening.

MRS. SOLNESS [*in alarm*]. No, no, no! Please God, I shall never see that! I'll write at once to the doctor—and I'm sure he won't let you do it.

SOLNESS. Why, Aline——!

MRS. SOLNESS. Oh, you know you're ill, Halvard. This *proves* it! Oh God—Oh God!

[*She goes hastily out to the right.*]

HILDA [*looks intently at him*]. Is it so, or is it not?

SOLNESS. That I turn dizzy?

HILDA. That *my* master builder *dares* not—*cannot*—climb as high as he builds?

SOLNESS. Is that the way you look at it?

HILDA. Yes.

SOLNESS. I believe there's scarcely a corner in me safe fr

HILDA [*looks towards the bow-window*]. Up there, th
there——

SOLNESS [*approaches her*]. You might have the topmc
the tower, Hilda—there you might live like a princess.

HILDA [*indefinably, between earnest and jest*]. Yes, that's what **you**
promised me.

SOLNESS. *Did* I really?

HILDA. Fie, Mr. Solness! You said, I should be a princess, and that
you would give me a kingdom. And then you went and——Well!

SOLNESS [*cautiously*]. Are you quite certain that this is not a dream
—a fancy, that has fixed itself in your mind?

HILDA [*sharply*]. Do you mean that you didn't do it?

SOLNESS. I scarcely know myself. [*More softly*] But now I know *so
much* for certain, that I——

HILDA. That you——? Say it at once!

SOLNESS. ——that I *ought* to have done it.

HILDA [*in a bold outburst*]. Don't tell me *you* can ever be dizzy!

SOLNESS. This evening, then, we'll hang up the wreath—Princess
Hilda.

HILDA [*with a bitter curve of the lips*]. Over your new home, yes.

SOLNESS. Over the new house, which will never be a *home* for *me*.
[*He goes out through the garden door.*]

HILDA [*looks straight in front of her with a far-away expression, and
whispers to herself. The only words audible are*]——frightfully
thrilling——

act 3

A large, broad veranda attached to SOLNESS's *dwelling-house.
Part of the house, with outer door leading to the veranda,
is seen to the left. A railing along the veranda to the right.
At the back, from the end of the veranda, a flight of steps
leads down to the garden below. Tall old trees in the garden
spread their branches over the veranda and towards the
house. Far to the right, in among the trees, a glimpse is
caught of the lower part of the new villa, with scaffolding
round so much as is seen of the tower. In the background
the garden is bounded by an old wooden fence. Outside the
fence, a street with low, tumble-down cottages.*

   Evening sky with sun-lit clouds.

On the veranda a garden bench stands along the wall of the house, and in front of the bench a long table. On the other side of the table, an arm-chair and some stools. All the furniture is of wicker-work.

MRS. SOLNESS, wrapped in a large white crape shawl, sits resting in the arm-chair and gazes over to the right. Shortly after, HILDA WANGEL comes up the flight of steps from the garden. She is dressed as in the last act and wears her hat. She has in her bodice a little nosegay of small common flowers.

MRS. SOLNESS [*turning her head a little*]. Have you been round the garden, Miss Wangel?

HILDA. Yes, I've been taking a look at it.

MRS. SOLNESS. And found some flowers too, I see.

HILDA. Yes, indeed. There are such heaps of them in among the bushes.

MRS. SOLNESS. Are there really? Still? You see I scarcely ever go there.

HILDA [*closer*]. What! Don't you take a run down into the garden every day, then?

MRS. SOLNESS [*with a faint smile*]. I don't "run" anywhere, nowadays.

HILDA. Well, but don't you go down now and then, to look at all the lovely things there?

MRS. SOLNESS. It has all become so strange to me. I'm almost afraid to see it again.

HILDA. Your own garden!

MRS. SOLNESS. I don't feel that it is *mine* any longer.

HILDA. What do you mean——?

MRS. SOLNESS. No, no, it *is* not—not as it was in my mother's and father's time. They have taken away so much—so much of the garden, Miss Wangel. Fancy—they've parcelled it out—and built houses for strangers—people that I don't know. And *they* can sit and look in upon me from their windows.

HILDA [*with a bright expression*]. Mrs. Solness?

MRS. SOLNESS. Yes?

HILDA. May I stay here with you a little?

MRS. SOLNESS. Yes, by all means, if you care to.

[HILDA *moves a stool close to the arm-chair and sits down.*]

HILDA. Ah—one can sit here and sun oneself like a cat.

MRS. SOLNESS [*lays her hand softly on* HILDA's *neck*]. It's nice of you to be willing to sit with *me*. I thought you wanted to go in to my husband.

HILDA. What should I want with him?

MRS. SOLNESS. To help him, I thought.

HILDA. No, thanks. And besides, he's not in. He's over there with his workmen. But he looked so fierce that I didn't dare to talk to him.

MRS. SOLNESS. He's so kind and gentle in reality.

HILDA. *He!*

MRS. SOLNESS. You don't really know him yet, Miss Wangel.

HILDA [*looks affectionately at her*]. Are you pleased at the thought of moving over to the new house?

MRS. SOLNESS. I *ought* to be pleased; for it's what Halvard wants——

HILDA. Oh, not just on that account, surely.

MRS. SOLNESS. Yes, yes, Miss Wangel; for it's simply my duty to submit myself to *him*. But very often it's dreadfully difficult to force one's mind to obedience.

HILDA. Yes, *that* must be difficult indeed.

MRS. SOLNESS. I can tell you it is—when one has so many faults as I have——

HILDA. When one has gone through so much as *you* have——

MRS. SOLNESS. How do you know about that?

HILDA. Your husband told me.

MRS. SOLNESS. To me he very seldom mentions these things.—Yes, I can tell you I've gone through more than enough trouble in my life, Miss Wangel.

HILDA [*looks sympathetically at her and nods slowly*]. Poor Mrs. Solness. First of all there was the fire——

MRS. SOLNESS [*with a sigh*]. Yes, everything that was *mine* was burnt.

HILDA. And then came what was worse.

MRS. SOLNESS [*looking inquiringly at her*]. Worse?

HILDA. The worst of all.

MRS. SOLNESS. What do you mean?

HILDA [*softly*]. You lost the two little boys.

MRS. SOLNESS. Oh yes, the boys. But you see, *that* was a thing apart. That was a dispensation of Providence; and in such things one can only bow in submission—yes, and be thankful, too.

HILDA. Then are you so?

MRS. SOLNESS. Not always, I'm sorry to say. I know well enough that it's my duty—but all the same I *cannot.*

HILDA. No, no, I think that's only natural.

MRS. SOLNESS. And often and often I have to remind myself that it was a righteous punishment for me—

HILDA. Why?

MRS. SOLNESS. Because I hadn't fortitude enough in misfortune.

HILDA. But I don't see that——

MRS. SOLNESS. Oh, no, no, Miss Wangel—don't talk to me any more about the two little boys. We ought to feel nothing but joy in thinking of *them;* for they are so happy—so happy now. No, it's the *small* losses in life that cut one to the heart—the loss of all that other people look upon as almost nothing.

HILDA [*lays her arms on* MRS. SOLNESS' *knees and looks at her affectionately*]. Dear Mrs. Solness—tell me what things you mean!

MRS. SOLNESS. As I say, only little things. All the old portraits were burnt on the walls. And all the old silk dresses were burnt, that had belonged to the family for generations and generations. And all mother's and grandmother's lace—that was burnt too. And only think —the jewels too! [*Sadly*] And then all the dolls.

HILDA. The dolls?

MRS. SOLNESS [*choking with tears*]. I had nine lovely dolls.

HILDA. And *they* were burnt too?

MRS. SOLNESS. All of them. Oh, it was hard—so hard for me.

HILDA. Had you put by all these dolls, then? Ever since you were little?

MRS. SOLNESS. I hadn't put them by. The dolls and I had gone on living together.

HILDA. After you were grown up?

MRS. SOLNESS. Yes, long after that.

HILDA. After you were married too?

MRS. SOLNESS. Oh yes, indeed. So long as he didn't see it.—But they were all burnt up, poor things. No one thought of saving them. Oh, it's so miserable to think of. You mustn't laugh at me, Miss Wangel.

HILDA. I'm not laughing in the least.

MRS. SOLNESS. For you see, in a certain sense there was life in them, too. I carried them under my heart—like little unborn children.

[DR. HERDAL, *with his hat in his hand, comes out through the door and observes* MRS. SOLNESS *and* HILDA.]

DR. HERDAL. Well, Mrs. Solness, so you're sitting out here catching cold?

MRS. SOLNESS. I find it so pleasant and warm here to-day.

DR. HERDAL. Yes, yes. But is there anything going on here? I got a note from you.

MRS. SOLNESS [*rises*]. Yes, there's something I must talk to you about.

DR. HERDAL. Very well; then perhaps we'd better go in. [*To* HILDA] Still in your mountaineering dress, Miss Wangel?

HILDA [*gayly, rising*]. Yes—in full uniform! But today I'm not going climbing and breaking my neck. We two will stop quietly below and look on, doctor.

DR. HERDAL. What are we to look on at?

MRS. SOLNESS [*softly, in alarm, to* HILDA]. Hush, hush—for God's sake! He's coming! Try to get that idea out of his head. And let us be friends, Miss Wangel. Don't you think we can?

HILDA [*throws her arms impetuously round* MRS. SOLNESS' *neck*]. O, if we only could!

MRS. SOLNESS [*gently disengages herself*]. There, there, there! There he comes, doctor. Let me have a word with you.

DR. HERDAL. Is it about *him*?

MRS. SOLNESS. Yes, to be sure it's about him. Do come in.

[*She and the doctor enter the house. Next moment* SOLNESS *comes up from the garden by the flight of steps. A serious look comes over* HILDA's *face.*]

SOLNESS [*glances at the house-door, which is closed cautiously from within*]. Have you noticed, Hilda, that as soon as I come, she goes?

HILDA. I've noticed that as soon as you come, you make her go.

SOLNESS. Perhaps so. But I cannot help it. [*Looks observantly at her*] Are you cold, Hilda? I think you look so.

HILDA. I've just come up out of a tomb.

SOLNESS. What do you mean by *that*?

HILDA. That I've got chilled through and through, Mr. Solness.

SOLNESS [*slowly*]. I believe I understand——

HILDA. What brings you up here just now?

SOLNESS. I caught sight of you from over there.

HILDA. But then you must have seen her too?

SOLNESS. I knew she would go at once if I came.

HILDA. Is it very painful for you that she should avoid you in this way?

SOLNESS. In one sense, it's a relief as well.

HILDA. Not to have her before your eyes?

SOLNESS. Yes.

HILDA. Not to be always seeing how heavily the loss of the little boys weighs upon her?

SOLNESS. Yes. Chiefly that.

[HILDA *drifts across the veranda with her hands behind her back, stops at the railing and looks out over the garden.*]

SOLNESS [*after a short pause*]. Did you have a long talk with her?

[HILDA *stands motionless and does not answer.*]

SOLNESS. Had you a long talk, I asked?

[HILDA *is silent as before.*]

SOLNESS. What was she talking about, Hilda?

[HILDA *continues silent.*]

SOLNESS. Poor Aline! I suppose it was about the little boys.

HILDA [*A nervous shudder runs through her; then she nods hurriedly once or twice*].

SOLNESS. She will never get over it—never in this world. [*Approaches her*] Now you're standing there again like a statue; just as you stood last night.

HILDA [*turns and looks at him with great serious eyes*]. I am going away.

SOLNESS [*sharply*]. Going away!

HILDA. Yes.

SOLNESS. But I won't allow you to.

HILDA. What am I to do *here* now?

SOLNESS. Simply to *be* here, Hilda!

HILDA [*measures him with a look*]. Oh, thank you. You know it wouldn't end there.

SOLNESS [*without consideration*]. So much the better.

HILDA [*vehemently*]. I *can't* do any harm to one I *know!* I can't take away anything that belongs to her.

SOLNESS. Who wants you to do that?

HILDA [*continuing*]. A stranger, yes! for that's quite a different thing. A person I've never set eyes on. But one that I've come into close contact with——! No! Oh no! Ugh!

SOLNESS. Yes, but I never proposed you should.

HILDA. Oh, Mr. Solness, you know quite well what the end of it would be. And that's why I'm going away.

SOLNESS. And what's to become of me when you're gone? What shall I have to live for *then?*—After that?

HILDA [*with the indefinable look in her eyes*]. It's surely not so hard for *you.* You have your duties to her. Live for those duties.

SOLNESS. Too late. These powers—these—these——

HILDA. ——devils——

SOLNESS. Yes, these devils! And the troll within me as well—they have drawn all the life-blood out of her. [*Laughs in desperation*] They did it for my *happiness*. Yes, yes! [*Sadly*] And now she's dead—for my sake. And I am chained alive to a dead woman [*In wild anguish*] I—I who *cannot* live without joy in life!

[HILDA *walks round the table and seats herself on the bench with her elbows on the table, and her head supported by her hands.*]

HILDA [*sits and looks at him awhile*]. What will you build next?

SOLNESS [*shakes his head*]. I don't believe I shall build much more.

HILDA. Not those cosy, happy homes for mother and father, and for the troop of children?

SOLNESS. I wonder whether there will be any use for such homes in the times that are coming.

HILDA. Poor Mr. Solness! And you have gone all these ten years—and staked your whole life—on that alone.

SOLNESS. Yes, you may well say so, Hilda.

HILDA [*with an outburst*]. Oh, it all seems to me so foolish—so foolish!

SOLNESS. All what?

HILDA. Not to be able to grasp at your own happiness—at your own life! Merely because some one you know happens to stand in the way!

SOLNESS. One whom you have no right to set aside.

HILDA. I wonder whether one really *hasn't* the right? And yet, and yet——. Oh! if one could only sleep the whole thing away!

[*She lays her arms flat down on the table, rests the left side of her head on her hand and shuts her eyes.*]

SOLNESS [*turns the arm-chair and sits down at the table*]. Had *you* a cosy, happy home—up with your father, Hilda?

HILDA [*without stirring, answers as if half asleep*]. I had only a cage.

SOLNESS. And you're determined not to return to it?

HILDA [*as before*]. The wild bird never wants to go into the cage.

SOLNESS. Rather range through the free air—

HILDA [*still as before*]. The bird of prey loves to range—

SOLNESS [*lets his eyes rest on her*]. If only one had the viking-spirit in life——

HILDA [*in her usual voice; opens her eyes but does not move*]. And the other thing? Say what *that* was!

SOLNESS. A robust conscience.

[HILDA *sits upon the bench with animation. Her eyes have once more the sparkling expression of gladness.*]

HILDA [*nods to him*]. I know what you're going to build next!

SOLNESS. Then you know more than I do, Hilda.

HILDA. Yes, builders are such stupid people.

SOLNESS. What is it to be then?

HILDA [*nods again*]. The castle.

SOLNESS. What castle?

HILDA. *My* castle, of course.

SOLNESS. Do you want a castle now?

HILDA. Don't you owe me a kingdom, I'd like to know?

SOLNESS. You say I do.

HILDA. Well—you admit you owe me this kingdom. And you can't have a kingdom without a royal castle, I should think!

SOLNESS [*more and more animated*]. Yes, they usually go together.

HILDA. Good! Then build it for me this moment!

SOLNESS [*laughing*]. Must you have that on the instant, too?

HILDA. Yes, to be sure! For the ten years are up now, and I'm not going to wait any longer. So—out with the castle, Mr. Solness!

SOLNESS. It's no light matter to owe you anything, Hilda.

HILDA. You should have thought of that before. It's too late now. So—[*tapping the table*]—the castle on the table! It's *my* castle. I will have it *at once!*

SOLNESS [*more seriously, leans over towards her, with his arms on the table*]. What sort of castle have you imagined, Hilda?

[*Her expression becomes more and more veiled. She seems gazing inwards at herself.*]

HILDA [*slowly*]. My castle shall stand on a height—on a very great height—with a clear outlook on all sides, so that I can see far—far around.

SOLNESS. And no doubt it's to have a high tower?

HILDA. A tremendously high tower. And at the very top of the tower there shall be a balcony. And I will stand out upon it——

SOLNESS [*involuntarily clutches at his forehead*]. How can you like to stand at such a dizzy height——?

HILDA. Yes, I will! Right up there will I stand and look down on the other people—on those that are building churches, and homes for mother and father and the troop of children. And *you* may come up and look on at it, too.

SOLNESS [*in a low tone*]. Is the builder to be allowed to come up beside the princess?

HILDA. If the builder *will*.

SOLNESS [*more softly*]. Then I think the builder will come.

HILDA [*nods*]. The builder—he'll come.

SOLNESS. But he'll never be able to build any more. Poor builder!

HILDA [*animated*]. Oh yes, he will! We two will set to work together. And then we'll build the loveliest—the very loveliest—thing in all the world.

SOLNESS [*intently*]. Hilda, tell me what that is!

HILDA [*looks smilingly at him, shakes her head a little, pouts, and speaks as if to a child*]. Builders—they are such very—very stupid people.

SOLNESS. Yes, no doubt they're stupid. But now tell me what it is—the loveliest thing in the world—that we two are to build together?

HILDA [*is silent a little while, then says with an indefinable expression in her eyes*]. Castles in the air.

SOLNESS. Castles in the air?

HILDA [*nods*]. Castles in the air, yes! Do you know what sort of thing a castle in the air is?

SOLNESS. It's the loveliest thing in the world, you say.

HILDA [*rises with vehemence, and makes a gesture of repulsion with her hand*]. Yes, to be sure it is! Castles in the air—they're so easy to take refuge in. And so easy to build, too—[*looks scornfully at him*]—especially for the builders who have a—a dizzy conscience.

SOLNESS [*rises*]. After this day we two will build together, Hilda.

HILDA [*with a half-dubious smile*]. A *real* castle in the air?

SOLNESS. Yes. One with a firm foundation under it.

[RAGNAR BROVIK *comes out from the house. He is carrying a large, green wreath with flowers and silken ribbons.*]

HILDA [*with an outburst of pleasure*]. The wreath! Oh, that'll be glorious!

SOLNESS [*in surprise*]. Have *you* brought the wreath, Ragnar?

RAGNAR. I promised the foreman I would.

SOLNESS [*relieved*]. Ah, then I suppose your father's better?

RAGNAR. No.

SOLNESS. Wasn't he cheered by what I wrote?

RAGNAR. It came too late.

SOLNESS. Too late!

RAGNAR. When she came with it he was unconscious. He had had a stroke.

SOLNESS. Why, then, you must go home to him! You must attend to your father!

RAGNAR. He doesn't need me any more.

SOLNESS. But surely you ought to be with him.

RAGNAR. *She* is sitting by his bed.

SOLNESS [*rather uncertainly*]. Kaia?

RAGNAR [*looking darkly at him*]. Yes—Kaia.

SOLNESS. Go home, Ragnar—both to him and to her. Give *me* the wreath.

RAGNAR [*suppresses a mocking smile*]. You don't mean that you yourself——

SOLNESS. I will take it down to them myself. [*Takes the wreath from him*] And now, you go home; we don't require you to-day.

RAGNAR. I know you don't require me any more; but today I shall stop.

SOLNESS. Well, stop then, since you're bent upon it.

HILDA [*at the railing*]. Mr. Solness, I will stand here and look on at you.

SOLNESS. At me!

HILDA. It will be fearfully thrilling.

SOLNESS [*in a low tone*]. We'll talk about that another time, Hilda.
[*He goes down the flight of steps with the wreath, and away through the garden.*]

HILDA [*looks after him, then turns to* RAGNAR]. You might at least have thanked him, I think.

RAGNAR. Thanked him? Ought I to have thanked *him?*

HILDA. Yes, of course you ought!

RAGNAR. I think it's rather you I ought to thank.

HILDA. How can you say such a thing?

RAGNAR [*without answering her*]. But I advise you to take care, Miss Wangel! For you don't know *him* rightly yet.

HILDA [*ardently*]. Oh, I know him better than any one!

RAGNAR [*laughs in exasperation*]. Thank him, when he's held me down year after year! When he made father disbelieve in me—made me disbelieve in myself. And all merely that he might——!

HILDA [*as if divining something*]. That he might——? Tell me at once!

RAGNAR. That he might keep her with him.

HILDA [*with a start towards him*]. The girl at the desk!

RAGNAR. Yes.

HILDA [*threateningly, clenching her hands*]. That is not true! You're telling falsehoods about him!

RAGNAR. I wouldn't believe it either until to-day—when she said so herself.

HILDA [*as if beside herself*]. *What* did she say? I *will* know! At once! at once!

RAGNAR. She said that he had taken possession of her mind—her whole mind—centred all her thoughts upon himself alone. She says that she can never leave him—that she will remain here, where *he* is——

HILDA [*with flashing eyes*]. She won't be allowed to!

RAGNAR [*as if feeling his way*]. Who won't allow her?

HILDA [*rapidly*]. *He* won't either!

RAGNAR. Oh no—I understand the whole thing now. After this she would merely be—in the way.

HILDA. You understand nothing—since you can talk like that! No, *I* will tell you why he kept hold of her.

RAGNAR. Well then, why?

HILDA. In order to keep hold of *you*.

RAGNAR. Has he told you so?

HILDA. No, but it is so. It *must* be so! [*Wildly*] I will—I *will* have it so!

RAGNAR. And at the very moment when you came—he let her go.

HILDA. It was *you*—*you* that he let go! What do you suppose he cares about strange women like her?

RAGNAR [*reflects*]. Is it possible that all this time he's been afraid of me?

HILDA. *He* afraid! I wouldn't be so conceited if I were you.

RAGNAR. Oh, he must have seen long ago that I had something in me, too. Besides—cowardly—that's just what he is, you see.

HILDA. He! Oh yes, I'm likely to believe *that*.

RAGNAR. In a certain sense he *is* cowardly—he, the great master builder. He's not afraid of robbing others of their life's happiness—as he has done both for my father and for me. But when it comes to climbing a paltry bit of scaffolding—he'll do anything rather than *that*.

HILDA. Oh, you should just have seen him high, high up—at the dizzy height where I once saw him.

RAGNAR. Did you see that?

HILDA. Yes, indeed I did. How free and great he looked as he stood and fastened the wreath to the church-vane!

RAGNAR. I know that he ventured that, *once* in his life—one solitary time. It's a tradition among us younger men. But no power on earth would induce him to do it again.

HILDA. To-day he will do it again!

RAGNAR [*scornfully*]. Yes, I daresay!

HILDA. We shall see it.

RAGNAR. That neither you nor I will see.

HILDA [*with uncontrollable vehemence*]. I *will* see it! I *will* and *must* see it!

RAGNAR. But he won't do it. He simply daren't do it. For you see he can't get over this infirmity—master builder though he be.

[MRS. SOLNESS *comes from the house on to the veranda.*]

MRS. SOLNESS [*looks around*]. Isn't he here? Where has he gone to?

RAGNAR. Mr. Solness is down with the men.

HILDA. He took the wreath with him.

MRS. SOLNESS [*terrified*]. Took the wreath with him! Oh God! Oh God! Brovik—you must go down to him! Get him to come back here!

RAGNAR. Shall I say you want to speak to him, Mrs. Solness?

MRS. SOLNESS. Oh yes, do! No, no—don't say that *I* want anything! You can say that somebody is here, and that he must come at once.

RAGNAR. Good. I will do so, Mrs. Solness.

[*He goes down the flight of steps and away through the garden.*]

MRS. SOLNESS. Oh, Miss Wangel, you can't think how anxious I feel about him.

HILDA. Is there anything in this to be so terribly frightened about?

MRS. SOLNESS. Oh yes; surely you can understand. Just think, if he were really to do it! If he should take it into his head to climb up the scaffolding!

HILDA [*eagerly*]. Do you think he will?

MRS. SOLNESS. Oh, one can never tell what he might take into his head. I'm afraid there's nothing he mightn't think of doing.

HILDA. Aha! Perhaps you think that he's—well——?

MRS. SOLNESS. Oh, I don't know what to think about him now. The doctor has been telling me all sorts of things; and putting it all together with several things I've heard him say——

[DR. HERDAL *looks out through the door.*]

DR. HERDAL. Isn't he coming soon?

MRS. SOLNESS. Yes, I think so. I've sent for him at any rate.

DR. HERDAL [*coming closer*]. I'm afraid you'll have to go in, my dear lady——

MRS. SOLNESS. Oh no! Oh no! I shall stay out here and wait for Halvard.

DR. HERDAL. But some ladies have just come to call on you——

MRS. SOLNESS. Good heavens, that too! And just at this moment!

DR. HERDAL. They say they positively must see the ceremony.

MRS. SOLNESS. Well, well, I suppose I must go to them after all. It's my duty.

HILDA. Can't you ask the ladies to go away?

MRS. SOLNESS. No; that would never do. Now that they're here, it's my duty to see them. But do you stay out here in the mean time, and receive him when he comes.

DR. HERDAL. And try to occupy his attention as long as possible——

MRS. SOLNESS. Yes, do, dear Miss Wangel. Keep as firm hold of him as ever you can.

HILDA. Wouldn't it be best for you to do that?

MRS. SOLNESS. Yes; God knows that is *my* duty. But when one has duties in so many directions——

DR. HERDAL [*looks towards the garden*]. There he's coming!

MRS. SOLNESS. And I have to go in!

DR. HERDAL [*to* HILDA]. Don't say anything about *my* being here.

HILDA. Oh no! I dare say I shall find something else to talk to Mr. Solness about.

MRS. SOLNESS. And be sure you keep firm hold of him. I believe *you* can do it best.

[MRS. SOLNESS *and* DR. HERDAL *go into the house.* HILDA *remains standing on the veranda.* SOLNESS *comes from the garden up the flight of steps.*]

SOLNESS. Somebody wants me, I hear.

HILDA. Yes; it's I, Mr. Solness.

SOLNESS. Oh, is it you, Hilda? I was afraid it might be Aline or the Doctor.

HILDA. You're very easily frightened, it seems!

SOLNESS. Do you think so?

HILDA. Yes; people say that you're afraid to climb about—on the scaffoldings, you know.

SOLNESS. Well, that's quite a special thing.

HILDA. Then it's true that you're afraid to do it.

SOLNESS. Yes, I am.

HILDA. Afraid of falling down and killing yourself?

SOLNESS. No, not of that.

HILDA. Of what then?

SOLNESS. I'm afraid of retribution, Hilda.

HILDA. Of retribution? [*Shakes her head*] I don't understand that.

SOLNESS. Sit down, and I'll tell you something.

HILDA. Yes, do—at once!

[*She sits on a stool by the railing, and looks expectantly at him.*]

SOLNESS [*throws his hat on the table*]. You know that I began by building churches.

HILDA [*nods*]. I know that well.

SOLNESS. For, you see, I came as a boy from a pious home in the country; and so it seemed to me that this church building was the noblest task I could set myself.

HILDA. Yes, yes.

SOLNESS. And I venture to say that I built those poor little churches with such honest and warm and heart-felt devotion that—that——

HILDA. That——? Well?

SOLNESS. Well, that I think he ought to have been pleased with me.

HILDA. *He?* What *he?*

SOLNESS. He who was to have the churches, of course! He to whose honor and glory they were dedicated.

HILDA. Oh, indeed! But are you certain, then, that—that he wasn't —pleased with you?

SOLNESS [*scornfully*]. *He* pleased with *me!* How can you talk so, Hilda? He who gave the troll in me leave to lord it just as it pleased. He who bade them be at hand to serve me, both day and night—all these—all these——

HILDA. Devils——

SOLNESS. Yes, of both kinds. Oh no, he made me feel clearly enough that he wasn't pleased with me. [*Mysteriously*] You see, that was really the reason why he made the old house burn down.

HILDA. Was that why?

SOLNESS. Yes, don't you understand? He wanted to give me the chance of becoming an accomplished master in my own sphere—so that I might build all the more glorious churches for him. At first I didn't understand what he was driving at; but all of a sudden it flashed upon me.

HILDA. When was that?

SOLNESS. It was when I was building the church-tower up at Lysanger.

HILDA. I thought so.

SOLNESS. For you see, Hilda—up there, amid those new surroundings, I used to go about musing and pondering within myself. Then I saw plainly why he had taken my little children from me. It was that I should have nothing else to attach myself to. No such thing as love and happiness, you understand. I was to be only a master builder —nothing else. And all my life long I was to go on building for him. [*Laughs*] But I can tell you nothing came of that.

HILDA. What did you do, then?

SOLNESS. First of all, I searched and tried my own heart——

HILDA. And then?

SOLNESS. Then I did the *impossible*—I no less than *he*.

HILDA. The impossible?

SOLNESS. I had never before been able to climb up to a great, free height. But that day, I did it.

HILDA [*leaping up*]. Yes, yes, you did!

SOLNESS. And when I stood there, high over everything, and was hanging the wreath over the vane, I said to him: Hear me now, thou Mighty One! From this day forward I will be a free builder— I too, in my sphere—just as thou in thine. I will never build any more churches for thee—only homes for human beings.

HILDA [*with great sparkling eyes*]. *That* was the song that I heard through the air!

SOLNESS. But afterwards his turn came.

HILDA. What do you mean?

SOLNESS [*looks disconsolately at her*]. Building homes for human beings is not worth sixpence, Hilda.

HILDA. Do you say *that* now?

SOLNESS. Yes, for now I *see* it. Men have no use for these homes of theirs—to be happy in. And I shouldn't have had any use for such a home, if I'd had one. [*With a quiet, bitter laugh*] See, that is the upshot of the whole affair, however far back I look. Nothing really built; nor anything sacrificed for the chance of building. Nothing, nothing! the whole is nothing!

HILDA. Then you will never build anything more?

SOLNESS [*with animation*]. On the contrary, I'm just going to begin.

HILDA. What, then? What will you build? Tell me at once!

SOLNESS. I believe there's only one possible dwelling-place for human happiness—and that's what I'm going to build now.

HILDA [*looks firmly at him*]. Mr. Solness—you mean our castles in the air.

SOLNESS. The castles in the air—yes.

HILDA. I'm afraid you would turn dizzy before we got half-way up.

SOLNESS. Not if I can mount hand in hand with you, Hilda.

HILDA [*with an expression of suppressed resentment*]. Only with me? Won't there be others of the party?

SOLNESS. Who else should there be?

HILDA. Oh—that girl—that Kaia at the desk. Poor thing—don't you want to take her with you too?

SOLNESS. Oho! Was it about her that Aline was talking to you?

HILDA. Is it so—yes or no?

SOLNESS [*vehemently*]. I won't answer such a question! You must believe in me, utterly and entirely!

HILDA. All these ten years I've believed in you so fully—so fully.

SOLNESS. You must go on believing in me!

HILDA. Then let me see you stand free and high up!

SOLNESS [*sadly*]. Oh, Hilda—it's not every day that I can do that.

HILDA [*passionately*]. I will have you do it! I will have it! [*Imploringly*] Just once more, Mr. Solness! Do the *impossible* once again!

SOLNESS [*stands and looks deep into her eyes*]. If I try it, Hilda, I will stand up there and talk to him as I did that time before.

HILDA [*in rising excitement*]. What will you say to him?

SOLNESS. I will say to him: Hear me, Mighty Lord—thou may'st judge me as seems best to thee. But hereafter I will build nothing but the loveliest thing in the world——

HILDA [*carried away*]. Yes—yes—yes!

SOLNESS. —build it together with a princess, whom I love——

HILDA. Yes, tell him that! Tell him that!

SOLNESS. Yes. And then I will say to him: Now I shall go down and throw my arms round her and kiss her——

HILDA. —many times! Say that!

SOLNESS. —many, many times, I will say.

HILDA. And then——?

SOLNESS. Then I will wave my hat—and come down to the earth—and do as I said to him.

HILDA [*with outstretched arms*]. Now I see you again as I did when there was song in the air!

SOLNESS [*looks at her with his head bowed*]. How have you become what you are, Hilda?

HILDA. How have you made me what I am?

SOLNESS [*shortly and firmly*]. The princess shall have her castle.

HILDA [*jubilant, clapping her hands*]. Oh, Mr. Solness——! My lovely, lovely castle. Our castle in the air!

SOLNESS. On a firm foundation.

[*In the street a crowd of people have assembled, vaguely seen through the trees. Music of wind-instruments is heard far away behind the new house.*]

[MRS. SOLNESS, *with a fur collar round her neck,* DOCTOR HERDAL, *with her white shawl on his arm, and some ladies, come out on the veranda.* RAGNAR BROVIK *comes at the same time up from the garden.*]

MRS. SOLNESS [*to* RAGNAR]. Are we to have music, too?

RAGNAR. Yes. It's the band of the Masons' Union. [*To* SOLNESS] The foreman asked me to tell you that he's ready now to go up with the wreath.

SOLNESS [*takes his hat*]. All right. I'll go down to him myself.

MRS. SOLNESS [*anxiously*]. What have you to do down there, Halvard?

SOLNESS [*curtly*]. I must be down below with the men.

MRS. SOLNESS. Yes, down below—only down below.

SOLNESS. That's where I always stand—on everyday occasions.

[*He goes down the flight of steps and away through the garden.*]

MRS. SOLNESS [*calls after him over the railing*]. But do beg the man to be careful when he goes up! Promise me that, Halvard!

DR. HERDAL [*to* MRS. SOLNESS]. Don't you see that I was right? He's given up all thought of that folly.

MRS. SOLNESS. Oh, what a relief! Twice workmen have fallen, and each time they were killed on the spot. [*Turns to* HILDA] Thank you, Miss Wangel, for having kept such a firm hold upon him. I should never have had my own way with him.

DR. HERDAL [*playfully*]. Yes, yes, Miss Wangel, you know how to keep firm hold on a man, when you give your mind to it.

[MRS. SOLNESS *and* DR. HERDAL *go up to the ladies, who are standing nearer to the steps and looking over the garden.* HILDA *remains standing beside the railing in the foreground.* RAGNAR *goes up to her.*]

RAGNAR [*with suppressed laughter, half whispering*]. Miss Wangel, do you see all those young fellows down in the street?

HILDA. Yes.

RAGNAR. They're my fellow-students come to look at the master.

HILDA. What do they want to look at *him* for?

RAGNAR. They want to see how he daren't climb to the top of his own house.

HILDA. Oh, *that's* what those boys want, is it?

RAGNAR [*spitefully and scornfully*]. He's kept us down so long, that man. Now we're going to see him keep quietly down below himself.

HILDA. You won't see that—not this time.

RAGNAR [*smiles*]. Indeed! Then where shall we see him?

HILDA. High—high up by the vane! That's where you'll see him!

RAGNAR [*laughs*]. Him! Oh yes, I daresay!

HILDA. His *will* is to reach the top—so at the top you shall see him.

RAGNAR. His *will* yes; that I can easily believe. But he simply *can't* do it. His head would swim round, long, long before he got half-way. He'd have to crawl down again on his hands and knees.

DR. HERDAL [*points across*]. Look! there goes the foreman up the ladders.

MRS. SOLNESS. And of course he's got the wreath to carry too. Oh, I do hope he'll be careful!

RAGNAR [*stares incredulously and shouts*]. Why, but it's——

HILDA [*breaking out in jubilation*]. It's the master builder himself.

MRS. SOLNESS [*screams with terror*]. Yes, it's Halvard! O my great God——! Halvard! Halvard!

DR. HERDAL. Hush! Don't shout to him!

MRS. SOLNESS [*half beside herself*]. I must go to him! I must bring him down again.

DR. HERDAL [*holds her*]. Don't move, any of you! Not a sound!

HILDA [*immovable, follows* SOLNESS *with her eyes*]. He climbs and climbs. Higher and higher! Higher and higher! Look! Just look!

RAGNAR [*breathless*]. He *must* turn now. He can't possibly help it.

HILDA. He climbs and climbs. He'll soon be at the top now.

MRS. SOLNESS. Oh, I shall die of terror. I can't bear to see it!

DR. HERDAL. Then don't look up at him.

HILDA. There, he's standing on the topmost planks! Right at the top!

DR. HERDAL. Nobody must move! Do you hear?

HILDA [*exulting, with quiet intensity*]. At last! At last! Now I see him great and free again!

RAGNAR [*almost voiceless*]. But this is im——

HILDA. So I have seen him all through these ten years. How secure he stands! Frightfully thrilling all the same. Look at him! Now he's hanging the wreath round the vane!

RAGNAR. I feel as if I were looking at something utterly impossible.

HILDA. Yes, it *is* the *impossible* that he's doing now! [*With the indefinable expression in her eyes*] Can you see any one else up there with him?

RAGNAR. There is no one else.

HILDA. Yes, there is one he is striving with.

RAGNAR. You are mistaken.

HILDA. Then do you hear no song in the air, either?

RAGNAR. It must be the wind in the tree-tops.

HILDA. *I* hear a song—a mighty song! [*Shouts in wild jubilation and glee*] Look, look! Now he's waving his hat! He's waving it to us down here! Oh, wave, wave back to him! For now it's finished! [*Tears the white shawl from the doctor, waves it, and shouts up to* SOLNESS] Hurrah for Master Builder Solness!

DR. HERDAL. Stop! Stop! For God's sake——!

[*The ladies on the veranda wave their pocket-handkerchiefs, and the shouts of "Hurrah" are taken up in the street below. Then they are suddenly silenced, and the crowd bursts out into a shriek of horror. A human body, with planks and fragments of wood, is vaguely perceived crashing down behind the trees.*]

MRS. SOLNESS AND THE LADIES [*at the same time*]. He's falling! He's falling!

[MRS. SOLNESS *totters, falls backwards, swooning, and is caught, amid cries and confusion, by the ladies. The crowd in the street breaks down the fence and storms into the garden. At the same time* DR. HERDAL, *too, rushes down thither. A short pause.*]

HILDA [*stares fixedly upwards, and says as if petrified*]. My Master Builder.

RAGNAR [*supports himself, trembling, against the railing*]. He must be dashed to pieces—killed on the spot.

ONE OF THE LADIES [*whilst* MRS. SOLNESS *is carried into the house*]. Run down for the doctor——

RAGNAR. I can't stir a foot——

ANOTHER LADY. Then call to some one!

RAGNAR [*tries to call out*]. How is it? Is he alive?

A VOICE [*below, in the garden*]. Mr. Solness is dead!

OTHER VOICES [*nearer*]. The head is all crushed.—He fell right into the quarry.

HILDA [*turns to* RAGNAR, *and says quietly*]. I can't see him up there now.

RAGNAR. This is terrible. So, after all, he could not do it.

HILDA [*as if in quiet spell-bound triumph*]. But he mounted right to the top. And I heard harps in the air. [*Waves her shawl in the air, and shrieks with wild intensity*] My—my Master Builder!

THE END

AUGUST STRINDBERG (1849–1912)

The tempestuous career of August Strindberg, the tormented Swede, would seem to confirm the popular conception of an artist as an eccentric, if not psychopathic, personality, unable or unwilling to live the substantial life of an average citizen. Psychoanalytic studies of the man since his death have credited him with most of the complexes known, and he was painfully aware of his own inadequacies for normal living. Out of the agony of his maladjustment he wrote the best of his seventy-odd plays, gyrating through most of the aesthetic philosophies of his time and creating new ones when he did not find them ready-made. If he still seems one of the most modern of writers, it is perhaps because our age is still living with nightmarish troubles comparable to those he suffered. If his dramas sear us still with their almost too painful conviction, it is because they had their origin in the driving necessity of overpowering experience. In addition, Strindberg happened to be an authentic genius, one of the few unmistakable titans in the modern theater.

Strindberg was his own best biographer. Halfway through his career he began to write a series of seven confessional works tracing the sources of his personality conflicts and the nature of his anguish with somewhat embarrassing frankness. All of them make fascinating, if also painful reading, and the most artistic of them, *The Confessions of a Fool,* is one of the most gripping novels ever written.

Strindberg's difficulties seem to have begun at his birth. His father, a shipping agent in Stockholm, had already had three children by August's mother, a former barmaid, before he married her just in time to make August's birth legitimate. His family frowned on the marriage, so that she lived out her days "a bondwoman," as her son called her, in her husband's house. She was a vulgar, coarse-grained woman lacking an understanding of her children, and the father was a man of sensual appetites and haughty aristocratic manners. The sensitive boy found his early home life almost intolerable. The decline of his father's fortunes added poverty to his other hardships, so that Strindberg grew up with ten other people huddled into a three-room apartment. If his mother was harsh and unkind to him, his older sister was overbearing and apparently sowed in his mind the first seeds of that suspicion and hatred of women that he was never to lose. Only his maternal grandmother, who also lived in the household, gave him any attention, but its effect was vitiated by her religious fanaticism, which led him to dream of a career as a Pietist preacher.

The death of his mother when he was thirteen did not help matters. Soon after, his father married a cold and unmotherly woman, who largely ignored August as he came to resent her. His longing for affection and sympathy was frustrated at every point in his early life and led to that curious conflict of desire and loathing that was to characterize his relations with women ever after. His need for them, greater than most men's, led him to fear and despise their power over him as a sign of his inner weakness and to imagine in them devilish designs to overpower and degrade him. In this state of mind was born his idea of love-hate as the driving passion between the sexes, the deadly duel into which sexual love must eventually develop as two people who are drawn to each other strive for conquest and domination. Strindberg's notion of these conflicting urges in man's nature anticipated one of the basic concepts of Freud's psychoanalysis.

His professional career was at first beset by frustrations as great as those in his emotional life. His education had been intermittent and unsatisfactory. Rebellious at school, he found his university career repeatedly interrupted by lack of funds. After one painful semester at the University of Upsala, he was forced to drop out and take a teaching position in the very school where he had endured mental agony as a child. Thereafter he drifted through at least six jobs of strikingly different kinds, in all of which he failed. Eventually he resumed his studies at the University of Stockholm, though he never earned a degree. He had already begun to write verses and plays, and when some of these found favor with publishers, he left the university with a characteristic blast at the place.

The most fortunate incident of his early career was his appointment to the post of Sinologist at the Royal Library in Stockholm in 1874. This brought a discipline and order into his life for eight years but left him leisure to study and write. His enthusiastic exploration of Scandinavian history led him to write his early historical dramas, comparable to the romantic works of Ibsen's first period, and a naturalistic novel, *The Red Room,* brought him a flurry of international attention in 1879. In 1882 he resigned his position and began a life of harassed wandering about the Continent, with periods of return to Sweden.

Soon after commencing work at the Stockholm library, Strindberg had met and fallen in love with Siri von Essen, the wife of a stiff and unsympathetic Swedish baron, who longed for escape from her marriage. Strindberg tried repeatedly to conquer his feeling for her, but they at last persuaded the husband to consent to a divorce. Strindberg's marriage to Siri lasted fourteen years (1877–1891) and produced three children, but they were years of mutual torture, for which our sympathies may well go out to the wife. Characteristically, he published in 1893 a fascinating but shocking account of their marriage, in which each savage argument in his defense must impress a thoughtful reader as evidence of his incipient insanity. In the same year he contracted a second marriage, which ended in divorce three years later. The last year of it he spent in a sanitorium in Paris, from which he emerged sufficiently improved to continue his writing. Thereafter his mental state fluctuated down to the time of his death. Yet he went through a third marriage (1901–1904) and was engaged to still a fourth woman shortly before his death. If Strindberg was hounded by an overpowering desire for a woman's love and sympathy, he seems also to have held a strange attraction for the sex.

The one obsession of his writings is his fanatical attack on woman, and especially on Ibsen's "new woman," who wished to usurp the place of man in society. In work after work he gave his almost hysterical description of the type, denying her own femininity, embracing lesbianism in her search for complete independence of man, utterly indifferent to morality in her feline war upon him. In *The Father,* one of the best-known of his domestic dramas, a selfish, possessive wife drives her husband insane gradually through her vicious insinuations, especially that the daughter he loves is not his own. When the old nurse, whom he had loved since babyhood, puts him into a straitjacket by deceiving him with memories of his swaddling clothes, the woman he had trusted longest in his life proves false and despicable. Fortunately for the effectiveness of his best plays, Strindberg was more objective and fair in his treatment of this savage theme than he intended to be. If his women are sinister harpies, his men are neurotic and weak, and his people, however abnormal and unpleasant, are more convincingly visualized than one might expect. Strindberg had an extraordinary grasp of abnormal psychology, intuitive rather than systematic, which is demonstrated in the characters he created in a naked and uninhibited form. In his expressionistic dramas he represented with grotesque reality the disintegration of the human personality under the pressures of modern life.

The various aesthetic periods of his career overlap a good deal and can be correlated with the intellectual influences upon him—his early romanticism with an interest in Rousseau, his naturalism with his passing enthusiasm for Nietzsche's philosophy of the superman, his mystical dramas with his absorption in Buddhism and the religious writings of Emanuel Swedenborg. But one can trace four rather than three fairly distinct stages in his evolution as a dramatist. The romanticism of his apprenticeship (1870–1885) is best represented by his historical drama about an early Swedish Lutheran, *Master Olof* (1872), and his folk fantasy, *The Wanderings of Lucky Per* (1883). His ugly naturalism (1887–1893) centered in a series of burning studies of the sex duel in love and marriage, of which the best known are *The Father* (1887) and *Miss Julia* (1888), the latter linked with his famous preface on the objectives of the movement. His mental collapse in 1893 during his second marriage made him unable to write plays for four years. When he emerged from the asylum and what he called the inferno of his life, he entered a third artistic period characterized by religious mysticism and an obsession with the supernatural (1897–1901). Here belong the first two parts of his trilogy *To Damascus* (1898), his "mystery" play *Advent* (1898), and *Easter* (1901). Significantly, he resumed the writing of historical dramas at this time with *Gustavus Vasa* (1899), dramas characterized by greater realism and maturity than his early works of this kind. In the last decade of his life he developed the dramatic style known as expressionism, which was to inspire a large school of writers. *A Dream Play* (1902) and *The Ghost Sonata* (1907) are his most powerful specimens of expressionistic writing.

But Strindberg was much too volatile a writer to be pigeonholed in neat periods. The last two cut across each other, and in the very middle of them appeared one of his most terrifying naturalistic dramas, *The Dance of Death* I, II (1901). His total output was staggering: about seventy-three plays in forty years, a testament to his breathless search for solace from his mental tortures through writing. In his final years, under the affectionate care of his daughter, he achieved a measure of peace, especially as he busied himself with a little theater of his own, the Intima Teatern, founded in Stockholm in 1906 with the aid of friends for the production of his own plays. Two years later he ceased writing, plagued by an illness that turned out to be cancer. He died peacefully with a Bible in his hand, murmuring, "Everything is atoned for." Though his countrymen had stood aghast and aloof for many of his books and plays, they finally honored his sixty-third birthday (1912) as a great public event, with gala performances of his plays, and his death with a funeral befitting a national hero. But Sweden's greatest writer never received the Nobel Prize—perhaps because he announced in advance, with characteristic bitterness, that he would never accept it.

AUGUST STRINDBERG

PREFACE TO MISS JULIA

LIKE almost all other art, that of the stage has long seemed to me a sort of *Biblia Pauperum,* or a Bible in pictures for those who cannot read what is written or printed. And in the same way the playwright has seemed to me a lay preacher spreading the thoughts of his time in a form so popular that the middle classes, from which theatrical audiences are mainly drawn, can know what is being talked about without troubling their brains too much. For this reason the theatre has always served as a grammar-school to young people, women, and those who have acquired a little knowledge, all of whom retain the capacity for deceiving themselves and being deceived—which means again that they are susceptible to illusions produced by the suggestions of the author. And for the same reason I have had a feeling that, in our time, when the rudimentary, incomplete thought processes operating through our fancy seem to be developing into reflection, research, and analysis, the theatre might stand on the verge of being abandoned as a decaying form, for the enjoyment of which we lack the requisite conditions. The prolonged theatrical crisis now prevailing throughout Europe speaks in favour of such a supposition, as well as the fact that, in the civilised countries producing the greatest thinkers of the age, namely, England and Germany, the drama is as dead as are most of the other fine arts.

In some other countries it has, however, been thought possible to create a new drama by filling the old forms with the contents of a new time. But, for one thing, there has not been time for the new thoughts to become so popularised that the public might grasp the questions raised; secondly, minds have been so inflamed by party conflicts that pure and disinterested enjoyment has been excluded from places where one's innermost feelings are violated and the tyranny of an applauding or hissing majority is exercised with the openness for which the theatre gives a chance; and, finally, there has been no new form devised for the new contents, and the new wine has burst the old bottles.

In the following drama I have not tried to do anything new—for that cannot be done—but I have tried to modernise the form in accordance with the demands which I thought the new men of a new time might be likely to make on this art. And with such a purpose in view, I have chosen, or surrendered myself to, a theme that might well be said to lie outside the partisan strife of the day: for the problem of social ascendancy or decline, of higher or lower, of better or worse, of men or women, is, has been, and will be of lasting interest. In selecting this theme from real life, as it was related to me a number of years ago, when the incident impressed me very deeply, I found it suited to a tragedy, because it can only make us sad to see a fortunately placed individual perish, and this must be the case in still higher degree when we see an entire family die out. But perhaps a time will arrive when we have become so developed, so enlightened, that we can remain indifferent before the spectacle of life, which now seems so brutal, so cynical, so heartless; when we have closed up those lower, unreliable instruments of thought which we call feelings, and which have been rendered not only superfluous but harmful by the final growth of our reflective organs.

The fact that the heroine arouses our pity depends only on our weakness in not being able to resist the sense of fear that the same fate could befall ourselves. And yet it is possible that a very sensitive spectator might fail to find satisfaction in this kind of pity, while the man believing in the future might demand some positive suggestion for the abolition of evil, or, in other words, some kind of programme. But, first of all, there is no absolute evil. That one family perishes is the fortune of another family, which thereby gets a chance to rise. And the alternation of ascent and descent constitutes one of life's main charms, as fortune is solely determined by comparison. And to the man with a programme, who wants to remedy the sad circumstance that the hawk eats the dove, and the flea eats the hawk, I have this question to put: why should it be remedied? Life is not so mathematically idiotic that it lets only the big eat the small, but it happens just as often that the bee kills the lion, or drives it to madness at least.

That my tragedy makes a sad impression on many is their own fault. When we grow strong as were the men of the first French revolution, then we shall receive an unconditionally good and joyful impression from seeing the national forests rid of rotting and superannuated trees that have stood too long in the way of others with equal right to a period of free growth—an impression good in the same way as that received from the death of one incurably diseased.

Not long ago they reproached my tragedy "The Father" with being too sad—just as if they wanted merry tragedies. Everybody is clamouring arrogantly for "the joy of life," and all theatrical managers are giving orders for farces, as if the joy of life consisted in being silly and picturing all human beings as so many sufferers from St. Vitus' dance or idiocy. I find the joy of life in its violent and cruel struggles, and my pleasure lies in knowing something and learning something. And for this reason I have selected an unusual but instructive case—an exception, in a word—but a great exception, proving the rule, which, of course, will provoke all lovers of the commonplace. And what also will offend simple brains is that my action cannot be traced back to a single motive, that the view-point is not always the same. An event in real life—and this discovery is quite recent—springs generally from a whole series of more or less deep-lying motives, but of these the spectator chooses as a rule the one his reason can master most easily, or else the one reflecting most favourably on his power of reasoning. A suicide is committed. Bad business, says the merchant. Unrequited love, say the ladies. Sickness, says the sick man. Crushed hopes, says the shipwrecked. But now it may be that the motive lay in all or none of these directions. It is possible that the one who is dead may have hid the main motive by pushing forward another meant to place his memory in a better light.

In explanation of *Miss Julia's* sad fate I have suggested many factors: her mother's fundamental instincts; her father's mistaken upbringing of the girl; her own nature, and the suggestive influence of her fiancé on a weak and degenerate brain; furthermore, and more directly: the festive mood of the Midsummer Eve; the absence of her father; her physical condition; her preoccupation with the animals; the excitation of the dance; the dusk of the night; the strongly aphrodisiacal influence of the flowers; and lastly the chance forcing the two of them together in a secluded room, to which must be added the aggressiveness of the excited man.

Thus I have neither been one-sidedly physiological nor one-sidedly psychological in my procedure. Nor have I merely delivered a moral preachment. This multiplicity of motives I regard as praiseworthy because it is in keeping with the views of our own time. And if others have done the same thing before me, I may boast of not being the sole inventor of my paradoxes—as all discoveries are named.

In regard to the character-drawing I may say that I have tried to make my figures rather "characterless," and I have done so for reasons I shall now state.

In the course of the ages the word character has assumed many meanings. Originally it signified probably the dominant ground-note in the complex mass of the self, and as such it was confused with temperament. Afterward it became the middle-class term for an automaton, so that an individual whose nature had come to a stand-still, or who had adapted himself to a certain part in life—who had ceased to grow, in a word—was named a character; while one remaining in a state of development—a skilful navigator on life's river, who did not sail with close-tied sheets, but knew when to fall off before the wind and when to luff again—was called lacking in character. And he was called so in a depreciatory sense, of course, because he was so hard to catch, to classify, and to keep track of. This middle-class notion about the immobility of the soul was transplanted to the stage, where the middle-class element has always held sway. There a character became synonymous with a gentleman fixed and finished once for all—one who invariably appeared drunk, jolly, sad. And for the purpose of characterisation nothing more was needed than some physical deformity like a clubfoot, a wooden leg, a red nose; or the person concerned was made to repeat some phrase like "That's capital!" or "Barkis is willin',"[1] or something of that kind. This manner of regarding human beings as homogeneous is preserved even by the great Molière. *Harpagon*[2] is nothing but miserly, although *Harpagon* might as well have been at once miserly and a financial genius, a fine father, and a public-spirited citizen. What is worse yet, his "defect" is of distinct advantage to his son-in-law and daughter, who are his heirs, and for that reason should not find fault with him, even if they have to wait a little for their wedding. I do not believe, therefore, in simple characters on the stage. And the summary judgments of the author upon men—this one stupid, and that one brutal, this one jealous, and that one stingy—should be challenged by the naturalists, who know the fertility of the soul-complex, and who realise that "vice" has a reverse very much resembling virtue.

[1] *Barkis is willin'. Barkis, a character in Dickens'* David Copperfield, *was always "willin'" to marry nurse Peggotty, and finally did. Dickens used the phrase repeatedly as a tag for Barkis's character.*
[2] *Harpagon. In Molière's play* The Miser, *Harpagon is an exaggerated specimen of a miser and nothing else.*

Because they are modern characters, living in a period of transition more hysterically hurried than its immediate predecessor at least, I have made my figures vacillating, out of joint, torn between the old and the new. And I do not think it unlikely that, through newspaper reading and overheard conversations, modern ideas may have leaked down to the strata where domestic servants belong.

My souls (or characters) are conglomerates, made up of past and present stages of civilisation, scraps of humanity, torn-off pieces of Sunday clothing turned into rags—all patched together as is the human soul itself. And I have furthermore offered a touch of evolutionary history by letting the weaker repeat words stolen from the stronger, and by letting different souls accept "ideas"—or suggestions, as they are called—from each other.

Miss Julia is a modern character, not because the manhating half-woman may not have existed in all ages, but because now, after her discovery, she has stepped to the front and begun to make a noise. The half-woman is a type coming more and more into prominence, selling herself nowadays for power, decorations, distinctions, diplomas, as formerly for money, and the type indicates degeneration. It is not a good type, for it does not last, but unfortunately it has the power of reproducing itself and its misery through one more generation. And degenerate men seem instinctively to make their selection from this kind of women, so that they multiply and produce indeterminate sexes to whom life is a torture. Fortunately, however, they perish in the end, either from discord with real life, or from the irresistible revolt of their suppressed instincts, or from foiled hopes of possessing the man. The type is tragical, offering us the spectacle of a desperate struggle against nature. It is also tragical as a Romantic inheritance dispersed by the prevailing Naturalism, which wants nothing but happiness: and for happiness strong and sound races are required.

But *Miss Julia* is also a remnant of the old military nobility which is now giving way to the new nobility of nerves and brain. She is a victim of the discord which a mother's "crime" produces in a family, and also a victim of the day's delusions, of the circumstances, of her defective constitution—all of which may be held equivalent to the old-fashioned fate or universal law. The naturalist has wiped out the idea of guilt, but he cannot wipe out the results of an action—punishment, prison, or fear—and for the simple reason that they remain without regard to his verdict. For fellow-beings that have been wronged are not so good-natured as those on the outside, who have not been wronged at all, can be without cost to themselves.

Even if, for reasons over which he could have no control, the father should forego his vengeance, the daughter would take vengeance upon herself, just as she does in the play, and she would be moved to it by that innate or acquired sense of honour which the upper classes inherit —whence? From the days of barbarism, from the original home of the Aryans, from the chivalry of the Middle Ages? It is beautiful, but it has become disadvantageous to the preservation of the race. It is this, the nobleman's *harakiri*—or the law of the inner conscience compelling the Japanese to cut open his own abdomen at the insult of another—which survives, though somewhat modified, in the duel, also a privilege of the nobility. For this reason the valet, *Jean,* continues to live, but *Miss Julia* cannot live on without honour. In so far as he lacks this life-endangering superstition about honour, the serf takes precedence of the earl, and in all of us Aryans there is something of the nobleman, or of Don Quixote, which makes us sympathise with the man who takes his own life because he has committed a dishonourable deed and thus lost his honour. And we are noblemen to the extent of suffering from seeing the earth littered with the living corpse of one who was once great—yes, even if the one thus fallen should rise again and make restitution by honourable deeds.

Jean, the valet, is of the kind that builds new stock—one in whom the differentiation is clearly noticeable. He was a cotter's child, and he has trained himself up to the point where the future gentleman has become visible. He has found it easy to learn, having finely developed senses (smell, taste, vision) and an instinct for beauty besides. He has already risen in the world, and is strong enough not to be sensitive about using other people's services. He has already become a stranger to his equals, despising them as so many outlived stages, but also fearing and fleeing them because they know his secrets, pry into his plans, watch his rise with envy, and look forward to his fall with pleasure. From this relationship springs his dual, indeterminate character, oscillating between love of distinction and hatred of those who have already achieved it. He says himself that he is an aristocrat, and has learned the secrets of good company. He is polished on the outside and coarse within. He knows already how to wear the frock-coat with ease, but the cleanliness of his body cannot be guaranteed.

He feels respect for the young lady, but he is afraid of *Christine,* who has his dangerous secrets in her keeping. His emotional callousness is sufficient to prevent the night's happenings from exercising a disturbing influence on his plans for the future. Having at once the slave's brutality and the master's lack of squeamishness, he can see blood without fainting, and he can also bend his back under a mishap until able to throw it off. For this reason he will emerge unharmed from the battle, and will probably end his days as the owner of a hotel. And if he does not become a Roumanian count, his son will probably go to a university, and may even become a county attorney.

Otherwise, he furnishes us with rather significant information as to the way in which the lower classes look at life from beneath—that is, when he speaks the truth, which is not often, as he prefers what seems favourable to himself to what is true. When *Miss Julia* suggests that the lower classes must feel the pressure from above very heavily, *Jean* agrees with her, of course, because he wants to gain her sympathy. But he corrects himself at once, the moment he realises the advantage of standing apart from the herd.

And *Jean* stands above *Miss Julia* not only because his fate is in ascendancy, but because he is a man. Sexually he is the aristocrat because of his male strength, his more finely developed senses, and his capacity for taking the initiative. His inferiority depends mainly on the temporary social environment in which he has to live, and which he probably can shed together with the valet's livery.

The mind of the slave speaks through his reverence for the count (as shown in the incident with the boots) and through his religious superstition. But he reveres the count principally as a possessor of that higher position toward which he himself is striving. And this reverence remains even when he has won the daughter of the house, and seen that the beautiful shell covered nothing but emptiness.

I don't believe that any love relation in a "higher" sense can spring up between two souls of such different quality. And for this reason I let *Miss Julia* imagine her love to be protective or commiserative in its origin. And I let *Jean* suppose that, under different social conditions, he might feel something like real love for her. I believe love to be like the hyacinth, which has to strike roots in darkness *before* it can bring forth a vigorous flower. In this case it shoots up quickly, bringing forth blossom and seed at once, and for that reason the plant withers so soon.

Christine, finally, is a female slave, full of servility and sluggishness acquired in front of the kitchen fire, and stuffed full of morality and religion that are meant to serve her at once as cloak and scapegoat. Her church-going has for its purpose to bring her quick and easy riddance of all responsibility for her domestic thieveries and to equip her with a new stock of guiltlessness. Otherwise she is a subordinate figure, and therefore purposely sketched in the same manner as the minister and the doctor in "The Father," whom I designed as ordinary human beings, like the common run of country ministers and country doctors. And if these accessory characters have seemed mere abstractions to some people, it depends on the fact that ordinary men are to a certain extent impersonal in the exercise of their callings. This means that they are without individuality, showing only one side of themselves while at work. And as long as the spectator does not feel the need of seeing them from other sides, my abstract presentation of them remains on the whole correct.

In regard to the dialogue, I want to point out that I have departed somewhat from prevailing traditions by not turning my figures into catechists who make stupid questions in order to call forth witty answers. I have avoided the symmetrical and mathematical construction of the French dialogue, and have instead permitted the minds to work irregularly as they do in reality, where, during conversation, the cogs of one mind seem more or less haphazardly to engage those of another one, and where no topic is fully exhausted. Naturally enough, therefore, the dialogue strays a good deal as, in the opening scenes, it acquires a material that later on is worked over, picked up again, repeated, expounded, and built up like the theme in a musical composition.

The plot is pregnant enough, and as, at bottom, it is concerned only with two persons, I have concentrated my attention on these, introducing only one subordinate figure, the cook, and keeping the unfortunate spirit of the father hovering above and beyond the action. I have done this because I believe I have noticed that the psychological processes are what interest the people of our own day more than anything else. Our souls, so eager for knowledge, cannot rest satisfied with seeing what happens, but must also learn how it comes to happen! What we want to see are just the wires, the machinery. We want to investigate the box with the false bottom, touch the magic ring in order to find the suture, and look into the cards to discover how they are marked.

In this I have taken for models the monographic novels of the brothers de Goncourt,[1] which have appealed more to me than any other modern literature.

Turning to the technical side of the composition, I have tried to abolish the division into acts. And I have done so because I have come

[1] **brothers de Goncourt.** Edmond de Goncourt (1822–1896) and Jules de Goncourt (1830–1870) collaborated on a series of naturalistic novels in the sixties, which gave the impression of everyday reality through an elaborate accumulation of carefully observed details.

to fear that our decreasing capacity for illusion might be unfavourably affected by intermissions during which the spectator would have time to reflect and to get away from the suggestive influence of the author-hypnotist. My play will probably last an hour and a half, and as it is possible to listen that length of time, or longer, to a lecture, a sermon, or a debate, I have imagined that a theatrical performance could not become fatiguing in the same time. As early as 1872, in one of my first dramatic experiments, "The Outlaw," I tried the same concentrated form, but with scant success. The play was written in five acts and wholly completed when I became aware of the restless, scattered effect it produced. Then I burned it, and out of the ashes rose a single, well-built act, covering fifty printed pages, and taking an hour for its performance. Thus the form of the present play is not new, but it seems to be my own, and changing æsthetical conventions may possibly make it timely.

My hope is still for a public educated to the point where it can sit through a whole-evening performance in a single act. But that point cannot be reached without a great deal of experimentation. In the meantime I have resorted to three art forms that are to provide resting-places for the public and the actors, without letting the public escape from the illusion induced. All these forms are subsidiary to the drama. They are the monologue, the pantomime, and the dance, all of them belonging originally to the tragedy of classical antiquity. For the monologue has sprung from the monody, and the chorus has developed into the ballet.

Our realists have excommunicated the monologue as improbable, but if I can lay a proper basis for it, I can also make it seem probable, and then I can use it to good advantage. It is probable, for instance, that a speaker may walk back and forth in his room practising his speech aloud; it is probable that an actor may read through his part aloud, that a servant-girl may talk to her cat, that a mother may prattle to her child, that an old spinster may chatter to her parrot, that a person may talk in his sleep. And in order that the actor for once may have a chance to work independently, and to be free for a moment from the author's pointer, it is better that the monologues be not written out, but just indicated. As it matters comparatively little what is said to the parrot or the cat, or in one's sleep—because it cannot influence the action—it is possible that a gifted actor, carried away by the situation and the mood of the occasion, may improvise such matters better than they could be written by the author, who cannot figure out in advance how much may be said, and how long the talk may last, without waking the public out of their illusions.

It is well known that, on certain stages, the Italian theatre has returned to improvisation and thereby produced creative actors—who, however, must follow the author's suggestions—and this may be counted a step forward, or even the beginning of a new art form that might well be called *productive*.

Where, on the other hand, the monologue would seem unreal, I have used the pantomime, and there I have left still greater scope for the actor's imagination—and for his desire to gain independent honours. But in order that the public may not be tried beyond endurance, I have permitted the music—which is amply warranted by the Midsummer Eve's dance—to exercise its illusory power while the dumb show lasts. And I ask the musical director to make careful selection of the music used for this purpose, so that incompatible moods are not induced by reminiscences from the last musical comedy or topical song, or by folk-tunes of too markedly ethnographical distinction.

The mere introduction of a scene with a lot of "people" could not have taken the place of the dance, for such scenes are poorly acted and tempt a number of grinning idiots into displaying their own smartness, whereby the illusion is disturbed. As the common people do not improvise their gibes, but use ready-made phrases in which stick some double meaning, I have not composed their lampooning song, but have appropriated a little known folk-dance which I personally noted down in a district near Stockholm. The words don't quite hit the point, but hint vaguely at it, and this is intentional, for the cunning (i.e., weakness) of the slave keeps him from any direct attack. There must, then, be no chattering clowns in a serious action, and no coarse flouting at a situation that puts the lid on the coffin of a whole family.

As far as the scenery is concerned, I have borrowed from impressionistic painting its asymmetry, its quality of abruptness, and have thereby in my opinion strengthened the illusion. Because the whole room and all its contents are not shown, there is a chance to guess at things—that is, our imagination is stirred into complementing our vision. I have made a further gain in getting rid of those tiresome exits by means of doors, especially as stage doors are made of canvas and swing back and forth at the lightest touch. They are not even capable of expressing the anger of an irate *pater familias* who, on leaving his home after a poor dinner, slams the door behind him "so that it shakes the whole house." (On the stage the house sways.) I have also contented myself with a single setting, and for the double purpose of making the figures become parts of their surroundings, and of breaking with the tendency toward luxurious scenery. But having only a single setting, one may demand to have it real. Yet nothing is more difficult than to get a room that looks something like a room, although the painter can easily enough produce waterfalls and flaming volcanoes. Let it go at canvas for the walls, but we might be done with the painting of shelves and kitchen utensils on the canvas. We have so much else on the stage that is conventional, and in which we are asked to believe, that we might at least be spared the too great effort of believing in painted pans and kettles.

I have placed the rear wall and the table diagonally across the stage in order to make the actors show full face and half profile to the audience when they sit opposite each other at the table. In the opera "Aida" I noticed an oblique background, which led the eye out into unseen prospects. And it did not appear to be the result of any reaction against the fatiguing right angle.

Another novelty well needed would be the abolition of the foot-lights. The light from below is said to have for its purpose to make the faces of the actors look fatter. But I cannot help asking: why must all actors be fat in the face? Does not this light from below tend to wipe out the subtler lineaments in the lower part of the face, and especially around the jaws? Does it not give a false appearance to the nose and cast shadows upward over the eyes? If this be not so, another thing is certain: namely, that the eyes of the actors suffer from the light, so that the effective play of their glances is precluded. Coming from below, the light strikes the retina in places generally protected (except in sailors, who have to see the sun reflected in the water), and for this reason one observes hardly anything but a vulgar rolling of the eyes, either sideways or upwards, toward the galleries, so that nothing but the white of the eye shows. Perhaps the same cause may account for the tedious blinking of which especially the actresses are guilty. And when anybody on the stage wants to use his eyes to speak with, no other way is left him but the poor one of staring straight at the public, with whom he or she then gets into direct communication out-side of the frame provided by the setting. This vicious habit has, rightly or wrongly, been named "to meet friends." Would it not be possible by means of strong side-lights (obtained by the employment of reflectors, for instance) to add to the resources already possessed by the actor? Could not his mimicry be still further strengthened by use of the greatest asset possessed by the face: the play of the eyes?

Of course, I have no illusions about getting the actors to play *for* the public and not *at* it, although such a change would be highly desirable. I dare not even dream of beholding the actor's back throughout an important scene, but I wish with all my heart that crucial scenes might not be played in the centre of the proscenium, like duets meant to bring forth applause. Instead, I should like to have them laid in the place indicated by the situation. Thus I ask for no revolutions, but only for a few minor modifications. To make a real room of the stage, with the fourth wall missing, and a part of the furniture placed back toward the audience, would probably produce a disturbing effect at present.

In wishing to speak of the facial make-up, I have no hope that the ladies will listen to me, as they would rather look beautiful than lifelike. But the actor might consider whether it be to his advantage to paint his face so that it shows some abstract type which covers it like a mask. Suppose that a man puts a markedly choleric line between the eyes, and imagine further that some remark demands a smile of this face fixed in a state of continuous wrath. What a horrible grimace will be the result? And how can the wrathful old man produce a frown on his false forehead, which is smooth as a billiard ball?

In modern psychological dramas, where the subtlest movements of the soul are to be reflected on the face rather than by gestures and noise, it would probably be well to experiment with strong side-light on a small stage, and with unpainted faces, or at least with a minimum of make-up.

If, in addition, we might escape the visible orchestra, with its disturbing lamps and its faces turned toward the public; if we could have the seats on the main floor (the orchestra or the pit) raised so that the eyes of the spectators would be above the knees of the actors; if we could get rid of the boxes with their tittering parties of diners; if we could also have the auditorium completely darkened during the performance; and if, first and last, we could have a small stage and a small house: then a new dramatic art might rise, and the theatre might at least become an institution for the entertainment of people with culture. While waiting for this kind of theatre, I suppose we shall have to write for the "ice-box," and thus prepare the repertory that is to come.

I have made an attempt. If it prove a failure, there is plenty of time to try over again.

MISS JULIA[1]

A Naturalistic Tragedy

CHARACTERS

Miss Julia, aged twenty-five
Jean, a valet, aged thirty
Christine, a cook, aged thirty-five

The action takes place on Midsummer Eve,[2] in the kitchen of the count's country house.

A large kitchen: the ceiling and the side walls are hidden by draperies and hangings. The rear wall runs diagonally across the stage, from the left side and away from the spectators. On this wall, to the left, there are two shelves full of utensils made of copper, iron, and tin. The shelves are trimmed with scalloped paper.
   A little to the right may be seen three-fourths of the big arched doorway leading to the outside. It has double glass doors, through which are seen a fountain with a cupid, lilac shrubs in bloom, and the tops of some Lombardy poplars.

[1] *Translated from the Swedish by Edwin Björkman.*
[2] *Midsummer Eve. In the northern lands of Europe the lightest day of the year was popularly celebrated in pagan times by a vigil or wake the preceding night, which became the Christian feast of St. John's Eve on June 23. This summer solstice festival is still in Scandinavian countries a time of all-night merry-making comparable to the Yule celebration of the winter solstice. It is romantically associated with midsummer madness and the appearance of supernatural beings. The festival inspired the best-known Swedish musical composition, Hugo Alfven's rhapsody,* Midsommarvaka.

On the left side of the stage is seen the corner of a big cookstove built of glazed bricks; also a part of the smoke-hood above it.

From the right protrudes one end of the servants' dining-table of white pine, with a few chairs about it.

The stove is dressed with bundled branches of birch. Twigs of juniper are scattered on the floor.

On the table end stands a big Japanese spice pot full of lilac blossoms.

An icebox, a kitchen-table, and a wash-stand.

Above the door hangs a big old-fashioned bell on a steel spring, and the mouthpiece of a speaking-tube[3] appears at the left of the door.

CHRISTINE *is standing by the stove, frying something in a pan. She has on a dress of light-coloured cotton, which she has covered up with a big kitchen apron.*

JEAN *enters, dressed in livery and carrying a pair of big, spurred riding-boots, which he places on the floor in such manner that they remain visible to the spectators.*

JEAN. To-night Miss Julia is crazy again; absolutely crazy.

CHRISTINE. So you're back again?

JEAN. I took the count to the station, and when I came back by the barn, I went in and had a dance, and there I saw the young lady leading the dance with the gamekeeper. But when she caught sight of me, she rushed right up to me and asked me to dance the ladies' waltz with her. And ever since she's been waltzing like—well, I never saw the like of it. She's crazy!

CHRISTINE. And has always been, but never the way it's been this last fortnight, since her engagement was broken.

JEAN. Well, what kind of a story was that anyhow? He's a fine fellow, isn't he, although he isn't rich? Ugh, but they're so full of notions. [*Sits down at the end of the table*] It's peculiar anyhow, that a young lady—hm!—would rather stay at home with the servants—don't you think?—than go with her father to their relatives!

CHRISTINE. Oh, I guess she feels sort of embarrassed by that rumpus with her fellow.

JEAN. Quite likely. But there was some backbone to that man just

---

[3] *speaking-tube. In elegant homes of the late Victorian era the family communicated with the servants' quarters by speaking-tubes in the walls.*

the same. Do you know how it happened, Christine? I saw it, although I didn't care to let on.

CHRISTINE. No, did you?

JEAN. Sure, I did. They were in the stable-yard one evening, and the young lady was training him, as she called it. Do you know what that meant? She made him leap over her horse-whip the way you teach a dog to jump. Twice he jumped and got a cut each time. The third time he took the whip out of her hand and broke it into a thousand bits. And then he got out.

CHRISTINE. So that's the way it happened! You don't say!

JEAN. Yes, that's how that thing happened. Well, Christine, what have you got that's tasty?

CHRISTINE [*serves from the pan and puts the plate before* JEAN]. Oh, just some kidney which I cut out of the veal roast.

JEAN [*smelling the food*]. Fine! That's my great *délice*. [*Feeling the plate*] But you might have warmed the plate.

CHRISTINE. Well, if you ain't harder to please than the count himself! [*Pulls his hair playfully.*]

JEAN [*irritated*]. Don't pull my hair! You know how sensitive I am.

CHRISTINE. Well, well, it was nothing but a love pull, you know.

[JEAN *eats.* CHRISTINE *opens a bottle of beer.*]

JEAN. Beer—on Midsummer Eve? No, thank you! Then I have something better myself. [*Opens a table-drawer and takes out a bottle of claret with yellow cap*] Yellow seal, mind you! Give me a glass—and you use those with stems when you drink it *pure*.

CHRISTINE [*returns to the stove and puts a small pàn on the fire*]. Heaven preserve her that gets you for a husband, Mr. Finicky!

JEAN. Oh, rot! You'd be glad enough to get a smart fellow like me. And I guess it hasn't hurt you that they call me your beau. [*Tasting the wine*] Good! Pretty good! Just a tiny bit too cold. [*He warms the glass with his hands.*] We got this at Dijon. It cost us four francs per litre, not counting the bottle. And there was the duty besides. What is it you're cooking—with that infernal smell?

CHRISTINE. Oh, it's some deviltry the young lady is going to give Diana.

JEAN. You should choose your words with more care, Christine. But why should you be cooking for a bitch on a holiday eve like this? Is she sick?

CHRISTINE. Ye-es, she is sick. She's been running around with the gatekeeper's pug—and now's there's trouble—and the young lady just won't hear of it.

JEAN. The young lady is too stuck up in some ways and not proud enough in others—just as was the countess while she lived. She was most at home in the kitchen and among the cows, but she would never drive with only one horse. She wore her cuffs till they were dirty, but she had to have cuff buttons with a coronet on them. And speaking of the young lady, she doesn't take proper care of herself and her person. I might say even that she's lacking in refinement. Just now, when she was dancing in the barn, she pulled the gamekeeper away from Anna and asked him herself to come and dance with her. We wouldn't act in that way. But that's just how it is: when upper-class people want to demean themselves, then they grow—mean! But she's splendid! Magnificent! Oh, such shoulders! And—and so on!

CHRISTINE. Oh, well, don't brag too much! I've heard Clara talking, who tends to her dressing.

JEAN. Pooh, Clara! You're always jealous of each other. I, who have been out riding with her— And then the way she dances!

CHRISTINE. Say, Jean, won't you dance with me when I'm done?

JEAN. Of course I will.

CHRISTINE. Do you promise?

JEAN. Promise? When I say so, I'll do it. Well, here's thanks for the good food. It tasted fine! [*Puts the cork back into the bottle.*]

JULIA [*appears in the doorway, speaking to somebody on the outside*]. I'll be back in a minute. You go right on in the meantime.

[JEAN *slips the bottle into the table-drawer and rises respectfully.*]

JULIA [*enters and goes over to* CHRISTINE *by the wash-stand*]. Well, is it done yet?

[CHRISTINE *signs to her that* JEAN *is present.*]

JEAN [*gallantly*]. The ladies are having secrets, I believe.

JULIA [*strikes him in the face with her handkerchief*]. That's for you, Mr. Pry!

JEAN. Oh, what a delicious odor that violet has!

JULIA [*with coquetry*]. Impudent! So you know something about perfumes also? And know pretty well how to dance— Now don't peep! Go away!

JEAN [*with polite impudence*]. Is it some kind of witches' broth the ladies are cooking on Midsummer Eve—something to tell fortunes by and bring out the lucky star in which one's future love is seen?

JULIA [*sharply*]. If you can see that, you'll have good eyes, indeed!

[*To* CHRISTINE] Put it in a pint bottle and cork it well. Come and dance a *schottische* with me now, Jean.

JEAN [*hesitatingly*]. I don't want to be impolite, but I had promised to dance with Christine this time——

JULIA. Well, she can get somebody else—can't you, Christine? Won't you let me borrow Jean from you?

CHRISTINE. That isn't for me to say. When Miss Julia is so gracious, it isn't for him to say no. You just go along, and be thankful for the honour, too!

JEAN. Frankly speaking, but not wishing to offend in any way, I cannot help wondering if it's wise for Miss Julia to dance twice in succession with the same partner, especially as the people here are not slow in throwing out hints——

JULIA [*flaring up*]. What is that? What kind of hints? What do you mean?

JEAN [*submissively*]. As you don't want to understand, I have to speak more plainly. It don't look well to prefer one servant to all the rest who are expecting to be honoured in the same unusual way——

JULIA. Prefer! What ideas! I'm surprised! I, the mistress of the house, deign to honour this dance with my presence, and when it so happens that I actually want to dance, I want to dance with one who knows how to lead, so that I am not made ridiculous.

JEAN. As you command, Miss Julia! I am at your service!

JULIA [*softened*]. Don't take it as a command. To-night we should enjoy ourselves as a lot of happy people, and all rank should be forgotten. Now give me your arm. Don't be afraid, Christine! I'll return your beau to you!

[JEAN *offers his arm to* MISS JULIA *and leads her out.*]

pantomime

Must be acted as if the actress were really alone in the place. When necessary she turns her back to the public. She should not look in the direction of the spectators, and she should not hurry as if fearful that they might become impatient.

CHRISTINE *is alone. A* schottische *tune played on a violin is heard faintly in the distance.*

While humming the tune, CHRISTINE *clears off the table*

after JEAN, *washes the plate at the kitchen-table, wipes it, and puts it away in a cupboard.*

Then she takes off her apron, pulls out a small mirror from one of the table-drawers and leans it against the flower jar on the table; lights a tallow candle and heats a hairpin, which she uses to curl her front hair.

Then she goes to the door and stands there listening. Returns to the table. Discovers the handkerchief which MISS JULIA *has left behind, picks it up, and smells it, spreads it out absent-mindedly and begins to stretch it, smooth it, fold it up, and so forth.*

JEAN [*enters alone*]. Crazy, that's what she is! The way she dances! And the people stand behind the doors and grin at her. What do you think of it, Christine?

CHRISTINE. Oh, she has her time now, and then she is always a little queer like that. But are you going to dance with me now?

JEAN. You are not mad at me because I disappointed you?

CHRISTINE. No!—Not for a little thing like that, you know! And also, I know my place——

JEAN [*putting his arm around her waist*]. You are a sensible girl, Christine, and I think you'll make a good wife——

JULIA [*enters and is unpleasantly surprised; speaks with forced gayety*]. Yes, you are a fine partner—running away from your lady!

JEAN. On the contrary, Miss Julia. I have, as you see, looked up the one I deserted.

JULIA [*changing tone*]. Do you know, there is nobody that dances like you!—But why do you wear your livery on an evening like this? Take it off at once!

JEAN. Then I must ask you to step outside for a moment, as my black coat is hanging right here.

[*Points toward the right and goes in that direction.*]

JULIA. Are you bashful on my account? Just to change a coat? Why don't you go into your own room and come back again? Or, you can stay right here, and I'll turn my back on you.

JEAN. With your permission, Miss Julia.

[*Goes further over to the right; one of his arms can be seen as he changes his coat.*]

JULIA [*to* CHRISTINE]. Are you and Jean engaged, that he's so familiar with you?

CHRISTINE. Engaged? Well, in a way. We call it that.

JULIA. Call it?

CHRISTINE. Well, Miss Julia, you have had a fellow of your own, and——

JULIA. We were really engaged——

CHRISTINE. But it didn't come to anything just the same——

[JEAN *enters, dressed in black frock coat and black derby.*]

JULIA. *Très gentil, Monsieur Jean! Très gentil!*[1]

JEAN. *Vous voulez plaisanter, Madame!*

JULIA. *Et vous voulez parler français!* Where did you learn it?

JEAN. In Switzerland, while I worked as *sommelier*[2] in one of the big hotels at Lucerne.

JULIA. But you look like a real gentleman in your frock coat! Charming! [*Sits down at the table.*]

JEAN. Oh, you flatter me.

JULIA [*offended*]. Flatter—you!

JEAN. My natural modesty does not allow me to believe that you could be paying genuine compliments to one like me, and so I dare to assume that you are exaggerating, or, as we call it, flattering.

JULIA. Where did you learn to use your words like that? You must have been to the theatre a great deal?

JEAN. That, too. I have been to a lot of places.

JULIA. But you were born in this neighbourhood?

JEAN. My father was a cotter[3] on the county attorney's property right by here, and I can recall seeing you as a child, although you, of course, didn't notice me.

JULIA. No, really!

JEAN. Yes, and I remember one time in particular—but of that I can't speak.

JULIA. Oh, yes, do! Why—just for once.

JEAN. No, really, I cannot do it now. Another time, perhaps.

JULIA. Another time is no time. Is it as bad as that?

JEAN. It isn't bad, but it comes a little hard. Look at that one! [*Points to* CHRISTINE, *who has fallen asleep on a chair by the stove.*]

---

[1] *Très gentil, etc.*
JULIA. *Very fine, Mr. John! Very fine!*
JEAN. *You want to joke, madame!*
JULIA. *And you want to speak French!*
[2] *sommelier, butler.*
[3] *cotter, a cottager or peasant.*

JULIA. She'll make a pleasant wife. And perhaps she snores, too.

JEAN. No, she doesn't, but she talks in her sleep.

JULIA [*cynically*]. How do you know?

JEAN [*insolently*]. I have heard it.

[*Pause during which they study each other.*]

JULIA. Why don't you sit down?

JEAN. It wouldn't be proper in your presence.

JULIA. But if I order you to do it?

JEAN. Then I obey.

JULIA. Sit down, then!—But wait a moment! Can you give me something to drink first?

JEAN. I don't know what we have got in the icebox. I fear it is nothing but beer.

JULIA. And you call that nothing? My taste is so simple that I prefer it to wine.

JEAN [*takes a bottle of beer from the icebox and opens it; gets a glass and a plate from the cupboard, and serves the beer*]. Allow me!

JULIA. Thank you. Don't you want some yourself?

JEAN. I don't care very much for beer, but if it is a command, of course——

JULIA. Command?—I should think a polite gentleman might keep his lady company.

JEAN. Yes, that's the way it should be. [*Opens another bottle and takes out a glass.*]

JULIA. Drink my health now!

[*JEAN hesitates.*]

JULIA. Are you bashful—a big, grown-up man?

JEAN [*kneels with mock solemnity and raises his glass*]. To the health of my liege lady!

JULIA. Bravo!—And now you must also kiss my shoe in order to get it just right.

[*JEAN hesitates a moment; then he takes hold of her foot and touches it lightly with his lips.*]

JULIA. Excellent! You should have been on the stage.

JEAN [*rising to his feet*]. This won't do any longer, Miss Julia. Somebody might see us.

JULIA. What would that matter?

JEAN. Oh, it would set the people talking—that's all! And if you only knew how their tongues were wagging up there a while ago——

JULIA. What did they have to say? Tell me—— Sit down now!

JEAN [*sits down*]. I don't want to hurt you, but they were using expressions—which cast reflections of a kind that—oh, you know it yourself! You are not a child, and when a lady is seen alone with a man, drinking—no matter if he's only a servant—and at night— then——

JULIA. Then what? And besides, we are not alone. Isn't Christine with us?

JEAN. Yes—asleep!

JULIA. Then I'll wake her. [*Rising*] Christine, are you asleep?

CHRISTINE [*in her sleep*]. Blub-blub-blub-blub!

JULIA. Christine!—Did you ever see such a sleeper.

CHRISTINE [*in her sleep*]. The count's boots are polished—put on the coffee—yes, yes, yes—my—my—pooh!

JULIA [*pinches her nose*]. Can't you wake up?

JEAN [*sternly*]. You shouldn't bother those that sleep.

JULIA [*sharply*]. What's that?

JEAN. One who has stood by the stove all day has a right to be tired at night. And sleep should be respected.

JULIA [*changing tone*]. It is fine to think like that, and it does you honour—I thank you for it. [*Gives* JEAN *her hand*] Come now and pick some lilacs for me.

[*During the following scene* CHRISTINE *wakes up. She moves as if still asleep and goes out to the right in order to go to bed.*]

JEAN. With you, Miss Julia?

JULIA. With me!

JEAN. But it won't do! Absolutely not!

JULIA. I can't understand what you are thinking of. You couldn't possibly imagine——

JEAN. No, not I, but the people.

JULIA. What? That I am fond of the valet?

JEAN. I am not at all conceited, but such things have happened—and to the people nothing is sacred.

JULIA. You are an aristocrat, I think.

JEAN. Yes, I am.

JULIA. And I am stepping down——

JEAN. Take my advice, Miss Julia, don't step down. Nobody will believe you did it on purpose. The people will always say that you fell down.

JULIA. I think better of the people than you do. Come and see if I am not right. Come along! [*She ogles him.*]

JEAN. You're mighty queer, do you know!

JULIA. Perhaps. But so are you. And for that matter, everything is queer. Life, men, everything—just a mush that floats on top of the water until it sinks, sinks down! I have a dream that comes back to me ever so often. And just now I am reminded of it. I have climbed to the top of a column and sit there without being able to tell how to get down again. I get dizzy when I look down, and I must get down, but I haven't the courage to jump off. I cannot hold on, and I am longing to fall, and yet I don't fall. But there will be no rest for me until I get down, no rest until I get down, down on the ground. And if I did reach the ground, I should want to get still further down, into the ground itself— Have you ever felt like that?

JEAN. No, my dream is that I am lying under a tall tree in a dark wood. I want to get up, up to the top, so that I can look out over the smiling landscape, where the sun is shining, and so that I can rob the nest in which lie the golden eggs. And I climb and climb, but the trunk is so thick and smooth, and it is so far to the first branch. But I know that if I could only reach that first branch, then I should go right on to the top as on a ladder. I have not reached it yet, but I am going to, if it only be in my dreams.

JULIA. Here I am chattering to you about dreams! Come along! Only into the park!

[*She offers her arm to him, and they go toward the door.*]

JEAN. We must sleep on nine midsummer flowers to-night, Miss Julia—then our dreams will come true.

[*They turn around in the doorway, and* JEAN *puts one hand up to his eyes.*]

JULIA. Let me see what you have got in your eye.

JEAN. Oh, nothing—just some dirt—it will soon be gone.

JULIA. It was my sleeve that rubbed against it. Sit down and let me help you. [*Takes him by the arm and makes him sit down; takes hold of his head and bends it backwards; tries to get out the dirt with a corner of her handkerchief.*] Sit still now, absolutely still! [*Slaps him on the hand*] Well, can't you do as I say? I think you are shaking—a big, strong fellow like you! [*Feels his biceps*] And with such arms!

JEAN [*ominously*]. Miss Julia!

JULIA. Yes, Monsieur Jean.

JEAN. *Attention! Je ne suis qu' un homme.*[1]

[1] *Attention! etc. Be careful! I'm only a man.*

JULIA. Can't you sit still!—There now! Now it's gone. Kiss my hand now, and thank me.

JEAN [*rising*]. Miss Julia, listen to me. Christine has gone to bed now——Won't you listen to me?

JULIA. Kiss my hand first.

JEAN. Listen to me!

JULIA. Kiss my hand first!

JEAN. All right, but blame nobody but yourself!

JULIA. For what?

JEAN. For what? Are you still a mere child at twenty-five? Don't you know that it is dangerous to play with fire?

JULIA. Not for me. I am insured.

JEAN [*boldly*]. No, you are not. And even if you were, there are inflammable surroundings to be counted with.

JULIA. That's you, I suppose?

JEAN. Yes. Not because I am I, but because I am a young man——

JULIA. Of handsome appearance—what an incredible conceit! A Don Juan, perhaps. Or a Joseph? On my soul, I think you are a Joseph!

JEAN. Do you?

JULIA. I fear it almost.

[JEAN *goes boldly up to her and takes her around the waist in order to kiss her.*]

JULIA [*gives him a cuff on the ear*]. Shame!

JEAN. Was that in play or in earnest?

JULIA. In earnest.

JEAN. Then you were in earnest a moment ago also. Your playing is too serious, and that's the dangerous thing about it. Now I am tired of playing, and I ask to be excused in order to resume my work. The count wants his boots to be ready for him, and it is after midnight already.

JULIA. Put away the boots.

JEAN. No, it's my work, which I am bound to do. But I have not undertaken to be your playmate. It's something I can never become ——I hold myself too good for it.

JULIA. You're proud!

JEAN. In some ways, and not in others.

JULIA. Have you ever been in love?

JEAN. We don't use that word. But I have been fond of a lot of girls, and once I was taken sick because I couldn't have the one I wanted:

sick, you know, like those princes in the Arabian Nights who cannot eat or drink for sheer love.

JULIA. Who was it?

[JEAN *remains silent.*]

JULIA. Who was it?

JEAN. You cannot make me tell you.

JULIA. If I ask you as an equal, ask you as—a friend: who was it?

JEAN. It was you.

JULIA [*sits down*]. How funny!

JEAN. Yes, as you say—it was ludicrous. That was the story, you see, which I didn't want to tell you a while ago. But now I am going to tell it. Do you know how the world looks from below—no, you don't. No more than do hawks and falcons, of whom we never see the back because they are always floating about high up in the sky. I lived in the cotter's hovel, together with seven other children, and a pig—out there on the grey plain, where there isn't a single tree. But from our windows I could see the wall around the count's park, and apple-trees above it. That was the Garden of Eden, and many fierce angels were guarding it with flaming swords. Nevertheless I and some other boys found our way to the Tree of Life—now you despise me?

JULIA. Oh, stealing apples is something all boys do.

JEAN. You may say so now, but you despise me nevertheless. However—once I got into the Garden of Eden with my mother to weed the onion beds. Near by stood a Turkish pavillion, shaded by trees and covered with honeysuckle. I didn't know what it was used for, but I had never seen a more beautiful building. People went in and came out again, and one day the door was left wide open. I stole up and saw the walls covered with pictures of kings and emperors, and the windows were hung with red, fringed curtains—now you know what I mean. I—[*breaks off a lilac sprig and holds it under* MISS JULIA's *nose*]—I had never been inside the manor, and I had never seen anything but the church—and this was much finer. No matter where my thoughts ran, they returned always—to that place. And gradually a longing arose within me to taste the full pleasure of—*enfin!*[1] I sneaked in, looked and admired. Then I heard somebody coming. There was only one way out for fine people, but for me there was another, and I could do nothing else but choose it.

[JULIA, *who has taken the lilac sprig, lets it drop on the table.*]

[1] *enfin! well!*

JEAN. Then I started to run, plunged through a hedge of raspberry bushes, chased right across a strawberry plantation, and came out on the terrace where the roses grow. There I caught sight of a pink dress and pair of white stockings—that was you! I crawled under a pile of weeds—right into it, you know—into stinging thistles and wet, ill-smelling dirt. And I saw you walking among the roses, and I thought: if it be possible for a robber to get into heaven and dwell with the angels, then it is strange that a cotter's child, here on God's own earth, cannot get into the park and play with the count's daughter.

JULIA [*sentimentally*]. Do you think all poor children have the same thoughts as you had in this case?

JEAN [*hesitatingly at first; then with conviction*]. If *all* poor—yes—of course. Of course!

JULIA. It must be a dreadful misfortune to be poor.

JEAN [*in a tone of deep distress and with rather exaggerated emphasis*]. Oh, Miss Julia! Oh!—A dog may lie on her ladyship's sofa; a horse may have his nose patted by the young lady's hand, but a servant—[*changing his tone*]—oh well, here and there you meet one made of different stuff, and he makes a way for himself in the world, but how often does it happen?—However, do you know what I did? I jumped into the mill brook with my clothes on, and was pulled out, and got a licking. But the next Sunday, when my father and the rest of the people were going over to my grandmother's, I fixed it so that I could stay at home. And then I washed myself with soap and hot water, and put on my best clothes, and went to church, where I could see you. I did see you, and went home determined to die. But I wanted to die beautifully and pleasantly, without any pain. And then I recalled that it was dangerous to sleep under an elder bush. We had a big one that was in full bloom. I robbed it of all its flowers, and then I put them in the big box where the oats were kept and lay down in them. Did you ever notice the smoothness of oats? Soft to the touch as the skin of the human body! However, I pulled down the lid and closed my eyes—fell asleep and was waked up a very sick boy. But I didn't die, as you can see. What I wanted—that's more than I can tell. Of course, there was not the least hope of winning you—but you symbolised the hopelessness of trying to get out of the class into which I was born.

JULIA. You narrate spendidly, do you know! Did you ever go to school?

JEAN. A little. But I have read a lot of novels and gone to the theatre a good deal. And besides, I have listened to the talk of better-class people, and from that I have learned most of all.

JULIA. Do you stand around and listen to what we are saying?

JEAN. Of course! And I have heard a lot, too, when I was on the box of the carriage, or rowing the boat. Once I heard you, Miss Julia, and one of your girl friends——

JULIA. Oh!— What was it you heard then?

JEAN. Well, it wouldn't be easy to repeat. But I was rather surprised, and I couldn't understand where you had learned all those words. Perhaps, at bottom, there isn't quite so much difference as they think between one kind of people and another.

JULIA. You ought to be ashamed of yourself! We don't live as you do when we are engaged.

JEAN [*looking hard at her*]. Is it so certain?— Well, Miss Julia, it won't pay to make yourself out so very innocent to me——

JULIA. The man on whom I bestowed my love was a scoundrel.

JEAN. That's what you always say—afterwards.

JULIA. Always?

JEAN. Always, I believe, for I have heard the same words used several times before, on similar occasions.

JULIA. What occasions?

JEAN. Like the one of which we were speaking. The last time——

JULIA [*rising*]. Stop! I don't want to hear any more!

JEAN. Nor did *she*—curiously enough! Well, then I ask permission to go to bed.

JULIA [*gently*]. Go to bed on Midsummer Eve?

JEAN. Yes, for dancing with that mob out there has really no attraction for me.

JULIA. Get the key to the boat and take me out on the lake—I want to watch the sunrise.

JEAN. Would that be wise?

JULIA. It sounds as if you were afraid of your reputation.

JEAN. Why not? I don't care to be made ridiculous, and I don't care to be discharged without a recommendation, for I am trying to get on in the world. And then I feel myself under a certain obligation to Christine.

JULIA. So it's Christine now——

JEAN. Yes, but it's you also— Take my advice and go to bed!

JULIA. Am I to obey you?

JEAN. For once—and for your own sake! The night is far gone. Sleepiness makes us drunk, and the head grows hot. Go to bed! And besides—if I am not mistaken—I can hear the crowd coming this way to look for me. And if we are found together here, you are lost!

CHORUS [*is heard approaching*].

> Through the fields come two ladies a-walking,
> Treederee-derallah, treederee-derah.
> And one has her shoes full of water,
> Treederee-derallah-lah.
>
> They're talking of hundreds of dollars,
> Treederee-derallah, treederee-derah.
> But have not between them a dollar,
> Treederee-derallah-lah.
>
> This wreath I give you gladly,
> Treederee-derallah, treederee-derah.
> But love another madly,
> Treederee-derallah-lah.

JULIA. I know the people, and I love them, just as they love me. Let them come, and you'll see.

JEAN. No, Miss Julia, they don't love you. They take your food and spit at your back. Believe me. Listen to me—can't you hear what they are singing?—No, don't pay any attention to it!

JULIA [*listening*]. What is it they are singing?

JEAN. Oh, something scurrilous. About you and me.

JULIA. How infamous! They ought to be ashamed! And the treachery of it!

JEAN. The mob is always cowardly. And in such a fight as this there is nothing to do but to run away.

JULIA. Run away? Where to? We cannot get out. And we cannot go into Christine's room.

JEAN. Oh, we cannot? Well, into my room, then! Necessity knows no law. And you can trust me, for I am your true and frank and respectful friend.

JULIA. But think only—think if they should look for you in there!

JEAN. I shall bolt the door. And if they try to break it open, I'll shoot!—Come! [*Kneeling before her*] Come!

JULIA [*meaningly*]. And you promise me——?

JEAN. I swear!

[MISS JULIA *goes quickly out to the right.* JEAN *follows her eagerly.*]

ballet

The peasants enter. They are decked out in their best and carry flowers in their hats. A fiddler leads them. On the table they place a barrel of small-beer and a keg of "brännvin," or white Swedish whiskey, both of them decorated with wreathes woven out of leaves. First they drink. Then they form in ring and sing and dance to the melody heard before:

"Through the fields come two ladies a-walking."

The dance finished, they leave singing.

JULIA [*Enters alone. On seeing the disorder in the kitchen, she claps her hands together. Then she takes out a powder-puff and begins to powder her face*].

JEAN [*enters in a state of exaltation*]. There you see! And you heard, didn't you? Do you think it possible to stay here?

JULIA. No, I don't think so. But what are we to do?

JEAN. Run away, travel, far away from here.

JULIA. Travel? Yes—but where?

JEAN. To Switzerland, the Italian lakes—you have never been there?

JULIA. No. Is the country beautiful?

JEAN. Oh! Eternal summer! Orange trees! Laurels! Oh!

JULIA. But then—what are we to do down there?

JEAN. I'll start a hotel, everything first class, including the customers.

JULIA. Hotel?

JEAN. That's the life, I tell you! Constantly new faces and new languages. Never a minute free for nerves or brooding. No trouble about what to do—for the work is calling to be done: night and day, bells that ring, trains that whistle, 'busses that come and go; and gold pieces raining on the counter all the time. That's the life for you!

JULIA. Yes, that is life. And I?

JEAN. The mistress of everything, the chief ornament of the house. With your looks—and your manners—oh, success will be assured! Enormous! You'll sit like a queen in the office and keep the slaves going by the touch of an electric button. The guests will pass in review before your throne and timidly deposit their treasures on your table. You cannot imagine how people tremble when a bill is presented to them—I'll salt the items, and you'll sugar them with your sweetest smiles. Oh, let us get away from here—[*pulling a time-table from his pocket*]—at once, with the next train! We'll be in Malmö at 6:30; in Hamburg at 8:40 to-morrow morning; in Frankfort and Basel a day later. And to reach Como by way of the St. Gotthard it will take us— let me see—three days. Three days!

JULIA. All that is all right. But you must give me some courage— Jean. Tell me that you love me. Come and take me in your arms.

JEAN [*reluctantly*]. I should like to—but I don't dare. Not in this house again. I love you—beyond doubt—or, can you doubt it, Miss Julia?

JULIA [*with modesty and true womanly feeling*]. Miss?—Call me Julia. Between us there can be no barriers hereafter. Call me Julia!

JEAN [*disturbed*]. I cannot! There will be barriers between us as long as we stay in this house—there is the past, and there is the count—and I have never met another person for whom I felt such respect. If I only catch sight of his gloves on a chair I feel small. If I only hear that bell up there, I jump like a shy horse. And even now, when I see his boots standing there so stiff and perky, it is as if something made my back bend. [*Kicking at the boots*] It's nothing but superstition and tradition hammered into us from childhood—but it can be as easily forgotten again. Let us only get to another country, where they have a republic, and you'll see them bend their backs double before my liveried porter. You see, backs have to be bent, but not mine. I wasn't born to that kind of thing. There's better stuff in me— character—and if I only get hold of the first branch, you'll see me do some climbing. To-day I am a valet, but next year I'll be a hotel owner. In ten years I can live on the money I have made, and then I'll go to Roumania and get myself an order. And I may—note that I say *may*—end my days as a count.

JULIA. Splendid, splendid!

JEAN. Yes, in Roumania the title of count can be had for cash, and so you'll be a countess after all. My countess!

JULIA. What do I care about all I now cast behind me! Tell me that you love me: otherwise—yes, what am I otherwise?

JEAN. I will tell you so a thousand times—later. But not here. And above all, no sentimentality, or everything will be lost. We must look at the matter in cold blood, like sensible people. [*Takes out a cigar, cuts off the point, and lights it*] Sit down there now, and I'll sit here, and then we'll talk as if nothing had happened.

JULIA [*in despair*]. Good Lord! Have you then no feelings at all?

JEAN. I? No one is more full of feeling than I am. But I know how to control myself.

JULIA. A while ago you kissed my shoe—and now!

JEAN [*severely*]. Yes, that was then. Now we have other things to think of.

JULIA. Don't speak harshly to me!

JEAN. No, but sensibly. One folly has been committed—don't let us commit any more! The count may be here at any moment, and before he comes our fate must be settled. What do you think of my plans for the future? Do you approve of them?

JULIA. They seem acceptable, on the whole. But there is one question: a big undertaking of that kind will require a big capital—have you got it?

JEAN [*chewing his cigar*]. I? Of course! I have my expert knowledge, my vast experience, my familiarity with several languages. That's the very best kind of capital, I should say.

JULIA. But it won't buy you a railroad ticket even.

JEAN. That's true enough. And that is just why I am looking for a backer to advance the needful cash.

JULIA. Where could you get one all of a sudden?

JEAN. It's for you to find him if you want to become my partner.

JULIA. I cannot do it, and I have nothing myself. [*Pause.*]

JEAN. Well, then that's off——

JULIA. And——

JEAN. Everything remains as before.

JULIA. Do you think I am going to stay under this roof as your concubine? Do you think I'll let the people point their fingers at me? Do you think I can look my father in the face after this? No, take me away from here, from all this humiliation and disgrace!—Oh, what have I done? My God, my God! [*Breaks into tears.*]

JEAN. So we have got around to that tune now!—What you have done? Nothing but what many others have done before you.

JULIA [*crying hysterically*]. And now you're despising me!—I'm falling, I'm falling!

JEAN. Fall down to me, and I'll lift you up again afterwards.

JULIA. What horrible power drew me to you? Was it the attraction which the strong exercises on the weak—the one who is rising on one who is falling? Or was it love? This—love! Do you know what love is?

JEAN. I? Well, I should say so! Don't you think I have been there before?

JULIA. Oh, the language you use, and the thoughts you think!

JEAN. Well, that's the way I was brought up, and that's the way I am. Don't get nerves now and play the exquisite, for now one of us is just as good as the other. Look here, my girl, let me treat you to a glass of something superfine.

[*He opens the table-drawer, takes out the wine bottle and fills up two glasses that have already been used.*]

JULIA. Where did you get that wine?

JEAN. In the cellar.

JULIA. My father's Burgundy!

JEAN. Well, isn't it good enough for the son-in-law?

JULIA. And I am drinking beer—I!

JEAN. It shows merely that I have better taste than you.

JULIA. Thief!

JEAN. Do you mean to tell on me?

JULIA. Oh, oh! The accomplice of a house thief! Have I been drunk, or have I been dreaming all this night? Midsummer Eve! The feast of innocent games——

JEAN. Innocent—hm!

JULIA [*walking back and forth*]. Can there be another human being on earth so unhappy as I am at this moment?

JEAN. But why should you be? After such a conquest? Think of Christine in there. Don't you think she has feelings also?

JULIA. I thought so a while ago, but I don't think so any longer. No, a menial is a menial——

JEAN. And a whore a whore!

JULIA [*on her knees, with folded hands*]. O God in heaven, make an end of this wretched life! Take me out of the filth into which I am sinking! Save me! Save me!

JEAN. I cannot deny that I feel sorry for you. When I was lying among the onions and saw you up there among the roses—I'll tell you now—I had the same nasty thoughts that all boys have.

JULIA. And you who wanted to die for my sake!

JEAN. Among the oats. That was nothing but talk.

JULIA. Lies in other words!

JEAN [*beginning to feel sleepy*]. Just about. I think I read the story in a paper, and it was about a chimney-sweep who crawled into a wood-box full of lilacs because a girl had brought suit against him for not supporting her kid——

JULIA. So that's the sort you are——

JEAN. Well, I had to think of something—for it's the high-faluting stuff that the women bite on.

JULIA. Scoundrel!

JEAN. Rot!

JULIA. And now you have seen the back of the hawk——

JEAN. Well, I don't know——

JULIA. And I was to be the first branch——

JEAN. But the branch was rotten——

JULIA. I was to be the sign in front of the hotel——

JEAN. And I the hotel——

JULIA. Sit at your counter, and lure your customers, and doctor your bills——

JEAN. No, that I should have done myself——

JULIA. That a human soul can be so steeped in dirt!

JEAN. Well, wash it off!

JULIA. You lackey, you menial, stand up when I talk to you!

JEAN. You lackey-love, you mistress of a menial—shut up and get out of here! You're the right one to come and tell me that I am vulgar. People of my kind would never in their lives act as vulgarly as you have acted to-night. Do you think any servant girl would go for a man as you did? Did you ever see a girl of my class throw herself at anybody in that way? I have never seen the like of it except among beasts and prostitutes.

JULIA [*crushed*]. That's right: strike me, step on me—I haven't deserved any better! I am a wretched creature. But help me! Help me out of this, if there be any way to do so!

JEAN [*in a milder tone*]. I don't want to lower myself by a denial of my share in the honour of seducing. But do you think a person in my place would have dared to raise his eyes to you, if the invitation to do so had not come from yourself? I am still sitting here in a state of utter surprise——

JULIA. And pride——

JEAN. Yes, why not? Although I must confess that the victory was too easy to bring with it any real intoxication.

JULIA. Strike me some more!

JEAN [*rising*]. No! Forgive me instead what I have been saying. I don't want to strike one who is disarmed, and least of all a lady. On one hand I cannot deny that it has given me pleasure to discover that what has dazzled us below is nothing but cat-gold; that the hawk is simply grey on the back also; that there is powder on the tender cheek; that there may be black borders on the polished nails; and that the handkerchief may be dirty, although it smells of perfume. But on the other hand it hurts me to have discovered that what I was striving to reach is neither better nor more genuine. It hurts me to see you sinking so low that you are far beneath your own cook—it hurts me as it hurts to see the Fall flowers beaten down by the rain and turned into mud.

JULIA. You speak as if you were already above me?

JEAN. Well, so I am. Don't you see: I could have made a countess of you, but you could never make me a count.

JULIA. But I am born of a count, and that's more than you can ever achieve.

JEAN. That's true. But I might be the father of counts—if——

JULIA. But you are a thief—and I am not.

JEAN. Thief is not the worst. There are other kinds still farther down. And then, when I serve in a house, I regard myself in a sense as a member of the family, as a child of the house, and you don't call it theft when children pick a few of the berries that load down the vines. [*His passion is aroused once more.*] Miss Julia, you are a magnificent woman, and far too good for one like me. You were swept along by a spell of intoxication, and now you want to cover up your mistake by making yourself believe that you are in love with me. Well, you are not, unless possibly my looks might tempt you—in which case your love is no better than mine. I could never rest satisfied with having you care for nothing in me but the mere animal, and your love I can never win.

JULIA. Are you so sure of that?

JEAN. You mean to say that it might be possible? That I might love you: yes, without doubt—for you are beautiful, refined [*goes up to her and takes hold of her hand*], educated, charming when you want to be so, and it is not likely that the flame will ever burn out in a man who has once been set on fire by you. [*Puts his arm around her waist*] You are like burnt wine with strong spices in it, and one of your kisses——

[*He tries to lead her away, but she frees herself gently from his hold.*]

JULIA. Leave me alone! In that way you cannot win me.

JEAN. How then?— Not in that way! Not by caresses and sweet words! Not by thought for the future, by escape from disgrace! How then?

JULIA. How? How? I don't know— Not at all! I hate you as I hate rats, but I cannot escape from you!

JEAN. Escape *with* me!

JULIA [*straightening up*]. Escape? Yes, we must escape!—But I am so tired. Give me a glass of wine.

[JEAN *pours out wine.*]

JULIA [*looks at her watch*]. But we must have a talk first. We have still some time left. [*Empties her glass and holds it out for more.*]

JEAN. Don't drink so much. It will go to your head.

JULIA. What difference would that make?

JEAN. What difference would it make? It's vulgar to get drunk— What was it you wanted to tell me?

JULIA. We must get away. But first we must have a talk—that is, I must talk, for so far you have done all the talking. You have told me about your life. Now I must tell you about mine, so that we know each other right to the bottom before we begin the journey together.

JEAN. One moment, pardon me! Think first, so that you don't regret it afterwards, when you have already given up the secrets of your life.

JULIA. Are you not my friend?

JEAN. Yes, at times—but don't rely on me.

JULIA. You only talk like that—and besides, my secrets are known to everybody. You see, my mother was not of noble birth, but came of quite plain people. She was brought up in the ideas of her time about equality, and woman's independence, and that kind of thing. And she had a decided aversion to marriage. Therefore, when my father proposed to her, she said she wouldn't marry him—and then she did it just the same. I came into the world—against my mother's wish, I have come to think. Then my mother wanted to bring me up in a perfectly natural state, and at the same time I was to learn everything that a boy is taught, so that I might prove that a woman is just as good as a man. I was dressed as a boy, and was taught how to handle a horse, but could have nothing to do with the cows. I had to groom and harness and go hunting on horseback. I was even forced to learn something about agriculture. And all over the estate men were set to do women's work, and women to do men's—with the result that everything went to pieces and we became the laughingstock of the whole neighbourhood. At last my father must have recovered from the spell cast over him, for he rebelled, and everything was changed to suit his own ideas. My mother was taken sick—what kind of sickness it was I don't know, but she fell often into convulsions, and she used to hide herself in the garret or in the garden, and sometimes she stayed out all night. Then came the big fire, of which you have heard. Th house, the stable, and the barn were burned down, and this under circumstances which made it look as if the fire had been set on purpose. For the disaster occurred the day after our insurance expired, and the money sent for renewal of the policy had been delayed by the messenger's carelessness, so that it came too late. [*She fills her glass again and drinks.*]

JEAN. Don't drink any more.

JULIA. Oh, what does it matter!—We were without a roof over our heads and had to sleep in the carriages. My father didn't know where to get money for the rebuilding of the house. Then my mother suggested that he try to borrow from a childhood friend of hers, a brick manufacturer living not far from here. My father got the loan, but was not permitted to pay any interest, which astonished him. And so the house was built up again. [*Drinks again*] Do you know who set fire to the house?

JEAN. Her ladyship, your mother!

JULIA. Do you know who the brick manufacturer was?

JEAN. Your mother's lover?

JULIA. Do you know to whom the money belonged?

JEAN. Wait a minute—no, that I don't know.

JULIA. To my mother.

JEAN. In other words, to the count, if there was no settlement.

JULIA. There was no settlement. My mother possessed a small fortune of her own which she did not want to leave in my father's control, so she invested it with—her friend.

JEAN. Who copped it.

JULIA. Exactly! He kept it. All this came to my father's knowledge. He couldn't bring suit; he couldn't pay his wife's lover; he couldn't prove that it was his wife's money. That was my mother's revenge because he had made himself master in his own house. At that time he came near shooting himself—it was even rumoured that he had tried and failed. But he took a new lease of life, and my mother had to pay for what she had done. I can tell you that those were five years I'll never forget! My sympathies were with my father, but I took my mother's side because I was not aware of the true circumstances. From her I learned to suspect and hate men—for she hated the whole sex, as you have probably heard—and I promised her on my oath that I would never become a man's slave.

JEAN. And so you became engaged to the County Attorney.

JULIA. Yes, in order that he should be my slave.

JEAN. And he didn't want to?

JULIA. Oh, he wanted, but I wouldn't let him. I got tired of him.

JEAN. Yes, I saw it—in the stable-yard.

JULIA. What did you see?

JEAN. Just that—how he broke the engagement.

JULIA. That's a lie! It was I who broke it. Did he say he did it, the scoundrel?

JEAN. Oh, he was no scoundrel, I guess. So you hate men, Miss Julia?

JULIA. Yes! Most of the time. But now and then—when the weakness comes over me—oh, what shame!

JEAN. And you hate me too?

JULIA. Beyond measure! I should like to kill you like a wild beast——

JEAN. As you make haste to shoot a mad dog. Is that right?

JULIA. That's right!

JEAN. But now there is nothing to shoot with—and there is no dog. What are we to do then?

JULIA. Go abroad.

JEAN. In order to plague each other to death?

JULIA. No—in order to enjoy ourselves: a couple of days, a week, as long as enjoyment is possible. And then—die!

JEAN. Die? How silly! Then I think it's much better to start a hotel.

JULIA [*without listening to* JEAN].—At Lake Como, where the sun is always shining, and the laurels stand green at Christmas, and the oranges are glowing.

JEAN. Lake Como is a rainy hole, and I could see no oranges except in the groceries. But it is a good place for tourists, as it has a lot of villas that can be rented to loving couples, and that's a profitable business—do you know why? Because they take a lease for six months—and then they leave after three weeks.

JULIA [*naïvely*]. Why after three weeks?

JEAN. Because they quarrel, of course. But the rent has to be paid just the same. And then you can rent the house again. And that way it goes on all the time, for there is plenty of love—even if it doesn't last long.

JULIA. You don't want to die with me?

JEAN. I don't want to die at all. Both because I am fond of living, and because I regard suicide as a crime against the Providence which has bestowed life on us.

JULIA. Do you mean to say that *you* believe in God?

JEAN. Of course, I do. And I go to church every other Sunday

Frankly speaking, now I am tired of all this, and now I am going to bed.

JULIA. So! And you think that will be enough for me? Do you know what you owe a woman that you have spoiled?

JEAN [*takes out his purse and throws a silver coin on the table*]. You're welcome! I don't want to be in anybody's debt.

JULIA [*pretending not to notice the insult*]. Do you know what the law provides——

JEAN. Unfortunately the law provides no punishment for a woman who seduces a man.

JULIA [*as before*]. Can you think of any escape except by our going abroad and getting married, and then getting a divorce?

JEAN. Suppose I refuse to enter into this *mésalliance?*

JULIA. *Mésalliance*——

JEAN. Yes, for me. You see, I have better ancestry than you, for nobody in my family was ever guilty of arson.

JULIA. How do you know?

JEAN. Well, nothing is known to the contrary, for we keep no pedigrees—except in the police bureau. But I have read about your pedigree in a book that was lying on the drawing-room table. Do you know who was your first ancestor? A miller who let his wife sleep with the king one night during the war with Denmark. I have no such ancestry. I have none at all, but I can become an ancestor myself.

JULIA. That's what I get for unburdening my heart to one not worthy of it; for sacrificing my family's honour——

JEAN. Dishonour! Well, what was it I told you? You shouldn't drink, for then you talk. And you *must* not talk!

JULIA. Oh, how I regret what I have done! How I regret it! If at least you loved me!

JEAN. For the last time: what do you mean? Am I to weep? Am I to jump over your whip? Am I to kiss you, and lure you down to Lake Como for three weeks, and so on? What am I to do? What do you expect? This is getting to be rather painful! But that's what comes from getting mixed up with women. Miss Julia! I see that you are unhappy; I know that you are suffering; but I cannot understand you. We never carry on like that. There is never any hatred between us. Love is to us a play, and we play at it when our work leaves us time to do so. But we have not the time to do so all day and all night, as you have. I believe you are sick—I am sure you are sick.

JULIA. You should be good to me—and now you speak like a human being.

JEAN. All right, but be human yourself. You spit on me, and then you won't let me wipe myself—on you!

JULIA. Help me, help me! Tell me only what I am to do—where I am to turn?

JEAN. O Lord, if I only knew that myself!

JULIA. I have been exasperated, I have been mad, but there ought to be some way of saving myself.

JEAN. Stay right here and keep quiet. Nobody knows anything.

JULIA. Impossible! The people know, and Christine knows.

JEAN. They don't know, and they would never believe it possible.

JULIA [*hesitating*]. But—it might happen again.

JEAN. That's true.

JULIA. And the results?

JEAN [*frightened*]. The results! Where was my head when I didn't think of that! Well, then there is only one thing to do—you must leave. At once! I can't go with you, for then everything would be lost, so you must go alone—abroad—anywhere!

JULIA. Alone? Where?— I can't do it.

JEAN. You must! And before the count gets back. If you stay, then you know what will happen. Once on the wrong path, one wants to keep on, as the harm is done anyhow. Then one grows more and more reckless—and at last it all comes out. So you must get away! Then you can write to the count and tell him everything, except that it was me. And he would never guess it. Nor do I think he would be very anxious to find out.

JULIA. I'll go if you come with me.

JEAN. Are you stark mad, woman? Miss Julia to run away with her valet! It would be in the papers in another day, and the count could never survive it.

JULIA. I can't leave! I can't stay! Help me! I am so tired, so fearfully tired. Give me orders! Set me going, for I can no longer think, no longer act——

JEAN. Do you see now what good-for-nothings you are! Why do you strut and turn up your noses as if you were the lords of creation? Well, I am going to give you orders. Go up and dress. Get some travelling money, and then come back again.

JULIA [*in an undertone*]. Come up with me!

JEAN. To your room? Now you're crazy again! [*Hesitates a moment*] No, you must go at once! [*Takes her by the hand and leads her out.*]

JULIA [*on her way out*]. Can't you speak kindly to me, Jean?

JEAN. An order must always sound unkind. Now you can find out how it feels!

[JULIA *goes out.* JEAN, *alone, draws a sigh of relief; sits down at the table; takes out a note-book and a pencil; figures aloud from time to time; dumb play until* CHRISTINE *enters dressed for church; she has a false shirt front and a white tie in one of her hands.*]

CHRISTINE. Goodness gracious, how the place looks! What have you been up to anyhow?

JEAN. Oh, it was Miss Julia who dragged in the people. Have you been sleeping so hard that you didn't hear anything at all?

CHRISTINE. I have been sleeping like a log.

JEAN. And dressed for church already?

CHRISTINE. Yes, didn't you promise to come with me to communion to-day?

JEAN. Oh, yes, I remember now. And there you've got the finery. Well, come on with it. [*Sits down;* CHRISTINE *helps him to put on the shirt front and the white tie. Pause.*]

JEAN [*sleepily*]. What's the text to-day?

CHRISTINE. Oh, about John the Baptist beheaded, I guess.

JEAN. That's going to be a long story, I'm sure. My, but you choke me! Oh, I'm so sleepy, so sleepy!

CHRISTINE. Well, what has been keeping you up all night? Why, man, you're just green in the face!

JEAN. I have been sitting here talking with Miss Julia.

CHRISTINE. She hasn't an idea of what's proper, that creature! [*Pause.*]

JEAN. Say, Christine.

CHRISTINE. Well?

JEAN. Isn't it funny anyhow, when you come to think of it? Her!

CHRISTINE. What is it that's funny?

JEAN. Everything! [*Pause.*]

CHRISTINE [*seeing the glasses on the table that are only half emptied*]. So you've been drinking together also?

JEAN. Yes.

CHRISTINE. Shame on you! Look me in the eye!

JEAN. Yes.

CHRISTINE. Is it possible? Is it possible?

JEAN [*after a moment's thought*]. Yes, it is!

CHRISTINE. Ugh! That's worse than I could ever have believed. It's awful!

JEAN. You are not jealous of her, are you?

CHRISTINE. No, not of her. Had it been Clara or Sophie, then I'd have scratched your eyes out. Yes, that's the way I feel about it, and I can't tell why. Oh my, but that was nasty!

JEAN. Are you mad at her then?

CHRISTINE. No, but at you! It was wrong of you, very wrong! Poor girl! No, I tell you, I don't want to stay in this house any longer, with people for whom it is impossible to have any respect.

JEAN. Why should you have any respect for them?

CHRISTINE. And you who are such a smarty can't tell that! You wouldn't serve people who don't act decently, would you? It's to lower oneself, I think.

JEAN. Yes, but it ought to be a consolation to us that they are not a bit better than we.

CHRISTINE. No, I don't think so. For if they're no better, then it's no use trying to get up to them. And just think of the count! Think of him who has had so much sorrow in his day! No, I don't want to stay any longer in this house—— And with a fellow like you, too. If it had been the County Attorney—if it had only been some one of her own sort——

JEAN. Now look here!

CHRISTINE. Yes, yes! You're all right in your way, but there's after all some difference between one kind of people and another— No, but this is something I'll never get over!— And the young lady who was so proud, and so tart to the men, that you couldn't believe she would ever let one come near her—and such a one at that! And she who wanted to have poor Diana shot because she had been running around with the gatekeeper's pug!— Well, I declare!— But I won't stay here any longer, and next October I get out of here.

JEAN. And then?

CHRISTINE. Well, as we've come to talk of that now, perhaps it would be just as well if you looked for something, seeing that we're going to get married after all.

JEAN. Well, what could I look for? As a married man I couldn't get a place like this.

CHRISTINE. No, I understand that. But you could get a job as a janitor, or maybe as a messenger in some government bureau. Of course, the public loaf is always short in weight, but it comes steady, and then there is a pension for the widow and the children——

JEAN [*making a face*]. That's good and well, but it isn't my style to think of dying all at once for the sake of wife and children. I must say that my plans have been looking toward something better than that kind of thing.

CHRISTINE. Your plans, yes—but you've got obligations also, and those you had better keep in mind!

JEAN. Now don't you get my dander up by talking of obligations! I know what I've got to do anyhow. [*Listening for some sound on the outside*] However, we've plenty of time to think of all this. Go in now and get ready, and then we'll go to church.

CHRISTINE. Who is walking around up there?

JEAN. I don't know, unless it be Clara.

CHRISTINE [*going out*]. It can't be the count, do you think, who's come home without anybody hearing him?

JEAN [*scared*]. The count? No, that isn't possible, for then he would have rung for me.

CHRISTINE [*as she goes out*]. Well, God help us all! Never have I seen the like of it!

[*The sun has risen and is shining on the tree tops in the park. The light changes gradually until it comes slantingly in through the windows.* JEAN *goes to the door and gives a signal.*]

JULIA [*enters in travelling dress and carrying a small bird-cage covered up with a towel; this she places on a chair*]. Now I am ready.

JEAN. Hush! Christine is awake.

JULIA [*showing extreme nervousness during the following scene*]. Did she suspect anything?

JEAN. She knows nothing at all. But, my heavens, how you look!

JULIA. How do I look?

JEAN. You're as pale as a corpse, and—pardon me, but your face is dirty.

JULIA. Let me wash it then— Now! [*She goes over to the washstand and washes her face and hands.*] Give me a towel— Oh!— That's the sun rising!

JEAN. And then the ogre bursts.

JULIA. Yes, ogres and trolls were abroad last night!— But listen, Jean. Come with me, for now I have the money.

JEAN [*doubtfully*]. Enough?

JULIA. Enough to start with. Come with me, for I cannot travel alone to-day. Think of it—Midsummer Day, on a stuffy train, jammed with people who stare at you—and standing still at stations when you want to fly. No, I cannot! I cannot! And then the memories will come: childhood memories of Midsummer Days, when the inside of the church was turned into a green forest—birches and lilacs; the dinner at the festive table with relatives and friends; the afternoon in the park, with dancing and music, flowers and games! Oh, you may run and run, but your memories are in the baggage-car, and with them remorse and repentance!

JEAN. I'll go with you—but at once, before it's too late. This very moment!

JULIA. Well, get dressed then. [*Picks up the cage.*]

JEAN. But no baggage! That would only give us away.

JULIA. No, nothing at all! Only what we can take with us in the car.

JEAN [*has taken down his hat*]. What have you got there? What is it?

JULIA. It's only my finch. I can't leave it behind.

JEAN. Did you ever! Dragging a bird-cage along with us! You must be raving mad! Drop the cage!

JULIA. The only thing I take with me from my home! The only living creature that loves me since Diana deserted me! Don't be cruel! Let me take it along!

JEAN. Drop the cage, I tell you! And don't talk so loud—Christine can hear us.

JULIA. No, I won't let it fall into strange hands. I'd rather have you kill it!

JEAN. Well, give it to me, and I'll wring its neck.

JULIA. Yes, but don't hurt it. Don't—no, I cannot!

JEAN. Let me—I can!

JULIA [*takes the bird out of the cage and kisses it*]. Oh, my little birdie, must it die and go away from its mistress!

JEAN. Don't make a scene, please. Don't you know it's a question of your life, of your future? Come, quick! [*Snatches the bird away from her, carries it to the chopping-block and picks up an axe.* MISS JULIA *turns away.*]

JEAN. You should have learned how to kill chickens instead of shooting with a revolver—[*brings down the axe*]—then you wouldn't have fainted for a drop of blood.

JULIA [*screaming*]. Kill me too! Kill me! You who can take the life of an innocent creature without turning a hair! Oh, I hate and despise you! There is blood between us! Cursed be the hour when I first met you! Cursed be the hour when I came to life in my mother's womb!

JEAN. Well, what's the use of all that cursing? Come on!

JULIA [*approaching the chopping-block as if drawn to it against her will*]. No, I don't want to go yet. I cannot—I must see—Hush! There's a carriage coming up the road. [*Listening without taking her eyes off the block and the axe*] You think I cannot stand the sight of blood. You think I am as weak as that—oh, I should like to see your blood, your brains, on that block there. I should like to see your whole sex swimming in blood like that thing there. I think I could drink out of your skull, and bathe my feet in your open breast, and eat your heart from the spit!— You think I am weak; you think I love you because the fruit of my womb was yearning for your seed; you think I want to carry your offspring under my heart and nourish it with my blood—bear your children and take your name! Tell me, you, what are you called anyhow? I have never heard your family name—and maybe you haven't any. I should become Mrs. "Hovel," or Mrs. "Backyard"—you dog there, that's wearing my collar; you lackey with my coat of arms on your buttons—and I should share with my cook, and be the rival of my own servant. Oh! Oh! Oh!— You think I am a coward and want to run away! No, now I'll stay—and let the lightning strike! My father will come home—will find his chiffonier opened—the money gone! Then he'll ring—twice for the valet—and then he'll send for the sheriff—and then I shall tell everything! Everything! Oh, but it will be good to get an end to it—if it only be the end! And then his heart will break, and he dies!—So there will be an end to all of us—and all will be quiet—peace—eternal rest!— And then the coat of arms will be shattered on the coffin—and the count's line will be wiped out—but the lackey's line goes on in the orphan asylum—wins laurels in the gutter, and ends in jail.

JEAN. There spoke the royal blood! Bravo, Miss Julia! Now you put the miller back in his sack!

[CHRISTINE *enters dressed for church and carrying a hymn-book in her hand.*]

JULIA [*hurries up to her and throws herself into her arms as if seeking protection*]. Help me, Christine! Help me against this man!

CHRISTINE [*unmoved and cold*]. What kind of performance is this on the Sabbath morning? [*Catches sight of the chopping-block*] My, what a mess you have made!— What's the meaning of all this? And the way you shout and carry on!

JULIA. You are a woman, Christine, and you are my friend. Beware of that scoundrel!

JEAN [*a little shy and embarrassed*]. While the ladies are discussing I'll get myself a shave. [*Slinks out to the right.*]

JULIA. You must understand me, and you must listen to me.

CHRISTINE. No, really, I don't understand this kind of trolloping. Where are you going in your travelling-dress—and he with his hat on—what?— What?

JULIA. Listen, Christine, listen, and I'll tell you everything——

CHRISTINE. I don't want to know anything——

JULIA. You must listen to me——

CHRISTINE. What is it about? Is it about this nonsense with Jean? Well, I don't care about it at all, for it's none of my business. But if you're planning to get him away with you, we'll put a stop to that!

JULIA [*extremely nervous*]. Please try to be quiet, Christine, and listen to me. I cannot stay here, and Jean cannot stay here—and so we must leave——

CHRISTINE. Hm, hm!

JULIA [*brightening up*]. But now I have got an idea, you know. Suppose all three of us should leave—go abroad—go to Switzerland and start a hotel together—I have money, you know—and Jean and I could run the whole thing—and you, I thought, could take charge of the kitchen— Wouldn't that be fine!— Say yes, now! And come along with us! Then everything is fixed!— Oh, say yes! [*She puts her arms around* CHRISTINE *and pats her.*]

CHRISTINE [*coldly and thoughtfully*]. Hm, hm!

JULIA [*presto tempo*]. You have never travelled, Christine—you must get out and have a look at the world. You cannot imagine what fun it is to travel on a train—constantly new people—new countries —and then we get to Hamburg and take in the Zoological Gardens in passing—that's what you like—and then we go to the theatres and to the opera—and when we get to Munich, there, you know, we have a lot of museums, where they keep Rubens and Raphael and all those big painters, you know— Haven't you heard of Munich, where King Louis[1] used to live—the king, you know, that went mad— And then we'll have a look at his castle—he has still some castles that are furnished just as in a fairy tale—and from there it isn't very far to Switzerland—and the Alps, you know—just think of the Alps, with snow on top of them in the middle of the summer—and there you have orange trees and laurels that are green all the year around——

[1] *King Louis. Ludwig II (1845–1886), the passionate friend and patron of Wagner, built the fantastic castle of Neuschwanstein high in the Bavarian Alps and decorated it with romantic pictures of Lohengrin, Tannhäuser, and Tristram and Iseult inspired by Wagner's operas.*

[JEAN *is seen in the right wing, sharpening his razor on a strop which he holds between his teeth and his left hand; he listens to the talk with a pleased mien and nods approval now and then.*]

JULIA [*tempo prestissimo*]. And then we get a hotel—and I sit in the office, while Jean is outside receiving tourists—and goes out marketing—and writes letters— That's a life for you— Then the train whistles, and the 'bus drives up, and it rings upstairs, and it rings in the restaurant—and then I make out the bills—and I am going to salt them,[2] too— You can never imagine how timid tourists are when they come to pay their bills! And you—you will sit like a queen in the kitchen. Of course, you are not going to stand at the stove yourself. And you'll have to dress neatly and nicely in order to show yourself to people—and with your looks—yes, I am not flattering you—you'll catch a husband some fine day—some rich Englishman, you know—for those fellows are so easy [*slowing down*] to catch—and then we grow rich—and we build us a villa at Lake Como—of course, it is raining a little in that place now and then—but [*limply*] the sun must be shining sometimes—although it looks dark—and—then—or else we can go home again—and come back—here—or some other place——

CHRISTINE. Tell me, Miss Julia, do you believe in all that yourself?

JULIA [*crushed*]. Do I believe in it myself?

CHRISTINE. Yes.

JULIA [*exhausted*]. I don't know: I believe no longer in anything. [*She sinks down on the bench and drops her head between her arms on the table.*] Nothing! Nothing at all!

CHRISTINE [*turns to the right, where* JEAN *is standing*]. So you were going to run away!

JEAN [*abashed, puts the razor on the table*]. Run away? Well, that's putting it rather strong. You have heard what the young lady proposes, and though she is tired out now by being up all night, it's a proposition that can be put through all right.

CHRISTINE. Now you tell me: did you mean me to act as cook for that one there——?

JEAN [*sharply*]. Will you please use decent language in speaking to your mistress! Do you understand?

CHRISTINE. Mistress!

JEAN. Yes!

2 *salt them, pad them with charges.*

CHRISTINE. Well, well! Listen to him!

JEAN. Yes, it would be better for you to listen a little more and talk a little less. Miss Julia is your mistress, and what makes you disrespectful to her now should make you feel the same way about yourself.

CHRISTINE. Oh, I have always had enough respect for myself——

JEAN. To have none for others!

CHRISTINE. —not to go below my own station. You can't say that the count's cook has had anything to do with the groom or the swineherd. You can't say anything of the kind!

JEAN. Yes, it's your luck that you have had to do with a gentleman.

CHRISTINE. Yes, a gentleman who sells the oats out of the count's stable!

JEAN. What's that to you who get a commission on the groceries and bribes from the butcher?

CHRISTINE. What's that?

JEAN. And so you can't respect your master and mistress any longer! You—you!

CHRISTINE. Are you coming with me to church? I think you need a good sermon on top of such a deed.

JEAN. No, I am not going to church to-day. You can go by yourself and confess your own deeds.

CHRISTINE. Yes, I'll do that, and I'll bring back enough forgiveness to cover you also. The Saviour suffered and died on the cross for all our sins, and if we go to him with a believing heart and a repentant mind, he'll take all our guilt on himself.

JULIA. Do you believe that, Christine?

CHRISTINE. It is my living belief, as sure as I stand here, and the faith of my childhood which I have kept since I was young, Miss Julia. And where sin abounds, grace[1] abounds too.

JULIA. Oh, if I had your faith! Oh, if——

CHRISTINE. Yes, but you don't get it without the special grace of God, and that is not bestowed on everybody——

JULIA. On whom is it bestowed then?

CHRISTINE. That's just the great secret of the work of grace, Miss Julia, and the Lord has no regard for persons, but there those that are last shall be the foremost——

JULIA. Yes, but that means he has regard for those that are last.

CHRISTINE [*going right on*]. —and it is easier for a camel to go

---

[1] *grace, the undeserved favor of God toward man.*

through a needle's eye than for a rich man to get into heaven. That's the way it is, Miss Julia. Now I am going, however—alone—and as I pass by, I'll tell the stableman not to let out the horses if anybody should like to get away before the count comes home. Good-bye!
[*Goes out.*]

JEAN. Well, ain't she a devil!— And all this for the sake of a finch!

JULIA [*apathetically*]. Never mind the finch!— Can you see any way out of this, any way to end it?

JEAN [*ponders*]. No!

JULIA. What would you do in my place?

JEAN. In your place? Let me see. As one of gentle birth, as a woman, as one who has—fallen. I don't know—yes, I do know!

JULIA [*picking up the razor with a significant gesture*]. Like this?

JEAN. Yes!— But please observe that I myself wouldn't do it, for there is a difference between us.

JULIA. Because you are a man and I a woman? What is the difference?

JEAN. It is the same—as—that between man and woman.

JULIA [*with the razor in her hand*]. I want to, but I cannot!— My father couldn't either, that time he should have done it.

JEAN. No, he should not have done it, for he had to get his revenge first.

JULIA. And now it is my mother's turn to revenge herself again, through me.

JEAN. Have you not loved your father, Miss Julia?

JULIA. Yes, immensely, but I must have hated him, too. I think I must have been doing so without being aware of it. But he was the one who reared me in contempt for my own sex—half woman and half man! Whose fault is it, this that has happened? My father's—my mother's—my own? My own? Why, I have nothing that is my own. I haven't a thought that didn't come from my father; not a passion that didn't come from my mother; and now this last—this about all human creatures being equal—I got that from him, my fiancé—whom I call a scoundrel for that reason! How can it be my own fault? To put the blame on Jesus, as Christine does—no, I am too proud for that, and know too much—thanks to my father's teachings— And that about a rich person not getting into heaven, it's just a lie, and Christine, who has money in the savings-bank, wouldn't get in anyhow. Whose is the fault?— What does it matter whose it is? For just the same I am the one who must bear the guilt and the results——

JEAN. Yes, but——

[*Two sharp strokes are rung on the bell.* MISS JULIA *leaps to her feet.* JEAN *changes his coat.*]

JEAN. The count is back. Think if Christine—— [*Goes to the speaking-tube, knocks on it, and listens.*]

JULIA. Now he has been to the chiffonier!

JEAN. It is Jean, your lordship! [*Listening again, the spectators being unable to hear what the count says*] Yes, your lordship! [*Listening*] Yes, your lordship! At once! [*Listening*] In a minute, your lordship! [*Listening*] Yes, yes! In half an hour!

JULIA [*with intense concern*]. What did he say? Lord Jesus, what did he say?

JEAN. He called for his boots and wanted his coffee in half an hour.

JULIA. In half an hour then! Oh, I am so tired. I can't do anything; can't repent, can't run away, can't stay, can't live—can't die! Help me now! Command me, and I'll obey you like a dog! Do me this last favour—save my honour, and save his name! You know what my will ought to do, and what it cannot do—now give me your will, and make me do it!

JEAN. I don't know why—but now I can't either—I don't understand— It is just as if this coat here made a— I cannot command you —and now, since I've heard the count's voice—now—I can't quite explain it—but— Oh, that damned menial is back in my spine again. I believe if the count should come down here, and if he should tell me to cut my own throat—I'd do it on the spot!

JULIA. Make believe that you are he, and that I am you!— You did some fine acting when you were on your knees before me—then you were the nobleman—or—have you ever been to a show and seen one who could hypnotize people?

[JEAN *makes a sign of assent.*]

JULIA. He says to his subject: get the broom. And the man gets it. He says: sweep. And the man sweeps.

JEAN. But then the other person must be asleep.

JULIA [*ecstatically*]. I am asleep already—there is nothing in the whole room but a lot of smoke—and you look like a stove—that looks like a man in black clothes and a high hat—and your eyes glow like coals when the fire is going out—and your face is a lump of white ashes. [*The sunlight has reached the floor and is now falling on* JEAN.] How warm and nice it is! [*She rubs her hands as if warming them before a fire.*] And so light—and so peaceful!

JEAN [*takes the razor and puts it in her hand*]. There's the broom!

Go now, while it is light—to the barn—and—— [*Whispers something in her ear.*]

JULIA [*awake*]. Thank you! Now I shall have rest! But tell me first —that the foremost also receive the gift of grace. Say it, even if you don't believe it.

JEAN. The foremost? No, I can't do that!— But wait—Miss Julia— I know! You are no longer among the foremost—now when you are among the—last!

JULIA. That's right. I am among the last of all: I am the very last. Oh!— But now I cannot go— Tell me once more that I must go!

JEAN. No, now I can't do it either. I cannot!

JULIA. And those that are foremost shall be the last.

JEAN. Don't think, don't think! Why, you are taking away my strength, too, so that I become a coward— What? I thought I saw the bell moving!— To be that scared of a bell! Yes, but it isn't only the bell—there is somebody behind it—a hand that makes it move—and something else that makes the hand move—but if you cover up your ears—just cover up your ears! Then it rings worse than ever! Rings and rings, until you answer it—and then it's too late—then comes the sheriff—and then—

[*Two quick rings from the bell.*]

JEAN [*shrinks together; then he straightens himself up*]. It's horrid! But there's no other end to it!— Go!

[JULIA *goes firmly out through the door.*]

CURTAIN

ANTON CHEKHOV (1860–1904)

The third of the titans of modern drama wrote only four masterpieces, concentrated into the last eight years of his short life. Unlike Ibsen and Strindberg, the Russian Chekhov did not think of himself as a playwright but as the author of over a thousand short stories which made him, with Poe and Maupassant, one of the inventors of that modern form and still one of its greatest masters. Yet his plays were no less original and gave the modern theater one of its few unmistakable styles, which has often been imitated in Europe and America, but seldom with success.

The naturalism of Chekhov comes closer to Zola's demand for a "slice of life" than do the more lurid and spectacular specimens of the school. The seeming formlessness of his picture of czarist society, with its full panel of differentiated characters going their various ways in near-indifference to each other, gives an almost disconcerting illusion of reality. The apparent artlessness of this method disguises the subtle planning of one of the soundest craftsmen in the history of the theater. His quiet, almost uneventful drama baffled his first actors and audiences and accounted for the failure of the first production of *The Seagull* in 1896 and Chekhov's determination never to write another play if he lived seven hundred years. Fortunately, he was soon seduced away from this resolve and lived to produce two further masterworks, which brought his career to a triumphant close.

The gentle, self-effacing Chekhov led an uneventful life, clouded by poor health but far from unhappy. His father, the son of a former serf, ran a small grocery store in a port town on the Azov Sea in southern Russia, and Anton had an early struggle with poverty that made him sympathetic to the underprivileged all his life. Yet he managed to study medicine at the University of Moscow and practiced it briefly among the poor—often, it is said, without charge. In 1890 he traveled across Siberia to the notorious prison camps of Sakhalin Island and published an account of his experiences.

But even in medical school he began to write short stories, and when he found a publisher for the first volume of them at the age of twenty-six, he retired from medical practice and devoted the rest of his life to writing. He had also written his first drama at the university, but he did not take up playwriting seriously until a dozen years later. Most of his early plays were one-act skits or farces, which are still amusing and show the comic side of Chekhov that is all too often overlooked in his full-length works.

The first of Chekhov's quartet of mature dramas, *Uncle Vanya,* was tried out in the provinces by a touring company and did not immediately reach a major theater. Hence it remained for *The Seagull* to introduce the dramatic art of Chekhov to St. Petersburg, the Russian capital at the time. Ineptly produced at the most conservative of the state theaters, the Alexandrinsky, it was hissed into supposed oblivion, and Chekhov retired in disgust. Yet at this very time Stanislavsky and Nemirovitch-Danchenko were founding their famous Moscow Art Theatre, dedicated to an ideal of ensemble playing and integrated staging that suited the dramatic style of Chekhov perfectly. They persuaded him to let them revive *The Seagull* during their first season in 1898, and under their knowing direction it was an unqualified success. When they next asked to do the Moscow premiere of *Uncle Vanya,* he was still reluctant to commit his fortunes entirely to the neophyte organization. But after the state theater demanded major changes in the script before it would produce the play, he gave it to the Art Theatre after all.

The success of this second production wed him to the organization for the rest of his days, a marriage that was most fortunate for both parties. Now he turned the tables on the state theaters and would not let the Alexandrinsky produce *Uncle Vanya* at all. *The Three Sisters* was done first at the Moscow Art Theatre in 1901 and *The Cherry Orchard* in 1904, a few months before his death. To make his tie with the organization even closer, he married one of its leading actresses, Olga Knipper, in 1901. Chekhov's last years were spent in his villa at Yalta in the Crimea, where he fought a losing battle with tuberculosis. He died at a small health resort in Germany.

It is customary to consider *The Cherry Orchard* the masterpiece of Chekhov, but many find it hard to choose among the last four plays, either in reading or in stage-production. The Chekhov plays have never ceased to attract the most distinguished actors, which is fortunate, since they are unusually dependent upon skillful production for their effectiveness.

The pattern of all four is much the same. In each we are introduced to a houseful of world-weary, frustrated, hopeless Russians, caught up in the dull routine of remote village life and only quietly rebellious, if rebellious at all. They are provincial middle-class people for the most part, but sufficiently educated to dream of a larger world in Moscow or St. Petersburg. Occasionally a glamorous figure from the capital or even from Paris, such as the actress and the novelist in *The Seagull,* appears among them, but most of Chekhov's characters are the typical land-owners, army officers, local merchants, schoolteachers, and doctors, with their wives and children, set against the background of governesses, valets, servants, and simple serfs that made up the fabric of the decaying social system of old Russia.

It is a stagnant aristocratic society, seemingly doomed to eventual extinction—in the rising middle class. (In reality, it met its end in the violent liquidation of proletarian revolution.) Chekhov voiced the prevailing sentiment of Russia in 1900 that there were too many such estates and villages such as those which form the setting of his plays and that the country needed urbanization and industrialization to bring it in step with western Europe. But Chekhov was no political propagandist, and we sense his opinions only indirectly in his portrayal of the futility of the kind of life the old system provided.

A Russian village of the nineteenth century was backward beyond anything that we can conceive of. Often many miles from a railway station, cut off from towns by unpaved and all but impassable roads, it languished in self-contained dullness, without newspapers, libraries, or any of the cultural minima of the typical American village. The privileged classes doomed to vegetate in this stultifying environment lived in boredom with each other, contracting loveless marriages within the group, getting on each other's nerves, and bemoaning the sterility of their lot. Such a life is Masha's in *The Seagull*.

Chekhov has been called the dramatist of inaction, because he shows us a group of such helpless souls bound down to inertia and all but incapable of decision. As an uncompromising realist, he photographs these pathetic, yet amiable people as a cross-section of a society in decay. His objective method subdues even the most arresting incidents, such as an attempted murder or suicide, to the grey tones of his picture as a whole. In *Uncle Vanya* the harassed hero finally brings himself to shoot at his enemy, but misses. In *The Seagull* Constantin's first attempt to kill himself ends in humiliating failure. Though a good many things do happen in these plays, Chekhov's style gives an impression of relentless calm. His people seem merely to sit about and talk interminably—not to each other but to themselves. Perhaps the greatest tragedy of their lives is that they are all self-centered and cannot communicate with each other. Each is a self-contained vessel, struggling ineffectually with his own problems, largely uninterested in the others, though tacitly aware that they share a common frustration and a common fate.

A sadness approaching pessimism enshrouds his plays, though relieved by a sly sense of humor and an exhilarating sense of humanity. Chekhov is an atmospheric playwright, who builds an enveloping mood out of tiny details, almost insignificant in themselves. In such a milieu, plot as we know it in the well-made play has little place, because by its very contrivance it would defeat the purpose of naturalism. *The Cherry Orchard* is the most plotless of all the plays, showing us nothing more than some effete, unrealistic aristocrats who can avoid financial ruin only through converting a part of their family estate into a colony of summer bungalows and who lose everything because they cannot bring themselves to face the issue or take the unpleasant step. They talk and reminisce and hope absurdly for a miracle to stave off their ruin. Epic in its study of the passing of an outmoded social order, it is the most difficult of the plays to read because of its perpetual stageful of characters, seemingly talking at tangents. To be appreciated, it must be seen on the stage.

Chekhov is melancholy but never morbid, and it is one of the indefinable powers of his art to stimulate rather than depress us with the most forlorn subjects. His whimsical humor is unfortunately too subtle and too Russian for most outsiders to grasp. But in the very negative picture that his plays present we can see a positive contradiction, an affirmation of life under another system—one that would encourage growth and self-fulfillment, and that is on its way.

ANTON CHEKHOV

THE SEAGULL[1]

A Comedy in Four Acts

CHARACTERS

*Irina (Irene) Nikolayevna Arkádina (Ar-káh-dee-na),[2] married
name Treplyov, an actress*

Konstantín Gavrilovich Treplyov, her son, a young man

Pyotr (Peter) Nikolayevich Sorin, her brother

*Nina (Neena) Mikhailovna Zaryechnaya, a young girl, daughter of a
rich landowner*

*Ilya Afanassyevich Shamráyev (Sham-ráh-yev), a retired army lieu-
tenant, Sorin's estate agent*

Polina (Pauline) Andreyevna, his wife

Masha (Mary), his daughter

Boris Alexandrovich Trigórin, a novelist

Yevgény (Eugene) Sergeyevich Dorn, a doctor

Semyon (Simon) Semyonovich Medvyédenko, a schoolmaster

Yakov (Jacob), a workman

Cook

Maid

---

[1] *Translated from the Russian by David Magarshack.*
[2] *Arkádina is Irina Treplyov's stage name, and she is therefore referred to throughout the play as Miss Arkádina*—Translator's note.

The action takes place on Sorin's country estate. Between Act 3 and Act 4 there is an interval of two years.

act 1

Part of the park on SORIN's *estate. A hastily erected stage for private theatricals stands across a broad avenue leading into the park to the lake. The view of the lake is completely concealed by the stage. To the right and the left of the stage— bushes. A few chairs, a little table.*

The sun has just set. YAKOV *and other workmen are busy on the stage behind the lowered curtain; sounds of hammering and coughing.*

MASHA *and* MEDVYEDENKO *come in from left, returning from a stroll.*

MEDVYEDENKO. Why do you always go about in black?

MASHA. Because I'm in mourning for my life. I'm unhappy.

MEDVYEDENKO. Why? [*Wonderingly*] I don't understand . . . I mean, you've got your health, and though your father is not rich, he's not badly off. My life is much harder than yours. I only get twenty-three roubles a month, and my insurance is deducted from that. But I don't wear mourning, do I?

[*They sit down.*]

MASHA. Money's not everything. Even a pauper can be happy.

MEDVYEDENKO. That may be all right in theory, but in practice it's quite a different matter. I have to provide for my mother, my two sisters, my little brother, and myself, and all on a salary of twenty-three roubles. We must eat and drink, mustn't we? And what with the price of tea and sugar—and tobacco . . . What a life!

MASHA [*throwing a glance at the stage*]. The play will be starting soon.

MEDVYEDENKO. Yes, Nina will be acting, and the play was written by Konstantín. They are in love. Tonight their souls will unite in an endeavour to give expression to the same artistic idea. But your soul and mine have no common points of contact. I'm in love with you. I long for you so terribly that I find it impossible to stay at home. Every day I walk four miles here and four miles back, but all I get from you is cold indifference. Well—I can't say I'm surprised at it. After all, I haven't any private income, and I have a large family to support . . . What's the use of marrying a man who can't even provide for himself?

MASHA. That's not important. [*Takes snuff*] I'm touched by your love, and I'm sorry I can't return it. That's all. [*Proffers her snuffbox*] Help yourself.

MEDVYEDENKO. No, thank you. I don't feel like it.

[*A pause.*]

MASHA. It's awfully close. I expect there'll be a thunderstorm to-night. You're constantly holding forth on some subject or other, or else talking about money. According to you, there can be no greater misfortune than poverty; but I'd a hundred times rather walk about in rags and beg than . . . However, I can hardly expect you to understand that.

[SORIN *and* KONSTANTIN *enter on right.*]

SORIN [*leaning on his cane*]. I don't know, my boy, but somehow or other the country never agrees with me, and I think it's pretty clear that I shall never get used to it now. Last night I went to bed at ten. This morning I woke up at nine, feeling as though my brains were glued to my skull from too much sleep. Anyway, I felt pretty awful, I can tell you. [*Laughs*] But after lunch I dropped off again, and now every bone in my body is aching—I feel wretched—I mean, after all . . .

KONSTANTIN. I suppose you really ought to live in town. [*Seeing* MASHA *and* MEDVYEDENKO] I say, you shouldn't be here, you know. I'll let you know when we're ready to start. Please go.

SORIN [*to* MASHA]. Will you please ask your father to tell them to let the dog off the chain. It goes on howling. It kept my sister awake last night.

MASHA. I'd rather you spoke to my father yourself about it. I'm sorry, but I'm not going to say anything to him. Please, don't ask me. [*To* MEDVYEDENKO] Let's go.

MEDVYEDENKO [*to* KONSTANTIN]. You won't forget to call us before it begins, will you?

[*Both go out.*]

SORIN. Well, I suppose that means the damned dog will be howling the whole night again. It's a funny thing, but I've never managed to live in the country as I liked. I used to get leave for twenty-eight days to come down here for a rest and so on, but the moment I arrived they'd start worrying me with all sorts of silly trifles so that on the very

first day I wished I'd never come . . . [*Laughs*] I've always been glad
to get away from here . . . But now that I've retired, I've nowhere to go.
I mean, after all—whether I like it or not, I've got to live here.

YAKOV [*to* KONSTANTIN]. We're going for a dip in the lake, sir.

KONSTANTIN. All right, but see that you're in your places in ten
minutes. [*Looks at his watch*] We shall be starting soon.

YAKOV. Very good, sir. [*Goes out.*]

KONSTANTIN [*examining the stage*]. Now there's a theatre for you!
The curtain, the first wing, then the second, and beyond that an open
space. No scenery. You look straight across towards the lake and the
horizon. The curtain goes up at exactly half past eight, just when the
moon is due to rise.

SORIN. Splendid!

KONSTANTIN. If Nina's late, then of course the whole effect will be
ruined. It's time she was here. Her father and stepmother don't let her
out of their sight. And she finds it as hard to get out of the house as to
break out of prison. [*Puts his uncle's cravat straight*] You do look an
awful mess, uncle. Hair and beard dishevelled. You should have had a
trim or something.

SORIN [*combing out his beard*]. Ah, dear boy, it's the tragedy of my
life. I used to look just the same when I was young. As though I were
always drunk. Women never cared for me. [*Sitting down*] Why's
your mother in such a bad temper?

KONSTANTIN. Why? Bored, I suppose. [*Sitting down beside Sorin*]
Jealous. Already she's against me, against the whole idea of the
performance, and against my play, because, you see, it's Nina who's
acting in it and not she. She doesn't know my play, but that doesn't
prevent her from hating it.

SORIN [*laughs*]. Good Lord, you do get strange ideas into your head,
don't you?

KONSTANTIN. Oh, no. I tell you she can't bear the thought that on
this tiny stage it will be Nina and not she who'll shine. [*Glances at his
watch*] Mother's a real psychological case. An amusing case, if you like.
She's undoubtedly talented, she's clever, she's capable of shedding bitter tears over a book, she'll recite you the whole of Nekrassov[1] by
heart, she'll nurse you when you're sick like an angel—but just try
praising Duse[2] in her presence! Dear me, no! She alone must be
praised, she alone must be written about, she alone must be acclaimed!

---

[1] *Nekrassov, Nikolai (1821–1877), the Russian poet.*
[2] *Duse, Eleonora (1859–1924), the great Italian actress.*

You have to be in raptures over her marvellous acting in *La Dame aux Camèlias*[1] or *Life's Dizzy Whirl*.[2] But in the country she doesn't find this constant adulation, so she feels bored, she's in a vile temper: we're all her enemies, it's all our fault! And then again she's terribly superstitious—afraid of three candles, of the number thirteen. She's mean. She has seventy thousand roubles in a bank at Odessa—I know that for a fact! But ask her to lend you some money, and she'll burst into tears.

SORIN. You've got it into your head that your mother dislikes your play, and you're getting agitated about it and—and so on. Calm down, my boy. Your mother adores you.

KONSTANTIN [*plucking the petals off a flower*]. She loves me, she loves me not. She loves me, she loves me not. She loves me, she loves me not! [*Laughs*] You see, mother doesn't love me. And no wonder! She wants to live, to love, to wear gay clothes, and here am I, a man of twenty-five, constantly reminding her that she's no longer young. When I'm away, she's only thirty-two; but when I'm with her—she's forty-three—that's why she hates me. Besides, she knows too that I don't recognise the theatre as an art at all. *She* loves the theatre: she thinks she's serving humanity and the sacred cause of art. But to me the modern theatre is nothing but a mass of prejudice and dead convention. When the curtain goes up and—by artificial light, in a room with three walls—these great actors and actresses, these priests and priestesses of sacred art, show how people eat, drink, and make love, move about, and wear their clothes—when they try to fish some moral from those dreary scenes and phrases, a cheap, smug, cosy little moral, a moral useful in the home—when in thousands of different ways they go on shoving the same old thing over and over again under my nose—then I run like hell, I run as Maupassant[3] ran from the Eiffel Tower which drove him to distraction by its horrible vulgarity.

SORIN. But you can't do without the theatre, my boy.

KONSTANTIN. What we want is new forms, uncle. New forms. We must have new forms. If we can't get them, I'd much rather have nothing at all. [*Looks at his watch*] I love my mother. I love her very much. But she leads a silly sort of life. Always running about with that novelist fellow.[4] Her name constantly bandied about in the newspapers.

---

[1] *La Dame aux Camèlias*, (*1852*), *the tragedy of Dumas fils called* Camille *in English.*

[2] *Life's Dizzy Whirl*, *a contemporary Russian drama by B. Markévitch.*

[3] *Maupassant, Guy de* (*1850–1893*), *the French short-story writer.*

[4] *that novelist fellow, that is, Trigórin.*

Oh, I'm so tired of it all! Still, I don't mind admitting that now and again I am influenced by the egoism of an ordinary mortal: you see, I resent the fact that my mother is a famous actress, and, you know, I can't help thinking sometimes that if only she were an ordinary woman, I'd have been a much happier man. Now, please, tell me, uncle, could there be anything more dreadful or more idiotic than, for instance, this sort of situation? Very often she has visitors who are all —everyone of them—celebrities of one sort or another: actors, writers. And among them all I alone am a nobody, and the only reason why they tolerate me is because I happen to be her son. And, really, who am I? What am I? I left the university in my third year, "owing to circumstances beyond our control," as they say in the papers. I have no particular talents: I have no money—not a penny; and so far as my social position is concerned, I'm still described on my passport as a Kiev artisan. My father, you know, was a native of Kiev and he was of humble birth, though that didn't prevent him from becoming a famous actor. So, as I was saying, when all those great actors and writers in her drawing-room are gracious enough to take notice of me, I cannot help feeling from the way they look at me that they are merely weighing up my own insignificance. I know what they are thinking, and I don't mind telling you I feel pretty small.

SORIN. By the way, tell me what kind of a chap is this novelist? I can't make him out. He never utters a word.

KONSTANTIN. Oh, he's an intelligent man, unaffected, a bit, you know, on the melancholy side. A very decent fellow. He won't be forty for a long time yet, but he's already famous and has everything he wants. As for his writings—well—what shall I say? Nice, charming, but—er—after Tolstoy and Zola you'd hardly want to read Trigórin.

SORIN. Well, you know, my boy, I can't help liking literary chaps. A long time ago I wanted to do two things passionately: I wanted to marry and I wanted to be a writer, but I'm afraid I failed in both my ambitions. Ah, well, I suppose it must be nice to be even a second-rate writer—I mean, after all—

KONSTANTIN [*listens*]. I think I hear footsteps [*Embraces his uncle*] Oh, I can't live without her! Even the sound of her footsteps is beautiful! Oh, I'm so happy, so deliriously happy! [*Goes quickly to meet* NINA *who enters*] My darling! My dearest . . .

NINA [*excitedly*]. I hope I'm not late. I'm not late, am I?

KONSTANTIN [*kissing her hand*]. No, no, of course not!

NINA. All day I've been worried. I was so frightened! I was simply terrified that my father wouldn't let me come. But he's just gone out with my stepmother. The sky's red—the moon's just rising—and— and I've been driving so fast, fast! [*Laughs*] Oh, I'm so thrilled! [*Presses* SORIN'S *hand warmly.*]

SORIN [*laughs*]. I do believe I can see tears in those pretty eyes of yours. Ha-ha! That's bad!

NINA. I'm afraid I did cry a little. Oh, I was in such a hurry! You can see for yourself how out of breath I am. I shall have to leave in half an hour. I mustn't be late. No, no, I can't stay. I can't. Please, please, don't try to keep me. Father doesn't know I'm here.

KONSTANTIN. Anyway, it's time we started. I'd better go and tell them.

SORIN. No, no. Don't you bother to go, my boy. I'll go. Right away. [*Goes to the right, singing*] "Into France two grenadiers—"[1] [*Looks round*] Once, you know, I started singing like that and an assistant public prosecutor said to me, "You've got a very powerful voice, sir—," then he thought a little and added, "—but it's rather unpleasant!" [*Laughs and goes out.*]

NINA. My father and his wife have forbidden me to come here. They say you're bohemians . . . They're afraid I might go on the stage . . . But I feel drawn here, to the lake, like a seagull. Oh, my heart is so full of you [*Looks round.*]

KONSTANTIN. We're quite alone.

NINA. I thought there was someone there . . .

KONSTANTIN. There's no one there. [*A kiss.*]

NINA. What tree is this?

KONSTANTIN. An elm.

NINA. Why is it so dark?

KONSTANTIN. Well—it's evening. Everything's getting dark. Don't dash away after the play, please don't.

NINA. I must.

KONSTANTIN. And what if I went to your place, Nina? I'd like to spend the whole night in your garden, looking at your window.

NINA. You'd better not. The watchman is sure to see you. Besides, our dog isn't used to you yet, and he'll start barking.

KONSTANTIN. I love you.

NINA. Sh-h . . .

KONSTANTIN [*hearing footsteps*]. Who's there? Is that you, Yakov?

YAKOV [*behind the stage*]. Yes, sir.

---

[1] *"Into France two grenadiers—," Heine's poem as set to music by Schumann or Wagner.*

KONSTANTIN. Take your places, everybody. It's time to begin. Is the moon rising?

YAKOV. Yes, sir.

KONSTANTIN. Got the methylated spirit? The sulphur? When the red eyes appear, there must be a smell of sulphur. [*To* NINA] You'd better go now. Everything's ready. Nervous?

NINA. I'm afraid I am rather. But it isn't your mother. Oh, no. I don't mind her a bit. But there's Trigórin and—I shall feel rather frightened and self-conscious acting in front of him, I'm afraid. He's such a famous writer ... Is he young?

KONSTANTIN. Yes.

NINA. His stories are so wonderful!

KONSTANTIN [*coldly*]. I don't know. I haven't read them.

NINA. It's so difficult to act in your play. There are no living people in it.

KONSTANTIN. Living people! Life should be shown not as it is, nor as it ought to be, but as we see it in our dreams!

NINA. But there is so little action in your play. Just talk. Besides, I think that in a play there ought certainly to be love.

[*Both walk off behind the stage.*]
[*Enter* PAULINE *and* DORN.]

PAULINE. It's getting damp. Do go back and put on your galoshes.

DORN. I'm hot.

PAULINE. You don't look after yourself properly. It's sheer stubbornness. You're a doctor and you know perfectly well that damp is bad for you, but it seems you want to make me miserable. Yesterday you deliberately spent the whole evening on the terrace ...

DORN [*hums*]. "Don't tell me my youth was my ruin—"[1]

PAULINE. You were so carried away by your conversation with Irene that you didn't even notice how chilly it was. You like her, don't you?

DORN. My dear, I'm fifty-five.

PAULINE. That doesn't mean anything. A man isn't old at fifty-five. You're well preserved and you're still attractive to women.

DORN. All right, so what do you want me to do?

PAULINE. You're all ready to prostrate yourselves before an actress. All of you!

DORN [*hums*]. —"Once more before thee—" If actors are liked in

[1] ***Don't tell me my youth was my ruin—.*** *The songs that Dorn hums from time to time were popular favorites of the period in Russia.*

society and treated differently from—shall I say?—tradespeople, that's as it should be. That's idealism.

PAULINE. Women have always fallen for you. They've always thrown themselves on your neck. Is that idealism too?

DORN [*shrugging his shoulders*]. Yes, why not? There was a lot that was good in the women's attitude towards me. What they liked most about me was that I was a jolly good doctor. Ten or fifteen years ago, you remember, I was the only decent obstetrician in the whole county. Then again I've always been an honest man.

PAULINE [*grasps him by the hand*]. Oh, my dearest!

DORN. Not so loud! They're coming.

[*Enter* MISS ARKADINA *arm in arm with* SORIN, TRIGORIN, SHAMRAYEV, MEDVYEDENKO *and* MASHA.]

SHAMRAYEV. She acted marvellously at the Poltava Fair in 1873. Phenomenal acting. Phenomenal! I don't suppose you happen to know, madam, where Chadin is now? Paul Chadin, the comic actor. He was inimitable as Rasplyúyev. Much better than Sadóvsky,[1] I assure you, dear lady. I wonder where he is now.

MISS ARKADINA. You keep asking me about antedeluvian actors! How should I know? [*Sits down.*]

SHAMRAYEV. Paul Chadin! There are no such actors now. The stage is no longer what it was, madam. In the old days we had mighty oaks; all we have now are tree-stumps.

DORN. It's true there aren't many geniuses left on our stage now, but I should say the general standard of acting is much higher than it used to be.

SHAMRAYEV. I'm afraid I don't agree with you, sir. However, I suppose it's all a matter of taste. *De gustibus aut bene, aut nihil.*[2]

[KONSTANTIN *comes out from behind the stage.*]

MISS ARKADINA [*to her son*]. When do you begin, dear?

KONSTANTIN. In another minute, mother. Please, have patience.

MISS ARKADINA [*recites from "Hamlet"*[3]].

---

[1] *Sadóvsky, Prov (1818–1872), famous for his interpretation of comic roles in the plays of Ostrovsky. Rasplyúyev is a character in the play,* The Wedding of Krechinskago, *by Sukhovo-Kobylin.*

[2] *De gustibus . . . nihil, a scrambling and corruption of two hackneyed Latin proverbs:* De gustibus [non est disputandum] (*There is no disputing about tastes*) *and* [De mortuis] nil nisi bonum (*Say nothing but good of the dead*).

[3] *"Hamlet." The speeches are from Act III, scene 4, in which Hamlet reproaches his mother for her evil life.*

> *O Hamlet, speak no more;*
> *Thou turn'st mine eyes into my very soul;*
> *And there I see such black and grained spots*
> *As will not leave their tinct.*

KONSTANTIN [*from "Hamlet"*].
> *Nay, but to live*
> *In the rank sweat of an enseamed bed,*
> *Stew'd in corruption, honeying and making love*
> *Over the nasty sty,—*
> [*A horn is sounded behind the stage.*]

KONSTANTIN. Ladies and gentlemen, the play is about to begin. Quiet, please, quiet! I begin. [*Taps with a stick and speaks in a loud voice*] O, ye venerable shades that hover over this lake at night-time, send us to sleep and let us dream of what will be in two hundred thousand years!

SORIN. There'll be nothing in two hundred thousand years.

KONSTANTIN. Very well, let them show us that nothing.

MISS ARKADINA. Let them. We are asleep.

[*The curtain goes up; the view of the lake is revealed; the moon above the horizon is reflected in the water;* NINA, *all in white, is sitting on a big stone.*]

NINA. Men, lions, eagles and peacocks,[1] horned stags, geese, spiders, silent fish that inhabit the waters, starfish, and creatures no eye can see—all living things, all living things, all living things, having completed their round of sorrow, are extinct . . . For thousands and thousands of years the earth has bórne no living creature upon it, and this poor moon lights its lamp in vain. No longer do the cranes waken in the meadow with a cry, and in the lime groves the drone of the May-beetles is heard no more. It is cold, cold, cold. Empty, empty, empty. Horror, horror, horror . . . [*A pause.*] The bodies of living creatures have dissolved into dust and eternal matter has transformed them into stones, into water, into clouds,—and their souls have all merged into one soul. That world-soul am I—I—. In me is the soul of Alexander the Great, of Caesar, of Shakespeare, of Napoleon, and the soul of the last leech. In me man's mind is merged with the instincts of animals, and I remember all, all, all . . . And every life I relive anew in myself—

[*Will-o'-the-wisps appear on the stage.*]

---

[1] *In the Russian text* kuropatki—*partridges, which introduces certain ludicrous associations in English which are not contained in the Russian*—Translator's note.

MISS ARKADINA [*softly*]. This is something decadent.

KONSTANTIN [*imploringly, and in a reproachful voice*]. Please, mother!

NINA. I am lonely, lonely. Once in a hundred years I open my lips to speak, and my voice re-echoes forlornly in this desert, and no one hears . . . And you, too, pale lights, do not hear me . . . The stagnant marsh gives birth to you before daybreak, and you wander until dawn—without thought, without will, without a flutter of life. Fearing lest life be born within you, Satan, the father of eternal matter, every moment produces a change of atoms within you, as he does in the stones and in the water, and you go on changing and changing. In the universe only the spirit abides, constant and unchangeable. [*A pause.*] Like a prisoner cast into a deep, empty well, I know not where I am, nor what awaits me. One thing only is not hidden from me: I know that in the hard and cruel struggle with Satan, the origin of all the forces of matter, I am destined to conquer, and that after that matter and spirit will blend harmoniously and the glory of eternal beauty will be achieved, and the Kingdom of Universal Will will come. But that will only come to pass when—little by little and after a long succession of centuries—the moon, and the bright dog-star,[1] and the earth have all turned to dust . . . Till then—horror, horror . . .

[*A pause; upon the background of the lake two red spots appear.*] Here comes Satan, my mighty adversary. I can see his terrible, blood-red eyes—

MISS ARKADINA. There's a smell of sulphur. Is that really necessary?

KONSTANTIN. Yes.

MISS ARKADINA [*laughs*]. That certainly is very effective!

KONSTANTIN. Mother!

NINA. He feels lost without man—

PAULINE [*to* DORN]. You've taken off your hat. Please, put it on, or you'll catch your death of cold.

MISS ARKADINA. Why, the doctor has only taken his hat off to the devil, the father of eternal matter!

KONSTANTIN [*flaring up, aloud*]. The play's finished! Enough! Curtain!

MISS ARKADINA. What are you so cross about?

KONSTANTIN. Enough! Curtain! Lower the curtain! [*Stamps*] Curtain! [*The curtain drops.*] Sorry, I forgot it's only a few chosen ones who can act and write plays. I've infringed the monopoly. I— I—

---

[1] *dog-star*, Sirius, the brightest star in the heavens.

[*Tries to say something, but waves his hand instead and goes out on left.*]

MISS ARKADINA. What's the matter with him?

SORIN. Really, Irene, you shouldn't wound a young man's pride like that, my dear.

MISS ARKADINA. But what did I say to him?

SORIN. You hurt his feelings.

MISS ARKADINA. But he told me himself that it was all a joke, so I treated his play as a joke.

SORIN. All the same—

MISS ARKADINA. Now it seems he has written a masterpiece. Well, well . . . So he has put on this play of his and nearly suffocated us with sulphur not for a joke, but as a demonstration! He wanted to show us how to write and what to act. Oh dear, this really is getting a bit too much! These constant sallies against me, these pinpricks— say what you like—would try anyone's patience. What a conceited, headstrong boy!

SORIN. He only wanted to please you.

MISS ARKADINA. So that's what he wanted to do, did he? Then why didn't he choose some ordinary play, instead of making us listen to that decadent drivel? Not that I mind listening even to drivel for the sake of a joke, but here we have all these new pretensions to new forms, to a new era in art. Well, I didn't notice any new forms at all but simply a vicious temperament.

TRIGORIN. Everyone writes as he likes and as he can.

MISS ARKADINA. Well, in that case let him write as he likes and as he can, only let him leave me in peace!

DORN. Jupiter, thou'rt angry . . .

MISS ARKADINA. I'm not Jupiter. I'm a woman. [*Lights a cigarette*] And I'm not angry. I just can't help feeling annoyed that a young man should be wasting his time so senselessly. I certainly didn't mean to hurt him . . .

MEDVYEDENKO. There's no justification for separating spirit from matter, for may not spirit itself be only an agglomeration of material atoms? [*Brightly, to* TRIGORIN] Why not write a play about a schoolmaster, sir? Somebody ought to write a play to show how one of us lives. Oh, it's a hard life, sir, a very hard life.

MISS ARKADINA. You're quite right, but don't let us talk of plays or atoms. It's such a lovely evening! Do you hear? People are singing. [*Listening*] How nice!

PAULINE. It's coming from the other side of the lake.

[*A pause.*]

MISS ARKADINA [*to* TRIGORIN]. Sit down beside me, please. Ten or fifteen years ago music and singing could be heard on the lake almost every night. It would never stop. There are six country houses on the shore of this lake. Oh, I can remember it all so well! Laughter, noise, shooting, and of course love affairs! Oh, those never ending love affairs! The matinée idol and general favourite of the ladies in those days was our dear doctor there [*motions with her head towards* DORN], Yevgény Dorn. He's a very handsome man still, but at that time he was simply irresistible. Oh dear, my conscience is beginning to trouble me. Why did I hurt my poor boy's feelings? I'm worried [*Aloud*] Konstantín! Darling! Konstantín!

MASHA. I'll go and look for him.

MISS ARKADINA. Please do, my dear.

MASHA [*goes to the left*]. Konstantín Co-ee! Konstantín! [*Goes out.*]

NINA [*coming out from behind the stage*]. It doesn't look as if we shall go on with the play, so I suppose I can come out. How do you do? [*Exchanges kisses with* MISS ARKADINA *and* PAULINE.]

SORIN. Brava! Brava!

MISS ARKADINA. Brava! Brava! We were charmed, my dear, charmed. With your figure and your lovely voice it's a wicked shame to bury yourself in the country. I'm sure you have talent! Why, of course, you have! You must go on the stage, my dear.

NINA. Oh, it's one of my fondest dreams! [*Sighing*] But I'm afraid it will never come true.

MISS ARKADINA. You never can tell, my dear. Let me introduce you —Boris Trigórin.

NINA. I'm so glad to meet you. [*Covered with confusion*] I'm always reading your books.

MISS ARKADINA [*making her sit down beside her*]. Don't be so shy, my dear. He may be a famous man, but he isn't at all conceited. Are you, dear? You see, he's shy himself.

DORN. I suppose we may raise the curtain now, mayn't we? It's giving me the creeps.

SHAMRAYEV [*aloud*]. Yakov, raise the curtain, there's a good lad!

[*The curtain goes up.*]

NINA [*to* TRIGORIN]. Don't you think it's rather a strange play?

TRIGORIN. I couldn't make head or tail of it. Still, I enjoyed watch-

ing it. You played so sincerely. And the scenery is lovely. [*A pause.*]
I expect there must be a lot of fish in that lake.

NINA. Yes . . . .

TRIGORIN. I love fishing. There's nothing that gives me more pleasure than to sit on the bank of a stream in the evening and watch the float.

NINA. But, surely, anyone who has experienced the joys of creation can't possibly enjoy anything else!

MISS ARKADINA [*laughing*]. Don't talk like that, my dear. When people say nice things to him, the poor lamb feels terribly embarrassed.

SHAMRAYEV. I remember in Moscow once—at the opera—the famous Silva took the lower C. As it happened, the bass of our cathedral choir was in the gallery at the time, and imagine our utter astonishment when we suddenly heard from the gallery: "Bravo, Silva!" a whole octave lower . . . Like this [*in a low bass*] "Bravo, Silva." The audience was entranced!

[*A pause.*]

DORN. Dead silence.

NINA. I'm afraid I must fly. Good-bye.

MISS ARKADINA. Why? Where are you off to so early? We shan't let you go, my dear.

NINA. Father's expecting me.

MISS ARKADINA. Goodness, what an awful man he is! [*They exchange kisses.*] Well, I suppose it can't be helped. I'm very sorry to let you go . . . .

NINA. If you knew how I hate to have to go.

MISS ARKADINA. Don't you think someone ought to see you home, my pet?

NINA [*frightened*]. Oh, no, no!

SORIN [*to* NINA, *in an imploring voice*]. Do stay!

NINA. I'm awfully sorry, but I can't.

SORIN. Please, stay for just one hour. Really, I mean to say—

NINA [*after thinking it over, tearfully*]. I can't. [*Shakes hands and hurries off.*]

MISS ARKADINA. Poor child, I'm sorry for her. I understand her mother left the whole of her huge fortune to her father, and now this young girl hasn't a farthing in the world, for her father has already made a will leaving everything to his second wife. Isn't it dreadful?

DORN. Yes, to do him justice, her father is a mean old rascal.

SORIN [*rubbing his cold hands*]. Let us go, too, ladies and gentlemen. It's getting damp. My legs ache.

MISS ARKADINA. Poor darling, they're like wooden legs. You can hardly drag them along. Well, come along, hapless old man! [*Takes his arm.*]

SHAMRAYEV [*offering his arm to his wife*]. Madam?

SORIN. There's that damned dog howling again! [*To* SHAMRAYEV] Will you kindly tell them to unchain that dog, sir?

SHAMRAYEV. I'm very sorry, sir, but it can't be done. You see, I am afraid of thieves breaking into the barn. I've got millet[1] there. [*To* MEDVYEDENKO *who is walking beside him*] Yes, my dear fellow, a whole octave lower: "Bravo, Silva!" Not that he was a professional singer, mind you. Good Lord, no! Just a plain church chorister.

MEDVYEDENKO. And what salary does a church chorister get?

[*All go out, except* DORN.]

DORN [*alone*]. I don't know, maybe I don't understand anything, or I've just gone off my head, but I liked the play. There's something in it. When that girl talked about loneliness, and again later on when the devil's red eyes appeared, my hands shook with excitement. Fresh, naïve . . . There he comes, I think. I must say something nice to him, congratulate him.

KONSTANTIN [*enters*]. All gone.

DORN. I'm here.

KONSTANTIN. Masha's looking for me all over the park. What a nuisance she is!

DORN. I liked your play very much, Konstantín. It's rather an unusual play, to be sure, and I haven't heard the end, but I couldn't help being gripped by it all the same. You've got talent, young man. You must persevere.

[KONSTANTIN *presses his hand warmly and embraces him impulsively.*]

DORN. Dear me, how overwrought you are! Tears in the eyes . . . Now, what did I want to say? Well, what I mean is that you've taken a subject out of the realm of abstract ideas. That's how it should be, because a work of art ought to express some great idea. For it is only the serious that is beautiful. How pale you are!

KONSTANTIN. So you think I ought to go on?

DORN. Why, of course! But, remember, deal only with what is important and eternal. You know, I can claim to have had an interesting and varied life. I have nothing to grumble about. But if I had ever experienced the ecstasy artists experience while creating, I should, I be-

---

[1] *millet, a seed-plant used for hay.*

lieve, have despised this material husk of mine and everything that goes with it. I should have left the earth as far behind as possible.

KONSTANTIN. Look here, doctor, I'm awfully sorry, but where's Nina?

DORN. And one more thing. There must be a clear, definite idea in every work of art. You ought to know *why* you're writing. If you don't, if you walk along this picturesque road without any definite aim, you're bound to lose your way, and your talent will be your ruin.

KONSTANTIN [*impatiently*]. Where's Nina?

DORN. She's gone home.

KONSTANTIN [*in despair*]. But what am I going to do? I want to see her—I must see her! I'm going—

[MASHA *comes in.*]

DORN [*to* KONSTANTIN]. Compose yourself, my friend.

KONSTANTIN. I'm going after her all the same. I must go.

MASHA. You'd better go indoors, Konstantín. Your mother's waiting for you. She's worried about you.

KONSTANTIN. Tell her I've gone away. And, please, leave me alone, all of you! Leave me alone, I say! Don't follow me about!

DORN. Come, come, old man, you mustn't carry on like that! You really shouldn't, you know . . . .

KONSTANTIN [*in a voice choked with tears*]. Good-bye doctor. Thank you. [*Goes out.*]

DORN [*sighs*]. Youth! Youth!

MASHA. When people have nothing better to say, they say, "Youth! Youth!" [*Takes snuff.*]

DORN [*takes the snuffbox away from her and throws it into the bushes*]. Disgusting habit! [*A pause.*] I believe they're playing the piano indoors. We'd better go in.

MASHA. Please, wait a moment!

DORN. Why? What is it?

MASHA. I'd like to tell you—I—I wanted to before. I must talk to someone . . . [*Agitatedly*] I dislike my father . . . but I—I am very fond of you. I don't know why, but I have a strong feeling that you're very close to me . . . So please help me. Help me or I shall do something silly, I shall make a mess of my life, I shall ruin it . . . Oh, I can't go on like this . . .

DORN. What's the matter? How can I help you?

MASHA. Oh, I'm so miserable! No one, no one knows how wretched I am! [*Puts her head on his chest. Softly.*] I love Konstantín!

DORN. How overwrought they all are! How overwrought! And so

much love, too . . . Oh, that spellbinding lake! [*Gently*] But what can I do, my dear child? What? . . . What? . . .

CURTAIN

act 2

A croquet lawn. The house with a large terrace in front of it is on the right; the lake, in which the blazing sun is reflected, can be seen on the left. Flower beds.

Midday. MISS ARKADINA, MASHA, *and* DORN *are sitting on a garden seat in the shade of an old lime tree on one side of the lawn.* DORN *has an open book on his knees.*

MISS ARKADINA [*to* MASHA]. Come on, let's stand up. [*Both get up.*] Let's stand side by side. You're twenty-two, aren't you? Well, I'm almost twice your age. Which would you say was the younger of us, Mr. Dorn?

DORN. Why, you, of course.

MISS ARKADINA. There you are . . . And why, pray? Because I work, because I'm wide-awake, because I'm always active, while you just sit about in the same old place and do nothing! Why, you're not alive at all! And another thing: I make it a strict rule never to look into the future, never to worry about old age or death. What will be, will be.

MASHA. Well, and I always feel as though I had been born ages ago. I drag my life like an endless train behind me. And very often I don't want to go on living at all. [*Sitting down*] Of course, that's all nonsense. I must pull myself together and shake it all off.

DORN [*hums softly*]. "Tell her, oh, tell her, my flowers sweet. . . ."[1]

MISS ARKADINA. Besides, I'm always well turned out, just like an Englishman. My dress and my hair are always *comme il faut*: I take jolly good care, my dear, that they should be. Do I ever go out of the house, even for a stroll in the garden, in an old blouse or with untidy hair. Never. Shall I tell you why I look so young? It's because I've never neglected my appearance, never let myself go, like some women . . . . [*Struts about the lawn with arms akimbo*] There—just look at me—fresh as paint! Could take the part of a girl of fifteen.

DORN. Of course, all the same, if you don't mind, I'd like to continue.

---

[1] *"Tell her . . . my flowers sweet—," the Flower Song from Gounod's* Faust.

[*Takes up the book*] We got up to the grain-dealer and the rats . . .

MISS ARKADINA. And the rats. Please go on. [*Sits down*] Or shall I? Yes, I think I will. Give me the book, please. It's my turn. [*Takes the book and scans the page*] And the rats—here we are [*Reads*] "And of course for society people to spoil novelists and try to draw them into their company is as dangerous as for a corn-dealer to breed rats in his barns. And yet they are undoubtedly sought after. So much so that when a society woman picks out an author she wishes to capture, she overwhelms him with compliments, she tries to meet his slightest wish, she does her best to please him . . ." Well, I suppose that may be the French way, but nothing of the sort ever happens here: we have no set programme. With us if a woman tries to capture a writer, she herself, if you please, usually falls head over ears in love with him first. We have no need to look far: take me and Trigórin, for instance . . .

[*Enter* SORIN, *leaning on his cane, and* NINA *with him;* MEDVYE-DENKO *wheels an empty invalid chair behind them.*]

SORIN [*in the fond voice with which one speaks to children*]. So we're happy, aren't we? Very happy? We're gay today, eh? After all? [*To his sister*] We're happy! Father and stepmother have gone off to Tver and we're free for three whole days.

NINA [*sits down beside* MISS ARKADINA *and embraces her*]. Yes, I'm awfully happy. Now I belong to you.

SORIN [*sits down in his bath-chair*]. She looks very sweet today, doesn't she?

MISS ARKADINA. Elegant, charming . . . My dear, I never dreamt you could dress like that! [*Kisses* NINA] But we shouldn't praise you too much, should we? It may bring you bad luck. Where's Mr. Trigórin?

NINA. He's by the bathing hut, fishing.

MISS ARKADINA. I can't understand how he doesn't get sick of it! [*Is about to continue reading.*]

NINA. What are you reading?

MISS ARKADINA. Maupassant's *On the Water,* my sweet. [*Reads a few lines to herself*] Well, the rest is neither interesting, nor true. [*Closes the book*] I'm awfully worried. Tell me, what's the matter with my son? Why is he so moody and bad-tempered? He spends days on the lake, and I hardly ever see him.

MASHA. He's not feeling very happy. [*To* NINA, *shyly*] Won't you read us something out of his play, please?

NINA [*shrugging*]. Do you really want me to? It's so dull!

MASHA [*restraining her eagerness*]. When he reads something himself, his eyes blaze and his face goes pale. He has such a beautiful, sad voice, and the looks of a poet.

[SORIN *can be heard snoring.*]

DORN. Pleasant dreams!

MISS ARKADINA. Peter! Dear!

SORIN. Eh?

MISS ARKADINA. Are you asleep?

SORIN. Me? Not a bit.

[*A pause.*]

MISS ARKADINA. You don't look after yourself, Peter. I wish to goodness you would.

SORIN. I'd be glad to, my dear. It's the doctor who won't do anything for me.

DORN. Do something for a man of sixty!

SORIN. And why not? Doesn't a man of sixty want to live?

DORN [*annoyed*]. Oh, very well, take some valerian drops!

MISS ARKADINA. I think he ought to go to some spa, don't you? I'm sure it would do him a lot of good.

DORN. Well, why not? Let him by all means. On the other hand, he needn't, if he doesn't want to.

MISS ARKADINA. You're a great help, aren't you?

DORN. Aren't I? Well, everything is really quite simple.

[*A pause.*]

MEDVYEDENKO. I think Mr. Sorin ought to give up smoking.

SORIN. Don't talk such rubbish, man!

DORN. Well, no. It isn't rubbish. Wine and tobacco rob a man of his personality. After a cigar or a glass of vodka you're no longer Mr. Sorin, but Mr. Sorin plus someone else. Your personality has become blurred, and you even think of yourself in the third person singular —as *he.*

SORIN [*laughs*]. You're a one to talk! You've had a good time in your life, haven't you? But what about me? I served in the law-courts for twenty-eight years, but never really lived. I don't know what real life is, so it isn't after all surprising that I should still be anxious to get all I can from life. You have had all that life could offer you, and that's why you're so ready to take a philosophic view of life. But I still want to live, and that's why I like to have a glass of sherry with my dinner, a cigar, and so on. That's all there is to it, sir.

DORN. A man ought to take life seriously. To worry about your health at the age of sixty, to regret that you haven't enjoyed yourself sufficiently in your youth, that sir, if you'll pardon my saying so, is sheer folly!

MASHA [*gets up*]. I suppose it's almost lunch-time. [*Walks lazily, limply*] My leg's gone to sleep ... [*Goes out.*]

DORN. Gone to put down a couple of drinks before lunch.

SORIN. The poor girl's life is so unhappy.

DORN. Nonsense, sir!

SORIN. You talk like a man who's had all he wanted from life.

MISS ARKADINA. Oh, what can be more boring than this delightful country boredom! Quiet, hot, nobody does anything, everybody's philosophizing ... How nice it is to be with you, my friends, how pleasant to listen to you, but how much nicer to be alone in an hotel room studying a part!

NINA [*ecstatically*]. Oh, it must be! I quite understand!

SORIN. Of course, life is much nicer in town. You sit in your study, your butler admits no one you don't want to see, there's the telephone, cabmen in the street, and so on.

DORN [*hums*]. "Tell her, oh, tell her, my flowers sweet...."

[*Enter* SHAMRAYEV, *followed by* PAULINE.]

SHAMRAYEV. Here they all are! Good afternoon, ladies and gentlemen. [*Kisses* MISS ARKADINA's *hand, then* NINA's] So glad to see you looking so well. [*To* MISS ARKADINA] My wife tells me that you're thinking of driving to town with her today. Is that right?

MISS ARKADINA. Yes, we were thinking of it.

SHAMRAYEV. H'm—I see ... Well, it's an excellent idea of course, but, pray, madam, how do you propose to get to town? I can't spare anyone to drive you there. We're bringing in the rye today, and everybody on the estate is busy in the fields. And, besides, what horses are you going to have?

MISS ARKADINA. What do I care what horses?

SORIN. We've got carriage horses, haven't we?

SHAMRAYEV [*growing agitated*]. Carriage horses? And where, pray, am I to get the collars for them? Where am I to get the collars? I must say this is really incredible. It's—it's phenomenal! No, madam, I'm very sorry, but I can't let you have any horses. I'm full of admiration for you as an actress, I'd gladly sacrifice ten years of my life for you, but I can't let you have any horses!

MISS ARKADINA. But what if I have to go? Well, really!

SHAMRAYEV. My dear lady, you've no idea what it means to run an estate!

MISS ARKADINA [*flaring up*]. That's an old story! If that's the case,

I'm leaving for Moscow today. Please tell them to hire horses for me in the village, or I shall walk to the station!

SHAMRAYEV [*flaring up*]. In that case I throw up my job. Find yourself another agent!

MISS ARKADINA. Every summer it's the same thing! Every summer I'm insulted here! I shall never come here again! Never! [*Goes out on left where the bathing hut is supposed to be; in another minute she can be seen entering the house;* TRIGORIN *follows her with rod and pail.*]

SORIN [*flaring up*]. The nerve of the man! What infernal cheek! Damned if I'm going to put up with it any longer! I mean, after all— Get me all my horses here this very minute!

NINA [*to* PAULINE]. Refuse a famous actress like Miss Arkádina! Isn't her slightest wish, her slightest whim even, more important than the whole of your estate? It's unbelievable!

PAULINE [*in despair*]. But what can I do? Please put yourself in my place, my dear. What can I do?

SORIN [*to* NINA]. Let's go to my sister . . . Let's all plead with her not to leave. Shall we, my dear? [*Looking in the direction in which* SHAMRAYEV *has gone*] What a brute! A real despot!

NINA [*preventing him from getting up*]. Sit still, please . . . We'll wheel you there. [*She and* MEDVYEDENKO *wheel the chair.*] Oh, this is dreadful, dreadful!

SORIN. Yes, indeed. It is dreadful . . . Still don't you worry, my dear, he won't go. I'll talk to him at once.

[*They go out; only* DORN *and* PAULINE *remain.*]

DORN. People are tiresome. Your husband ought to have been kicked out of here long ago, but I suppose it'll all end in that old woman Sorin and his sister apologising to him. You'll see.

PAULINE. He's sent the carriage horses into the fields, too. Every day the same rows! If you knew how it upsets me! It makes me ill. Look, I'm shaking all over . . . I can't bear his coarseness. [*Imploringly*] Eugene, my dearest darling, please take me away with you! Our time is passing. We're no longer young. Don't let's pretend and lie any more now that we have so few years left to us . . .

[*A pause.*]

DORN. I'm fifty-five, my dear. It's too late for me to change my life.

PAULINE. That's not why you refuse to take me away. You've got other women who mean as much to you as I do, haven't you? You can't have them all at your house, can you? I quite understand. I'm sorry, you must think me an awful nuisance.

[NINA *appears near the house; she is picking flowers.*]

DORN. You know I don't.

PAULINE. I can't help being jealous. I don't suppose you can very well avoid women, being a doctor, can you? I understand.

DORN [*to* NINA *who walks up to them*]. What's happening there?

NINA. Irene is crying, and Mr. Sorin has an attack of asthma.

DORN [*getting up*]. I suppose I'd better go and give the pair of them some valerian drops.

NINA [*gives him the flowers*]. They're for you, doctor.

DORN. Thank you very much.[1] [*Walks off in the direction of the house.*]

PAULINE [*going with him*]. What lovely flowers! [*Near the house in a strangled voice*] Give me those flowers! Give me those flowers! [*Taking the flowers, she tears them up and throws them away; both go into the house.*]

NINA [*alone*]. How strange to see a famous actress crying because of some silly trifle! And isn't it even stranger that a famous writer should spend all day fishing and be so pleased because he has caught two chub? And so popular a writer, too, a writer whose name appears constantly in the papers, whose photographs are sold in the shops, whose works are translated into foreign languages! And I imagined famous people would be proud and unapproachable! I thought that they despised the mob, and that they used their fame and popularity only to avenge themselves on it for worshipping rank and wealth. But it appears they cry, fish, play cards, laugh, and lose their tempers just like anybody else!

KONSTANTIN [*enters hatless with a gun and a dead seagull*]. Are you alone here?

NINA. Yes.

[KONSTANTIN *lays the seagull at her feet.*]

NINA. What does it mean?

KONSTANTIN. I did a vile thing today: I killed this seagull. Allow me to lay it at your feet.

NINA. What's the matter with you? [*Picks up the seagull and gazes at it.*]

KONSTANTIN [*after a pause*]. I shall kill myself in the same way soon.

NINA. You look so strange. I hardly know you.

KONSTANTIN. That's not surprising. I hardly know you. Your atti-

---

[1] *in the text:* Merci bien—Translator's note.

tude towards me has changed. You look so coldly at me. My presence seems to make you feel uncomfortable.

NINA. You've grown so irritable lately. Whatever I do is wrong. It's so hard to understand you, almost as though you were talking in symbols. And I expect this seagull is some kind of a symbol too. I'm sorry, but I don't understand it. [*Puts seagull down on the bench*] I'm afraid I'm too unsophisticated to understand you.

KONSTANTIN. It goes back to the evening when my play was such a dismal flop, doesn't it? Women never forgive a failure. I have burnt my play, every page of it. Oh, if only you knew how unhappy I am! Your sudden indifference is so awful, so incredible! It is as if I woke up and found the lake had suddenly run dry, vanished under the ground. You said just now that you were not sophisticated enough to understand me. Oh, what is there to understand? My play was a failure. You despise my work. You think me worthless, commonplace, like hundreds of others . . . [*Stamping*] How well I understand it, how well! Oh, my head, my head! My brain feels as though it had been pierced with a red-hot nail. To hell with it, and with my pride which is sucking at my life-blood, sucking away at it like a serpent. [*Seeing* TRIGORIN *who is walking towards them, reading a book*] There comes real genius! Walks like Hamlet, and with a book, too! [*Mimicking*] "Words, words, words . . ."[1] Look, this sun is still miles away from you, and already you're smiling. Your gaze has melted in its rays. Good-bye, I won't be in your way. [*Walks away quickly.*]

TRIGORIN [*writing in his note-book*]. Takes snuff and drinks vodka. Always wears black. The schoolmaster is in love with her.

NINA. Good afternoon, Mr. Trigórin.

TRIGORIN. Good afternoon. I'm afraid we shall probably be leaving today. Events, you know, have taken rather an unexpected turn. So I don't think we're likely to meet again. A pity. I don't often meet charming young girls now. I hardly know what a girl of eighteen or nineteen is feeling or thinking about. That's why the girls in my stories are usually so unconvincing. I wish I could put myself in your place just for one hour to find out what you're thinking about and what you're really like.

NINA. And I wish I could be in your place.

TRIGORIN. Why?

NINA. To find out what it is like to be a famous and gifted writer.

---

[1] *"Words, words, words . . . ," as Hamlet replies to the inquisitive Polonius in Act II, scene 2.*

What does it feel like to be famous? How does the fact that you're so popular affect you?

TRIGORIN. How does it affect me? Why, I don't believe it affects me at all. I—I've never thought of it. [*Thinking it over*] Well, if you really want to know it's one of two things: either you are exaggerating my fame or it's something I'm hardly aware of.

NINA. But when you read about yourself in the papers?

TRIGORIN. When I'm praised, I like it, and when I'm abused, I'm upset for a day or two.

NINA. How wonderful the world is! If only you knew how I envy you! The fate of people is so different. Some live dreary, miserable, narrow lives, everyone just like everyone else, and all terribly unhappy. But others—you, for instance, you—the one in a million and fated to live such interesting, bright, happy lives, lives which are worth while, which are full of significance. Oh, I'm sure you must be very happy . . .

TRIGORIN. Me? [*Shrugging*] Well, I wonder . . . You talk about fame, happiness, some bright, interesting life, but—I hope you won't mind my saying so—to me all these fine words are just like honey which I detest. I'm afraid you're very kind and—so very young!

NINA. But your life must be wonderful!

TRIGORIN. Must it? What is there particularly good about it? [*Looks at his watch*] Afraid I must go in now. Have to do some writing. Sorry, but I'm busy . . . . [*Laughs*] I'm afraid you've touched me on a raw spot, and I'm beginning to get a bit worked up and cross. However, let's talk. Let's talk about my bright and beautiful life . . . Well, where shall we begin? [*After a little thought*] There are certain ideas which take possession of a man's mind so completely that he can't shake them off. For instance, a man may be obsessed day and night by the thought of the moon. Well, I too have my own moon. Day and night one tormenting thought takes complete possession of me—I must write, I must write! I must . . . I must! No sooner do I finish one story than for some unknown reason I must start on another, then a third, a fourth, and so on. I go on writing incessantly, without a break, and there seems to be no other way for it. Well, tell me what is there so bright and beautiful about that? It's a crazy sort of life! Even now while talking to you I can't forget for one single moment that there is an unfinished story waiting for me in my room. Do you see that cloud? Looks remarkably like a grand piano, doesn't it? Well, the moment I saw it, the thought flashed through my mind that I mustn't forget to mention somewhere in my story that a cloud looking like a grand piano sailed across the sky. I catch a whiff of heliotrope: A-ha, I say to myself, quick, make a mental note: a cloying scent, the widow's colour—must remember to mention that in a description of a summer evening. I eagerly snap up every word, every sentence, you or I may utter just for the sake of locking them away in my literary lumber-room—who knows, they may come in useful one day! When my work's done I rush off to the theatre, or go away to do a bit of fishing. There, at least, one would have thought, I could take a rest and forget my work. But not a bit of it! A heavy iron cannon-ball is already turning round and round in my head—an idea for a new story! It drags me back to my desk, and off I go again: write, write, write! And so it goes on and on, and I can find no rest from myself. I feel that I am consuming my own life, that for the honey I give away to someone I don't know, I gather up the pollen from my best flowers, tear the flowers themselves and crush them under my feet. Don't you think I'm just stark staring mad? Do my friends and those dear and near to me treat me like a normal human being? "Ah, what are you writing now, old man? What masterpiece are you going to bestow upon us next?" And so it goes on and on. Always the same thing, over and over again. And I cannot help feeling that all the attention my acquaintances bestow upon me, all their praises and cries of ecstatic delight—that all that is nothing but a piece of the most elaborate deception. They deceive me, as a doctor deceives a patient, and I assure you that sometimes I'm positively afraid that at any moment they may quietly steal up behind me, seize and drag me off to a lunatic asylum. Even when I was embarking on my literary career, in those best and dearest years of my youth, life was one long drawn-out agony to me. A minor writer, especially when he's unlucky, can't help feeling awkward, clumsy, unwanted. His nerves are frayed, they're always at breaking point. He feels himself drawn irresistibly to people who have some connexion with art and literature—unrecognised, ignored by everybody, too shy to look people straight in the face, like an incurable gambler without money. I'd never met any of my readers, but for some reason I always imagined them to be sceptical and hostile. I was afraid of a theatre audience. It terrified me. And every time I put on a new play I had the odd feeling that the dark people in the audience were my enemies and the fair ones coldly indifferent. Oh, it was awful! It really was simply torture!

NINA. But, surely, inspiration and the very act of creative work must give you moments of ecstasy and happiness!

TRIGORIN. Well, yes, in a way. When I'm writing, I feel happy. And I enjoy reading the proofs. But the moment my book is published, I'm in despair. I realise that it isn't what I wanted, that the whole thing is a mistake, that I shouldn't have written it at all. And I feel worried. I feel rotten—rotten! [*Laughing*] Well, the public reads it: "Yes, yes—very charming stuff, clever! Very charming, but it's a far cry to Tolstoy!" or "Excellent, but Turgenev's *Fathers and Sons*[1] is better!" And so to my dying day everything will be charming and clever, charming and clever, nothing more. And when I'm dead, my friends, as they walk past my grave, will say "Here lies Trigórin. He was a good writer, but not as good as Turgenev."

NINA. Excuse me, but I don't agree with you. You're simply spoilt by success.

TRIGORIN. What success? I never liked my own stuff. No, I'm most certainly not fond of myself as a writer. The worst of it is that I am in a kind of daze, and often I scarcely know myself what I am writing . . . Now, I like this stretch of water, I like the trees, the sky. I appreciate nature. It arouses passion in me and an irresistible longing to write. But after all, I am not just a descriptive writer. I also happen to be a citizen. I love my country, my people. And I can't help feeling that if I am a writer, I must speak of the people, I must speak of their sufferings, of their future. I must speak of science, of the rights of man and so on and so forth. So I talk about everything, I'm always in a hurry, I'm being pushed on all sides. People prod me on, they are angry with me. I rush about. Here, there, everywhere. Like a fox with the hounds in full cry after it. And I can see that life and knowledge are getting further and further away from me, that I'm lagging behind more and more, like the peasant who tried to overtake a train. So that in the end I'm beginning to feel that all I am good for is descriptive stuff, and in everything else, I'm false, false, false to the marrow of my bones.

NINA. You've been overworking, and I don't suppose you have either the time or the wish to realise your own importance. What does it matter that you are dissatisfied with yourself? Everybody thinks you're great and wonderful! If I were such a writer as you, I'd dedicate my whole life to the people, but I'd realise at the same time that they could only be happy by raising themselves to my level, and I'm sure it would draw me along in a chariot.

[1] *Fathers and Sons, the most popular novel of Ivan Turgenev (1818–1883).*

TRIGORIN. Well, as for the chariot—I'm not Agamemnon,[1] am I? [*Both smile.*]

NINA. For the happiness of being a writer or an actress, I'd gladly put up with the disapproval of my relations and friends, endure poverty and disappointment, live in an attic, eat nothing but dry bread. I would suffer agonies from the realisation of my own shortcomings, but I'd also demand fame . . . real, resounding fame! . . . [*Buries her face in her hands*] Oh, my head's spinning . . . .

MISS ARKADINA'S VOICE [*from within the house*]. Boris!

TRIGORIN. They're calling me . . . I suppose I shall have to go in and pack. Lord, how I wish I could stay! [*Looks round at the lake*] How glorious it is! What a lovely spot!

NINA. Do you see the house and the garden on the other side of the lake?

TRIGORIN. Yes.

NINA. That was my mother's house. I was born there. I've spent all my life on the banks of this lake and I know every little island on it.

TRIGORIN. You have a nice place here. [*Seeing the seagull*] And what's this?

NINA. A seagull. Konstantín shot it.

TRIGORIN. A beautiful bird. No, I don't want to leave, not really. I wonder if you could persuade Irene to stay? [*Writes something down in his note-book.*]

NINA. What are you writing?

TRIGORIN. Oh, nothing. Just making a note . . . Got an idea— [*Putting away his note-book*] An idea for a short story: a young girl has lived in a house on the shore of a lake since her childhood, a young girl like you; she loves the lake like a seagull, and she's as free and happy as a seagull. Then a man comes along, sees her, and—just for the fun of it—destroys her, like the seagull here.

[*A pause.*]

[MISS ARKADINA *appears at the window.*]

MISS ARKADINA. Boris, where are you?

TRIGORIN. Coming! [*As he walks towards the house, he turns round a few times to look at* NINA. *Stops by the window, to* MISS ARKADINA] Well?

MISS ARKADINA. We're staying.

[TRIGORIN *goes into the house.*]

---

[1] *Agamemnon, the King of Mycenae and leader of the ancient Greeks in the Trojan War.*

NINA [*goes up to the footlights; after a moment's reflection*].
A dream!

CURTAIN

act 3

Dining-room in SORIN'S *country house. On right and left—
doors. A sideboard. A medicine chest. A table in the middle
of the room. A suitcase and hat-boxes. Signs of preparations
for a journey.*

    TRIGORIN *is having lunch.* MASHA *stands by the table.*

MASHA. I'm telling you all this as a writer. You can use it if you like.
I'll be quite frank with you: If he had hurt himself badly, I
shouldn't have gone on living another minute. But that doesn't mean
that I haven't any courage. As a matter of fact, I've made up my mind
to tear this love out of my heart—tear it out by the roots.

TRIGORIN. How do you propose to do that?

MASHA. By getting married. I'm marrying Simon Medvyédenko.

TRIGORIN. The schoolmaster?

MASHA. Yes.

TRIGORIN. I don't see why you should.

MASHA. To love without hope, to wait for years and years for something to happen—no, thank you . . . Once I get married, I shan't
have time to think of love. New worries will make me forget my
unhappy past. And, anyway, it will be a change. Shall we have another?

TRIGORIN. Don't you think you've had enough?

MASHA. Good Lord, no! [*Fills a glass for each of them*] Don't look
at me like that! Women drink more often than you think. A few,
like me, drink openly, but most of them drink in secret. Yes, and it's
always vodka or brandy. [*Clinks glasses*] Cheers! You're a nice man,
Mr. Trigórin. Easy to get on with. I'm sorry you're going. [*They
drink.*]

TRIGORIN. So am I.

MASHA. Why don't you ask her to stay?

TRIGORIN. No use, she won't stay now. Her son's behaving rather tactlessly. First he tries to shoot himself, and now I'm told he wants to challenge me to a duel. And what for? Sulks, snorts, preaches new forms . . . Isn't there room enough in the world for everybody? For the new as well as the old? Why get in each other's way?

MASHA. Well, I suppose it's jealousy, too. However, it's none of my business.

[*A pause.* YAKOV *crosses the room from left to right with a suitcase; Nina comes in and stands by the window.*]

MASHA. My schoolmaster isn't particularly clever, but he is a good sort, and as poor as a church mouse. He's very much in love with me. I'm sorry for him. And I'm sorry for his old mother, too . . . Well, let me wish you the best of luck. Don't think too badly of me. [*Shakes him warmly by the hand*] Thank you for your kindness and your sympathy. Send me your books and don't forget to autograph them. Only please don't inscribe them "To my dear—" etc., but simply "To Mary, the world forgetting, and by the world forgot." Good-bye! [*Goes out.*]

NINA [*holding out her clenched fist to* TRIGORIN]. Odd or even?

TRIGORIN. Even.

NINA [*sighing*]. Wrong. I've only one pea in my hand. I was trying to find out whether to go on the stage or not. I wish someone would advise me what to do.

TRIGORIN. I'm afraid it's something you'll have to decide for yourself.

[*A pause.*]

NINA. You're going away and—I don't suppose we shall ever see each other again. I'd like you to accept this little medallion as a keepsake. I had your initials engraved on it—and on the other side the title of your book: "Days and Nights."

TRIGORIN. How sweet! [*Kisses the medallion*] What a lovely present!

NINA. I hope you'll think of me sometimes.

TRIGORIN. I will. I shall think of you as you were on that lovely day —remember?—a week ago, when you wore that summer frock . . . We had a long talk and—there was a white seagull lying on the seat.

NINA [*thoughtfully*]. Yes, a seagull . . .

[*A pause.*]

We can't talk here any more . . . Someone's coming. Please, let me have two minutes before you go. Please, do . . .

[*Goes out on left; at the same time* MISS ARKADINA, SORIN, *in a frock-coat with a star of some order on it, followed by* YAKOV *busy with the luggage, enter on the right.*]

MISS ARKADINA. I wish you'd stay at home, Peter. With your rheumatism and at your age you oughtn't to go gallivanting about. [*To* TRIGORIN] Who left the room just now? Nina?

TRIGORIN. Yes.

MISS ARKADINA. Sorry we disturbed you . . . [*Sits down*] Well, I think I have packed everything. My goodness, I'm worn out.

TRIGORIN [*reads the inscription on the medallion*]. "Days and Nights," page one hundred and twenty-one, lines eleven and twelve.

YAKOV [*clearing the table*]. Am I to pack your fishing rods too, sir?

TRIGORIN. Yes, I may need them again. But the books you can give away to anyone you like.

YAKOV. Very good, sir.

TRIGORIN [*to himself*]. Page one hundred and twenty-one, lines eleven and twelve. I wonder what there is in those lines [*To* MISS ARKADINA] Have you got my books in the house?

MISS ARKADINA. Yes, you'll find them in my brother's study, in the corner book-case.

TRIGORIN. Page one hundred and twenty-one—[*Goes out.*]

MISS ARKADINA. Really, Peter dear, I do wish you'd stay at home . . .

SORIN. You're going away and I shall find it awfully dull here without you.

MISS ARKADINA. And what about the town? I bet there's nothing in particular happening there.

SORIN. No, perhaps not, but it'll make a change. [*Laughs*] They're going to lay the foundation stone of the rural council building, and all that sort of thing . . . You see, my dear, I'm thoroughly fed up with this silly sort of life. Want to liven up a bit, if only for an hour or two. Been on the shelf too long, like an old pipe. I've ordered the carriage for one o'clock. We shall leave together.

MISS ARKADINA [*after a pause*]. Very well, but don't fret too much when you come back. Don't catch cold. Look after my son. Take care of him. Get some sense into his head. [*A pause.*] Here I'm going away, and I shall never know why he tried to shoot himself. I believe the main reason was jealousy, and the sooner I take Trigórin away from here, the better.

SORIN. Well, I don't know. I daresay, there were other reasons, too. And no wonder. He's young, intelligent, living in the country, in some God-forsaken hole with no money, no position, and no future. Nothing to do. Ashamed of doing nothing and afraid of it. I'm very fond of him, my dear, and I think he's fond of me too, but all the same—I mean, after all, he can't help feeling that he isn't of any use here, that he is a poor relation, a dependant. It's—I mean, it's pretty obviously, isn't it? His vanity—

MISS ARKADINA. Oh, what a trial that boy is to me! [*Reflectively*] I wish he'd get himself some job. In the Civil Service, or something.

SORIN [*whistles, then diffidently*]. I think it wouldn't be a bad idea if you—er—if you'd let him have a little money. You see, he should really—I mean, he does want some decent clothes badly, and—so on. The poor fellow has been wearing the same old coat for the last three years. Walks about without an overcoat . . . [*Laughs*] And I don't suppose it would be such a bad thing for the young man to have a little fun—go abroad for a while . . . It wouldn't cost a lot, would it?

MISS ARKADINA. Well, I don't know. I suppose I might manage a new suit for him, but as for going abroad— No, I'm afraid that's quite out of the question. As a matter of fact, I don't think I could even afford the money for a suit just now. [*Firmly*] I haven't any money!

[SORIN *laughs.*]

MISS ARKADINA. I have no money!

SORIN [*whistling*]. I see. Forgive me, my dear. Don't be angry with me. I—I believe you . . . You're such a warmhearted generous woman.

MISS ARKADINA [*crying*]. I have no money!

SORIN. Of course if I had any money, I'd give him some myself, but I haven't got anything—not a penny! [*Laughs*] My agent grabs all my pension and spends it on the estate. He rears cattle, keeps bees, and all my money just goes down the drain. The damned bees die, the damned cows die, and when I ask for a carriage, the horses are wanted for something else . . .

MISS ARKADINA. Of course I have some money, but you must realise that I'm an actress. Why, my dresses alone are enough to ruin me.

SORIN. You're very kind, my dear. I—I respect you . . . Indeed, I do. Oh dear, I—I'm afraid—I—I'm not feeling well again—[*swaying*] my head's going round and round—[*holding on to the table*] afraid I—I'm going to—faint—and—so on.

MISS ARKADINA [*frightened*]. Peter! My dear! [*Trying to support him*] Peter, darling! [*Shouts*] Help! Help!

[*Enter* KONSTANTIN *with a dark bandage on his head, followed by* MEDVYEDENKO.]

MISS ARKADINA. He's going to faint!

SORIN. Oh, it's nothing—nothing. [*Smiles and has a drink of water*] It's passed off—and—so on.

KONSTANTIN [*to his mother*]. Don't be alarmed, mother. It's nothing serious. Uncle often has these attacks now. [*To his uncle*] You ought to go and lie down for a bit, uncle.

SORIN. Yes, for a bit . . . But I'm going to town all the same . . . I'll lie down for a bit, and then I'll go . . . I mean, it's pretty obvious, isn't it . . . [*Walks to the door, leaning on his cane.*]

MEDVYEDENKO [*taking his arm*]. Do you know the riddle,[1] sir? In the morning on all fours, in the afternoon on two, in the evening on three . . .

SORIN [*laughs*]. That's right. And at night on his back. Thank you, I can manage myself now . . .

MEDVYEDENKO. Good Lord, sir, this is no time to stand on ceremony, is it?

[SORIN *and* MEDVYEDENKO *go out.*]

MISS ARKADINA. Oh, he gave me such a fright!

KONSTANTIN. It isn't good for him to live in the country. He frets too much. I wish you'd feel munificent for once, mother, and lend him fifteen hundred or two thousand roubles. Then he could manage a whole year in town.

MISS ARKADINA. I have no money. I'm an actress, not a banker.

[*A pause.*]

KONSTANTIN. Please change the bandage for me, mother. You do it so beautifully.

MISS ARKADINA [*takes some iodoform and a box with bandages from the medicine chest*]. The doctor is late today, isn't he?

KONSTANTIN. Yes. Promised to be here at ten, and now it's twelve already.

MISS ARKADINA. Sit down, dear. [*Takes the bandage off his head*] You look as if you were wearing a turban. Yesterday a stranger in the kitchen asked what nationality you were. Your wound has almost healed up. Just a little scar left. [*Kisses his head*] You won't do anything so stupid again while I'm away, will you?

KONSTANTIN. No, mother. I did it in a moment of black despair, when I lost control of myself. It won't happen again. [*Kisses her hand*] You've got clever fingers, mother. I remember long ago when you were still acting on the Imperial stage—I was a little boy then—there was a fight in our yard, and a washerwoman who lived in our house was badly hurt. Remember? She was unconscious when they

---

[1] *the riddle, the famous riddle of man with which the Sphinx of Thebes taxed visitors to the city. Oedipus guessed the riddle, whereupon the sphinx committed suicide.*

picked her up. You looked after her, gave her her medicine and bathed her children. Don't you remember?

MISS ARKADINA. I don't. [*Puts on a fresh bandage.*]

KONSTANTIN. Two ballet dancers lived in our house at the time. They used to come and have coffee with you ...

MISS ARKADINA. Oh yes, I remember that.

KONSTANTIN. They were such pious women, weren't they? [*A pause.*] Lately, I mean these last few days, mother, I've loved you as I used to love you when I was a little boy: so dearly and so tenderly. I've no one left in the whole world now except you, mother. Only why, oh why, are you so much under the influence of that man?

MISS ARKADINA. You don't understand him, Konstantín. He's one of the most honourable men I've ever known ...

KONSTANTIN. Yet when he was told I was going to challenge him to a duel, his honour did not prevent his playing the coward, did it? He's running away. What an ignominious flight!

MISS ARKADINA. What utter nonsense! It was I who asked him to leave.

KONSTANTIN. A most honourable man! Here you and I are almost quarrelling over him, and he's probably somewhere in the drawing-room or the garden—laughing at us, broadening Nina's mind, doing his best to convince her once and for all that he is a genius.

MISS ARKADINA. You seem to enjoy saying all sorts of disagreeable things to me. I tell you I think very highly of him, and I'd thank you not to speak badly of him in my presence.

KONSTANTIN. And I don't! You want me to regard him as a genius. Well, I'm very sorry, mother, but the truth is his books make me sick!

MISS ARKADINA. You're jealous. Mediocrities who cherish absurdly grand ideas about themselves, naturally turn up their noses at men of real genius. Much good does it do them, I must say!

KONSTANTIN [*ironically*]. Men of real genius! [*Angrily*] I've got more genius than any of you, if it comes to that! [*Tears the bandage off his head*] You purveyors of stale ideas have scrambled to the top in the world of art and, according to you, only what you yourselves do is legitimate and genuine. You stifle and persecute everything else. I don't acknowledge your authority! I don't care a damn for you or for him!

MISS ARKADINA. You decadent, you! ...

KONSTANTIN. Go to your precious theatre and act in your miserable, third-rate plays!

MISS ARKADINA. Never in my life have I acted in third-rate plays!

Leave me alone, will you? You couldn't even write the words for some cheap revue. You Kiev artisan! You parasite!

KONSTANTIN. Miser!

MISS ARKADINA. Tramp!

[KONSTANTIN *sinks into a chair and weeps quietly.*]

MISS ARKADINA. Nonentity! [*After pacing the room in agitation*] Don't cry, please. You mustn't cry, my dear . . . [*Crying*] Please, don't . . . [*Kisses his forehead, cheeks, and head*] Oh, my darling, please forgive me . . . Forgive your silly mother. I'm so unhappy. Please, please forgive me, dear.

KONSTANTIN [*embracing her*]. Oh, mother, if only you knew. I've lost everything. She doesn't love me, and now I can't write any more . . . All my hopes are shattered . . .

MISS ARKADINA. Don't give up, my darling . . . Everything will come right. He'll be gone soon, and she'll fall in love with you again. [*Wiping his tears*] There, there—stop crying. We've made it up now, haven't we?

KONSTANTIN [*kissing her hands*]. Yes, mother.

MISS ARKADINA [*gently*]. Won't you make it up with him too, my dear? You don't really want to challenge him to a duel, do you? . . . The whole thing's so silly, darling!

KONSTANTIN. All right, only don't ask me to meet him, mother. It would be too painful—I couldn't stand it [*Enter* TRIGORIN] Here he comes . . . . I'll go now . . . [*Replaces the bandages, etc., quickly in the medicine chest*] The doctor will do up the bandage . . .

TRIGORIN [*turning over the pages of the book*]. Page one hundred and twenty-one—lines eleven and twelve . . . Here it is . . . [*Reads*] "If my life should ever be of any use to you, come and take it."

[KONSTANTIN *picks up the bandage from the floor and goes out.*]

MISS ARKADINA [*glancing at the clock*]. The carriage will soon be here.

TRIGORIN [*to himself*]. If my life should ever be of any use to you, come and take it.

MISS ARKADINA. You've finished packing, I hope?

TRIGORIN [*impatiently*]. Yes, yes . . . [*Musing*] Why does that appeal from so pure a heart fill me with sadness? Why does my heart contract with pain? . . . If my life should be of any use to you, come and take it. [*To* MISS ARKADINA] Please, let's stay for just one more day!

[MISS ARKADINA *shakes her head.*]

TRIGORIN. Please, let's.

MISS ARKADINA. My dear, I know what's keeping you here. But please take yourself in hand. You're slightly infatuated. Do quieten down.

TRIGORIN. You, too, should be quiet, sensible, wise. I entreat you, look upon this as a true friend. [*Presses her hand*] You're capable of sacrifice. Be my friend, set me free . . . .

MISS ARKADINA [*in great agitation*]. Are you so much in love with her?

TRIGORIN. I feel strongly drawn to her! Perhaps this is just what I need.

MISS ARKADINA. The love of a provincial miss? Oh, how little you know yourself!

TRIGORIN. Sometimes people walk in their sleep. Well, I feel like that now. Here I am talking to you, and yet I seem to be asleep and dreaming of her . . . Sweet dreams—oh, such wonderful dreams have taken possession of me! . . . Set me free, please!

MISS ARKADINA [*trembling*]. No, no! . . . I'm an ordinary woman. You mustn't talk iike that to me . . . Don't torment me. Boris . . . I'm frightened . . .

TRIGORIN. If you really want to, you needn't be ordinary. The love of a young girl—delightful, poetic, carrying you away into a world of dreams—can there be any greater happiness on earth? I have never known a love like that . . . As a young man I never had time: I was too busy running from one editorial office to another, trying to earn a bare living . . . But it is here, this love, it has come to me at last! It beckons to me . . . I'd be a fool to run away from it!

MISS ARKADINA [*angrily*]. You're quite out of your mind!

TRIGORIN. Well, what if I am?

MISS ARKADINA. All of you seem to have conspired to torment me today. [*Bursts out crying.*]

TRIGORIN [*clutches at his head*]. She doesn't understand! She doesn't want to understand!

MISS ARKADINA. Am I so old and ugly that you can talk to me about other women without the slightest embarrassment? [*Embracing and kissing him*] Oh, you've gone out of your senses! Oh, my darling, my dear, my beautiful one! . . You—you're the last page of my life! [*Goes down on her knees*] Oh, my joy, my pride, my happiness! . . . [*Embracing his knees*] If you forsake me now, if you leave me for only one hour, I shall not survive it! I shall go mad! Oh, my darling, my dearest love, my master!

TRIGORIN. Someone may come in! [*Helps her to get up.*]

MISS ARKADINA. Let them come. I'm not ashamed of my love for you! [*Kisses his hands*] My dearest treasure, why do such a desperate thing? You want to behave like a madman, but I don't want you to. I won't let you . . . [*Laughs*] You're mine—mine! . . . This forehead is mine, these eyes are mine, this lovely silky hair is mine! . . . You're all mine. Oh, you're so gifted, so clever. You're the greatest of all our modern writers. You're Russia's only hope . . . You have so much sincerity, simplicity, freshness, healthy humour . . . With one stroke of your pen you can express what is most significant and typical of any person and place. Your characters are so wonderfully alive. One can't read you without delight. You think I'm exaggerating? Flattering you? Well, look into my eyes! . . . Please, please! . . . Do I look as if I were telling you lies? Well, you see! I alone know how to appreciate you, I alone am telling you the truth! Oh, my darling, my precious darling! . . . You will come with me, won't you? You won't leave me, will you?

TRIGORIN. I have no will of my own . . . . I never had one . . . . . Listless, flabby, always submissive. No! no woman can possibly care for a man like me! Take me away with you, carry me off, only for heaven's sake don't let me out of your sight for a single moment!

MISS ARKADINA [*to herself*]. Now he's mine! [*Cheerfully, as though nothing had happened*] But of course if you like, you can stay. I'll go by myself and you can join me later. In a week perhaps. Why, indeed, should you be in such a hurry?

TRIGORIN. No, we'd better go together.

MISS ARKADINA. As you wish. If you really want to, then by all means let's go together.

[*A pause.*]
[TRIGORIN *jots something down in his note-book.*]

MISS ARKADINA. What are you writing?

TRIGORIN. A phrase I heard this morning. I liked it very much . . . "A glitter of girls" . . . It may come in useful. [*Stretching himself*] So we are going, are we? Oh dear, more railway carriages, stations, refreshment bars, mutton chops, talk . . .

SHAM RAYEV [*enters*]. I have the honour to announce with the utmost regret, dear lady, that the carriage is at the door. Time you left for the station. The train is due at five past two. So you won't forget to let me know where the actor Suzdáltsev is now, will you? Is he alive? Is he well? There was a time when we used to go out drinking together, he and I . . . He was inimitable in "The Mail Robbery" . . Inimitable! The tragedian Izmáylov used to appear with him at

Yelissavetgrád. He was a remarkable man, too, quite remarkable.
. . . No need to be in a hurry, dear lady. You've still got another five
minutes. Once they acted two conspirators in a melodrama, and,
when they were suddenly discovered, Izmáylov had to say, "We've
been caught in a trap!" but instead he said "We've been trapped in a
caught!" [*Roars with laughter*] Trapped in a caught!

[*While he is speaking,* YAKOV *busies himself with the suitcases,
the maid brings* MISS ARKADINA *her hat, coat, umbrella and gloves;
they all assist her to put on her things. The cook peeps through
the door on the left and, after a little while, comes in diffidently.
Enter* PAULINE, *followed by* SORIN *and* MEDVYEDENKO.]

PAULINE [*with a little basket*]. I brought you some plums for the
journey, my dear. They're delicious. You might like to have some in
the train . . .

MISS ARKADINA. Thank you. It's very kind of you, my dear.

PAULINE. Good-bye, my dear. I'm sorry if everything wasn't quite
all right. [*Bursts into tears.*]

MISS ARKADINA [*embracing her*]. Everything was perfect, everything! But, please, don't cry. That certainly isn't right.

PAULINE. We're growing old!

MISS ARKADINA. Well, my dear, we can't help that, can we?

SORIN [*in overcoat with cape, with his hat and a cane in his hand,
comes in through door on left; crossing the room*]. We'd better hurry,
my dear, or we shall miss our train. I mean, after all—I'm going to
get into the carriage. [*Goes out.*]

MEDVYEDENKO. I think I'll walk to the station to see you off . . . If I
walk fast enough, I can get there in time . . . [*Goes out.*]

MISS ARKADINA. Good-bye, my dears . . . If we are alive and well, we
shall meet again next summer . . . [*The maid,* YAKOV, *and the cook
kiss her hands.*] Thank you for everything. [*Gives the cook a rouble*]
Here's a rouble[1] for the three of you.

THE COOK. Thank you kindly, madam. A happy journey to you.
You've been very good to us.

YAKOV. May the Lord bless you, madam. Good luck, madam.

SHAMRAYEV. Don't forget to drop us a line, dear lady. Good-bye,
Mr. Trigórin.

MISS ARKADINA. Where's Konstantín? Tell him I'm going. I must
say good-bye to him. Well, good-bye to you all. Good-bye. [*To*

---

[1] *rouble, equivalent at the time to $.51; hardly a munificent gift for three serv-
ants.*

YAKOV] I've given cook a rouble. It's for the three of you.

[*All go out on right. The stage is empty. Behind the scenes the usual farewell noises. The maid comes back, takes the basket of plums from the table and goes out again.*]

TRIGORIN [*coming back*]. I've forgotten my stick. It must be on the terrace. [*Goes towards the door on left where he meets* NINA *who is coming in*] Is that you? .. We're leaving ...

NINA. I knew we'd meet again. [*Excitedly*] Mr. Trigórin, I've made up my mind once and for all: I'm taking the plunge—I'm going on the stage. I shan't be here tomorrow. I'm running away from home, I'm leaving everything, I'm starting a new life. I'm leaving for Moscow—like you. We shall meet there.

TRIGORIN [*looking round*]. Stop at the "Slav Bazaar." And let me know at once ... Molchánovka, Grokhólsky's House ... Sorry, I must run.

[*A pause.*]

NINA. One moment, please! ...

TRIGORIN [*in an undertone*]. You're so lovely ... Oh, I'm so happy that we shall meet each other soon. [*She lays her head on his chest.*] I shall see your wonderful bright eyes again, your sweet, tender smile, your dear face, your look of angelic purity .. Oh, my dear!

[*A lingering kiss.*]

CURTAIN

act 4

There is an interval of two years between the third and the fourth acts.

One of the drawing-rooms in SORIN'S *country-house converted into a study by* KONSTANTIN. *To the right and left— doors leading into the inner rooms. Straight in front a french window leading on to the terrace. In addition to the usual drawing-room furniture, a writing desk in corner on right, a Turkish divan by the door on the left, a bookcase, books on window-sills and chairs.*

Evening. One lamp is burning under a lampshade. The room is only dimly lit. The trees rustle outside and the wind is howling in the chimney. The night-watchman knocks.

MEDVYEDENKO *and* MASHA *enter.*

MASHA [*calling*]. Konstantín! Konstantín! [*looking round*] There's no one here. Every minute the old man keeps asking: where's Konstantín? where's Konstantín? ... He can't live without him ...

MEDVYEDENKO. He's afraid of being left alone. [*Listening*] What beastly weather! It's been like this for two days.

MASHA [*turning up the lamp*]. There are waves on the lake. Great big ones.

MEDVYEDENKO. It's dark in the garden. I wish to goodness they'd tell someone to knock down that stage in the park. There it stands, bare and hideous like a skeleton, the curtain flapping in the wind. As I passed it yesterday evening, I thought I could hear someone crying there.

MASHA. You do imagine things, don't you?

[*A pause.*]

MEDVYEDENKO. Let's go home, Masha.

MASHA [*shakes her head*]. I'm staying here for the night.

MEDVYEDENKO [*imploringly*]. Please let's go, Masha. The baby must be starving.

MASHA. Don't be silly, Simon. Nurse won't let him starve.

[*A pause.*]

MEDVYEDENKO. It's a shame. Three nights now he's been without his mother.

MASHA. You're getting an awful bore, Simon. Before we were married at least you used to hold forth on every imaginable subject, but now all one hears from you is: baby—come home, baby—come home.

MEDVYEDENKO. Let's go, Masha.

MASHA. You go yourself.

MEDVYEDENKO. Your father won't let me have a horse.

MASHA. He will. You ask him, and see if he won't.

MEDVYEDENKO. Well, I suppose I might as well ask him. But you will be coming home tomorrow, won't you?

MASHA [*takes snuff*]. All right, I'll come tomorrow. Do stop worrying me now, will you?

Enter KONSTANTIN *and* PAULINE, KONSTANTIN *carrying pillows and blankets, and* PAULINE *sheets. They lay them on the Turkish divan. Then* KONSTANTIN *goes to his desk and sits down.*]

MASHA. What is it for, mother?

PAULINE. Mr. Sorin wants his bed made up in Konstantín's study.

MASHA. Let me do it. [*Lays the bed.*]

PAULINE [*sighs*]. The old man is getting more like a baby every day ...

[*Goes up to writing desk and, leaning on her elbow, looks at the manuscript; a pause.*]

MEDVYEDENKO. I'd better be going. Good-bye, Masha. [*Kisses his wife's hand*] Good-bye, mother. [*Tries to kiss his mother-in-law's hand.*]

PAULINE. All right! For goodness sake, go!

MEDVYEDENKO. Good-bye Konstantín.

[KONSANTIN *offers him his hand in silence.* MEDVYEDENKO *goes out.*]

PAULINE [*looking at the manuscript*]. No one ever thought you'd be a real writer one day, Konstantín. Now, thank God, you're even getting money from the magazines. [*Smooths his hair*] And you've grown so handsome, too! Dear, dear Konstantín, please try to be more kind to my Masha!

MASHA [*making the bed*]. Do leave him alone, mother.

PAULINE [*to* KONSTANTIN]. She's such a nice girl. [*A pause*] All a woman wants, Konstantín, is that a man should look kindly at her. Don't I know it from my own experience?

[KONSTANTIN *gets up from his desk and leaves the room without a word.*]

MASHA. Now you've made him angry. Why do you pester him, mother?

PAULINE. I'm sorry for you, my child.

MASHA. A lot of good that does.

PAULINE. My heart's been bleeding for you, dear. Do you suppose I don't see what's going on? I understand everything!

MASHA. It's just silly nonsense, mother. It's only in novels you read about unhappy love. It's nothing. The only sensible thing to do is not to brood over it, not to sit about waiting for something to happen ... If you're silly enough to fall in love with a man who doesn't care a pin for you, then you must be able to get over it. They've promised to transfer Simon to another district. As soon as we have moved, I shall forget all about this ... I shall tear it out of my heart by the roots ...

[*In the next room but one someone is playing a melancholy waltz.*]

PAULINE. Konstantín is playing the piano. That means he's unhappy.

MASHA [*dances a few waltz steps noiselessly*]. The chief thing, mother, is not to see him. I wish they'd give Simon his transfer. I'm sure I'd forget Konstantín within a month. All this is so damn silly!

[*The door on left opens.* DORN *and* MEDVYEDENKO *wheel in* SORIN *in his invalid chair.*]

MEDVYEDENKO. I've six people to provide for now, and flour is two copecks a pound.

DORN. What a life, eh?

MEDVYEDENKO. It's all very well for you to laugh. You're rolling in money.

DORN. Rolling in money, am I? My dear chap, I've been in medical practice now for thirty years—damned troublesome practice it was, too, for there was not a moment either by day or by night when I could call my soul my own. Well, do you know how much money I've saved up in all these years? Two thousand roubles! And that I spent during my recent trip abroad. No, sir. I've nothing.

MASHA [*to her husband*]. Haven't you gone yet?

MEDVYEDENKO [*guiltily*]. Well, how can I when he won't let me have a horse.

MASHA [*with bitter disappointment, in an undertone*]. Oh, how I wish I'd never set eyes on you!

[*The bath-chair comes to a stop in the left half of the room;* PAULINE, MASHA, *and* DORN *sit down beside it,* MEDVYEDENKO, *with a hang-dog expression, walks off to the other end of the room.*]

DORN. I see you've made a lot of changes here. You've turned this drawing-room into a study!

MASHA. Konstantín finds it much more convenient to work here. You see, he can walk out into the garden whenever he likes and do his thinking there.

[*The night-watchman knocks.*]

SORIN. Where's my sister?

DORN. Gone to the station to meet Trigórin. She should be back soon.

SORIN. I suppose if you thought it necessary to send for my sister, I must be pretty bad. [*After a moment's silence*] How do you like that? Here I am seriously ill, and they won't give me any medicine!

DORN. Well, what would you like? Valerian drops? Bicarbonate of soda? Quinine?

SORIN. There he goes again! Bless my soul, what an awful trial that man is! [*Motioning his head towards the divan*] Has that bed been made up for me?

PAULINE. Yes, Mr. Sorin. It's for you.

SORIN. Thank you.

DORN [*hums*]. "The moon is sailing across the sky at night—"

SORIN. I've thought of a damned good idea for a short story for Konstantín. Now, let me see. Yes. It's title will be: The Man Who Wanted To. You see, when I was young I wanted to become a writer —and I didn't. I wanted to speak well—and I spoke abominably: [*mimicking himself*] "I mean—I mean to say—and so on and so forth —I—er—this, and I—er—that." Sometimes I'd go on babbling like that for hours till I'd be in a regular sweat. I wanted to marry—and I didn't. I always wanted to live in town—and here I am ending my days in the country. And so on.

DORN. You wanted to become a State Councillor—and you did.

SORIN [*laughs*]. I'm afraid I didn't want to become that. It just happened.

DORN. You must admit that to express dissatisfaction with life at sixty-two is a bit ungenerous.

SORIN. What a damned obstinate fellow you are! Can't you understand? I want to live.

DORN. That's sheer folly. According to the laws of nature, every life must come to an end.

SORIN. You talk like a man who has had his fill of everything. You've had all you wanted and so you can be philosophic about life. It makes no difference to you. But I daresay even you will be frightened all right when your time comes to die.

DORN. The fear of death, sir, is an animal fear . . . We must do our best to overcome it. Only those who believe in life everlasting are consciously afraid to die, but what they're really afraid of is their sins. But you, sir, are, in the first place, an unbeliever, and, in the second, what sort of sins could you have committed? Served in the Ministry of Justice for twenty-five years? That's all, isn't it?

SORIN [*laughs*]. Twenty-eight, my dear sir, twenty-eight . . .

[*Enter* KONSTANTIN *and sits down at* SORIN's *feet.* MASHA *never takes her eyes off him.*]

DORN. I'm afraid we must be interfering with Konstantín's work.

KONSTANTIN. No, not at all.

[*A pause.*]

MEDVYEDENKO. May I ask you, doctor, which city you liked best abroad.

DORN. Genoa.

KONSTANTIN. Why Genoa?

DORN. Because the crowds in the streets of Genoa are so wonderful.

Whenever you leave your hotel in the evening, the streets are swarming with people. You move about aimlessly in the crowd, swept along this way and that, up and down the street, you live with it, you acquire, as it were, a collective personality and you begin to believe that there really is such a thing as a world-soul, like the one Nina once acted in your play. Incidentally, where is Nina now? Where is she and how is she getting on?

KONSTANTIN. I believe she's quite well.

DORN. I was told she'd been leading a rather peculiar sort of life. What exactly did happen?

KONSTANTIN. Oh, it's a long story, doctor.

DORN. All right, make it short then.

[*A pause.*]

KONSTANTIN. She ran away from home and went to live with Trigórin. You know that, don't you?

DORN. Yes, I know that.

KONSTANTIN. She had a child. The child died. Trigórin got tired of her and went back to his old love, as might have been expected. Not that he had really ever broken with her, but being the spineless character he is, he managed to make the best of both worlds and, as far as I can gather, made a complete mess of Nina's private life.

DORN. And her stage career?

KONSTANTIN. Her stage career was even a worse failure, I believe. Her first appearance on the stage was at a holiday resort near Moscow. She then went on tour in the provinces. At that particular time I never lost sight of her, and for some months I used to follow her about wherever she went. She always took big parts, but her acting was crude, without a trace of refinement. She'd tear a passion to tatters, and her gestures were melodramatic. Now and then she would utter a cry that showed some talent, or she would do a death scene really well—but those were only moments.

DORN. So she has some talent after all?

KONSTANTIN. I don't know. It's hard to say. I suppose she must have. I saw her of course, but she would not see me. I was never admitted to her hotel room. I realised how she felt, and I did not insist on a meeting. [*A pause.*] Well, what more do you want to know? Later, after I had returned home, I used to get letters from her. Warm, sensible, interesting letters. She never complained, but I could feel she was terribly unhappy: every line showed very clearly that her nerves were dreadfully strained. And she seemed a little unhinged, too. Always signed herself "The Seagull." In Pushkin's

"Water Nymph"[1] the miller calls himself a raven, and so she went on repeating in her letters that she was a seagull. She's here now.

DORN. How do you mean—here?

KONSTANTIN. She's staying at an inn in the town. She's been there for the last five days. I nearly went to see her, but Masha has been there and it seems she won't see anyone. Medvyédenko assures me that he saw her yesterday afternoon walking across a field about a mile and a half from here.

MEDVYEDENKO. Yes, I saw her. She was walking in that direction, towards the town. I spoke to her and asked her why she had not been to see us. She said she'd come.

KONSTANTIN. She'll never come. [*A pause.*] Her father and step-mother will have nothing to do with her. They've stationed men everywhere on their estate to make sure she doesn't get near the house. [*Walks away with the doctor to the writing desk*] How awfully easy it is, doctor, to be a philosopher on paper, and how damned difficult it is to be one in life!

SORIN. She was such a sweet girl!

DORN. I beg your pardon?

SORIN. I said she was a very sweet girl. State Councillor Sorin, sir, was even in love with her for a time.

DORN. You old rake!

[SHAMRAYEV *is heard laughing.*]

PAULINE. I believe they've come back from the station.

KONSTANTIN. Yes, I can hear mother.

[*Enter* MISS ARKADINA *and* TRIGORIN, *followed by* SHAMRAYEV].

SHAMRAYEV [*as he comes in*]. We're growing older and older, madam, falling, as they say, into the sere and yellow, but you're as young as ever . . . Gay clothes, vivacious, exquisite!

MISS ARKADINA. You want to bring me bad luck again, you awful man!

TRIGORIN [*to* SORIN]. How do you do, sir? Why are you always ill? That's very naughty of you! [*Seeing* MASHA, *joyfully*] Why, hullo Mary!

MASHA. So you recognised me? [*Presses his hand.*]

TRIGORIN. Married?

MASHA. Ages ago.

TRIGORIN. Happy? [*Exchanges bows with* DORN *and* MEDVYEDENKO,

---

[1] *Pushkin's "Water Nymph,"* the unfinished *drama* Rusalka *by the Russian poet Alexander Pushkin (1799–1837).*

then approaches KONSTANTIN *diffidently*] Your mother has told me that you've forgotten the past and are no longer angry with me.

[KONSTANTIN *holds out his hand to him.*]

MISS ARKADINA [*to her son*]. Boris has brought you the magazine with your new story.

KONSTANTIN [*accepting the magazine, to* TRIGORIN]. Thank you. It's very kind of you, I'm sure.

[*They sit down.*]

TRIGORIN. Your admirers want to be remembered to you . . . You'd be surprised how interested they are in you in Petersburg and Moscow. They're always asking me all sorts of questions about you. What you are like, how old you are, whether you are dark or fair. For some reason they all assume that you can't be young. And no one knows your real name as you write under a pseudonym. You're as mysterious as the Man in the Iron Mask.[1]

KONSTANTIN. Will you be staying long?

TRIGORIN. No, afraid not. I'm thinking of leaving for Moscow to-morrow. I'm anxious to finish my novel and I've promised to contribute something to a collection of short stories. As you see, it's the old, old story.

[*While they are talking,* MISS ARKADINA *and* PAULINE *place a card table in the middle of the room and open it out;* SHAMRAYEV *lights candles and sets chairs. A game of lotto is brought out of the bookcase.*]

TRIGORIN. I'm afraid the weather hasn't been very kind to me. The wind's ferocious. If it drops by the morning I'll do a bit of fishing in the lake. And come to think of it, I might as well take a walk round the garden too. I'd like to have a look at that place where—you remember?—your play was acted. I've got a very good plot for a story. All I need is to refresh my memory a little: get the local colour right, you know.

MASHA [*to her father*]. Please, father, let Simon have a horse, he's got to go home.

SHAMRAYEV [*mimicking her*]. Horse—home! [*Sternly*] Don't you realise the horses have just been to the station? You don't want me to send them out again in this weather, do you?

MASHA. But there are other horses . . . [*Seeing that her father*

---

[1] *Man in the Iron Mask, a famous prisoner of the French government of Louis XIV, who was treated with respect by his jailers during nearly twenty-five years of imprisonment but never allowed to remove his mask for fear of revealing his identity.*

makes no reply, she waves her hand.] What's the use—

MEDVYEDENKO. I don't mind walking home, Masha. I don't, really I don't . . .

PAULINE [*sighs*]. Walk in such weather? [*sitting down to the card table*] Shall we start, ladies and gentlemen?

MEDVYEDENKO. It's only four miles. Good-bye, dear. [*Kisses his wife's hand*] Good-bye, mother. [*His mother-in-law holds out her hand reluctantly for him to kiss.*] I wouldn't trouble anyone if it weren't for the baby—[*Bows to the company*] Good-bye. [*Slinks out guiltily.*]

SHAMRAYEV. He'll get there all right. He's not a general, is he?

PAULINE [*raps on the table*]. Please, ladies and gentlemen, don't let's waste time. Dinner will be served soon.

[*SHAMRAYEV, MASHA, and DORN sit down at the card table.*]

MISS ARKADINA [*to* TRIGORIN]. During the long autumn evenings we always play lotto here. Look, it's the same old lotto mother used to play with us when we were children. Wouldn't you like to join us in a game before dinner? [*Sits down with* TRIGORIN *at the card table*] It's not a very exciting game, but it's not bad once you get into it. [*Deals out three cards to each.*]

KONSTANTIN [*turning the pages of the magazine*]. He's read his own story, but he hasn't even cut the pages of mine. [*Puts the magazine down on the desk, then goes to the door on left; as he passes his mother, he kisses her on the head.*]

MISS ARKADINA. And what about you, darling?

KONSTANTIN. No, thank you, mother, I don't feel like it, somehow. I'll go out for a stroll. [*Goes out.*]

MISS ARKADINA. The stake is ten copecks. Put it down for me, doctor, will you?

DORN. Certainly, madam.

MASHA. Have you all put down your stakes? I begin . . . Twenty-two!

MISS ARKADINA. Got it.

MASHA. Three!

DORN. Right.

MASHA. Have you put three down? Eight! Eighty-one! Ten!

SHAMRAYEV. Don't be in such a hurry!

MISS ARKADINA. What a wonderful reception I had in Kharkov! My goodness, my head's still swimming!

MASHA. Thirty-four!

[*A melancholy waltz is played behind the scenes.*]

MISS ARKADINA. The students gave me an ovation. Three baskets of flowers, two bouquets, and look at that! [*Takes a brooch off her dress and throws it on the table.*]

SHAMRAYEV. Ah, now that is something!

MASHA. Fifty!

DORN. Did you say fifty?

MISS ARKADINA. I wore a lovely dress . . . Say what you like, but I do know how to dress.

PAULINE. Konstantín's playing again. Poor boy, he's unhappy.

SHAMRAYEV. They've been going for him in the papers, I see.

MASHA. Seventy-seven!

MISS ARKADINA. Why worry about it?

TRIGORIN. He's unlucky, poor fellow. Seems quite unable to find his own individual style. He writes such queer stuff, so vague. At times it almost reminds you of the ravings of a lunatic. Not one living character!

MASHA. Eleven!

MISS ARKADINA [*looking round at* SORIN]. Are you bored, Peter dear? [*A pause.*] He's asleep.

DORN. State Councillor Sorin is peacefully asleep.

MASHA. Seven! Ninety!

TRIGORIN. Do you think I'd ever have written anything, if I'd lived in a country house like this, by a lake? I'd have conquered this mania of mine and spent all my days fishing.

MASHA. Twenty-eight!

TRIGORIN. To catch a ruff or a perch, why, that's my idea of heaven!

DORN. Well, and I believe in Konstantín. There's something in him! Yes, there's something in him! He thinks in images, his stories are vivid, brilliant. They affect me strongly. A great pity, though, he doesn't seem to have any definite aim. He produces an impression, and that's all. But you can't go far by merely producing an impression. Are you glad your son's a writer, Miss Arkádina?

MISS ARKADINA. I'm ashamed to confess it, doctor, but I haven't read any of his things yet. I can never find the time.

MASHA. Twenty-six!

[KONSTANTIN *comes in quietly and goes to his desk.*]

SHAMRAYEV [*to* TRIGORIN]. I forgot to tell you, Mr. Trigórin. We've still got something here of yours.

TRIGORIN. Oh? What?

SHAMRAYEV. You remember the seagull Konstantín shot down some time ago? Well, you asked me to have it stuffed for you.

TRIGORIN. Did I? I don't remember. [*Thinking*] No, I don't remember.

MASHA. Sixty-six! One!

KONSTANTIN [*flings open the window and listens*]. How dark it is! I wonder why I'm feeling so restless!

MISS ARKADINA. Konstantín, dear, shut the window! There's an awful draught.

[KONSTANTIN *closes the window.*]

MASHA. Eighty-eight!

TRIGORIN. My game, ladies and gentlemen.

MISS ARKADINA [*gaily*]. Bravo! Bravo!

SHAMRAYEV. Bravo!

MISS ARKADINA. What marvellous luck that man has! He always wins. [*Gets up*] Now let's go and have something to eat. Our great man hasn't had any lunch today. We'll carry on with the game after dinner. [*To her son*] Leave your manuscripts, dear. Let's go in to dinner.

KONSTANTIN. I don't want to, mother. I'm not hungry.

MISS ARKADINA. As you wish, dear. [*Wakes* SORIN] Dinner, Peter, dear! [*Takes* SHAMRAYEV's *arm*] Let me tell you about the marvellous reception I had in Kharkov.

[PAULINE *puts out the candles on the table; then she and* DORN *wheel the chair. All go out by door on left;* KONSTANTIN *alone remains on the stage, sitting at his desk.*]

KONSTANTIN [*preparing to write; runs through what he has written already*]. I've talked so much about new forms, but I can't help feeling that little by little I'm lapsing into clichés myself. [*Reads*] "The poster on the wooden fence, announced . . . A pale face, framed by dark hair" . . . Announced, framed—it's so trite! [*Crosses it out*] I'd better begin where the hero is awakened by the patter of rain and cross out the rest. The description of the moonlight evening is too long and much too precious. Trigórin has his methods all nicely worked out. He finds it easy. The neck of a broken bottle gleaming on the mill-dam, the black shadow of the water-wheel— and there's your moonlight night all ready for you. But I have to bring in the tremulous light, the gently twinkling stars, and the distant strains of the piano dying away in the still, scented air . . . Oh, it's dreadful! [*A pause.*] New forms! No! I'm coming more and more to believe that it isn't old or new forms that matter; what matters is that one should write without thinking about forms at all;

what matters is that whatever one has to say should come straight from the heart! [*There's a knock at the window nearest to the desk.*] What's that? [*Looks out of the window*] Can't see a thing . . . [*Opens french window and looks out into the garden*] Someone ran down the steps. [*Calls*] Who's there? [*Goes out into the garden; he can be heard walking rapidly on the terrace; presently he comes back with* NINA.] Nina! Nina!

[NINA *lays her head on his chest and sobs softly.*]

KONSTANTIN [*moved*]. Nina! Oh, my darling, it's you—you. I had a feeling you'd come. All day I've been so awfully restless. [*Takes off her hat and cloak*] Oh, my darling, my precious darling, so you've come! Don't let's cry, don't!

NINA. There's someone here.

KONSTANTIN. There's no one, no one.

NINA. Lock the doors. Someone may come in.

KONSTANTIN. No one will come in.

NINA. I know your mother's here. Please, lock the doors . . .

KONSTANTIN [*locks the door on right, going to door on left*]. There's no lock on this door. I'll put a chair against it. [*Puts an arm-chair against the door*] Don't be afraid. No one will come in.

NINA [*scanning his face intently*]. Come, let me look at you. [*Looking round the room*] Warm, nice . . . This used to be a drawing-room before. Do you find me much changed?

KONSTANTIN. Oh, Nina, it's strange to be seeing you again. Why wouldn't you let me see you? Why haven't you come all this time? I know you've been living here almost a week . . . I've been to your hotel several times a day. I stood under your window like a beggar.

NINA. I was afraid you might hate me. Every night I dream that you look and look at me and don't recognise me. Oh, if only you knew! Ever since I returned I've been coming here . . . to walk by the lake. I've been near the house many times, but I couldn't bring myself to go in. Let's sit down. [*They sit down.*] Let's sit and talk and talk. Oh, it's so nice here, cosy, warm . . . Listen, how the wind howls! There's a passage in Turgenev—"Happy is he who on a night like this has a roof over his head, a warm corner—" I'm a seagull—no, that's not what I was going to say. [*Rubs her forehead*] I'm sorry— what was I saying? Oh, yes. Turgenev. "And may the Lord help all homeless wanderers." . . . Never mind. [*Sobs.*]

KONSTANTIN. Nina, darling, there you go again . . . Nina!

NINA. It's nothing. I feel much better now . . . I haven't cried for two years. Late last night I went to see if our stage was still in the park. Well, it turned out it was still there. Then I cried for the first time for two years, and I felt much better, my heart grew lighter. See? I'm not crying any more. [*Takes his hand*] And so you're a writer now . . . You—a writer, and I—an actress . . . It seems we're right in it now, the two of us . . . Oh, I used to be so happy! I'd wake up like a child, bright and early, as merry as a lark. I loved you. I dreamt of fame. And now? Early tomorrow morning I shall have to leave for Yeletz. Travel third class—with peasants. And in Yeletz the better class tradesmen will pester me with their attentions. Life is sordid.

KONSTANTIN. Why are you going to Yeletz?

NINA. I've an engagement there for the whole winter. I shall have to go soon.

KONSTANTIN. Oh, Nina, I cursed you, hated you, tore up your letters and photographs, but every minute I was conscious that I belonged to you, that my heart was yours for ever. I find it impossible, Nina, to stop loving you. Ever since I lost you and my stories began to appear in print, life has been unbearable to me. I suffered agonies, agonies . . . It was as though I were an old man of ninety. I prayed for you to come back, I kissed the ground you had walked on. Wherever I looked, I saw your dear face, your sweet smile, which brought so much sunshine into the best years of my life . . .

NINA [*bewildered*]. Why does he talk like this? Why does he talk like this?

KONSTANTIN. I am alone in the world, Nina. I have no one whose affection might warm me. I'm cold, cold, as though I lived in some underground dungeon, and everything I write is dry, harsh, gloomy. Please, stay Nina, I implore you! Or let me go away with you!

[NINA *quickly puts on her hat and cloak.*]

KONSTANTIN. Nina, why? For God's sake—[*Looks at her as she puts her things on; a pause.*]

NINA. My cab is waiting for me at the gate . . . Don't see me out, please. I'll find my way alone . . . [*Bursts into tears*] Could you give me some water, please?

KONSTANTIN [*gives* NINA *a glass of water*]. Where are you going now?

NINA. To the town. [*Pause.*] Is your mother here?

KONSTANTIN. Yes, she's here . . . Uncle was taken ill on Thursday, so we wired her to come.

NINA. Why did you say that you kissed the ground on which I'd walked? I deserve to be killed. [*Bends over the table*] Oh, I'm so tired! I want to rest—rest! [*Raises her head*] I'm a seagull. No, that's not it. I'm an actress. Yes! [*Hearing* MISS ARKADINA *and* TRIGORIN *laughing, she listens for a minute, then runs to the door on left and looks through the keyhole*] So he's here too . . . [*Returning to* KONSTANTIN] Oh, well—it doesn't matter. No, he didn't believe in the theatre. He was always laughing at my dreams, and little by little I stopped believing in them and lost heart . . . Besides, I had the worries of love to cope with, jealousy, constant anxiety for my little one . . . I grew trivial, cheap. And I acted badly . . . Didn't know what to do with my hands, how to stand on the stage, how to control my voice. Oh, you've no idea what it feels like to know that you're acting abominably! I'm a seagull—no, that's not it. Remember you shot a seagull? A man came along, saw it, and—just for the fun of it —destroyed it . . . An idea for a short story . . . No, I don't mean that . . . [*Rubs her forehead*] What was I saying? I was talking about the stage. Well, I'm different now . . . I'm a real actress now. I enjoy my acting. I revel in it. The stage intoxicates me. I feel that I am—peerless. But now, while I've been here, I've been walking about a lot and thinking—thinking—and feeling that the powers of my mind and soul are growing stronger every day . . . Now I know, now I understand, my dear, that in our calling, whether we act on the stage or write, what matters is not fame, nor glory, nor the things I used to dream of. No. What matters is knowing how to endure. Know how to bear your cross and have faith. I have faith, and it no longer hurts so much. And when I think of my calling, I'm no longer afraid of life.

KONSTANTIN [*sadly*]. You have found your path in life. You know which way you are going. But I am still whirled about in a maze of dreams and images, without knowing what it is all about or who wants it. I have no faith, and I do not know what my calling is.

NINA [*listening*]. Sh-sh— I'm going. Good-bye. When I'm a famous actress, come and see me in a play. Promise? And now . . . —[*Presses his hand*] It's late. I can hardly stand on my feet—I'm worn out—famished . . .

KONSTANTIN. Won't you stay and have some supper? Please, do . . .

NINA. No, thank you. I can't. I can't. Please, don't see me off. I'll find my way alone . . My cab isn't far from here . . . So she brought him with her? Oh well, it doesn't matter really. When you see Trigórin don't say anything to him . . . I love him. I love him more than ever. An idea for a short story. I love him. I love him passionately. I love him to distraction. Oh, how beautiful everything was before, my dear. Remember? What a bright, glorious, happy life! Our feelings for each other were like sweet, exquisite flowers . . . Remember? . . . [*Recites*] "Men, lions, eagles and peacocks, horned stags, geese, spiders, silent fish that inhabit the water, starfish, and creatures no eye can see—all living things, all living things, all living things, having completed their round of sorrow, are extinct. For thousands and thousands of years the earth has borne no living creature upon it, and this poor moon lights its lamp in vain. No longer do the cranes waken in the meadow with a cry, and in the lime groves the drone of May-beetles is heard no more" . . . [*Embraces* KONSTANTIN *impulsively and runs out through the french window.*]

KONSTANTIN [*after a pause*]. I hope no one sees her in the garden and tells mother about it. It's sure to upset mother.

[*During the next two minutes* KONSTANTIN *tears up all his manuscripts and throws them under the desk; then he unlocks the door on right and goes out.*]

DORN [*trying to open the door on left*]. Extraordinary! The door seems to be locked. [*Enters and puts arm-chair in its place*] An obstacle race!

[*Enter* MISS ARKADINA *and* PAULINE, *followed by* YAKOV *carrying a tray with bottles, and* MASHA; *then* SHAMRAYEV *and* TRIGORIN.]

MISS ARKADINA. Put the claret and the beer for Mr. Trigórin here on the table, please. We can have our drinks while we play. Come on, sit down everybody, please.

PAULINE [*to* YAKOV]. Bring the tea at once, Yakov.

[PAULINE *lights the candles. They all sit down to the card table.*]

SHAMRAYEV [*leading* TRIGORIN *to the bookcase*]. Here's the thing I mentioned to you before . . . [*Takes out the stuffed seagull*] Your order, sir.

TRIGORIN [*gazing at the seagull*]. Don't remember! [*After a moment's thought*] Don't remember!

[*A shot behind the scenes on the right; they all start.*]

MISS ARKADINA [*frightened*]. What was that?

DORN. It's nothing. I expect something must have gone off in my medicine-chest. Please, don't be alarmed. [*Goes out at door on right and returns in half a minute*] Just as I thought. A bottle of ether has gone off. [*Hums*] "Once more before thee I stand enchanted—"

MISS ARKADINA [*sitting down to the table*]. Heavens, what a fright it gave me! It reminded me how—[*Covers her face with her hands*] Oh dear, for a moment everything went black before my eyes . . .

DORN [*turning the pages of the magazine, to* TRIGORIN]. There was an article published here about two months ago—a letter from America—and I meant, incidentally, to ask you about it—[*puts his arm round* TRIGORIN's *waist and leads him to the footlights*]—as I'm rather interested in this question. [*Lowering his voice, in an undertone*] Get Miss Arkádina away from here somehow. You see, Konstantín has shot himself.

CURTAIN

BERNARD SHAW (1856-1950)

Through three generations Bernard Shaw was the Great Gadfly of the English-speaking world, stinging his contemporaries with witty exposure of their hypocritical morality and outmoded institutions as Socrates and Voltaire had done in ages past. Shaw the social philosopher, the rational minister to a dishonest and ailing society, often seemed to exploit the drama for his special purposes of lecture and reform, and yet his ample genius found room for a superb art of characterization, plot development, and even poetic expression that converted the comedy of ideas into exciting theater. Today he is the most popular dramatist on the American stage, and revivals of his plays outnumber those of Shakespeare, whose romantic playmaking he often savagely disparaged.

Shaw was an Irishman who, like Oscar Wilde and George Moore, found the little world of Irish nationalism too provincial for his tastes and talents. The son of an impecunious and dissipated agricultural agent in Dublin, he developed in his youth an intensely puritanical outlook in reaction against his father's irresponsibility, embracing temperance and vegetarianism in his own life, to say nothing of the antivivisection and antivaccination views revealed in *The Doctor's Dilemma*. But his mother, an accomplished musician, guided young Shaw's education in the arts and encouraged his avid reading. He finished his formal education at fifteen, whereupon he was apprenticed to a Dublin land agent at less than a pound (then about five dollars) a month. After five years of service with the prospect of only a modest income, he departed for London, where his mother was teaching music after having left her husband.

Shaw's discouraging experience with business in Dublin and his nine years of struggle for recognition in London crystallized his criticism of the British economic system, which was strongly influenced by his reading of Henry George and Karl Marx. In 1884 he joined the Fabian Society, a socialist organization dedicated to reform through democratic action, and began to give speeches and write political tracts for the cause. He never relinquished his socialist views and irritated his well-wishers in later years by his continued support of the Soviet Union; but his active participation in political affairs ended around the turn of the century.

Meanwhile, his literary apprenticeship proceeded apace. He wrote five unsuccessful novels in the early eighties and began a career in journalism as critic of books and plays, art and music, that extended through the nineties. It was the era of Ibsen's first influence on the English stage, and Shaw proclaimed in *The Quintessence of Ibsenism* (1891) his enthusiastic support of the new realistic drama of social criticism. He had already begun a play, and when it was finally produced in 1892 as *Widowers' Houses,* it proved to be a vigorous attack on the cynical landlord system that encouraged slums, a polemical drama that carried Ibsen a good step further in social protest. In its forthright exposure of a specific evil of modern society, it made Pinero's stiff-necked dramas of demi-mondaines seem timid and inconsequential. It was staged in J. T. Grein's little Independent Theatre in London, which thus had the honor of launching the greatest British dramatist of modern times upon his long career.

Although no major play of Shaw's is without its thought content, a clear pattern of development away from particular social criticism to more general issues appears in them. He began with such daring dramas as *Mrs. Warren's Profession* (privately produced in 1902), a frank discussion of prostitution, which shocked Victorian decorum, won the censor's ban, and convinced the English public that Shaw was a dangerous radical bent on destroying vested interests and discussing the unmentionable on the stage.

But he soon followed these "unpleasant" plays with comparatively pleasant ones, which examined more general issues in wryly humorous terms. His pacifism took in *Arms*

and the Man (1894) the form of a playful satire of war and
warriors, so innocuous that it inspired the libretto of the
operetta, *The Chocolate Soldier*. In *Candida* (1894) he
began that scrutiny of love and marriage which would be
continued in *Man and Superman* (1903), *Getting Married*
(1908), and other plays. Yet Shaw did not actually repeat
himself. His famous prefaces, often competing in length
with the plays themselves, reveal in pungent essay form
the ideas that inspired his dramas. However gay and witty
the dialogue may be, however humorous the treatment of
character in the works of this second group, we leave the
theater with the conviction that an important idea has been
discussed and an important opinion expressed about it. Shaw
has himself said: "My method is to take the utmost trouble
to find the right thing to say, and then to say it with the
utmost levity."

From time to time throughout his career Shaw wrote
also plays of history, but they do not differ in purpose or
method from his plays of contemporary life. As if to
attack the Shakespearian tradition, which had demanded a
romantic treatment for historical subject matter, he shows
us figures out of the past as recognizable human beings, not
deflated or debunked but freed from the coating of heroism
or villainy which history and historical dramatists may
have given them. The phenomenal success of Shaw's *Caesar and Cleopatra* and Shakespeare's *Antony and Cleopatra*
in parallel revivals in 1951 was due in part to the fascinating
experience of studying two approaches to historical drama,
realistic and romantic, on successive evenings. Contrary to
what some might imagine, Shaw's humanizing of Caesar
enhanced rather than destroyed our respect for the great
Roman.

In *The Devil's Disciple* (1900) a patriot of the American revolution is frustrated in an attempt at heroic self-
sacrifice by the worldly common sense of the British com-
mander, General Johnny Burgoyne. In *Androcles and the
Lion* (1912) we find a group of early Christian martyrs to
have been extremely human people. Shaw ended the brilliant
middle period of his career with his masterpiece, but hardly
his most typical play, *Saint Joan* (1923). To his rational and
intimate picture of historical character he added here the

spiritual transfiguration only dimly predicted in his earlier work.

As if exhausted by the effort of writing his finest work, Shaw waited six years before publishing another play, and when it appeared—*The Apple Cart* (1929)—it began to be clear that the septuagenarian had passed his prime. Although he wrote industriously for twenty years more, his capacity for talk gradually submerged his dramatic instincts, and his later plays had a diminishing success on the stage. They were of no one kind, but one remembers especially the eccentric conversation pieces, such as *Too True to Be Good* (1932), *On the Rocks* (1933), and *Geneva* (1938), in which he sacrificed plot and character to a witty and penetrating discussion of various issues in modern life. The very danger that he had avoided so successfully through his great period overtook him at last. Those who had argued that his plays were mere debates and his characters mere mouthpieces for ideas now had reason on their side.

But the repeated revivals of his best plays disprove any such estimate of his work as a whole. If there are already classics in modern drama, a good share of them lie in Shaw's amazing output. He created a new dramatic type in the comedy of ideas. His was essentially a comic genius, as successful criticism of life almost inevitably takes a satiric form. Without the humorous or witty slant an attack on society degenerates into misanthropy and despair. Shaw was no misanthrope; indeed, he remained an optimist about man's future to the end. His materialism did not dehumanize man but showed him the way to self-betterment. He is therefore as cheerful to read as he is stimulating.

THE DOCTOR'S DILEMMA

act 1

On the 15th June 1903, in the early forenoon, a medical student, surname REDPENNY, *Christian name unknown and of no importance, sits at work in a doctor's consulting-room. He devils for the doctor by answering his letters, acting as his domestic laboratory assistant, and making himself indispensable generally, in return for unspecified advantages involved by intimate intercourse with a leader of his profession, and amounting to an informal apprenticeship and a temporary affiliation.* REDPENNY *is not proud, and will do anything he is asked without reservation of his personal dignity if he is asked in a fellow-creaturely way. He is a wide-open-eyed, ready, credulous, friendly, hasty youth, with his hair and clothes in reluctant transition from the untidy boy to the tidy doctor.*

REDPENNY *is interrupted by the entrance of an old serving-woman who has never known the cares, the preoccupations, the responsibilities, jealousies, and anxieties of personal beauty. She has the complexion of a never-washed gypsy, incurable by any detergent; and she has, not a regular beard and moustaches, which could at least be trimmed and waxed into a masculine presentableness, but a whole crop of small beards and moustaches, mostly springing from moles all over her face. She carries a duster and toddles about meddlesomely, spying out dust so diligently that whilst she is flicking off one speck she is already looking elsewhere for another. In conversation she has the same trick, hardly ever looking at the person she is addressing except when she is excited. She has only one manner, and that is the manner of an old family nurse to a child just after it has learnt to walk. She has used her ugliness to secure indulgences unattainable by Cleopatra or Fair Rosamund, and has the further great advantage over them that age in-*

creases her qualification instead of impairing it. Being an industrious, agreeable, and popular old soul, she is a walking sermon on the vanity of feminine prettiness. Just as RED-PENNY *has no discovered Christian name, she has no discovered surname, and is known throughout the doctors' quarter between Cavendish Square and the Marylebone Road[1] simply as* EMMY.

The consulting-room has two windows looking on Queen Anne Street. Between the two is a marble-topped console, with haunched gilt legs ending in sphinx claws. The huge pier-glass[2] which surmounts it is mostly disabled from reflection by elaborate painting on its surface of palms, ferns, lilies, tulips, and sunflowers. The adjoining wall contains the fireplace, with two arm-chairs before it. As we happen to face the corner we see nothing of the other two walls. On the right of the fireplace, or rather on the right of any person facing the fireplace, is the door. On its left is the writing-table at which REDPENNY *sits. It is an untidy table with a microscope, several test tubes, and a spirit lamp standing up through its litter of papers. There is a couch in the middle of the room, at right angles to the console, and parallel to the fireplace. A chair stands between the couch and the window. Another in the corner. Another at the other end of the windowed wall. The windows have green Venetian blinds and rep curtains;[3] and there is a gasalier;[4] but it is a convert to electric lighting. The wall paper and carpets are mostly green, coeval with the gasalier and the Venetian blinds. The house, in fact, was so well furnished in the middle of the XIXth century that it stands unaltered to this day and is still quite presentable.*

EMMY [*entering and immediately beginning to dust the couch*]. Theres a lady bothering me to see the doctor.

REDPENNY [*distracted by the interruption*]. Well, she cant see the doctor. Look here: whats the use of telling you that the doctor

---

[1] *Cavendish Square . . . Marylebone Road,* the boundaries of the area inhabited by fashionable medical specialists.

[2] *pier-glass,* a long, narrow mirror designed to fit between two windows.

[3] *rep curtains,* curtains of a fabric with transverse line markings on the face.

[4] *gasalier,* a frame hung from the ceiling, holding a number of gas burners.

cant take any new patients, when the moment a knock comes to the door, in you bounce to ask whether he can see somebody?

EMMY. Who asked you whether he could see somebody?

REDPENNY. You did.

EMMY. I said theres a lady bothering me to see the doctor. That isnt asking. Its telling.

REDPENNY. Well, is the lady bothering you any reason for you to come bothering me when I'm busy?

EMMY. Have you seen the papers?

REDPENNY. No.

EMMY. Not seen the birthday honors?[1]

REDPENNY [*beginning to swear*]. What the—

EMMY. Now, now, ducky!

REDPENNY. What do you suppose I care about the birthday honors? Get out of this with your chattering. Dr Ridgeon will be down before I have these letters ready. Get out.

EMMY. Dr Ridgeon wont never be down any more, young man. [*She detects dust on the console and is down on it immediately.*]

REDPENNY [*jumping up and following her*]. What?

EMMY. He's been made a knight. Mind you dont go Dr Ridgeon-ing him in them letters. Sir Colenso Ridgeon is to be his name now.

REDPENNY. I'm jolly glad.

EMMY. I never was so taken aback. I always thought his great discoveries was fudge (let alone the mess of them) with his drops of blood and tubes full of Maltese fever and the like. Now he'll have a rare laugh at me.

REDPENNY. Serve you right! It was like your cheek to talk to him about science. [*He returns to his table and resumes his writing.*]

EMMY. Oh, I dont think much of science; and neither will you when youve lived as long with it as I have. Whats on my mind is answering the door. Old Sir Patrick Cullen has been here already and left first congratulations—hadnt time to come up on his way to the hospital, but was determined to be first—coming back, he said. All the rest will be here too: the knocker will be going all day. What I'm afraid of is that the doctor'll want a footman like all the rest, now that he's Sir Colenso. Mind: dont you go putting him up to it, ducky; for he'll never have any comfort with anybody but me to answer the door. I know who to let in and who to keep out. And that reminds me of the poor lady. I think he ought to see her. She's

---

[1] *birthday honors, the annual list conferring honors, such as knighthood, on distinguished subjects of the English king, issued on his birthday.*

just the kind that puts him in a good temper. [*She dusts* RED-PENNY'S *papers.*]

REDPENNY. I tell you he cant see anybody. Do go away, Emmy. How can I work with you dusting all over me like this?

EMMY. I'm not hindering you working—if you call writing letters working. There goes the bell. [*She looks out of the window.*] A doctor's carriage. Thats more congratulations. [*She is going out when* SIR COLENSO RIDGEON *enters.*] Have you finished your two eggs, sonny?

RIDGEON. Yes.

EMMY. Have you put on your clean vest?

RIDGEON. Yes.

EMMY. Thats my ducky diamond! Now keep yourself tidy and dont go messing about and dirtying your hands: the people are coming to congratulate you. [*She goes out.*]

[SIR COLENSO RIDGEON *is a man of fifty who has never shaken off his youth. He has the off-handed manner and the little audacities of address which a shy and sensitive man acquires in breaking himself in to intercourse with all sorts and conditions of men. His face is a good deal lined; his movements are slower than, for instance,* REDPENNY'S; *and his flaxen hair has lost its lustre; but in figure and manner he is more the young man than the titled physician. Even the lines in his face are those of overwork and restless scepticism, perhaps partly of curiosity and appetite, rather than of age. Just at present the announcement of his knighthood in the morning papers makes him specially self-conscious, and consequently specially off-hand with* REDPENNY.]

RIDGEON. Have you seen the papers? Youll have to alter the name in the letters if you havnt.

REDPENNY. Emmy has just told me. I'm awfully glad. I—

RIDGEON. Enough, young man, enough. You will soon get accustomed to it.

REDPENNY. They ought to have done it years ago.

RIDGEON. They would have; only they couldnt stand Emmy opening the door, I daresay.

EMMY [*at the door, announcing*]. Dr Shoemaker. [*She withdraws.*]

[*A middle-aged gentleman, well dressed, comes in with a friendly but propitiatory air, not quite sure of his reception. His combination of soft manners and responsive kindliness,*

*with a certain unseizable reserve and a familiar yet foreign
chiselling of feature, reveal the Jew: in this instance the
handsome gentlemanly Jew, gone a little pigeon-breasted and
stale after thirty, as handsome young Jews often do, but still
decidedly good-looking.*]

THE GENTLEMAN. Do you remember me? Schutzmacher. University College school and Belsize Avenue. Loony Schutzmacher, you know.

RIDGEON. What! Loony! [*He shakes hands cordially.*] Why, man, I thought you were dead long ago. Sit down. [SCHUTZMACHER *sits on the couch:* RIDGEON *on the chair between it and the window.*] Where have you been these thirty years?

SCHUTZMACHER. In general practice, until a few months ago. Ive retired.

RIDGEON. Well done, Loony! I wish *I* could afford to retire. Was your practice in London?

SCHUTZMACHER. No.

RIDGEON. Fashionable coast practice, I suppose.

SCHUTZMACHER. How could I afford to buy a fashionable practice?[1] I hadnt a rap.[2] I set up in a manufacturing town in the midlands in a little surgery at ten shillings a week.

RIDGEON. And made your fortune?

SCHUTZMACHER. Well, I'm pretty comfortable. I have a place in Hertfordshire besides our flat in town. If you ever want a quiet Saturday to Monday, I'll take you down in my motor at an hour's notice.

RIDGEON. Just rolling in money! I wish you rich g.p.'s[3] would teach me how to make some. Whats the secret of it?

SCHUTZMACHER. Oh, in my case the secret was simple enough, though I suppose I should have got into trouble if it had attracted any notice. And I'm afraid youll think it rather infra dig.[4]

RIDGEON. Oh, I have an open mind. What was the secret?

---

[1] *to buy a fashionable practice. In England it was the custom for a medical
graduate who could afford it to buy out the practice of a retiring physician, since
the inhabitants of the district controlled by that physician were required to
patronize him and his successors for their routine medical problems. The price of
the practice would depend on the wealth of the inhabitants of the district, so that
a high initial investment would guarantee a proportionately high income.*
[2] *rap, an Irish counterfeit halfpenny. Cf. I don't care a rap.*
[3] *g.p.'s, general practitioners.*
[4] *infra dig, infra dignitatem, beneath one's dignity.*

SCHUTZMACHER. Well, the secret was just two words.

RIDGEON. Not Consultation Free, was it?

SCHUTZMACHER [*shocked*]. No, no. Really!

RIDGEON [*apologetic*]. Of course not. I was only joking.

SCHUTZMACHER. My two words were simply Cure Guaranteed.

RIDGEON [*admiring*]. Cure Guaranteed!

SCHUTZMACHER. Guaranteed. After all, thats what everybody wants from a doctor, isnt it?

RIDGEON. My dear Loony, it was an inspiration. Was it on the brass plate?

SCHUTZMACHER. There was no brass plate. It was a shop window: red, you know, with black lettering. Doctor Leo Schutzmacher, L.R.C.P. M.R.C.S.[1] Advice and medicine sixpence. Cure Guaranteed.

RIDGEON. And the guarantee proved sound nine times out of ten, eh?

SCHUTZMACHER [*rather hurt at so moderate an estimate*]. Oh, much oftener than that. You see, most people get well all right if they are careful and you give them a little sensible advice. And the medicine really did them good. Parrish's Chemical Food: phosphates, you know. One tablespoonful to a twelve-ounce bottle of water: nothing better, no matter what the case is.

RIDGEON. Redpenny: make a note of Parrish's Chemical Food.

SCHUTZMACHER. I take it myself, you know, when I feel run down. Good-bye. You dont mind my calling, do you? Just to congratulate you.

RIDGEON. Delighted, my dear Loony. Come to lunch on Saturday next week. Bring your motor and take me down to Hertford.

SCHUTZMACHER. I will. We shall be delighted. Thank you. Good-bye. [*He goes out with* RIDGEON, *who returns immediately.*]

REDPENNY. Old Paddy Cullen was here before you were up, to be the first to congratulate you.

RIDGEON. Indeed. Who taught you to speak of Sir Patrick Cullen as old Paddy Cullen, you young ruffian?

REDPENNY. You never call him anything else.

RIDGEON. Not now that I am Sir Colenso. Next thing, you fellows will be calling me old Colly Ridgeon.

REDPENNY. We do, at St Anne's.

[1] *L.R.C.P. M.R.C.S., Licentiate of the Royal College of Physicians, Member of the Royal College of Surgeons.*

RIDGEON. Yach! Thats what makes the medical student the most disgusting figure in modern civilization. No veneration, no manners —no—

EMMY [*at the door, announcing*]. Sir Patrick Cullen. [*She retires.*]

[SIR PATRICK CULLEN[1] *is more than twenty years older than* RIDGEON, *not yet quite at the end of his tether, but near it and resigned to it. His name, his plain, downright, sometimes rather arid common sense, his large build and stature, the absence of those odd moments of ceremonial servility by which an old English doctor sometimes shews you what the status of the profession was in England in his youth, and an occasional turn of speech, are Irish; but he has lived all his life in England and is thoroughly acclimatized. His manner to* RIDGEON, *whom he likes, is whimsical and fatherly: to others he is a little gruff and uninviting, apt to substitute more or less expressive grunts for articulate speech, and generally indisposed, at his age, to make much social effort. He shakes* RIDGEON's *hand and beams at him cordially and jocularly.*]

SIR PATRICK. Well, young chap. Is your hat too small for you, eh?

RIDGEON. Much too small. I owe it all to you.

SIR PATRICK. Blarney, my boy. Thank you all the same. [*He sits in one of the arm-chairs near the fireplace.* RIDGEON *sits on the couch.*] Ive come to talk to you a bit. [*To* REDPENNY] Young man: get out.

REDPENNY. Certainly, Sir Patrick [*He collects his papers and makes for the door.*]

SIR PATRICK. Thank you. Thats a good lad. [REDPENNY *vanishes.*] They all put up with me, these young chaps, because I'm an old man, a real old man, not like you. Youre only beginning to give yourself the airs of age. Did you ever see a boy cultivating a moustache? Well, a middle-aged doctor cultivating a grey head is much the same sort of spectacle.

RIDGEON. Good Lord! yes: I suppose so. And I thought that the days of my vanity were past. Tell me: at what age does a man leave off being a fool?

SIR PATRICK. Remember the Frenchman who asked his grandmother at what age we get free from the temptations of love. The old woman said she didn't know. [RIDGEON *laughs.*] Well, I make

[1] *Sir Patrick Cullen. Much of the description suggests Shaw himself, as many of Sir Patrick's utterances will.*

you the same answer. But the world's growing very interesting to me now, Colly.

RIDGEON. You keep up your interest in science, do you?

SIR PATRICK. Lord! yes. Modern science is a wonderful thing. Look at your great discovery! Look at all the great discoveries! Where are they leading to? Why, right back to my poor dear old father's ideas and discoveries. He's been dead now over forty years. Oh, it's very interesting.

RIDGEON. Well, theres nothing like progress, is there?

SIR PATRICK. Dont misunderstand me, my boy. I'm not belittling your discovery. Most discoveries are made regularly every fifteen years; and it's fully a hundred and fifty since yours was made last. Thats something to be proud of. But your discovery's not new. It's only inoculation. My father practised inoculation until it was made criminal in eighteen-forty. That broke the poor old man's heart, Colly: he died of it. And now it turns out that my father was right after all. Youve brought us back to inoculation.

RIDGEON. I know nothing about smallpox. My line is tuberculosis and typhoid and plague. But of course the principle of all vaccines is the same.

SIR PATRICK. Tuberculosis? M-m-m-m! Youve found out how to cure consumption, eh?

RIDGEON. I believe so.

SIR PATRICK. Ah yes. It's very interesting. What is it the old cardinal says in Browning's play? "I have known four and twenty leaders of revolt."[1] Well, Ive known over thirty men that found out how to cure consumption. Why do people go on dying of it, Colly? Devilment, I suppose. There was my father's old friend George Boddington of Sutton Coldfield. He discovered the open-air cure in eighteen-forty. He was ruined and driven out of his practice for only opening the windows; and now we wont let a consumptive patient have as much as a roof over his head. Oh, it's very very interesting to an old man.

RIDGEON. You old cynic, you dont believe a bit in my discovery.

SIR PATRICK. No, no: I dont go quite so far as that, Colly. But still, you remember Jane Marsh?

RIDGEON. Jane Marsh? No.

SIR PATRICK. You dont!

RIDGEON. No.

[1] "I have . . . revolt!" "I have known three-and-twenty leaders of revolts!" Robert Browning, *A Soul's Tragedy*, *Act II*.

SIR PATRICK. You mean to tell me you dont remember the woman with the tuberculous ulcer on her arm?

RIDGEON [*enlightened*]. Oh, your washerwoman's daughter. Was her name Jane Marsh? I forgot.

SIR PATRICK. Perhaps youve forgotten also that you undertook to cure her with Koch's[1] tuberculin.

RIDGEON. And instead of curing her, it rotted her arm right off. Yes: I remember. Poor Jane! However, she makes a good living out of that arm now by shewing it at medical lectures.

SIR PATRICK. Still, that wasnt quite what you intended, was it?

RIDGEON. I took my chance of it.

SIR PATRICK. Jane did, you mean.

RIDGEON. Well, it's always the patient who has to take the chance when an experiment is necessary. And we can find out nothing without experiment.

SIR PATRICK. What did you find out from Jane's case?

RIDGEON. I found out that the inoculation that ought to cure sometimes kills.

SIR PATRICK. I could have told you that. Ive tried these modern inoculations a bit myself. Ive killed people with them; and Ive cured people with them; but I gave them up because I never could tell which I was going to do.

RIDGEON [*taking a pamphlet from a drawer in the writing-table and handing it to him*]. Read that the next time you have an hour to spare; and youll find out why.

SIR PATRICK [*grumbling and fumbling for his spectacles*]. Oh, bother your pamphlets. Whats the practice of it? [*Looking at the pamphlet*] Opsonin? What the devil is opsonin?

RIDGEON. Opsonin is what you butter the disease germs with to make your white blood corpuscles eat them. [*He sits down again on the couch.*]

SIR PATRICK. Thats not new. Ive heard this notion that the white corpuscles—what is it that whats his name?—Metchnikoff[2]—calls them?

RIDGEON. Phagocytes.

SIR PATRICK. Aye, phagocytes: yes, yes, yes. Well, I heard this

<hr/>

[1] *Koch,* Robert Koch (*1843–1910*), *the German bacteriologist who identified the bacillus of tuberculosis, but whose tuberculin proved unsuccessful in treating the disease.*

[2] *Metchnikoff,* Ilya Metchnikoff (*1845–1916*), *the Russian biologist who discovered the rôle of the phagocytes in combating germ diseases.*

theory that the phagocytes eat up the disease germs years ago: long before you came into fashion. Besides, they dont always eat them.

RIDGEON. They do when you butter them with opsonin.

SIR PATRICK. Gammon.

RIDGEON. No: it's not gammon. What it comes to in practice is this. The phagocytes wont eat the microbes unless the microbes are nicely buttered for them. Well, the patient manufactures the butter for himself all right; but my discovery is that the manufacture of that butter, which I call opsonin, goes on in the system by ups and downs—Nature being always rhythmical, you know—and that what the inoculation does is to stimulate the ups or downs, as the case may be. If we had inoculated Jane Marsh when her butter factory was on the up-grade, we should have cured her arm. But we got in on the down-grade and lost her arm for her. I call the up-grade the positive phase and the down-grade the negative phase. Everything depends on your inoculating at the right moment. Inoculate when the patient is in the negative phase and you kill: inoculate when the patient is in the positive phase and you cure.

SIR PATRICK. And pray how are you to know whether the patient is in the positive or the negative phase?

RIDGEON. Send a drop of the patient's blood to the laboratory at St. Anne's;[1] and in fifteen minutes I'll give you his opsonin index in figures. If the figure is one, inoculate and cure: if it's under point eight, inoculate and kill. Thats my discovery: the most important that has been made since Harvey discovered the circulation of the blood. My tuberculosis patients dont die now.

SIR PATRICK. And mine do when my inoculation catches them in the negative phase, as you call it. Eh?

RIDGEON. Precisely. To inject a vaccine into a patient without first testing his opsonin is as near murder as a respectable practitioner can get. If I wanted to kill a man I should kill him that way.

EMMY [*looking in*]. Will you see a lady that wants her husband's lungs cured?

RIDGEON [*impatiently*]. No. Havnt I told you I will see nobody? [*To* SIR PATRICK] I live in a state of siege ever since it got about that I'm a magician who can cure consumption with a drop of serum. [*To* EMMY] Dont come to me again about people who have no appointments. I tell you I can see nobody.

EMMY. Well, I'll tell her to wait a bit.

[1] *St. Anne's, a hospital.*

RIDGEON [*furious*]. Youll tell her I cant see her, and send her away: do you hear?

EMMY [*unmoved*]. Well, will you see Mr Cutler Walpole? He dont want a cure: he only wants to congratulate you.

RIDGEON. Of course. Shew him up. [*She turns to go.*] Stop. [*To* SIR PATRICK] I want two minutes more with you between ourselves. [*To* EMMY] Emmy: ask Mr Walpole to wait just two minutes, while I finish a consultation.

EMMY. Oh, he'll wait all right. He's talking to the poor lady. [*She goes out.*]

SIR PATRICK. Well? what is it?

RIDGEON. Dont laugh at me. I want your advice.

SIR PATRICK. Professional advice?

RIDGEON. Yes. Theres something the matter with me. I dont know what it is.

SIR PATRICK. Neither do I. I suppose youve been sounded.[1]

RIDGEON. Yes, of course. Theres nothing wrong with any of the organs: nothing special, anyhow. But I have a curious aching: I dont know where: I cant localize it. Sometimes I think it's my heart: sometimes I suspect my spine. It doesnt exactly hurt me; but it unsettles me completely. I feel that something is going to happen. And there are other symptoms. Scraps of tunes come into my head that seem to me very pretty, though theyre quite commonplace.

SIR PATRICK. Do you hear voices?

RIDGEON. No.

SIR PATRICK. I'm glad of that. When my patients tell me that theyve made a greater discovery than Harvey, and that they hear voices, I lock them up.

RIDGEON. You think I'm mad! Thats just the suspicion that has come across me once or twice. Tell me the truth: I can bear it.

SIR PATRICK. Youre sure there are no voices?

RIDGEON. Quite sure.

SIR PATRICK. Then it's only foolishness.

RIDGEON. Have you ever met anything like it before in your practice?

SIR PATRICK. Oh, yes: often. It's very common between the ages of seventeen and twenty-two. It sometimes comes on again at forty or thereabouts. Youre a bachelor, you see. It's not serious—if youre careful.

---

[1] *sounded, to examine the lungs of a patient by having him emit sounds.*

RIDGEON. About my food?

SIR PATRICK. No: about your behavior. Theres nothing wrong with your spine; and theres nothing wrong with your heart; but theres something wrong with your common sense. Youre not going to die; but you may be going to make a fool of yourself. So be careful.

RIDGEON. I see you dont believe in my discovery. Well, sometimes I dont believe in it myself. Thank you all the same. Shall we have Walpole up?

SIR PATRICK. Oh, have him up. [RIDGEON *rings*.] He's a clever operator, is Walpole, though he's only one of your chloroform surgeons. In my early days, you made your man drunk; and the porters and students held him down; and you had to set your teeth and finish the job fast. Nowadays you work at your ease; and the pain doesnt come until afterwards, when youve taken your cheque and rolled up your bag and left the house. I tell you, Colly, chloroform has done a lot of mischief. It's enabled every fool to be a surgeon.

RIDGEON [*to* EMMY, *who answers the bell*]. Shew Mr Walpole up.

EMMY. He's talking to the lady.

RIDGEON [*exasperated*]. Did I not tell you—

[EMMY *goes out without heeding him. He gives it up, with a shrug, and plants himself with his back to the console, leaning resignedly against it.*]

SIR PATRICK. I know your Cutler Walpoles and their like. Theyve found out that a man's body's full of bits and scraps of old organs he has no mortal use for. Thanks to chloroform, you can cut half a dozen of them out without leaving him any the worse, except for the illness and the guineas it costs him. I knew the Walpoles well fifteen years ago. The father used to snip off the ends of people's uvulas for fifty guineas, and paint throats with caustic every day for a year at two guineas a time. His brother-in-law extirpated tonsils for two hundred guineas until he took up women's cases at double the fees. Cutler himself worked hard at anatomy to find something fresh to operate on; and at last he got hold of something he calls the nuciform sac, which he's made quite the fashion. People pay him five hundred guineas to cut it out. They might as well get their hair cut for all the difference it makes; but I suppose they feel important after it. You cant go out to dinner now without your neighbor bragging to you of some useless operation or other.

EMMY [*announcing*]. Mr Cutler Walpole. [*She goes out.*]

[CUTLER WALPOLE[1] *is an energetic, unhesitating man of forty, with a cleanly modelled face, very decisive and symmetrical about the shortish, salient, rather pretty nose, and the three trimly turned corners made by his chin and jaws. In comparison with* RIDGEON's *delicate broken lines, and* SIR PATRICK's *softly rugged aged ones, his face looks machine-made and beeswaxed; but his scrutinizing, daring eyes give it life and force. He seems never at a loss, never in doubt: one feels that if he made a mistake he would make it thoroughly and firmly. He has neat, well-nourished hands, short arms, and is built for strength and compactness rather than for height. He is smartly dressed with a fancy waistcoat, a richly colored scarf secured by a handsome ring, ornaments on his watch chain, spats on his shoes, and a general air of the well-to-do sportsman about him. He goes straight across to* RIDGEON *and shakes hands with him.*]

WALPOLE. My dear Ridgeon, best wishes! heartiest congratulations! You deserve it.

RIDGEON. Thank you.

WALPOLE. As a man, mind you. You deserve it as a man. The opsonin is simple rot, as any capable surgeon can tell you; but we're all delighted to see your personal qualities officially recognized. Sir Patrick: how are you? I sent you a paper lately about a little thing I invented: a new saw. For shoulder blades.

SIR PATRICK [*meditatively*]. Yes: I got it. It's a good saw: a useful, handy instrument.

WALPOLE [*confidently*]. I knew youd see its points.

SIR PATRICK. Yes: I remember that saw sixty-five years ago.

WALPOLE. What!

SIR PATRICK. It was called a cabinetmaker's jimmy then.

WALPOLE. Get out! Nonsense! Cabinetmaker be—

RIDGEON. Never mind him, Walpole. He's jealous.

WALPOLE. By the way, I hope I'm not disturbing you two in anything private.

RIDGEON. No no. Sit down. I was only consulting him. I'm rather out of sorts. Overwork, I suppose.

WALPOLE [*swiftly*]. I know whats the matter with you. I can see it in your complexion. I can feel it in the grip of your hand.

[1] *Cutler Walpole. Most of the characters' names carry amusing suggestions of what they stand for.*

RIDGEON. What is it?

WALPOLE. Blood-poisoning.

RIDGEON. Blood-poisoning! Impossible.

WALPOLE. I tell you, blood-poisoning. Ninety-five per cent of the human race suffer from chronic blood-poisoning, and die of it. It's as simple as A.B.C. Your nuciform sac is full of decaying matter—undigested food and waste products—rank ptomaines. Now you take my advice, Ridgeon. Let me cut it out for you. Youll be another man afterwards.

SIR PATRICK. Dont you like him as he is?

WALPOLE. No I dont. I dont like any man who hasnt a healthy circulation. I tell you this: in an intelligently governed country people wouldnt be allowed to go about with nuciform sacs, making themselves centres of infection. The operation ought to be compulsory: it's ten times more important than vaccination.

SIR PATRICK. Have you had your own sac removed, may I ask?

WALPOLE [*triumphantly*]. I havnt got one. Look at me! Ive no symptoms. I'm as sound as a bell. About five per cent of the population havnt got any; and I'm one of the five per cent. I'll give you an instance. You know Mrs Jack Foljambe: the smart Mrs Foljambe? I operated at Easter on her sister-in-law, Lady Gorran, and found she had the biggest sac I ever saw: it held about two ounces. Well, Mrs Foljambe had the right spirit—the genuine hygienic instinct. She couldnt stand her sister-in-law being a clean, sound woman, and she simply a whited sepulchre. So she insisted on my operating on her, too. And by George, sir, she hadnt any sac at all. Not a trace! Not a rudiment!! I was so taken aback—so interested, that I forgot to take the sponges out, and was stitching them up inside her when the nurse missed them. Somehow, I'd made sure she'd have an exceptionally large one. [*He sits down on the couch, squaring his shoulders and shooting his hands out of his cuffs as he sets his knuckles akimbo.*]

EMMY [*looking in*]. Sir Ralph Bloomfield Bonington.

[*A long and expectant pause follows this announcement. All look to the door; but there is no* SIR RALPH.]

RIDGEON [*at last*]. Where is he?

EMMY [*looking back*]. Drat him, I thought he was following me. He's stayed down to talk to that lady.

RIDGEON [*exploding*]. I told you to tell that lady—[EMMY *vanishes.*]

WALPOLE [*jumping up again*]. Oh, by the way, Ridgeon, that reminds me. Ive been talking to that poor girl. It's her husband; and she thinks it's a case of consumption: the usual wrong diagnosis: these damned general practitioners ought never to be allowed to touch a patient except under the orders of a consultant. She's been describing his symptoms to me; and the case is as plain as a pikestaff: bad blood-poisoning. Now she's poor. She cant afford to have him operated on. Well, you send him to me: I'll do it for nothing. Theres room for him in my nursing home. I'll put him straight, and feed him up and make her happy. I like making people happy. [*He goes to the chair near the window.*]

EMMY [*looking in*]. Here he is.

[SIR RALPH BLOOMFIELD BONINGTON *wafts himself into the room. He is a tall man, with a head like a tall and slender egg. He has been in his time a slender man; but now, in his sixth decade, his waistcoat has filled out somewhat. His fair eyebrows arch good-naturedly and uncritically. He has a most musical voice; his speech is a perpetual anthem; and he never tires of the sound of it. He radiates an enormous self-satisfaction, cheering, reassuring, healing by the mere incompatibility of disease or anxiety with his welcome presence. Even broken bones, it is said, have been known to unite at the sound of his voice: he is a born healer, as independent of mere treatment and skill as any Christian scientist. When he expands into oratory or scientific exposition, he is as energetic as* WALPOLE; *but it is with a bland, voluminous, atmospheric energy, which envelops its subject and its audience, and makes interruption or inattention impossible, and imposes veneration and credulity on all but the strongest minds. He is known in the medical world as B. B.; and the envy roused by his success in practice is softened by the conviction that he is, scientifically considered, a colossal humbug: the fact being that, though he knows just as much (and just as little) as his contemporaries, the qualifications that pass muster in common men reveal their weakness when hung on his egregious personality.*]

B. B. Aha! Sir Colenso. Sir Colenso, eh? Welcome to the order of knighthood.

RIDGEON [*shaking hands*]. Thank you, B. B.

B. B. What! Sir Patrick! And how are we to-day? a little chilly? a little stiff? but hale and still the cleverest of us all. [SIR PATRICK *grunts.*] What! Walpole! the absent-minded beggar: eh?

WALPOLE. What does that mean?

B. B. Have you forgotten the lovely opera singer I sent you to have that growth taken off her vocal cords?

WALPOLE [*springing to his feet*]. Great heavens, man, you dont mean to say you sent her for a throat operation!

B. B. [*archly*]. Aha! Ha ha! Aha! [*Trilling like a lark as he shakes his finger at Walpole*] You removed her nuciform sac. Well, well! force of habit! force of habit! Never mind, ne-e-e-ver mind. She got back her voice after it, and thinks you the greatest surgeon alive; and so you are, so you are, so you are.

WALPOLE [*in a tragic whisper, intensely serious*]. Blood-poisoning. I see. I see. [*He sits down again.*]

SIR PATRICK. And how is a certain distinguished family[1] getting on under your care, Sir Ralph?

B. B. Our friend Ridgeon will be gratified to hear that I have tried his opsonin treatment on little Prince Henry[2] with complete success.

RIDGEON [*startled and anxious*]. But how——

B. B. [*continuing*]. I suspected typhoid: the head gardener's boy had it; so I just called at St Anne's one day and got a tube of your very excellent serum. You were out, unfortunately.

RIDGEON. I hope they explained to you carefully——

B. B. [*waving away the absurd suggestion*]. Lord bless you, my dear fellow, I didnt need any explanations. I'd left my wife in the carriage at the door; and I'd no time to be taught my business by your young chaps. I know all about it. Ive handled these anti-toxins ever since they first came out.

RIDGEON. But theyre not anti-toxins; and theyre dangerous unless you use them at the right time.

B. B. Of course they are. Everything is dangerous unless you take it at the right time. An apple at breakfast does you good: an apple at bedtime upsets you for a week. There are only two rules for anti-toxins. First, dont be afraid of them: second, inject them a quarter of an hour before meals, three times a day.

RIDGEON [*appalled*]. Great heavens, B. B., no, no, no.

B. B. [*sweeping on irresistibly*]. Yes, yes, yes, Colly. The proof of the pudding is in the eating, you know. It was an immense success. It acted like magic on the little prince. Up went his temperature; off to bed I packed him; and in a week he was all right again, and

[1] *distinguished family, the royal family.*
[2] *Prince Henry, born in 1900, Duke of Gloucester and uncle of Queen Elizabeth II.*

absolutely immune from typhoid for the rest of his life. The family were very nice about it: their gratitude was quite touching; but I said they owed it all to you, Ridgeon; and I am glad to think that your knighthood is the result.

RIDGEON. I am deeply obliged to you. [*Overcome, he sits down on the chair near the couch.*]

B. B. Not at all, not at all. Your own merit. Come! come! come! dont give way.

RIDGEON. It's nothing. I was a little giddy just now. Overwork, I suppose.

WALPOLE. Blood-poisoning.

B. B. Overwork! Theres no such thing. I do the work of ten men. Am I giddy? No. NO. If youre not well, you have a disease. It may be a slight one; but it's a disease. And what is a disease? The lodgment in the system of a pathogenic germ, and the multiplication of that germ. What is the remedy? A very simple one. Find the germ and kill it.

SIR PATRICK. Suppose theres no germ?

B. B. Impossible, Sir Patrick: there must be a germ: else how could the patient be ill?

SIR PATRICK. Can you shew me the germ of overwork?

B. B. No; but why? Why? Because, my dear Sir Patrick, though the germ is there, it's invisible. Nature has given it no danger signal for us. These germs—these bacilli—are translucent bodies, like glass, like water. To make them visible you must stain them. Well, my dear Paddy, do what you will, some of them wont stain. They wont take cochineal: they wont take methylene blue: they wont take gentian violet: they wont take any coloring matter. Consequently, though we know, as scientific men, that they exist, we cannot see them. But can you disprove their existence? Can you conceive the disease existing without them? Can you, for instance, shew me a case of diphtheria without the bacillus?

SIR PATRICK. No; but I'll shew you the same bacillus, without the disease, in your own throat.

B. B. No, not the same, Sir Patrick. It is an entirely different bacillus; only the two are, unfortunately, so exactly alike that you cannot see the difference. You must understand, my dear Sir Patrick, that every one of these interesting little creatures has an imitator. Just as men imitate each other, germs imitate each other. There is the genuine diphtheria bacillus discovered by Lœffler;[1]

[1] *Lœffler, Friedrich Lœffler (1852–1915), German bacteriologist.*

and there is the pseudo-bacillus, exactly like it, which you could find, as you say, in my own throat.

SIR PATRICK. And how do you tell one from the other?

B. B. Well, obviously, if the bacillus is the genuine Lœffler, you have diphtheria; and if it's the pseudo-bacillus, youre quite well. Nothing simpler. Science is always simple and always profound. It is only the half-truths that are dangerous. Ignorant faddists pick up some superficial information about germs; and they write to the papers and try to discredit science. They dupe and mislead many honest and worthy people. But science has a perfect answer to them on every point.

> A little learning is a dangerous thing:
> Drink deep; or taste not the Pierian spring.[1]

I mean no disrespect to your generation, Sir Patrick: some of you old stagers did marvels through sheer professional intuition and clinical experience; but when I think of the average men of your day, ignorantly bleeding and cupping and purging, and scattering germs over their patients from their clothes and instruments, and contrast all that with the scientific certainty and simplicity of my treatment of the little prince the other day, I cant help being proud of my own generation: the men who were trained on the germ theory, the veterans of the great struggle over Evolution in the seventies. We may have our faults; but at least we are men of science. That is why I am taking up your treatment, Ridgeon, and pushing it. It's scientific. [*He sits down on the chair near the couch.*]

EMMY [*at the door, announcing*]. Dr Blenkinsop.

[*DR BLENKINSOP is in very different case from the others. He is clearly not a prosperous man. He is flabby and shabby, cheaply fed and cheaply clothed. He has the lines made by a conscience between his eyes, and the lines made by continual money worries all over his face, cut all the deeper as he has seen better days, and hails his well-to-do colleagues as their contemporary and old hospital friend, though even in this he has to struggle with the diffidence of poverty and relegation to the poorer middle class.*]

Pierian spring. *A spring in Pieria, a district sacred to the Greek Muses or Pierides; hence, the fountain of learning. Pope's famous saw from* An Essay on Criticism *applies to B. B. only too well.*

RIDGEON. How are you, Blenkinsop?

BLENKINSOP. Ive come to offer my humble congratulations. Oh dear! all the great guns are before me.

B. B. [*patronizing, but charming*]. How d'ye do, Blenkinsop? How d'ye do?

BLENKINSOP. And Sir Patrick, too! [SIR PATRICK *grunts*.]

RIDGEON. Youve met Walpole, of course?

WALPOLE. How d'ye do?

BLENKINSOP. It's the first time Ive had that honor. In my poor little practice there are no chances of meeting you great men. I know nobody but the St Anne's men of my own day. [*To* RIDGEON] And so youre Sir Colenso. How does it feel?

RIDGEON. Foolish at first. Dont take any notice of it.

BLENKINSOP. I'm ashamed to say I havnt a notion what your great discovery is; but I congratulate you all the same for the sake of old times.

B. B. [*shocked*]. But, my dear Blenkinsop, you used to be rather keen on science.

BLENKINSOP. Ah, I used to be a lot of things. I used to have two or three decent suits of clothes, and flannels to go up the river on Sundays. Look at me now: this is my best; and it must last til Christmas. What can I do? Ive never opened a book since I was qualified thirty years ago. I used to read the medical papers at first; but you know how soon a man drops that; besides, I cant afford them; and what are they after all but trade papers, full of advertisements? Ive forgotten all my science: whats the use of my pretending I havnt? But I have great experience: clinical experience; and bedside experience is the main thing, isnt it?

B. B. No doubt; always provided, mind you, that you have a sound scientific theory to correlate your observations at the bedside. Mere experience by itself is nothing. If I take my dog to the bedside with me, he sees what I see. But he learns nothing from it. Why? Because he's not a scientific dog.

WALPOLE. It amuses me to hear you physicians and general practitioners talking about clinical experience. What do you see at the bedside but the outside of the patient? Well: it isnt his outside thats wrong, except perhaps in skin cases. What you want is a daily familiarity with people's insides; and that you can only get at the operating table. I know what I'm talking about: I've been a surgeon and a consultant for twenty years; and I've never known a general practitioner right in his diagnosis yet. Bring them a perfectly simple case; and they diagnose cancer, and arthritis, and appendicitis, and every other itis, when any really experienced surgeon can see that it's a plain case of blood-poisoning.

BLENKINSOP. Ah, it's easy for you gentlemen to talk; but what would you say if you had my practice? Except for the workmen's clubs, my patients are all clerks and shopmen. They darent be ill: they cant afford it. And when they break down, what can I do for them? You can send your people to St Moritz or to Egypt, or recommend horse exercise or motoring or champagne jelly or complete change and rest for six months. *I* might as well order my people a slice of the moon. And the worst of it is, I'm too poor to keep well myself on the cooking I have to put up with. Ive such a wretched digestion; and I look it. How am I to inspire confidence? [*He sits disconsolately on the couch.*]

RIDGEON [*restlessly*]. Dont, Blenkinsop: it's too painful. The most tragic thing in the world is a sick doctor.

WALPOLE. Yes, by George: its like a bald-headed man trying to sell a hair restorer. Thank God I'm a surgeon!

B. B. [*sunnily*]. I am never sick. Never had a day's illness in my life. Thats what enables me to sympathize with my patients.

WALPOLE [*interested*]. What! youre never ill!

B. B. Never.

WALPOLE. Thats interesting. I believe you have no nuciform sac. If you ever do feel at all queer, I should very much like to have a look.

B. B. Thank you, my dear fellow; but I'm too busy just now.

RIDGEON. I was just telling them when you came in, Blenkinsop, that I have worked myself out of sorts.

BLENKINSOP. Well, it seems presumptuous of me to offer a prescription to a great man like you; but still I have great experience; and if I might recommend a pound of ripe greengages every day half an hour before lunch, I'm sure youd find a benefit. Theyre very cheap.

RIDGEON. What do you say to that, B. B.?

B. B. [*encouragingly*]. Very sensible, Blenkinsop: very sensible indeed. I'm delighted to see that you disapprove of drugs.

SIR PATRICK [*grunts*]!

B. B. [*archly*]. Aha! Haha! Did I hear from the fireside armchair the bow-wow of the old school defending its drugs? Ah, believe me, Paddy, the world would be healthier if every chemist's shop in England were demolished. Look at the papers! full of scandalous advertisements of patent medicines! a huge commercial system of quackery and poison. Well, whose fault is it? Ours. I say, ours. We set the example. We spread the superstition. We taught the people to believe in bottles of doctor's stuff; and now they buy it at the stores instead of consulting a medical man.

WALPOLE. Quite true. I've not prescribed a drug for the last fifteen years.

B. B. Drugs can only repress symptoms: they cannot eradicate disease. The true remedy for all diseases is Nature's remedy. Nature and Science are at one, Sir Patrick, believe me; though you were taught differently. Nature has provided, in the white corpuscles as you call them—in the phagocytes as we call them—a natural means of devouring and destroying all disease germs. There is at bottom only one genuinely scientific treatment for all diseases, and that is to stimulate the phagocytes. Stimulate the phagocytes. Drugs are a delusion. Find the germ of the disease; prepare from it a suitable anti-toxin; inject it three times a day quarter of an hour before meals; and what is the result? The phagocytes are stimulated; they devour the disease; and the patient recovers—unless, of course, he's too far gone. That, I take it, is the essence of Ridgeon's discovery.

SIR PATRICK [*dreamily*]. As I sit here, I seem to hear my poor old father talking again.

B. B. [*rising in incredulous amazement*]. Your father! But, Lord bless my soul, Paddy, your father must have been an older man than you.

SIR PATRICK. Word for word almost, he said what you say. No more drugs. Nothing but inoculation.

B. B. [*almost contemptuously*]. Inoculation! Do you mean smallpox inoculation?

SIR PATRICK. Yes. In the privacy of our family circle, sir, my father used to declare his belief that smallpox inoculation was good, not only for smallpox, but for all fevers.

B. B. [*suddenly rising to the new idea with immense interest and excitement*]. What! Ridgeon: did you hear that? Sir Patrick: I am more struck by what you have just told me than I can well express. Your father, sir, anticipated a discovery of my own. Listen, Walpole. Blenkinsop: attend one moment. You will all be intensely interested in this. I was put on the track by accident. I had a typhoid case and a tetanus case side by side in the hospital: a beadle[1] and a city missionary.[2] Think of what that meant for them, poor fellows! Can a beadle be dignified with typhoid? Can a missionary be eloquent with lockjaw? No. NO. Well, I got some typhoid anti-toxin from Ridgeon and a tube of Muldooley's anti-tetanus serum. But the missionary jerked all my things off the table in one of his paroxysms; and in replacing them I put Ridgeon's tube where Mul-dooley's ought to have been. The consequence was that I inoculated the typhoid case for tetanus and the tetanus case for typhoid. [*The doctors look greatly concerned.* B. B., *undamped, smiles trium-phantly.*] Well, they recovered. THEY RECOVERED. Except for a touch of St Vitus's dance the missionary's as well to-day as ever; and the beadle's ten times the man he was.

BLENKINSOP. Ive known things like that happen. They cant be explained.

B. B. [*severely*]. Blenkinsop: there is nothing that cannot be explained by science. What did I do? Did I fold my hands helplessly and say that the case could not be explained? By no means. I sat down and used my brains. I thought the case out on scientific principles. I asked myself why didnt the missionary die of typhoid on top of tetanus, and the beadle of tetanus on top of typhoid? Theres a problem for you, Ridgeon. Think, Sir Patrick. Reflect, Blenkinsop. Look at it without prejudice, Walpole. What is the real work of the anti-toxin? Simply to stimulate the phagocytes. Very well. But so long as you stimulate the phagocytes, what does it matter which particular sort of serum you use for the purpose? Haha! Eh? Do you see? Do you grasp it? Ever since that Ive used all sorts of anti-toxins absolutely indiscriminately, with perfectly satis-factory results. I inoculated the little prince with your stuff, Ridgeon, because I wanted to give you a lift; but two years ago I tried the experiment of treating a scarlet fever case with a sample of hy-drophobia serum from the Pasteur Institute, and it answered capi-tally. It stimulated the phagocytes; and the phagocytes did the rest. That is why Sir Patrick's father found that inoculation cured all fevers. It stimulated the phagocytes. [*He throws himself into his chair, exhausted with the triumph of his demonstration, and beams magnificently on them.*]

EMMY [*looking in*]. Mr Walpole: your motor's come for you; and it's frightening Sir Patrick's horses; so come along quick.

[1] beadle, *a petty official whose duty it is to keep order in church.*
city missionary, *such as a Salvation Army worker.*

WALPOLE [*rising*]. Good-bye, Ridgeon.

RIDGEON. Good-bye; and many thanks.

B. B. You see my point, Walpole?

EMMY. He cant wait, Sir Ralph. The carriage will be into the area if he dont come.

WALPOLE. I'm coming. [*To* B. B.] Theres nothing in your point: phagocytosis is pure rot: the cases are all blood-poisoning; and the knife is the real remedy. Bye-bye, Sir Paddy. Happy to have met you, Mr. Blenkinsop. Now, Emmy. [*He goes out, followed by* EMMY.]

B. B. [*sadly*]. Walpole has no intellect. A mere surgeon. Wonderful operator; but, after all, what is operating? Only manual labor. Brain — BRAIN remains master of the situation. The nuciform sac is utter nonsense: theres no such organ. It's a mere accidental kink in the membrane, occurring in perhaps two-and-a-half per cent of the population. Of course I'm glad for Walpole's sake that the operation is fashionable; for he's a dear good fellow; and after all, as I always tell people, the operation will do them no harm: indeed, Ive known the nervous shake-up and the fortnight in bed do people a lot of good after a hard London season; but still it's a shocking fraud. [*Rising*] Well, I must be toddling. Good-bye, Paddy [SIR PATRICK *grunts.*] good-bye, good-bye. Good-bye, my dear Blenkinsop, good-bye! Good-bye, Ridgeon. Dont fret about your health: you know what to do: if your liver is sluggish, a little mercury never does any harm. If you feel restless, try bromide. If that doesnt answer, a stimulant, you know: a little phosphorus and strychnine. If you cant sleep, trional, trional, trion—

SIR PATRICK [*drily*]. But no drugs, Colly, remember that.

B. B. [*firmly*]. Certainly not. Quite right, Sir Patrick. As temporary expedients, of course; but as treatment, no, NO. Keep away from the chemist's shop, my dear Ridgeon, whatever you do.

RIDGEON [*going to the door with him*]. I will. And thank you for the knighthood. Good-bye.

B. B. [*stopping at the door, with the beam in his eye twinkling a little*]. By the way, who's your patient?

RIDGEON. Who?

B. B. Downstairs. Charming woman. Tuberculous husband.

RIDGEON. Is she there still?

EMMY [*looking in*]. Come on, Sir Ralph: your wife's waiting in the carriage.

B. B. [*suddenly sobered*]. Oh! Good-bye. [*He goes out almost precipitately.*]

RIDGEON. Emmy: is that woman there still? If so, tell her once for all that I cant and wont see her. Do you hear?

EMMY. Oh, she aint in a hurry: she doesnt mind how long she waits. [*She goes out.*]

BLENKINSOP. I must be off, too: every half-hour I spend away from my work costs me eighteen pence. Good-bye, Sir Patrick.

SIR PATRICK. Good-bye. Good-bye.

RIDGEON. Come to lunch with me some day this week.

BLENKINSOP. I cant afford it, dear boy; and it would put me off my own food for a week. Thank you all the same.

RIDGEON [*uneasy at* BLENKINSOP's *poverty*]. Can I do nothing for you?

BLENKINSOP. Well, if you have an old frock-coat to spare? you see what would be an old one for you would be a new one for me; so remember me the next time you turn out your wardrobe. Good-bye. [*He hurries out.*]

RIDGEON [*looking after him*]. Poor chap! [*Turning to* SIR PATRICK] So thats why they made me a knight! And thats the medical profession!

SIR PATRICK. And a very good profession, too, my lad. When you know as much as I know of the ignorance and superstition of the patients, youll wonder that we're half as good as we are.

RIDGEON. We're not a profession: we're a conspiracy.

SIR PATRICK. All professions are conspiracies against the laity. And we cant all be geniuses like you. Every fool can get ill; but every fool cant be a good doctor: there are not enough good ones to go round. And for all you know, Bloomfield Bonington kills less people than you do.

RIDGEON. Oh, very likely. But he really ought to know the difference between a vaccine and an anti-toxin. Stimulate the phagocytes! The vaccine doesnt affect the phagocytes at all. He's all wrong: hopelessly, dangerously wrong. To put a tube of serum into his hands is murder: simple murder.

EMMY [*returning*]. Now, Sir Patrick. How long more are you going to keep them horses standing in the draught?

SIR PATRICK. Whats that to you, you old catamaran?

EMMY. Come, come, now! none of your temper to me. And it's time for Colly to get to his work.

RIDGEON. Behave yourself, Emmy. Get out.

EMMY. Oh, I learnt how to behave myself before I learnt you to do it. I know what doctors are: sitting talking together about themselves when they ought to be with their poor patients. And I know what horses are, Sir Patrick. I was brought up in the country. Now be good; and come along.

SIR PATRICK [*rising*]. Very well, very well, very well. Good-bye, Colly. [*He pats* RIDGEON *on the shoulder and goes out, turning for a moment at the door to look meditatively at* EMMY *and say, with grave conviction*] You are an ugly old devil, and no mistake.

EMMY [*highly indignant, calling after him*]. Youre no beauty yourself. [*To* RIDGEON, *much flustered*] Theyve no manners: they think they can say what they like to me; and you set them on, you do. I'll teach them their places. Here now: are you going to see that poor thing or are you not?

RIDGEON. I tell you for the fiftieth time I wont see anybody. Send her away.

EMMY. Oh, I'm tired of being told to send her away. What good will that do her?

RIDGEON. Must I get angry with you, Emmy?

EMMY [*coaxing*]. Come now: just see her for a minute to please me: theres a good boy. She's given me half-a-crown. She thinks it's life and death to her husband for her to see you.

RIDGEON. Values her husband's life at half-a-crown!

EMMY. Well, it's all she can afford, poor lamb. Them others think nothing of half-a-sovereign[1] just to talk about themselves to you, the sluts! Besides, she'll put you in a good temper for the day, because it's a good deed to see her; and she's the sort that gets round you.

RIDGEON. Well, she hasnt done so badly. For half-a-crown she's had a consultation with Sir Ralph Bloomfield Bonington and Cutler Walpole. Thats six guineas[2] to start with. I dare say she's consulted Blenkinsop too: thats another eighteenpence.[3]

EMMY. Then youll see her for me, wont you?

RIDGEON. Oh, send her up and be hanged. [EMMY *trots out, satisfied.* RIDGEON *calls*] Redpenny!

---

[1] *half-a-crown . . . half-a-sovereign,* $.60 *vs.* $2.43, *both of which sums had at least triple their present buying power.*

[2] *six guineas,* $30.60.

[3] *eighteenpence,* $.35.

REDPENNY [*appearing at the door*]. What is it?

RIDGEON. Theres a patient coming up. If she hasnt gone in five minutes, come in with an urgent call from the hospital for me. You understand: she's to have a strong hint to go.

REDPENNY. Right O! [*He vanishes.*]

[RIDGEON *goes to the glass, and arranges his tie a little.*]

EMMY [*announcing*]. Mrs Doobidad [RIDGEON *leaves the glass and goes to the writing-table.*]

[*The lady comes in.* EMMY *goes out and shuts the door.* RIDGEON, *who has put on an impenetrable and rather distant professional manner, turns to the lady, and invites her, by a gesture, to sit down on the couch.*]

[MRS DUBEDAT *is beyond all demur an arrestingly good-looking young woman. She has something of the grace and romance of a wild creature, with a good deal of the elegance and dignity of a fine lady.* RIDGEON, *who is extremely susceptible to the beauty of women, instinctively assumes the defensive at once, and hardens his manner still more. He has an impression that she is very well dressed; but she has a figure on which any dress would look well, and carries herself with the unaffected distinction of a woman who has never in her life suffered from those doubts and fears as to her social position which spoil the manners of most middling people. She is tall, slender, and strong; has dark hair, dressed so as to look like hair and not like a bird's nest or a pantaloon's wig[1] (fashion wavering just then between these two models); has unexpectedly narrow, subtle, dark-fringed eyes that alter her expression disturbingly when she is excited and flashes them wide open; is softly impetuous in her speech and swift in her movements; and is just now in mortal anxiety. She carries a portfolio.*]

MRS DUBEDAT [*in low urgent tones*]. Doctor—

RIDGEON [*curtly*]. Wait. Before you begin, let me tell you at once that I can do nothing for you. My hands are full. I sent you that message by my old servant. You would not take that answer.

MRS DUBEDAT. How could I?

RIDGEON. You bribed her.

MRS DUBEDAT. I—

[1] *a pantaloon's wig, the wig of the comic old pantomime character, Pantaloon.*

RIDGEON. That doesnt matter. She coaxed me to see you. Well, you must take it from me now that with all the good will in the world, I cannot undertake another case.

MRS DUBEDAT. Doctor: you must save my husband. You must. When I explain to you, you will see that you must. It is not an ordinary case, not like any other case. He is not like anybody else in the world: oh, believe me, he is not. I can prove it to you: [*fingering her portfolio*] I have brought some things to shew you. And you can save him: the papers say you can.

RIDGEON. Whats the matter? Tuberculosis?

MRS DUBEDAT. Yes. His left lung—

RIDGEON. Yes: you neednt tell me about that.

MRS DUBEDAT. You can cure him, if only you will. It is true that you can, isnt it? [*In great distress*] Oh, tell me, please.

RIDGEON [*warningly*]. You are going to be quiet and self-possessed, arnt you?

MRS DUBEDAT. Yes. I beg your pardon. I know I shouldnt— [*Giving way again*] Oh, please, say that you can; and then I shall be all right.

RIDGEON [*huffily*]. I am not a curemonger: if you want cures, you must go to the people who sell them. [*Recovering himself, ashamed of the tone of his own voice*] But I have at the hospital ten tuberculous patients whose lives I believe I can save.

MRS DUBEDAT. Thank God!

RIDGEON. Wait a moment. Try to think of those ten patients as ten shipwrecked men on a raft—a raft that is barely large enough to save them—that will not support one more. Another head bobs up through the waves at the side. Another man begs to be taken aboard. He implores the captain of the raft to save him. But the captain can only do that by pushing one of his ten off the raft and drowning him to make room for the new comer. That is what you are asking me to do.

MRS DUBEDAT. But how can that be? I dont understand. Surely—

RIDGEON. You must take my word for it that it is so. My laboratory, my staff, and myself are working at full pressure. We are doing our utmost. The treatment is a new one. It takes time, means, and skill; and there is not enough for another case. Our ten cases are already chosen cases. Do you understand what I mean by chosen?

MRS DUBEDAT. Chosen. No: I cant understand.

RIDGEON [*sternly*]. You must understand. Youve got to understand and to face it. In every single one of those ten cases I have had to consider, not only whether the man could be saved, but whether he was worth saving. There were fifty cases to choose from; and forty had to be condemned to death. Some of the forty had young wives and helpless children. If the hardness of their cases could have saved them they would have been saved ten times over. Ive no doubt your case is a hard one: I can see the tears in your eyes [*she hastily wipes her eyes*]: I know that you have a torrent of entreaties ready for me the moment I stop speaking; but it's no use. You must go to another doctor.

MRS DUBEDAT. But can you give me the name of another doctor who understands your secret?

RIDGEON. I have no secret: I am not a quack.

MRS DUBEDAT. I beg your pardon: I didnt mean to say anything wrong. I dont understand how to speak to you. Oh, pray dont be offended.

RIDGEON [*again a little ashamed*]. There! there! never mind. [*He relaxes and sits down.*] After all, I'm talking nonsense: I daresay I am a quack, a quack with a qualification. But my discovery is not patented.

MRS DUBEDAT. Then can any doctor cure my husband? Oh, why dont they do it? I have tried so many: I have spent so much. If only you would give me the name of another doctor.

RIDGEON. Every man in this street is a doctor. But outside myself and the handful of men I am training at St Anne's, there is nobody as yet who has mastered the opsonin treatment. And we are full up? I'm sorry; but that is all I can say. [*Rising*] Good morning.

MRS DUBEDAT [*suddenly and desperately taking some drawings from her portfolio*]. Doctor: look at these. You understand drawings: you have good ones in your waiting-room. Look at them. They are his work.

RIDGEON. It's no use my looking. [*He looks, all the same.*] Hallo! [*He takes one to the window and studies it.*] Yes: this is the real thing. Yes, yes. [*He looks at another and returns to her.*] These are very clever. Theyre unfinished, arnt they?

MRS DUBEDAT. He gets tired so soon. But you see, dont you, what a genius he is? You see that he is worth saving. Oh, doctor, I married him just to help him to begin: I had money enough to tide him over the hard years at the beginning—to enable him to follow his inspiration until his genius was recognized. And I was useful to him as a model: his drawings of me sold quite quickly.

RIDGEON. Have you got one?

MRS DUBEDAT [*producing another*]. Only this one. It was the first.

RIDGEON [*devouring it with his eyes*]. Thats a wonderful drawing. Why is it called Jennifer?

MRS DUBEDAT. My name is Jennifer.

RIDGEON. A strange name.

MRS DUBEDAT. Not in Cornwall. I am Cornish. It's only what you call Guinevere.

RIDGEON [*repeating the names with a certain pleasure in them*]. Guinevere. Jennifer. [*Looking again at the drawing*] Yes: it's really a wonderful drawing. Excuse me; but may I ask is it for sale? I'll buy it.

MRS DUBEDAT. Oh, take it. It's my own: he gave it to me. Take it. Take them all. Take everything; ask anything; but save him. You can: you will: you must.

REDPENNY [*entering with every sign of alarm*]. Theyve just telephoned from the hospital that youre to come instantly—a patient on the point of death. The carriage is waiting.

RIDGEON [*intolerantly*]. Oh, nonsense: get out. [*Greatly annoyed*] What do you mean by interrupting me like this?

REDPENNY. But—

RIDGEON. Chut! cant you see I'm engaged? Be off.

[REDPENNY, *bewildered, vanishes.*]

MRS DUBEDAT [*rising*]. Doctor: one instant only before you go—

RIDGEON. Sit down. It's nothing.

MRS DUBEDAT. But the patient. He said he was dying.

RIDGEON. Oh, he's dead by this time. Never mind. Sit down.

MRS DUBEDAT [*sitting down and breaking down*]. Oh, you none of you care. You see people die every day.

RIDGEON [*petting her*]. Nonsense! it's nothing: I told him to come in and say that. I thought I should want to get rid of you

MRS DUBEDAT [*shocked at the falsehood*]. Oh!

RIDGEON [*continuing*]. Dont look so bewildered: theres nobody dying.

MRS DUBEDAT. My husband is.

RIDGEON [*pulling himself together*]. Ah, yes: I had forgotten your husband. Mrs Dubedat: you are asking me to do a very serious thing?

MRS DUBEDAT. I am asking you to save the life of a great man

RIDGEON. You are asking me to kill another man for his sake

for as surely as I undertake another case, I shall have to hand back one of the old ones to the ordinary treatment. Well, I dont shrink from that. I have had to do it before; and I will do it again if you can convince me that his life is more important than the worst life I am now saving. But you must convince me first.

MRS DUBEDAT. He made those drawings; and they are not the best—nothing like the best; only I did not bring the really best: so few people like them. He is twenty-three: his whole life is before him. Wont you let me bring him to you? wont you speak to him? wont you see for yourself?

RIDGEON. Is he well enough to come to a dinner at the Star and Garter at Richmond?

MRS DUBEDAT. Oh yes. Why?

RIDGEON. I'll tell you. I am inviting all my old friends to a dinner to celebrate my knighthood—youve seen about it in the papers, havnt you?

MRS DUBEDAT. Yes, oh yes. That was how I found out about you.

RIDGEON. It will be a doctors' dinner; and it was to have been a bachelors' dinner. I'm a bachelor. Now if you will entertain for me, and bring your husband, he will meet me; and he will meet some of the most eminent men in my profession: Sir Patrick Cullen, Sir Ralph Bloomfield Bonington, Cutler Walpole, and others. I can put the case to them; and your husband will have to stand or fall by what we think of him. Will you come?

MRS DUBEDAT. Yes, of course I will come. Oh, thank you, thank you. And may I bring some of his drawings—the really good ones?

RIDGEON. Yes. I will let you know the date in the course of to-morrow. Leave me your address.

MRS DUBEDAT. Thank you again and again. You have made me so happy: I know you will admire him and like him. This is my address. [*She gives him her card.*]

RIDGEON. Thank you. [*He rings.*]

MRS DUBEDAT [*embarrassed*]. May I—is there—should I—I mean—[*She blushes and stops in confusion.*]

RIDGEON. Whats the matter?

MRS DUBEDAT. Your fee for this consultation?

RIDGEON. Oh, I forgot that. Shall we say a beautiful drawing of his favorite model for the whole treatment, including the cure?

MRS DUBEDAT. You are very generous. Thank you. I know you will cure him. Good-bye.

RIDGEON. I will. Good-bye. [*They shake hands.*] By the way, you know, dont you, that tuberculosis is catching. You take every precaution, I hope.

MRS DUBEDAT. I am not likely to forget it. They treat us like lepers at the hotels.

EMMY [*at the door*]. Well, deary: have you got round him?

RIDGEON. Yes. Attend to the door and hold your tongue.

EMMY. Thats a good boy. [*She goes out with* MRS DUBEDAT.]

RIDGEON [*alone*]. Consultation free. Cure guaranteed. [*He heaves a great sigh.*]

act 2

After dinner on the terrace at the Star and Garter, Richmond. Cloudless summer night; nothing disturbs the stillness except from time to time the long trajectory of a distant train and the measured clucking of oars coming up from the Thames in the valley below. The dinner is over; and three of the eight chairs are empty. SIR PATRICK, *with his back to the view, is at the head of the square table with* RIDGEON. *The two chairs opposite them are empty. On their right come, first, a vacant chair, and then one very fully occupied by* B. B., *who basks blissfully in the moonbeams. On their left,* SCHUTZMACHER *and* WALPOLE. *The entrance to the hotel is on their right, behind* B. B. *The five men are silently enjoying their coffee and cigarets, full of food, and not altogether void of wine.*

MRS DUBEDAT, wrapped up for departure, comes in. They rise, except SIR PATRICK; *but she takes one of the vacant places at the foot of the table, next* B. B.; *and they sit down again.*

MRS DUBEDAT [*as she enters*]. Louis will be here presently. He is shewing Dr Blenkinsop how to work the telephone. [*She sits.*] Oh, I am so sorry we have to go. It seems such a shame, this beautiful night. And we have enjoyed ourselves so much.

RIDGEON. I dont believe another half-hour would do Mr Dubedat a bit of harm.

SIR PATRICK. Come now, Colly, come! come! none of that. You take your man home, Mrs Dubedat; and get him to bed before eleven.

B. B. Yes, yes. Bed before eleven. Quite right, quite right. Sorry to lose you, my dear lady; but Sir Patrick's orders are the laws of—er—of Tyre and Sidon.[1]

WALPOLE. Let me take you home in my motor.

SIR PATRICK. No. You ought to be ashamed of yourself, Walpole. Your motor will take Mr and Mrs Dubedat to the station, and quite far enough too for an open carriage at night.

MRS DUBEDAT. Oh, I am sure the train is best.

RIDGEON. Well, Mrs Dubedat, we have had a most enjoyable evening.

WALPOLE. Most enjoyable.

B. B. Delightful. Charming. Unforgettable.

MRS DUBEDAT [*with a touch of shy anxiety*]. What did you think of Louis? Or am I wrong to ask?

RIDGEON. Wrong! Why, we are all charmed with him.

WALPOLE. Delighted.

B. B. Most happy to have met him. A privilege, a real privilege.

SIR PATRICK [*grunts*]!

MRS DUBEDAT [*quickly*]. Sir Patrick: are you uneasy about him?

SIR PATRICK [*discreetly*]. I admire his drawings greatly, maam.

MRS DUBEDAT. Yes; but I meant—

RIDGEON. You shall go away quite happy. He's worth saving. He must and shall be saved.

[MRS DUBEDAT *rises and gasps with delight, relief, and grati-tude. They all rise except* SIR PATRICK *and* SCHUTZMACHER, *and come reassuringly to her.*]

B. B. Certainly, cer-tainly.

WALPOLE. Theres no real difficulty, if only you know what to do.

MRS DUBEDAT. Oh, how can I ever thank you! From this night I can begin to be happy at last. You dont know what I feel. [*She sits down in tears. They crowd about her to console her.*]

B. B. My dear lady: come come! come come! [*very persuasively*] come come!

WALPOLE. Dont mind us. Have a good cry.

RIDGEON. No: dont cry. Your husband had better not know that weve been talking about him.

MRS DUBEDAT [*quickly pulling herself together*]. No, of course not. Please dont mind me. What a glorious thing it must be to be a doctor! [*They laugh.*] Dont laugh. You dont know what youve

---

[1] *Tyre and Sidon*, the Biblical cities, fabulous for their luxury.

done for me. I never knew until now how deadly afraid I was—
how I had come to dread the worst. I never dared let myself know.
But now the relief has come: now I know.

[LOUIS DUBEDAT *comes from the hotel, in his overcoat, his
throat wrapped in a shawl. He is a slim young man of 23,
physically still a stripling, and pretty, though not effeminate.
He has turquoise blue eyes, and a trick of looking you
straight in the face with them, which, combined with a frank
smile, is very engaging. Although he is all nerves, and
very observant and quick of apprehension, he is not in the
least shy. He is younger than* JENNIFER; *but he patronizes
her as a matter of course. The doctors do not put him out
in the least: neither* SIR PATRICK'S *years nor* BLOOMFIELD BON-
INGTON'S *majesty have the smallest apparent effect on him:
he is as natural as a cat: he moves among men as most men
move among things, though he is intentionally making himself agreeable to them on this occasion. Like all people who
can be depended on to take care of themselves, he is welcome
company; and his artist's power of appealing to the imagination gains him credit for all sorts of qualities and powers,
whether he possesses them or not.*]

LOUIS [*pulling on his gloves behind* RIDGEON'S *chair*]. Now,
Jinny-Gwinny: the motor has come round.

RIDGEON. Why do you let him spoil your beautiful name like
that, Mrs Dubedat?

MRS DUBEDAT. Oh, on grand occasions I am Jennifer.

B. B. You are a bachelor: you do not understand these things,
Ridgeon. Look at me [*They look.*] I also have two names. In
moments of domestic worry, I am simple Ralph. When the sun
shines in the home, I am Beedle-Deedle-Dumkins. Such is married
life! Mr Dubedat: may I ask you to do me a favor before you go.
Will you sign your name to this menu card, under the sketch you
have made of me?

WALPOLE. Yes; and mine too, if you will be so good.

LOUIS. Certainly. [*He sits down and signs the cards.*]

MRS DUBEDAT. Wont you sign Dr Schutzmacher's for him, Louis?

LOUIS. I dont think Dr Schutzmacher is pleased with his portrait.
I'll tear it up. [*He reaches across the table for* SCHUTZMACHER'S
menu card, and is about to tear it. SCHUTZMACHER *makes no sign.*]

RIDGEON. No, no: if Loony doesnt want it, I do.

LOUIS. I'll sign it for you with pleasure. [*He signs and hands it to* RIDGEON.] Ive just been making a little note of the river to-night: it will work up into something good. [*He shews a pocket sketch-book.*] I think I'll call it the Silver Danube.

B. B. Ah, charming, charming.

WALPOLE. Very sweet. Youre a nailer at pastel.[1]

[LOUIS *coughs, first out of modesty, then from tuberculosis.*]

SIR PATRICK. Now then, Mr Dubedat: youve had enough of the night air. Take him home, maam.

MRS DUBEDAT. Yes. Come, Louis.

RIDGEON. Never fear. Never mind. I'll make that cough all right.

B. B. We will stimulate the phagocytes. [*With tender effusion, shaking her hand*] Good-night, Mrs Dubedat. Good-night. Good-night.

WALPOLE. If the phagocytes fail, come to me. I'll put you right.

LOUIS. Good-night, Sir Patrick. Happy to have met you.

SIR PATRICK. 'Night. [*Half a grunt*]

MRS DUBEDAT. Good-night, Sir Patrick.

SIR PATRICK. Cover yourself well up. Dont think your lungs are made of iron because theyre better than his. Good-night.

MRS DUBEDAT. Thank you. Nothing hurts me. Good-night.

[LOUIS *goes out through the hotel without noticing* SCHUTZ-MACHER. MRS DUBEDAT *hesitates, then bows to him.* SCHUTZ-MACHER *rises and bows formally, German fashion. She goes out, attended by* RIDGEON. *The rest resume their seats, ruminating or smoking quietly.*]

B. B. [*harmoniously*]. Dee-lightful couple! Charming woman! Gifted lad! Remarkable talent! Graceful outlines! Perfect evening! Great success! Interesting case! Glorious night! Exquisite scenery! Capital dinner! Stimulating conversation! Restful outing! Good wine! Happy ending! Touching gratitude! Lucky Ridgeon—

RIDGEON [*returning*]. What's that? Calling me, B. B.? [*He goes back to his seat next* SIR PATRICK.]

B. B. No, no. Only congratulating you on a most successful evening! Enchanting woman! Thorough breeding! Gentle nature! Refined—

[BLENKINSOP *comes from the hotel and takes the empty chair next* RIDGEON.]

BLENKINSOP. I'm so sorry to have left you like this, Ridgeon; but it was a telephone message from the police. Theyve found half a

---

[1] *a nailer at pastel, a man exceptionally good at pastel painting.*

milkman at our level crossing[1] with a prescription of mine in its pocket. Wheres Mr Dubedat?

RIDGEON. Gone.

BLENKINSOP [*rising, very pale*]. Gone!

RIDGEON. Just this moment—

BLENKINSOP. Perhaps I could overtake him— [*He rushes into the hotel.*]

WALPOLE [*calling after him*]. He's in the motor, man, miles off. You cant— [*Giving it up*] No use.

RIDGEON. Theyre really very nice people. I confess I was afraid the husband would turn out an appalling bounder. But he's almost as charming in his way as she is in hers. And theres no mistake about his being a genius. It's something to have got a case really worth saving. Somebody else will have to go; but at all events it will be easy to find a worse man.

SIR PATRICK. How do you know?

RIDGEON. Come now, Sir Paddy, no growling. Have something more to drink.

SIR PATRICK. No, thank you.

WALPOLE. Do you see anything wrong with Dubedat, B. B.?

B. B. Oh, a charming young fellow. Besides, after all, what could be wrong with him? Look at him. What could be wrong with him?

SIR PATRICK. There are two things that can be wrong with any man. One of them is a cheque. The other is a woman. Until you know that a man's sound on these two points, you know nothing about him.

B. B. Ah, cynic, cynic!

WALPOLE. He's all right as to the cheque, for a while at all events. He talked to me quite frankly before dinner as to the pressure of money difficulties on an artist. He says he has no vices and is very economical, but that theres one extravagance he cant afford and yet cant resist; and that is dressing his wife prettily. So I said, bang plump out, "Let me lend you twenty pounds, and pay me when your ship comes home." He was really very nice about it. He took it like a man; and it was a pleasure to see how happy it made him, poor chap.

B. B. [*who has listened to* WALPOLE *with growing perturbation*]. But—but—but—when was this, may I ask?

WALPOLE. When I joined you that time down by the river.

[1] *level crossing, a road and a train track crossing on the same level.*

B. B. But, my dear Walpole, he had just borrowed ten pounds from me.

WALPOLE. What!

SIR PATRICK [*grunts*]!

B. B. [*indulgently*]. Well, well, it was really hardly borrowing; for he said heaven only knew when he could pay me. I couldnt refuse. It appears that Mrs Dubedat has taken a sort of fancy to me—

WALPOLE [*quickly*]. No: it was to me.

B. B. Certainly not. Your name was never mentioned between us. He is so wrapped up in his work that he has to leave her a good deal alone; and the poor innocent young fellow—he has of course no idea of my position or how busy I am—actually wanted me to call occasionally and talk to her.

WALPOLE. Exactly what he said to me!

B. B. Pooh! Pooh pooh! Really, I must say. [*Much disturbed, he rises and goes up to the balustrade, contemplating the landscape vexedly.*]

WALPOLE. Look here, Ridgeon! this is beginning to look serious.

[BLENKINSOP, *very anxious and wretched, but trying to look unconcerned, comes back.*]

RIDGEON. Well, did you catch him?

BLENKINSOP. No. Excuse my running way like that. [*He sits down at the foot of the table, next* BLOOMFIELD BONINGTON'S *chair.*]

WALPOLE. Anything the matter?

BLENKINSOP. Oh no. A trifle—something ridiculous. It cant be helped. Never mind.

RIDGEON. Was it anything about Dubedat?

BLENKINSOP [*almost breaking down*]. I ought to keep it to myself, I know. I cant tell you, Ridgeon, how ashamed I am of dragging my miserable poverty to your dinner after all your kindness. It's not that you wont ask me again; but it's so humiliating. And I did so look forward to one evening in my dress clothes (theyre still presentable, you see) with all my troubles left behind, just like old times.

RIDGEON. But what has happened?

BLENKINSOP. Oh, nothing. It's too ridiculous, I had just scraped up four shillings for this little outing; and it cost me one-and-four-pence to get here. Well, Dubedat asked me to lend him half-a-crown to tip the chambermaid of the room his wife left her wraps in, and for the cloakroom. He said he only wanted it for five minutes, as she had his purse. So of course I lent it to him. And he's forgotten to pay me. I've just tuppence to get back with.

RIDGEON. Oh, never mind that—

BLENKINSOP [*stopping him resolutely*]. No: I know what youre going to say; but I wont take it. Ive never borrowed a penny; and I never will. Ive nothing left but my friends; and I wont sell them. If none of you were to be able to meet me without being afraid that my civility was leading up to the loan of five shillings, there would be an end of everything for me. I'll take your old clothes, Colly, sooner than disgrace you by talking to you in the street in my own; but I wont borrow money. I'll train it as far as the twopence will take me; and I'll tramp the rest.

WALPOLE. Youll do the whole distance in my motor. [*They are all greatly relieved; and* WALPOLE *hastens to get away from the painful subject by adding*] Did he get anything out of you, Mr Schutzmacher?

SCHUTZMACHER [*shakes his head in a most expressive negative*].

WALPOLE. You didn't appreciate his drawing, I think.

SCHUTZMACHER. Oh yes I did. I should have liked very much to have kept the sketch and got it autographed.

B. B. But why didnt you?

SCHUTZMACHER. Well, the fact is, when I joined Dubedat after his conversation with Mr Walpole, he said that the Jews were the only people who knew anything about art, and that though he had to put up with your Philistine twaddle, as he called it, it was what I said about the drawings that really pleased him. He also said that his wife was greatly struck with my knowledge, and that she always admired Jews. Then he asked me to advance him £50 on the security of the drawings.

B. B.		No, no. Positively! Seriously!
WALPOLE	[*All exclaiming together*]	What! Another fifty!
BLENKINSOP		Think of that!
SIR PATRICK		[*grunts*]!

SCHUTZMACHER. Of course I couldnt lend money to a stranger like that.

B. B. I envy you the power to say No, Mr Schutzmacher. Of course, I knew I oughtnt to lend money to a young fellow in that way; but I simply hadnt the nerve to refuse. I couldnt very well, you know, could I?

SCHUTZMACHER. I dont understand that. *I* felt that I couldnt very well lend it.

WALPOLE. What did he say?

SCHUTZMACHER. Well, he made a very uncalled-for remark about a Jew not understanding the feelings of a gentleman. I must say you Gentiles are very hard to please. You say we are no gentlemen when we lend money; and when we refuse to lend it you say just the same. I didnt mean to behave badly. As I told him, I might have lent it to him if he had been a Jew himself.

SIR PATRICK [*with a grunt*]. And what did he say to that?

SCHUTZMACHER. Oh, he began trying to persuade me that he was one of the chosen people—that his artistic faculty shewed it, and that his name was as foreign as my own. He said he didnt really want £50; that he was only joking; that all he wanted was a couple of sovereigns.

B. B. No, no, Mr Schutzmacher. You invented the last touch. Seriously, now?

SCHUTZMACHER. No. You cant improve on Nature in telling stories about gentlemen like Mr Dubedat.

BLENKINSOP. You certainly do stand by one another, you chosen people, Mr Schutzmacher.

SCHUTZMACHER. Not at all. Personally, I like Englishmen better than Jews, and always associate with them. Thats only natural, because, as I am a Jew, theres nothing interesting in a Jew to me, whereas there is always something interesting and foreign in an Englishman. But in money matters it's quite different. You see, when an Englishman borrows, all he knows or cares is that he wants money; and he'll sign anything to get it, without in the least understanding it, or intending to carry out the agreement if it turns out badly for him. In fact, he thinks you a cad if you ask him to carry it out under such circumstances. Just like the Merchant of Venice, you know. But if a Jew makes an agreement, he means to keep it and expects you to keep it. If he wants money for a time, he borrows it and knows he must pay it at the end of the time. If he knows he cant pay, he begs it as a gift.

RIDGEON. Come, Loony! do you mean to say that Jews are never rogues and thieves?

SCHUTZMACHER. Oh, not at all. But I was not talking of criminals. I was comparing honest Englishmen with honest Jews.

[*One of the hotel maids, a pretty, fair-haired woman of about 25, comes from the hotel, rather furtively. She accosts* RIDGEON.]

THE MAID. I beg your pardon, sir—

RIDGEON. Eh?

THE MAID. I beg pardon, sir. It's not about the hotel. I'm not allowed to be on the terrace; and I should be discharged if I were seen speaking to you, unless you were kind enough to say you called me to ask whether the motor has come back from the station yet.

WALPOLE. Has it?

THE MAID. Yes, sir.

RIDGEON. Well, what do you want?

THE MAID. Would you mind, sir, giving me the address of the gentleman that was with you at dinner?

RIDGEON [*sharply*]. Yes, of course I should mind very much. You have no right to ask.

THE MAID. Yes, sir, I know it looks like that. But what am I to do?

SIR PATRICK. Whats the matter with you?

THE MAID. Nothing, sir. I want the address: thats all.

B. B. You mean the young gentleman?

THE MAID. Yes, sir: that went to catch the train with the woman he brought with him.

RIDGEON. The woman! Do you mean the lady who dined here? the gentleman's wife?

THE MAID. Dont believe them, sir. She cant be his wife. I'm his wife.

B. B.	[*in amazed remonstrance*]. My good girl!
RIDGEON	You his wife!
WALPOLE	What! whats that? Oh, this is getting perfectly fascinating, Ridgeon.

THE MAID. I could run upstairs and get you my marriage lines in a minute, sir, if you doubt my word. He's Mr Louis Dubedat, isnt he?

RIDGEON. Yes.

THE MAID. Well, sir, you may believe me or not; but I'm the lawful Mrs Dubedat.

SIR PATRICK. And why arnt you living with your husband?

THE MAID. We couldnt afford it, sir. I had thirty pounds saved; and we spent it all on our honeymoon in three weeks, and a lot more that he borrowed. Then I had to go back into service, and he went to London to get work at his drawing; and he never wrote me a line or sent me an address. I never saw nor heard of him again until I caught sight of him from the window going off in the motor with that woman.

SIR PATRICK. Well, thats two wives to start with.

B. B. Now upon my soul I dont want to be uncharitable; but really I'm beginning to suspect that our young friend is rather careless.

SIR PATRICK. Beginning to think! How long will it take you, man, to find out that he's a damned young blackguard?

BLENKINSOP. Oh, thats severe, Sir Patrick, very severe. Of course it's bigamy; but still he's very young; and she's very pretty. Mr Walpole: may I spunge on you for another of those nice cigarets of yours? [*He changes his seat for the one next* WALPOLE.]

WALPOLE. Certainly. [*He feels in his pockets.*] Oh bother! Where—? [*Suddenly remembering*] I say: I recollect now: I passed my cigaret case to Dubedat and he didnt return it. It was a gold one.

THE MAID. He didnt mean any harm: he never thinks about things like that, sir. I'll get it back for you, sir, if youll tell me where to find him.

RIDGEON. What am I to do? Shall I give her the address or not?

SIR PATRICK. Give her your own address; and then we'll see. [*To the maid*] Youll have to be content with that for the present, my girl. [RIDGEON *gives her his card.*] Whats your name?

THE MAID. Minnie Tinwell, sir.

SIR PATRICK. Well, you write him a letter to care of this gentleman; and it will be sent on. Now be off with you.

THE MAID. Thank you, sir. I'm sure you wouldnt see me wronged. Thank you all, gentlemen; and excuse the liberty. [*She goes into the hotel. They watch her in silence.*]

RIDGEON [*when she is gone*]. Do you realize, you chaps, that we have promised Mrs Dubedat to save this fellow's life?

BLENKINSOP. Whats the matter with him?

RIDGEON. Tuberculosis.

BLENKINSOP [*interested*]. And can you cure that?

RIDGEON. I believe so.

BLENKINSOP. Then I wish youd cure me. My right lung is touched, I'm sorry to say.

RIDGEON			What! your lung is going!
B. B.			My dear Blenkinsop, what do you tell me? [*Full of concern for Blenkinsop, he comes back from the balustrade.*]
		[*all together*]	
SIR PATRICK			Eh? Eh? whats that?
WALPOLE			Hullo! you mustnt neglect this, you know.

BLENKINSOP [*putting his fingers in his ears*]. No, no: it's no use. I know what youre going to say: Ive said it often to others. I cant afford to take care of myself; and theres an end of it. If a fortnight's holiday would save my life, I'd have to die. I shall get on as others have to get on. We cant all go to St Moritz or to Egypt, you know, Sir Ralph. Dont talk about it.

[*Embarrassed silence*]

SIR PATRICK [*grunts and looks hard at* RIDGEON]!

SCHUTZMACHER [*looking at his watch and rising*]. I must go. It's been a very pleasant evening, Colly. You might let me have my portrait if you dont mind. I'll send Mr Dubedat that couple of sovereigns for it.

RIDGEON [*giving him the menu card*]. Oh dont do that, Loony. I dont think he'd like that.

SCHUTZMACHER. Well, of course I shant if you feel that way about it. But I dont think you understand Dubedat. However, perhaps thats because I'm a Jew. Good-night, Dr Blenkinsop. [*Shaking hands*]

BLENKINSOP. Good-night, sir—I mean—Good-night.

SCHUTZMACHER [*waving his hand to the rest*]. Good-night, everybody.

WALPOLE
B. B.
SIR PATRICK
RIDGEON } Good-night.

[B. B. *repeats the salutation several times, in varied musical tones.* SCHUTZMACHER *goes out.*]

SIR PATRICK. It's time for us all to move. [*He rises and comes between* BLENKINSOP *and* WALPOLE. RIDGEON *also rises.*] Mr Walpole: take Blenkinsop home: he's had enough of the open air cure for to-night. Have you a thick overcoat to wear in the motor, Dr Blenkinsop?

BLENKINSOP. Oh, theyll give me some brown paper in the hotel; and a few thicknesses of brown paper across the chest are better than any fur coat.

WALPOLE. Well, come along. Good-night, Colly. Youre coming with us, arnt you, B. B.?

B. B. Yes: I'm coming. [WALPOLE *and* BLENKINSOP *go into the hotel.*] Good-night, my dear Ridgeon. [*Shaking hands affectionately.*] Dont let us lose sight of your interesting patient and his very charming wife. We must not judge him too hastily, you know. [*With unction*] G o o o o o o o o o d-night, Paddy. Bless you, dear old chap. [SIR PATRICK *utters a formidable grunt.* B. B. *laughs and pats him indulgently on the shoulder.*] Good-night. Good-night. Good-night. Good-night. [*He good-nights himself into the hotel.*]

[*The others have meanwhile gone without ceremony.* RIDGEON *and* SIR PATRICK *are left alone together.* RIDGEON, *deep in thought, comes down to* SIR PATRICK.]

SIR PATRICK. Well, Mr Savior of Lives: which is it to be? that honest decent man Blenkinsop, or that rotten blackguard of an artist, eh?

RIDGEON. It's not an easy case to judge, is it? Blenkinsop's an honest decent man; but is he any use? Dubedat's a rotten blackguard; but he's a genuine source of pretty and pleasant and good things.

SIR PATRICK. What will he be a source of for that poor innocent wife of his, when she finds him out?

RIDGEON. Thats true. Her life will be a hell.

SIR PATRICK. And tell me this. Suppose you had this choice put before you: either to go through life and find all the pictures bad but all the men and women good, or to go through life and find all the pictures good and all the men and women rotten. Which would you choose?

RIDGEON. Thats a devilishly difficult question, Paddy. The pictures are so agreeable, and the good people so infernally disagreeable and mischievous, that I really cant undertake to say offhand which I should prefer to do without.

SIR PATRICK. Come come! none of your cleverness with me: I'm too old for it. Blenkinsop isnt that sort of good man; and you know it.

RIDGEON. It would be simpler if Blenkinsop could paint Dubedat's pictures.

SIR PATRICK. It would be simpler still if Dubedat had some of Blenkinsop's honesty. The world isnt going to be made simple for you, my lad: you must take it as it is. Youve to hold the scales between Blenkinsop and Dubedat. Hold them fairly.

RIDGEON. Well, I'll be as fair as I can. I'll put into one scale all the pounds Dubedat has borrowed, and into the other all the half-crowns that Blenkinsop hasnt borrowed.

SIR PATRICK. And youll take out of Dubedat's scale all the faith he has destroyed and the honor he has lost, and youll put into Blenkinsop's scale all the faith he has justified and the honor he has created.

RIDGEON. Come come, Paddy! none of your claptrap with me: I'm too sceptical for it. I'm not at all convinced that the world wouldnt be a better world if everybody behaved as Dubedat does than it is now that everybody behaves as Blenkinson does.

SIR PATRICK. Then why dont you behave as Dubedat does?

RIDGEON. Ah, that beats me. Thats the experimental test. Still, it's a dilemma. It's a dilemma. You see theres a complication we havnt mentioned.

SIR PATRICK. Whats that?

RIDGEON. Well, if I let Blenkinsop die, at least nobody can say I did it because I wanted to marry his widow.

SIR PATRICK. Eh? Whats that?

RIDGEON. Now if I let Dubedat die, I'll marry his widow.

SIR PATRICK. Perhaps she wont have you, you know.

RIDGEON [*with a self-assured shake of the head*]. I've a pretty good flair for that sort of thing. I know when a woman is interested in me. She is.

SIR PATRICK. Well, sometimes a man knows best; and sometimes he knows worst. Youd much better cure them both.

RIDGEON. I cant. I'm at my limit. I can squeeze in one more case, but not two. I must choose.

SIR PATRICK. Well, you must choose as if she didnt exist: thats clear.

RIDGEON. Is that clear to you? Mind: it's not clear to me. She troubles my judgment.

SIR PATRICK. To me, it's a plain choice between a man and a lot of pictures.

RIDGEON. It's easier to replace a dead man than a good picture.

SIR PATRICK. Colly: when you live in an age that runs to pictures and statues and plays and brass bands because its men and women are not good enough to comfort its poor aching soul, you should thank Providence that you belong to a profession which is a high and great profession because its business is to heal and mend men and women.

RIDGEON. In short, as a member of a high and great profession, I'm to kill my patient.

SIR PATRICK. Dont talk wicked nonsense. You cant kill him. But you can leave him in other hands.

RIDGEON. In B. B.'s, for instance: eh? [*Looking at him significantly.*]

SIR PATRICK [*demurely facing his look*]. Sir Ralph Bloomfield Bonington is a very eminent physician.

RIDGEON. He is.

SIR PATRICK. I'm going for my hat.

[RIDGEON *strikes the bell as* SIR PATRICK *makes for the hotel. A waiter comes.*]

RIDGEON [*to the waiter*]. My bill, please.

WAITER. Yes, sir. [*He goes for it.*]

act 3

In DUBEDAT's *studio. Viewed from the large window the outer door is in the wall on the left at the near end. The door leading to the inner rooms is in the opposite wall, at the far end. The facing wall has neither window nor door. The plaster on all the walls is uncovered and undecorated, except by scrawlings of charcoal sketches and memoranda. There is a studio throne (a chair on a dais) a little to the left, opposite the inner door, and an easel to the right, opposite the outer door, with a dilapidated chair at it. Near the easel and against the wall is a bare wooden table with bottles and jars of oil and medium, paint-smudged rags, tubes of color, brushes, charcoal, a small lay figure,[1] a kettle and spirit-lamp, and other odds and ends. By the table is a sofa, littered with drawing blocks, sketch-books, loose sheets of paper, newspapers, books, and more smudged rags. Next the outer door is an umbrella and hat stand, occupied partly by* LOUIS' *hats and cloak and muffler, and partly by odds and ends of costumes. There is an old piano stool on the near side of this door. In the corner near the inner door is a little tea-table. A lay figure, in a cardinal's robe and hat, with an hour-glass in one hand and a scythe slung on its back, smiles with inane malice at* LOUIS, *who, in a milkman's smock much smudged with colors, is painting a piece of brocade which he has draped about his wife. She is*

[1] *lay figure, an adjustable wooden figure of the human body used as a model frame by artists.*

sitting on the throne, not interested in the painting, and appealing to him very anxiously about another matter.

MRS DUBEDAT. Promise.

LOUIS [*putting on a touch of paint with notable skill and care and answering quite perfunctorily*]. I promise, my darling.

MRS DUBEDAT. When you want money, you will always come to me.

LOUIS. But it's so sordid, dearest. I hate money. I cant keep always bothering you for money, money, money. Thats what drives me sometimes to ask other people, though I hate doing it.

MRS DUBEDAT. It is far better to ask me, dear. It gives people a wrong idea of you.

LOUIS. But I want to spare your little fortune, and raise money on my own work. Dont be unhappy, love: I can easily earn enough to pay it all back. I shall have a one-man-show next season; and then there will be no more money troubles. [*Putting down his palette*] There! I mustnt do any more on that until it's bone-dry; so you may come down.

MRS DUBEDAT [*throwing off the drapery as she steps down, and revealing a plain frock of tussore silk*]. But you have promised, remember, seriously and faithfully, never to borrow again until you have first asked me.

LOUIS. Seriously and faithfully. [*Embracing her*] Ah, my love, how right you are! how much it means to me to have you by me to guard me against living too much in the skies. On my solemn oath, from this moment forth I will never borrow another penny.

MRS DUBEDAT [*delighted*]. Ah, thats right. Does his wicked worrying wife torment him and drag him down from the clouds. [*She kisses him.*] And now, dear, wont you finish those drawings for Maclean?

LOUIS. Oh, they dont matter. Ive got nearly all the money from him in advance.

MRS DUBEDAT. But, dearest, that is just the reason why you should finish them. He asked me the other day whether you really intended to finish them.

LOUIS. Confound his impudence! What the devil does he take me for? Now that just destroys all my interest in the beastly job. Ive a good mind to throw up the commission, and pay him back his money.

MRS DUBEDAT. We cant afford that, dear. You had better finish the drawings and have done with them. I think it is a mistake to accept money in advance.

LOUIS. But how are we to live?

MRS DUBEDAT. Well, Louis, it is getting hard enough as it is, now that they are all refusing to pay except on delivery.

LOUIS. Damn these fellows! they think of nothing and care for nothing but their wretched money.

MRS DUBEDAT. Still, if they pay us, they ought to have what they pay for.

LOUIS [*coaxing*]. There now: thats enough lecturing for to-day. Ive promised to be good, havnt I?

MRS DUBEDAT [*putting her arms round his neck*]. You know that I hate lecturing, and that I dont for a moment misunderstand you, dear, dont you?

LOUIS [*fondly*]. I know. I know. I'm a wretch; and youre an angel. Oh, if only I were strong enough to work steadily, I'd make my darling's house a temple, and her shrine a chapel more beautiful than was ever imagined. I cant pass the shops without wrestling with the temptation to go in and order all the really good things they have for you.

MRS DUBEDAT. I want nothing but you, dear. [*She gives him a caress, to which he responds so passionately that she disengages herself.*] There! be good now: remember that the doctors are coming this morning. Isnt it extraordinarily kind of them, Louis, to insist on coming? all of them, to consult about you?

LOUIS [*coolly*]. Oh, I daresay they think it will be a feather in their cap to cure a rising artist. They wouldnt come if it didnt amuse them, anyhow. [*Someone knocks at the door.*] I say: it's not time yet, is it?

MRS DUBEDAT. No, not quite yet.

LOUIS [*opening the door and finding* RIDGEON *there*]. Hello, Ridgeon. Delighted to see you. Come in.

MRS DUBEDAT [*shaking hands*]. It's so good of you to come, doctor.

LOUIS. Excuse this place, wont you? It's only a studio, you know: theres no real convenience for living here. But we pig along somehow, thanks to Jennifer.

MRS DUBEDAT. Now I'll run away. Perhaps later on, when youre finished with Louis, I may come in and hear the verdict. [RIDGEON *bows rather constrainedly.*] Would you rather I didnt?

RIDGEON. Not at all. Not at all.

[MRS DUBEDAT *looks at him, a little puzzled by his formal manner; then goes into the inner room.*]

LOUIS [*flippantly*]. I say: dont look so grave. Theres nothing awful going to happen, is there?

RIDGEON. No.

LOUIS. Thats all right. Poor Jennifer has been looking forward to your visit more than you can imagine. Shes taken quite a fancy to you, Ridgeon. The poor girl has nobody to talk to: I'm always painting. [*Taking up a sketch*] Theres a little sketch I made of her yesterday.

RIDGEON. She shewed it to me a fortnight ago when she first called on me.

LOUIS [*quite unabashed*]. Oh! did she? Good Lord! how time does fly! I could have sworn I'd only just finished it. It's hard for her here, seeing me piling up drawings and nothing coming in for them. Of course I shall sell them next year fast enough, after my one-man-show; but while the grass grows the steed starves. I hate to have her coming to me for money, and having none to give her. But what can I do?

RIDGEON. I understood that Mrs Dubedat had some property of her own.

LOUIS. Oh yes, a little; but how could a man with any decency of feeling touch that? Suppose I did, what would she have to live on if I died? I'm not insured: cant afford the premiums. [*Picking out another drawing*] How do you like that?

RIDGEON [*putting it aside*]. I have not come here to-day to look at your drawings. I have more serious and pressing business with you.

LOUIS. You want to sound my wretched lung. [*With impulsive candor*] My dear Ridgeon: I'll be frank with you. Whats the matter in this house isnt lungs but bills. It doesnt matter about me; but Jennifer has actually to economize in the matter of food. Youve made us feel that we can treat you as a friend. Will you lend us a hundred and fifty pounds?

RIDGEON. No.

LOUIS [*surprised*]. Why not?

RIDGEON. I am not a rich man; and I want every penny I can spare and more for my researches.

LOUIS. You mean youd want the money back again.

RIDGEON. I presume people sometimes have that in view when they lend money.

LOUIS [*after a moment's reflection*]. Well, I can manage that for you. I'll give you a cheque—or see here: theres no reason why you shouldnt have your bit too: I'll give you a cheque for two hundred.

RIDGEON. Why not cash the cheque at once without troubling me?

LOUIS. Bless you! they wouldnt cash it: I'm overdrawn as it is. No: the way to work it is this. I'll postdate the cheque next October. In October Jennifer's dividends come in. Well, you present the cheque. It will be returned marked "refer to drawer" or some rubbish of that sort. Then you can take it to Jennifer, and hint that if the cheque isnt taken up at once I shall be put in prison. She'll pay you like a shot. Youll clear £50; and youll do me a real service; for I do want the money very badly, old chap, I assure you.

RIDGEON [*staring at him*]. You see no objection to the transaction; and you anticipate none from me!

LOUIS. Well, what objection can there be? It's quite safe. I can convince you about the dividends.

RIDGEON. I mean on the score of its being—shall I say dishonorable?

LOUIS. Well, of course I shouldnt suggest it if I didnt want the money.

RIDGEON. Indeed! Well, you will have to find some other means of getting it.

LOUIS. Do you mean that you refuse?

RIDGEON. Do I mean—! [*Letting his indignation loose*] Of course I refuse, man. What do you take me for? How dare you make such a proposal to me?

LOUIS. Why not?

RIDGEON. Faugh! You would not understand me if I tried to explain. Now, once for all, I will not lend you a farthing. I should be glad to help your wife; but lending you money is no service to her.

LOUIS. Oh well, if youre in earnest about helping her, I'll tell you what you might do. You might get your patients to buy some of my things, or to give me a few portrait commissions.

RIDGEON. My patients call me in as a physician, not as a commercial traveller.

[*A knock at the door.* LOUIS *goes unconcernedly to open it, pursuing the subject as he goes.*]

LOUIS. But you must have great influence with them. You must know such lots of things about them—private things that they wouldnt like to have known. They wouldnt dare to refuse you.

RIDGEON [*exploding*]. Well, upon my—

[LOUIS *opens the door, and admits* SIR PATRICK, SIR RALPH, *and* WALPOLE.]

RIDGEON [*proceeding furiously*]. Walpole: Ive been here hardly ten minutes; and already he's tried to borrow £150 from me. Then he proposed that I should get the money for him by blackmailing his wife; and youve just interrupted him in the act of suggesting that I should blackmail my patients into sitting to him for their portraits.

LOUIS. Well, Ridgeon, if this is what you call being an honorable man! I spoke to you in confidence.

SIR PATRICK. We're all going to speak to you in confidence, young man.

WALPOLE [*hanging his hat on the only peg left vacant on the hat-stand*]. We shall make ourselves at home for half an hour, Dubedat. Dont be alarmed: youre a most fascinating chap; and we love you.

LOUIS. Oh, all right, all right. Sit down—anywhere you can. Take this chair, Sir Patrick. [*Indicating the one on the throne*] Up-z-z-z! [*Helping him up:* SIR PATRICK *grunts and enthrones himself.*] Here you are, B. B. [SIR RALPH *glares at the familiarity; but* LOUIS, *quite undisturbed, puts a big book and a sofa cushion on the dais, on* SIR PATRICK's *right; and* B. B. *sits down, under protest.*] Let me take your hat. [*He takes* B. B.'s *hat unceremoniously, and substitutes it for the cardinal's hat on the head of the lay figure, thereby ingeniously destroying the dignity of the conclave. He then draws the piano stool from the wall and offers it to* WALPOLE.] You dont mind this, Walpole, do you? [WALPOLE *accepts the stool, and puts his hand into his pocket for his cigaret case. Missing it, he is reminded of his loss.*]

WALPOLE. By the way, I'll trouble you for my cigaret case, if you dont mind?

LOUIS. What cigaret case?

WALPOLE. The gold one I lent you at the Star and Garter.

LOUIS [*surprised*]. Was that yours?

WALPOLE. Yes.

LOUIS. I'm awfully sorry, old chap. I wondered whose it was. I'm sorry to say this is all thats left of it. [*He hitches up his smock; produces a card from his waistcoat pocket; and hands it to Walpole.*]

WALPOLE. A pawn ticket!

LOUIS [*reassuringly*]. It's quite safe: he cant sell it for a year, you know. I say, my dear Walpole, I am sorry. [*He places his hand ingenuously on* WALPOLE'S *shoulder and looks frankly at him.*]

WALPOLE [*sinking on the stool with a gasp*]. Dont mention it. It adds to your fascination.

RIDGEON [*who has been standing near the easel*]. Before we go any further, you have a debt to pay, Mr Dubedat.

LOUIS. I have a precious lot of debts to pay, Ridgeon. I'll fetch you a chair. [*He makes for the inner door.*]

RIDGEON [*stopping him*]. You shall not leave the room until you pay it. It's a small one; and pay it you must and shall. I dont so much mind your borrowing £10 from one of my guests and £20 from the other—

WALPOLE. I walked into it, you know. I offered it.

RIDGEON. —they could afford it. But to clean poor Blenkinsop out of his last half-crown was damnable. I intend to give him that half-crown and to be in a position to pledge him my word that you paid it. I'll have that out of you, at all events.

B. B. Quite right, Ridgeon. Quite right. Come, young man! down with the dust. Pay up.

LOUIS. Oh, you neednt make such a fuss about it. Of course I'll pay it. I had no idea the poor fellow was hard up. I'm as shocked as any of you about it. [*Putting his hand into his pocket*] Here you are. [*Finding his pocket empty*] Oh, I say, I havnt any money on me just at present. Walpole: would you mind lending me half-a-crown just to settle his.

WALPOLE. Lend you half— [*His voice faints away.*]

LOUIS. Well, if you dont, Blenkinsop wont get it; for I havnt a rap: you may search my pockets if you like.

WALPOLE. Thats conclusive. [*He produces half-a-crown.*]

LOUIS [*passing it to* RIDGEON]. There! I'm really glad thats settled: it was the only thing that was on my conscience. Now I hope youre all satisfied.

SIR PATRICK. Not quite, Mr Dubedat. Do you happen to know a young woman named Minnie Tinwell?

LOUIS. Minnie! I should think I do; and Minnie knows me too. She's a really nice good girl, considering her station. Whats become of her?

WALPOLE. It's no use bluffing, Dubedat. Weve seen Minnie's marriage lines.

LOUIS [*coolly*]. Indeed? Have you seen Jennifer's?

RIDGEON [*rising in irrepressible rage*]. Do you dare insinuate that Mrs Dubedat is living with you without being married to you?

LOUIS. Why not?

B. B.		[*echoing him in*		Why not!
SIR PATRICK		*various tones of*		Why not!
RIDGEON		*scandalized*		Why not!
WALPOLE		*amazement*]		Why not!

LOUIS. Yes, why not? Lots of people do it: just as good people as you. Why dont you learn to think, instead of bleating and baahing like a lot of sheep when you come up against anything youre not accustomed to? [*Contemplating their amazed faces with a chuckle*] I say: I should like to draw the lot of you now: you do look jolly foolish. Especially you, Ridgeon. I had you that time, you know.

RIDGEON. How, pray?

LOUIS. Well, you set up to appreciate Jennifer, you know. And you despise me, dont you?

RIDGEON [*curtly*]. I loathe you. [*He sits down again on the sofa.*]

LOUIS. Just so. And yet you believe that Jennifer is a bad lot because you think I told you so.

RIDGEON. Were you lying?

LOUIS. No; but you were smelling out a scandal instead of keeping your mind clean and wholesome. I can just play with people like you. I only asked you had you seen Jennifer's marriage lines; and you concluded straight away that she hadnt got any. You dont know a lady when you see one.

B. B. [*majestically*]. What do you mean by that, may I ask?

LOUIS. Now, I'm only an immoral artist; but if youd told me that Jennifer wasnt married, I'd have had the gentlemanly feeling and artistic instinct to say that she carried her marriage certificate in her face and in her character. But you are all moral men; and Jennifer is only an artist's wife—probably a model; and morality consists in suspecting other people of not being legally married. Arnt you ashamed of yourselves? Can one of you look me in the face after it?

WALPOLE. It's very hard to look you in the face, Dubedat; you have such a dazzling cheek. What about Minnie Tinwell, eh?

LOUIS. Minnie Tinwell is a young woman who has had three weeks of glorious happiness in her poor little life, which is more than most girls in her position get, I can tell you. Ask her whether she'd take it back if she could. She's got her name into history, that girl. My little sketches of her will be fought for by collectors at Christie's.[1] She'll have a page in my biography. Pretty good, that, for a still-room[2] maid at a seaside hotel, I think. What have you fellows done for her to compare with that?

RIDGEON. We havnt trapped her into a mock marriage and deserted her.

LOUIS. No: you wouldnt have the pluck. But dont fuss yourselves. *I* didnt desert little Minnie. We spent all our money—

WALPOLE. All her money. Thirty pounds.

LOUIS. I said all our money: hers and mine too. Her thirty pounds didnt last three days. I had to borrow four times as much to spend on her. But I didnt grudge it; and she didnt grudge her few pounds either, the brave little lassie. When we were cleaned out, we'd had enough of it: you can hardly suppose that we were fit company for longer than that: I an artist, and she quite out of art and literature and refined living and everything else. There was no desertion, no misunderstanding, no police court or divorce court sensation for you moral chaps to lick your lips over at breakfast. We just said, Well, the money's gone: weve had a good time that can never be taken from us; so kiss; part good friends; and she back to service, and I back to my studio and my Jennifer, both the better and happier for our holiday.

WALPOLE. Quite a little poem, by George!

B. B. If you had been scientifically trained, Mr Dubedat, you would know how very seldom an actual case bears out a principle. In medical practice a man may die when, scientifically speaking, he ought to have lived. I have actually known a man die of a disease from which he was, scientifically speaking, immune. But that does not affect the fundamental truth of science. In just the same way, in moral cases, a man's behavior may be quite harmless and even beneficial, when he is morally behaving like a scoundrel. And he may do great harm when he is morally acting on the highest principles. But that does not affect the fundamental truth of morality.

SIR PATRICK. And it doesnt affect the criminal law on the subject of bigamy.

LOUIS. Oh bigamy! bigamy! bigamy! What a fascination any-

Christie's, the famous art auctioneer's in London.
still-room, a pantry.

thing connected with the police has for you all, you moralists! Ive proved to you that you were utterly wrong on the moral point: now I'm going to shew you that youre utterly wrong on the legal point; and I hope it will be a lesson to you not to be so jolly cocksure next time.

WALPOLE. Rot! You were married already when you married her; and that settles it.

LOUIS. Does it! Why cant you think? How do you know she wasnt married already too?

B. B.	[*all*	Walpole! Ridgeon!
RIDGEON	*crying*	This is beyond everything.
WALPOLE	*out*	Well, damn me!
SIR PATRICK	*together*]	You young rascal.

LOUIS [*ignoring their outcry*]. She was married to the steward of a liner. He cleared out and left her; and she thought, poor girl, that it was the law that if you hadnt heard of your husband for three years you might marry again. So as she was a thoroughly respectable girl and refused to have anything to say to me unless we were married I went through the ceremony to please her and to preserve her self-respect.

RIDGEON. Did you tell her you were already married?

LOUIS. Of course not. Dont you see that if she had known, she wouldnt have considered herself my wife? You dont seem to understand, somehow.

SIR PATRICK. You let her risk imprisonment in her ignorance of the law?

LOUIS. Well, *I* risked imprisonment for her sake. I could have been had up for it just as much as she. But when a man makes a sacrifice of that sort for a woman, he doesnt go and brag about it to her; at least, not if he's a gentleman.

WALPOLE. What are we to do with this daisy!

LOUIS [*impatiently*]. Oh, go and do whatever the devil you please. Put Minnie in prison. Put me in prison. Kill Jennifer with the disgrace of it all. And then, when youve done all the mischief you can, go to church and feel good about it. [*He sits down pettishly on the old chair at the easel, and takes up a sketching block, on which he begins to draw.*]

WALPOLE. He's got us.

SIR PATRICK [*grimly*]. He has.

B. B. But is he to be allowed to defy the criminal law of the land?

SIR PATRICK. The criminal law is no use to decent people. I

only helps blackguards to blackmail their families. What are we family doctors doing half our time but conspiring with the family solicitor to keep some rascal out of jail and some family out of disgrace?

B. B. But at least it will punish him.

SIR PATRICK. Oh yes: itll punish him. Itll punish not only him but everybody connected with him, innocent and guilty alike. Itll throw his board and lodging on our rates and taxes for a couple of years, and then turn him loose on us a more dangerous blackguard than ever. Itll put the girl in prison and ruin her: itll lay his wife's life waste. You may put the criminal law out of your head once for all: it's only fit for fools and savages.

LOUIS. Would you mind turning your face a little more this way, Sir Patrick. [SIR PATRICK *turns indignantly and glares at him.*] Oh, thats too much.

SIR PATRICK. Put down your foolish pencil, man; and think of your position. You can defy the laws made by men; but there are other laws to reckon with. Do you know that youre going to die?

LOUIS. We're all going to die, arnt we?

WALPOLE. We're not all going to die in six months.

LOUIS. How do you know?

[*This for B. B. is the last straw. He completely loses his temper and begins to walk excitedly about.*]

B. B. Upon my soul, I will not stand this. It is in questionable taste under any circumstances or in any company to harp on the subject of death; but it is a dastardly advantage to take of a medical man. [*Thundering at DUBEDAT*] I will not allow it, do you hear?

LOUIS. Well, I didnt begin it: you chaps did. It's always the way with the inartistic professions: when theyre beaten in argument they fall back on intimidation. I never knew a lawyer yet who didnt threaten to put me in prison sooner or later. I never knew a parson who didnt threaten me with damnation. And now you threaten me with death. With all your tall talk youve only one real trump in your hand, and thats Intimidation. Well, I'm not a coward; so it's no use with me.

B. B. [*advancing upon him*]. I'll tell you what you are, sir. Youre a scoundrel.

LOUIS. Oh, I dont mind you calling me a scoundrel a bit. It's only a word: a word that you dont know the meaning of. What is a scoundrel?

B. B. You are a scoundrel, sir.

LOUIS. Just so. What is a scoundrel? I am. What am I? A scoundrel. It's just arguing in a circle. And you imagine youre a man of science!

B. B. I—I—I—I have a good mind to take you by the scruff of your neck, you infamous rascal, and give you a sound thrashing.

LOUIS. I wish you would. Youd pay me something handsome to keep it out of court afterwards. [B. B., *baffled, flings away from him with a snort.*] Have you any more civilities to address to me in my own house? I should like to get them over before my wife comes back. [*He resumes his sketching.*]

RIDGEON. My mind's made up. When the law breaks down, honest men must find a remedy for themselves. I will not lift a finger to save this reptile.

B. B. That is the word I was trying to remember. Reptile.

WALPOLE. I cant help rather liking you, Dubedat. But you certainly are a thoroughgoing specimen.

SIR PATRICK. You know our opinion of you now, at all events.

LOUIS [*patiently putting down his pencil*]. Look here. All this is no good. You dont understand. You imagine that I'm simply an ordinary criminal.

WALPOLE. Not an ordinary one, Dubedat. Do yourself justice.

LOUIS. Well, youre on the wrong tack altogether. I'm not a criminal. All your moralizings have no value for me. I dont believe in morality. I'm a disciple of Bernard Shaw.

SIR PATRICK ⎱ ⎰ [*puzzled*]. Eh?

B. B. ⎰ ⎱ [*waving his hand as if the subject were now disposed of*]. Thats enough: I wish to hear no more.

LOUIS. Of course I havnt the ridiculous vanity to set up to be exactly a Superman;[1] but still, it's an ideal that I strive towards just as any other man strives towards his idea.

B. B. [*intolerant*]. Dont trouble to explain. I now understand you perfectly. Say no more, please. When a man pretends to discuss science, morals, and religion, and then avows himself a follower of a notorious and avowed anti-vaccinationist, there is nothing more to be said. [*Suddenly putting in an effusive saving clause in parenthesis to* RIDGEON] Not, my dear Ridgeon, that I believe in

---

[1] *Superman, a jocular reference to a concept in Shaw's play,* Man and Superman.

vaccination in the popular sense any more than you do: I neednt tell you that. But there are things that place a man socially; and anti-vaccination is one of them. [*He resumes his seat on the dais.*]

SIR PATRICK. Bernard Shaw? I never heard of him. He's a Methodist preacher, I suppose.

LOUIS [*scandalized*]. No, no. He's the most advanced man now living: he isnt anything.

SIR PATRICK. I assure you, young man, my father learnt the doctrine of deliverance from sin from John Wesley's[1] own lips before you or Mr Shaw were born. It used to be very popular as an excuse for putting sand in sugar and water in milk. Youre a sound Methodist, my lad; only you dont know it.

LOUIS [*seriously annoyed for the first time*]. It's an intellectual insult. I dont believe theres such a thing as sin.

SIR PATRICK. Well, sir, there are people who dont believe theres such a thing as disease either. They call themselves Christian Scientists, I believe. Theyll just suit your complaint. We can do nothing for you. [*He rises.*] Good afternoon to you.

LOUIS [*running to him piteously*]. Oh dont get up, Sir Patrick. Dont go. Please dont. I didnt mean to shock you, on my word. Do sit down again. Give me another chance. Two minutes more: thats all I ask.

SIR PATRICK [*surprised by this sign of grace, and a little touched*]. Well— [*He sits down.*]—

LOUIS [*gratefully*]. Thanks awfully.

SIR PATRICK [*continuing*].—I dont mind giving you two minutes more. But dont address yourself to me; for Ive retired from practice; and I dont pretend to be able to cure your complaint. Your life is in the hands of these gentlemen.

RIDGEON. Not in mine. My hands are full. I have no time and no means available for this case.

SIR PATRICK. What do you say, Mr Walpole?

WALPOLE. Oh, I'll take him in hand: I dont mind. I feel perfectly convinced that this is not a moral case at all: it's a physical one. Theres something abnormal about his brain. That means, probably, some morbid condition affecting the spinal cord. And that means the circulation. In short, it's clear to me that he's suffering from an obscure form of blood-poisoning, which is almost certainly due to

[1] *John Wesley (1703–1791), the founder of Methodism.*

an accumulation of ptomaines in the nuciform sac. I'll remove the sac—

LOUIS [*changing color*]. Do you mean, operate on me? Ugh! No, thank you.

WALPOLE. Never fear: you wont feel anything. Youll be under an anæsthetic, of course. And it will be extraordinarily interesting.

LOUIS. Oh, well, if it would interest you, and if it wont hurt, thats another matter. How much will you give me to let you do it?

WALPOLE [*rising indignantly*]. How much! What do you mean?

LOUIS. Well, you dont expect me to let you cut me up for nothing, do you?

WALPOLE. Will you paint my portrait for nothing?

LOUIS. No; but I'll give you the portrait when it's painted; and you can sell it afterwards for perhaps double the money. But I cant sell my nuciform sac when youve cut it out.

WALPOLE. Ridgeon: did you ever hear anything like this! [*To* LOUIS] Well, you can keep your nuciform sac, and your tubercular lung, and your diseased brain: Ive done with you. One would think I was not conferring a favor on the fellow! [*He returns to his stool in high dudgeon.*]

SIR PATRICK. That leaves only one medical man who has not withdrawn from your case, Mr Dubedat. You have nobody left to appeal to now but Sir Ralph Bloomfield Bonington.

WALPOLE. If I were you, B. B., I shouldnt touch him with a pair of tongs. Let him take his lungs to the Brompton Hospital. They wont cure him; but theyll teach him manners.

B. B. My weakness is that I have never been able to say No, even to the most thoroughly undeserving people. Besides, I am bound to say that I dont think it is possible in medical practice to go into the question of the value of the lives we save. Just consider, Ridgeon. Let me put it to you, Paddy. Clear your mind of cant, Walpole.

WALPOLE [*indignantly*]. My mind is perfectly clear of cant.

B. B. Quite so. Well now, look at my practice. It is what I suppose you would call a fashionable practice, a smart practice, a practice among the best people. You ask me to go into the question of whether my patients are of any use either to themselves or anyone else. Well, if you apply any scientific test known to me, you will achieve a reductio ad absurdum. You will be driven to the conclusion that the majority of them would be, as my friend Mr J. M. Barrie has tersely phrased it, better dead. Better dead.

There are exceptions, no doubt. For instance, there is the court, an essentially social-democratic institution, supported out of public funds by the public because the public wants it and likes it. My court patients are hard-working people who give satisfaction, undoubtedly. Then I have a duke or two whose estates are probably better managed than they would be in public hands. But as to most of the rest, if I once began to argue about them, unquestionably the verdict would be, Better dead. When they actually do die, I sometimes have to offer that consolation, thinly disguised, to the family. [*Lulled by the cadences of his own voice, he becomes drowsier and drowsier.*] The fact that they spend money so extravagantly on medical attendance really would not justify me in wasting my talents—such as they are—in keeping them alive. After all, if my fees are high, I have to spend heavily. My own tastes are simple: a camp bed, a couple of rooms, a crust, a bottle of wine; and I am happy and contented. My wife's tastes are perhaps more luxurious; but even she deplores an expenditure the sole object of which is to maintain the state my patients require from their medical attendant. The—er—er—er— [*Suddenly waking up*] I have lost the thread of these remarks. What was I talking about, Ridgeon?

RIDGEON. About Dubedat.

B. B. Ah yes. Precisely. Thank you. Dubedat, of course. Well, what is our friend Dubedat? A vicious and ignorant young man with a talent for drawing.

LOUIS. Thank you. Dont mind me.

B. B. But then, what are many of my patients? Vicious and ignorant young men without a talent for anything. If I were to stop to argue about their merits I should have to give up three-quarters of my practice. Therefore I have made it a rule not so to argue. Now, as an honorable man, having made that rule as to paying patients, can I make an exception as to a patient who, far from being a paying patient, may more fitly be described as a borrowing patient. No. I say No. Mr Dubedat: your moral character is nothing to me. I look at you from a purely scientific point of view. To me you are simply a field of battle in which an invading army of tubercle bacilli struggles with a patriotic force of phagocytes. Having made a promise to your wife, which my principles will not allow me to break, to stimulate those phagocytes, I will stimulate them. And I take no further responsibility. [*He flings himself back in his seat exhausted.*]

SIR PATRICK. Well, Mr Dubedat, as Sir Ralph has very kindly offered to take charge of your case, and as the two minutes I promised you are up, I must ask you to excuse me. [*He rises.*]

LOUIS. Oh, certainly. Ive quite done with you. [*Rising and holding up the sketch block*] There! While youve been talking, Ive been doing. What is there left of your moralizing? Only a little carbonic acid gas which makes the room unhealthy. What is there left of my work? That. Look at it.

[RIDGEON *rises to look at it.*]

SIR PATRICK [*who has come down to him from the throne*]. You young rascal, was it drawing me you were?

LOUIS. Of course. What else?

SIR PATRICK [*takes the drawing from him and grunts approvingly*]. Thats rather good. Dont you think so, Colly?

RIDGEON. Yes. So good that I should like to have it.

SIR PATRICK. Thank you; but I should like to have it myself. What d'ye think, Walpole?

WALPOLE [*rising and coming over to look*]. No, by Jove: *I* must have this.

LOUIS. I wish I could afford to give it to you, Sir Patrick. But I'd pay five guineas sooner than part with it.

RIDGEON. Oh, for that matter, I will give you six for it.

WALPOLE. Ten.

LOUIS. I think Sir Patrick is morally entitled to it, as he sat for it. May I send it to your house, Sir Patrick, for twelve guineas?

SIR PATRICK. Twelve guineas! Not if you were President of the Royal Academy, young man. [*He gives him back the drawing decisively and turns away, taking up his hat.*]

LOUIS [*to* B. B.]. Would you like to take it at twelve, Sir Ralph?

B. B. [*coming between* LOUIS *and* WALPOLE]. Twelve guineas? Thank you: I'll take it at that. [*He takes it and presents it to* SIR PATRICK.] Accept it from me, Paddy; and may you long be spared to contemplate it.

SIR PATRICK. Thank you. [*He puts the drawing into his hat.*]

B. B. I needn't settle with you now, Mr Dubedat: my fees will come to more than that. [*He also retrieves his hat.*]

LOUIS [*indignantly*]. Well, of all the mean—[*Words fail him!*] I'd let myself be shot sooner than do a thing like that. I consider youve stolen that drawing.

SIR PATRICK [*drily*]. So weve converted you to a belief in morality after all, eh?

LOUIS. Yah! [*To* WALPOLE] I'll do another one for you, Walpole, if youll let me have the ten you promised.

WALPOLE. Very good. I'll pay on delivery.

LOUIS. Oh! What do you take me for? Have you no confidence in my honor?

WALPOLE. None whatever.

LOUIS. Oh well, of course if you feel that way, you cant help it. Before you go, Sir Patrick, let me fetch Jennifer. I know she'd like to see you, if you dont mind. [*He goes to the inner door.*] And now, before she comes in, one word. Youve all been talking here pretty freely about me—in my own house too. *I* dont mind that: I'm a man and can take care of myself. But when Jennifer comes in, please remember that she's a lady, and that you are supposed to be gentlemen. [*He goes out.*]

WALPOLE. Well!!! [*He gives the situation up as indescribable, and goes for his hat.*]

RIDGEON. Damn his impudence!

B. B. I shouldnt be at all surprised to learn that he's well connected. Whenever I meet dignity and self-possession without any discoverable basis, I diagnose good family.

RIDGEON. Diagnose artistic genius, B. B. Thats what saves his self-respect.

SIR PATRICK. The world is made like that. The decent fellows are always being lectured and put out of countenance by the snobs.

B. B. [*altogether refusing to accept this*]. *I* am not out of countenance. I should like, by Jupiter, to see the man who could put me out of countenance. [*Jennifer comes in.*] Ah, Mrs Dubedat! And how are we to-day?

MRS DUBEDAT [*shaking hands with him*]. Thank you all so much for coming. [*She shakes* WALPOLE's *hand.*] Thank you, Sir Patrick [*She shakes* SIR PATRICK's.] Oh, life has been worth living since I have known you. Since Richmond I have not known a moment's fear. And it used to be nothing but fear. Wont you sit down and tell me the result of the consultation?

WALPOLE. I'll go, if you dont mind, Mrs Dubedat. I have an appointment. Before I go, let me say that I am quite agreed with my colleagues here as to the character of the case. As to the cause and the remedy, thats not my business: I'm only a surgeon; and these gentlemen are physicians and will advise you. I may have my own views: in fact I have them; and they are perfectly well known to my colleagues. If I am needed—and needed I shall be finally—they know where to find me; and I am always at your service. So for to-day, good-bye. [*He goes out, leaving Jennifer much puzzled by his unexpected withdrawal and formal manner.*]

SIR PATRICK. I also will ask you to excuse me, Mrs Dubedat.

RIDGEON [*anxiously*]. Are you going?

SIR PATRICK. Yes: I can be of no use here; and I must be getting back. As you know, maam, I'm not in practice now; and I shall not be in charge of the case. It rests between Sir Colenso Ridgeon and Sir Ralph Bloomfield Bonington. They know my opinion. Good afternoon to you, maam. [*He bows and makes for the door.*]

MRS DUBEDAT [*detaining him*]. Theres nothing wrong, is there? You dont think Louis is worse, do you?

SIR PATRICK. No: he's not worse. Just the same as at Richmond.

MRS DUBEDAT. Oh, thank you: you frightened me. Excuse me.

SIR PATRICK. Dont mention it, maam. [*He goes out.*]

B. B. Now, Mrs Dubedat, if I am to take the patient in hand—

MRS DUBEDAT [*apprehensively, with a glance at* RIDGEON]. You! But I thought that Sir Colenso—

B. B. [*beaming with the conviction that he is giving her a most gratifying surprise*]. My dear lady, your husband shall have Me.

MRS DUBEDAT. But—

B. B. Not a word: it is a pleasure to me, for your sake. Sir Colenso Ridgeon will be in his proper place, in the bacteriological laboratory. *I* shall be in my proper place, at the bedside. Your husband shall be treated exactly as if he were a member of the royal family. [MRS DUBEDAT *uneasy, again is about to protest.*] No gratitude: it would embarrass me, I assure you. Now, may I ask whether you are particularly tied to these apartments. Of course, the motor has annihilated distance; but I confess that if you were rather nearer to me, it would be a little more convenient.

MRS DUBEDAT. You see, this studio and flat are self-contained. I have suffered so much in lodgings. The servants are so frightfully dishonest.

B. B. Ah! Are they? Are they? Dear me!

MRS DUBEDAT. I was never accustomed to lock things up. And I missed so many small sums. At last a dreadful thing happened. I missed a five-pound note. It was traced to the housemaid; and she actually said Louis had given it to her. And he wouldnt let me do anything: he is so sensitive that these things drive him mad.

B. B. Ah—hm—ha—yes—say no more, Mrs Dubedat: you shall not move. If the mountain will not come to Mahomet, Mahomet must come to the mountain. Now I must be off. I will write and make an appointment. We shall begin stimulating the phagocytes on—on—probably on Tuesday next; but I will let you know. Depend on me; dont fret; eat regularly; sleep well; keep your spirits up; keep the patient cheerful; hope for the best; no tonic like a charming woman; no medicine like cheerfulness; no resource like science; good-bye, good-bye, good-bye. [*Having shaken hands— she being too overwhelmed to speak—he goes out, stopping to say to* RIDGEON] On Tuesday morning send me down a tube of some really stiff anti-toxin. Any kind will do. Dont forget. Good-bye, Colly. [*He goes out.*]

RIDGEON. You look quite discouraged again. [*She is almost in tears.*] Whats the matter? Are you disappointed?

MRS DUBEDAT. I know I ought to be very grateful. Believe me, I am very grateful. But—but—

RIDGEON. Well?

MRS DUBEDAT. I had set my heart on your curing Louis.

RIDGEON. Well, Sir Ralph Bloomfield Bonington—

MRS DUBEDAT. Yes, I know, I know. It is a great privilege to have him. But oh, I wish it had been you. I know it's unreasonable; I cant explain; but I had such a strong instinct that you would cure him. I dont—I cant feel the same about Sir Ralph. You promised me. Why did you give Louis up?

RIDGEON. I explained to you. I cannot take another case.

MRS DUBEDAT. But at Richmond?

RIDGEON. At Richmond I thought I could make room for one more case. But my old friend Dr Blenkinsop claimed that place. His lung is attacked.

MRS DUBEDAT [*attaching no importance whatever to* BLENKINSOP]. Do you mean that elderly man—that rather silly—

RIDGEON [*sternly*]. I mean the gentleman that dined with us: an excellent and honest man, whose life is as valuable as anyone else's. I have arranged that I shall take his case, and that Sir Ralph Bloomfield Bonington shall take Mr Dubedat's.

MRS DUBEDAT [*turning indignantly on him*]. I see what it is. Oh! it is envious, mean, cruel. And I thought that you would be above such a thing.

RIDGEON. What do you mean?

MRS DUBEDAT. Oh, do you think I dont know? do you think it

has never happened before? Why does everybody turn against him? Can you not forgive him for being superior to you? for being cleverer? for being braver? for being a great artist?

RIDGEON. Yes: I can forgive him for all that.

MRS DUBEDAT. Well, have you anything to say against him? I have challenged everyone who has turned against him—challenged them face to face to tell me any wrong thing he has done, any ignoble thought he has uttered. They have always confessed that they could not tell me one. I challenge you now. What do you accuse him of?

RIDGEON. I am like all the rest. Face to face, I cannot tell you one thing against him.

MRS DUBEDAT [*not satisfied*]. But your manner is changed. And you have broken your promise to me to make room for him as your patient.

RIDGEON. I think you are a little unreasonable. You have had the very best medical advice in London for him; and his case has been taken in hand by a leader of the profession. Surely—

MRS DUBEDAT. Oh, it is so cruel to keep telling me that. It seems all right; and it puts me in the wrong. But I am not in the wrong. I have faith in you; and I have no faith in the others. We have seen so many doctors: I have come to know at last when they are only talking and can do nothing. It is different with you. I feel that you know. You must listen to me, doctor. [*With sudden misgiving*] Am I offending you by calling you doctor instead of remembering your title?

RIDGEON. Nonsense. I am a doctor. But mind you dont call Walpole one.

MRS DUBEDAT. I dont care about Mr Walpole: it is you who must befriend me. Oh, will you please sit down and listen to me just for a few minutes. [*He assents with a grave inclination, and sits on the sofa. She sits on the easel chair.*] Thank you. I wont keep you long; but I must tell you the whole truth. Listen. I know Louis as nobody else in the world knows him or ever can know him. I am his wife. I know he has little faults: impatiences, sensitivenesses, even little selfishnesses that are too trivial for him to notice. I know that he sometimes shocks people about money because he is so utterly above it, and cant understand the value ordinary people set on it. Tell me: did he—did he borrow any money from you?

RIDGEON. He asked me for some—once.

MRS DUBEDAT [*tears again in her eyes*]. Oh, I am so sorry—so sorry. But he will never do it again: I pledge you my word for that. He has given me his promise: here in this room just before you came; and he is incapable of breaking his word. That was his only real weakness; and now it is conquered and done with for ever.

RIDGEON. Was that really his only weakness?

MRS DUBEDAT. He is perhaps sometimes weak about women, because they adore him so, and are always laying traps for him. And of course when he says he doesnt believe in morality, ordinary pious people think he must be wicked. You can understand, cant you, how all this starts a great deal of gossip about him, and gets repeated until even good friends get set against him?

RIDGEON. Yes: I understand.

MRS DUBEDAT. Oh, if you only knew the other side of him as I do! Do you know, doctor, that if Louis dishonored himself by a really bad action, I should kill myself.

RIDGEON. Come! dont exaggerate.

MRS DUBEDAT. I should. You dont understand that, you east country people.

RIDGEON. You did not see much of the world in Cornwall, did you?

MRS DUBEDAT [*naïvely*]. Oh yes. I saw a great deal every day of the beauty of the world—more than you ever see here in London. But I saw very few people, if that is what you mean. I was an only child.

RIDGEON. That explains a good deal.

MRS DUBEDAT. I had a great many dreams; but at last they all came to one dream.

RIDGEON [*with half a sigh*]. Yes, the usual dream.

MRS DUBEDAT [*surprised*]. Is it usual?

RIDGEON. As I guess. You havnt yet told me what it was.

MRS DUBEDAT. I didnt want to waste myself. I could do nothing myself; but I had a little property and I could help with it. I had even a little beauty: dont think me vain for knowing it. I knew that men of genius always had a terrible struggle with poverty and neglect at first. My dream was to save one of them from that, and bring some charm and happiness into his life. I prayed Heaven to send me one. I firmly believe that Louis was guided to me in answer to my prayer. He was no more like the other men I had met than the Thames Embankment is like our Cornish coasts. He saw everything that I saw, and drew it for me. He understood everything. He came to me like a child. Only fancy, doctor: he never even wanted to marry me: he never thought of the things other men think of! I had to propose it myself. Then he said he had no money. When I told him I had some, he said "Oh, all right," just like a boy. He is still like that, quite unspoiled, a man in his thoughts, a great poet and artist in his dreams, and a child in his ways. I gave him myself and all I had that he might grow to his full height with plenty of sunshine. If I lost faith in him, it would mean the wreck and failure of my life. I should go back to Cornwall and die. I could show you the very cliff I should jump off. You must cure him: you must make him quite well again for me. I know that you can do it and that nobody else can. I implore you not to refuse what I am going to ask you to do. Take Louis yourself; and let Sir Ralph cure Dr Blenkinsop.

RIDGEON [*slowly*]. Mrs Dubedat: do you really believe in my knowledge and skill as you say you do?

MRS DUBEDAT. Absolutely. I do not give my trust by halves.

RIDGEON. I know that. Well, I am going to test you—hard. Will you believe me when I tell you that I understand what you have just told me; that I have no desire but to serve you in the most faithful friendship; and that your hero must be preserved to you.

MRS DUBEDAT. Oh forgive me. Forgive what I said. You will preserve him to me.

RIDGEON. At all hazards. [*She kisses his hand. He rises hastily.*] No: you have not heard the rest. [*She rises too.*] You must believe me when I tell you that the one chance of preserving the hero lies in Louis being in the care of Sir Ralph.

MRS DUBEDAT [*firmly*]. You say so: I have no more doubt: I believe you. Thank you.

RIDGEON. Good-bye. [*She takes his hand.*] I hope this will be a lasting friendship.

MRS DUBEDAT. It will. My friendships end only with death.

RIDGEON. Death ends everything, doesnt it? Good-bye. [*With a sigh and a look of pity at her which she does not understand, he goes.*]

act 4

The studio. The easel is pushed back to the wall. Cardinal Death, holding his scythe and hour-glass like a sceptre and

globe, sits on the throne. On the hat-stand hang the hats of
SIR PATRICK *and* BLOOMFIELD BONINGTON. WALPOLE, *just
come in, is hanging up his beside them. There is a knock.
He opens the door and finds* RIDGEON *there.*

WALPOLE. Hallo, Ridgeon!
   [*They come into the middle of the room together, taking off
   their gloves.*]
RIDGEON. Whats the matter? Have you been sent for, too?
WALPOLE. Weve all been sent for. Ive only just come: I havnt
seen him yet. The charwoman says that old Paddy Cullen has
been here with B. B. for the last half-hour. [SIR PATRICK, *with bad
news in his face, enters from the inner room.*] Well: whats up?
SIR PATRICK. Go in and see. B. B. is in there with him.
   [WALPOLE *goes.* RIDGEON *is about to follow him; but* SIR
   PATRICK *stops him with a look.*]
RIDGEON. What has happened?
SIR PATRICK. Do you remember Jane Marsh's arm?
RIDGEON. Is that whats happened?
SIR PATRICK. Thats whats happened. His lung has gone like
Jane's arm. I never saw such a case. He has got through three
months galloping consumption in three days.
RIDGEON. B. B. got in on the negative phase.
SIR PATRICK. Negative or positive, the lad's done for. He wont
last out the afternoon. He'll go suddenly: Ive often seen it.
RIDGEON. So long as he goes before his wife finds him out, *I*
dont care. I fully expected this.
SIR PATRICK [*drily*]. It's a little hard on a lad to be killed
because his wife has too high an opinion of him. Fortunately few
of us are in any danger of that.
   [SIR RALPH *comes from the inner room and hastens between
   them, humanely concerned, but professionally elate and com-
   municative.*]
B. B. Ah, here you are, Ridgeon. Paddy's told you, of course.
RIDGEON. Yes.
B. B. It's an enormously interesting case. You know, Colly, by
Jupiter, if I didnt know as a matter of scientific fact that I'd been
stimulating the phagocytes, I should say I'd been stimulating the
other things. What is the explanation of it, Sir Patrick? How do
you account for it, Ridgeon? Have we over-stimulated the phagocytes? Have they not only eaten up the bacilli, but attacked and

destroyed the red corpuscles as well? a possibility suggested by the patient's pallor. Nay, have they finally begun to prey on the lungs themselves? Or on one another? I shall write a paper about this case.

[WALPOLE *comes back, very serious, even shocked. He comes between* B. B. *and* RIDGEON.]

WALPOLE. Whew! B. B.: youve done it this time.

B. B. What do you mean?

WALPOLE. Killed him. The worst case of neglected blood-poisoning I ever saw. It's too late now to do anything. He'd die under the anæsthetic.

B. B. [*offended*]. Killed! Really, Walpole, if your monomania were not well known, I should take such an expression very seriously.

SIR PATRICK. Come come! When youve both killed as many people as I have in my time youll feel humble enough about it. Come and look at him, Colly.

[RIDGEON *and* SIR PATRICK *go into the inner room.*]

WALPOLE. I apologize, B. B. But it's blood-poisoning.

B. B. [*recovering his irresistible good nature*]. My dear Walpole, everything is blood-poisoning. But upon my soul, I shall not use any of that stuff of Ridgeon's again. What made me so sensitive about what you said just now is that, strictly between ourselves, Ridgeon has cooked our young friend's goose.

[JENNIFER, *worried and distressed, but always gentle, comes between them from the inner room. She wears a nurse's apron.*]

MRS DUBEDAT. Sir Ralph: what am I to do? That man who insisted on seeing me, and sent in word that his business was important to Louis, is a newspaper man. A paragraph appeared in the paper this morning saying that Louis is seriously ill; and this man wants to interview him about it. How can people be so brutally callous?

WALPOLE [*moving vengefully towards the door*]. You just leave me to deal with him!

MRS DUBEDAT [*stopping him*]. But Louis insists on seeing him: he almost began to cry about it. And he says he cant bear his room any longer. He says he wants to—[*she struggles with a sob*]—to die in his studio. Sir Patrick says let him have his way: it can do no harm. What shall we do?

B. B. [*encouragingly*]. Why, follow Sir Patrick's excellent advice, of course. As he says, it can do him no harm; and it will no doubt do him good—a great deal of good. He will be much the better for it.

MRS DUBEDAT [*a little cheered*]. Will you bring the man up here, Mr Walpole, and tell him that he may see Louis, but that he mustnt exhaust him by talking? [WALPOLE *nods and goes out by the outer door.*] Sir Ralph: dont be angry with me; but Louis will die if he stays here. I must take him to Cornwall. He will recover there.

B. B. [*brightening wonderfully, as if* DUBEDAT *were already saved*]. Cornwall! The very place for him! Wonderful for the lungs. Stupid of me not to think of it before. You are his best physician after all, dear lady. An inspiration! Cornwall: of course, yes, yes, yes.

MRS DUBEDAT [*comforted and touched*]. You are so kind, Sir Ralph. But dont give me much hope or I shall cry; and Louis cant bear that.

B. B. [*gently putting his protecting arm round her shoulders*]. Then let us come back to him and help to carry him in. Cornwall! of course, of course. The very thing! [*They go together into the bedroom.*]

[WALPOLE *returns with* THE NEWSPAPER MAN, *a cheerful, affable young man who is disabled for ordinary business pursuits by a congenital erroneousness which renders him incapable of describing accurately anything he sees, or understanding or reporting accurately anything he hears. As the only employment in which these defects do not matter is journalism (for a newspaper, not having to act on its descriptions and reports, but only to sell them to idly curious people, has nothing but honor to lose by inaccuracy and unveracity), he has perforce become a journalist, and has to keep up an air of high spirits through a daily struggle with his own illiteracy and the precariousness of his employment. He has a notebook, and occasionally attempts to make a note; but as he cannot write shorthand, and does not write with ease in any hand, he generally gives it up as a bad job before he succeeds in finishing a sentence.*]

THE NEWSPAPER MAN [*looking round and making indecisive attempts at notes*]. This is the studio, I suppose.

WALPOLE. Yes.

THE NEWSPAPER MAN [*wittily*]. Where he has his models, eh?

WALPOLE [*grimly irresponsive*]. No doubt.

THE NEWSPAPER MAN. Cubicle, you said it was?

WALPOLE. Yes, tubercle.

THE NEWSPAPER MAN. Which way do you spell it: is it c-u-b-i-c-a-l or c-l-e?

WALPOLE. Tubercle, man, not cubical. [*Spelling it for him*] T-u-b-e-r-c-l-e.

THE NEWSPAPER MAN. Oh! tubercle. Some disease, I suppose. I thought he had consumption. Are you one of the family or the doctor?

WALPOLE. I'm neither one nor the other. I am Mister Cutler Walpole. Put that down. Then put down Sir Colenso Ridgeon.

THE NEWSPAPER MAN. Pigeon?

WALPOLE. Ridgeon. [*Contemptuously snatching his book*] Here: youd better let me write the names down for you: youre sure to get them wrong. That comes of belonging to an illiterate profession, with no qualifications and no public register.[1] [*He writes the particulars.*]

THE NEWSPAPER MAN. Oh, I say: you have got your knife into us, havnt you?

WALPOLE [*vindictively*]. I wish I had: I'd make a better man of you. Now attend. [*Shewing him the book*] These are the names of the three doctors. This is the patient. This is the address. This is the name of the disease. [*He shuts the book with a snap which makes the journalist blink, and returns it to him.*] Mr Dubedat will be brought in here presently. He wants to see you because he doesnt know how bad he is. We'll allow you to wait a few minutes to humor him; but if you talk to him, out you go. He may die at any moment.

THE NEWSPAPER MAN [*interested*]. Is he as bad as that? I say: I am in luck to-day. Would you mind letting me photograph you? [*He produces a camera.*] Could you have a lancet or something in your hand?

WALPOLE. Put it up. If you want my photograph you can get it in Baker Street in any of the series of celebrities.

THE NEWSPAPER MAN. But theyll want to be paid. If you wouldnt mind [*fingering the camera*]—?

WALPOLE. I would. Put it up, I tell you. Sit down there and be quiet.

[1] *no qualification . . . register,* that is, no official examination and licensing.

[THE NEWSPAPER MAN *quickly sits down on the piano stool as* DUBEDAT, *in an invalid's chair, is wheeled in by* MRS DUBEDAT *and* SIR RALPH. *They place the chair between the dais and the sofa, where the easel stood before.* LOUIS *is not changed as a robust man would be; and he is not scared. His eyes look larger; and he is so weak physically that he can hardly move, lying on his cushions with complete languor; but his mind is active: it is making the most of his condition, finding voluptuousness in languor and drama in death. They are all impressed, in spite of themselves, except* RIDGEON, *who is implacable.* B. B. *is entirely sympathetic and forgiving.* RIDGEON *follows the chair with a tray of milk and stimulants.* SIR PATRICK, *who accompanies him, takes the tea-table from the corner and places it behind the chair for the tray.* B. B. *takes the easel chair and places it for* JENNIFER *at* DUBEDAT's *side, next the dais, from which the lay figure ogles the dying artist.* B. B. *then returns to* DUBEDAT's *left.* JENNIFER *sits.* WALPOLE *sits down on the edge of the dais.* RIDGEON *stands near him.*]

LOUIS [*blissfully*]. Thats happiness. To be in a studio! Happiness!

MRS DUBEDAT. Yes, dear. Sir Patrick says you may stay here as long as you like.

LOUIS. Jennifer.

MRS DUBEDAT. Yes, my darling.

LOUIS. Is the newspaper man here?

THE NEWSPAPER MAN [*glibly*]. Yes, Mr Dubedat: I'm here, at your service. I represent the press. I thought you might like to let us have a few words about—about—er—well, a few words on your illness, and your plans for the season.

LOUIS. My plans for the season are very simple. I'm going to die.

MRS DUBEDAT [*tortured*]. Louis—dearest—

LOUIS. My darling: I'm very weak and tired. Dont put on me the horrible strain of pretending that I dont know. Ive been lying there listening to the doctors—laughing to myself. They know. Dearest: dont cry. It makes you ugly; and I cant bear that. [*She dries her eyes and recovers herself with a proud effort.*] I want you to promise me something.

MRS DUBEDAT. Yes, yes: you know I will. [*Imploringly*] Only, my love, my love, dont talk: it will waste your strength.

LOUIS. No: it will only use it up. Ridgeon: give me something to

keep me going for a few minutes—not one of your confounded
anti-toxins, if you dont mind. I have some things to say before I go.

RIDGEON [*looking at* SIR PATRICK]. I suppose it can do no harm?
[*He pours out some spirit, and is about to add soda water when*
SIR PATRICK *corrects him.*]

SIR PATRICK. In milk. Dont set him coughing.

LOUIS [*after drinking*]. Jennifer.

MRS DUBEDAT. Yes, dear.

LOUIS. If theres one thing I hate more than another, it's a widow.
Promise me that youll never be a widow.

MRS DUBEDAT. My dear, what do you mean?

LOUIS. I want you to look beautiful. I want people to see in
your eyes that you were married to me. The people in Italy used
to point at Dante and say "There goes the man who has been in
hell." I want them to point at you and say "There goes a woman
who has been in heaven." It has been heaven, darling, hasnt it—
sometimes?

MRS DUBEDAT. Oh yes, yes. Always, always.

LOUIS. If you wear black and cry, people will say "Look at that
miserable woman: her husband made her miserable."

MRS DUBEDAT. No, never. You are the light and the blessing of
my life. I never lived until I knew you.

LOUIS [*his eyes glistening*]. Then you must always wear beautiful dresses and splendid magic jewels. Think of all the wonderful
pictures I shall never paint. [*She wins a terrible victory over a sob.*]
Well, you must be transfigured with all the beauty of those pictures. Men must get such dreams from seeing you as they never
could get from any daubing with paints and brushes. Painters
must paint you as they never painted any mortal woman before.
There must be a great tradition of beauty, a great atmosphere
of wonder and romance. That is what men must always think of
when they think of me. That is the sort of immortality I want.
You can make that for me, Jennifer. There are lots of things you
dont understand that every woman in the street understands; but
you can understand that and do it as nobody else can. Promise me
that immortality. Promise me you will not make a little hell of
crape and crying and undertaker's horrors and withering flowers
and all that vulgar rubbish.

MRS DUBEDAT. I promise. But all that is far off, dear. You are
to come to Cornwall with me and get well. Sir Ralph says so.

LOUIS. Poor old B. B.!

B. B. [*affected to tears, turns away and whispers to* SIR PATRICK]. Poor fellow! Brain going.

LOUIS. Sir Patrick's there, isnt he?

SIR PATRICK. Yes, yes. I'm here.

LOUIS. Sit down, wont you? It's a shame to keep you standing about.

SIR PATRICK. Yes, yes. Thank you. All right.

LOUIS. Jennifer.

MRS DUBEDAT. Yes, dear.

LOUIS [*with a strange look of delight*]. Do you remember the burning bush?

MRS DUBEDAT. Yes, yes. Oh, my dear, how it strains my heart to remember it now!

LOUIS. Does it? It fills me with joy. Tell them about it.

MRS DUBEDAT. It was nothing—only that once in my old Cornish home we lit the first fire of the winter; and when we looked through the window we saw the flames dancing in a bush in the garden.

LOUIS. Such a color! Garnet color. Waving like silk. Liquid lovely flame flowing up through the bay leaves, and not burning them. Well, I shall be a flame like that. I'm sorry to disappoint the poor little worms; but the last of me shall be the flame in the burning bush. Whenever you see the flame, Jennifer, that will be me. Promise me that I shall be burnt.

MRS DUBEDAT. Oh, if I might be with you, Louis!

LOUIS. No: you must always be in the garden when the bush flames. You are my hold on the world: you are my immortality. Promise.

MRS DUBEDAT. I'm listening. I shall not forget. You know that I promise.

LOUIS. Well, thats about all; except that you are to hang my pictures at the one-man show. I can trust your eye. You wont let anyone else touch them.

MRS DUBEDAT. You can trust me.

LOUIS. Then theres nothing more to worry about, is there? Give me some more of that milk. I'm fearfully tired; but if I stop talking I shant begin again. [SIR RALPH *gives him a drink. He takes it and looks up quaintly.*] I say, B. B., do you think anything would stop you talking?

B. B. [*almost unmanned*]. He confuses me with you, Paddy. Poor fellow! Poor fellow!

LOUIS [*musing*]. I used to be awfully afraid of death; but now it's come I have no fear; and I'm perfectly happy. Jennifer.

MRS DUBEDAT. Yes, dear?

LOUIS. I'll tell you a secret. I used to think that our marriage was all an affectation, and that I'd break loose and run away some day. But now that I'm going to be broken loose whether I like it or not, I'm perfectly fond of you, and perfectly satisfied because I'm going to live as part of you and not as my troublesome self.

MRS DUBEDAT [*heartbroken*]. Stay with me, Louis. Oh, dont leave me, dearest.

LOUIS. Not that I'm selfish. With all my faults I dont think Ive ever been really selfish. No artist can: Art is too large for that. You will marry again, Jennifer.

MRS DUBEDAT. Oh, how can you, Louis?

LOUIS [*insisting childishly*]. Yes, because people who have found marriage happy always marry again. Ah, *I* shant be jealous. [*Slyly*] But dont talk to the other fellow too much about me: he wont like it. [*Almost chuckling*] *I* shall be your lover all the time; but it will be a secret from him, poor devil!

SIR PATRICK. Come! youve talked enough. Try to rest awhile.

LOUIS [*wearily*]. Yes: I'm fearfully tired; but I shall have a long rest presently. I have something to say to you fellows. Youre all there, arnt you? I'm too weak to see anything but Jennifer's bosom. That promises rest.

RIDGEON. We are all here.

LOUIS [*startled*]. That voice sounded devilish. Take care, Ridgeon: my ears hear things that other people's ears cant. Ive been thinking—thinking. I'm cleverer than you imagine.

SIR PATRICK [*whispering to* RIDGEON]. Youve got on his nerves, Colly. Slip out quietly.

RIDGEON [*apart to* SIR PATRICK]. Would you deprive the dying actor of his audience?

LOUIS [*his face lighting up faintly with mischievous glee*]. I heard that, Ridgeon. That was good. Jennifer, dear: be kind to Ridgeon always; because he was the last man who amused me.

RIDGEON [*relentless*]. Was I?

LOUIS. But it's not true. It's you who are still on the stage. I'm half way home already.

MRS DUBEDAT [*to* RIDGEON]. What did you say?

LOUIS [*answering for him*]. Nothing, dear. Only one of those little secrets that men keep among themselves. Well, all you chaps have thought pretty hard things of me, and said them.

B. B. [*quite overcome*]. No, no, Dubedat. Not at all.

LOUIS. Yes, you have. I know what you all think of me. Dont imagine I'm sore about it. I forgive you.

WALPOLE [*involuntarily*]. Well, damn me! [*Ashamed*] I beg your pardon.

LOUIS. That was old Walpole, I know. Dont grieve, Walpole. I'm perfectly happy. I'm not in pain. I dont want to live. Ive escaped from myself. I'm in heaven, immortal in the heart of my beautiful Jennifer. I'm not afraid, and not ashamed. [*Reflectively, puzzling it out for himself weakly*] I know that in an accidental sort of way, struggling through the unreal part of life, I havnt always been able to live up to my ideal. But in my own real world I have never done anything wrong, never denied my faith, never been untrue to myself. Ive been threatened and blackmailed and insulted and starved. But Ive played the game. Ive fought the good fight. And now it's all over, theres an indescribable peace. [*He feebly folds his hands and utters his creed*] I believe in Michael Angelo, Velasquez, and Rembrandt; in the might of design, the mystery of color, the redemption of all things by Beauty everlasting, and the message of Art that has made these hands blessed. Amen. Amen. [*He closes his eyes and lies still.*]

MRS DUBEDAT [*breathless*]. Louis: are you—

[WALPOLE *rises and comes quickly to see whether he is dead.*]

LOUIS. Not yet, dear. Very nearly, but not yet. I should like to rest my head on your bosom; only it would tire you.

MRS DUBEDAT. No, no, no, darling: how could you tire me? [*She lifts him so that he lies in her bosom.*]

LOUIS. Thats good. Thats real.

MRS DUBEDAT. Dont spare me, dear. Indeed indeed you will not tire me. Lean on me with all your weight.

LOUIS [*with a sudden half return of his normal strength and comfort*]. Jinny Gwinny: I think I shall recover after all.

[SIR PATRICK *looks significantly at* RIDGEON, *mutely warning him that this is the end.*]

MRS DUBEDAT [*hopefully*]. Yes, yes: you shall.

LOUIS. Because I suddenly want to sleep. Just an ordinary sleep.

MRS DUBEDAT [*rocking him*]. Yes, dear. Sleep. [*He seems to go to sleep.* WALPOLE *makes another movement. She protests.*]

Sh-sh: please dont disturb him. [*His lips move.*] What did you say, dear? [*In great distress*] I cant listen without moving him. [*His lips move again:* WALPOLE *bends down and listens.*]

WALPOLE. He wants to know is the newspaper man here.

THE NEWSPAPER MAN [*excited; for he has been enjoying himself enormously*]. Yes, Mr Dubedat. Here I am.

[WALPOLE *raises his hand warningly to silence him.* SIR RALPH *sits down quietly on the sofa and frankly buries his face in his handkerchief.*]

MRS DUBEDAT [*with great relief*]. Oh thats right, dear: dont spare me: lean with all your weight on me. Now you are really resting.

[SIR PATRICK *quickly comes forward and feels* LOUIS' *pulse; then takes him by the shoulders.*]

SIR PATRICK. Let me put him back on the pillow, maam. He will be better so.

MRS DUBEDAT [*piteously*]. Oh no, please, please, doctor. He is not tiring me; and he will be so hurt when he wakes if he finds I have put him away.

SIR PATRICK. He will never wake again. [*He takes the body from her and replaces it in the chair.* RIDGEON, *unmoved, lets down the back and makes a bier of it.*]

MRS DUBEDAT [*who has unexpectedly sprung to her feet, and stands dry-eyed and stately*]. Was that death?

WALPOLE. Yes.

MRS DUBEDAT [*with complete dignity*]. Will you wait for me a moment. I will come back. [*She goes out.*]

WALPOLE. Ought we to follow her? Is she in her right senses?

SIR PATRICK [*with quiet conviction*]. Yes. Shes all right. Leave her alone. She'll come back.

RIDGEON [*callously*]. Let us get this thing out of the way before she comes.

B. B. [*rising, shocked*]. My dear Colly! The poor lad! He died splendidly.

SIR PATRICK. Aye! that is how the wicked die.

> For there are no bands in their death;
> But their strength is firm:
> They are not in trouble as other men.

No matter: it's not for us to judge. He's in another world now.

WALPOLE. Borrowing his first five-pound note there, probably.

RIDGEON. I said the other day that the most tragic thing in the world is a sick doctor. I was wrong. The most tragic thing in the world is a man of genius who is not also a man of honor.

[RIDGEON *and* WALPOLE *wheel the chair into the recess.*]

THE NEWSPAPER MAN [*to* SIR RALPH]. I thought it shewed a very nice feeling, his being so particular about his wife going into proper mourning for him and making her promise never to marry again.

B. B. [*impressively*]. Mrs Dubedat is not in a position to carry the interview any further. Neither are we.

SIR PATRICK. Good afternoon to you.

THE NEWSPAPER MAN. Mrs Dubedat said she was coming back.

B. B. After you have gone.

THE NEWSPAPER MAN. Do you think she would give me a few words on How It Feels to be a Widow? Rather a good title for an article, isnt it?

B. B. Young man: if you wait until Mrs Dubedat comes back, you will be able to write an article on How It Feels to be Turned Out of the House.

THE NEWSPAPER MAN [*unconvinced*]. You think she'd rather not—

B. B. [*cutting him short*]. Good day to you. [*Giving him a visiting-card*] Mind you get my name correctly. Good day.

THE NEWSPAPER MAN. Good day. Thank you. [*Vaguely trying to read the card*] Mr—

B. B. No, not Mister. This is your hat, I think. [*Giving it to him*] Gloves? No, of course: no gloves. Good day to you. [*He edges him out at last; shuts the door on him; and returns to* SIR PATRICK *as* RIDGEON *and* WALPOLE *come back from the recess,* WALPOLE *crossing the room to the hat-stand, and* RIDGEON *coming between* SIR RALPH *and* SIR PATRICK.] Poor fellow! Poor young fellow! How well he died! I feel a better man, really.

SIR PATRICK. When youre as old as I am, youll know that it matters very little how a man dies. What matters is, how he lives. Every fool that runs his nose against a bullet is a hero nowadays, because he dies for his country. Why dont he live for it to some purpose?

B. B. No, please, Paddy: dont be hard on the poor lad. Not now, not now. After all, was he so bad? He had only two failings: money and women. Well, let us be honest. Tell the truth, Paddy. Dont be hypocritical, Ridgeon. Throw off the mask, Walpole. Are these two matters so well arranged at present that a disregard of the usual arrangements indicates real depravity?

WALPOLE. I dont mind his disregarding the usual arrangements. Confound the usual arrangements! To a man of science theyre beneath contempt both as to money and women. What I mind is his disregarding everything except his own pocket and his own fancy. He didnt disregard the usual arrangements when they paid him. Did he give us his pictures for nothing? Do you suppose he'd have hesitated to blackmail me if I'd compromised myself with his wife? Not he.

SIR PATRICK. Dont waste your time wrangling over him. A blackguard's a blackguard; an honest man's an honest man; and neither of them will ever be at a loss for a religion or a morality to prove that their ways are the right ways. It's the same with nations, the same with professions, the same all the world over and always will be.

B. B. Ah, well, perhaps, perhaps, perhaps. Still, de mortuis nil nisi bonum.[1] He died extremely well, remarkably well. He has set us an example: let us endeavor to follow it rather than harp on the weaknesses that have perished with him. I think it is Shakespear who says that the good that most men do lives after them: the evil lies interréd with their bones. Yes: interréd with their bones. Believe me, Paddy, we are all mortal. It is the common lot, Ridgeon. Say what you will, Walpole, Nature's debt must be paid. If tis not to-day, twill be tomorrow.

> To-morrow and to-morrow and to-morrow
> After life's fitful fever they sleep well
> And like this insubstantial bourne from which
> No traveller returns
> Leave not a wrack behind.

[WALPOLE *is about to speak, but* B. B., *suddenly and vehemently proceeding, extinguishes him.*]

> Out, out, brief candle:
> For nothing canst thou to damnation add
> The readiness is all.[2]

[1] *de . . . bonum,* [*speak*] *nothing but good of the dead.*
[2] *Tomorrow and tomorrow, etc., a jumble of quotations from* Macbeth, Hamlet, *and* The Tempest.

WALPOLE [*gently; for* B. B.'s *feeling, absurdly expressed as it is, is too sincere and humane to be ridiculed*]. Yes, B. B. Death makes people go on like that. I dont know why it should; but it does. By the way, what are we going to do? Ought we to clear out; or had we better wait and see whether Mrs Dubedat will come back?

SIR PATRICK. I think we'd better go. We can tell the charwoman what to do.

[*They take their hats and go to the door.*]

MRS DUBEDAT [*coming from the inner door wonderfully and beautifully dressed, and radiant, carrying a great piece of purple silk, handsomely embroidered, over her arm*]. I'm so sorry to have kept you waiting.

SIR PATRICK	[*amazed, all*	Dont mention it, madam.
B. B.	*together in*	Not at all, not at all.
RIDGEON	*a confused*	By no means.
WALPOLE	*murmur*]	It doesnt matter in the least.

MRS DUBEDAT [*coming to them*]. I felt that I must shake hands with his friends once before we part to-day. We have shared together a great privilege and a great happiness. I dont think we can ever think of ourselves as ordinary people again. We have had a wonderful experience; and that gives us a common faith, a common ideal, that nobody else can quite have. Life will always be beautiful to us: death will always be beautiful to us. May we shake hands on that?

SIR PATRICK [*shaking hands*]. Remember: all letters had better be left to your solicitor. Let him open everything and settle everything. Thats the law, you know.

MRS DUBEDAT. Oh, thank you: I didnt know.

[SIR PATRICK *goes.*]

WALPOLE. Good-bye. I blame myself: I should have insisted on operating. [*He goes.*]

B. B. I will send the proper people: they will know what to do: you shall have no trouble. Good-bye, my dear lady. [*He goes.*]

RIDGEON. Good-bye. [*He offers his hand.*]

MRS DUBEDAT [*drawing back with gentle majesty*]. I said his friends, Sir Colenso. [*He bows and goes.*]

[*She unfolds the great piece of silk, and goes into the recess to cover her dead.*]

act 5

*One of the smaller Bond Street Picture Galleries. The en-
trance is from a picture shop. Nearly in the middle of the
gallery there is a writing-table, at which the* SECRETARY, *fash-
ionably dressed, sits with his back to the entrance, correcting
catalogue proofs. Some copies of a new book are on the
desk, also the* SECRETARY's *shining hat and a couple of
magnifying glasses. At the side, on his left, a little behind
him, is a small door marked* PRIVATE. *Near the same side
is a cushioned bench parallel to the walls, which are covered with* DUBEDAT's *works. Two screens, also covered with
drawings, stand near the corners right and left of the
entrance.*

*JENNIFER, beautifully dressed and apparently very happy
and prosperous, comes into the gallery through the private
door.*

JENNIFER. Have the catalogues come yet, Mr Danby?

THE SECRETARY. Not yet.

JENNIFER. What a shame! It's a quarter past: the private view
will begin in less than half an hour.

THE SECRETARY. I think I'd better run over to the printers to
hurry them up.

JENNIFER. Oh, if you would be so good, Mr Danby. I'll take your
place while youre away.

THE SECRETARY. If anyone should come before the time dont take
any notice. The commissionaire wont let anyone through unless he
knows him. We have a few people who like to come before the
crowd—people who really buy; and of course we're glad to see them.
Have you seen the notices in Brush and Crayon and in The Easel?

JENNIFER [*indignantly*]. Yes: most disgraceful. They write quite
patronizingly, as if they were Mr Dubedat's superiors. After all
the cigars and sandwiches they had from us on the press day,
and all they drank, I really think it is infamous that they should
write like that. I hope you have not sent them tickets for to-day.

THE SECRETARY. Oh, they wont come again: theres no lunch to-
day. The advance copies of your book have come. [*He indicates
the new books.*]

JENNIFER [*pouncing on a copy, wildly excited*]. Give it to me. Oh! excuse me a moment. [*She runs away with it through the private door.*]

> [*The* SECRETARY *takes a mirror from his drawer and smartens himself before going out.* RIDGEON *comes in.*]

RIDGEON. Good morning. May I look round, as usual, before the doors open?

THE SECRETARY. Certainly, Sir Colenso. I'm sorry the catalogues have not come: I'm just going to see about them. Heres my own list, if you dont mind.

RIDGEON. Thanks. Whats this? [*He takes up one of the new books.*]

THE SECRETARY. Thats just come in. An advance copy of Mrs Dubedat's Life of her late husband.

RIDGEON [*reading the title*]. The Story of a King of Men. By His Wife. [*He looks at the portrait frontispiece.*] Ay: there he is. You knew him here, I suppose.

THE SECRETARY. Oh, we knew him. Better than she did, Sir Colenso, in some ways, perhaps.

RIDGEON. So did I. [*They look significantly at one another.*] I'll take a look round.

> [*The* SECRETARY *puts on the shining hat and goes out.* RIDGEON *begins looking at the pictures. Presently he comes back to the table for a magnifying glass, and scrutinizes a drawing very closely. He sighs; shakes his head, as if constrained to admit the extraordinary fascination and merit of the work; then marks the* SECRETARY's *list. Proceeding with his survey, he disappears behind the screen.* JENNIFER *comes back with her book. A look round satisfies her that she is alone. She seats herself at the table and admires the memoir—her first printed book—to her heart's content.* RIDGEON *re-appears, face to the wall, scrutinizing the drawings. After using his glass again, he steps back to get a more distant view of one of the larger pictures. She hastily closes the book at the sound; looks round; recognizes him; and stares, petrified. He takes a further step back which brings him nearer to her.*]

RIDGEON [*shaking his head as before, ejaculates*]. Clever brute! [*She flushes as though he had struck her. He turns to put the glass down on the desk, and finds himself face to face with her intent gaze.*] I beg your pardon. I thought I was alone.

JENNIFER [*controlling herself, and speaking steadily and meaningly*]. I am glad we have met, Sir Colenso Ridgeon. I met Dr Blenkinsop yesterday. I congratulate you on a wonderful cure.

RIDGEON [*can find no words: makes an embarrassed gesture of assent after a moment's silence, and puts down the glass and the* SECRETARY's *list on the table*].

JENNIFER. He looked the picture of health and strength and prosperity. [*She looks for a moment at the walls, contrasting* BLENKINSOP's *fortune with the artist's fate.*]

RIDGEON [*in low tones, still embarrassed*]. He has been fortunate.

JENNIFER. Very fortunate. His life has been spared.

RIDGEON. I mean that he has been made a Medical Officer of Health. He cured the Chairman of the Borough Council very successfully.

JENNIFER. With your medicines?

RIDGEON. No. I believe it was with a pound of ripe greengages.

JENNIFER [*with deep gravity*]. Funny!

RIDGEON. Yes. Life does not cease to be funny when people die any more than it ceases to be serious when people laugh.

JENNIFER. Dr Blenkinsop said one very strange thing to me.

RIDGEON. What was that?

JENNIFER. He said that private practice in medicine ought to be put down by law. When I asked him why, he said that private doctors were ignorant licensed murderers.

RIDGEON. That is what the public doctor always thinks of the private doctor. Well, Blenkinsop ought to know. He was a private doctor long enough himself. Come! you have talked at me long enough. Talk to me. You have something to reproach me with. There is reproach in your face, in your voice: you are full of it. Out with it.

JENNIFER. It is too late for reproaches now. When I turned and saw you just now, I wondered how you could come here coolly to look at his pictures. You answered the question. To you, he was only a clever brute.

RIDGEON [*quivering*]. Oh, dont. You know I did not know you were here.

JENNIFER [*raising her head a little with a quite gentle impulse of pride*]. You think it only mattered because I heard it. As if it could touch me, or touch him! Dont you see that what is really dreadful is that to you living things have no souls.

RIDGEON [*with a sceptical shrug*]. The soul is an organ I have not come across in the course of my anatomical work.

JENNIFER. You know you would not dare to say such a silly thing as that to anybody but a woman whose mind you despise. If you dissected me you could not find my conscience. Do you think I have got none?

RIDGEON. I have met people who had none.

JENNIFER. Clever brutes? Do you know, doctor, that some of the dearest and most faithful friends I ever had were only brutes! You would have vivisected them. The dearest and greatest of all my friends had a sort of beauty and affectionateness that only animals have. I hope you may never feel what I felt when I had to put him into the hands of men who defend the torture of animals because they are only brutes.

RIDGEON. Well, did you find us so very cruel, after all? They tell me that though you have dropped me, you stay for weeks with the Bloomfield Boningtons and the Walpoles. I think it must be true, because they never mention you to me now.

JENNIFER. The animals in Sir Ralph's house are like spoiled children. When Mr Walpole had to take a splinter out of the mastiff's paw, I had to hold the poor dog myself; and Mr Walpole had to turn Sir Ralph out of the room. And Mrs Walpole has to tell the gardener not to kill wasps when Mr Walpole is looking. But there are doctors who are naturally cruel; and there are others who get used to cruelty and are callous about it. They blind themselves to the souls of animals; and that blinds them to the souls of men and women. You made a dreadful mistake about Louis; but you would not have made it if you had not trained yourself to make the same mistake about dogs. You saw nothing in them but dumb brutes; and so you could see nothing in him but a clever brute.

RIDGEON [*with sudden resolution*]. I made no mistake whatever about him.

JENNIFER. Oh, doctor!

RIDGEON [*obstinately*]. I made no mistake whatever about him.

JENNIFER. Have you forgotten that he died?

RIDGEON [*with a sweep of his hand towards the pictures*]. He is not dead. He is there. [*Taking up the book*] And there.

JENNIFER [*springing up with blazing eyes*]. Put that down. How dare you touch it?

[RIDGEON, *amazed at the fierceness of the outburst, puts it down with a deprecatory shrug. She takes it up and looks at it as if he had profaned a relic.*]

RIDGEON. I am very sorry. I see I had better go.

JENNIFER [*putting the book down*]. I beg your pardon. I—I forgot myself. But it is not yet—it is a private copy.

RIDGEON. But for me it would have been a very different book.

JENNIFER. But for you it would have been a longer one.

RIDGEON. You know then that I killed him?

JENNIFER [*suddenly moved and softened*]. Oh, doctor, if you acknowledge that—if you have confessed it to yourself—if you realize what you have done, then there is forgiveness. I trusted in your strength instinctively at first; then I thought I had mistaken callousness for strength. Can you blame me? But if it was really strength—if it was only such a mistake as we all make sometimes—it will make me so happy to be friends with you again.

RIDGEON. I tell you I made no mistake. I cured Blenkinsop: was there any mistake there?

JENNIFER. He recovered. Oh, dont be foolishly proud, doctor. Confess to a failure, and save our friendship. Remember, Sir Ralph gave Louis your medicine; and it made him worse.

RIDGEON. I cant be your friend on false pretences. Something has got me by the throat: the truth must come out. I used that medicine myself on Blenkinsop. It did not make him worse. It is a dangerous medicine: it cured Blenkinsop: it killed Louis Dubedat. When I handle it, it cures. When another man handles it, it kills—sometimes.

JENNIFER [*naïvely: not yet taking it all in*]. Then why did you let Sir Ralph give it to Louis?

RIDGEON. I'm going to tell you. I did it because I was in love with you.

JENNIFER [*innocently surprised*]. In lo—You! an elderly man!

RIDGEON [*thunderstruck, raising his fists to heaven*]. Dubedat: thou art avenged! [*He drops his hands and collapses on the bench.*] I never thought of that. I suppose I appear to you a ridiculous old fogey.

JENNIFER. But surely—I did not mean to offend you, indeed—but you must be at least twenty years older than I am.

RIDGEON. Oh, quite. More, perhaps. In twenty years you will understand how little difference that makes.

JENNIFER. But even so, how could you think that I—his wife—could ever think of you—

RIDGEON [*stopping her with a nervous waving of his fingers*]. Yes, yes, yes, yes: I quite understand: you neednt rub it in.

JENNIFER. But—oh, it is only dawning on me now—I was so surprised at first—do you dare to tell me that it was to gratify a miserable jealousy that you deliberately—oh! oh! you murdered him.

RIDGEON. I think I did. It really comes to that.

> Thou shalt not kill, but needst not strive
> Officiously to keep alive.[1]

I suppose—yes: I killed him.

JENNIFER. And you tell me that! to my face! callously! You are not afraid!

RIDGEON. I am a doctor: I have nothing to fear. It is not an indictable offence to call in B. B. Perhaps it ought to be; but it isnt.

JENNIFER. I did not mean that. I meant afraid of my taking the law into my own hands, and killing you.

RIDGEON. I am so hopelessly idiotic about you that I should not mind it a bit. You would always remember me if you did that.

JENNIFER. I shall remember you always as a little man who tried to kill a great one.

RIDGEON. Pardon me. I succeeded.

JENNIFER [*with quiet conviction*]. No. Doctors think they hold the keys of life and death; but it is not their will that is fulfilled. I dont believe you made any difference at all.

RIDGEON. Perhaps not. But I intended to.

JENNIFER [*looking at him amazedly: not without pity*]. And you tried to destroy that wonderful and beautiful life merely because you grudged him a woman whom you could never have expected to care for you!

RIDGEON. Who kissed my hands. Who believed in me. Who told me her friendship lasted until death.

JENNIFER. And whom you were betraying.

RIDGEON. No. Whom I was saving.

JENNIFER [*gently*]. Pray, doctor, from what?

RIDGEON. From making a terrible discovery. From having your life laid waste.

JENNIFER. How?

Thou . . . alive, from Arthur Hugh Clough's The Latest Decalogue.

RIDGEON. No matter. I have saved you. I have been the best friend you ever had. You are happy. You are well. His works are an imperishable joy and pride for you.

JENNIFER. And you think that is your doing. Oh doctor, doctor! Sir Patrick is right: you do think you are a little god. How can you be so silly? You did not paint those pictures which are my imperishable joy and pride: you did not speak the words that will always be heavenly music in my ears. I listen to them now whenever I am tired or sad. That is why I am always happy.

RIDGEON. Yes, now that he is dead. Were you always happy when he was alive?

JENNIFER [*wounded*]. Oh, you are cruel, cruel. When he was alive I did not know the greatness of my blessing. I worried meanly about little things. I was unkind to him. I was unworthy of him.

RIDGEON [*laughing bitterly*]. Ha!

JENNIFER. Dont insult me: dont blaspheme. [*She snatches up the book and presses it to her heart in a paroxysm of remorse, exclaiming*] Oh, my King of Men!

RIDGEON. King of Men! Oh, this is too monstrous, too grotesque. We cruel doctors have kept the secret from you faithfully; but it is like all secrets: it will not keep itself. The buried truth germinates and breaks through to the light.

JENNIFER. What truth?

RIDGEON. What truth! Why, that Louis Dubedat, King of Men, was the most entire and perfect scoundrel, the most miraculously mean rascal, the most callously selfish blackguard that ever made a wife miserable.

JENNIFER [*unshaken: calm and lovely*]. He made his wife the happiest woman in the world, doctor.

RIDGEON. No: by all thats true on earth, he made his widow the happiest woman in the world; but it was I who made her a widow. And her happiness is my justification and my reward. Now you know what I did and what I thought of him. Be as angry with me as you like: at least you know me as I really am. If you ever come to care for an elderly man, you will know what you are caring for.

JENNIFER [*kind and quiet*]. I am not angry with you any more, Sir Colenso. I knew quite well that you did not like Louis, but it is not your fault: you dont understand: that is all. You never could have believed in him. It is just like your not believing in my religion: it is a sort of sixth sense that you have not got. And —[*with a gentle reassuring movement towards him*]—dont think that you have shocked me so dreadfully. I know quite well what you mean by his selfishness. He sacrificed everything for his art. In a certain sense he had even to sacrifice everybody—

RIDGEON. Everybody except himself. By keeping that back he lost the right to sacrifice you, and gave me the right to sacrifice him. Which I did.

JENNIFER [*shaking her head, pitying his error*]. He was one of the men who know what women know: that self-sacrifice is vain and cowardly.

RIDGEON. Yes, when the sacrifice is rejected and thrown away. Not when it becomes the food of godhead.

JENNIFER. I dont understand that. And I cant argue with you: you are clever enough to puzzle me, but not to shake me. You are so utterly, so wildly wrong; so incapable of appreciating Louis—

RIDGEON. Oh! [*Taking up the* SECRETARY's *list*] I have marked five pictures as sold to me.

JENNIFER. They will not be sold to you. Louis' creditors insisted on selling them; but this is my birthday; and they were all bought in for me this morning by my husband.

RIDGEON. By whom?!!!

JENNIFER. By my husband.

RIDGEON [*gabbling and stuttering*]. What husband? Whose husband? Which husband? Whom? how? what? Do you mean to say that you have married again?

JENNIFER. Do you forget that Louis disliked widows, and that people who have married happily once always marry again?

RIDGEON. Then I have committed a purely disinterested murder!

[*The* SECRETARY *returns with a pile of catalogues.*]

THE SECRETARY. Just got the first batch of catalogues in time. The doors are open.

JENNIFER [*to* RIDGEON, *politely*]. So glad you like the pictures, Sir Colenso. Good morning.

RIDGEON. Good morning. [*He goes towards the door; hesitates; turns to say something more; gives it up as a bad job; and goes.*]

JOHN MILLINGTON SYNGE
(1871-1909)

Although the Abbey Theatre in Dublin and the whole
Irish dramatic movement are properly linked with the revolution that brought independence from English rule, the
Abbey was never in its heyday a mere instrument of the
patriots, and some of its most notable achievements aroused
stormy opposition from the more militant republicans.
Since a majority of its best dramatists, such as Yeats, Synge,
and O'Casey, were of the small Protestant minority and
wrote in English rather than in Gaelic, they were viewed
with suspicion by the sensitive nationalists, who were on the
lookout for any slight to the fair name of Ireland. Yet, cosmopolitan though some of the playwrights were and critical
of the extravagant patriotism of their countrymen, they
form an authentic national school in contrast to the Irish
expatriates, such as Shaw, George Moore, and St. John Ervine, who chose to identify themselves with the main
stream of English literature.

As the poet Yeats, who was the guiding spirit of the
Abbey through its first thirty-five years, envisioned it, the
Irish theater was to be a national institution in that it took
poetic inspiration from the Irish peasantry and their folklore. It was the primitive beauty of his native land and its
wild rustic people that attracted the sophisticate home from
London and the aesthetic circles of the Continent. His early
plays, highly romantic in mood, apply the artistic methods
of some contemporary French writers, notably Maeter-
linck, to the fresh and vital material that he found in
Ireland.

His example spurred the greatest Irish playwright of the prerevolutionary generation, John Millington Synge, who added to Yeats' poetic power a dramatic sense that the older writer seldom displayed. Like Yeats, he came from a middle-class Protestant family and enjoyed a gentleman's education that centered in the arts and took him eventually to Germany and France and the life of a cosmopolitan aesthete. It was in Paris that Yeats came upon him in March 1898, studying Racine, imitating French decadents in his verses, and supporting himself precariously with free-lance journalism for English papers. Yeats had only recently given up his own sojourn among the *fin-de-siècle* writers of London and was engaged in launching the Irish Literary Theatre with the assistance of Lady Gregory. Filled with a new enthusiasm for his native country, Yeats persuaded Synge that his literary prospects and inspiration lay in his unspoiled homeland rather than in imitation of foreign traditions.

Two months later Synge left France for the primitive Aran Islands in Galway Bay off the west coast of Ireland, where the transformation in his work that Yeats had predicted soon began to take place. The simple life and the poetic speech of the picturesque islanders fascinated him, as he tells us in his revealing book of sketches called *The Aran Islands*. Thereafter, through the eleven years of life that remained to him, he was to spend part of each year in Ireland getting to know other rural areas in County Kerry, and Wicklow and Connemara, and the Blasket Islands off the Kerry coast. Another delightful volume of essays, *In Wicklow* and *In West Kerry,* provided further background for his plays.

Synge was one of the original directors of the Abbey Theatre, which gave its first performance on December 27, 1904. But his services to Irish drama were to be cut short by his last illness less than five years later. Never in robust health, he underwent an operation in 1908 for what turned out to be a hopeless cancer. At the time of his death in 1909, he was at work on a new play, a romantic tragedy on a legendary subject, *Deirdre of the Sorrows,* which some critics now consider his best work.

Few writers have achieved so considerable a reputation with so slight an output. Synge's dramatic works comprise only three plays in three acts, one in two acts, and two in one act; yet together they create an unforgettable world of romantic enchantment. He would have us believe that they all but wrote themselves, that his plots were derived from actual incidents that came to his attention as he lived among the peasants, and that the rich poetic speech of his characters was a faithful transcript of the language they spoke. He tells of listening through a chink in the wall of his room in a peasant house to the conversation of his simple hosts, recording their characteristic expressions and verbal rhythms to insure the authenticity of his dialogue. Always an enthusiast for accuracy, he demanded the most meticulous attention to scenery, properties, and costumes. Such concern for detail suggests the methods of the naturalists, photographing their glimpses of life with cold objectivity; and admittedly there is a strong infusion of realism in the romantic pictures of his rustics. This blending of diverse elements provides one source of his appeal.

But Synge was a poet by nature and a dramatist only by training, so that there is more of his own imagination in his works than his methods would suggest. As director of his plays, he developed a sure grasp of stagecraft. The actor W. G. Fay has recalled how carefully he would rehearse the company, repeating sentences aloud over and over to hit upon the precise effect he wanted. Again, as an intellectual cosmopolitan who turned deliberately to the primitive for inspiration, he intensified the romantic quality of his material. However picturesque the Irish peasants may have been, they could not have achieved the continuous flow of music and fancy that Synge has given them. But as a reticent, somewhat sardonic observer of life, Synge had also a strain of disillusionment, even cynicism, in his nature, which led him to unconventional interpretations of Irish character highly offensive to the touchy nationalists of Dublin.

His first produced play, *The Shadow of the Glen* (1903), portrayed a lonely young wife who left her irascible, suspicious older husband to find peace on the road with a passing tramp. This aspersion of Irish womanhood and implied attack upon the institution of marriage, as it was considered, aroused the ire of a good segment of the Abbey's public. *The Tinker's Wedding* (1907), Synge's poorest play, gave so undignified a picture of a priest that the theater's directorate did not dare produce it until after his death. But the greatest storm of protest fell upon his masterpiece of folk-comedy, *The Playboy of the Western World* (1907), which was greeted with roughhouse and pandemonium in both Ireland and America. It tells the droll tale of a commonplace youth who is hailed as a hero in a remote village because of his admission that he has killed his father. The women in particular are overpowered by the glamor of this "playboy," until his father suddenly turns up very much alive and the villagers recoil from the son in disillusionment. The ironic suggestion that the romantic Irishman cannot distinguish true heroism from false and has no clear-cut moral sense rocked more than one theater in the days when the play was new. Today its humor seems more whimsical than shocking, and we marvel that the shy, reserved Synge could have been capable of such high spirits. *Riders to the Sea* is more typical of this essentially serious writer, but the *Playboy* should be read as well to fill out one's impression of the scope of his talents. His province was a limited one, but he explored it fully.

JOHN MILLINGTON SYNGE

RIDERS TO THE SEA

PERSONS

Maurya, an old woman
Bartley, her son
Cathleen, her daughter
Nora, a younger daughter
Men and Women

SCENE: *An Island off the West of Ireland.*
Cottage kitchen, with nets, oil-skins, spinning-wheel, some new boards standing by the wall, etc. CATHLEEN, *a girl of about twenty, finishes kneading cake, and puts it down in the pot-oven by the fire; then wipes her hands, and begins to spin at the wheel.* NORA, *a young girl, puts her head in at the door.*

NORA [*in a low voice*]. Where is she?

CATHLEEN. She's lying down, God help her, and may be sleeping, if she's able.

[NORA *comes in softly, and takes a bundle from under her shawl.*]

CATHLEEN [*spinning the wheel rapidly*]. What is it you have?

NORA. The young priest is after bringing them. It's a shirt and a plain stocking were got off a drowned man in Donegal.

[CATHLEEN *stops her wheel with a sudden movement, and leans out to listen.*]

NORA. We're to find out if it's Michael's they are, some time herself will be down looking by the sea.

CATHLEEN. How would they be Michael's, Nora? How would he go the length of that way to the far north?

NORA. The young priest says he's known the like of it. "If it's Michael's they are," says he, "you can tell herself he's got a clean burial by the grace of God, and if they're not his, let no one say a word about them, for she'll be getting her death," says he, "with crying and lamenting."

[*The door which* NORA *half closed is blown open by a gust of wind.*]

CATHLEEN [*looking out anxiously*]. Did you ask him would he stop Bartley going this day with the horses to the Galway fair?

NORA. "I won't stop him," says he, "but let you not be afraid. Herself does be saying prayers half through the night, and the Almighty God won't leave her destitute," says he, "with no son living."

CATHLEEN. Is the sea bad by the white rocks, Nora?

NORA. Middling bad, God help us. There's a great roaring in the west, and it's worse it'll be getting when the tide's turned to the wind. [*She goes over to the table with the bundle.*] Shall I open it now?

CATHLEEN. Maybe she'd wake up on us, and come in before we'd done. [*Coming to the table*] It's a long time we'll be, and the two of us crying.

NORA [*goes to the inner door and listens*]. She's moving about on the bed. She'll be coming in a minute.

CATHLEEN. Give me the ladder, and I'll put them up in the turf-loft,[1] the way she won't know of them at all, and maybe when the tide turns she'll be going down to see would he be floating from the east.

[*They put the ladder against the gable of the chimney;* CATHLEEN *goes up a few steps and hides the bundle in the turf-loft.* MAURYA *comes from the inner room.*]

MAURYA [*looking up at* CATHLEEN *and speaking querulously*]. Isn't it turf enough you have for this day and evening?

CATHLEEN. There's a cake baking at the fire for a short space—

[1] *turf-loft, a store-place for slabs of peat dug for use as fuel.*

[*throwing down the turf*]—and Bartley will want it when the tide turns if he goes to Connemara.

[NORA *picks up the turf and puts it round the pot-oven.*]

MAURYA [*sitting down on a stool at the fire*]. He won't go this day with the wind rising from the south and west. He won't go this day, for the young priest will stop him surely.

NORA. He'll not stop him, mother, and I heard Eamon Simon and Stephen Pheety and Colum Shawn saying he would go.

MAURYA. Where is he itself?

NORA. He went down to see would there be another boat sailing in the week, and I'm thinking it won't be long till he's here now, for the tide's turning at the green head, and the hooker's tacking[1] from the east.

CATHLEEN. I hear some one passing the big stones.

NORA [*looking out*]. He's coming now, and he in a hurry.

BARTLEY [*comes in and looks round the room; speaking sadly and quietly*]. Where is the bit of new rope, Cathleen, was bought in Connemara?

CATHLEEN [*coming down*]. Give it to him, Nora; it's on a nail by the white boards. I hung it up this morning, for the pig with the black feet was eating it.

NORA [*giving him a rope*]. Is that it, Bartley?

MAURYA. You'd do right to leave that rope, Bartley, hanging by the boards. [BARTLEY *takes the rope.*] It will be wanting in this place, I'm telling you, if Michael is washed up tomorrow morning, or the next morning, or any morning in the week, for it's a deep grave we'll make him by the grace of God.

BARTLEY [*beginning to work with the rope*]. I've no halter the way I can ride down on the mare, and I must go now quickly. This is the one boat going for two weeks or beyond it, and the fair will be a good fair for horses I heard them saying below.

MAURYA. It's a hard thing they'll be saying below if the body is washed up and there's no man in it to make the coffin, and I after giving a big price for the finest white boards you'd find in Connemara. [*She looks round at the boards.*]

BARTLEY. How would it be washed up, and we after looking each day for nine days, and a strong wind blowing a while back from the west and south?

---

[1] *the hooker's tacking. A hooker is a one-masted fishing smack. To tack is to make a run obliquely against the wind.*

MAURYA. If it wasn't found itself, that wind is raising the sea, and there was a star up against the moon, and it rising in the night. If it was a hundred horses, or a thousand horses you had itself, what is the price of a thousand horses against a son where there is one son only?

BARTLEY [*working at the halter, to* CATHLEEN]. Let you go down each day, and see the sheep aren't jumping in on the rye, and if the jobber comes you can sell the pig with the black feet if there is a good price going.

MAURYA. How would the like of her get a good price for a pig?

BARTLEY [*to* CATHLEEN]. If the west wind holds with the last bit of the moon let you and Nora get up weed enough for another cock for the kelp.[1] It's hard set we'll be from this day with no one in it but one man to work.

MAURYA. It's hard set we'll be surely the day you're drownd'd with the rest. What way will I live and the girls with me, and I an old woman looking for the grave?

[BARTLEY *lays down the halter, takes off his old coat, and puts on a newer one of the same flannel.*]

BARTLEY [*to* NORA]. Is she coming to the pier?

NORA [*looking out*]. She's passing the green head and letting fall her sails.

BARTLEY [*getting his purse and tobacco*]. I'll have half an hour to go down, and you'll see me coming again in two days, or in three days, or maybe in four days if the wind is bad.

MAURYA [*turning round to the fire, and putting her shawl over her head*]. Isn't it a hard and cruel man won't hear a word from an old woman, and she holding him from the sea?

CATHLEEN. It's the life of a young man to be going on the sea, and who would listen to an old woman with one thing and she saying it over?

BARTLEY [*taking the halter*]. I must go now quickly. I'll ride down on the red mare, and the gray pony'll run behind me. . . . The blessing of God on you. [*He goes out.*]

MAURYA [*crying out as he is in the door*]. He's gone now, God spare us, and we'll not see him again. He's gone now, and when the black night is falling I'll have no son left me in the world.

CATHLEEN. Why wouldn't you give him your blessing and he look-

---

[1] *get . . . kelp, get up enough seaweed for another stack to be burned into kelp, the ash used as a fertilizer.*

ing round in the door? Isn't it sorrow enough is on every one in this house without your sending him out with an unlucky word behind him, and a hard word in his ear?

[MAURYA *takes up the tongs and begins raking the fire aimlessly without looking round.*]

NORA [*turning toward her*]. You're taking away the turf from the cake.

CATHLEEN [*crying out*]. The Son of God forgive us, Nora, we're after forgetting his bit of bread. [*She comes over to the fire.*]

NORA. And it's destroyed[1] he'll be going till dark night, and he after eating nothing since the sun went up.

CATHLEEN [*turning the cake out of the oven*]. It's destroyed he'll be, surely. There's no sense left on any person in a house where an old woman will be talking forever.

[MAURYA *sways herself on her stool.*]

CATHLEEN [*cutting off some of the bread and rolling it in a cloth; to* MAURYA]. Let you go down now to the spring well and give him this and he passing. You'll see him then and the dark word will be broken, and you can say "God speed you," the way he'll be easy in his mind.

MAURYA [*taking the bread*]. Will I be in it as soon as himself?

CATHLEEN. If you go now quickly.

MAURYA [*standing up unsteadily*]. It's hard set I am to walk.

CATHLEEN [*looking at her anxiously*]. Give her the stick, Nora, or maybe she'll slip on the big stones.

NORA. What stick?

CATHLEEN. The stick Michael brought from Connemara.

MAURYA [*taking a stick* NORA *gives her*]. In the big world the old people do be leaving things after them for their sons and children, but in this place it is the young men do be leaving things behind for them that do be old. [*She goes out slowly.* NORA *goes over to the ladder.*]

CATHLEEN. Wait, Nora, maybe she'd turn back quickly. She's that sorry, God help her, you wouldn't know the thing she'd do.

NORA. Is she gone round by the bush?

CATHLEEN [*looking out*]. She's gone now. Throw it down quickly, for the Lord knows when she'll be out of it again.

NORA [*getting the bundle from the loft*]. The young priest said

---

[1] *destroyed, half-dead.*

he'd be passing tomorrow, and we might go down and speak to him below if it's Michael's they are surely.

CATHLEEN [*taking the bundle*]. Did he say what way they were found?

NORA [*coming down*]. "There were two men," says he, "and they rowing round with poteen before the cocks crowed, and the oar of one of them caught the body, and they passing the black cliffs of the north."

CATHLEEN [*trying to open the bundle*]. Give me a knife, Nora, the string's perished with the salt water, and there's a black knot on it you wouldn't loosen in a week.

NORA [*giving her a knife*]. I've heard tell it was a long way to Donegal.

CATHLEEN [*cutting the string*]. It is surely. There was a man in here a while ago—the man sold us that knife—and he said if you set off walking from the rocks beyond, it would be seven days you'd be in Donegal.

NORA. And what time would a man take, and he floating?

[CATHLEEN *opens the bundle and takes out a bit of a stocking. They look at them eagerly.*]

CATHLEEN [*in a low voice*]. The Lord spare us, Nora! isn't it a queer hard thing to say if it's his they are surely?

NORA. I'll get his shirt off the hook the way we can put the one flannel on the other. [*She looks through some clothes hanging in the corner.*] It's not with them, Cathleen, and where will it be?

CATHLEEN. I'm thinking Bartley put it on him in the morning, for his own shirt was heavy with the salt in it. [*Pointing to the corner*] There's a bit of a sleeve was of the same stuff. Give me that and it will do.

[NORA *brings it to her and they compare the flannel.*]

CATHLEEN. It's the same stuff, Nora; but if it is itself aren't there great rolls of it in the shops of Galway, and isn't it many another man may have a shirt of it as well as Michael himself?

NORA [*who has taken up the stocking and counted the stitches, crying out*]. It's Michael, Cathleen, it's Michael; God spare his soul, and what will herself say when she hears this story, and Bartley on the sea?

CATHLEEN [*taking the stocking*]. It's a plain stocking.

NORA. It's the second one of the third pair I knitted, and I put up threescore stitches, and I dropped four of them.

CATHLEEN [*counts the stitches*]. It's that number is in it. [*Crying out*] Ah, Nora, isn't it a bitter thing to think of him floating that way to the far north, and no one to keen[1] him but the black hags that do be flying on the sea?

NORA [*swinging herself round, and throwing out her arms on the clothes*]. And isn't it a pitiful thing when there is nothing left of a man who was a great rower and fisher, but a bit of an old shirt and a plain stocking?

CATHLEEN [*after an instant*]. Tell me is herself coming, Nora? I hear a little sound on the path.

NORA [*looking out*]. She is, Cathleen. She's coming up to the door.

CATHLEEN. Put these things away before she'll come in. Maybe it's easier she'll be after giving her blessing to Bartley, and we won't let on we've heard anything the time he's on the sea.

NORA [*helping* CATHLEEN *to close the bundle*]. We'll put them here in the corner.

[*They put them into a hole in the chimney corner.* CATHLEEN *goes back to the spinning-wheel.*]

NORA. Will she see it was crying I was?

CATHLEEN. Keep your back to the door the way the light'll not be on you.

[NORA *sits down at the chimney corner, with her back to the door.* MAURYA *comes in very slowly, without looking at the girls, and goes over to her stool at the other side of the fire. The cloth with the bread is still in her hand. The girls look at each other, and* NORA *points to the bundle of bread.*]

CATHLEEN [*after spinning for a moment*]. You didn't give him his bit of bread?

[MAURYA *begins to keen softly, without turning round.*]

CATHLEEN. Did you see him riding down?

[MAURYA *goes on keening.*]

CATHLEEN [*a little impatiently*]. God forgive you; isn't it a better thing to raise your voice and tell what you seen, than to be making lamentation for a thing that's done? Did you see Bartley, I'm saying to you.

MAURYA [*with a weak voice*]. My heart's broken from this day.

CATHLEEN [*as before*]. Did you see Bartley?

MAURYA. I seen the fearfulest thing.

---

[1] *keen*, to make the Irish wail, or lamentation, for the dead.

CATHLEEN [*leaves her wheel and looks out*]. God forgive you; he's riding the mare now over the green head, and the gray pony behind him.

MAURYA [*starts, so that her shawl falls back from her head and shows her white tossed hair. With a frightened voice*]. The gray pony behind him.

CATHLEEN [*coming to the fire*]. What is it ails you, at all?

MAURYA [*speaking very slowly*]. I've seen the fearfulest thing any person has seen, since the day Bride Dara[1] seen the dead man with a child in his arms.

CATHLEEN AND NORA. Uah. [*They crouch down in front of the old woman at the fire.*]

NORA. Tell us what it is you seen.

MAURYA. I went down to the spring well, and I stood there saying a prayer to myself. Then Bartley came along, and he riding on the red mare with the gray pony behind him. [*She puts up her hands, as if to hide something from her eyes.*] The Son of God spare us, Nora!

CATHLEEN. What is it you seen?

MAURYA. I seen Michael himself.

CATHLEEN [*speaking softly*]. You did not, mother; it wasn't Michael you seen, for his body is after being found in the far north, and he's got a clean burial by the grace of God.

MAURYA [*a little defiantly*]. I'm after seeing him this day, and he riding and galloping. Bartley came first on the red mare; and I tried to say, "God speed you," but something choked the words in my throat. He went by quickly; and "the blessing of God on you," says he, and I could say nothing. I looked up then, and I crying, at the gray pony, and there was Michael upon it—with fine clothes on him, and new shoes on his feet.

CATHLEEN [*begins to keen*]. It's destroyed we are from this day. It's destroyed, surely.

NORA. Didn't the young priest say the Almighty God wouldn't leave her destitute with no son living?

MAURYA [*in a low voice, but clearly*]. It's little the like of him knows of the sea. . . . Bartley will be lost now, and let you call in Eamon and make me a good coffin out of the white boards, for I won't live after them. I've had a husband, and a husband's father,

---

[1] *Bride Dara, possibly an allusion to St. Bride (Bridget) of Kill-dara (Kildare), though Mr. Padraic Colum assures the editor of this volume that the story is an invention of Synge's.*

and six sons in this house—six fine men, though it was a hard birth I had with every one of them and they coming to the world—and some of them were found and some of them were not found, but they're gone now the lot of them. . . . There were Stephen, and Shawn, were lost in the great wind, and found after in the Bay of Gregory of the Golden Mouth, and carried up the two of them on the one plank, and in by that door. [*She pauses for a moment, the girls start as if they heard something through the door that is half open behind them.*]

NORA [*in a whisper*]. Did you hear that, Cathleen? Did you hear a noise in the northeast?

CATHLEEN [*in a whisper*]. There's some one after crying out by the seashore.

MAURYA [*continues without hearing anything*]. There was Sheamus and his father, and his own father again, were lost in a dark night, and not a stick or sign was seen of them when the sun went up. There was Patch after was drowned out of a curagh[1] that turned over. I was sitting here with Bartley, and he a baby, lying on my two knees, and I seen two women, and three women, and four women coming in, and they crossing themselves, and not saying a word. I looked out then, and there were men coming after them, and they holding a thing in the half of a red sail, and water dripping out of it—it was a dry day, Nora—and leaving a track to the door. [*She pauses again with her hand stretched out toward the door. It opens softly and old women begin to come in, crossing themselves on the threshold, and kneeling down in front of the stage with red petticoats over their heads.*]

MAURYA [*half in a dream, to* CATHLEEN]. Is it Patch, or Michael, or what is it at all?

CATHLEEN. Michael is after being found in the far north, and when he is found there how could he be here in this place?

MAURYA. There does be a power of young men floating round in the sea, and what way would they know if it was Michael they had, or another man like him, for when a man is nine days in the sea, and the wind blowing, it's hard set his own mother would be to say what man was it.

CATHLEEN. It's Michael, God spare him, for they're after sending us a bit of his clothes from the far north. [*She reaches out and*

---

[1] *curagh, a coracle, i.e., a small, basketlike wicker boat, covered formerly with hides, but now with tarred canvas.*

hands MAURYA *the clothes that belonged to* MICHAEL. MAURYA *stands up slowly, and takes them in her hands.* NORA *looks out.*]

NORA. They're carrying a thing among them and there's water dripping out of it and leaving a track by the big stones.

CATHLEEN [*in a whisper to the women who have come in*]. Is it Bartley it is?

ONE OF THE WOMEN. It is surely, God rest his soul.

[*Two younger women come in and pull out the table. Then men carry in the body of* BARTLEY, *laid on a plank, with a bit of a sail over it, and lay it on the table.*]

CATHLEEN [*to the women, as they are doing so*]. What way was he drowned?

ONE OF THE WOMEN. The gray pony knocked him into the sea, and he was washed out where there is a great surf on the white rocks.

[MAURYA *has gone over and knelt down at the head of the table. The women are keening softly and swaying themselves with a slow movement.* CATHLEEN *and* NORA *kneel at the other end of the table. The men kneel near the door.*]

MAURYA [*raising her head and speaking as if she did not see the people around her*]. They're all gone now, and there isn't anything more the sea can do to me. . . . I'll have no call now to be up crying and praying when the wind breaks from the south, and you can hear the surf is in the east, and the surf is in the west, making a great stir with the two noises, and they hitting one on the other. I'll have no call now to be going down and getting Holy Water in the dark nights after Samhain,[1] and I won't care what way the sea is when the other women will be keening. [*To* NORA] Give me the Holy Water, Nora, there's a small sup still on the dresser.

[NORA *gives it to her.*]

MAURYA [*drops* MICHAEL'S *clothes across* BARTLEY'S *feet, and sprinkles the Holy Water over him*]. It isn't that I haven't prayed for you, Bartley, to the Almighty God. It isn't that I haven't said prayers in the dark night till you wouldn't know what I'd be saying; but it's a great rest I'll have now, and it's time surely. It's a great rest I'll have now, and great sleeping in the long nights after Samhain, if it's only a bit of wet flour we do have to eat, and maybe a fish that would be stinking. [*She kneels down again, crossing herself, and saying prayers under her breath.*]

---

[1] *Samhain, an annual pagan festival corresponding roughly to Halloween.*

CATHLEEN [*to an old man*]. Maybe yourself and Eamon would make a coffin when the sun rises. We have fine white boards herself bought, God help her, thinking Michael would be found, and I have a new cake you can eat while you'll be working.

THE OLD MAN [*looking at the boards*]. Are there nails with them?

CATHLEEN. There are not, Colum; we didn't think of the nails.

ANOTHER MAN. It's a great wonder she wouldn't think of the nails, and all the coffins she's seen made already.

CATHLEEN. It's getting old she is, and broken.

[MAURYA *stands up again very slowly and spreads out the pieces of* MICHAEL's *clothes beside the body, sprinkling them with the last of the Holy Water.*]

NORA [*in a whisper to* CATHLEEN]. She's quiet now and easy; but the day Michael was drowned you could hear her crying out from this to the spring well. It's fonder she was of Michael, and would any one have thought that?

CATHLEEN [*slowly and clearly*]. An old woman will be soon tired with anything she will do, and isn't it nine days herself is after crying and keening, and making great sorrow in the house?

MAURYA [*puts the empty cup mouth downwards on the table, and lays her hands together on* BARTLEY's *feet*]. They're all together this time, and the end is come. May the Almighty God have mercy on Bartley's soul, and on Michael's soul, and on the souls of Sheamus and Patch, and Stephen and Shawn—[*bending her head*]; and may He have mercy on my soul, Nora, and on the soul of every one is left living in the world. [*She pauses, and the keen rises a little more loudly from the women, then sinks away.*]

MAURYA [*continuing*]. Michael has a clean burial in the far north, by the grace of the Almighty God. Bartley will have a fine coffin out of the white boards, and a deep grave surely. What more can we want than that? No man at all can be living forever, and we must be satisfied. [*She kneels down again and the curtain falls slowly.*]

SEAN O'CASEY (1884–   )

Sean O'Casey has had a unique career among contemporary playwrights. Born into extreme poverty and largely self-educated, he early developed artistic and political convictions to which he has been resolutely true at the cost of estrangement from his Irish compatriots and from the professional theater as a whole. His refusal to compromise his political views or his artistic aims has made him for thirty years the great unproduced dramatist of our theater, who has nevertheless continued to write, undiscouraged by the indifference of producers to his later works. His great reputation rests very largely on two masterpieces out of his first years of writing, works which made him the worthy successor to Synge in the Irish dramatic movement.

O'Casey's early life is brilliantly revealed in his leisurely autobiographical books, *I Knock at the Door* (1939), *Pictures in the Hallway* (1942), *Drums Under the Windows* (1946), *Inishfallen, Fare Thee Well* (1949), *Rose and Crown* (1952), and *Sunset and Evening Star* (1954). His youth was beset with difficulties which were to postpone his debut as a playwright until the age of forty. He grew up in just such a tenement as he pictures in *Juno and the Paycock*, and the best of his dramatic characters are faithful and salty re-creations of types that he knew in the Dublin slums. After he lost his father at the age of three, his mother undertook to rear her large family, but could provide only the meanest shelter and an inadequate diet for the growing children. As a result, O'Casey has been sickly throughout his life and suffered from a painful eye disease, which impaired his sight severely. His three years of schooling barely taught him to read and write, but when he went out to work at the age of thirteen, he conceived a great ambition to learn and to express himself. Using the cast-off textbooks of his older brothers and sisters, he became acquainted with the best English authors, especially Shakespeare, and gradually developed a lively literary style of his own.

O'Casey's self-education was one expression of a fierce pride that his humble, poverty-stricken existence long frustrated. Between thirteen and forty he held a variety of laboring jobs, or rather he did not hold them, for his explosive temper and sensitive nature frequently embroiled him with his bosses. His first position, as a handyman in a hardware store, earned him four shillings (one dollar) a week for ten hours of work a day. Later he worked twelve hours a day with a pick and shovel on a road-building crew. His bitter sense of social injustice led him to open defiance of the system under which he lived, and he angrily embraced the Communist point of view in politics. Although he participated at first in the Irish national movement, he became convinced that mere freedom from England would not solve the problems of the Irish working class. Indeed, he came to see rabid nationalism as a false god leading the Irish people away from their ultimate goal of economic liberation. The biography of O'Casey is almost a case study in the making of a radical. In any case, his satiric skepticism of the Irish patriots and their followers accounted for the stormy reception of his early play, *The Plough and the Stars,* at the Abbey Theatre.

Yet the objectives of *The Shadow of a Gunman* (1923), *Juno and the Paycock* (1924), and *The Plough and the Stars* (1926) are primarily artistic, above all to give an accurate picture of life in the Dublin slums, with its extremes of boisterous humor and bitter tragedy. His style is severely naturalistic, in contrast to the near-symbolism of much of Synge, and yet it captures the richness of the Irish temperament, its extravagant romanticism and cold-blooded or fatalistic acceptance of calamity. Like the best of Irish writers over many generations, he displays a prodigal gift of language, which unearths the music and metaphor of poetry in the common speech of his countrymen.

From these inimitable plays O'Casey went on to experiment with his own brand of expressionism in *The Silver Tassie* and *Within the Gates*. The brutal pacifism of the former and the unconventional moralizing of the latter led to a sharp break with the Abbey Theatre and his former public. Thereafter he was to live in England. These were the last of his plays to receive notable productions in London or New York. *The Star Turns Red* and *Red Roses for Me* applied his individual style to revolutionary themes, and *Oak Leaves and Lavender* took his readers into a bewildering world of fantasy. *The Bishop's Bonfire* (1955) and *The Drums of Father Ned* (1960), despite their whimsical humor, show the septuagenarian's loss of contact with the stage.

Yet the integrity of these later plays is undeniable, and to the imaginative reader they offer a fascinating picture of the evolution of a major talent. The early plays, however, should be read first as the most memorable realistic dramas that Ireland has produced.

SEAN O'CASEY

JUNO AND THE PAYCOCK

CHARACTERS

"Captain" Jack Boyle
Juno Boyle, his wife
Johnny Boyle ⎫
Mary Boyle ⎬ *their children*   ⎫ *Residents in*
"Joxer" Daly ⎭   ⎬ *the Tenement*
Mrs. Maisie Madigan   ⎭
"Needle" Nugent, a tailor
Mrs. Tancred ⎭
Jerry Devine
Charlie Bentham, a school teacher
An Irregular Mobilizer
Two Irregulars
A Coal-block Vendor
A Sewing Machine Man
Two Furniture Removal Men
Two Neighbors

Scene

Act One—The living apartment of a two-roomed tenancy of the
    Boyle family, in a tenement house in Dublin.

Act Two—The same.

Act Three—The same.

A few days elapse between Acts One and Two, and two months
between Acts Two and Three.

During Act Three the curtain is lowered for a few minutes to
denote the lapse of one hour.

The period of the play is 1922.[1]

act 1

The living room of a two-room tenancy occupied by the
BOYLE family in a tenement house in Dublin. Left, a door
leading to another part of the house; left of door a window
looking into the street; at back a dresser; farther to right at
back, a window looking into the back of the house. Between
the window and the dresser is a picture of the Virgin; below
the picture, on a bracket, is a crimson bowl in which a floating votive light is burning. Farther to the right is a small
bed partly concealed by cretonne hangings strung on a
twine. To the right is the fireplace; near the fireplace is a
door leading to the other room. Beside the fireplace is a box
containing coal. On the mantelshelf is an alarm clock lying
on its face. In a corner near the window looking into the
back is a galvanized bath. A table and some chairs. On the
table are breakfast things for one. A teapot is on the hob[2]

---

[1] 1922, the first year of the Irish Free State, when the wounds of the civil war
were fresh and the extreme republicans under De Valera were fighting against
their countrymen for complete independence from England.
[2] hob, a metal stand level with the grate in a fireplace, used to keep kettles, etc.,
warm.

*and a fryingpan stands inside the fender.[1] There are a few
books on the dresser and one on the table. Leaning against
the dresser is a long-handled shovel—the kind invariably
used by laborers when turning concrete or mixing mortar.*
JOHNNY BOYLE *is sitting crouched beside the fire.* MARY
*with her jumper off—it is lying on the back of a chair—is
arranging her hair before a tiny mirror perched on the table.
Beside the mirror is stretched out the morning paper, which
she looks at when she isn't gazing into the mirror. She is a
well-made and good-looking girl of twenty-two. Two forces
are working in her mind—one, through the circumstances
of her life, pulling her back; the other, through the influence of books she has read, pushing her forward. The opposing forces are apparent in her speech and her manners, both
of which are degraded by her environment, and improved
by her acquaintance—slight though it be—with literature.
The time is early forenoon.*

MARY [*looking at the paper*]. On a little by-road, out beyant
Finglas, he was found.

[MRS. BOYLE *enters by door on right; she has been shopping
and carries a small parcel in her hand. She is forty-five years of
age, and twenty years ago she must have been a pretty woman;
but her face has now assumed that look which ultimately
settles down upon the faces of the women of the working-
class: a look of listless monotony and harassed anxiety, blending with an expression of mechanical resistance. Were circumstances favorable, she would probably be a handsome,
active, and clever woman.*]

MRS. BOYLE. Isn't he come in yet?

MARY. No, mother.

MRS. BOYLE. Oh, he'll come in when he likes; struttin' about the
town like a paycock with Joxer, I suppose. I hear all about Mrs. Tancred's son is in this mornin's paper.

MARY. The full details are in it this mornin'; seven wounds he
had—one entherin' the neck, with an exit wound beneath the left
shoulder-blade; another in the left breast penethratin' the heart,
an' . . .

JOHNNY [*springing up from the fire*]. Oh, quit that readin', for

[1] *fender, a metal frame placed in front of a fireplace to protect the room from
falling coals.*

God's sake! Are yous losin' all your feelin's? It'll soon be that none of yous'll read anythin' that's not about butcherin'! [*He goes quickly into the room on left.*]

MARY. He's gettin' very sensitive, all of a sudden!

MRS. BOYLE. I'll read it myself, Mary, by an' by, when I come home. Everybody's sayin' that he was a die-hard[1]—thanks be to God that Johnny had nothin' to do with him this long time. . . . [*Opening the parcel and taking out some sausages, which she places on a plate*] Ah, then, if that father o' yours doesn't come in soon for his breakfast, he may go without any; I'll not wait much longer for him.

MARY. Can't you let him get it himself when he comes in?

MRS. BOYLE. Yes, an' let him bring in Joxer Daly along with him? Ay, that's what he'd like, an' that's what he's waitin' for—till he thinks I'm gone to work, an' then sail in with the boul'[2] Joxer, to burn all the coal an' dhrink all the tea in the place, to show them what a good Samaritan he is! But I'll stop here till he comes in, if I have to wait till to-morrow mornin'.

VOICE OF JOHNNY INSIDE. Mother!

MRS. BOYLE. Yis?

VOICE OF JOHNNY. Bring us in a dhrink o' wather.

MRS. BOYLE. Bring in that fella a dhrink o' wather, for God's sake, Mary.

MARY. Isn't he big an' able enough to come out an' get it himself?

MRS. BOYLE. If you weren't well yourself you'd like somebody to bring you in a dhrink o' wather. [*She brings in drink and returns.*]

MRS. BOYLE. Isn't it terrible to have to be waitin' this way! You'd think he was bringin' twenty poun's a week into the house the way he's going on. He wore out the Health Insurance long ago, he's afther wearin' out the unemployment dole, an', now, he's thryin' to wear out me! An' constantly singin', no less, when he ought always to be on his knees offerin' up a Novena[3] for a job!

MARY [*tying a ribbon, fillet-wise around her head*]. I don't like this ribbon, ma; I think I'll wear the green—it looks betther than the blue.

MRS. BOYLE. Ah, wear whatever ribbon you like, girl, only don't be botherin' me. I don't know what a girl on strike wants to be

---

[1] *die-hard, one who favored renewing the war with England for complete independence and union with the seven northern counties of Ireland.*
[2] *boul', bold, shameless.*
[3] *Novena, a nine days' prayer.*

wearin' a ribbon round her head for or silk stockin's on her legs either; it's wearin' them things that make the employers think they're givin' yous too much money.

MARY. The hour is past now when we'll ask the employers' permission to wear what we like.

MRS. BOYLE. I don't know why you wanted to walk out for Jennie Claffey; up to this you never had a good word for her.

MARY. What's the use of belongin' to a Trades Union if you won't stand up for your principles? Why did they sack her? It was a clear case of victimization. We couldn't let her walk the streets, could we?

MRS. BOYLE. No, of course yous couldn't—yous wanted to keep her company. Wan victim wasn't enough. When the employers sacrifice wan victim, the Trades Unions go wan betther be sacrificin' a hundred.

MARY. It doesn't matther what you say, ma—a principle's a principle.

MRS. BOYLE. Yis; an' when I go into oul' Murphy's to-morrow, an' he gets to know that, instead o' payin' all, I'm goin' to borry more, what'll he say when I tell him a principle's a principle? What'll we do if he refuses to give us any more on tick?[1]

MARY. He daren't refuse—if he does, can't you tell him he's paid?

MRS. BOYLE. It's lookin' as if he was paid, whether he refuses or no.

[JOHNNY *appears at the door on left. He can be plainly seen now; he is a thin delicate fellow, something younger than* MARY. *He has evidently gone through a rough time. His face is pale and drawn; there is a tremulous look of indefinite fear in his eyes. The left sleeve of his coat is empty, and he walks with a slight halt.*]

JOHNNY. I was lyin' down; I thought yous were gone. Oul' Simon Mackay is thrampin' about like a horse over me head, an' I can't sleep with him—they're like thunder-claps in me brain! The curse o'—God forgive me for goin' to curse!

MRS. BOYLE. There, now; go back an' lie down agan, an' I'll bring you in a nice cup o' tay.

JOHNNY. Tay, tay, tay! You're always thinkin' o' tay. If a man was dyin', you'd thry to make him swally a cup o' tay! [*He goes back.*]

[1] *on tick, on credit.*

MRS. BOYLE. I don't know what's goin' to be done with him. The bullet he got in the hip in Easter Week[1] was bad enough, but the bomb that shatthered his arm in the fight in O'Connell Street put the finishin' touch on him. I knew he was makin' a fool of himself. God knows I went down on me bended knees to him not to go agen the Free State.

MARY. He stuck to his principles, an', no matther how you may argue, ma, a principle's a principle.

VOICE OF JOHNNY. Is Mary goin' to stay here?

MARY. No, I'm not goin' to stay here; you can't expect me to be always at your beck an' call, can you?

VOICE OF JOHNNY. I won't stop here be meself!

MRS. BOYLE. Amn't I nicely handicapped with the whole o' yous! I don't know what any o' yous ud do without your ma. [*To* JOHNNY] Your father'll be here in a minute, an' if you want anythin', he'll get it for you.

JOHNNY. I hate assin' him for anythin'. . . . He hates to be assed to stir. . . . Is the light lightin' before the picture o' the Virgin?

MRS. BOYLE. Yis, yis! The wan inside to St. Anthony isn't enough, but he must have another wan to the Virgin here!

[JERRY DEVINE *enters hastily. He is about twenty-five, well set, active, and earnest. He is a type, becoming very common now in the Labor Movement, of a mind knowing enough to make the mass of his associates, who know less, a power, and too little to broaden that power for the benefit of all.* MARY *seizes her jumper and runs hastily into room left.*]

JERRY [*breathless*]. Where's the Captain, Mrs. Boyle; where's the Captain?

MRS. BOYLE. You may well ass a body that: he's wherever Joxer Daly is—dhrinkin' in some snug[2] or another.

JERRY. Father Farrell is just afther stoppin' to tell me to run up an' get him to go to the new job that's goin' on in Rathmines; his cousin is foreman o' the job, an' Father Farrell was speakin' to him about poor Johnny an' his father bein' idle so long, an' the foreman told Father Farrell to send the Captain up an' he'd give him a start— I wondher where I'd find him?

MRS. BOYLE. You'll find he's ayther in Ryan's or Foley's.

---

[1] *Easter Week, the time of the bloody rebellion of the Citizen Army in Dublin in 1916.*

[2] *snug, a public house or saloon bar.*

JERRY. I'll run round to Ryan's—I know it's a great house o' Joxer's. [*He rushes out.*]

MRS. BOYLE [*piteously*]. There now, he'll miss that job, or I know for what! If he gets win' o' the word, he'll not come back till evenin', so that it'll be too late. There'll never be any good got out o' him so long as he goes with that shouldher-shruggin' Joxer. I killin' meself workin', an' he sthruttin' about from mornin' till night like a paycock!

[*The steps of two persons are heard coming up a flight of stairs. They are the footsteps of* CAPTAIN BOYLE *and* JOXER. CAPTAIN BOYLE *is singing in a deep, sonorous, self-honoring voice.*]

THE CAPTAIN. Sweet Spirit, hear me prayer! Hear ... oh ... hear ... me prayer ... hear, oh, hear ... oh, he ... ar ... oh, he ... ar ... me ... pray ... er!

JOXER [*outside*]. Ah, that's a darlin' song, a daaarlin' song!

MRS. BOYLE [*viciously*]. Sweet spirit hear his prayer! Ah, then, I'll take me solemn affeydavey, it's not for a job he's prayin'! [*She sits down on the bed so that the cretonne hangings hide her from the view of those entering.*]

[THE CAPTAIN *comes slowly in. He is a man of about sixty; stout, gray-haired, and stocky. His neck is short, and his head looks like a stone ball that one sometimes sees on top of a gate-post. His cheeks, reddish-purple, are puffed out, as if he were always repressing an almost irrepressible ejaculation. On his upper lip is a crisp, tightly cropped moustache; he carries himself with the upper part of his body slightly thrown back, and his stomach slightly thrust forward. His walk is a slow, consequential strut. His clothes are dingy, and he wears a faded seaman's cap with a glazed peak.*]

BOYLE [*to* JOXER, *who is still outside*]. Come on, come on in, Joxer; she's gone out long ago, man. If there's nothing else to be got, we'll furrage out a cup o' tay, anyway. It's the only bit I get in comfort when she's away. 'Tisn't Juno should be her pet name at all, but Deirdre of the Sorras,[1] for she's always grousin'.

[JOXER *steps cautiously into the room. He may be younger than* THE CAPTAIN *but he looks a lot older. His face is like a bundle*

---

[1] *Deirdre of the Sorras, the ill-starred heroine of the old Irish folk tale, Deirdre of the Sorrows, who brought death to her lover and his two brothers and then committed suicide.*

of crinkled paper; his eyes have a cunning twinkle; he is spare and loosely built; he has a habit of constantly shrugging his shoulders with a peculiar twitching movement, meant to be ingratiating. His face is invariably ornamented with a grin.]

JOXER. It's a terrible thing to be tied to a woman that's always grousin'. I don't know how you stick it—it ud put years on me. It's a good job she has to be so ofen away, for—[*with a shrug*]—when the cat's away, the mice can play!

BOYLE [*with a commanding and complacent gesture*]. Pull over to the fire, Joxer, an' we'll have a cup o' tay in a minute.

JOXER. Ah, a cup o' tay's a darlin' thing, a daaarlin' thing—the cup that cheers but doesn't . . .

[JOXER's *rhapsody is cut short by the sight of* JUNO *coming forward and confronting the two cronies. Both are stupefied.*]

MRS. BOYLE [*with sweet irony—poking the fire, and turning her head to glare at* JOXER]. Pull over to the fire, Joxer Daly, an' we'll have a cup o' tay in a minute! Are you sure, now, you wouldn't like an egg?

JOXER. I can't stop, Mrs. Boyle; I'm in a desperate hurry, a desperate hurry.

MRS. BOYLE. Pull over to the fire, Joxer Daly; people is always far more comfortabler here than they are in their own place.

[JOXER *makes hastily for the door.* BOYLE *stirs to follow him; thinks of something to relieve the situation—stops, and says suddenly*]

BOYLE. Joxer!

JOXER [*at door ready to bolt*]. Yis?

BOYLE. You know the foreman o' that job that's goin' on down in Killesther, don't you, Joxer?

JOXER [*puzzled*]. Foreman—Killesther?

BOYLE [*with a meaning look*]. He's a butty o' yours, isn't he?

JOXER [*the truth dawning on him*]. The foreman at Killesther—oh yis, yis. He's an oul' butty o' mine—oh, he's a darlin' man, a daarlin' man.

BOYLE. Oh, then, it's a sure thing. It's a pity we didn't go down at breakfast first thing this mornin'—we might ha' been working now; but you didn't know it then.

JOXER [*with a shrug*]. It's betther late than never.

BOYLE. It's nearly time we got a start, anyhow; I'm fed up knockin' round, doin' nothin'. He promised you—gave you the straight tip?

JOXER. Yis. "Come down on the blow o' dinner," says he, "an' I'll start you, an' any friend you like to brin' with you." Ah, says I, you're a darlin' man, a daaarlin' man.

BOYLE. Well, it couldn't come at a betther time—we're a long time waitin' for it.

JOXER. Indeed we were; but it's a long lane that has no turnin'.

BOYLE. The blow up for dinner is at one—wait till I see what time it 'tis. [*He goes over to the mantelpiece, and gingerly lifts the clock.*]

MRS. BOYLE. Min' now, how you go on fiddlin' with that clock—you know the least little thing sets it asthray.

BOYLE. The job couldn't come at a betther time; I'm feelin' in great fettle, Joxer. I'd hardly believe I ever had a pain in me legs, an' last week I was nearly crippled with them.

JOXER. That's betther an' betther; ah, God never shut wan door but he opened another!

BOYLE. It's only eleven o'clock; we've lashins o' time. I'll slip on me oul' moleskins[1] afther breakfast, an' we can saunter down at our ayse. [*Putting his hand on the shovel*] I think, Joxer, we'd betther bring our shovels?

JOXER. Yis, Captain, yis; it's betther to go fully prepared an' ready for all eventualities. You bring your long-tailed shovel, an' I'll bring me navvy.[2] We mighten' want them, an', then agen, we might: for want of a nail the shoe was lost, for want of a shoe the horse was lost, an' for want of a horse the man was lost—aw, that's a darlin' proverb, a daarlin' . . .

[*As* JOXER *is finishing his sentence,* MRS. BOYLE *approaches the door and* JOXER *retreats hurriedly. She shuts the door with a bang.*]

BOYLE [*suggestively*]. We won't be long pullin' ourselves together agen when I'm working for a few weeks. [MRS. BOYLE *takes no notice.*] The foreman on the job is an oul' butty o' Joxer's; I have an idea that I know him meself. [*Silence*] . . . There's a button off the back o' me moleskin trousers. . . . If you leave out a needle an' thread I'll sew it on meself. . . . Thanks be to God, the pains in me legs is gone, anyhow!

MRS. BOYLE [*with a burst*]. Look here, Mr. Jacky Boyle, them yarns won't go down with Juno. I know you an' Joxer Daly of an

---

[1] *moleskins, trousers made of a heavy fabric with a thick nap.*
[2] *navvy, an implement for excavation, used by a navvy, or common laborer.*

oul' date, an', if you think you're able to come it over me with them fairy tales, you're in the wrong shop.

BOYLE [*coughing subduedly to relieve the tenseness of the situation*]. U-u-u-ugh.

MRS. BOYLE. Butty o' Joxer's! Oh, you'll do a lot o' good as long as you continue to be a butty o' Joxer's!

BOYLE. U-u-u-ugh.

MRS. BOYLE. Shovel! Ah, then, me boyo, you'd do far more work with a knife an' fork than ever you'll do with a shovel! If there was e'er a genuine job goin' you'd be dh'other way about—not able to lift your arms with the pains in your legs! Your poor wife slavin' to keep the bit in your mouth, an' you gallivantin' about all the day like a paycock!

BOYLE. It ud be betther for a man to be dead, betther for a man to be dead.

MRS. BOYLE [*ignoring the interruption*]. Everybody callin' you "Captain," an' you only wanst on the wather, in an oul' collier from here to Liverpool, when anybody, to listen or look at you, ud take you for a second Christo For Columbus!

BOYLE. Are you never goin' to give us a rest?

MRS. BOYLE. Oh, you're never tired o' lookin' for a rest.

BOYLE. D'ye want to dhrive me out o' the house?

MRS. BOYLE. It ud be easier to dhrive you out o' the house than to dhrive you into a job. Here, sit down an' take your breakfast—it may be the last you'll get, for I don't know where the next is goin' to come from.

BOYLE. If I get this job we'll be all right.

MRS. BOYLE. Did ye see Jerry Devine?

BOYLE [*testily*]. No, I didn't see him.

MRS. BOYLE. No, but you seen Joxer. Well, he was here lookin' for you.

BOYLE. Well, let him look!

MRS. BOYLE. Oh, indeed, he may well look, for it ud be hard for him to see you, an' you stuck in Ryan's snug.

BOYLE. I wasn't in Ryan's snug—I don't go into Ryan's.

MRS. BOYLE. Oh, is there a mad dog there? Well, if you weren't in Ryan's you were in Foley's.

BOYLE. I'm telling you for the last three weeks I haven't tasted a dhrop of intoxicatin' liquor. I wasn't in ayther wan snug or dh'other—I could swear that on a prayer-book—I'm as innocent as the child unborn!

MRS. BOYLE. Well, if you'd been in for your breakfast you'd ha' seen him.

BOYLE [*suspiciously*]. What does he want me for?

MRS. BOYLE. He'll be back any minute an' then you'll soon know.

BOYLE. I'll dhrop out an' see if I can meet him.

MRS. BOYLE. You'll sit down an' take your breakfast, an' let me go to me work, for I'm an hour late already waitin' for you.

BOYLE. You needn't ha' waited, for I'll take no breakfast—I've a little spirit left in me still!

MRS. BOYLE. Are you goin' to have your breakfast—yes or no?

BOYLE [*too proud to yield*]. I'll have no breakfast—yous can keep your breakfast. [*Plaintively*] I'll knock out a bit somewhere, never fear.

MRS. BOYLE. Nobody's goin' to coax you—don't think that. [*She vigorously replaces the pan and the sausages in the press.*[1]]

BOYLE. I've a little spirit left in me still.

[JERRY DEVINE *enters hastily.*]

JERRY. Oh, here you are at last! I've been searchin' for you everywhere. The foreman in Foley's told me you hadn't left the snug with Joxer ten minutes before I went in.

MRS. BOYLE. An' he swearin' on the holy prayer-book that he wasn't in no snug!

BOYLE [*to* JERRY]. What business is it o' yours whether I was in a snug or no? What do you want to be gallopin' about afther me for? Is a man not to be allowed to leave his house for a minute without havin' a pack o' spies, pimps, an' informers cantherin' at his heels?

JERRY. Oh, you're takin' a wrong view of it, Mr. Boyle; I simply was anxious to do you a good turn. I have a message for you from Father Farrell: he says that if you go to the job that's on in Rathmines, an' ask for Foreman Mangan, you'll get a start.

BOYLE. That's all right, but I don't want the motions of me body to be watched the way an asthronomer ud watch a star. If you're folleyin' Mary aself, you've no pereeogative to be folleyin' me. [*Suddenly catching his thigh*] U-ugh, I'm afther gettin' a terrible twinge in me right leg!

MRS. BOYLE. Oh, it won't be very long now till it travels into your left wan. It's miraculous that whenever he scents a job in front of him, his legs begin to fail him! Then, me bucko, if you lose this chance, you may go an' furrage for yourself!

[1] *press, cupboard.*

JERRY. This job'll last for some time too, Captain, an' as soon as the foundations are in, it'll be cushy enough.

BOYLE. Won't it be a climbin' job? How d'ye expect me to be able to go up a ladder with these legs? An', if I get up aself, how am I goin' to get down agen?

MRS. BOYLE [*viciously*]. Get wan o' the laborers to carry you down in a hod! You can't climb a laddher, but you can skip like a goat into a snug!

JERRY. I wouldn't let meself be let down that easy, Mr. Boyle; a little exercise, now, might do you all the good in the world.

BOYLE. It's a docthor you should have been, Devine—maybe you know more about the pains in me legs than meself that has them?

JERRY [*irritated*]. Oh, I know nothin' about the pains in your legs; I've brought the message that Father Farrell gave me, an' that's all I can do.

MRS. BOYLE. Here, sit down an' take your breakfast, an' go an' get ready; an' don't be actin' as if you couldn't pull a wing out of a dead bee.

BOYLE. I want no breakfast, I tell you; it ud choke me afther all that's been said. I've a little spirit left in me still.

MRS. BOYLE. Well, let's see your spirit, then, an' go in at wanst an' put on your moleskin trousers!

BOYLE [*moving towards the door on left*]. It ud be betther for a man to be dead! U-ugh! There's another twinge in me other leg! Nobody but meself knows the sufferin' I'm goin' through with the pains in these legs o' mine! [*He goes into the room on left as MARY comes out with her hat in her hand.*]

MRS. BOYLE. I'll have to push off now, for I'm terrible late already, but I was determined to stay an' hunt that Joxer this time. [*She goes off.*]

JERRY. Are you going out, Mary?

MARY. It looks like it when I'm putting on my hat, doesn't it?

JERRY. The bitther word agen, Mary.

MARY. You won't allow me to be friendly with you; if I thry, you deliberately misundherstand it.

JERRY. I didn't always misundherstand it; you were ofen delighted to have the arms of Jerry around you.

MARY. If you go on talkin' like this, Jerry Devine, you'll make me hate you!

JERRY. Well, let it be either a weddin' or a wake! Listen, Mary, I'm standin' for the Secretaryship of our Union. There's only one opposin' me; I'm popular with all the men, an' a good speaker—all are sayin' that I'll get elected.

MARY. Well?

JERRY. The job's worth three hundred an' fifty pounds a year, Mary. You an' I could live nice an' cosily on that; it would lift you out o' this place an' . . .

MARY. I haven't time to listen to you now—I have to go. [*She is going out when* JERRY *bars the way*.]

JERRY [*appealingly*]. Mary, what's come over you with me for the last few weeks? You hardly speak to me, an' then only a word with a face o' bittherness on it. Have you forgotten, Mary, all the happy evenin's that were as sweet as the scented hawthorn that sheltered the sides o' the road as we saunthered through the country?

MARY. That's all over now. When you get your new job, Jerry, you won't be long findin' a girl far betther than I am for your sweetheart.

JERRY. Never, never, Mary! No matther what happens you'll always be the same to me.

MARY. I must be off; please let me go, Jerry.

JERRY. I'll go a bit o' the way with you.

MARY. You needn't, thanks; I want to be by meself.

JERRY [*catching her arm*]. You're goin' to meet another fella; you've clicked with some one else, me lady!

MARY. That's no concern o' yours, Jerry Devine; let me go!

JERRY. I saw yous comin' out o' the Cornflower Dance Class, an' you hangin' on his arm—a thin, lanky strip of a Micky Dazzler,[1] with a walkin'-stick an' gloves!

VOICE OF JOHNNY [*loudly*]. What are you doin' there—pullin' about everything!

VOICE OF BOYLE [*loudly and viciously*]. I'm puttin' on me moleskin trousers!

MARY. You're hurtin' me arm! Let me go, or I'll scream, an' then you'll have the oul' fella out on top of us!

JERRY. Don't be so hard on a fella, Mary, don't be so hard.

BOYLE [*appearing at the door*]. What's the meanin' of all this hillabaloo?

MARY. Let me go, let me go!

BOYLE. D'ye hear me—what's all this hillabaloo about?

JERRY [*plaintively*]. Will you not give us one kind word, one kind word, Mary?

[1] *Micky Dazzler, dude.*

BOYLE. D'ye hear me talkin' to yous? What's all this hillabaloo for?

JERRY. Let me kiss your hand, your little, tiny, white hand!

BOYLE. Your little, tiny, white hand—are you takin' leave o' your senses, man?

[MARY *breaks away and rushes out.*]

BOYLE. This is nice goin's on in front of her father!

JERRY. Ah, dhry up, for God's sake! [*He follows* MARY.]

BOYLE. Chiselurs[1] don't care a damn now about their parents, they're bringin' their fathers' gray hairs down with sorra to the grave, an' laughin' at it, laughin' at it. Ah, I suppose it's just the same everywhere—the whole worl's in a state o' chassis![2] [*He sits by the fire.*] Breakfast! Well, they can keep their breakfast for me. Not if they went down on their bended knees would I take it—I'll show them I've a little spirit left in me still! [*He goes over to the press, takes out a plate and looks at it.*] Sassige! Well, let her keep her sassige. [*He returns to the fire, takes up the teapot and gives it a gentle shake.*] The tea's wet right enough. [*A pause; he rises, goes to the press, takes out the sausage, puts it on the pan, and puts both on the fire. He attends the sausage with a fork.*]

BOYLE [*singing*].

When the robins nest agen,
And the flowers are in bloom,
When the Springtime's sunny smile seems to banish all sorrow an'
    gloom;
Then me bonny blue-ey'd lad, if me heart be true till then—
He's promised he'll come back to me,
When the robins nest agen!

[*He lifts his head at the high note, and then drops his eyes to the pan.*]

BOYLE [*singing*].

When the . . .

[*Steps are heard approaching; he whips the pan off the fire and puts it under the bed, then sits down at the fire. The door opens and a bearded man looking in says*] You don't happen to want a sewin' machine?

BOYLE [*furiously*]. No, I don't want e'er a sewin' machine! [*He returns the pan to the fire, and commences to sing again.*]

---

[1] *Chiselurs, children.*
[2] *chassis, Captain Boyle's unintentional malapropism for "chaos."*

BOYLE [*singing*].
When the robins nest agen,
And the flowers they are in bloom,
He's . . .

[*A thundering knock is heard at the street door.*]

BOYLE. There's a terrible tatheraraa—that's a stranger—that's nobody belongin' to the house.

[*Another loud knock*]

JOXER [*sticking his head in at the door*]. Did ye hear them tatherarahs?

BOYLE. Well, Joxer, I'm not deaf.

JOHNNY [*appearing in his shirt and trousers at the door on left; his face is anxious and his voice is tremulous*]. Who's that at the door; who's that at the door? Who gave that knock—d'ye yous hear me—are yous deaf or dhrunk or what?

BOYLE [*to* JOHNNY]. How the hell do I know who 'tis? Joxer, stick your head out o' the window an' see.

JOXER. An' mebbe get a bullet in the kisser? Ah, none o' them tricks for Joxer! It's betther to be a coward than a corpse!

BOYLE [*looking cautiously out of the window*]. It's a fella in a thrench coat.

JOHNNY. Holy Mary, Mother o' God, I . . .

BOYLE. He's goin' away—he must ha' got tired knockin'.

[JOHNNY *returns to the room on left.*]

BOYLE. Sit down an' have a cup o' tay, Joxer.

JOXER. I'm afraid the missus ud pop in on us agen before we'd know where we are. Somethin's tellin' me to go at wanst.

BOYLE. Don't be superstitious, man; we're Dublin men, an' not boyos that's only afther comin' up from the bog o' Allen[1]—though if she did come in, right enough, we'd be caught like rats in a thrap.

JOXER. An' you know the sort she is—she wouldn't listen to reason—an' wanse bitten twice shy.

BOYLE [*going over to the window at back*]. If the worst came to the worst, you could dart out here, Joxer; it's only a dhrop of a few feet to the roof of the return room,[2] an' the first minute she goes into dh'other room, I'll give you the bend,[3] an' you can slip in an' away.

[1] *bog o' Allen, the great central turf (peat) bog of Ireland, sparsely settled and uncultivated. Its inhabitants are considered extremely uncouth and ignorant.*
[2] *the return room, a wing of the building.*
[3] *give you the bend, give you the sign.*

JOXER [*yielding to the temptation*]. Ah, I won't stop very long anyhow. [*Picking up a book from the table*] Whose is the buk?

BOYLE. Aw, one o' Mary's; she's always readin' lately—nothin' but thrash, too. There's one I was lookin' at dh'other day: three stories, The Doll's House, Ghosts, an' The Wild Duck[1]—buks only fit for chiselurs!

JOXER. Didja ever rade *Elizabeth, or Th' Exile o' Sibayria* . . . ah, it's a darlin' story, a daarlin' story!

BOYLE. You eat your sassige, an' never min' *Th' Exile o' Sibayria.* [*Both sit down;* BOYLE *fills out[2] tea, pours gravy on* JOXER'S *plate, and keeps the sausage for himself.*]

JOXER. What are you wearin' your moleskin trousers for?

BOYLE. I have to go to a job, Joxer. Just afther you'd gone, Devine kem runnin' in to tell us that Father Farrell said if I went down to the job that's goin' on in Rathmines I'd get a start.

JOXER. Be the holy, that's good news!

BOYLE. How is it good news? I wondher if you were in my condition, would you call it good news?

JOXER. I thought . . .

BOYLE. You thought! You think too sudden sometimes, Joxer. D'ye know, I'm hardly able to crawl with the pains in me legs!

JOXER. Yis, yis; I forgot the pains in your legs. I know you can do nothin' while they're at you.

BOYLE. You forgot; I don't think any of yous realize the state I'm in with the pains in me legs. What ud happen if I had to carry a bag o' cement?

JOXER. Ah, any man havin' the like of them pains id be down an' out, down an' out.

BOYLE. I wouldn't mind if he had said it to meself; but, no, oh no, he rushes in an' shouts it out in front o' Juno, an' you know what Juno is, Joxer. We all know Devine knows a little more than the rest of us, but he doesn't act as if he did; he's a good boy, sober, able to talk an' all that, but still . . .

JOXER. Oh ay; able to argufy, but still . . .

BOYLE. If he's runnin' afther Mary, aself, he's not goin' to be runnin' afther me. Captain Boyle's able to take care of himself.

---

[1] The Doll's House, Ghosts, The Wild Duck, *the social dramas of Ibsen, considered very radical forty years before this time.*
[2] *fills out, pours out.*

Afther all, I'm not gettin' brought up on Virol.[1] I never heard him usin' a curse; I don't believe he was ever dhrunk in his life—sure he's not like a Christian at all!

JOXER. You're afther takin' the word out o' me mouth—afther all, a Christian's natural, but he's unnatural.

BOYLE. His oul' fella was just the same—a Wicklow[2] man.

JOXER. A Wicklow man! That explains the whole thing. I've met many a Wicklow man in me time, but I never met wan that was any good.

BOYLE. "Father Farrell," says he, "sent me down to tell you." Father Farrell! . . . D'ye know, Joxer, I never like to be beholden to any o' the clergy.

JOXER. It's dangerous, right enough.

BOYLE. If they do anything for you, they'd want you to be livin' in the Chapel. . . . I'm goin' to tell you somethin', Joxer, that I wouldn't tell to anybody else—the clergy always had too much power over the people in this unfortunate country.

JOXER. You could sing that if you had an air to it!

BOYLE [*becoming enthusiastic*]. Didn't they prevent the people in '47[3] from seizin' the corn, an' they starvin'; didn't they down Parnell;[4] didn't they say that hell wasn't hot enough nor eternity long enough to punish the Fenians?[5] We don't forget, we don't forget them things, Joxer. If they've taken everything else from us, Joxer, they've left us our memory.

JOXER [*emotionally*]. For mem'ry's the only friend that grief can call its own, that grief . . . can . . . call . . . its own!

BOYLE. Father Farrell's beginnin' to take a great intherest in Captain Boyle; because of what Johnny did for his country, says he to me wan day. It's a curious way to reward Johnny be makin' his poor oul' father work. But, that's what the clergy want, Joxer—work, work, work for me an' you; havin' us mulin' from mornin' till night, so that they may be in betther fettle when they come hoppin' round for their dues! Job! Well, let him give his job to wan

---

[1] *Virol, a proprietary tonic.*

[2] *Wicklow, an eastern county of Ireland, just south of Dublin.*

[3] *in '47. The Irish potato famine was at its worst in 1847.*

[4] *Parnell, Charles Stewart Parnell (1846–1891), the Irish leader whose attempt to gain home rule for Ireland was discredited by a private scandal.*

[5] *Fenians, the Fenian Brotherhood, a secret organization founded in York in 1856, whose objective was to secure home rule for Ireland.*

of his hymn-singin', prayer-spoutin', craw-thumpin' Confraternity men![1]

[*The voice of a coal-block vendor*[2] *is heard chanting in the street.*]

VOICE OF COAL VENDOR. Blocks . . . coal-blocks! Blocks . . . coal-blocks!

JOXER. God be with the young days when you were steppin' the deck of a manly ship, with the win' blowin' a hurricane through the masts, an' the only sound you'd hear was, "Port your helm!" an' the only answer, "Port it is, sir!"

BOYLE. Them was days, Joxer, them was days. Nothin' was too hot or too heavy for me then. Sailin' from the Gulf o' Mexico to the Antanartic Ocean. I seen things, I seen things, Joxer, that no mortal man should speak about that knows his Catechism. Ofen, an' ofen, when I was fixed to the wheel with a marlinspike, an' the win's blowin' fierce an' the waves lashin' an' lashin', till you'd think every minute was goin' to be your last, an' it blowed, an' blowed—blew is the right word, Joxer, but blowed is what the sailors use. . . .

JOXER. Aw, it's a darlin' word, a daarlin' word.

BOYLE. An', as it blowed an' blowed, I ofen looked up at the sky an' assed meself the question—what is the stars, what is the stars?

VOICE OF COAL VENDOR. Any blocks, coal-blocks; blocks, coal-blocks!

JOXER. Ah, that's the question, that's the question—what is the stars?

BOYLE. An' then, I'd have another look, an' I'd ass meself—what is the moon?

JOXER. Ah, that's the question—what is the moon, what is the moon?

[*Rapid steps are heard coming towards the door.* BOYLE *makes desperate efforts to hide everything;* JOXER *rushes to the window in a frantic effort to get out;* BOYLE *begins to innocently lilt—"Oh, me darlin' Jennie, I will be thrue to thee," when the door is opened, and the black face of the* COAL VENDOR *appears.*]

THE COAL VENDOR. D'yes want any blocks?

---

[1] **Confraternity men,** *members of a voluntary association of Catholics, established to promote special works of charity or piety.*
[2] **coal-block vendor,** *street vendor of synthetic blocks of coal and pitch, used as fuel.*

BOYLE [*with a roar*]. No, we don't want any blocks!

JOXER [*coming back with a sigh of relief*]. That's afther puttin' the heart across me—I could ha' sworn it was Juno. I'd betther be goin', Captain; you couldn't tell the minute Juno'd hop in on us.

BOYLE. Let her hop in; we may as well have it out first as at last. I've made up me mind—I'm not goin' to do only what she damn well likes.

JOXER. Them sentiments does you credit, Captain; I don't like to say anything as between man an' wife, but I say as a butty, as a butty, Captain, that you've stuck it too long, an' that it's about time you showed a little spunk.

> How can a man die betther than facin' fearful odds,
> For th' ashes of his fathers an' the temples of his gods.

BOYLE. She has her rights—there's no one denyin' it, but haven't I me rights too?

JOXER. Of course you have—the sacred rights o' man!

BOYLE. To-day, Joxer, there's goin' to be issued a proclamation be me, establishin' an independent Republic, an' Juno'll have to take an oath of allegiance.

JOXER. Be firm, be firm, Captain; the first few minutes'll be the worst:—if you gently touch a nettle it'll sting you for your pains; grasp it like a lad of mettle, an' as soft as silk remains!

VOICE OF JUNO OUTSIDE. Can't stop, Mrs. Madigan—I haven't a minute!

JOXER [*flying out of the window*]. Holy God, here she is!

BOYLE [*packing the things away with a rush in the press*]. I knew that fella ud stop till she was in on top of us! [*He sits down by the fire.*]

[*JUNO enters hastily; she is flurried and excited.*]

JUNO. Oh, you're in—you must have been only afther comin' in?

BOYLE. No, I never went out.

JUNO. It's curious, then, you never heard the knockin'. [*She puts her coat and hat on bed.*]

BOYLE. Knockin'? Of course I heard the knockin'.

JUNO. An' why didn't you open the door, then? I suppose you were so busy with Joxer that you hadn't time.

BOYLE. I haven't seen Joxer since I seen him before. Joxer! What ud bring Joxer here?

JUNO. D'ye mean to tell me that the pair of yous wasn't collogin'[1] together here when me back was turned?

BOYLE. What ud we be collogin' together about? I have somethin' else to think of besides collogin' with Joxer. I can swear on all the holy prayer-books . . .

MRS. BOYLE. That you weren't in no snug! Go on in at wanst now, an' take aff that moleskin trousers o' yours, an' put on a collar an' tie to smarten yourself up a bit. There's a visitor comin' with Mary in a minute, an' he has great news for you.

BOYLE. A job, I suppose; let us get wan first before we start lookin' for another.

MRS. BOYLE. That's the thing that's able to put the win' up you. Well, it's no job, but news that'll give you the chance o' your life.

BOYLE. What's all the mystery about?

MRS. BOYLE. G'win an' take off the moleskin trousers when you're told!

[BOYLE *goes into room on left.* MRS. BOYLE *tidies up the room, puts the shovel under the bed, and goes to the press.*]

MRS. BOYLE. Oh, God bless us, looka the way everything's thrun about! Oh, Joxer was here, Joxer was here!

[MARY *enters with* CHARLIE BENTHAM; *he is a young man of twenty-five, tall, good-looking, with a very high opinion of himself generally. He is dressed in a brown coat, brown knee-breeches, gray stockings, a brown sweater, with a deep blue tie; he carries gloves and a walking-stick.*]

MRS. BOYLE [*fussing round*]. Come in, Mr. Bentham; sit down, Mr. Bentham, in this chair; it's more comfortabler than that, Mr. Bentham. Himself'll be here in a minute; he's just takin' off his trousers.

MARY. Mother!

BENTHAM. Please don't put yourself to any trouble, Mrs. Boyle— I'm quite all right here, thank you.

MRS. BOYLE. An' to think of you knowin' Mary, an' she knowin' the news you had for us, an' wouldn't let on; but it's all the more welcomer now, for we were on our last lap!

VOICE OF JOHNNY INSIDE. What are you kickin' up all the racket for?

BOYLE [*roughly*]. I'm takin' off me moleskin trousers!

JOHNNY. Can't you do it, then, without lettin' th' whole house

---

[1] *collogin', talking.*

know you're takin' off your trousers? What d'ye want puttin' them on an' takin' them off again?

BOYLE. Will you let me alone, will you let me alone? Am I never goin' to be done thryin' to please th' whole o' yous?

MRS. BOYLE [*to* BENTHAM]. You must excuse th' state o' th' place, Mr. Bentham; th' minute I turn me back that man o' mine always makes a litther o' th' place, a litther o' th' place.

BENTHAM. Don't worry, Mrs. Boyle; it's all right, I assure . . .

BOYLE [*inside*]. Where's me braces; where in th' name o' God did I leave me braces. . . . Ay, did you see where I put me braces?

JOHNNY [*inside, calling out*]. Ma, will you come in here an' take da away ou' o' this or he'll dhrive me mad.

MRS. BOYLE [*going towards door*]. Dear, dear, dear, that man'll be lookin' for somethin' on th' day o' Judgment. [*Looking into room and calling to* BOYLE] Look at your braces, man, hangin' round your neck!

BOYLE [*inside*]. Aw, Holy God!

MRS. BOYLE [*calling*]. Johnny, Johnny, come out here for a minute.

JOHNNY. Oh, leave Johnny alone, an' don't be annoyin' him!

MRS. BOYLE. Come on, Johnny, till I inthroduce you to Mr. Bentham. [*To* BENTHAM] Me son, Mr. Bentham; he's afther goin' through the mill. He was only a chiselur of a Boy Scout in Easter Week, when he got hit in the hip; and his arm was blew off in the fight in O'Connell Street. [JOHNNY *comes in.*] Here he is, Mr. Bentham; Mr. Bentham, Johnny. None can deny he done his bit for Irelan', if that's going to do him any good.

JOHNNY [*boastfully*]. I'd do it agen, ma, I'd do it agen; for a principle's a principle.

MRS. BOYLE. Ah, you lost your best principle, me boy, when you lost your arm; them's the only sort o' principles that's any good to a workin' man.

JOHNNY. Ireland only half free'll never be at peace while she has a son left to pull a trigger.

MRS. BOYLE. To be sure, to be sure—no bread's a lot betther than half a loaf. [*Calling loudly in to* BOYLE] Will you hurry up there?

[BOYLE *enters in his best trousers, which aren't too good, and looks very uncomfortable in his collar and tie.*]

MRS. BOYLE. This is me husband; Mr. Boyle, Mr. Bentham.

BENTHAM. Ah, very glad to know you, Mr. Boyle. How are you?

BOYLE. Ah, I'm not too well at all; I suffer terrible with pains in me legs. Juno can tell you there what . . .

MRS. BOYLE. You won't have many pains in your legs when you hear what Mr. Bentham has to tell you.

BENTHAM. Juno! What an interesting name! It reminds one of Homer's glorious story of ancient gods[1] and heroes.

BOYLE. Yis, doesn't it? You see, Juno was born an' christened in June; I met her in June; we were married in June, an' Johnny was born in June, so wan day I says to her, "You should ha' been called Juno," an' the name stuck to her ever since.

MRS. BOYLE. Here, we can talk o' them things agen; let Mr. Bentham say what he has to say now.

BENTHAM. Well, Mr. Boyle, I suppose you'll remember a Mr. Ellison of Santry—he's a relative of yours, I think.

BOYLE [*viciously*]. Is it that prognosticator an' procrastinator! Of course I remember him.

BENTHAM. Well, he's dead, Mr. Boyle . . .

BOYLE. Sorra many'll[2] go into mournin' for him.

MRS. BOYLE. Wait till you hear what Mr. Bentham has to say, an' then, maybe, you'll change your opinion.

BENTHAM. A week before he died he sent for me to write his will for him. He told me that there were two only that he wished to leave his propery to: his second cousin Michael Finnegan of Santry, and John Boyle, his first cousin of Dublin.

BOYLE [*excitedly*]. Me, is it me, me?

BENTHAM. You, Mr. Boyle; I'll read a copy of the will that I have here with me, which has been duly filed in the Court of Probate. [*He takes a paper from his pocket and reads*]

6th February, 1922

This is the last Will and Testament of William Ellison, of Santry, in the County of Dublin. I hereby order and wish my property to be sold and divided as follows—

£20 to the St. Vincent De Paul Society.

£60 for Masses for the repose of my soul [5s. for Each Mass].

The rest of my property to be divided between my first and second cousins.

---

[1] *ancient gods. Juno was the Roman goddess of womanhood, who figures largely in Virgil's* Aeneid. *It is her Greek counterpart, Hera, who appears in Homer's* Iliad.

[2] *Sorra many, not many. Cf. precious few.*

I hereby appoint Timothy Buckly, of Santry, and Hugh Brierly, of Coolock, to be my Executors.

[*Signed*] WILLIAM ELLISON TIMOTHY BUCKLY
HUGH BRIERLY CHARLES BENTHAM, N.T.

BOYLE [*eagerly*]. An' how much'll be comin' out of it, Mr. Bentham?

BENTHAM. The Executors told me that half of the property would be anything between £1500 and £2000.

MARY. A fortune, father, a fortune!

JOHNNY. We'll be able to get out o' this place now, an' go somewhere we're not known.

MRS. BOYLE. You won't have to trouble about a job for a while, Jack.

BOYLE [*fervently*]. I'll never doubt the goodness o' God agen.

BENTHAM. I congratulate you, Mr. Boyle. [*They shake hands.*]

BOYLE. An' now, Mr. Bentham, you'll have to have a wet.

BENTHAM. A wet?

BOYLE. A wet—a jar—a boul!

MRS. BOYLE. Jack, you're speakin' to Mr. Bentham, an' not to Joxer.

BOYLE [*solemnly*]. Juno . . . Mary . . . Johnny . . . we'll have to go into mournin' at wanst. . . . I never expected that poor Bill ud die so sudden. . . . Well, we all have to die some day . . . you, Juno, to-day . . . an' me, maybe, to-morrow. . . . It's sad, but it can't be helped. . . . Requiescat in pace . . . or, usin' our oul' tongue like St. Patrick or St. Briget, Guh sayeree jeea ayera!

MARY. Oh, father, that's not Rest in Peace; that's God save Ireland.

BOYLE. U-u-ugh, it's all the same—isn't it a prayer? . . . Juno, I'm done with Joxer; he's nothin' but a prognosticator an' a . . .

JOXER [*climbing angrily through the window and bounding into the room*]. You're done with Joxer, are you? Maybe you thought I'd stop on the roof all the night for you! Joxer out on the roof with the win' blowin' through him was nothin' to you an' your friend with the collar an' tie!

MRS. BOYLE. What in the name o' God brought you out on the roof; what were you doin' there?

JOXER [*ironically*]. I was dhreamin' I was standin' on the bridge of a ship, an' she sailin' the Antartic Ocean, an' it blowed, an' blowed, an' I lookin' up at the sky an' sayin', what is the stars, what is the stars?

MRS. BOYLE [*opening the door and standing at it*]. Here, get ou'
o' this, Joxer Daly; I was always thinkin' you had a slate off.[1]

JOXER [*moving to the door*]. I have to laugh every time I look
at the deep sea sailor; an' a row on a river ud make him sea-sick!

BOYLE. Get ou' o' this before I take the law into me own hands!

JOXER [*going out*]. Say aw rewaeawr, but not good-by. Lookin'
for work, an' prayin' to God he won't get it. [*He goes.*]

MRS. BOYLE. I'm tired tellin' you what Joxer was; maybe now you
see yourself the kind he is.

BOYLE. He'll never blow the froth off a pint o' mine agen, that's
a sure thing. Johnny . . . Mary . . . you're to keep yourselves to yourselves for the future. Juno, I'm done with Joxer. . . . I'm a new
man from this out. . . . [*Clasping* JUNO's *hand, and singing emotionally*]

> Oh, me darlin' Juno, I will be thrue to thee;
> Me own, me darlin' Juno, you're all the world to me.

CURTAIN

act 2

SCENE: *The same, but the furniture is more plentiful, and of
a vulgar nature. A glaringly upholstered arm-chair and
lounge; cheap pictures and photos everywhere. Every available spot is ornamented with huge vases filled with artificial
flowers. Crossed festoons of colored paper chains stretch
from end to end of ceiling. On the table is an old attaché
case.[2] It is about six in the evening, and two days after the
First Act.* BOYLE, *in his shirt sleeves, is voluptuously
stretched on the sofa; he is smoking a clay pipe. He is half
asleep. A lamp is lighted on the table. After a few moments'
pause the voice of* JOXER *is heard singing softly outside at
the door—"Me pipe I'll smoke, as I dhrive me moke[3]—are
you there, Mor . . . ee . . . ar . . . i . . . teeel"*

---

[1] *a slate off, that is, off your roof (a bit crazy). Cf. a screw loose.*
[2] *attaché case, a small leather case used for carrying papers.*
[3] *moke, donkey.*

BOYLE [*leaping up, takes a pen in his hand and busies himself with papers*]. Come along, Joxer, me son, come along.

JOXER [*putting his head in*]. Are you be yourself?

BOYLE. Come on, come on; that doesn't matther; I'm masther now, an' I'm going to remain masther.

[JOXER *comes in.*]

JOXER. How d'ye feel now, as a man o' money?

BOYLE [*solemnly*]. It's a responsibility, Joxer, a great responsibility.

JOXER. I suppose 'tis now, though you wouldn't think it.

BOYLE. Joxer, han' me over that attackey case on the table there. [JOXER *hands the case.*] Ever since the Will was passed I've run hundhreds o' dockyments through me han's—I tell you, you have to keep your wits about you. [*He busies himself with papers.*]

JOXER. Well, I won't disturb you; I'll dhrop in when . . .

BOYLE [*hastily*]. It's all right, Joxer, this is the last one to be signed to-day. [*He signs a paper, puts it into the case, which he shuts with a snap, and sits back pompously in the chair.*] Now, Joxer, you want to see me; I'm at your service—what can I do for you, me man?

JOXER. I've just dhropped in with the £3:5s. that Mrs. Madigan riz on the blankets an' table for you, an' she says you're to be in no hurry payin' it back.

BOYLE. She won't be long without it; I expect the first cheque for a couple o' hundhred any day. There's the five bob for yourself —go on, take it, man; it'll not be the last you'll get from the Captain. Now an' agen we have our differ, but we're there together all the time.

JOXER. Me for you, an' you for me, like the two Musketeers.

BOYLE. Father Farrell stopped me to-day an' tole me how glad he was I fell in for the money.

JOXER. He'll be stoppin' you ofen enough now; I suppose it was "Mr." Boyle with him?

BOYLE. He shuk me be the han'. . . .

JOXER [*ironically*]. I met with Napper Tandy, an' he shuk me by the han'![1]

BOYLE. You're seldom asthray, Joxer, but you're wrong shipped

[1] *I met . . . han', the first line of the celebrated patriotic song,* The Wearing of the Green. *James Napper Tandy (1740–1803) was an Irish patriot associated with Wolfe Tone in founding the United Irishmen in 1791.*

this time. What you're sayin' of Father Farrell is very near to blasfeemey. I don't like any one to talk disrespectful of Father Farrell.

JOXER. You're takin' me up wrong Captain; I wouldn't let a word be said agen Father Farrell—the heart o' the rowl, that's what he is; I always said he was a darlin' man, a daarlin' man.

BOYLE. Comin' up the stairs who did I meet but that bummer, Nugent. "I seen you talkin' to Father Farrell," says he, with a grin on him. "He'll be folleyin' you," says he, "like a Guardian Angel from this out"—all the time the oul' grin on him, Joxer.

JOXER. I never seen him yet but he had that oul' grin on him!

BOYLE. "Mr. Nugent," says I, "Father Farrell is a man o' the people, an', as far as I know the History o' me country, the priests was always in the van of the fight for Irelan's freedom."

JOXER [*fervently*].
Who was it led the van, Soggart Aroon?[1]
Since the fight first began, Soggart Aroon?

BOYLE. "Who are you tellin'?" says he. "Didn't they let down the Fenians, an' didn't they do in Parnell? An' now . . ." "You ought to be ashamed o' yourself," says I, interruptin' him, "not to know the History o' your country." An' I left him gawkin' where he was.

JOXER. Where ignorance 's bliss 'tis folly to be wise; I wondher did he ever read the Story o' Irelan'.

BOYLE. Be J. L. Sullivan?[2] Don't you know he didn't.

JOXER. Ah, it's a darlin' buk, a daarlin' buk!

BOYLE. You'd betther be goin', now, Joxer, his Majesty, Bentham, 'll be here any minute, now.

JOXER. Be the way things is lookin', it'll be a match between him an' Mary. She's thrun over Jerry altogether. Well, I hope it will, for he's a darlin' man.

BOYLE. I'm glad you think so—I don't. [*Irritably*] What's darlin' about him?

JOXER [*nonplussed*]. I only seen him twiced; if you want to know me, come an' live with me.

BOYLE. He's too ignified for me—to hear him talk you'd think

---

[1] *Soggart Aroon*, Soggarth is Irish for priest, Aroon an Irish term of affection. The "beloved priest" in question was a certain Father Murphy, who took a leading part in the rebellion of 1798. The line is from a popular ballad in his honor. See M. J. F. McCarthy, Priests and People in Ireland (1902).

[2] *J. L. Sullivan.* Boyle is referring to The Story of Ireland by A. M. Sullivan, a well-known Irish nationalist and Member of Parliament, but he confuses the author's name with that of the famous boxer.

he knew as much as a Boney's Oraculum. He's given up his job as teacher, an' is goin' to become a solicitor in Dublin—he's been studyin' law. I suppose he thinks I'll set him up, but he's wrong shipped. An' th' other fella—Jerry's as bad. The two o' them ud give you a pain in your face, listenin' to them; Jerry believin' in nothin,' an' Bentham believin' in everythin'. One that says all is God an' no man; an' th' other that says all is man an' no God!

JOXER. Well, I'll be off now.

BOYLE. Don't forget to dhrop down afther a while; we'll have a quiet jar,[1] an' a song or two.

JOXER. Never fear.

BOYLE. An' tell Mrs. Madigan that I hope we'll have the pleasure of her organization at our little enthertainment.

JOXER. Righto; we'll come down together. [*He goes out.*]

[JOHNNY *comes from room on left, and sits down moodily at the fire.* BOYLE *looks at him for a few moments, and shakes his head. He fills his pipe.*]

VOICE OF JUNO AT THE DOOR. Open the door, Jack; this thing has me nearly kilt with the weight.

[BOYLE *opens the door.* JUNO *enters carrying the box of a gramophone, followed by* MARY *carrying the horn, and some parcels.* JUNO *leaves the box on the table and flops into a chair.*]

JUNO. Carryin' that from Henry Street was no joke.

BOYLE. U-u-ugh, that's a grand lookin' insthrument—how much was it?

JUNO. Pound down, an' five to be paid at two shillin's a week.

BOYLE. That's reasonable enough.

JUNO. I'm afraid we're runnin' into too much debt; first the furniture, an' now this.

BOYLE. The whole lot won't be much out of £2000.

MARY. I don't know what you wanted a gramophone for—I know Charlie hates them; he says they're destructive of real music.

BOYLE. Desthructive of music—that fella ud give you a pain in your face. All a gramophone wants is to be properly played; its thrue wondher is only felt when everythin's quiet—what a gramophone wants is dead silence!

MARY. But, father, Jerry says the same; afther all, you can only appreciate music when your ear is properly trained.

[1] *jar, tankard of beer.*

BOYLE. That's another fella ud give you a pain in your face. Properly thrained! I suppose you couldn't appreciate football unless your fut was properly thrained.

MRS. BOYLE [*to* MARY]. Go on in ower that an' dress, or Charlie 'll be in on you, an' tea nor nothin 'll be ready.

[MARY *goes into room left.*]

MRS. BOYLE [*arranging table for tea*]. You didn't look at our new gramophone, Johnny?

JOHNNY. 'Tisn't gramophones I'm thinking of.

MRS. BOYLE. An' what is it you're thinkin' of, allanna?[1]

JOHNNY. Nothin', nothin', nothin'.

MRS. BOYLE. Sure, you must be thinkin' of somethin'; it's yourself that has yourself the way y'are; sleepin' wan night in me sisther's, an' the nex' in your father's brother's—you'll get no rest goin' on that way.

JOHNNY. I can rest nowhere, nowhere, nowhere.

MRS. BOYLE. Sure, you're not thryin' to rest anywhere.

JOHNNY. Let me alone, let me alone, let me alone, for God's sake.

[*A knock at street door.*]

MRS. BOYLE [*in a flutter*]. Here he is; here's Mr. Bentham!

BOYLE. Well, there's room for him; it's a pity there's not a brass band to play him in.

MRS. BOYLE. We'll han' the tea round, an' not be clusthered round the table, as if we never seen nothin'.

[*Steps are heard approaching, and* JUNO, *opening the door, allows* BENTHAM *to enter.*]

JUNO. Give your hat an' stick to Jack, there . . . sit down, Mr. Bentham . . . no, not there . . . in th' easy chair be the fire . . . there, that's bether. Mary'll be out to you in a minute.

BOYLE [*solemnly*]. I seen be the paper this mornin' that Consols[2] was down half per cent. That's serious, min' you, an' shows the whole counthry's in a state o' chassis.

MRS. BOYLE. What's Consols, Jack?

BOYLE. Consols? Oh, Consols is—oh, there's no use tellin' women what Consols is—th' wouldn't undherstand.

---

[1] *allanna, an Irish term of endearment.*
[2] *Consols, an abbreviation of* Consolidated Annuities, *the government securities of Great Britain resulting from the consolidation in 1751 of many securities into one stock, which originally bore interest at 3 per cent. For a number of years' before the time of the play the interest had been 2½ per cent, but the quoted value of the stock had fluctuated a great deal.*

BENTHAM. It's just as you were saying, Mr. Boyle . . .

[MARY *enters charmingly dressed.*]

BENTHAM. Oh, good evening, Mary; how pretty you're looking!

MARY [*archly*]. Am I?

BOYLE. We were just talkin' when you kem in, Mary. I was tellin' Mr. Bentham that the whole counthry's in a state o' chassis.

MARY [*to* BENTHAM]. Would you prefer the green or the blue ribbon round me hair, Charlie?

MRS. BOYLE. Mary, your father's speakin'.

BOYLE [*rapidly*]. I was jus' tellin' Mr. Bentham that the whole counthry's in a state o' chassis.

MARY. I'm sure you're frettin', da, whether it is or no.

MRS. BOYLE. With all our churches an' religions, the worl's not a bit the betther.

BOYLE [*with a commanding gesture*]. Tay!

[MARY *and* MRS. BOYLE *dispense the tea.*]

MRS. BOYLE. An' Irelan's takin' a leaf out o' the worl's buk; when we got the makin' of our own laws I thought we'd never stop to look behind us, but instead of that we never stopped to look before us! If the people ud folley up their religion betther there'd be a betther chance for us—what do you think, Mr. Bentham?

BENTHAM. I'm afraid I can't venture to express an opinion on that point, Mrs. Boyle; dogma has no attraction for me.

MRS. BOYLE. I forgot you didn't hold with us: what's this you said you were?

BENTHAM. A Theosophist, Mrs. Boyle.

MRS. BOYLE. An' what in the name o' God's a Theosophist?

BOYLE. A Theosophist, Juno, 's a—tell her, Mr. Bentham, tell her.

BENTHAM. It's hard to explain in a few words: Theosophy's founded on The Vedas, the religious books of the East. Its central theme is the existence of an all-pervading Spirit—the Life-Breath. Nothing really exists but this one Universal Life-Breath. And whatever even seems to exist separately from this Life-Breath, doesn't really exist at all. It is all vital force in man, in all animals, and in all vegetation. This Life-Breath is called the Prawna.

MRS. BOYLE. The Prawna! What a comical name!

BOYLE. Prawna; yis, the Prawna. [*Blowing gently through his lips*] That's the Prawna!

MRS. BOYLE. Whist, whist, Jack.

BENTHAM. The happiness of man depends upon his sympathy with this Spirit. Men who have reached a high state of excellence are called Yogi. Some men become Yogi in a short time, it may take others millions of years.

BOYLE. Yogi! I seen hundhreds of them in the streets o' San Francisco.

BENTHAM. It is said by these Yogi that if we practise certain mental exercises that we would have powers denied to others—for instance, the faculty of seeing things that happen miles and miles away.

MRS. BOYLE. I wouldn't care to meddle with that sort o' belief; it's a very curious religion, altogether.

BOYLE. What's curious about it? Isn't all religions curious? If they weren't you wouldn't get any one to believe them. But religions is passin' away—they've had their day like everything else. Take the real Dublin people, f'rinstance: they know more about Charlie Chaplin an' Tommy Mix[1] than they do about SS. Peter an' Paul!

MRS. BOYLE. You don't believe in ghosts, Mr. Bentham?

MARY. Don't you know he doesn't, mother?

BENTHAM. I don't know that, Mary. Scientists are beginning to think that what we call ghosts are sometimes seen by persons of a certain nature. They say that sensational actions, such as the killing of a person, demand great energy, and that that energy lingers in the place where the action occurred. People may live in the place and see nothing, when some one may come along whose personality has some peculiar connection with the energy of the place, and, in a flash, the person sees the whole affair.

JOHNNY [*rising swiftly, pale and affected*]. What sort o' talk is this to be goin' on with? Is there nothin' betther to be talkin' about but the killin' o' people? My God, isn't it bad enough for these things to happen without talkin' about them! [*He hurriedly goes into the room on left.*]

BENTHAM. Oh, I'm very sorry, Mrs. Boyle; I never thought . . .

MRS. BOYLE [*apologetically*]. Never mind, Mr. Bentham, he's very touchy.

[*A frightened scream is heard from* JOHNNY *inside.*]

MRS. BOYLE. Mother of God, what's that?

[*He rushes out again, his face pale, his lips twitching, his limbs trembling.*]

JOHNNY. Shut the door, shut the door, quick, for God's sake!

---

[1] *Tommy Mix*, Tom Mix, the favorite cowboy star of the period.

Great God, have mercy on me! Blessed Mother o' God, shelter me, shelther your son!

MRS. BOYLE [*catching him in her arms*]. What's wrong with you? What ails you? Sit down, sit down, here, on the bed . . . there now . . . there now.

MARY. Johnny, Johnny, what ails you?

JOHNNY. I seen him, I seen him . . . kneelin' in front o' the statue . . . merciful Jesus, have pity on me!

MRS. BOYLE [*to* BOYLE]. Get him a glass o' whisky . . . quick, man, an' don't stand gawkin'.

[BOYLE *gets the whisky.*]

JOHNNY. Sit here, sit here, mother . . . between me an' the door.

MRS. BOYLE. I'll sit beside you as long as you like, only tell me what was it came across you at all?

JOHNNY [*after taking some drink*]. I seen him. . . . I seen Robbie Tancred kneelin' down before the statue . . . an' the red light shinin' on him . . . an' when I went in . . . he turned an' looked at me . . . an' I seen the woun's bleedin' in his breast. . . . Oh, why did he look at me like that . . . it wasn't my fault that he was done in. . . . Mother o' God, keep him away from me!

MRS. BOYLE. There, there, child, you've imagined it all. There was nothin' there at all—it was the red light you seen, an' the talk we had put all the rest into your head. Here, dhrink more o' this— it'll do you good. . . . An', now, stretch yourself down on the bed for a little. [*To* BOYLE] Go in, Jack, an' show him it was only in his own head it was.

BOYLE [*making no move*]. E-e-e-eh; it's all nonsense; it was only a shadda he saw.

MARY. Mother o' God, he made me heart lep!

BENTHAM. It was simply due to an overwrought imagination— we all get that way at times.

MRS. BOYLE. There, dear, lie down in the bed, an' I'll put the quilt across you . . . e-e-e-eh, that's it . . . you'll be as right as the mail in a few minutes.

JOHNNY. Mother, go into the room an' see if the light's lightin' before the statue.

MRS. BOYLE [*to* BOYLE]. Jack, run in, an' see if the light's lightin' before the statue.

BOYLE [*to* MARY]. Mary, slip in an' see if the light's lightin' before the statue.

[MARY *hesitates to go in.*]

BENTHAM. It's all right; Mary, I'll go.

[*He goes into the room; remains for a few moments, and returns.*]

BENTHAM. Everything's just as it was—the light burning bravely before the statue.

BOYLE. Of course; I knew it was all nonsense.

[*A knock at the door.*]

BOYLE [*going to open the door*]. E-e-e-eh.

[*He opens it, and* JOXER, *followed by* MRS. MADIGAN, *enters.* MRS. MADIGAN *is a strong, dapper little woman of about forty-five; her face is almost always a widespread smile of complacency. She is a woman who, in manner at least, can mourn with them that mourn, and rejoice with them that do rejoice. When she is feeling comfortable, she is inclined to be reminiscent; when others say anything, or following a statement made by herself, she has a habit of putting her head a little to one side, and nodding it rapidly several times in succession, like a bird pecking at a hard berry. Indeed, she has a good deal of the bird in her, but the bird instinct is by no means a melodious one. She is ignorant, vulgar, and forward, but her heart is generous withal. For instance, she would help a neighbor's sick child; she would probably kill the child, but her intentions would be to cure it; she would be more at home helping a drayman to lift a fallen horse. She is dressed in a rather soiled gray dress and a vivid purple blouse; in her hair is a huge comb, ornamented with huge colored beads. She enters with a gliding step, beaming smile, and nodding head.* BOYLE *receives them effusively.*]

BOYLE. Come on in, Mrs. Madigan; come on in; I was afraid you weren't comin'. . . . [*Slyly*] There's some people able to dhress, ay, Joxer?

JOXER. Fair as the blossoms that bloom in the May, an' sweet as the scent of the new mown hay. . . . Ah, well she may wear them.

MRS. MADIGAN [*looking at* MARY]. I know some as are as sweet as the blossoms that bloom in the May—oh, no names, no pack dhrill![1]

BOYLE. An', now, I'll inthroduce the pair o' yous to Mary's intended: Mr. Bentham, this is Mrs. Madigan, an oul' back-parlor neighbor, that, if she could help it at all, ud never see a body shuk![2]

[1] *pack dhrill, a military punishment.*
[2] *a body shuk, a person taken advantage of.*

BENTHAM [*rising, and tentatively shaking the hand of* MRS. MADIGAN]. I'm sure, it's a great pleasure to know you, Mrs. Madigan.

MRS. MADIGAN. An' I'm goin' to tell you, Mr. Bentham, you're goin' to get as nice a bit o' skirt in Mary, there, as ever you seen in your puff.[1] Not like some of the dhressed up dolls that's knockin' about lookin' for men when it's a skelpin'[2] they want. I remember as well as I remember yesterday, the day she was born—of a Tuesday, the 25th o' June, in the year 1901, at thirty-three minutes past wan in the day be Foley's clock, the pub at the corner o' the street. A cowld day it was too, for the season o' the year, an' I remember sayin' to Joxer, there, who I met comin' up th' stairs, that the new arrival in Boyle's ud grow up a hardy chiselur if it lived, an' that she'd be somethin' one o' these days that nobody suspected, an' so signs on it, here she is to-day, goin' to be married to a young man lookin' as if he'd be fit to commensurate in any position in life it ud please God to call him!

BOYLE [*effusively*]. Sit down, Mrs. Madigan, sit down, me oul' sport. [*To* BENTHAM] This is Joxer Daly, Past Chief Ranger of the Dear Little Shamrock Branch of the Irish National Foresters, an oul' front-top neighbor, that never despaired, even in the darkest days of Ireland's sorra.

JOXER. Nil desperandum,[3] Captain, nil desperandum.

BOYLE. Sit down, Joxer, sit down. The two of us was ofen in a tight corner.

MRS. BOYLE. Ay, in Foley's snug!

JOXER. An' we kem out of it flyin', we kem out of it flyin', Captain.

BOYLE. An', now, for a dhrink—I know yous won't refuse an oul' friend.

MRS. MADIGAN [*to* JUNO]. Is Johnny not well, Mrs. . . .

MRS. BOYLE [*warningly*]. S-s-s-sh.

MRS. MADIGAN. Oh, the poor darlin'.

BOYLE. Well, Mrs. Madigan, is it tea or what?

MRS. MADIGAN. Well, speakin' for meself, I jus' had me tea a minute ago, an' I'm afraid to dhrink any more—I'm never the same when I dhrink too much tay. Thanks, all the same, Mr. Boyle.

BOYLE. Well, what about a bottle o' stout or a dhrop o' whisky?

---

[1] *in your puff* (*of breath*); *hence, in your life.*
[2] *skelpin'*, *spanking.*
[3] Nil desperandum. *There is nothing to despair about. Horace, Odes I, vii, 27.*

MRS. MADIGAN. A bottle o' stout ud be a little too heavy for me stummock afther me tay. . . . A-a-ah, I'll thry the ball o' malt.

[BOYLE *prepares the whisky.*]

MRS. MADIGAN. There's nothin' like a ball o' malt occasional like —too much of it isn't good. [*To* BOYLE, *who is adding water*] Ah, God, Johnny, don't put too much wather on it! [*She drinks.*] I suppose yous'll be lavin' this place.

BOYLE. I'm looking for a place near the sea; I'd like the place that you might say was me cradle, to be me grave as well. The sea is always callin' me.

JOXER. She is callin', callin', callin', in the win' an' on the sea.

BOYLE. Another dhrop o' whisky, Mrs. Madigan?

MRS. MADIGAN. Well, now, it ud be hard to refuse seein' the suspicious times that's in it.[1]

BOYLE [*with a commanding gesture*]. Song! . . . Juno . . . Mary . . . "Home to Our Mount'ins"!

MRS. MADIGAN [*enthusiastically*]. Hear, hear!

JOXER. Oh, tha's a darlin' song, a daarlin' song!

MARY [*bashfully*]. Ah, no, da; I'm not in a singin' humor.

MRS. MADIGAN. Gawn with you, child, an' you only goin' to be married; I remember as well as I remember yesherday—it was on a lovely August evenin', exactly, accordin' to date, fifteen years ago, come the Tuesday folleyin' the nex' that's comin' on, when me own man (the Lord be good to him) an' me was sittin' shy together in a doty[2] little nook on a counthry road, adjacent to The Stiles. "That'll scratch your lovely, little white neck," says he, ketchin' hould of a danglin' bramble branch, holdin' clusters of the loveliest flowers you ever seen, an' breakin' it off, so that his arm fell, accidental like, roun' me waist, an' as I felt it tightenin', an' tightenin', an' tightenin', I thought me buzzum was every minute goin' to burst out into a roystherin' song about

The little green leaves that were shakin' on the threes,
The gallivantin' butterflies, an' buzzin' o' the bees!

BOYLE. Ordher for the song!

JUNO. Come on, Mary—we'll do our best.

[JUNO *and* MARY *stand up, and choosing a suitable position, sing simply* "Home to Our Mountains." *They bow to company, and return to their places.*]

[1] *that's in it,* that we are living in.
[2] *doty,* fit for doting, or making love.

BOYLE [*emotionally, at the end of song*]. Lull . . . me . . . to . . . rest!

JOXER [*clapping his hands*]. Bravo, bravo! Darlin' girulls, darlin' girulls!

MRS. MADIGAN. Juno, I never seen you in betther form.

BENTHAM. Very nicely rendered indeed.

MRS. MADIGAN. A noble call, a noble call!

MRS. BOYLE. What about yourself, Mrs. Madigan?

[*After some coaxing,* MRS. MADIGAN *rises, and in a quavering voice sings the following verse*]

If I were a blackbird I'd whistle and sing;
I'd follow the ship that my thrue love was in;
An' on the top riggin', I'd there build me nest,
An' at night I would sleep on me Willie's white breast!

[*Becoming husky, amid applause, she sits down.*]

MRS. MADIGAN. Ah, me voice is too husky now, Juno; though I remember the time when Maisie Madigan could sing like a nightingale at matin' time. I remember as well as I remember yesterday, at a party given to celebrate the comin' of the first chiselur to Annie an' Benny Jimeson—who was the barber, yous may remember, in Henrietta Street, that, afther Easter Week, hung out a green, white an' orange[1] pole, an', then, when the Tans started their Jazz dancin', whipped it in agen, an' stuck out a red, white an' blue wan instead, givin' as an excuse that a barber's pole was strictly non-political—singin' "An' You'll Remember Me," with the top notes quiverin' in a dead hush of pethrified attention, folleyed by a clappin' o' han's that shuk the tumblers on the table, an' capped be Jimeson, the barber, sayin' that it was the best rendherin' of "You'll Remember Me" he ever heard in his natural![2]

BOYLE [*peremptorily*]. Ordher for Joxer's song!

JOXER. Ah, no, I couldn't; don't ass me, Captain.

BOYLE. Joxer's song, Joxer's song—give us wan of your shut-eyed wans.

[JOXER *settles himself in his chair; takes a drink; clears his throat; solemnly closes his eyes, and begins to sing in a very querulous voice*]

[1] *green, white an' orange,* the colors of the flag of the Irish Free State. Red, white, and blue are the colors of the British flag, which the barber revived when the Black-and-Tan English guard arrived.
[2] *natural,* his natural born life.

She is far from the lan' where her young hero sleeps,
An' lovers around her are sighing
> [*He hesitates.*]

An' lovers around her are sighin' . . . sighin' . . . sighin' . . .
> [*A pause*]

BOYLE [*imitating* JOXER].

> And lovers around her are sighing!

What's the use of you thryin' to sing the song if you don't know it?

MARY. Thry another one, Mr. Daly—maybe you'd be more fortunate.

MRS. MADIGAN. Gawn, Joxer, thry another wan.

JOXER [*starting again*].

I have heard the mavis[1] singin' his love song to the morn;
I have seen the dew-dhrop clingin' to the rose jus' newly born; but
. . . but . . . [*frantically*] to the rose jus' newly born . . .
newly born . . . born.

JOHNNY. Mother, put on the gramophone, for God's sake, an' stop Joxer's bawlin'.

BOYLE [*commandingly*]. Gramophone! . . . I hate to see fellas thryin' to do what they're not able to do. [BOYLE *arranges the gramophone, and is about to start it, when voices are heard of persons descending the stairs.*]

MRS. BOYLE [*warningly*]. Whisht, Jack, don't put it on, don't put it on yet; this must be poor Mrs. Tancred comin' down to go to the hospital—I forgot all about them bringin' the body to the church to-night. Open the door, Mary, an' give them a bit o' light.

> [MARY *opens the door, and* MRS. TANCRED—*a very old woman, obviously shaken by the death of her son—appears, accompanied by several neighbors. The first few phrases are spoken before they appear.*]

FIRST NEIGHBOR. It's a sad journey we're goin' on, but God's good, an' the Republicans won't be always down.

MRS. TANCRED. Ah, what good is that to me now? Whether they're up or down—it won't bring me darlin' boy from the grave.

MRS. BOYLE. Come in an' have a hot cup o' tay, Mrs. Tancred, before you go.

MRS. TANCRED. Ah, I can take nothin' now, Mrs. Boyle—I won't be long afther him.

---

[1] *mavis,* a song thrush.

FIRST NEIGHBOR. Still an' all, he died a noble death, an' we'll bury him like a king.

MRS. TANCRED. An' I'll go on livin' like a pauper. Ah, what's the pains I suffered bringin' him into the world to carry him to his cradle, to the pains I'm sufferin' now, carryin' him out o' the world to bring him to his grave!

MARY. It would be better for you not to go at all, Mrs. Tancred, but to stay at home beside the fire with some o' the neighbors.

MRS. TANCRED. I seen the first of him, an' I'll see the last of him.

MRS. BOYLE. You'd want a shawl, Mrs. Tancred; it's a cowld night, an' the win's blowin' sharp.

MRS. MADIGAN [*rushing out*]. I've a shawl above.

MRS. TANCRED. Me home is gone, now; he was me only child, an' to think that he was lyin' for a whole night stretched out on the side of a lonely counthry lane, with his head, his darlin' head, that I ofen kissed an' fondled, half hidden in the wather of a runnin' brook. An' I'm told he was the leadher of the ambush where me nex' door neighbor, Mrs. Mannin', lost her Free State soldier son. An' now here's the two of us oul' women, standin' one on each side of a scales o' sorra, balanced be the bodies of our two dead darlin' sons. [MRS. MADIGAN *returns, and wraps a shawl around her.*] God bless you, Mrs. Madigan. . . . [*She moves slowly towards the door.*] Mother o' God, Mother o' God, have pity on the pair of us! . . . O Blessed Virgin, where were you when me darlin' son was riddled with bullets, when me darlin' son was riddled with bullets! . . . Sacred Heart of the Crucified Jesus, take away our hearts o' stone . . . an' give us hearts o' flesh! . . . Take away this murdherin' hate . . . an' give us Thine own eternal love!

[*They pass out of the room.*]

MRS. BOYLE [*explanatorily to* BENTHAM]. That was Mrs. Tancred of the two-pair back; her son was found, e'er yesterday, lyin' out beyant Finglas riddled with bullets. A die-hard he was, be all accounts. He was a nice quiet boy, but lattherly he went to hell, with his Republic first, an' Republic last, an' Republic over all. He ofen took tea with us here, in the oul' days, an' Johnny, there, an' him used to be always together.

JOHNNY. Am I always to be havin' to tell you that he was no friend o' mine? I never cared for him, an' he could never stick me. It's not because he was Commandant of the Battalion that I was Quarther-Masther of, that we were friends.

MRS. BOYLE. He's gone, now—the Lord be good to him! God

help his poor oul' creature of a mother, for no matther whose friend or enemy he was, he was her poor son.

BENTHAM. The whole thing is terrible, Mrs. Boyle; but the only way to deal with a mad dog is to destroy him.

MRS. BOYLE. An' to think of me forgettin' about him bein' brought to the church to-night, an' we singin' an' all, but it was well we hadn't the gramophone goin', anyhow.

BOYLE. Even if we had aself, we've nothin' to do with these things, one way or t'other. That's the Government's business, an' let them do what we're payin' them for doin'.

MRS. BOYLE. I'd like to know how a body's not to mind these things; look at the way they're afther leavin' the people in this very house. Hasn't the whole house, nearly, been massacreed? There's young Mrs. Dougherty's husband with his leg off; Mrs. Travers that had her son blew up be a mine in Inchegeela, in Co. Cork; Mrs. Mannin' that lost wan of her sons in an ambush a few weeks ago, an' now, poor Mrs. Tancred's only child gone West with his body made a collandher of. Sure, if it's not our business, I don't know whose business it is.

BOYLE. Here, there, that's enough about them things; they don't affect us, an' we needn't give a damn. If they want a wake, well, let them have a wake. When I was a sailor, I was always resigned to meet with a wathery grave; an', if they want to be soldiers, well, there's no use o' them squealin' when they meet a soldier's fate.

JOXER. Let me like a soldier fall—me breast expandin' to th' ball!

MRS. BOYLE. In wan way, she deserves all she got; for lately, she let th' die-hards make an open house of th' place; an' for th' last couple of months, either when th' sun was risin', or when th' sun was settin', you had C.I.D. men[1] burstin' into your room, assin' you where were you born, where were you christened, where were you married, an' where would you be buried!

JOHNNY. For God's sake, let us have no more o' this talk.

MRS. MADIGAN. What about Mr. Boyle's song before we start th' gramophone?

MARY [*getting her hat, and putting it on*]. Mother, Charlie and I are goin' out for a little sthroll.

MRS. BOYLE. All right, darlin'.

---

[1] *C.I.D. men, Criminal Investigation Department men from Scotland Yard. Since these detectives did not operate in Ireland after 1921, the expression means Irishmen acting like British police agents against their countrymen.*

BENTHAM [*going out with* MARY]. We won't be long away, Mrs. Boyle.

MRS. MADIGAN. Gwan, Captain, gwan.

BOYLE. E-e-e-e-eh, I'd want to have a few more jars in me, before I'd be in fettle for singin'.

JOXER. Give us that poem you writ t'other day. [*To the rest*] Aw, it's a darlin' poem, a daarlin' poem.

MRS. BOYLE. God bless us, is he startin' to write poetry!

BOYLE [*rising to his feet*]. E-e-e-e-eh. [*He recites in an emotional, consequential manner the following verses*]

Shawn an' I were friends, sir, to me he was all in all.
His work was very heavy and his wages were very small.
None betther on th' beach as Docker, I'll go bail,
'Tis now I'm feelin' lonely, for to-day he lies in jail.
He was not what some call pious—seldom at church or prayer;
For the greatest scoundrels I know, sir, goes every Sunday there.
Fond of his pint—well, rather, but hated the Boss by creed
But never refused a copper to comfort a pal in need.

E-e-e-e-eh. [*He sits down.*]

MRS. MADIGAN. Grand, grand; you should folley that up, you should folley that up.

JOXER. It's a daarlin' poem!

BOYLE [*delightedly*]. E-e-e-e-eh.

JOHNNY. Are yous goin' to put on th' gramophone to-night, or are yous not?

MRS. BOYLE. Gwan, Jack, put on a record.

MRS. MADIGAN. Gwan, Captain, gwan.

BOYLE. Well, yous'll want to keep a dead silence. [*He sets a record, starts the machine, and it begins to play "If you're Irish, come into the Parlor." As the tune is in full blare, the door is suddenly opened by a brisk, little bald-headed man, dressed circumspectly in a black suit; he glares fiercely at all in the room; he is* "NEEDLE" NUGENT, *a tailor. He carries his hat in his hand.*]

NUGENT [*loudly, above the noise of the gramophone*]. Are yous goin' to have that thing bawlin' an' the funeral of Mrs. Tancred's son passin' the house? Have none of yous any respect for the Irish people's National regard for the dead?

[BOYLE *stops the gramophone.*]

MRS. BOYLE. Maybe, Needle Nugent, it's nearly time we had a little less respect for the dead, an' a little more regard for the livin'.

MRS. MADIGAN. We don't want you, Mr. Nugent, to teach us what we learned at our mother's knee. You don't look yourself as if you were dyin' of grief; if y'ass Maisie Madigan anything, I'd call you a real thrue die-hard an' live-soft Republican, attendin' Republican funerals in the day, an' stoppin' up half the night makin' suits for the Civic Guards!

[*Persons are heard running down to the street, some saying, "Here it is, here it is."* NUGENT *withdraws, and the rest, except* JOHNNY, *go to the window looking into the street, and look out. Sounds of a crowd coming nearer are heard; a portion are singing*]

> To Jesus' Heart all burning
> With fervent love for men,
> My heart with fondest yearning
> Shall raise its joyful strain.
> While ages course along,
> Blest be with loudest song,
> The Sacred Heart of Jesus
> By every heart and tongue.

MRS. BOYLE. Here's the hearse, here's the hearse!

BOYLE. There's t'oul' mother walkin' behin' the coffin.

MRS. MADIGAN. You can hardly see the coffin with the wreaths.

JOXER. Oh, it's a darlin' funeral, a daarlin' funeral!

MRS. MADIGAN. We'd have a betther view from the street.

BOYLE. Yes—this place ud give you a crick in your neck.

[*They leave the room, and go down.* JOHNNY *sits moodily by the fire.*]

[*A young man enters; he looks at* JOHNNY *for a moment.*]

THE YOUNG MAN. Quarther-Masther Boyle.

JOHNNY [*with a start*]. The Mobilizer!

THE YOUNG MAN. You're not at the funeral?

JOHNNY. I'm not well.

THE YOUNG MAN. I'm glad I've found you; you were stoppin' at your aunt's; I called there but you'd gone. I've to give you an ordher to attend a Battalion Staff meetin' the night afther to-morrow.

JOHNNY. Where?

THE YOUNG MAN. I don't know; you're to meet me at the Pillar at eight o'clock; then we're to go to a place I'll be told of to-night; there we'll meet a mothor that'll bring us to the meeting.

They think you might be able to know somethin' about them that
gave the bend where Commandant Tancred was shelterin'.'

JOHNNY. I'm not goin', then. I know nothin' about Tancred.

THE YOUNG MAN [*at the door*]. You'd betther come for your
own sake—remember your oath.

JOHNNY [*passionately*]. I won't go! Haven't I done enough for
Ireland! I've lost me arm, an' me hip's desthroyed so that I'll never
be able to walk right agen! Good God, haven't I done enough for
Ireland?

THE YOUNG MAN. Boyle, no man can do enough for Ireland! [*He
goes.*]

[*Faintly in the distance the crowd is heard saying*]

Hail, Mary, full of grace, the Lord is with Thee;
Blessed art Thou amongst women, and blessed, etc.

CURTAIN

act 3

SCENE: *The same as Act Two. It is about half-past six on a
November evening; a bright fire is burning in the grate;*
MARY, *dressed to go out, is sitting on a chair by the fire,
leaning forward, her hands under her chin, her elbows on
her knees. A look of dejection, mingled with uncertain
anxiety, is on her face. A lamp, turned low, is lighting on the
table. The votive light under the picture of the Virgin
gleams more redly than ever.* MRS. BOYLE *is putting on her
hat and coat. It is two months later.*

MRS. BOYLE. An' has Bentham never even written to you since—
not one line for the past month?

MARY [*tonelessly*]. Not even a line, mother.

MRS. BOYLE. That's very curious. . . . What came between the two
of yous at all? To leave you so sudden, an' yous so great together.
. . . To go away t' England, an' not to even leave you his address. . . .
The way he was always bringin' you to dances, I thought he was
mad afther you. Are you sure you said nothin' to him?

MARY. No, mother—at least nothing that could possibly explain
his givin' me up.

MRS. BOYLE. You know you're a bit hasty at times, Mary, an' say things you shouldn't say.

MARY. I never said to him what I shouldn't say, I'm sure of that.

MRS. BOYLE. How are you sure of it?

MARY. Because I love him with all my heart and soul, mother. Why, I don't know; I often thought to myself that he wasn't the man poor Jerry was, but I couldn't help loving him, all the same.

MRS. BOYLE. But you shouldn't be frettin' the way you are; when a woman loses a man, she never knows what she's afther losin', to be sure, but, then, she never knows what she's afther gainin', either. You're not the one girl of a month ago—you look like one pinin' away. It's long ago I had a right to bring you to the doctor, instead of waitin' till to-night.

MARY. There's no necessity, really, mother, to go to the doctor; nothing serious is wrong with me—I'm run down and disappointed, that's all.

MRS. BOYLE. I'll not wait another minute; I don't like the look of you at all. . . . I'm afraid we made a mistake in throwin' over poor Jerry. . . . He'd have been betther for you than that Bentham.

MARY. Mother, the best man for a woman is the one for whom she has the most love, and Charlie had it all.

MRS. BOYLE. Well, there's one thing to be said for him—he couldn't have been thinkin' of the money, or he wouldn't ha' left you . . . it must ha' been somethin' else.

MARY [*wearily*]. I don't know . . . I don't know, mother . . . only I think. . . .

MRS. BOYLE. What d'ye think?

MARY. I imagine . . . he thought . . . we weren't . . . good enough for him.

MRS. BOYLE. An' what was he himself, only a school teacher? Though I don't blame him for fightin' shy of people like that Joxer fella an' that oul' Madigan wan—nice sort o' people for your father to inthroduce to a man like Mr. Bentham. You might have told me all about this before now, Mary; I don't know why you like to hide everything from your mother; you knew Bentham, an' I'd ha' known nothin' about it if it hadn't bin for the Will; an' it was only to-day, afther long coaxin', that you let out that he'd left you.

MARY. It would have been useless to tell you—you wouldn't understand.

MRS. BOYLE [*hurt*]. Maybe not. . . . Maybe I wouldn't understand. . . . Well, we'll be off now. [*She goes over to door left, and speaks to* BOYLE *inside.*] We're goin' now to the doctor's. Are you goin' to get up this evenin'?

BOYLE [*from inside*]. The pains in me legs is terrible! It's me should be poppin' off to the doctor instead o' Mary, the way I feel.

MRS. BOYLE. Sorra mend you! A nice way you were in last night—carried in in a frog's march, dead to the world. If that's the way you'll go on when you get the money it'll be the grave for you, an asylum for me and the Poorhouse for Johnny.

BOYLE. I thought you were goin'?

MRS. BOYLE. That's what has you as you are—you can't bear to be spoken to. Knowin' the way we are, up to our ears in debt, it's a wondher you wouldn't ha' got up to go to th' solicitor's an' see if we could ha' gettin' a little o' the money even.

BOYLE [*shouting*]. I can't be goin' up there night, noon, an' mornin', can I? He can't give the money till he gets it, can he? I can't get blood out of a turnip, can I?

MRS. BOYLE. It's nearly two months since we heard of the Will, an' the money seems as far off as ever. . . . I suppose you know we owe twenty poun's to oul' Murphy?

BOYLE. I've a faint recollection of you tellin' me that before.

MRS. BOYLE. Well, you'll go over to the shop yourself for the things in future—I'll face him no more.

BOYLE. I thought you said you were goin'?

MRS. BOYLE. I'm goin' now; come on, Mary.

BOYLE. Ey, Juno, ey!

MRS. BOYLE. Well, what d'ye want now?

BOYLE. Is there e'er a bottle o' stout left?

MRS. BOYLE. There's two o' them here still.

BOYLE. Show us in one o' them an' leave t'other there till I get up. An' throw us in the paper that's on the table, an' the bottle o' Sloan's Liniment that's in th' drawer.

MRS. BOYLE [*getting the liniment and the stout*]. What paper is it you want—the *Messenger*?

BOYLE. *Messenger! The News o' the World!*[1]

[MRS. BOYLE *brings in the things asked for and comes out again.*]

MRS. BOYLE [*at door*]. Mind the candle, now, an' don't turn the house over our heads. I left t'other bottle o' stout on the table. [*She*

---

[1] **Messenger . . . World.** The News of the World *is a sensational paper specializing in murders and scandals, in contrast to the conservative* Messenger.

puts bottle of stout on table. She goes out with MARY. *A cork is heard popping inside.*]

[*A pause; then outside the door is heard the voice of* JOXER *lilting softly:* "*Me pipe I'll smoke, as I dhrive me moke . . . are you . . . there . . . More . . . aar . . . i . . . tee!*" *A gentle knock is heard and, after a pause, the door opens, and* JOXER, *followed by* NUGENT, *enters.*]

JOXER. Be God, they must be all out; I was thinkin' there was somethin' up when he didn't answer the signal. We seen Juno an' Mary goin', but I didn't see him, an' it's very seldom he escapes me.

NUGENT. He's not goin' to escape me—he's not goin' to be let go to the fair altogether.

JOXER. Sure, the house couldn't hould them lately; an' he goin' about like a mastherpiece of the Free State counthry; forgettin' their friends; forgettin' God—wouldn't even lift his hat passin' a chapel! Sure they were bound to get a dhrop! An' you really think there's no money comin' to him afther all?

NUGENT. Not as much as a red rex,[1] man; I've been a bit anxious this long time over me money, an' I went up to the solicitor's to find out all I could—ah, man, they were goin' to throw me down the stairs. They toul' me that the oul' cock himself had the stairs worn away comin' up afther it, an' they black in the face tellin' him he'd get nothin'. Some way or another that the Will is writ he won't be entitled to get as much as a make![2]

JOXER. Ah, I thought there was somethin' curious about the whole thing; I've bin havin' sthrange dhreams for the last couple o' weeks. An' I notice that that Bentham fella doesn't be comin' here now—there must be somethin' on the mat there too. Anyhow, who, in the name o' God, ud leave anythin' to that oul' bummer? Sure it ud be unnatural. An' the way Juno an' him's been throwin' their weight about for the last few months! Ah, him that goes a borrowin' goes a sorrowin'!

NUGENT. Well, he's not goin' to throw his weight about in the suit I made for him much longer. I'm tellin' you seven poun's aren't to be found growin' on the bushes these days.

JOXER. An' there isn't hardly a neighbor in the whole street that hasn't lent him money on the strength of what he was goin' to get, but they're after backing the wrong horse. Wasn't it a mercy o' God that I'd nothin' to give him! The softy I am, you know, I'd ha'

[1] *rex, penny, from the emblem of the king* ("*rex*") *on the coin.*
[2] *a make, a halfpenny.*

lent him me last juice! I must have had somebody's good prayers. Ah, afther all, an honest man's the noblest work o' God!

[BOYLE *coughs inside.*]

JOXER. Whisht, damn it, he must be inside in bed.

NUGENT. Inside o' bed or outside of it he's goin' to pay me for that suit, or give it back—he'll not climb up my back as easily as he thinks.

JOXER. Gwan in at wanst, man, an' get it off him, an' don't be a fool.

NUGENT [*going to door left, opening it and looking in*]. Ah, don't disturb yourself, Mr. Boyle; I hope you're not sick?

BOYLE. Th' oul' legs, Mr. Nugent, th' oul' legs.

NUGENT. I just called over to see if you could let me have anything off the suit?

BOYLE. E-e-e-eh, how much is this it is?

NUGENT. It's the same as it was at the start—seven poun's.

BOYLE. I'm glad you kem, Mr. Nugent; I want a good heavy top-coat—Irish frieze,[1] if you have it. How much would a top-coat like that be now?

NUGENT. About six poun's.

BOYLE. Six poun's—six an' seven, six an' seven is thirteen—that'll be thirteen poun's I'll owe you.

[JOXER *slips the bottle of stout that is on the table into his pocket.* NUGENT *rushes into the room, and returns with suit on his arm; he pauses at the door.*]

NUGENT. You'll owe me no thirteen poun's. Maybe you think you're bether able to owe it than pay it!

BOYLE [*frantically*]. Here, come back to hell ower that—where're you goin' with them clothes o' mine?

NUGENT. Where am I goin' with them clothes o' yours? Well, I like your damn cheek!

BOYLE. Here, what am I goin' to dhress meself in when I'm goin' out?

NUGENT. What do I care what you dhress yourself in? You can put yourself in a bolsther cover, if you like. [*He goes towards the other door, followed by* JOXER.]

JOXER. What'll he dhress himself in! Gentleman Jack an' his frieze coat!

[*They go out.*]

---

[1] *Irish frieze, a coarse woolen cloth, usually with a nap.*

BOYLE [*inside*]. Ey, Nugent, ey, Mr. Nugent, Mr. Nugent! [*After a pause* BOYLE *enters hastily, buttoning the braces of his moleskin trousers; his coat and vest are on his arm; he throws these on a chair and hurries to the door on right.*]

BOYLE. Ey, Mr. Nugent, Mr. Nugent!

JOXER [*meeting him at the door*]. What's up, what's wrong, Captain?

BOYLE. Nugent's been here an' took away me suit—the only things I had to go out in!

JOXER. Tuk your suit—for God's sake! An' what were you doin' while he was takin' them?

BOYLE. I was in bed when he stole in like a thief in the night, an' before I knew even what he was thinkin' of, he whipped them from the chair, an' was off like a redshank![1]

JOXER. An' what, in the name of God, did he do that for?

BOYLE. What did he do it for? How the hell do I know what he done it for? Jealousy an' spite, I suppose.

JOXER. Did he not say what he done it for?

BOYLE. Amn't I afther tellin' you that he had them whipped up an' was gone before I could open me mouth?

JOXER. That was a very sudden thing to do; there mus' be somethin' behin' it. Did he hear anythin', I wondher?

BOYLE. Did he hear anythin'?—you talk very queer, Joxer—what could he hear?

JOXER. About you not gettin' the money, in some way or t'other?

BOYLE. An' what ud prevent me from gettin' th' money?

JOXER. That's jus' what I was thinkin'—what ud prevent you from gettin' the money—nothin', as far as I can see.

BOYLE [*looking round for bottle of stout with an exclamation*]. Aw, holy God!

JOXER. What's up, Jack?

BOYLE. He must have afther lifted the bottle o' stout that Juno left on the table!

JOXER [*horrified*]. Ah, no, ah, no! He wouldn't be afther doin' that, now.

BOYLE. An' who done it then? Juno left a bottle o' stout here, an' it's gone—it didn't walk, did it?

JOXER. Oh, that's shockin'; ah, man's inhumanity to man makes countless thousands mourn![2]

---

[1] *redshank, a duck.*

[2] *man's . . . mourn!* From Man Was Made to Mourn *by Robert Burns.*

MRS. MADIGAN [*appearing at the door*]. I hope I'm not disturbin' you in any discussion on your forthcomin' legacy—if I may use the word—an' that you'll let me have a barny[1] for a minute or two with you, Mr. Boyle.

BOYLE [*uneasily*]. To be sure, Mrs. Madigan—an oul' friend's always welcome.

JOXER. Come in the evenin', come in th' mornin'; come when you're assed, or come without warnin', Mrs. Madigan.

BOYLE. Sit down, Mrs. Madigan.

MRS. MADIGAN [*ominously*]. Th' few words I have to say can be said standin'. Puttin' aside all formularies, I suppose you remember me lendin' you some time ago three poun's that I raised on blankets an' furniture in me uncle's?

BOYLE. I remember it well. I have it recorded in me book—three poun's five shillin's from Maisie Madigan, raised on articles pawned; an', item: fourpence, given to make up the price of a pint, on th' principle that no bird ever flew on wan wing; all to be repaid at par, when the ship comes home.

MRS. MADIGAN. Well, ever since I shoved in the blankets I've been perishing with th' cowld, an' I've decided, if I'll be too hot in th' nex' world aself, I'm not goin' to be too cowld in this wan; an' consequently, I want me three poun's, if you please.

BOYLE. This is a very sudden demand, Mrs. Madigan, an' can't be met; but I'm willin' to give you a receipt in full, in full.

MRS. MADIGAN. Come on, out with th' money, an' don't be jackactin'.[2]

BOYLE. You can't get blood out of a turnip, can you?

MRS. MADIGAN [*rushing over and shaking him*]. Gimme me money, y'oul' reprobate, or I'll shake the worth of it out of you!

BOYLE. Ey, houl' on, there; houl' on, there! You'll wait for your money now, me lassie!

MRS. MADIGAN [*looking around the room and seeing the gramophone*]. I'll wait for it, will I? Well, I'll not wait long; if I can't get th' cash, I'll get th' worth of it. [*She catches up the gramophone.*]

BOYLE. Ey, ey, there, wher'r you goin' with that?

MRS. MADIGAN. I'm goin' to th' pawn to get me three quid[3] five

[1] *barny, chat.*
[2] *jack-actin', playing the fool.*
[3] *three quid, three pounds.*

shillin's; I'll brin' you th' ticket, an' then you can do what you like, me bucko.

BOYLE. You can't touch that, you can't touch that! It's not my property, an' it's not ped for yet!

MRS. MADIGAN. So much th' betther. It'll be an ayse to me conscience, for I'm takin' what doesn't belong to you. You're not goin' to be swankin' it like a paycock with Maisie Madigan's money—I'll pull some o' th' gorgeous feathers out o' your tail! [*She goes off with the gramophone.*]

BOYLE. What's th' world comin' to at all? I ass you, Joxer Daly, is there any morality left anywhere?

JOXER. I wouldn't ha' believed it, only I seen it with me own two eyes. I didn't think Maisie Madigan was that sort of a woman; she has either a sup taken, or she's heard somethin'.

BOYLE. Heard somethin'—about what, if it's not any harm to ass you?

JOXER. She must ha' heard some rumor or other that you weren't goin' to get th' money.

BOYLE. Who says I'm not goin' to get th' money?

JOXER. Sure, I know—I was only sayin'.

BOYLE. Only sayin' what?

JOXER. Nothin'.

BOYLE. You were goin' to say somethin', don't be a twisther.[1]

JOXER [*angrily*]. Who's a twisther?

BOYLE. Why don't you speak your mind, then?

JOXER. You never twisted yourself—no, you wouldn't know how!

BOYLE. Did you ever know me to twist; did you ever know me to twist?

JOXER [*fiercely*]. Did you ever do anythin' else! Sure, you can't believe a word that comes out o' your mouth.

BOYLE. Here, get out, ower o' this;[2] I always knew you were a prognosticator an' a procrastinator!

JOXER [*going out as* JOHNNY *comes in*]. The anchor's weighed, farewell, re . . . mem . . . ber . . . me. Jacky Boyle, Esquire, infernal rogue an' damned liar!

JOHNNY. Joxer an' you at it agen?—when are you goin' to have a little respect for yourself, an' not be always makin' a show of us all?

---

[1] *twisther, a liar or swindler.*
[2] *ower o' this, enough of this.*

BOYLE. Are you goin' to lecture me now?

JOHNNY. Is mother back from the doctor yet, with Mary?

[MRS. BOYLE *enters; it is apparent from the serious look on her face that something has happened. She takes off her hat and coat without a word and puts them by. She then sits down near the fire, and there is a few moments' pause.*]

BOYLE. Well, what did the doctor say about Mary?

MRS. BOYLE [*in an earnest manner and with suppressed agitation*]. Sit down here, Jack; I've something to say to you . . . about Mary.

BOYLE [*awed by her manners*]. About . . . Mary?

MRS. BOYLE. Close that door there and sit down here.

BOYLE [*closing the door*]. More throuble in our native land, is it? [*He sits down.*] Well, what is it?

MRS. BOYLE. It's about Mary.

BOYLE. Well, what about Mary—there's nothin' wrong with her, is there?

MRS. BOYLE. I'm sorry to say there's a gradle wrong with her.

BOYLE. A gradle wrong with her! [*Peevishly*] First Johnny an' now Mary; is the whole house goin' to become an hospital! It's not consumption is it?

MRS. BOYLE. No . . . it's not consumption . . . it's worse.

JOHNNY. Worse! Well, we'll have to get her into some place ower this, there's no one here to mind her.

MRS. BOYLE. We'll all have to mind her now. You might as well know now, Johnny, as another time. [*To* BOYLE] D'ye know what the doctor said to me about her, Jack?

BOYLE. How ud I know—I wasn't there, was I?

MRS. BOYLE. He told me to get her married at wanst.

BOYLE. Married at wanst! An' why did he say the like o' that?

MRS. BOYLE. Because Mary's goin' to have a baby in a short time.

BOYLE. Goin' to have a baby!—my God, what'll Bentham say when he hears that?

MRS. BOYLE. Are you blind, man, that you can't see that it was Bentham that has done this wrong to her?

BOYLE [*passionately*]. Then he'll marry her, he'll have to marry her!

MRS. BOYLE. You know he's gone to England, an' God knows where he is now.

BOYLE. I'll folley him, I'll folley him, an' bring him back, an' make him do her justice. The scoundrel, I might ha' known what he was, with his yogees an' his prawna!

MRS. BOYLE. We'll have to keep it quiet till we see what we can do.

BOYLE. Oh, isn't this a nice thing to come on top o' me, an' the state I'm in! A pretty show I'll be to Joxer an' to that oul' wan, Madigan! Amn't I afther goin' through enough without havin' to go through this!

MRS. BOYLE. What you an' I'll have to go through'll be nothin' to what poor Mary'll have to go through; for you an' me is middlin' old, an' most of our years is spent; but Mary'll have maybe forty years to face an' handle, an' every wan of them'll be tainted with a bitther memory.

BOYLE. Where is she? Where is she till I tell her off? I'm tellin' you when I'm done with her she'll be a sorry girl!

MRS. BOYLE. I left her in me sisther's till I came to speak to you. You'll say nothin' to her, Jack; ever since she left school she's earned her livin', an' your fatherly care never throubled the poor girl.

BOYLE. Gwan, take her part agen her father! But I'll let you see whether I'll say nothin' to her or no! Her an' her readin'! That's more o' th' blasted nonsense that has the house fallin' down on top of us! What did th' likes of her, born in a tenement house, want with readin'? Her readin's afther bringin' her to a nice pass—oh, it's madnin', madnin', madnin'!

MRS. BOYLE. When she comes back say nothin' to her, Jack, or she'll leave this place.

BOYLE. Leave this place! Ay, she'll leave this place, an' quick too!

MRS. BOYLE. If Mary goes, I'll go with her.

BOYLE. Well, go with her! Well, go, th' pair o' yous! I lived before I seen yous, an' I can live when yous are gone. Isn't this a nice thing to come rollin' in on top o' me afther all your prayin' to St. Anthony an' The Little Flower. An' she's a child o' Mary, too—I wonder what'll the nuns think of her now? An' it'll be bellows'd[1] all over th' disthrict before you could say Jack Robinson; an' whenever I'm seen they'll whisper, "That's th' father of Mary Boyle that had th' kid be th' swank she used to go with; d'ye know, d'ye know?" To be sure they'll know—more about it than I will meself!

JOHNNY. She should be dhriven out o' th' house she's brought disgrace on!

[1] *bellows'd, noised.*

MRS. BOYLE. Hush, you, Johnny. We needn't let it be bellows'd all over the place; all we've got to do is to leave this place quietly an' go somewhere where we're not known, an' nobody'll be th' wiser.

BOYLE. You're talkin' like a two-year-oul', woman. Where'll we get a place ou' o' this?—places aren't that easily got.

MRS. BOYLE. But, Jack, when we get the money . . .

BOYLE. Money—what money?

MRS. BOYLE. Why, oul' Ellison's money, of course.

BOYLE. There's no money comin' from oul' Ellison, or any one else. Since you've heard of wan throuble, you might as well hear of another. There's no money comin' to us at all—the Will's a wash out!

MRS. BOYLE. What are you sayin', man—no money?

JOHNNY. How could it be a wash out?

BOYLE. The boyo that's afther doin' it to Mary done it to me as well. The thick made out the Will wrong; he said in th' Will, only first cousin an' second cousin, instead of mentionin' our names, an' now any one that thinks he's a first cousin or second cousin t'oul' Ellison can claim the money as well as me, an' they're springin' up in hundreds, an' comin' from America an' Australia, thinkin' to get their whack out of it, while all the time the lawyers is gobblin' it up, till there's not as much as ud buy a stockin' for your lovely daughter's baby!

MRS. BOYLE. I don't believe it, I don't believe it, I don't believe it!

JOHNNY. Why did you say nothin' about this before?

MRS. BOYLE. You're not serious, Jack; you're not serious!

BOYLE. I'm tellin' you the scholar, Bentham, made a banjax[1] o' th' Will; instead o' sayin', "th' rest o' me property to be divided between me first cousin, Jack Boyle, an' me second cousin, Mick Finnegan, o' Santhry," he writ down only, "me first an' second cousins," an' the world an' his wife are afther th' property now.

MRS. BOYLE. Now, I know why Bentham left poor Mary in th' lurch; I can see it all now—oh, is there not even a middlin' honest man left in th' world?

JOHNNY [*to* BOYLE]. An' you let us run into debt, an' you borreyed money from everybody to fill yourself with beer! An' now, you tell us the whole thing's a wash out! Oh, if it's thrue, I'm done with you, for you're worse than me sisther Mary!

---

[1] *banjax, botch, mess.*

BOYLE. You hole yur tongue, d'ye hear? I'll not take any lip from you. Go an' get Bentham if you want satisfaction for all that's afther happenin' us.

JOHNNY. I won't hole me tongue, I won't hole me tongue! I'll tell you what I think of you, father an' all as you are . . . you . . .

MRS. BOYLE. Johnny, Johnny, Johnny, for God's sake, be quiet!

JOHNNY. I'll not be quiet, I'll not be quiet; he's a nice father, isn't he? Is it any wondher Mary went asthray, when . . .

MRS. BOYLE. Johnny, Johnny, for my sake be quiet—for your mother's sake!

BOYLE. I'm goin' out now to have a few dhrinks with th' last few makes I have, an' tell that lassie o' yours not to be here when I come back; for if I lay me eyes on her, I'll lay me han's on her, an' if I lay me han's on her, I won't be accountable for me actions!

JOHNNY. Take care somebody doesn't lay his han's on you— y'oul' . . .

MRS. BOYLE. Johnny, Johnny!

BOYLE [*at door, about to go out*]. Oh, a nice son, an' a nicer daughter, I have. [*Calling loudly upstairs*] Joxer, Joxer, are you there?

JOXER [*from a distance*]. I'm here, More . . . ee . . . aar . . . i . . . tee!

BOYLE. I'm goin' down to Foley's—are you comin'?

JOXER. Come with you? With that sweet call me heart is stirred; I'm only waiting for the word, an' I'll be with you, like a bird!

[BOYLE *and* JOXER *pass the door going out.*]

JOHNNY [*throwing himself on the bed*]. I've a nice sisther, an' a nice father, there's no bettin' on it. I wish to God a bullet or a bomb had whipped me ou' o' this long ago! Not one o' yous, not one o' yous, have any thought for me!

MRS. BOYLE [*with passionate remonstrance*]. If you don't whisht,[1] Johnny, you'll drive me mad. Who has kep' th' home together for the past few years—only me. An' who'll have to bear th' biggest part o' this throuble but me—but whinin' an' whingin'[2] isn't goin' to do any good.

JOHNNY. You're to blame yourself for a gradle of it—givin' him his own way in everything, an' never assin' to check him, no matther what he done. Why didn't you look afther th' money? why . . .

[1] *whisht, be quiet.*
[2] *whingin'. "Whinge" is a dialectal equivalent of "whine." (See* Oxford English Dictionary.)

[*There is a knock at the door;* MRS. BOYLE *opens it;* JOHNNY *rises on his elbow to look and listen; two men enter.*]

FIRST MAN. We've been sent up be th' Manager of the Hibernian Furnishing Co., Mrs. Boyle, to take back the furniture that was got a while ago.

MRS. BOYLE. Yous'll touch nothin' here—how do I know who yous are?

FIRST MAN [*showing a paper*]. There's the ordher, ma'am. [*Reading*] A chest o' drawers, a table, wan easy an' two ordinary chairs; wan mirror; wan chesterfield divan, an' a wardrobe an' two vases. [*To his comrade*] Come on, Bill, it's afther knockin' off time already.

JOHNNY. For God's sake, mother, run down to Foley's an' bring father back, or we'll be left without a stick.

[*The men carry out the table.*]

MRS. BOYLE. What good would it be? You heard what he said before he went out.

JOHNNY. Can't you thry? He ought to be here, an' the like of this goin' on.

[MRS. BOYLE *puts a shawl around her, as* MARY *enters.*]

MARY. What's up, mother? I met men carryin' away the table, an' everybody's talking about us not gettin' the money after all.

MRS. BOYLE. Everythin's gone wrong, Mary, everythin'. We're not gettin' a penny out o' the Will, not a penny—I'll tell you all when I come back; I'm goin' for your father. [*She runs out.*]

JOHNNY [*to* MARY, *who has sat down by the fire*]. It's a wondher you're not ashamed to show your face here, afther what has happened.

[JERRY *enters slowly; there is a look of earnest hope on his face. He looks at* MARY *for a few moments.*]

JERRY [*softly*]. Mary!

[MARY *does not answer.*]

JERRY. Mary, I want to speak to you for a few moments, may I? [MARY *remains silent;* JOHNNY *goes slowly into room on left.*]

JERRY. Your mother has told me everything, Mary, and I have come to you. . . . I have come to tell you, Mary, that my love for you is greater and deeper than ever. . . .

MARY [*with a sob*]. Oh, Jerry, Jerry, say no more; all that is over now; anything like that is impossible now!

JERRY. Impossible! Why do you talk like that, Mary?

MARY. After all that has happened.

JERRY. What does it matter what has happened? We are young enough to be able to forget all those things. [*He catches her hand.*] Mary, Mary, I am pleading for your love. With Labor, Mary, humanity is above everything; we are the Leaders in the fight for a new life. I want to forget Bentham, I want to forget that you left me—even for a while.

MARY. Oh, Jerry, Jerry, you haven't the bitter word of scorn for me after all.

JERRY [*passionately*]. Scorn! I love you, love you, Mary!

MARY [*rising, and looking him in the eyes*]. Even though . . .

JERRY. Even though you threw me over for another man; even though you gave me many a bitter word!

MARY. Yes, yes, I know; but you love me, even though . . . even though . . . I'm . . . goin' . . . goin' . . . [*He looks at her questioningly, and fear gathers in his eyes.*] Ah, I was thinkin' so. . . . You don't know everything!

JERRY [*poignantly*]. Surely to God, Mary, you don't mean that . . . that . . . that . . .

MARY. Now you know all, Jerry; now you know all!

JERRY. My God, Mary, have you fallen as low as that?

MARY. Yes, Jerry, as you say, I have fallen as low as that.

JERRY. I didn't mean it that way, Mary . . . it came on me so sudden, that I didn't mind what I was sayin'. . . . I never expected this—your mother never told me. . . . I'm sorry . . . God knows, I'm sorry for you, Mary.

MARY. Let us say no more, Jerry; I don't blame you for thinkin' it's terrible. . . . I suppose it is. . . . Everybody'll think the same. . . . It's only as I expected—your humanity is just as narrow as the humanity of the others.

JERRY. I'm sorry, all the same. . . . I shouldn't have troubled you. . . . I wouldn't if I'd known . . . if I can do anything for you . . . Mary . . . I will. [*He turns to go, and halts at the door.*]

MARY. Do you remember, Jerry, the verses you read when you gave the lecture in the Socialist Rooms some time ago, on Humanity's Strife with Nature?

JERRY. The verses—no; I don't remember them.

MARY. I do. They're runnin' in me head now—

> An' we felt the power that fashion'd
> All the lovely things we saw,

That created all the murmur
Of an everlasting law,
Was a hand of force an' beauty,
With an eagle's tearin' claw.

Then we saw our globe of beauty
Was an ugly thing as well,
A hymn divine whose chorus
Was an agonizin' yell;
Like the story of a demon,
That an angel had to tell.

Like a glowin' picture by a
Hand unsteady, brought to ruin;
Like her craters, if their deadness
Could give life unto the moon;
Like the agonizing horror
Of a violin out of tune.

[*There is a pause, and* DEVINE *goes slowly out.*]

JOHNNY [*returning*]. Is he gone?

MARY. Yes.

[*The two men re-enter.*]

FIRST MAN. We can't wait any longer for t'oul fella—sorry, Miss, but we have to live as well as th' nex' man.

[*They carry out some things.*]

JOHNNY. Oh, isn't this terrible! . . . I suppose you told him everything . . . couldn't you have waited for a few days . . . he'd have stopped th' takin' of the things, if you'd kep' your mouth shut. Are you burnin' to tell every one of the shame you've brought on us?

MARY [*snatching up her hat and coat*]. Oh, this is unbearable! [*She rushes out.*]

FIRST MAN [*re-entering*]. We'll take the chest o' drawers next —it's the heaviest.

[*The votive light flickers for a moment, and goes out.*]

JOHNNY [*in a cry of fear*]. Mother o' God, the light's afther goin' out!

FIRST MAN. You put the win' up me the way you bawled that time. The oil's all gone, that's all.

JOHNNY [*with an agonizing cry*]. Mother o' God, there's a shot I'm afther gettin'!

FIRST MAN. What's wrong with you, man? Is it a fit you're takin'?

JOHNNY. I'm after feelin' a pain in me breast, like the tearin' by of a bullet!

FIRST MAN. He's goin' mad—it's a wondher they'd leave a chap like that here be himself.

[*Two* IRREGULARS *enter swiftly; they carry revolvers; one goes over to* JOHNNY; *the other covers the two furniture men.*]

FIRST IRREGULAR [*to the men, quietly and incisively*]. Who are you—what are yous doin' here—quick!

FIRST MAN. Removin' furniture that's not paid for.

IRREGULAR. Get over to the other end of the room an' turn your faces to the wall—quick.

[*The two men turn their faces to the wall, with their hands up.*]

SECOND IRREGULAR [*to* JOHNNY]. Come on, Sean Boyle, you're wanted; some of us have a word to say to you.

JOHNNY. I'm sick, I can't—what do you want with me?

SECOND IRREGULAR. Come on, come on; we've a distance to go, an' haven't much time—come on.

JOHNNY. I'm an oul' comrade—yous wouldn't shoot an oul' comrade.

SECOND IRREGULAR. Poor Tancred was an oul' comrade o' yours, but you didn't think o' that when you gave him away to the gang that sent him to his grave. But we've no time to waste; come on—here, Dermot, ketch his arm. [*To* JOHNNY] Have you your beads?

JOHNNY. Me beads! Why do you ass me that, why do you ass me that?

SECOND IRREGULAR. Go on, go on, march!

JOHNNY. Are yous goin' to do in a comrade—look at me arm, I lost it for Ireland.

SECOND IRREGULAR. Commandant Tancred lost his life for Ireland.

JOHNNY. Sacred Heart of Jesus, have mercy on me! Mother o' God, pray for me—be with me now in the agonies o' death! . . . Hail, Mary, full o' grace . . . the Lord is . . . with Thee.

[*They drag out* JOHNNY BOYLE, *and the curtain falls. When it rises again the most of the furniture is gone.* MARY *and* MRS. BOYLE, *one on each side, are sitting in a darkened room, by the fire; it is an hour later.*]

MRS. BOYLE. I'll not wait much longer . . . what did they bring

him away in the mothor for? Nugent says he thinks they had guns
... is me throubles never goin' to be over? ... If anything ud happen
to poor Johnny, I think I'd lost me mind. .... I'll go to the Police
Station, surely they ought to be able to do somethin'.

[*Below is heard the sound of voices.*]

MRS. BOYLE. Whisht, is that something? Maybe, it's your father,
though when I left him in Foley's he was hardly able to lift his head.
Whisht!

[*A knock at the door, and the voice of* MRS. MADIGAN, *speaking
very softly*]

Mrs. Boyle, Mrs. Boyle.

[MRS. BOYLE *opens the door.*]

MRS. MADIGAN. Oh, Mrs. Boyle, God an' His Blessed Mother be
with you this night!

MRS. BOYLE [*calmly*]. What is it, Mrs. Madigan? It's Johnny—
something about Johnny.

MRS. MADIGAN. God send it's not, God send it's not Johnny!

MRS. BOYLE. Don't keep me waitin', Mrs. Madigan; I've gone
through so much lately that I feel able for anything.

MRS. MADIGAN. Two polismen below wantin' you.

MRS. BOYLE. Wantin' me; an' why do they want me?

MRS. MADIGAN. Some poor fella's been found, an' they think it's,
it's ...

MRS. BOYLE. Johnny, Johnny!

MARY [*with her arms round her mother*]. Oh, mother, mother,
me poor, darlin' mother.

MRS. BOYLE. Hush, hush, darlin'; you'll shortly have your own
throuble to bear. [*To* MRS. MADIGAN] An' why do the polis think
it's Johnny, Mrs. Madigan?

MRS. MADIGAN. Because one o' the doctors knew him when he
was attendin' with his poor arm.

MRS. BOYLE. Oh, it's thrue, then, it's Johnny, it's me son, me own
son!

MARY. Oh, it's thrue, it's thrue what Jerry Devine says—there
isn't a God, there isn't a God; if there was He wouldn't let these
things happen!

MRS. BOYLE. Mary, Mary, you mustn't say them things. We'll
want all the help we can get from God an' His Blessed Mother
now! These things have nothin' to do with the Will o' God. Ah,
what can God do agen the stupidity o' men!

MRS. MADIGAN. The polis want you to go with them to the hospital to see the poor body—they're waitin' below.

MRS. BOYLE. We'll go. Come, Mary, an' we'll never come back here agen. Let your father furrage for himself now; I've done all I could an' it was all no use—he'll be hopeless till the end of his days. I've got a little room in me sisther's where we'll stop till your throuble is over, an' then we'll work together for the sake of the baby.

MARY. My poor little child that'll have no father!

MRS. BOYLE. It'll have what's far betther—it'll have two mothers.

[*A rough voice shouting from below*]

Are yous goin' to keep us waitin' for yous all night?

MRS. MADIGAN [*going to the door, and shouting down*]. Take your hour,[1] there, take your hour! If yous are in such a hurry, skip off, then, for nobody wants you here—if they did yous wouldn't be found. For you're the same as yous were undher the British Government—never where yous are wanted! As far as I can see, the Polis as Polis, in this city, is Null an' Void!

MRS. BOYLE. We'll go, Mary, we'll go; you to see your poor dead brother, an' me to see me poor dead son!

MARY. I dhread it, mother, I dhread it!

MRS. BOYLE. I forgot, Mary, I forgot; your poor oul' selfish mother was only thinkin' of herself. No, no, you mustn't come—it wouldn't be good for you. You go on to me sisther's an' I'll face th' ordeal meself. Maybe I didn't feel sorry enough for Mrs. Tancred when her poor son was found as Johnny's been found now—because he was a Die-hard! Ah, why didn't I remember that then he wasn't a Die-hard or a Stater,[2] but only a poor dead son! It's well I remember all that she said—an' it's my turn to say it now: What was the pain I suffered, Johnny, bringin' you into the world to carry you to your cradle to the pains I'll suffer carryin' you out o' the world to bring you to your grave! Mother o' God, Mother of' God, have pity on us all! Blessed Virgin, where were you when me darlin' son was riddled with bullets, when me darlin' son was riddled with bullets? Sacred Heart o' Jesus, take away our hearts o' stone, and give us hearts o' flesh! Take away this murdherin'

---

[1] *take your hour, i.e., your time.*
[2] *a Die-hard or a Stater, one who still demands an independent republic or one who accepts the Irish Free State within the British Empire.*

hate, an' give us Thine own eternal love! [*They all go slowly out.*]

    [*There is a pause; then a sound of shuffling steps on the stairs outside. The door opens and* BOYLE *and* JOXER, *both of them very drunk, enter.*]

BOYLE. I'm able to go no farther. . . . Two polis, ey . . . what were they doin' here, I wondher? . . . Up to no good, anyhow . . . an' Juno an' that lovely daughter o' mine with them. [*Taking a sixpence from his pocket and looking at it*] Wan single, solitary tanner left out of all I borreyed. . . . [*He lets it fall.*] The last o' the Mohicans. . . . The blinds is down, Joxer, the blinds is down!

JOXER [*walking unsteadily across the room, and anchoring at the bed*]. Put all . . . your throubles . . . in your oul' kit bag . . . an' smile . . . smile . . . smile!

BOYLE. The counthry'll have to steady itself . . . it's goin' . . . to hell. . . . Where'r all . . . the chairs . . . gone to . . . steady itself, Joxer. . . . Chairs'll . . . have to . . . steady themselves. . . . No matther . . . what any one may . . . say. . . . Irelan' sober . . . is Irelan' . . . free.

JOXER [*stretching himself on the bed*]. Chains . . . an' . . . slaveree[1] . . . that's a darlin' motto . . . a daaarlin' . . . motto!

BOYLE. If th' worst comes . . . to th' worse . . . I can join a . . . flyin' . . . column. . . . I done . . . me bit . . . in Easther Week . . . had no business . . . to . . . be . . . there . . . but Captain Boyle's Captain Boyle!

JOXER. Breathes there a man with soul . . . so . . . de . . . ad . . . this . . . me . . . o . . . wn, me nat . . . ive l . . . an'!

BOYLE [*subsiding into a sitting posture on the floor*]. Commandant Kelly died . . . in them . . . arms . . . Joxer. . . . Tell me Volunteer Butties . . . says he . . . that . . . I died for . . . Irelan'!

JOXER. D'jever rade Willie . . . Reilly . . . an' his . . . own . . . Colleen . . . Bawn?[2] It's a darlin' story, a daarlin' story!

BOYLE. I'm telling you . . . Joxer . . . th' whole worl's . . . in a terr . . . ible state o' . . . chassis!

CURTAIN

---

[1] *Chains . . . slaveree.* "*Is life so dear, or peace so sweet, as to be purchased at the price of chains and slavery?*" Patrick Henry, *Speech in the Virginia Convention of Delegates, 1775.*

[2] *Willie Reilly . . . Colleen Bawn, characters in the Irish folk ballad,* Willy Reilly. *See Stevenson,* Home Book of Verse.

EUGENE O'NEILL (1888-1953)

Though no one playwright was responsible for the sudden flowering of American drama in the twenties, Eugene O'Neill towered above his contemporaries with his titanic individuality, his bold experimentation, and his prolific production during the fifteen years after the First World War. Only O'Neill earned an international reputation for our drama, which was based not only on his commanding stature as a writer but also on his close ties with the European tradition from Strindberg to the German expressionists. He gave a Continental cast to our stage in his restless exploration of new dramatic techniques, and if he founded no school and had no imitators, it was in part because his styles were too personal and too varied to be copied, in part because they were themselves derived from European writers whose work had never been much at home in the theaters of England and America. The dramas of this dedicated and somberly brooding spirit ranged from amazing successes to embarrassing failures, both commercially and artistically. Half of his plays are mercifully forgotten today, but the others, covering every period of his career, provide an exciting study in self-expression and self-fulfillment. Above all, they reveal a sure sense of theatrical know-how which enabled him to attain the most unlikely triumphs with uncompromising plays that tax the intellect and the patience of his audiences to the breaking point.

This sense of the stage may well have sprung from his background, for O'Neill actually grew up in the theater. The son of the famous romantic actor James O'Neill, who traveled the country from one end to the other in *The*

Count of Monte Cristo, he was literally born on Broadway, in a hotel where his parents were staying during the theater season. The O'Neills summered at New London, Connecticut, which was home to the growing boy. The devout Catholicism of his mother and his early education in Catholic schools may be revealed in the strong current of mysticism in his plays and in his persistent quest for spiritual peace amid the disturbing realities of modern life.

His expulsion from Princeton for a freshman escapade in 1907 began a decade of seemingly aimless living, in which he was slowly finding himself through a great variety of experiences in many parts of the Western Hemisphere. He prospected for gold in Honduras in 1909 and struck nothing but a case of malaria. He worked intermittently in his father's touring company as actor and stage manager. Most influential of all his experiences was his turn as a merchant seaman on several ships, where he gained that understanding of the sailor's life that was to inspire his first acted plays, the *S. S. Glencairn* series. Stranded in Buenos Aires, he worked as a clerk in the Argentine offices of several American firms. He took to drink and dissipation there and later lived for a time among the derelicts in Jimmy the Priest's saloon on the New York waterfront, which formed the setting of his last play produced on Broadway, *The Iceman Cometh.*

Gradually the urge to write took possession of O'Neill, and he went to work as a reporter and columnist on a newspaper in his old home of New London. The praise of his editor first encouraged him to concentrate upon creative work. At this turning point in his career he contracted tuberculosis, and during his long convalescence in a sanatorium at Wallingford, Connecticut, his reading in the older playwrights focused his ambition on the drama. This year of 1913-1914, then, saw the completion of his youthful exploration of life. Thereafter he was directed by a purposeful creative energy that drove him on through experiment and triumph in the theater until his sudden retirement in 1933.

But five years of apprenticeship lay ahead before his first première in a Broadway theater. Feeling the need of technical discipline he studied for a year (1914-1915) with George Pierce Baker in his "47 Workshop" at Harvard, and then joined the Provincetown Players, who gave summer performances at their tiny Wharf Theatre on Cape Cod, Massachusetts, and winter performances on a little stage down in the Greenwich Village section of New York City. At Provincetown in 1916 O'Neill saw his first play produced, a one-acter in the *S. S. Glencairn* series called *Bound East for Cardiff*. In part because of the interruption of the First World War, it was not until February 2, 1920, that the first of his full-length plays, *Beyond the Horizon,* was staged in a Broadway theater. This date marks conveniently, if inaccurately, the new drama's conquest of the professional stage. But O'Neill continued to present his plays at the Provincetown Playhouse in the Village until its demise in 1929. Thereafter he was taken over by the Theatre Guild, which was in a position to provide adequate productions for his most taxing works, such as *Strange Interlude* and *Mourning Becomes Electra.*

Some playwrights have seemed to work within a very narrow area, perfecting a formula or two to be repeated in play after play. Such were Philip Barry and S. N. Behrman. O'Neill, on the other hand, has seemed to write with a driving fear of repeating himself. Every modern dramatic style—realism, naturalism, romanticism, symbolism, expressionism—is represented in his work, as well as most of the dramatic types from the gloomy naturalistic tragedy of *Beyond the Horizon* and the historical romance of *The Fountain* to folk comedy in *Ah, Wilderness!* and social satire in *Marco Millions.* His success in experimenting with bizarre technical devices—the masks of *The Great God Brown,* the asides and soliloquies of *Strange Interlude,* the trilogy form of *Mourning Becomes Electra,* the alter ego character in *Days Without End*—seldom moved him to try the same thing a second time. Each represented an artistic challenge to be met, but once the problem was solved, he would move on to a new one. It would almost seem that the badge of an O'Neill play is its differentness from all other plays by O'Neill.

Actually, nearly all of his works betray a strong affinity with each other, which lies not in the formal matters of the type of play, style, and technical experiment, but in the enveloping mood of the play and the undercurrent of moral idea that obsesses them. In the most ambitious and provocative study of O'Neill's work that has yet appeared, R. D. Skinner has traced what he calls "a poet's quest" for resolution of the moral conflicts of modern man in a world dedicated to materialism. This full-length critical analysis undoubtedly ascribes a more consistent design to O'Neill's plays than he was himself aware of, but it does not falsify the facts in arguing for an underlying pattern of ideas that may reveal a cycle of question and answer in the mind, or the conscience, of the artist himself.

O'Neill was a highly subjective writer who put nearly all of his own problems and experiences into his plays. Not only did he include the superficial happenings of his life: his New England background in the locale of *Desire Under the Elms* and *Mourning Becomes Electra;* his sea voyages in the *S. S. Glencairn* plays and the sea and sailor motifs in a host of others, especially *Anna Christie;* the tuberculosis sanatorium that forms the setting of *The Straw;* or Jimmy the Priest's of *The Iceman Cometh*—but his works also showed signs of influence by authors who impressed him: the Greek dramatists who inspired in part *The Great God Brown* and *Mourning Becomes Electra;* Freud and the psychoanalysts who honeycomb O'Neill's drama, particularly *Strange Interlude* and *Mourning Becomes Electra;* and above all August Strindberg, whose shocking interpretation of the sex duel appeared especially in O'Neill's early plays, like *Before Breakfast, Beyond the Horizon, Welded,* and *All God's Chillun Got Wings.*

At the end of his life, *Long Day's Journey Into Night* (1957), another naturalistic double-decker, came closest of all his dramas to outright autobiography. It projected out of his youth a savage reminiscence of his family at their summer home in Connecticut, representing his father as a pompous, parsimonious, hard-drinking, passé stage star, his mother as a pathetic dreamer, addicted to narcotics because of the father's stinginess in giving her responsible physicians, his older brother as an obnoxious alcoholic windbag, and himself as a pale, bewildered, half-formed young man. The picture was certainly jaundiced, but the drama, in its depressing way, is overpowering. Despite the physical agony of his last years, O'Neill never lost his grip on the stage.

Beyond these obvious ties with his personal life, O'Neill's plays suggest his trial of soul and his abiding concern with the problem of good and evil in the cold-steel world of *Dynamo*. Being both an Irishman and a Catholic by background, he possessed that curious combination of mysticism and almost Calvinist conscience that has haunted so much of modern Irish literature. Despite the testimony of *Days Without End,* O'Neill never returned to the faith of his fathers, but he was temperamentally unable to accept the godless materialism of our century, which dwarfs the dignity of man and tries to dispel the mystery of the universe. For O'Neill the revolution wrought by physical science and psychoanalysis did not destroy the realities of older periods of man's spiritual life but gave him a new understanding of their meaning. To the interpretation of these spiritual realities he brought not simply the soul-baring realism of Strindberg and Freud, but also the cumulated tradition of centuries of inquiry. He believed that facing the truth about the nature of man, however unpleasant, must precede any final security. Like Socrates he must know before he can find contentment and rest. Like Dante he must go through the inferno of horror and disillusionment to reach the truth and the eventual peace of the spirit.

EUGENE O'NEILL

DESIRE UNDER THE ELMS

CHARACTERS

Ephraim Cabot
Simeon
Peter   } *his sons*
Eben
Abbie Putnam
Young Girl, two Farmers, the Fiddler, a Sheriff, and other folk from the neighboring farms.

The action of the entire play takes place in, and immediately outside of, the Cabot farmhouse in New England, in the year 1850. The south end of the house faces front to a stone wall with a wooden gate at center opening on a country road. The house is in good condition but in need of paint. Its walls are a sickly grayish, the green of the shutters faded. Two enormous elms are on each side of the house. They bend their trailing branches down over the roof. They appear to protect and at the same time subdue. There is a sinister maternity in their aspect, a crushing, jealous absorption. They have developed from their intimate contact with the life of man in the house an appalling humaneness. They brood oppressively over the house. They are like exhausted women resting their sagging breasts and hands and hair on its roof, and when it rains their tears trickle down monotonously and rot on the shingles.

There is a path running from the gate around the right corner of the house to the front door. A narrow porch is on this side. The end wall facing us has two windows in its upper story, two larger ones on the floor below. The two upper are those of the father's bedroom and that of the brothers. On the left, ground floor, is the kitchen—on the right, the parlor, the shades of which are always drawn down.

part 1, scene 1

Exterior of the farmhouse. It is sunset of a day at the beginning of summer in the year 1850. There is no wind and everything is still. The sky above the roof is suffused with deep colors, the green of the elms glows, but the house is in shadow, seeming pale and washed out by contrast.

A door opens and EBEN CABOT comes to the end of the porch and stands looking down the road to the right. He has a large bell in his hand and this he swings mechanically, awakening a deafening clangor. Then he puts his hands on his hips and stares up at the sky. He sighs with a puzzled awe and blurts out with halting appreciation.

EBEN. God! Purty! [*His eyes fall and he stares about him frowningly. He is twenty-five, tall and sinewy. His face is well-formed, good-looking, but its expression is resentful and defensive. His defiant, dark eyes remind one of a wild animal's in captivity. Each day is a cage in which he finds himself trapped but inwardly unsubdued. There is a fierce repressed vitality about him. He has black hair, mustache, a thin curly trace of beard. He is dressed in rough farm clothes.*

He spits on the ground with intense disgust, turns and goes back into the house.

[SIMEON *and* PETER *come in from their work in the fields. They are tall men, much older than their half-brother (*SIMEON *is thirty-nine and* PETER *thirty-seven), built on a squarer, simpler model, fleshier in body, more bovine and homelier in face, shrewder and more practical. Their shoulders stoop a bit from years of farm work. They clump heavily along in their clumsy*

[*thick-soled boots caked with earth. Their clothes, their faces, hands, bare arms and throats are earth-stained. They smell of earth. They stand together for a moment in front of the house and, as if with the one impulse, stare dumbly up at the sky, leaning on their hoes. Their faces have a compressed, unresigned expression. As they look upward, this softens.*]

SIMEON [*grudgingly*]. Purty.

PETER. Ay-eh.

SIMEON [*suddenly*]. Eighteen year ago.

PETER. What?

SIMEON. Jenn. My woman. She died.

PETER. I'd fergot.

SIMEON. I rec'lect—now an' agin. Makes it lonesome. She'd hair long's a hoss' tail—an' yaller like gold!

PETER. Waal—she's gone. [*This with indifferent finality—then after a pause*] They's gold in the West, Sim.

SIMEON [*still under the influence of sunset—vaguely*]. In the sky?

PETER. Waal—in a manner o' speakin'—thar's the promise. [*Growing excited*] Gold in the sky—in the West—Golden Gate—Californi-a!—Goldest West!—fields o' gold!

SIMEON [*excited in his turn*]. Fortunes layin' just atop o' the ground waitin' t' be picked! Solomon's mines, they says! [*For a moment they continue looking up at the sky—then their eyes drop.*]

PETER [*with sardonic bitterness*]. Here—it's stones atop o' the ground—stones atop o' stones—makin' stone walls—year atop o' year—him 'n' yew 'n' me 'n' then Eben—makin' stone walls fur him to fence us in!

SIMEON. We've wuked. Give our strength. Give our years. Plowed 'em under in the ground—[*he stamps rebelliously*]—rottin'—makin' soil for his crops! [*A pause.*] Waal—the farm pays good for hereabouts.

PETER. If we plowed in Californi-a, they'd be lumps o' gold in the furrow!

SIMEON. Californi-a's t'other side o' earth, a'most. We got t' calc'late—

PETER [*after a pause*]. 'Twould be hard fur me, too, to give up what we've 'arned here by our sweat. [*A pause,* EBEN *sticks his head out of the dining-room window, listening.*]

SIMEON. Ay-eh. [*A pause*] Mebbe—he'll die soon.

PETER [*doubtfully*]. Mebbe.

SIMEON. Mebbe—fur all we knows—he's dead now.

PETER. Ye'd need proof.

SIMEON. He's been gone two months—with no word.

PETER. Left us in the fields an evenin' like this. Hitched up an' druv off into the West. That's plum onnateral. He hain't never been off this farm 'ceptin' t' the village in thirty year or more, not since he married Eben's maw. [*A pause. Shrewdly*] I calc'late we might git him declared crazy by the court.

SIMEON. He skinned 'em too slick. He got the best o' all on 'em. They'd never b'lieve him crazy. [*A pause.*] We got t' wait—till he's under ground.

EBEN [*with a sardonic chuckle*]. Honor thy father! [*They turn, startled, and stare at him. He grins, then scowls.*] I pray he's died. [*They stare at him. He continues matter-of-factly.*] Supper's ready.

SIMEON *and* PETER [*together*]. Ay-eh.

EBEN [*gazing up at the sky*]. Sun's downin' purty.

SIMEON *and* PETER [*together*]. Ay-eh. They's gold in the West.

EBEN. Ay-eh. [*Pointing*] Yonder atop o' the hill pasture, ye mean?

SIMEON *and* PETER [*together*]. In Californi-a!

EBEN. Hunh? [*Stares at them indifferently for a second, then drawls*] Waal—supper's gittin' cold. [*He turns back into kitchen.*]

SIMEON [*startled—smacks his lips*]. I air hungry!

PETER [*sniffing*]. I smells bacon!

SIMEON [*with hungry appreciation*]. Bacon's good!

PETER [*in same tone*]. Bacon's bacon! [*They turn, shouldering each other, their bodies bumping and rubbing together as they hurry clumsily to their food, like two friendly oxen toward their evening meal. They disappear around the right corner of house and can be heard entering the door.*]

CURTAIN

part 1, scene 2

The color fades from the sky. Twilight begins. The interior of the kitchen is now visible. A pine table is at center, a cookstove in the right rear corner, four rough wooden chairs, a tallow candle on the table. In the middle of the rear wall is fastened a big advertising poster with a ship in full sail and the word "California" in big letters. Kitchen utensils hang from nails. Everything is neat and in order but the atmos-

phere is of a men's camp kitchen rather than that of a home.
    Places for three are laid. EBEN *takes boiled potatoes and bacon from the stove and puts them on the table, also a loaf of bread and a crock of water.* SIMEON *and* PETER *shoulder in, slump down in their chairs without a word.* EBEN *joins them. The three eat in silence for a moment, the two elder as naturally unrestrained as beasts of the field,* EBEN *picking at his food without appetite, glancing at them with a tolerant dislike.*

SIMEON [*suddenly turns to* EBEN]. Looky here! Ye'd oughtn't t' said that, Eben.

PETER. 'Twa'n't righteous.

EBEN. What?

SIMEON. Ye prayed he'd died.

EBEN. Waal—don't yew pray it? [*A pause.*]

PETER. He's our Paw.

EBEN [*violently*]. Not mine!

SIMEON [*dryly*]. Ye'd not let no one else say that about yer Maw! Ha! [*He gives one abrupt sardonic gufflaw.* PETER *grins.*]

EBEN [*very pale*]. I meant—I hain't his'n—I hain't like him—he hain't me!

PETER [*dryly*]. Wait till ye've growed his age!

EBEN [*intensely*]. I'm Maw—every drop o' blood! [*A pause. They stare at him with indifferent curiosity.*]

PETER [*reminiscently*]. She was good t' Sim 'n' me. A good Step-maw's scurse.

SIMEON. She was good t' everyone.

EBEN [*greatly moved, gets to his feet and makes an awkward bow to each of them—stammering*]. I be thankful t'ye. I'm her—her heir. [*He sits down in confusion.*]

PETER [*after a pause—judicially*]. She was good even t' him.

EBEN [*fiercely*]. An' fur thanks he killed her!

SIMEON [*after a pause*]. No one never kills nobody. It's allus somethin'. That's the murderer.

EBEN. Didn't he slave Maw t' death?

PETER. He slaved himself t' death. He's slaved Sim 'n' me 'n' yew t' death—on'y none o' us hain't died—yit.

SIMEON. It's somethin'—drivin' him—t' drive us!

EBEN [*vengefully*]. Waal—I hold him t' jedgment! [*Then scornfully*] Somethin'! What's somethin'?

SIMEON. Dunno.

EBEN [*sardonically*]. What's drivin' yew to Californi-a, mebbe? [*They look at him in surprise.*] Oh, I've heerd ye! [*Then, after a pause*] But ye'll never go t' the gold fields!

PETER [*assertively*]. Mebbe!

EBEN. Whar'll ye git the money?

PETER. We kin walk. It's an a'mighty ways—Californi-a—but if yew was t' put all the steps we've walked on this farm end t' end we'd be in the moon!

EBEN. The Injuns'll skulp ye on the plains.

SIMEON [*with grim humor*]. We'll mebbe make 'em pay a hair fur a hair!

EBEN [*decisively*]. But t'ain't that. Ye won't never go because ye'll wait here fur yer share o' the farm, thinkin' allus he'll die soon.

SIMEON [*after a pause*]. We've a right.

PETER. Two-thirds belongs t' us.

EBEN [*jumping to his feet*]. Ye've no right! She wa'n't yewr Maw! It was her farm! Didn't he steal it from her? She's dead. It's my farm.

SIMEON [*sardonically*]. Tell that t' Paw—when he comes! I'll bet ye a dollar he'll laugh—fur once in his life. Ha! [*He laughs himself in one single mirthless bark.*]

PETER [*amused in turn, echoes his brother*]. Ha!

SIMEON [*after a pause*]. What've ye got held agin us, Eben? Year after year it's skulked in yer eye—somethin'.

PETER. Ay-eh.

EBEN. Ay-eh. They's somethin'. [*Suddenly exploding*] Why didn't ye never stand between him 'n' my Maw when he was slavin' her to her grave—t' pay her back fur the kindness she done t' yew? [*There is a long pause. They stare at him in surprise.*]

SIMEON. Waal—the stock'd got t' be watered.

PETER. 'R they was woodin' t' do.

SIMEON. 'R plowin'.

PETER. 'R hayin'.

SIMEON. 'R spreadin' manure.

PETER. 'R weedin'.

SIMEON. 'R prunin'.

PETER. 'R milkin'.

EBEN [*breaking in harshly*]. An' makin' walls—stone atop o' stone —makin' walls till yer heart's a stone ye heft up out o' the way o' growth onto a stone wall t' wall in yer heart!

SIMEON [*matter-of-factly*]. We never had no time t' meddle.

PETER [*to* EBEN]. Yew was fifteen afore yer Maw died—an' big fur yer age. Why didn't ye never do nothin'?

EBEN [*harshly*]. They was chores t' do, wa'n't they? [*A pause— then slowly*] It was on'y arter she died I come to think o' it. Me cookin' —doin' her work—that made me know her, suffer her sufferin'—she'd come back t' help—come back t' bile potatoes—come back t' fry bacon—come back t' bake biscuits—come back all cramped up t' shake the fire, an' carry ashes, her eyes weepin' an' bloody with smoke an' cinders same's they used t' be. She still comes back—stands by the stove thar in the evenin'—she can't find it nateral sleepin' an' restin' in peace. She can't git used t' bein' free—even in her grave.

SIMEON. She never complained none.

EBEN. She'd got too tired. She'd got too used t' bein' too tired. That was what he done. [*With vengeful passion*] An' sooner'r later, I'll meddle. I'll say the thin's I didn't say then t' him! I'll yell 'em at the top o' my lungs. I'll see t' it my Maw gits some rest an' sleep in her grave! [*He sits down again, relapsing into a brooding silence. They look at him with a queer indifferent curiosity.*]

PETER [*after a pause*]. Whar in tarnation d'ye s'pose he went, Sim?

SIMEON. Dunno. He druv off in the buggy, all spick an' span, with the mare all breshed an' shiny, druv off clackin' his tongue an' wavin' his whip. I remember it right well. I was finishin' plowin', it was spring an' May an' sunset, an' gold in the West, an' he druv off into it. I yells "Whar ye goin', Paw?" an' he hauls up by the stone wall a jiffy. His old snake's eyes was glitterin' in the sun like he'd been drinkin' a jugful an' he says with a mule's grin: "Don't ye run away till I come back!"

PETER. Wonder if he knowed we was wantin' fur Californi-a?

SIMEON. Mebbe. I didn't say nothin' and he says, lookin' kinder queer an' sick: "I been hearin' the hens cluckin' an' the roosters crowin' all the durn day. I been listenin' t' the cows lowin' an' everythin' else kickin' up till I can't stand it no more. It's spring an' I'm feelin' damned," he says. "Damned like an old bare hickory tree fit on'y fur burnin'," he says. An' then I calc'late I must've looked a mite hopeful, fur he adds real spry and vicious: "But don't git no fool idee I'm dead. I've sworn t' live a hundred an' I'll do it, if on'y t' spite yer sinful greed! An' now I'm ridin' out t' learn God's message t' me in the spring, like the prophets done. An' yew git back t' yer plowin'," he says. An' he druv off singin' a hymn. I thought he was drunk—'r I'd stopped him goin'.

EBEN [*scornfully*]. No, ye wouldn't! Ye're scared o' him. He's stronger—inside—than both o' ye put together!

PETER [*sardonically*]. An' yew—be yew Samson?

EBEN. I'm gittin' stronger. I kin feel it growin' in me—growin' an' growin'—till it'll bust out—! [*He gets up and puts on his coat and a hat. They watch him, gradually breaking into grins.* EBEN *avoids their eyes sheepishly.*] I'm goin' out fur a spell—up the road.

PETER. T' the village?

SIMEON. T' see Minnie?

EBEN [*defiantly*]. Ay-eh!

PETER [*jeeringly*]. The Scarlet Woman!

SIMEON. Lust—that's what's growin' in ye!

EBEN. Waal—she's purty!

PETER. She's been purty fur twenty year!

SIMEON. A new coat o' paint'll make a heifer out of forty.

EBEN. She hain't forty!

PETER. If she hain't, she's teeterin' on the edge.

EBEN [*desperately*]. What d'yew know—

PETER. All they is . . . Sim knew her—an' then me arter—

SIMEON. An' Paw kin tell yew somethin' too! He was fust!

EBEN. D'ye mean t' say he . . . ?

SIMEON [*with a grin*]. Ay-eh! We air his heirs in everythin'!

EBEN [*intensely*]. That's more to it! That grows on it! It'll bust soon! [*Then violently*] I'll go smash my fist in her face! [*He pulls open the door in rear violently.*]

SIMEON [*with a wink at* PETER—*drawlingly*]. Mebbe—but the night's wa'm—purty—by the time ye git thar mebbe ye'll kiss her instead!

PETER. Sart'n he will! [*They both roar with coarse laughter.* EBEN *rushes out and slams the door—then the outside front door— comes around the corner of the house and stands still by the gate, staring up at the sky.*]

SIMEON [*looking after him*]. Like his Paw.

PETER. Dead spit an' image!

SIMEON. Dog'll eat dog!

PETER. Ay-eh. [*Pause. With yearning*] Mebbe a year from now we'll be in Californi-a.

SIMEON. Ay-eh. [*A pause. Both yawn.*] Let's git t'bed. [*He blows out the candle. They go out door in rear.* EBEN *stretches his arms up to the sky—rebelliously.*]

EBEN. Waal—thar's a star, an' somewhar's they's him, an' here's me, an' thar's Min up the road—in the same night. What if I does kiss her? She's like t'night, she's soft 'n' wa'm, her eyes kin wink like a star, her mouth's wa'm, her arms're wa'm, she smells like a wa'm plowed field, she's purty . . . Ay-eh! By God A'mighty she's purty, an' I don't give a damn how many sins she's sinned afore mine or who's she's sinned 'em with, my sin's as purty as any one on 'em! [*He strides off down the road to the left.*]

part 1, scene 3

It is the pitch darkness just before dawn. EBEN *comes in from the left and goes around to the porch, feeling his way, chuckling bitterly and cursing half-aloud to himself.*

EBEN. The cussed old miser! [*He can be heard going in the front door. There is a pause as he goes upstairs, then a loud knock on the bedroom door of the brothers.*] Wake up!

SIMEON [*startledly*]. Who thar?

EBEN [*pushing open the door and coming in, a lighted candle in his hand. The bedroom of the brothers is revealed. Its ceiling is the sloping roof. They can stand upright only close to the center dividing wall of the upstairs.* SIMEON *and* PETER *are in a double bed, front.* EBEN'S *cot is to the rear.* EBEN *has a mixture of silly grin and vicious scowl on his face*]. I be!

PETER [*angrily*]. What in hell's-fire . . . ?

EBEN. I got news fur ye! Ha! [*He gives one abrupt sardonic guffaw.*]

SIMEON [*angrily*]. Couldn't ye hold it 'til we'd got our sleep?

EBEN. It's nigh sunup. [*Then explosively*] He's gone an' married agen!

SIMEON *and* PETER [*explosively*]. Paw?

EBEN. Got himself hitched to a female 'bout thirty-five—an' purty, they says . . .

SIMEON [*aghast*]. It's a durn lie!

PETER. Who says?

SIMEON. They been stringin' ye!

EBEN. Think I'm a dunce, do ye? The hull village says. The preacher from New Dover, he brung the news—told it t'our preacher —New Dover, that's whar the old loon got himself hitched—that's whar the woman lived—

PETER [*no longer doubting—stunned*]. Waal...!

SIMEON [*the same*]. Waal...!

EBEN [*sitting down on a bed—with vicious hatred*]. Ain't he a devil out o' hell? It's jest t' spite us—the damned old mule!

PETER [*after a pause*]. Everythin'll go t' her now.

SIMEON. Ay-eh [*A pause—dully*] Waal—if it's done—

PETER. It's done us. [*Pause—then persuasively*] They's gold in the fields o' Californi-a, Sim. No good a-stayin' here now.

SIMEON. Jest what I was a-thinkin'. [*Then with decision*] S'well fust's last! Let's light out and git this mornin'.

PETER. Suits me.

EBEN. Ye must like walkin'.

SIMEON [*sardonically*]. If ye'd grow wings on us we'd fly thar!

EBEN. Ye'd like ridin' better—on a boat, wouldn't ye? [*Fumbles in his pocket and takes out a crumpled sheet of foolscap*] Waal, if ye sign this ye kin ride on a boat. I've had it writ out an' ready in case ye'd ever go. It says fur three hundred dollars t' each ye agree yewr shares o' the farm is sold t' me. [*They look suspiciously at the paper. A pause.*]

SIMEON [*wonderingly*]. But if he's hitched agen—

PETER. An' whar'd yew git that sum o' money, anyways?

EBEN [*cunningly*]. I know whar it's hid. I been waitin'—Maw told me. She knew whar it lay fur years, but she was waitin' ... It's her'n—the money he hoarded from her farm an' hid from Maw. It's my money by rights now.

PETER. Whar's it hid?

EBEN [*cunningly*]. Whar yew won't never find it without me. Maw spied on him—'r she'd never knowed. [*A pause. They look at him suspiciously, and he at them.*] Waal, is it fa'r trade?

SIMEON. Dunno.

PETER. Dunno.

SIMEON [*looking at window*]. Sky's grayin'.

PETER. Ye better start the fire, Eben.

SIMEON. An' fix some vittles.

EBEN. Ay-eh. [*Then with a forced jocular heartiness*] I'll git ye a good one. If ye're startin' t' hoof it t' Californi-a ye'll need somethin' that'll stick t' yer ribs. [*He turns to the door, adding meaningly*] But ye kin ride on a boat if ye'll swap. [*He stops at the door and pauses. They stare at him.*]

SIMEON [*suspiciously*]. Whar was ye all night?

EBEN [*defiantly*]. Up t' Min's. [*Then slowly*] Walkin' thar, fust I felt 's if I'd kiss her; then I got a-thinkin' o' what ye'd said o' him an' her an' I says, I'll bust her nose fur that! Then I got t' the village an' heerd the news an' I got madder'n hell an' run all the way t' Min's not knowin' what I'd do—[*He pauses—then sheepishly but more defiantly*] Waal—when I seen her, I didn't hit her—nor I didn't kiss her nuther—I begun t' beller like a calf an' cuss at the same time, I was so durn mad—an' she got scared—an' I jest grabbed holt an' tuk her! [*Proudly*] Yes, sirree! I tuk her. She may've been his'n—an' your'n, too—but she's mine now!

SIMEON [*dryly*]. In love, air yew?

EBEN [*with lofty scorn*]. Love! I don't take no stock in sech slop!

PETER [*winking at* SIMEON]. Mebbe Eben's aimin' t' marry, too.

SIMEON. Min'd make a true faithful he'pmeet! [*They snicker.*]

EBEN. What do I care fur her—'ceptin' she's round an' wa'm? The p'int is she was his'n—an' now she belongs t' me! [*He goes to the door—then turns—rebelliously.*] An' Min hain't sech a bad un. They's worse'n Min in the world, I'll bet ye! Wait'll we see this cow the Old Man's hitched t'! She'll beat Min, I got a notion! [*He starts to go out.*]

SIMEON [*suddenly*]. Mebbe ye'll try t' make her your'n, too?

PETER. Ha! [*He gives a sardonic laugh of relish at this idea.*]

EBEN [*spitting with disgust*]. Her—here—sleepin' with him—stealin' my Maw's farm! I'd as soon pet a skunk 'r kiss a snake! [*He goes out. The two stare after him suspiciously. A pause. They listen to his steps receding.*]

PETER. He's startin' the fire.

SIMEON. I'd like t' ride t' Californi-a—but—

PETER. Min might o' put some scheme in his head.

SIMEON. Mebbe it's all a lie 'bout Paw marryin'. We'd best wait an' see the bride.

PETER. An' don't sign nothin' till we does!

SIMEON. Nor till we've tested it's good money! [*Then with a grin*] But if Paw's hitched we'd be sellin' Eben somethin' we'd never git nohow!

PETER. We'll wait an' see. [*Then with sudden vindictive anger*] An' till he comes, let's yew 'n' me not wuk a lick, let Eben tend to thin's if he's a mind t', let's us jest sleep an' eat an' drink likker, an' let the hull damned farm go t' blazes!

SIMEON [*excitedly*]. By God, we've 'arned a rest! We'll play rich fur a change. I hain't a-goin' to stir outa bed till breakfast's ready.

PETER. An' on the table!

SIMEON [*after a pause—thoughtfully*]. What d' ye calc'late she'll be like—our new Maw? Like Eben thinks?

PETER. More'n likely.

SIMEON [*vindictively*]. Waal—I hope she's a she-devil that'll make him wish he was dead an' livin' in the pit o' hell fur comfort!

PETER [*fervently*]. Amen!

SIMEON [*imitating his father's voice*]. "I'm ridin' out t' learn God's message t' me in the spring like the prophets done," he says. I'll bet right then an' thar he knew plumb well he was goin' whorin', the stinkin' old hypocrite!

part 1, scene 4

Same as Scene 2—shows the interior of the kitchen with a lighted candle on table. It is gray dawn outside. SIMEON *and* PETER *are just finishing their breakfast.* EBEN *sits before his plate of untouched food, brooding frowningly.*

PETER [*glancing at him rather irritably*]. Lookin' glum don't help none.

SIMEON [*sarcastically*]. Sorrowin' over his lust o' the flesh!

PETER [*with a grin*]. Was she yer fust?

EBEN [*angrily*]. None o' yer business. [*A pause.*] I was thinkin' o' him. I got a notion he's gittin' near—I kin feel him comin' on like yew kin feel malaria chill afore it takes ye.

PETER. It's too early yet.

SIMEON. Dunno. He'd like t' catch us nappin'—jest t' have somethin' t' hoss us 'round over.

PETER [*mechanically gets to his feet.* SIMEON *does the same*]. Waal —let's git t' wuk. [*They both plod mechanically toward the door before they realize. Then they stop short.*]

SIMEON [*grinning*]. Ye're a cussed fool, Pete—and I be wuss! Let him see we hain't wukin'! We don't give a durn!

PETER [*as they go back to the table*]. Not a damned durn! It'll serve t' show him we're done with him. [*They sit down again.* EBEN *stares from one to the other with surprise.*]

SIMEON [*grins at him*]. We're aimin' t' start bein' lilies o' the field.

PETER. Nary a toil 'r spin 'r lick o' wuk do we put in!

SIMEON. Ye're sole owner—till he comes—that's what ye wanted. Waal, ye got t' be sole hand, too.

PETER. The cows air bellerin'. Ye better hustle at the milkin'.

EBEN [*with excited joy*]. Ye mean ye'll sign the paper?

SIMEON [*dryly*]. Mebbe.

PETER. Mebbe.

SIMEON. We're considerin'. [*Peremptorily*] Ye better git t' wuk.

EBEN [*with queer excitement*]. It's Maw's farm agen! It's my farm! Them's my cows! I'll milk my durn fingers off fur cows o' mine! [*He goes out door in rear, they stare after him indifferently.*]

SIMEON. Like his Paw.

PETER. Dead spit 'n' image!

SIMEON. Waal—let dog eat dog! [EBEN *comes out of front door and around the corner of the house. The sky is beginning to grow flushed with sunrise.* EBEN *stops by the gate and stares around him with glowing, possessive eyes. He takes in the whole farm with his embracing glance of desire.*]

EBEN. It's purty! It's damned purty! It's mine! [*He suddenly throws his head back boldly and glares with hard, defiant eye at the sky.*] Mine, d'ye hear? Mine! [*He turns and walks quickly off left, rear, toward the barn. The two brothers light their pipes.*]

SIMEON [*putting his muddy boots up on the table, tilting back his chair, and puffing defiantly*]. Waal—this air solid comfort—fur once.

PETER. Ay-eh. [*He follows suit. A pause. Unconsciously they both sigh.*]

SIMEON [*suddenly*]. He never was much o' a hand at milkin', Eben wa'n't.

PETER [*with a snort*]. His hands air like hoofs! [*A pause.*]

SIMEON. Reach down the jug thar! Let's take a swaller. I'm feelin' kind o' low.

PETER. Good idee! [*He does so—gets two glasses—they pour out drinks of whisky.*] Here's t' the gold in Californi-a!

SIMEON. An' luck t' find it! [*They drink—puff resolutely—sigh—take their feet down from the table.*]

PETER. Likker don't 'pear t' sot right.

SIMEON. We hain't used t' it this early. [*A pause. They become very restless.*]

PETER. Gittin' close in this kitchen.

SIMEON [*with immense relief*]. Let's git a breath o' air. [*They arise briskly and go out rear—appear around house and stop by the gate. They stare up at the sky with a numbed appreciation.*]

PETER. Purty!

SIMEON. Ay-eh. Gold's t' the East now.

PETER. Sun's startin' with us fur the Golden West.

SIMEON [*staring around the farm, his compressed face tightened, unable to conceal his emotion*]. Waal—it's our last mornin'—mebbe.

PETER [*the same*]. Ay-eh.

SIMEON [*stamps his foot on the earth and addresses it desperately*]. Waal—ye've thirty year o' me buried in ye—spread out over ye—blood an' bone an' sweat—rotted away—fertilizin' ye—richin' yer soul— prime manure, by God, that's what I been t' ye!

PETER. Ay-eh! An' me!

SIMEON. An' yew, Peter. [*He sighs—then spits.*] Waal—no use'n cryin' over spilt milk.

PETER. They's gold in the West—an' freedom, mebbe. We been slaves t' stone walls here.

SIMEON [*defiantly*]. We hain't nobody's slaves from this out—nor no thin's slaves nuther. [*A pause—restlessly*] Speakin' o' milk, wonder how Eben's managin'?

PETER. I s'pose he's managin'.

SIMEON. Mebbe we'd ought t' help—this once.

PETER. Mebbe. The cows knows us.

SIMEON. An' likes us. They don't know him much.

PETER. An' the hosses, an' pigs, an' chickens. They don't know him much.

SIMEON. They knows us like brothers—an' likes us! [*Proudly*] Hain't we raised 'em t' be fust-rate, number one prize stock?

PETER. We hain't—not no more.

SIMEON [*dully*]. I was fergittin'. [*Then resignedly*] Waal, let's go help Eben a spell an' git waked up.

PETER. Suits me. [*They are starting off down left, rear, for the barn when* EBEN *appears from there hurrying toward them, his face excited.*]

EBEN [*breathlessly*]. Waal—har they be! The old mule an' the bride! I seen 'em from the barn down below at the turnin'.

PETER. How could ye tell that far?

EBEN. Hain't I as far-sight as he's near-sight? Don't I know the mare 'n' buggy, an' two people settin' in it? Who else . . . ? An' I tell ye I kin feel 'em a-comin', too! [*He squirms as if he had the itch.*]

PETER [*beginning to be angry*]. Waal—let him do his own unhitchin'!

SIMEON [*angry in his turn*]. Let's hustle in an' git our bundles an' be a-goin' as he's a-comin'. I don't want never t' step inside the door agen arter he's back. [*They both start back around the corner of the house.* EBEN *follows them.*]

EBEN [*anxiously*]. Will ye sign it afore ye go?

PETER. Let's see the color o' the old skinflint's money an' we'll sign. [*They disappear left. The two brothers clump upstairs to get their bundles.* EBEN *appears in the kitchen, runs to the window, peers out, comes back and pulls up a strip of flooring in under stove, takes out a canvas bag and puts it on table, then sets the floorboard back in place. The two brothers appear a moment after. They carry old carpet bags.*]

EBEN [*puts his hand on bag guardingly*]. Have ye signed?

SIMEON [*shows paper in his hand*]. Ay-eh [*Greedily*] Be that the money?

EBEN [*opens bag and pours out pile of twenty-dollar gold pieces*]. Twenty-dollar pieces—thirty on 'em. Count 'em. [PETER *does so, arranging them in stacks of five, biting one or two to test them.*]

PETER. Six hundred. [*He puts them in bag and puts it inside his shirt carefully.*]

SIMEON [*handing paper to* EBEN]. Har ye be.

EBEN [*after a glance, folds it carefully and hides it under his shirt—gratefully*]. Thank yew.

PETER. Thank yew fur the ride.

SIMEON. We'll send ye a lump o' gold fur Christmas. [*A pause.* EBEN *stares at them and they at him.*]

PETER [*awkwardly*]. Waal—we're a-goin'.

SIMEON. Comin' out t' the yard?

EBEN. No. I'm waitin' in here a spell. [*Another silence. The brothers edge awkwardly to the door in rear—then turn and stand.*]

SIMEON. Waal—good-by.

PETER. Good-by.

EBEN. Good-by. [*They go out. He sits down at the table, faces the stove and pulls out the paper. He looks from it to the stove. His face, lighted up by the shaft of sunlight from the window, has an expression of trance. His lips move. The two brothers come out to the gate.*]

PETER [*looking off toward barn*]. Thar he be—unhitchin'.

SIMEON [*with a chuckle*]. I'll bet ye he's riled!

PETER. An' thar she be.

SIMEON. Let's wait 'n' see what our new Maw looks like.

PETER [*with a grin*]. An' give him our partin' cuss!

SIMEON [*grinning*]. I feel like raisin' fun. I feel light in my head an' feet.

PETER. Me, too. I feel like laffin' till I'd split up the middle.

SIMEON. Reckon it's the likker?

PETER. No. My feet feel itchin' t' walk an, walk—an' jump high over thin's—an' . . . .

SIMEON. Dance? [*A pause.*]

PETER [*puzzled*]. It's plumb onnateral.

SIMEON [*a light coming over his face*]. I calc'late it's 'cause school's out. It's holiday. Fur once we're free!

PETER [*dazedly*]. Free?

SIMEON. The halter's broke—the harness is busted—the fence bars is down—the stone walls air crumblin' an' tumblin'! We'll be kickin' up an' tearin' away down the road!

PETER [*Drawing a deep breath—oratorically*]. Anybody that wants this stinkin' old rock-pile of a farm kin hev it. 'Tain't our'n, no sirree!

SIMEON [*takes the gate off its hinges and puts it under his arm*]. We harby 'bolishes shet gates an' open gates, an' all gates, by thunder!

PETER. We'll take it with us fur luck an' let 'er sail free down some river.

SIMEON [*as a sound of voices comes from left, rear*]. Har they comes! [*The two brothers congeal into two stiff, grim-visaged statues.* EPHRAIM CABOT *and* ABBIE PUTNAM *come in.* CABOT *is seventy-five, tall and gaunt, with great, wiry, concentrated power, but stoop-shouldered from toil. His face is as hard as if it were hewn out of a boulder, yet there is a weakness in it, a petty pride in its own narrow strength. His eyes are small, close together, and extremely near-sighted, blinking continually in the effort to focus on objects, their stare having a straining, ingrowing quality. He is dressed in his dismal black Sunday suit.* ABBIE *is thirty-five, buxom, full of vitality. Her round face is pretty but marred by its rather gross sensuality. There is strength and obstinacy in her jaw, a hard determination in her eyes, and about her whole personality the same unsettled, untamed, desperate quality which is so apparent in* EBEN.]

CABOT [*as they enter—a queer strangled emotion in his dry cracking voice*]. Har we be t' hum, Abbie.

ABBIE [*with lust for the word*]. Hum! [*Her eyes gloating on the house without seeming to see the two stiff figures at the gate.*] It's purty—purty! I can't b'lieve it's r'ally mine.

CABOT [*sharply*]. Yewr'n? Mine! [*He stares at her penetratingly. She stares back. He adds relentingly.*] Our'n—mebbe! It was lonesome too long. I was growin' old in the spring. A hum's got t' hev a woman.

ABBIE [*her voice taking possession*]. A woman's got t' hev a hum!

CABOT [*nodding uncertainly*]. Ay-eh. [*Then irritably*] Whar be they? Ain't thar nobody about—'r wukin'—r' nothin'?

ABBIE [*sees the brothers. She returns their stare of cold appraising contempt with interest—slowly*]. Thar's two men loafin' at the gate an' starin' at me like a couple o' strayed hogs.

CABOT [*straining his eyes*]. I kin see 'em—but I can't make out. . . .

SIMEON. It's Simeon.

PETER. It's Peter.

CABOT [*exploding*]. Why hain't ye wukin'?

SIMEON [*dryly*]. We're waitin' t' welcome ye hum—yew an' the bride!

CABOT [*confusedly*]. Huh? Waal—this be yer new Maw, boys. [*She stares at them and they at her.*]

SIMEON [*turns away and spits contemptuously*]. I see her!

PETER [*spits also*]. An' I see her!

ABBIE [*with the conqueror's conscious superiority*]. I'll go in an' look at *my* house. [*She goes slowly around to porch.*]

SIMEON [*with a snort*]. *Her* house!

PETER [*calls after her*]. Ye'll find Eben inside. Ye better not tell him it's *yewr* house.

ABBIE [*mouthing the name*]. Eben. [*Then quietly*] I'll tell Eben.

CABOT [*with a contemptuous sneer*]. Ye needn't heed Eben. Eben's a dumb fool—like his Maw—soft an' simple!

SIMEON [*with his sardonic burst of laughter*]. Ha! Eben's a chip o' yew—spit 'n' image—hard 'n' bitter's a hickory tree! Dog'll eat dog. He'll eat ye yet, old man!

CABOT [*commandingly*]. Ye git t' wuk!

SIMEON [*as ABBIE disappears in house—winks at PETER and says tauntingly*]. So that thar's our new Maw, be it? Whar in hell did ye dig her up? [*He and PETER laugh.*]

PETER. Ha! Ye'd better turn her in the pen with the other sows. [*They laugh uproariously, slapping their thighs.*]

CABOT [*so amazed at their effrontery that he stutters in confusion*]. Simeon! Peter! What's come over ye? Air ye drunk?

SIMEON. We're free, old man—free o' yew an' the hull damned farm! [*They grow more and more hilarious and excited.*]

PETER. An' we're startin' out fur the gold fields o' Californi-a!

SIMEON. Ye kin take this place an' burn it!

PETER. An' bury it—fur all we cares!

SIMEON. We're free, old man! [*He cuts a caper.*]

PETER. Free! [*He gives a kick in the air.*]

SIMEON [*in a frenzy*]. Whoop!

PETER. Whoop! [*They do an absurd Indian war dance about the old man who is petrified between rage and the fear that they are insane.*]

SIMEON. We're free as Injuns! Lucky we don't sculp ye!

PETER. An' burn yer barn an' kill the stock!

SMEON. An' rape yer new woman! Whoop! [*He and* PETER *stop their dance, holding their sides, rocking with wild laughter.*]

CABOT [*edging away*]. Lust fur gold—fur the sinful, easy gold o' Californi-a! It's made ye mad!

SIMEON [*tauntingly*]. Wouldn't ye like us to send ye back some sinful gold, ye old sinner?

PETER. They's gold besides what's in Californi-a! [*He retreats back beyond the vision of the old man and takes the bag of money and flaunts it in the air above his head, laughing.*]

SIMEON. And sinfuller, too!

PETER. We'll be voyagin' on the sea! Whoop! [*He leaps up and down.*]

SIMEON. Livin' free! Whoop! [*He leaps in turn.*]

CABOT [*suddenly roaring with rage*]. My cuss on ye!

SIMEON. Take our'n in trade fur it! Whoop!

CABOT. I'll hev ye both chained up in the asylum!

PETER. Ye old skinflint! Good-by!

SIMEON. Ye old blood sucker! Good-by!

CABOT. Go afore I . . . !

PETER. Whoop! [*He picks a stone from the road.* SIMEON *does the same.*]

SIMEON. Maw'll be in the parlor.

PETER. Ay-eh! One! Two!

CABOT [*frightened*]. What air ye . . . ?

PETER. Three! [*They both throw, the stones hitting the parlor window with a crash of glass, tearing the shade.*]

SIMEON. Whoop!

PETER. Whoop!

CABOT [*in a fury now, rushing toward them*]. If I kin lay hands on ye—I'll break yer bones fur ye! [*But they beat a capering retreat before him,* SIMEON *with the gate still under his arm.* CABOT *comes back, panting with impotent rage. Their voices as they go off take up the song of the gold-seekers to the old tune of "Oh, Susannah!"*]

> "I jumped aboard the Liza ship,
>   And traveled on the sea,
>   And every time I thought of home
>   I wished it wasn't me!
>   Oh! Californi-a,
>   That's the land fur me!
>   I'm off to Californi-a!
>   With my wash bowl on my knee."

[*In the meantime, the window of the upper bedroom on right is raised and* ABBIE *sticks her head out. She looks down at* CABOT—*with a sigh of relief.*]

ABBIE. Waal—that's the last o' them two, hain't it? [*He doesn't answer. Then in possessive tones*] This here's a nice bedroom, Ephraim. It's a r'al nice bed. Is it my room, Ephraim?

CABOT [*grimly—without looking up*]. Our'n! [*She cannot control a grimace of aversion and pulls back her head slowly and shuts the window. A sudden horrible thought seems to enter* CABOT's *head.*] They been up to somethin'! Mebbe—mebbe they've pizened the stock—'r something'! [*He almost runs off down toward the barn. A moment later the kitchen door is slowly pushed open and* ABBIE *enters. For a moment she stands looking at* EBEN. *He does not notice her at first. Her eyes take him in penetratingly with a calculating appraisal of his strength as against hers. But under this her desire is dimly awakened by his youth and good looks. Suddenly he becomes conscious of her presence and looks up. Their eyes meet. He leaps to his feet, glowering at her speechlessly.*]

ABBIE [*in her most seductive tones which she uses all through this scene*]. Be you—Eben? I'm Abbie—[*She laughs.*] I mean, I'm yer new Maw.

EBEN [*viciously*]. No, damn ye!

ABBIE [*as if she hadn't heard—with a queer smile*]. Yer Paw's spoke a lot o' yew. . . .

EBEN. Ha!

ABBIE. Ye mustn't mind him. He's an old man. [*A long pause. They stare at each other.*] I don't want t' pretend playin' Maw t' ye, Eben. [*Admiringly*] Ye're too big an' too strong fur that. I want t' be frens with ye. Mebbe with me fur a fren ye'd find ye'd like livin' here better. I kin make it easy fur ye with him, mebbe. [*With a scornful sense of power*] I calc'late I kin get him t' do most anythin' fur me.

EBEN [*with bitter scorn*]. Ha! [*They stare again,* EBEN *obscurely moved, physically attracted to her—in forced stilted tones*] Yew kin go t' the devil!

ABBIE [*calmly*]. If cussin' me does ye good, cuss all ye've a mind t'. I'm all prepared t' have ye agin me—at fust. I don't blame ye nuther. I'd feel the same at any stranger comin' t' take my Maw's place. [*He shudders. She is watching him carefully.*] Yew must've cared a lot fur yewr Maw, didn't ye? My Maw died afore I'd growed. I don't remember her none. [*A pause.*] But yew won't hate me long, Eben. I'm not the wust in the world—an' yew an' me've got a lot in common. I kin tell that by lookin' at ye. Waal—I've had a hard life, too— oceans o' trouble an' nuthin' but wuk fur reward. I was a orphan early an' had t' wuk fur others in other folks' hums. Then I married an' he turned out a drunken spreer an' so he had to wuk fur others an' me too agen in other folks' hums, an' the baby died, an' my husband got sick an' died too, an' I was glad sayin' now I'm free fur once, on'y I diskivered right away all I was free fur was t' wuk agen in other folks' hums, doin' other folks' wuk till I'd most give up hope o' ever doin' my own wuk in my own hum, an' then your Paw come. . . . [CABOT *appears returning from the barn. He comes to the gate and looks down the road the brothers have gone. A faint strain of their retreating voices is heard:* "Oh, Californi-a! That's the place for me." *He stands glowering, his fist clenched, his face grim with rage.*]

EBEN [*fighting against his growing attraction and sympathy— harshly*]. An' bought yew—like a harlot! [*She is stung and flushes angrily. She has been sincerely moved by the recital of her troubles. He adds furiously:*] An' the price he's payin' ye—this farm—was my Maw's, damn ye!—an' mine now!

ABBIE [*with a cool laugh of confidence*]. Yewr'n? We'll see 'bout that! [*Then strongly*] Waal—what if I did need a hum? What else'd I marry an old man like him fur?

EBEN [*maliciously*]. I'll tell him ye said that!

ABBIE [*smiling*]. I'll say ye're lyin' a-purpose—an' he'll drive ye off the place!

EBEN. Ye devil!

ABBIE [*defying him*]. This be my farm—this be my hum—this be my kitchen—!

EBEN [*furiously, as if he were going to attack her*]. Shut up, damn ye!

ABBIE [*walks up to him—a queer coarse expression of desire in her face and body—slowly*]. An' upstairs—that be my bedroom—an' my bed! [*He stares into her eyes, terribly confused and torn. She adds softly:*] I hain't bad nor mean—'ceptin' fur an enemy—but I got t' fight fur what's due me out o' life, if I ever 'spect t' git it. [*Then putting her hand on his arm—seductively*] Let's yew 'n' me be frens, Eben.

EBEN [*stupidly—as if hypnotized*]. Ay-eh. [*Then furiously flinging off her arm*] No, ye durned old witch! I hate ye! [*He rushes out the door.*]

ABBIE [*looks after him smiling satisfiedly—then half to herself, mouthing the word*]. Eben's nice. [*She looks at the table, proudly.*] I'll wash up *my* dishes now. [EBEN *appears outside, slamming the door behind him. He comes around corner, stops on seeing his father, and stands staring at him with hate.*]

CABOT [*raising his arms to heaven in the fury he can no longer control*]. Lord God o' Hosts, smite the undutiful sons with Thy wust cuss!

EBEN [*breaking in violently*]. Yew 'n' yewr God! Allus cussin' folks—allus naggin' 'em!

CABOT [*oblivious to him—summoningly*]. God o' the old! God o' the lonesome!

EBEN [*mockingly*]. Naggin' His sheep t' sin! T' hell with yewr God! [CABOT *turns. He and* EBEN *glower at each other.*]

CABOT [*harshly*]. So it's yew. I might've knowed it. [*Shaking his finger threateningly at him*] Blasphemin' fool! [*Then quickly*] Why hain't ye t' wuk?

EBEN. Why hain't yew? They've went. I can't wuk it all alone.

CABOT [*contemptuously*]. Nor noways! I'm wuth ten o' ye yit, old's I be! Ye'll never be more'n half a man! [*Then, matter-of-factly*] Waal—let's git t' the barn. [*They go. A last faint note of the "Californi-a" song is heard from the distance.* ABBIE *is washing her dishes.*]

CURTAIN

part 2, scene 1

The exterior of the farmhouse, as in Part 1—a hot Sunday afternoon two months later. ABBIE, *dressed in her best, is discovered sitting in a rocker at the end of the porch. She rocks listlessly, enervated by the heat, staring in front of her with bored, half-closed eyes.*

EBEN *sticks his head out of his bedroom window. He looks around furtively and tries to see—or hear—if anyone is on the porch, but although he has been careful to make no noise, Abbie has sensed his movement. She stops rocking, her face grows animated and eager, she waits attentively.* EBEN *seems to feel her presence, he scowls back his thoughts of her and spits with exaggerated disdain—then withdraws back into the room.* ABBIE *waits, holding her breath as she listens with passionate eagerness for every sound within the house.*

EBEN *comes out. Their eyes meet. His falter, he is confused, he turns away and slams the door resentfully. At this gesture,* ABBIE *laughs tantalizingly, amused but at the same time piqued and irritated. He scowls, strides off the porch to the path and starts to walk past her to the road with a grand swagger of ignoring her existence. He is dressed in his store suit, spruced up, his face shines from soap and water.* ABBIE *leans forward on her chair, her eyes hard and angry now, and, as he passes her, gives a sneering, taunting chuckle.*

EBEN [*stung—turns on her furiously*]. What air yew cacklin' 'bout?

ABBIE [*triumphant*]. Yew!

EBEN. What about me?

ABBIE. Ye look all slicked up like a prize bull.

EBEN [*with a sneer*]. Waal—ye hain't so durned purty yerself, be ye? [*They stare into each other's eyes, his held by hers in spite of himself, hers glowingly possessive. Their physical attraction becomes a palpable force quivering in the hot air.*]

ABBIE [*softly*]. Ye don't mean that, Eben. Ye may think ye mean it, mebbe, but ye don't. Ye can't. It's agin nature, Eben. Ye been fightin' yer nature ever since the day I come—tryin' t' tell yerself I hain't purty t'ye. [*She laughs a low humid laugh without taking her eyes from his. A pause—her body squirms desirously—she murmurs languorously.*] Hain't the sun strong an' hot? Ye kin feel it burnin' into the earth—Nature—makin' thin's grow—bigger 'n' bigger—burnin' inside ye—makin' ye want t' grow—into somethin' else—till ye're jined with it—an' it's yourn—but it owns ye, too—an' makes ye grow bigger—like a tree—like them elums—[*She laughs again softly, holding his eyes. He takes a step toward her, compelled against his will.*] Nature'll beat ye, Eben. Ye might's well own up t' it fust 's last.

EBEN [*trying to break from her spell—confusedly*]. If Paw'd hear ye goin' on. . . . [*Resentfully*] But ye've made such a damned idjit out o' the old devil . . . ! [ABBIE *laughs.*]

ABBIE. Waal—hain't it easier fur yew with him changed softer?

EBEN [*defiantly*]. No. I'm fightin' him—fightin' yew—fightin' fur Maw's rights t' her hum! [*This breaks her spell for him. He glowers at her.*] An' I'm onto ye. Ye hain't foolin' me a mite. Ye're aimin' t' swaller up everythin' an' make it your'n. Waal, you'll find I'm a heap sight bigger hunk nor yew kin chew! [*He turns from her with a sneer.*]

ABBIE [*trying to regain her acendancy—seductively*]. Eben!

EBEN. Leave me be! [*He starts to walk away.*]

ABBIE [*more commandingly*]. Eben!

EBEN [*stops—resentfully*]. What d'ye want?

ABBIE [*trying to conceal a growing excitement*]. Whar air ye goin'?

EBEN [*with malicious nonchalance*]. Oh—up the road a spell.

ABBIE. T' the village?

EBEN [*airily*]. Mebbe.

ABBIE [*excitedly*]. T' see that Min, I s'pose?

EBEN. Mebbe.

ABBIE [*weakly*]. What d'ye want t' waste time on her fur?

EBEN [*revenging himself now—grinning at her*]. Ye can't beat Nature, didn't ye say? [*He laughs and again starts to walk away.*]

ABBIE [*bursting out*]. An ugly old hake!

EBEN [*with a tantalizing sneer*]. She's purtier'n yew be!

ABBIE. That every wuthless drunk in the country has. . . .

EBEN [*tauntingly*]. Mebbe—but she's better'n yew. She owns up fa'r 'n' squar' t' her doin's.

ABBIE [*furiously*]. Don't ye dare compare. . . .

EBEN. She don't go sneakin' an' stealin'—what's mine.

ABBIE [*savagely seizing on his weak point*]. Your'n? Yew mean—my farm?

EBEN. I mean the farm yew sold yerself fur like any other old whore—my farm!

ABBIE [*stung—fiercely*]. Ye'll never live t' see the day when even a stinkin' weed on it'll belong t' ye! [*Then in a scream*] Git out o' my sight! Go on t' yer slut—disgracin' yer Paw 'n' me! I'll git yer Paw t' horsewhip ye off the place if I want t'! Ye're only livin' here 'cause I tolerate ye! Git along! I hate the sight o' ye! [*She stops, panting and glaring at him.*]

EBEN [*returning her glance in kind*]. An' I hate the sight o' yew! [*He turns and strides off up the road. She follows his retreating figure with concentrated hate. Old* CABOT *appears coming up from the barn. The hard, grim expression of his face has changed. He seems in some queer way softened, mellowed. His eyes have taken on a strange, incongruous dreamy quality. Yet there is no hint of physical weakness about him—rather he looks more robust and younger.* ABBIE *sees him and turns away quickly with unconcealed aversion. He comes slowly up to her.*]

CABOT [*mildly*]. War yew an' Eben quarrelin' agen?

ABBIE [*shortly*]. No.

CABOT. Ye was talkin' a'mighty loud. [*He sits down on the edge of porch.*]

ABBIE [*snappishly*]. If ye heered us they hain't no need askin' questions.

CABOT. I didn't hear what ye said.

ABBIE [*relieved*]. Waal—it wa'n't nothin' t' speak on.

CABOT [*after a pause*]. Eben's queer.

ABBIE [*bitterly*]. He's the dead spit 'n' image o' yew!

CABOT [*queerly interested*]. D'ye think so, Abbie? [*After a pause, ruminatingly*] Me 'n' Eben's allus fit 'n' fit. I never could b'ar him noways. He's so thunderin' soft—like his Maw.

ABBIE [*scornfully*]. Ay-eh! 'Bout as soft as yew be!

CABOT [*as if he hadn't heard*]. Mebbe I been too hard on him.

ABBIE [*jeeringly*]. Waal—ye're gettin' soft now—soft as slop! That's what Eben was sayin'.

CABOT [*his face instantly grim and ominous*]. Eben was sayin'? Waal, he'd best not do nothin' t' try me 'r he'll soon diskiver. . . . [*A pause. She keeps her face turned away. His gradually softens. He stares up at the sky.*] Purty, hain't it?

ABBIE [*crossly*]. I don't see nothin' purty.

CABOT. The sky. Feels like a wa'm field up thar.

ABBIE [*sarcastically*]. Air yew aimin' t' buy up over the farm too? [*She snickers contemptuously.*]

CABOT [*strangely*]. I'd like t' own my place up thar. [*A pause.*]

I'm gittin' old, Abbie, I'm gittin' ripe on the bough. [*A pause. She stares at him mystified. He goes on.*] It's allus lonesome cold in the house—even when it's bilin' hot outside. Hain't yew noticed?

ABBIE. No.

CABOT. It's wa'm down t' the barn—nice smellin' an' warm—with the cows. [*A pause.*] Cows is queer.

ABBIE. Like yew?

CABOT. Like Eben. [*A pause.*] I'm gittin' t' feel resigned t' Eben—jest as I got t' feel 'bout his Maw. I'm gittin' t' learn to b'ar his soft-ness—jest like her'n. I calc'late I c'd a'most take t' him—if he wa'n't sech a dumb fool! [*A pause.*] I s'pose it's old age a-creepin' in my bones.

ABBIE [*indifferently*]. Waal—ye hain't dead yet.

CABOT [*roused*]. No, I hain't, yew bet—not by a hell of a sight—I'm sound 'n' tough as hickory! [*Then moodily*] But arter three score and ten the Lord warns ye t' prepare. [*A pause.*] That's why Eben's come in my head. Now that his cussed sinful brothers is gone their path t' hell, they's no one left but Eben.

ABBIE [*resentfully*]. They's me, hain't they? [*Agitatedly*] What's all this sudden likin' ye tuk to Eben? Why don't ye say nothin' 'bout me? Hain't I yer lawful wife?

CABOT [*simply*]. Ay-eh. Ye be. [*A pause—he stares at her desirously—his eyes grow avid—then with a sudden movement he seizes her hands and squeezes them, declaiming in a queer camp meeting preacher's tempo:*] Yew air my Rose o' Sharon! Behold, yew air fair; yer eyes air doves; yer lips air like scarlet; yer two breasts air like two fawns; yer navel be like a round goblet; yer belly be like a heap o' wheat. . . . [*He covers her hand with kisses. She does not seem to notice. She stares before her with hard angry eyes.*]

ABBIE [*jerking her hands away—harshly*]. So ye're plannin' t' leave the farm t' Eben, air ye?

CABOT [*dazedly*]. Leave. . . ? [*Then with resentful obstinacy*] I hain't a-givin' it t' no one!

ABBIE [*remorselessly*]. Ye can't take it with ye.

CABOT [*thinks a moment—then reluctantly*]. No, I calc'late not. [*After a pause—with a strange passion*] But if I could, I would, by the Etarnal! 'R if I could, in my dyin' hour, I'd set it afire an' watch it burn—this house an' every ear o' corn an' every tree down t' the last blade o' hay! I'd sit an' know it was all a-dying with me an' no one else'd ever own what was mine, what I'd made out o' nothin' with my own sweat 'n' blood! [*A pause—then he adds with a queer affection.*] 'Ceptin' the cows. Them I'd turn free.

ABBIE [*harshly*]. An' me?

CABOT [*with a queer smile*]. Ye'd be turned free, too.

ABBIE [*furiously*]. So that's the thanks I git fur marryin' ye—t' have ye change kind to Eben who hates ye, an' talk o' turnin' me out in the road.

CABOT [*hastily*]. Abbie! Ye know I wa'n't ...

ABBIE [*vengefully*]. Just let me tell ye a thing or two 'bout Eben. Whar's he gone? T' see that harlot, Min! I tried fur t' stop him. Disgracin' yew an' me—on the Sabbath, too!

CABOT [*rather guiltily*]. He's a sinner—nateral-born. It's lust eatin' his heart.

ABBIE [*enraged beyond endurance—wildly vindictive*]. An' his lust fur me! Kin ye find excuses fur that?

CABOT [*stares at her—after a dead pause*]. Lust—fur yew?

ABBIE [*defiantly*]. He was tryin' t' make love t' me—when ye heerd us quarrelin'.

CABOT [*stares at her—then a terrible expression of rage comes over his face—he springs to his feet shaking all over*]. By the A'mighty God—I'll end him!

ABBIE [*frightened now for* EBEN]. No! Don't ye!

CABOT [*violently*]. I'll git the shotgun an' blow his soft brains t' the top o' them elums!

ABBIE [*throwing her arms around him*]. No, Ephraim!

CABOT [*pushing her away violently*]. I will, by God!

ABBIE [*in a quieting tone*]. Listen, Ephraim. 'Twa'n't nothin' bad—on'y a boy's foolin'—'twa'n't meant serious—jest jokin' an' teasin'. ...

CABOT. Then why did ye say—lust?

ABBIE. It must hev sounded wusser'n I meant. An' I was mad at thinkin'—ye'd leave him the farm.

CABOT [*quieter but still grim and cruel*]. Waal then, I'll horsewhip him off the place if that much'll content ye.

ABBIE [*reaching out and taking his hand*]. No. Don't think o' me! Ye mustn't drive him off. 'Tain't sensible. Who'll ye get to help ye on the farm? They's no one hereabouts.

CABOT [*considers this—then nodding his appreciation*]. Ye got a head on ye. [*Then irritably*] Waal, let him stay. [*He sits down on the edge of the porch. She sits beside him. He murmurs contemptu-*

ously:] I oughn't git riled so—at that 'ere fool calf. [*A pause.*] But har's the p'int. What son o' mine'll keep on here t' the farm—when the Lord does call me? Simeon an' Peter air gone t' hell—an' Eben's follerin' 'em.

ABBIE. They's me.

CABOT. Ye're on'y a woman.

ABBIE. I'm yewr wife.

CABOT. That hain't me. A son is me—my blood—mine. Mine ought t' git mine. An' then it's still mine—even though I be six foot under. D'ye see?

ABBIE [*giving him a look of hatred*]. Ay-eh. I see. [*She becomes very thoughtful, her face growing shrewd, her eyes studying* CABOT *craftily.*]

CABOT. I'm gittin' old—ripe on the bough. [*Then with a sudden forced reassurance*] Not but what I hain't a hard nut t' crack even yet—an' fur many a year t' come! By the Etarnal, I kin break most o' the young fellars' backs at any kind o' work any day o' the year!

ABBIE [*suddenly*]. Mebbe the Lord'll give *us* a son.

CABOT [*turns and stares at her eagerly*]. Ye mean—a son—t' me 'n' yew?

ABBIE [*with a cajoling smile*]. Ye're a strong man yet, hain't ye? 'Tain't noways impossible, be it? We know that. Why d'ye stare so? Hain't ye never thought o' that afore? I been thinkin' o' it all along. Ay-eh—an' I been prayin' it'd happen, too.

CABOT [*his face growing full of joyous pride and a sort of religious ecstasy*]. Ye been prayin', Abbie?—fur a son?—t' us?

ABBIE. Ay-eh. [*With a grim resolution*] I want a son now.

CABOT [*excitedly clutching both of her hands in his*]. It'd be the blessin' o' God, Abbie the blessin' o' God A'mighty on me—in my old age—in my lonesomeness! They hain't nothin' I wouldn't do fur ye then, Abbie. Ye'd hev on'y t' ask it—anythin' ye'd a mind t'!

ABBIE [*interrupting*]. Would ye will the farm t' me then—t' me an' it . . . ?

CABOT [*vehemently*]. I'd do anythin' ye axed, I tell ye! I swar it! May I be everlastin' damned t' hell if I wouldn't! [*He sinks to his knees pulling her down with him. He trembles all over with the fervor of his hopes.*] Pray t' the Lord agen, Abbie. It's the Sabbath! I'll jine ye! Two prayers air better nor one. "An' God hearkened unto Rachel"! An' God hearkened unto Abbie! Pray, Abbie! Pray fur him to hearken! [*He bows his head, mumbling. She pretends to do likewise but gives him a side glance of scorn and triumph.*]

part 2, scene 2

*About eight in the evening. The interior of the two bedrooms on the top floor is shown—*EBEN *is sitting on the side of his bed in the room on the left. On account of the heat he has taken off everything but his undershirt and pants. His feet are bare. He faces front, brooding moodily, his chin propped on his hands, a desperate expression on his face.*

In the other room CABOT *and* ABBIE *are sitting side by side on the edge of their bed, an old four-poster with feather mattress. He is in his night shirt, she in her nightdress. He is still in the queer, excited mood into which the notion of a son has thrown him. Both rooms are lighted dimly and flickeringly by tallow candles.*

CABOT. The farm needs a son.

ABBIE. I need a son.

CABOT. Ay-eh. Sometimes ye air the farm an' sometimes the farm be yew. That's why I clove t' ye in my lonesomeness. [*A pause. He pounds his knee with his fist.*] Me an' the farm has got t' beget a son!

ABBIE. Ye'd best go t' sleep. Ye're gittin' thin's all mixed.

CABOT [*with an impatient gesture*]. No, I hain't. My mind's clear's a well. Ye don't know me, that's it. [*He stares hopelessly at the floor.*]

ABBIE [*indifferently*]. Mebbe. [*In the next room* EBEN *gets up and paces up and down distractedly.* ABBIE *hears him. Her eyes fasten on the intervening wall with concentrated attention.* EBEN *stops and stares. Their hot glances seem to meet through the wall. Unconsciously he stretches out his arms for her and she half rises. Then aware, he mutters a curse at himself and flings himself face downward on the bed, his clenched fists above his head, his face buried in the pillow.* ABBIE *relaxes with a faint sigh but her eyes remain fixed on the wall; she listens with all her attention for some movement from* EBEN.]

CABOT [*suddenly raises his head and looks at her—scornfully*]. Will ye ever know me—'r will any man 'r woman? [*Shaking his head*] No. I calc'late 't wa'n't t' be. [*He turns away.* ABBIE *looks at the wall. Then, evidently unable to keep silent about his thoughts, without looking at his wife, he puts out his hand and clutches her knee. She starts violently, looks at him, sees he is not watching her, concentrates again on the wall and pays no attention to what he says.*] Listen, Abbie. When I come here fifty odd year ago—I was jest twenty an' the strongest an' hardest ye ever seen—ten times as strong an' fifty times as hard as Eben. Waal—this place was nothin' but fields o' stones. Folks laughed when I tuk it. They couldn't know what I knowed. When ye kin make corn sprout out o' stones, God's livin' in yew! They wa'n't strong enuf fur that! They reckoned God was easy. They laughed. They don't laugh no more. Some died hereabouts. Some went West an' died. They're all under ground—fur follerin' arter an easy God. God hain't easy. [*He shakes his head slowly.*] An' I growed hard. Folks kept allus sayin' he's a hard man like 'twas sinful t' be hard, so's at last I said back at 'em: Waal then, by thunder, ye'll git me hard an' see how ye like it! [*Then suddenly*] But I give in t' weakness once. 'Twas arter I'd been here two year. I got weak—despairful—they was so many stones. They was a party leavin', givin' up, goin' West. I jined 'em. We tracked on 'n' on. We come t' broad medders, plains, whar the soil was black an' rich as gold. Nary a stone. Easy. Ye'd on'y to plow an' sow an' then set an' smoke yer pipe an' watch thin's grow. I could o' been a rich man—but somethin' in me fit me an' fit me—the voice o' God sayin': "This hain't wuth nothin' t' Me. Get ye back t' hum!" I got afeerd o' that voice an' I lit out back t' hum here, leavin' my claim an' crops t' whoever'd a mind t' take 'em. Ay-eh. I actoolly give up what was rightful mine! God's hard, not easy! God's in the stones! Build my church on a rock —out o' stones an' I'll be in them! That's what He meant t' Peter! [*He sighs heavily—a pause.*] Stones. I picked 'em up an' piled 'em into walls. Ye kin read the years o' my life in them walls, every day a hefted stone, climbin' over the hills up and down, fencin' in the fields that was mine, whar I'd made thin's grow out o' nothin'—like the will o' God, like the servant o' His hand. It wa'n't easy. It was hard an' He made me hard fur it. [*He pauses.*] All the time I kept gittin' lonesomer. I tuk a wife. She bore Simeon an' Peter. She was a good woman. She wuked hard. We was married twenty year. She never knowed me. She helped but she never knowed what she was helpin'. I was allus lonesome. She died. After that it wa'n't so lonesome fur a spell. [*A pause.*] I lost count o' the years. I had no time t' fool away countin' 'em. Sim an' Peter helped. The farm growed. It was all mine! When I thought o' that I didn't feel lonesome. [*A pause.*] But ye can't hitch yer mind t' one thin' day an' night. I tuk another wife—Eben's Maw. Her folks was contestin' me at law over my deeds t' the farm—my farm! That's why Eben keeps a'talkin' his fool talk o' this bein' his Maw's farm. She bore Eben. She was purty—but soft. She tried t' be hard. She couldn't. She never knowed me nor nothin'. It was lonesomer 'n hell with her. After a matter o' sixteen odd years, she died. [*A pause.*] I lived with the boys. They hated me 'cause I was hard. I hated them 'cause they was soft. They coveted the farm without knowin' what it meant. It made me bitter 'n wormwood. It aged me—them coveting what I'd made fur mine. Then this spring the call come—the voice o' God cryin' in my wilderness, in my lonesomeness—t' go out an' seek an' find! [*Turning to her with strange passion*] I sought ye an' I found ye! Yew air my Rose o' Sharon! Yer eyes air like . . . . [*She has turned a blank face, resentful eyes to his. He stares at her for a moment—then harshly*] Air ye any the wiser fur all I've told ye?

ABBIE [*confusedly*]. Mebbe.

CABOT [*pushing her away from him—angrily*]. Ye don't know nothin'—nor never will. If ye don't hev a son t' redeem ye . . . [*This in a tone of cold threat.*]

ABBIE [*resentfully*]. I've prayed, hain't I?

CABOT [*bitterly*]. Pray agen—fur understandin'!

ABBIE [*a veiled threat in her tone*]. Ye'll have a son out o' me, I promise ye.

CABOT. How kin ye promise?

ABBIE. I got second-sight mebbe. I kin foretell. [*She gives a queer smile.*]

CABOT. I believe ye have. Ye give me the chills sometimes. [*He shivers.*] It's cold in this house. It's oneasy. They's thin's pokin' about in the dark—in the corners. [*He pulls on his trousers, tucking in his night shirt, and pulls on his boots.*]

ABBIE [*surprised*]. Whar air ye goin'?

CABOT [*queerly*]. Down whar it's restful—whar it's warm—down t' the barn. [*Bitterly*] I kin talk t' the cows. They know. They know the farm an' me. They'll give me peace. [*He turns to go out the door.*]

ABBIE [*a bit frightenedly*]. Air ye ailin' tonight, Ephraim?

CABOT. Growin'. Growin' ripe on the bough. [*He turns and goes, his boots clumping down the stairs.* EBEN *sits up with a start, listening.* ABBIE *is conscious of his movement and stares at the wall.* CABOT *comes out of the house around the corner and stands by the gate, blinking at the sky. He stretches up his hands in a tortured gesture.*] God A'mighty, call from the dark! [*He listens as if expecting an answer. Then his arms drop, he shakes his head and plods off toward the barn.* EBEN *and* ABBIE *stare at each other through the wall.* EBEN *sighs heavily and* ABBIE *echoes it. Both become terribly nervous, uneasy. Finally* ABBIE *gets up and listens, her ear to the wall. He acts as if he saw every move she was making, he becomes resolutely still. She seems driven into a decision—goes out the door in rear determinedly. His eyes follow her. Then as the door of his room is opened softly, he turns away, waits in an attitude of strained fixity.* ABBIE *stands for a second staring at him, her eyes burning with desire. Then with a little cry she runs over and throws her arms about his neck, she pulls his head back and covers his mouth with kisses. At first, he submits dumbly; then he puts his arms about her neck and returns her kisses, but finally, suddenly aware of his hatred, he hurls her away from him, springing to his feet. They stand speechless and breathless, panting like two animals.*]

ABBIE [*at last—painfully*]. Ye shouldn't, Eben—ye shouldn't—I'd make ye happy!

EBEN [*harshly*]. I don't want t' be happy—from yew!

ABBIE [*helplessly*]. Ye do, Eben! Ye do! Why d'ye lie?

EBEN [*viciously*]. I don't take t'ye, I tell ye! I hate the sight o' ye!

ABBIE [*with an uncertain troubled laugh*]. Waal, I kissed ye anyways—an' ye kissed back—yer lips was burnin'—ye can't lie 'bout that! [*Intensely*] If ye don't care, why did ye kiss me back—why was yer lips burnin'?

EBEN [*wiping his mouth*]. It was like pizen on 'em [*Then tauntingly*] When I kissed ye back, mebbe I thought 'twas someone else.

ABBIE [*wildly*]. Min?

EBEN. Mebbe.

ABBIE [*torturedly*]. Did ye go t' see her? Did ye r'ally go? I thought ye mightn't. Is that why ye throwed me off jest now?

EBEN [*sneeringly*]. What if it be?

ABBIE [*raging*]. Then ye're a dog, Eben Cabot!

EBEN [*threateningly*]. Ye can't talk that way t' me!

ABBIE [*with a shrill laugh*]. Can't I? Did ye think I was in love with ye—a weak thin' like yew? Not much! I on'y wanted ye fur a purpose o' my own—an' I'll hev ye fur it yet 'cause I'm stronger'n yew be!

EBEN [*resentfully*]. I knowed well it was on'y part o' yer plan t' swaller everythin'!

ABBIE [*tauntingly*]. Mebbe!

EBEN [*furious*]. Git out o' my room!

ABBIE. This air my room an' ye're on'y hired help!

EBEN [*threateningly*]. Git out afore I murder ye!

ABBIE [*quite confident now*]. I hain't a mite afeerd. Ye want me, don't ye? Yes, ye do! An' yer Paw's son'll never kill what he wants! Look at yer eyes! They's lust fur me in 'em, burnin' 'em up! Look at yer lips now! They're tremblin' an' longin' t' kiss me, an' yer teeth t' bite [*He is watching her now with a horrible fascination. She laughs a crazy triumphant laugh.*] I'm a-goin' t' make all o' this hum my hum! They's one room hain't mine yet, but it's a-goin' t' be tonight. I'm a-goin' down now an' light up! [*She makes him a mocking bow.*] Won't ye come courtin' me in the best parlor, Mister Cabot?

EBEN [*staring at her—horribly confused—dully*]. Don't ye dare! It hain't been opened since Maw died an' was laid out thar! Don't ye . . . ! [*But her eyes are fixed on his so burningly that his will seems to wither before hers. He stands swaying toward her helplessly.*]

ABBIE [*holding his eyes and putting all her will into her words as she backs out the door*]. I'll expect ye afore long, Eben.

EBEN [*stares after her for a while, walking toward the door. A light appears in the parlor window. He murmurs*]. In the parlor? [*This seems to arouse connotations for he comes back and puts on his white shirt, collar, half ties the tie mechanically, puts on coat, takes his hat, stands barefooted looking about him in bewilderment, mutters wonderingly:*] Maw! Whar air yew? [*Then goes slowly toward the door in rear.*

part 2, scene 3

A few minutes later. The interior of the parlor is shown. A grim, repressed room like a tomb in which the family has been interred alive. ABBIE *sits on the edge of the horsehair sofa. She has lighted all the candles and the room is revealed in all its preserved ugliness. A change has come over the woman. She looks awed and frightened now, ready to run away.*

The door is opened and EBEN *appears. His face wears an expression of obsessed confusion. He stands staring at her, his arms hanging disjointedly from his shoulders, his feet bare, his hat in his hand.*

ABBIE [*after a pause—with a nervous, formal politeness*]. Won't ye set?

EBEN [*dully*]. Ay-eh. [*Mechanically he places his hat carefully on the floor near the door and sits stiffly beside her on the edge of the sofa. A pause. They both remain rigid, looking straight ahead with eyes full of fear.*]

ABBIE. When I fust came in—in the dark—they seemed somethin' here.

EBEN [*simply*]. Maw.

ABBIE. I kin still feel—somethin'....

EBEN. It's Maw.

ABBIE. At fust I was feered o' it. I wanted t' yell an' run. Now—since yew come—seems like it's growin' soft an' kind t' me. [*Addressing the air—queerly*] Thank yew.

EBEN. Maw allus loved me.

ABBIE. Mebbe it knows I love yew too. Mebbe that makes it kind t' me.

EBEN [*dully*]. I dunno. I should think she'd hate ye.

ABBIE [*with certainty*]. No. I kin feel it don't—not no more.

EBEN. Hate ye fur stealin' her place—here in her hum—settin' in her parlor whar she was laid— [*He suddenly stops, staring stupidly before him.*]

ABBIE. What is it, Eben?

EBEN [*in a whisper*]. Seems like Maw didn't want me t' remind ye.

ABBIE [*excitedly*]. I knowed, Eben! It's kind t' me! It don't b'ar me no grudges fur what I never knowed an' couldn't help!

EBEN. Maw b'ars him a grudge.

ABBIE. Waal, so does all o' us.

EBEN. Ay-eh. [*With passion*] I does, by God!

ABBIE [*taking one of his hands in hers and patting it*]. Thar! Don't git riled thinkin' o' him. Think o' yer Maw who's kind t' us. Tell me about ycr Maw, Eben.

EBEN. They hain't nothin' much. She was kind. She was good.

ABBIE [*putting one arm over his shoulder. He does not seem to notice—passionately*]. I'll be kind an' good t' ye!

EBEN. Sometimes she used t' sing fur me.

ABBIE. I'll sing fur ye!

EBEN. This was her hum. This was her farm.

ABBIE. This is my hum! This is my farm!

EBEN. He married her t' steal 'em. She was soft an' easy. He couldn't 'preciate her.

ABBIE. He can't 'preciate me!

EBEN. He murdered her with his hardness.

ABBIE. He's murderin' me!

EBEN. She died. [*A pause.*] Sometimes she used to sing fur me. [*He bursts into a fit of sobbing.*]

ABBIE [*both her arms around him—with wild passion*]. I'll sing fur ye! I'll die fur ye! [*In spite of her overwhelming desire for him, there is a sincere maternal love in her manner and voice—a horribly frank mixture of lust and mother love.*] Don't cry, Eben! I'll take yer Maw's place! I'll be everythin' she was t' ye! Let me kiss ye, Eben! [*She pulls his head around. He makes a bewildered pretense of resistance. She is tender.*] Don't be afeered! I'll kiss ye pure, Eben— same 's if I was a Maw t' ye—an' ye kin kiss me back 's if yew was my son—my boy—sayin' good-night t' me! Kiss me, Eben. [*They kiss in restrained fashion. Then suddenly wild passion overcomes her. She kisses him lustfully again and again and he flings his arms about her and returns her kisses. Suddenly, as in the bedroom, he frees himself from her violently and springs to his feet. He is trembling all over, in a strange state of terror.* ABBIE *strains her arms toward him with fierce pleading.*] Don't ye leave me, Eben! Can't ye see it hain't enuf—lovin' ye like a Maw—can't ye see it's got t' be that an' more—much more—a hundred times more—fur me t' be happy—fur yew t' be happy?

EBEN [*to the presence he feels in the room*]. Maw! Maw! What d'ye want? What air ye tellin' me?

ABBIE. She's tellin' ye t' love me. She knows I love ye an' I'll be good t' ye. Can't ye feel it? Don't ye know? She's tellin' ye t' love me, Eben!

EBEN. Ay-eh. I feel—mebbe she—but—I can't figger out—why— when ye've stole her place—here in her hum—in the parlor whar she was—

ABBIE [*fiercely*]. She knows I love ye!

EBEN [*his face suddenly lighting up with a fierce triumphant grin*]. I see it! I sees why. It's her vengeance on him—so's she kin rest quiet in her grave!

ABBIE [*wildly*]. Vengeance o' God on the hull o' us! What d'we give a durn? I love ye, Eben! God knows I love ye! [*She stretches out her arms for him.*]

EBEN [*throws himself on his knees beside the sofa and grabs her in his arms—releasing all his pent-up passion*]. An' I love yew, Abbie!— now I kin say it! I been dyin' fur want o' ye—every hour since ye come! I love ye! [*Their lips meet in a fierce, bruising kiss.*]

part 2, scene 4

Exterior of the farmhouse. It is just dawn. The front door at right is opened and EBEN *comes out and walks around to the gate. He is dressed in his working clothes. He seems changed. His face wears a bold and confident expression, he is grinning to himself with evident satisfaction. As he gets near the gate, the window of the parlor is heard opening and the shutters are flung back and* ABBIE *sticks her head out. Her hair tumbles over her shoulders in disarray, her face is flushed, she looks at* EBEN *with tender, languorous eyes and calls softly.*

ABBIE. Eben. [*As he turns—playfully*] Jest one more kiss afore ye go. I'm goin' to miss ye fearful all day.

EBEN. An' me yew, ye kin bet! [*He goes to her. They kiss several times. He draws away, laughingly.*] Thar. That's enuf, hain't it? Ye won't hev none left fur next time.

ABBIE. I got a million o' 'em left fur yew! [*Then a bit anxiously*] D'ye r'ally love me, Eben?

EBEN [*emphatically*]. I like ye better'n any gal I ever knowed! That's gospel!

ABBIE. Likin' hain't lovin'.

EBEN. Waal then—I love ye. Now air yew satisfied?

ABBIE. Ay-eh, I be. [*She smiles at him adoringly.*]

EBEN. I better git t' the barn. The old critter's liable t' suspicion an' come sneakin' up.

ABBIE [*with a confident laugh*]: Let him! I kin allus pull the wool over his eyes. I'm goin' t' leave the shutters open and let in the sun 'n' air. This room's been dead long enuf. Now it's goin' t' be my room!

EBEN [frowning]: Ay-eh.

ABBIE [*hastily*]. I meant—our room.

EBEN. Ay-eh.

ABBIE. We made it our'n last night, didn't we? We give it life— our lovin' did. [*A pause.*]

EBEN [*with a strange look*]. Maw's gone back t' her grave. She kin sleep now.

ABBIE. May she rest in peace! [*Then tenderly rebuking*] Ye oughtn't t' talk o' sad thin's—this mornin'.

EBEN. It jest come up in my mind o' itself.

ABBIE. Don't let it. [*He doesn't answer. She yawns.*] Waal, I'm a-goin' t' steal a wink o' sleep. I'll tell the Old Man I hain't feelin' pert. Let him git his own vittles.

EBEN. I see him comin' from the barn. Ye better look smart an' git upstairs.

ABBIE. Ay-eh. Good-by. Don't fergit me. [*She throws him a kiss. He grins—then squares his shoulders and awaits his father confidently.* CABOT *walks slowly up from the left, staring up at the sky with a vague face.*]

EBEN [*jovially*]. Mornin', Paw. Star-gazin' in daylight?

CABOT. Purty, hain't it?

EBEN [*looking around him possessively*]. It's a durned purty farm.

CABOT. I mean the sky.

EBEN [*grinning*]. How d'ye know? Them eyes o' your'n can't see that fur. [*This tickles his humor and he slaps his thigh and laughs.*] Ho-ho! That's a good un!

CABOT [*grimly sarcastic*]. Ye're feelin' right chipper, hain't ye? Whar'd ye steal the likker?

EBEN [*good-naturedly*]. 'Tain't likker. Jest life. [*Suddenly holding out his hand—soberly*] Yew 'n' me is quits. Let's shake hands.

CABOT [*suspiciously*]. What's come over ye?

EBEN. Then don't. Mebbe it's jest as well. [*A moment's pause.*] What's come over me? [*Queerly*] Didn't ye feel her passin'—goin' back t' her grave?

CABOT [*dully*]. Who?

EBEN. Maw. She kin rest now an' sleep content. She's quits with ye.

CABOT [*confusedly*]. I rested. I slept good—down with the cows. They know how t' sleep. They're teachin' me.

EBEN [*suddenly jovial again*]. Good fur the cows! Waal—ye better git t' work.

CABOT [*grimly amused*]. Air yew bossin' me, ye calf?

EBEN [*beginning to laugh*]. Ay-eh! I'm bossin' yew! Ha-ha-ha! see how ye like it! Ha-ha-ha! I'm the prize rooster o' this roost. Ha-ha-ha! [*He goes off toward the barn laughing.*]

CABOT [*looks after him with scornful pity*]. Soft-headed. Like his Maw. Dead spit 'n' image. No hope in him! [*He spits with contemptuous disgust.*] A born fool! [*Then matter-of-factly*] Waal—I'm gittin' peckish. [*He goes toward door.*]

CURTAIN

part 3, scene 1

A night in late spring the following year. The kitchen and the two bedrooms upstairs are shown. The two bedrooms are dimly lighted by a tallow candle in each. EBEN *is sitting on the side of the bed in his room, his chin propped on his fists, his face a study of the struggle he is making to understand his conflicting emotions. The noisy laughter and music from below where a kitchen dance is in progress annoy and distract him. He scowls at the floor.*

In the next room a cradle stands beside the double bed.

In the kitchen all is festivity. The stove has been taken down to give more room to the dancers. The chairs, with wooden benches added, have been pushed back against the walls. On these are seated, squeezed in tight against one another, farmers and their wives and their young folks of both sexes from the neighboring farms. They are all chattering and laughing loudly. They evidently have some secret joke in common. There is no end of winking, of nudging, of meaning nods of the head toward CABOT *who, in a state of extreme hilarious excitement increased by the amount he has drunk, is standing near the rear door where there is a small keg of whisky and serving drinks to all the men. In the left corner, front, dividing the attention with her husband,* ABBIE *is sitting in a rocking chair, a shawl wrapped about her shoulders. She is very pale, her face is thin and drawn, her eyes are fixed anxiously on the open door in rear as if waiting for someone.*

The musician is tuning up his fiddle, seated in the far right corner. He is a lanky young fellow with a long, weak face. His pale eyes blink incessantly and he grins about him slyly with a greedy malice.

ABBIE [*suddenly turning to a young girl on her right*]. Whar's Eben?

YOUNG GIRL [*eying her scornfully*]. I dunno, Mrs. Cabot. I hain't seen Eben in ages. [*Meaningly*] Seems like he's spent most o' his time t' hum since yew come.

ABBIE [*vaguely*]. I tuk his Maw's place.

YOUNG GIRL. Ay-eh. So I heerd. [*She turns away to retail this bit of gossip to her mother sitting next to her.* ABBIE *turns to her left to a big stoutish middle-aged man whose flushed face and staring eyes show the amount of "likker" he has consumed.*]

ABBIE. Ye hain't seen Eben, hev ye?

MAN. No, I hain't. [*Then he adds with a wink*] If yew hain't, who would?

ABBIE. He's the best dancer in the county. He'd ought t' come an' dance.

MAN [*with a wink*]. Mebbe he's doin' the dutiful an' walkin' the kid t' sleep. It's a boy, hain't it?

ABBIE [*nodding vaguely*]. Ay-eh—born two weeks back—purty's a picter.

MAN. They all is—t' their Maws. [*Then in a whisper, with a nudge and a leer*] Listen, Abbie—if ye ever git tired o' Eben, remember me! Don't fergit now! [*He looks at her uncomprehending face for a second—then grunts disgustedly.*] Waal—guess I'll likker agin. [*He goes over and joins* CABOT *who is arguing noisily with an old farmer over cows. They all drink.*]

ABBIE [*this time appealing to nobody in particular*]. Wonder what Eben's a-doin'? [*Her remark is repeated down the line with many a guffaw and titter until it reaches the fiddler. He fastens his blinking eyes on* ABBIE.]

FIDDLER [*raising his voice*]. Bet I kin tell ye, Abbie, what Eben's doin'! He's down t' the church offerin' up prayers o' thanksgivin'. [*They all titter expectantly.*]

MAN. What fur? [*Another titter.*]

FIDDLER. 'Cause unto him a—[*he hesitates just long enough*]—brother is born! [*a roar of laughter. They all look from* ABBIE *to* CABOT. *She is oblivious, staring at the door.* CABOT, *although he hasn't heard the words, is irritated by the laughter and steps forward, glaring about him. There is an immediate silence.*]

CABOT. What're ye all bleatin' about—like a flock o' goats? Why don't ye dance, damn ye? I axed ye here t' dance—t' eat, drink an' be merry—an' thar ye set cacklin' like a lot o' wet hens with the pip! Ye've swilled my likker an' guzzled my vittles like hogs, hain't ye? Then dance fur me, can't ye? That's fa'r an' squar', hain't it? [*A grumble of resentment goes around but they are all evidently in too much awe of him to express it openly.*]

FIDDLER [*slyly*]. We're waitin' fur Eben. [*A suppressed laugh.*]

CABOT [*with a fierce exultation*]. T'hell with Eben! Eben's done fur now! I got a new son! [*His mood switching with drunken sud-*

denness] But ye needn't t' laugh at Eben, none o' ye! He's my blood, if he be a dumb fool. He's better nor any o' yew! He kin do a day's work a'most up t' what I kin—an' that'd put any o' yew pore critters t' shame!

FIDDLER. An' he kin do a good night's work, too! [*A roar of laughter.*]

CABOT. Laugh, ye damn fools! Ye're right jist the same, Fiddler. He kin work day an' night too, like I kin, if need be!

OLD FARMER [*from behind the keg where he is weaving drunkenly back and forth—with great simplicity*]. They hain't many t' touch ye, Ephraim—a son at seventy-six. That's a hard man fur ye! I be on'y sixty-eight an' I couldn't do it. [*A roar of laughter in which* CABOT *joins uproariously.*]

CABOT [*slapping him on the back*]. I'm sorry fur ye, Hi. I'd never suspicion sech weakness from a boy like yew!

OLD FARMER. An' I never reckoned yew had it in ye nuther, Ephraim. [*There is another laugh.*]

CABOT [*suddenly grim*]. I got a lot in me—a hell of a lot—folks don't know on. [*Turning to the* FIDDLER] Fiddle 'er up, durn ye! Give 'em somethin' t' dance t'! What air ye, an ornament? Hain't this a celebration? Then grease yer elbow an' go it!

FIDDLER [*seizes a drink which the* OLD FARMER *holds out to him and downs it*]. Here goes! [*He starts to fiddle "Lady of the Lake."* Four young fellows and four girls form in two lines and dance a square dance. The FIDDLER shouts directions for the different movements, keeping his words in the rhythm of the music and interspersing them with jocular personal remarks to the dancers themselves. The people seated along the walls stamp their feet and clap their hands in unison. CABOT is especially active in this respect. Only ABBIE remains apathetic, staring at the door as if she were alone in a silent room.*]

FIDDLER. Swing your partner t' the right! That's it, Jim! Give her a b'ar hug! Her Maw hain't lookin'. [*Laughter.*] Change partners! That suits ye, don't it, Essie, now ye got Reub afore ye? Look at her redden up, will ye! Waal, life is short an' so's love, as the feller says. [*Laughter.*]

CABOT [*excitedly, stamping his foot*]. Go it, boys! Go it, gals!

FIDDLER [*with a wink at the others*]. Ye're the spryest seventy-six ever I sees, Ephraim! Now if ye'd on'y good eye-sight . . . ! [*Suppressed laughter. He gives* CABOT *no chance to retort but roars.*] Promenade! Ye're walkin' like a bride down the aisle, Sarah! Waal, while they's life they's allus hope. I've heerd tell. Swing your partner to the left! Gosh A'mighty, look at Johnny Cook high-steppin'! They hain't goin' t' be much strength left fur howin' in the corn lot t'morrow. [*Laughter.*]

CABOT. Go it! Go it! [*Then suddenly, unable to restrain himself any longer, he prances into the midst of the dancers, scattering them, waving his arms about wildly.*] Ye're all hoofs! Git out o' my road! Give me room! I'll show ye dancin'. Ye're all too soft! [*He pushes them roughly away. They crowd back toward the walls, muttering, looking at him resentfully.*]

FIDDLER [*jeeringly*]. Go it, Ephraim! Go it! [*He starts "Pop Goes the Weasel," increasing the tempo with every verse until at the end he is fiddling crazily as fast as he can go.*]

CABOT [*starts to dance, which he does very well and with tremendous vigor. Then he begins to improvise, cuts incredibly grotesque capers, leaping up and cracking his heels together, prancing around in a circle with body bent in an Indian war dance, then suddenly straightening up and kicking as high as he can with both legs. He is like a monkey on a string. And all the while he intersperses his antics with shouts and derisive comments*]. Whoop! Here's dancin' fur ye! Whoop! See that! Seventy-six, if I'm a day! Hard as iron yet! Beatin' the young 'uns like I allus done! Look at me! I'd invite ye t' dance on my hundredth birthday on'y ye'll all be dead by then. Ye're a sickly generation! Yer hearts air pink, not red! Yer veins is full o' mud an' water! I be the on'y man in the county! Whoop! See that! I'm a Injun! I've killed Injuns in the West afore ye was born—an' skulped 'em too! They's a arrer wound on my backside I c'd show ye! The hull tribe chased me. I outrun 'em all—with the arrer stuck in me! An' I tuk vengeance on 'em. Ten eyes fur an yew! He kin do a day's work a'most up t' what I kin kick the ceilin' off the room! Whoop!

FIDDLER [*stops playing—exhaustedly*]. God A'mighty, I got enuf. Ye got the devil's strength in ye.

CABOT [*delightedly*]. Did I beat yew, too? Wa'al, ye played smart. Hev a swig. [*He pours whisky for himself and* FIDDLER. *They drink. The others watch* CABOT *silently with cold, hostile eyes. There is a dead pause. The* FIDDLER *rests.* CABOT *leans against the keg, panting, glaring around him confusedly. In the room above,* EBEN *gets to his feet and tiptoes out the door in rear, appearing a moment later in the other bedroom. He moves silently, even frightenedly, toward the cradle and stands there looking down at the baby. His face is as vague as his reactions are confused, but there is a trace of tenderness, of interested discovery. At the same moment that he reaches the cradle,* ABBIE *seems to sense something. She gets up weakly and goes to* CABOT]

ABBIE. I'm goin' up t' the baby.

CABOT [*with real solicitude*]. Air ye able fur the stairs? D'ye want me t' help ye, Abbie?

ABBIE. No. I'm able. I'll be down agen soon.

CABOT. Don't ye git wore out! He needs ye, remember—our son does! [*He grins affectionately, patting her on the back. She shrinks from his touch.*]

ABBIE [*dully*]. Don't—tech me. I'm goin'—up. [*She goes.* CABOT *looks after her. A whisper goes around the room.* CABOT *turns. It ceases. He wipes his forehead streaming with sweat. He is breathing pantingly.*]

CABOT. I'm a-goin' out t' git fresh air. I'm feelin' a mite dizzy. Fiddle up thar! Dance, all o' ye! Here's likker fur them as wants it. Enjoy yerselves. I'll be back. [*He goes, closing the door behind him.*]

FIDDLER [*sarcastically*]. Don't hurry none on our account! [*A suppressed laugh. He imitates* ABBIE.] Whar's Eben? [*More laughter.*]

A WOMAN [*loudly*]. What's happened in this house is plain as the nose on yer face! [ABBIE *appears in the doorway upstairs and stands looking in surprise and adoration at* EBEN *who does not see her.*]

A MAN. Ssshh! He's li'ble t' be listenin' at the door. That'd be like him. [*Their voices die to an intensive whispering. Their faces are concentrated on this gossip. A noise as of dead leaves in the wind comes from the room.* CABOT *has come out from the porch and stands by the gate, leaning on it, staring at the sky blinkingly.* ABBIE *comes across the room silently.* EBEN *does not notice her until quite near.*]

EBEN [*starting*]. Abbie!

ABBIE. Ssshh! [*She throws her arms around him. They kiss—then bend over the cradle together.*] Ain't he purty?—dead spit 'n' image o' yew!

EBEN [*pleased*]. Air he? I can't tell none.

ABBIE. E-zactly like!

EBEN [*frowningly*]. I don't like this. I don't like lettin' on what's mine's his'n. I been doin' that all my life. I'm gittin' t' the end o' b'arin' it!

ABBIE [*putting her finger on his lips*]. We're doin' the best we kin. We got t' wait. Somethin's bound t' happen. [*She puts her arms around him.*] I got t' go back.

EBEN. I'm goin' out. I can't b'ar it with the fiddle playin' an' the laughin'.

ABBIE. Don't git feelin' low. I love ye, Eben. Kiss me [*He kisses her. They remain in each other's arms.*]

CABOT [*at the gate, confusedly*]. Even the music can't drive it out—somethin'. Ye kin feel it droppin' off the elums, climbin' up the roof, sneakin' down the chimney, pokin' in the corners! They's no peace in houses, they's no rest livin' with folks. Somethin's always livin' with ye. [*With a deep sigh*] I'll go t' the barn an' rest a spell. [*He goes wearily toward the barn.*]

FIDDLER [*tuning up*]. Let's celebrate the old skunk gittin' fooled! We kin have some fun now he's went. [*He starts to fiddle "Turkey in the Straw." There is real merriment now. The young folks get up to dance.*]

part 3, scene 2

*A half hour later—exterior—*EBEN *is standing by the gate looking up at the sky, an expression of dumb pain bewildered by itself on his face.* CABOT *appears, returning from the barn, walking wearily, his eyes on the ground. He sees* EBEN *and his whole mood immediately changes. He becomes excited, a cruel, triumphant grin comes to his lips, he strides up and slaps* EBEN *on the back. From within comes the whining of the fiddle and the noise of stamping feet and laughing voices.*

CABOT. So har ye be!

EBEN [*startled, stares at him with hatred for a moment—then dully*]. Ay-eh.

CABOT [*surveying him jeeringly*]. Why hain't ye been in t' dance? They was all axin' fur ye.

EBEN. Let 'em ax!

CABOT. They's a hull passel o' purty gals.

EBEN. T' hell with 'em!

CABOT. Ye'd ought t' be marryin' one o' 'em soon.

EBEN. I hain't marryin' no one.

CABOT. Ye might 'arn a share o' a farm that way.

EBEN [*with a sneer*]. Like yew did, ye mean? I hain't that kind.

CABOT [*stung*]. Ye lie! 'Twas yer Maw's folks aimed t' steal my farm from me.

EBEN. Other folks don't say so. [*After a pause—defiantly*] An' I got a farm, anyways!

CABOT [*derisively*]. Whar?

EBEN [*stamps a foot on the ground*]. Har!

CABOT [*throws his head back and laughs coarsely*]. Ho-ho! Ye hev, hev ye? Waal, that's a good un!

EBEN [*controlling himself—grimly*]. Ye'll see!

CABOT [*stares at him suspiciously, trying to make him out—a pause —then with scornful confidence*]. Ay-eh. I'll see. So'll ye. It's ye that's blind—blind as a mole underground. [EBEN *suddenly laughs, one short sardonic bark: "Ha." A pause.* CABOT *peers at him with re-newed suspicion.*] Whar air ye hawin' 'bout? [EBEN *turns away with-out answering.* CABOT *grows angry.*] God A'mighty, yew air a dumb dunce! They's nothin' in that thick skull o' your'n but noise—like a empty keg it be! [EBEN *doesn't seem to hear*—CABOT's *rage grows.*] Yewr farm! God A'mighty! If ye wa'n't a born donkey ye'd know ye'll never own stick nor stone on it, specially now arter him bein' born. It's his'n, I tell ye—his'n arter I die—but I'll live a hundred jest t' fool ye all—an' he'll be growed then—yewr age a'most! [EBEN *laughs again his sardonic "Ha." This drives* CABOT *into a fury.*] Ha? Ye think ye kin git 'round that someways, do ye? Waal, it'll be her'n, too—Abbie's—ye won't git 'round her—she knows yer tricks —she'll be too much fur ye—she wants the farm her'n—she was afeerd o' ye—she told me ye was sneakin' 'round tryin' t' make love t' her t' git her on yer side . . . ye . . . ye mad fool, ye! [*He raises his clenched fists threateningly.*]

EBEN [*is confronting him choking with rage*]. Ye lie, ye old skunk! Abbie never said no sech thing!

CABOT [*suddenly triumphant when he sees how shaken* EBEN *is*]. She did. An' I says, I'll blow his brains t' the top o' them elums—an' she says no, that hain't sense, who'll ye git t' help ye on the farm in his place—an' then she says yew'n me ought t' have a son—I know we kin, she says—an' I says, if we do, ye kin have anythin' I've got ye've a mind t'. An' she says, I wants Eben cut off so's this farm'll be mine when ye die! [*With terrible gloating*] An' that's what's hap-pened, hain't it? An' the farm's her'n! An' the dust o' the road—that's you'rn! Ha! Now who's hawin'?

EBEN [*has been listening, petrified with grief and rage—suddenly laughs wildly and brokenly*]. Ha-ha-ha! So that's her sneakin' game

—all along!—like I suspicioned at fust—t' swaller it all—an' me, too
. . . ! [*Madly*] I'll murder her! [*He springs toward the porch but*
CABOT *is quicker and gets in between.*]

CABOT. No, ye don't!

EBEN. Git out o' my road! [*He tries to throw* CABOT *aside. They
grapple in what becomes immediately a murderous struggle. The
old man's concentrated strength is too much for* EBEN. CABOT *gets
one hand on his throat and presses him back across the stone wall.
At the same moment,* ABBIE *comes out on the porch. With a stifled cry
she runs toward them.*]

ABBIE. Eben! Ephraim! [*She tugs at the hand on* EBEN's *throat.*]
Let go, Ephraim! Ye're chokin' him!

CABOT [*removes his hand and flings* EBEN *sideways full length on
the grass, gasping and choking. With a cry,* ABBIE *kneels beside him,
trying to take his head on her lap, but he pushes her away.* CABOT
stands looking down with fierce triumph]. Ye needn't t've fret, Abbie,
I wa'n't aimin' t' kill him. He hain't wuth hangin' fur—not by a hell
of a sight! [*More and more triumphantly*] Seventy-six an' him not
thirty yit—an' look whar he be fur thinkin' his Paw was easy! No,
by God, I hain't easy! An' him upstairs, I'll raise him t' be like
me! [*He turns to leave them.*] I'm goin' in an' dance!—sing an' celebrate! [*He walks to the porch—then turns with a great grin.*] I don't
calc'late it's left in him, but if he gits pesky, Abbie, ye jest sing out.
I'll come a-runnin' an' by the Etarnal, I'll put him across my knee an'
birch him! Ha-ha-ha! [*He goes into the house laughing. A moment
later his loud "whoop" is heard.*]

ABBIE [*tenderly*]. Eben. Air ye hurt? [*she tries to kiss him but he
pushes her violently away and struggles to a sitting position.*]

EBEN [*gaspingly*]. T'hell—with ye!

ABBIE [*not believing her ears*]. It's me, Eben—Abbie—don't ye
know me?

EBEN [*glowering at her with hatred*]. Ay-eh—I know ye—now!
[*He suddenly breaks down, sobbing weakly.*]

ABBIE [*fearfully*]. Eben—what's happened t' ye—why did ye look
at me 's if ye hated me?

EBEN [*violently, between sobs and gasps*]. I do hate ye! Ye're a
whore—a damn trickin' whore!

ABBIE [*shrinking back horrified*]. Eben! Ye don't know what
ye're sayin'!

EBEN [*scrambling to his feet and following her—accusingly*]. Ye're
nothin' but a stinkin' passel o' lies! Ye've been lyin' t' me every word

ye spoke, day an' night, since we fust—done it. Ye've kept sayin' ye loved me. . . .

ABBIE [*frantically*]. I do love ye! [*She takes his hand but he flings hers away.*]

EBEN [*unheeding*]. Ye've made a fool o' me—a sick, dumb fool—a-purpose! Ye've been on'y playin' yer sneakin', stealin' game all along—gittin' me t' lie with ye so's ye'd hev a son he'd think was his'n, an' makin' him promise he'd give ye the farm and let me eat dust, if ye did git him a son! [*Staring at her with anguished, bewildered eyes*] They must be a devil livin' in ye! 'Tain't human t' be as bad as that be!

ABBIE [*stunned—dully*]. He told yew . . . ?

EBEN. Hain't it true? It hain't no good in yew lyin'.

ABBIE [*pleadingly*]. Eben, listen—ye must listen—it was long ago—afore we done nothin'—yew was scornin' me—goin' t' see Min—when I was lovin' ye—an' I said it t' him t' git vengeance on ye!

EBEN [*unheedingly. With tortured passion*]. I wish ye was dead! I wish I was dead along with ye afore this come! [*Ragingly*] But I'll git my vengeance too! I'll pray Maw t' come back t' help me—t' put her cuss on yew an' him!

ABBIE [*brokenly*]. Don't ye, Eben! Don't ye! [*She throws herself on her knees before him, weeping.*] I didn't mean t' do bad t'ye! Fergive me, won't ye?

EBEN [*not seeming to hear her—fiercely*]. I'll git squar' with the old skunk—an' yew! I'll tell him the truth 'bout the son he's so proud o'! Then I'll leave ye here t' pizen each other—with Maw comin' out o' her grave at nights—an' I'll go t' the gold fields o' Californi-a whar Sim an' Peter be!

ABBIE [*terrified*]. Ye won't—leave me? Ye can't!

EBEN [*with fierce determination*]. I'm a-goin', I tell ye! I'll git rich thar an' come back an' fight him fur the farm he stole—an' I'll kick ye both out in the road—t' beg an' sleep in the woods—an' yer son along with ye—t' starve an' die! [*He is hysterical at the end.*]

ABBIE [*with a shudder—humbly*]. He's yewr son, too, Eben.

EBEN [*torturedly*]. I wish he never was born! I wish he'd die this minit! I wish I'd never sot eyes on him! It's him—yew havin' him—a purpose t' steal—that's changed everythin'!

ABBIE [*gently*]. Did ye believe I loved ye—afore he come?

EBEN. Ay-eh—like a dumb ox!

ABBIE. An' ye don't believe no more?

EBEN. B'lieve a lyin' thief! Ha!

ABBIE [*shudders—then humbly*]. An did ye r'ally love me afore?

EBEN [*brokenly*]. Ay-eh—an' ye was trickin' me!

ABBIE. An' ye don't love me now!

EBEN [*violently*]. I hate ye, I tell ye!

ABBIE. An' ye're truly goin' West—goin' t' leave me—all account o' him being born?

EBEN. I'm a-goin' in the mornin'—or may God strike me t' hell!

ABBIE [*after a pause—with a dreadful cold intensity—slowly*]. If that's what his comin's done t' me—killin' yewr love—takin' yew away—my on'y joy—the on'y joy I've ever knowed—like heaven t' me—purtier'n heaven—then I hate him, too, even if I be his Maw!

EBEN [*bitterly*]. Lies! Ye love him! He'll steal the farm fur ye! [*Brokenly*] But 'tain't the farm so much—not no more—it's yew foolin' me—gittin' me t' love ye—lyin' yew loved me—jest t' git a son t' steal!

ABBIE [*distractedly*]. He won't steal! I'd kill him fust! I do love ye! I'll prove t' ye ... !

EBEN [*harshly*]. Tain't no use lyin' no more. I'm deaf t' ye! [*He turns away.*] I hain't seein' ye agen. Good-by!

ABBIE [*pale with anguish*]. Hain't ye even goin' t' kiss me—not once—arter all we loved?

EBEN [*in a hard voice*]. I hain't wantin' t' kiss ye never agen! I'm wantin' t' forgit I ever sot eyes on ye!

ABBIE. Eben!—ye mustn't—wait a spell—I want t' tell ye ...

EBEN. I'm a-goin' in t' git drunk. I'm a-goin' t' dance.

ABBIE [*clinging to his arm—with passionate earnestness*]. If I could make it—'s if he'd never come up between us—if I could prove t' ye I wa'n't schemin' t' steal from ye—so's everythin' could be jest the same with us, lovin' each other jest the same, kissin' an' happy the same's we've been happy afore he come—if I could do it—ye'd love me agen, wouldn't ye? Ye'd kiss me agen? Ye wouldn't never leave me, would ye?

EBEN [*moved*]. I calc'late not. [*Then shaking her hand off his arm—with a bitter smile*] But ye hain't God, be ye?

ABBIE [*exultantly*]. Remember ye've promised! [*Then with strange intensity*] Mebbe I kin take back one thin' God does!

EBEN [*peering at her*]. Ye're gittin' cracked, hain't ye? [*Then going towards door*] I'm a-goin' t' dance.

ABBIE [*calls after him intensely*]. I'll prove t' ye! I'll prove I love ye better'n. . . . [*He goes in the door, not seeming to hear. She remains standing where she is, looking after him—then she finishes desperately:*] Better'n everythin' else in the world!

part 3, scene 3

Just before dawn in the morning—shows the kitchen and CABOT's *bedroom. In the kitchen, by the light of a tallow candle on the table,* EBEN *is sitting, his chin propped on his hands, his drawn face blank and expressionless. His carpetbag is on the floor beside him. In the bedroom, dimly lighted by a small whale-oil lamp,* CABOT *lies asleep.* ABBIE *is bending over the cradle, listening, her face full of terror yet with an undercurrent of desperate triumph. Suddenly, she breaks down and sobs, appears about to throw herself on her knees beside the cradle; but the old man turns restlessly, groaning in his sleep, and she controls herself, and shrinking away from the cradle with a gesture of horror, backs swiftly toward the door in rear and goes out. A moment later she comes into the kitchen and, running to* EBEN, *flings her arms about his neck and kisses him wildly. He hardens himself, he remains unmoved and cold, he keeps his eyes straight ahead.*

ABBIE [*hysterically*]. I done it, Eben! I told ye I'd do it! I've proved I love ye—better'n everythin'—so's ye can't never doubt me no more!

EBEN [*dully*]. Whatever ye done, it hain't no good now.

ABBIE [*wildly*]. Don't ye say that! Kiss me, Eben, won't ye? I need ye t' kiss me arter what I done! I need ye t' say ye love me!

EBEN [*kisses her without emotion—dully*]. That's fur good-by. I'm a-goin' soon.

ABBIE. No! No! Ye won't go—not now!

EBEN [*going on with his own thoughts*]. I been a-thinkin'—an' I hain't goin' t' tell Paw nothin'. I'll leave Maw t' take vengeance on ye. If I told him, the old skunk'd jest be stinkin' mean enuf to take it out on that baby. [*His voice showing emotion in spite of him*] An' I don't want nothin' bad t' happen t' him. He hain't t' blame fur yew. [*He adds with a certain queer pride:*] An' he looks like me! An' by God, he's mine! An' some day I'll be a-comin' back an' . . . !

ABBIE [*too absorbed in her own thoughts to listen to him—*

pleadingly]. They's no cause fur ye t' go now—they's no sense—it's all the same's it was—they's nothin' come b'tween us now—arter what I done!

EBEN [*something in her voice arouses him. He stares at her a bit frightenedly*]. Ye look mad, Abbie. What did ye do?

ABBIE. I—I killed him, Eben.

EBEN [*amazed*]. Ye killed him?

ABBIE [*dully*]. Ay-eh.

EBEN [*recovering from his astonishment—savagely*]. An' serves him right! But we got t' do somethin' quick t' make it look s'if the old skunk'd killed himself when he was drunk. We kin prove by 'em all how drunk he got.

ABBIE [*wildly*]. No! No! Not him! [*Laughing distractedly*] But that's what I ought t' done, hain't it? I oughter killed him instead! Why didn't ye tell me?

EBEN [*appalled*]. Instead? What d'ye mean?

ABBIE. Not him.

EBEN [*his face grown ghastly*]. Not—not that baby!

ABBIE [*dully*]. Ay-eh!

EBEN [*falls to his knees as if he'd been struck—his voice trembling with horror*]. Oh, God A'mighty! A'mighty God! Maw, whar was ye, why didn't ye stop her?

ABBIE [*simply*]. She went back t' her grave that night we fust done it, remember? I hain't felt her about since. [*A pause.* EBEN *hides his head in his hands, trembling all over as if he had the ague. She goes on dully:*] I left the piller over his little face. Then he killed himself. He stopped breathin'. [*She begins to weep softly.*]

EBEN [*rage beginning to mingle with grief*]. He looked like me. He was mine, damn ye!

ABBIE [*slowly and brokenly*]. I didn't want t' do it. I hated myself fur doin' it. I loved him. He was so purty—dead spit 'n' image o' yew. But I loved yew more—an' yew was goin' away—far off whar I'd never see ye agen, never kiss ye, never feel ye pressed agin me agen—an' ye said ye hated me fur havin' him—ye said ye hated him an' wished he was dead—ye said if it hadn't been fur him comin' it'd be the same's afore between us.

EBEN [*unable to endure this, springs to his feet in a fury, threatening her, his twitching fingers seeming to reach out for her throat*]. Ye lie! I never said—I never dreamed ye'd—I'd cut off my head afore I'd hurt his finger!

ABBIE [*piteously, sinking on her knees*]. Eben, don't ye look at me like that—hatin' me—not after what I done fur ye—fur us—so's we could be happy agen—

EBEN [*furiously now*]. Shut up, or I'll kill ye! I see yer game now— the same old sneakin' trick—ye're aimin' t' blame me fur the murder ye done!

ABBIE [*moaning—putting her hands over her ears*]. Don't ye, Eben! Don't ye! [*She grasps his legs.*]

EBEN [*his mood suddenly changing to horror, shrinks away from her*]. Don't ye tech me! Ye're pizen! How could ye—t' murder a pore little critter—Ye must've swapped yer soul t' hell! [*Sudden raging*] Ha! I kin see why ye done it! Not the lies ye jest told—but 'cause ye wanted t' steal agen—steal the last thin' ye'd left me—my part o' him —no, the hull o' him—ye saw he looked like me—ye knowed he was all mine—an' ye couldn't b'ar it—I know ye! Ye killed him fur bein' mine! [*All this has driven him almost insane. He makes a rush past her for the door—then turns—shaking both fists at her, violently.*] But I'll take vengeance now! I'll git the Sheriff! I'll tell him everythin'! Then I'll sing "I'm off to Californi-a!" an' go—gold—Golden Gate— gold sun—fields o' gold in the West! [*This last he half shouts, half croons incoherently, suddenly breaking off passionately.*] I'm a-goin' fur the Sheriff t' come an' git ye! I want ye tuk away, locked up from me! I can't stand t' luk at ye! Murderer an' thief 'r not, ye still tempt me! I'll give ye up t' the Sheriff! [*He turns and runs out, around the corner of house, panting and sobbing, and breaks into a swerving sprint down the road.*]

ABBIE [*struggling to her feet, runs to the door, calling after him*]. I love ye, Eben! I love ye! [*She stops at the door weakly, swaying, about to fall.*] I don't care what ye do—if ye'll on'y love me agen— [*She falls limply to the floor in a faint.*]

part 3, scene 4

About an hour later. Same as Scene 3. Shows the kitchen and CABOT's bedroom. It is after dawn. The sky is brilliant with the sunrise. In the kitchen, ABBIE sits at the table, her body limp and exhausted, her head bowed down over her arms, her face hidden. Upstairs, CABOT is still asleep but awakens with a start. He looks toward the window and gives a snort of surprise and irritation—throws back the

*covers and begins hurriedly pulling on his clothes. Without
looking behind him, he begins talking to* ABBIE *whom he
supposes beside him.*

CABOT. Thunder 'n' lightnin', Abbie! I hain't slept this late in fifty
year! Looks 's if the sun was full riz a'most. Must've been the dancin'
an' likker. Must be gittin' old. I hope Eben's t'wuk. Ye might've tuk
the trouble t' rouse me, Abbie. [*He turns—sees no one there—surprised.*] Waal—whar air she? Gittin' vittles, I calc'late. [*He tiptoes to
the cradle and peers down—proudly*] Mornin', sonny. Purty's a picter!
Sleepin' sound. He don't beller all night like most o' 'em. [*He goes
quietly out the door in rear—a few moments later enters kitchen—
sees* ABBIE—*with satisfaction*] So thar ye be. Ye got any vittles cooked?
ABBIE [*without moving*]. No.
CABOT [*coming to her, almost sympathetically*]. Ye feelin' sick?
ABBIE. No.
CABOT [*pats her on shoulder. She shudders*]. Ye'd best lie down a
spell. [*Half jocularly*] Yer son'll be needin' ye soon. He'd ought t'
wake up with a gnashin' appetite, the sound way he's sleepin'.
ABBIE [*shudders—then in a dead voice*]. He ain't never goin' to
wake up.
CABOT [*jokingly*]. Takes after me this mornin'. I ain't slept so late
in . . .
ABBIE. He's dead.
CABOT [*stares at her—bewilderedly*]. What . . .
ABBIE. I killed him.
CABOT [*stepping back from her—aghast*]. Air ye drunk—'r
crazy—'r . . . !
ABBIE [*suddenly lifts her head and turns on him—wildly*]. I killed
him, I tell ye! I smothered him. Go up an' see if ye don't b'lieve me!
[CABOT *stares at her a second, then bolts out the rear door, can be
heard bounding up the stairs, and rushes into the bedroom and
over to the cradle.* ABBIE *has sunk back lifelessly into her former
position.* CABOT *puts his hand down on the body in the crib. An expression of fear and horror comes over his face.*]
CABOT [*shrinking away—tremblingly*]. God A'mighty! God
A'mighty. [*He stumbles out the door—in a short while returns to
the kitchen—comes to* ABBIE, *the stunned expression still on his face
—hoarsely*] Why did ye do it? Why? [*As she doesn't answer, he
grabs her violently by the shoulder and shakes her.*] I ax ye why ye
done it! Ye'd better tell me'r . . . !

ABBIE [*gives him a furious push which sends him staggering back and springs to her feet—with wild rage and hatred*]. Don't ye dare tech me! What right hev ye t' question me 'bout him? He wa'n't yewr son! Think I'd have a son by yew? I'd die fust! I hate the sight o' ye an' allus did! It's yew I should've murdered, if I'd had good sense! I hate ye! I love Eben. I did from the fust. An' he was Eben's son—mine an' Eben's—not your'n!

CABOT [*stands looking at her dazedly—a pause—finding his words with an effort—dully*]. That was it—what I felt—pokin' round the corners—while ye lied—holdin' yerself from me—sayin' ye'd a'ready conceived— [*He lapses into crushed silence—then with a strange emotion*] He's dead, sart'n. I felt his heart. Pore little critter! [*He blinks back one tear, wiping his sleeve across his nose.*]

ABBIE [*hysterically*]. Don't ye! Don't ye! [*She sobs unrestrainedly.*]

CABOT [*with a concentrated effort that stiffens his body into a rigid line and hardens his face into a stony mask—through his teeth to himself*]. I got t' be—like a stone—a rock o' jedgment! [*A pause. He gets complete control over himself—harshly*] If he was Eben's, I be glad he air gone! An' mebbe I suspicioned it all along. I felt they was somethin' onnateral—somewhars—the house got so lonesome—an' cold—drivin' me down t' the barn—t' the beasts o' the field. . . . Ay-eh. I must've suspicioned—somethin'. Ye didn't fool me—not altogether, leastways—I'm too old a bird—growin' ripe on the bough. . . . [*He becomes aware he is wandering, straightens again, looks at ABBIE with a cruel grin.*] So ye'd liked t' hev murdered me 'stead o' him, would ye? Waal, I'll live to a hundred! I'll live t' see ye hung! I'll deliver ye up t' the jedgment o' God an' the law! I'll git the Sheriff now. [*Starts for the door.*]

ABBIE [*dully*]. Ye needn't. Eben's gone fur him.

CABOT [*amazed*]. Eben—gone fur the Sheriff?

ABBIE. Ay-eh.

CABOT. T' inform agen ye?

ABBIE. Ay-eh.

CABOT [*considers this—a pause—then in a hard voice*]. Waal, I'm thankful fur him savin' me the trouble. I'll git t' wuk. [*He goes to the door—then turns—in a voice full of strange emotion*] He'd ought t' been my son, Abbie. Ye'd ought t' loved me. I'm a man. If ye'd loved me, I'd never told no Sheriff on ye no matter what ye did, if they was t' brile me alive!

ABBIE [*defensively*]. They's more to it nor yew know, makes him tell.

CABOT [*dryly*]. Fur yewr sake, I hope they be. [*He goes out—comes around to the gate—stares up at the sky. His control relaxes. For a moment he is old and weary. He murmurs despairingly:*] God A'mighty, I be lonesomer'n ever! [*He hears running footsteps from the left, immediately is himself again.* EBEN *runs in, panting exhaustedly, wild-eyed and mad looking. He lurches through the gate.* CABOT *grabs him by the shoulder.* EBEN *stares at him dumbly.*] Did ye tell the Sheriff?

EBEN [*nodding stupidly*]. Ay-eh.

CABOT [*gives him a push away that sends him sprawling—laughing with withering contempt*]. Good fur ye! A prime chip o' yer Maw ye be! [*He goes toward the barn, laughing harshly.* EBEN *scrambles to his feet. Suddenly* CABOT *turns—grimly threatening*] Git off this farm when the Sheriff takes her—or, by God, he'll have t' come back an' git me fur murder, too! [*He stalks off.* EBEN *does not appear to have heard him. He runs to the door and comes into the kitchen.* ABBIE *looks up with a cry of anguished joy.* EBEN *stumbles over and throws himself on his knees beside her—sobbing brokenly.*]

EBEN. Fergive me!

ABBIE [*happily*]. Eben! [*She kisses him and pulls his head over against her breast.*]

EBEN. I love ye! Fergive me!

ABBIE [*ecstatically*]. I'd fergive ye all the sins in hell fur sayin' that! [*She kisses his head, pressing it to her with a fierce passion of possession.*]

EBEN [*brokenly*]. But I told the Sheriff. He's comin' fur ye!

ABBIE. I kin b'ar what happens t' me—now!

EBEN. I woke him up. I told him. He says, wait 'til I git dressed. I was waiting. I got to thinkin' o' yew. I got to thinkin' how I'd loved ye. It hurt like somethin' was bustin' in my chest an' head. I got t' cryin'. I knowed sudden I loved ye yet, an' allus would love ye!

ABBIE [*caressing his hair—tenderly*]. My boy, hain't ye?

EBEN. I begun t' run back. I cut across the fields an' through the woods. I thought ye might have time t' run away—with me—an' . . .

ABBIE [*shaking her head*]. I got t' take my punishment—t' pay fur my sin.

EBEN. Then I want t' share it with ye.

ABBIE. Ye didn't do nothin'.

EBEN. I put it in yer head. I wisht he was dead! I as much as urged ye t' do it!

ABBIE. No. It was me alone!

EBEN. I'm as guilty as yew be! He was the child o' our sin.

ABBIE [*lifting her head as if defying God*]. I don't repent that sin! I hain't askin' God t' fergive that!

EBEN. Nor me—but it led up t' the other—an' the murder ye did, ye did 'count o' me—an' it's my murder, too, I'll tell the Sheriff—an' if ye deny it, I'll say we planned it t'gether—an' they'll all b'lieve me, fur they suspicion everythin' we've done, an' it'll seem likely an' true to 'em. An' it is true—way down. I did help ye—somehow.

ABBIE [*laying her head on his—sobbing*]. No! I don't want yew t' suffer!

EBEN. I got t' pay fur my part o' the sin! An' I'd suffer wuss leavin' ye, goin' West, thinkin' o' ye day an' night, bein' out when yew was in—[*lowering his voice*]—'r bein' alive when yew was dead. [*A pause.*] I want t' share with ye, Abbie—prison 'r death 'r hell 'r anythin'! [*He looks into her eyes and forces a trembling smile.*] If I'm sharin' with ye, I won't feel lonesome, leastways.

ABBIE [*weakly*]. Eben! I won't let ye! I can't let ye!

EBEN [*kissing her—tenderly*]. Ye can't he'p yerself. I got ye beat fur once!

ABBIE [*forcing a smile—adoringly*]. I hain't beat—s'long's I got ye!

EBEN [*hears the sound of feet outside*]. Ssshh! Listen! They've come t' take us!

ABBIE. No, it's him. Don't give him no chance to fight ye, Eben. Don't say nothin'—no matter what he says. An' I won't neither. [*It is* CABOT. *He comes up from the barn in a great state of excitement and strides into the house and then into the kitchen.* EBEN *is kneeling beside* ABBIE, *his arm around her, hers around him. They stare straight ahead.*]

CABOT [*stares at them, his face hard. A long pause—vindictively*]. Ye make a slick pair o' murderin' turtle doves! Ye'd ought t' be both hung on the same limb an' left thar t' swing in the breeze an' rot—a warnin' t' old fools like me t' b'ar their lonesomeness alone—an' fur young fools like ye t' hobble their lust. [*A pause. The excitement returns to his face, his eyes snap, he looks a bit crazy.*] I couldn't work today. I couldn't take no interest. T' hell with the farm! I'm leavin' it! I've turned the cows an' other stock loose! I've druv 'em into the woods whar they kin be free! By freein' 'em, I'm freein' myself! I'm quittin' here today! I'll set fire t' house an' barn an' watch 'em burn, an' I'll leave yer Maw t' haunt the ashes, an' I'll will the fields back t' God, so that nothin' human kin never touch 'em! I'll be a-goin' to

Californi-a—t' jine Simeon an' Peter—true sons o' mine if they be dumb fools—an' the Cabots'll find Solomon's Mines t'gether! [*He suddenly cuts a mad caper.*] Whoop! What was the song they sung? "Oh, Californi-a! That's the land fur me." [*He sings this—then gets on his knees by the floor-board under which the money was hid.*] An' I'll sail thar on one o' the finest clippers I kin find! I've got the money! Pity ye didn't know whar this was hidden so's ye could steal ... [*He has pulled up the board. He stares—feels—stares again. A pause of dead silence. He slowly turns, slumping into a sitting position on the floor, his eyes like those of a dead fish, his face the sickly green of an attack of nausea. He swallows painfully several times—forces a weak smile at last.*] So—ye did steal it!

EBEN [*emotionlessly*]. I swapped it t' Sim an' Peter fur their share o' the farm—t' pay their passage t' Californi-a.

CABOT [*with one sardonic*]. Ha! [*He begins to recover. Gets slowly to his feet—strangely*] I calc'late God give it to 'em—not yew! God's hard, not easy! Mebbe they's easy gold in the West but it hain't God's gold. It hain't fur me. I kin hear His voice warnin' me agen t' be hard an' stay on my farm. I kin see his hand usin' Eben t' steal t' keep me from weakness. I kin feel I be in the palm o' His hand, His fingers guidin' me. [*A pause—then he mutters sadly:*] It's a-goin' t' be lonesomer now than ever it war afore—an' I'm gittin' old, Lord— ripe on the bough. ... [*Then stiffening*] Waal—what d'ye want? God's lonesome, hain't He? God's hard an' lonesome! [*A pause. The* SHERIFF *with two men comes up the road from the left. They move cautiously to the door. The* SHERIFF *knocks on it with the butt of his pistol.*]

SHERIFF. Open in the name o' the law! [*They start.*]

CABOT. They've come fur ye. [*He goes to the rear door.*] Come in, Jim! [*The three men enter.* CABOT *meets them in doorway.*] Jest a minit, Jim. I got 'em safe here. [*The* SHERIFF *nods. He and his companions remain in the doorway.*]

EBEN [*suddenly calls*]. I lied this mornin', Jim. I helped her to do it. Ye kin take me, too.

ABBIE [*brokenly*]. No!

CABOT. Take 'em both. [*He comes forward—stares at* EBEN *with a trace of grudging admiration.*] Purty good—fur yew! Waal, I got t' round up the stock. Good-by.

EBEN. Good-by.

ABBIE. Good-by. [CABOT *turns and strides past the men—comes out and around the corner of the house, his shoulders squared, his face stony, and stalks grimly toward the barn. In the meantime the* SHERIFF *and men have come into the room.*]

SHERIFF [*embarrassedly*]. Waal—we'd best start.

ABBIE. Wait. [*Turns to* EBEN.] I love ye, Eben.

EBEN. I love ye, Abbie. [*They kiss. The three men grin and shuffle embarrassedly.* EBEN *takes* ABBIE's *hand. They go out the door in rear, the men following, and come from the house, walking hand in hand to the gate.* EBEN *stops there and points to the sunrise sky.*] Sun's a-risin'. Purty, hain't it?

ABBIE. Ay-eh. [*They both stand for a moment looking up raptly in attitudes strangely aloof and devout.*]

SHERIFF [*looking around at the farm enviously—to his companion*]. It's a jim-dandy farm, no denyin'. Wished I owned it!

CURTAIN

THE END

W. SOMERSET MAUGHAM
(1874-   )

Somerset Maugham has had the common misfortune of popular writers that his public refused to take him seriously as an artist when he was actually very much in earnest. During a tireless career of more than half a century devoted to entertaining his contemporaries, he has occasionally extended himself to a searching biographical novel, such as *Of Human Bondage* (1915) and *The Moon and Sixpence* (1919), or a somber play of contemporary problems, such as *The Unknown* (1920) and *For Services Rendered* (1932). But his critics have persisted in considering him a facile practitioner of literature, the craftsman of twenty books of ingenious stories and as many drawing-room plays. In his frank and wise autobiographical works, *The Summing Up* (1938) and *A Writer's Notebook* (1949), which should be read by all would-be writers, Maugham cannot conceal his chagrin at being dismissed as a superior journeyman, or his abiding concern for his posthumous reputation.

Actually, the bulk of his work reveals both the virtues and the limitations of the successful professional writer. He does not deny the implications of the term, but insists that the code of such a writer demands a careful training in his craft and an integrity in choice of subject matter and treatment that can be measured against the rough-hewn inspiration of the instinctive author. For Maugham this means especially a clean, lucid prose style, a methodical grasp of form, an urbane polish, and a sophisticated wit. His suave professionalism springs as much from his detached and somewhat cynical temperament and his cosmopolitan experience as from the careful apprentice-ship of his youth. Those who esteem him most highly may pass over most of his books as filler for a long career, but they cannot ignore their importance as the training ground for his infallible competence and as a calculated means of achieving leisure for his more important writing.

Maugham's life and works are all of one piece. The mark of the great world was upon him even in his child-hood, which he passed mostly in Paris, where his father was legal advisor to the British embassy. He spoke French be-fore English, and though not of a wealthy family, enjoyed the advantages of education and worldly experience associ-ated with the young of the upper classes. Still, his child-hood was clouded by difficulties that re-enforced his ex-tremely stoic nature. Orphaned at ten, he was reared by a stern uncle in England, a dry clergyman who intended him for a career in the church. Incapacitated by his small stature and incipient tuberculosis for sports and an active physical life, cut off from his fellows by a painful stammer that he was never to lose, Maugham grew up a reticent, introspec-tive youth, who longed for freedom to live as he chose. After a year at Heidelberg that helped to shape his philosophy of life, he studied medicine for six years at St. Thomas' Hospital in London and qualified as a physician and sur-geon. Except for a year's internship in the Lambeth slums, he never practiced, but we can assume that this scientific training sharpened his almost clinical observation of human beings and his highly unidealistic approach to himself and the world. When a novel called *Liza of Lambeth* (1897) that he had written as an interne found a publisher, he abandoned medicine for the profession of literature and began a parade of successes that continued into his seventies.

Realistically aware of the importance of money to his way of life, Maugham turned from his somewhat grim early work to drawing-room plays that made him a favorite of upper-class theater audiences. Perfecting a dra-matic formula in the tradition of the English comedy of manners, he was soon earning so much from the stage that he could travel the world as he chose and satisfy his curi-osity about exotic lands. The Far East and the South Seas were to figure largely in the work of his middle period, but he was equally enthusiastic about Spain. In later years he became a member of the international set, enjoying a round of cosmopolitan living in London and New York, but especially in his sumptuous villa on the French Riviera. Though apparently a man of infinite leisure to travel and read and enjoy the good things of life, he continued his methodical work-habits, turning out an extraordinary amount of writing.

Even as he passed seventy and had written *The Summing Up* of his life, it became clear that he "often took leave but was loth to depart." Obsessed with a fear that he might outstay his welcome, he folded his affairs one by one. The drama was the first field from which he formally retired, when the failure of *Sheppey* in London in 1933 convinced him that he was no longer in touch with the public that patronizes the theater. But as he neared eighty this "very old party," as he humorously called himself, proved by the continued success of his books that he had not lost his hold upon his readers. Through outliving everyone else in his generation, he became by default the dean of English authors.

W. SOMERSET MAUGHAM

THE CONSTANT WIFE

CHARACTERS

Constance	*Martha*
John Middleton, F.R.C.S.	*Barbara*
Bernard Kersal	*Mortimer Durham*
Mrs. Culver	*Bentley*
Marie-Louise	

The action of the play takes place in John's house in Harley Street.

act 1

CONSTANCE'S *drawing-room. It is a room furnished with singularly good taste.* CONSTANCE *has a gift for decoration and has made this room of hers both beautiful and comfortable.*

It is afternoon.

MRS. CULVER *is seated alone. She is an elderly lady with a pleasant face and she is dressed in walking costume. The door is opened and* BENTLEY *the butler introduces* MARTHA CULVER. *This is her daughter and a fine young woman.*

BENTLEY. Miss Culver. [*He goes out.*]

MARTHA [*with astonishment*]. Mother.

MRS. CULVER [*very calmly*]. Yes, darling.

MARTHA. You're the last person I expected to find here. You never told me you were coming to see Constance.

MRS. CULVER [*good-humouredly*]. I didn't intend to till I saw in your beady eye that *you* meant to. I thought I'd just as soon be here first.

MARTHA. Bentley says she's out.

MRS. CULVER. Yes. . . . Are you going to wait?

MARTHA. Certainly.

MRS. CULVER. Then I will, too.

MARTHA. That'll be very nice.

MRS. CULVER. Your words are cordial, but your tone is slightly frigid, my dear.

MARTHA. I don't know what you mean by that, mother.

MRS. CULVER. My dear, we've known one another a great many years, haven't we? More than we always find it convenient to mention.

MARTHA. Not at all. I'm thirty-two. I'm not in the least ashamed of my age. Constance is thirty-six.

MRS. CULVER. And yet we still think it worth while to be a trifle disingenuous with one another. Our sex takes a natural pleasure in dissimulation.

MARTHA. I don't think anyone can accuse me of not being frank.

MRS. CULVER. Frankness of course is the pose of the moment. It is often a very effective screen for one's thoughts.

MARTHA. I think you're being faintly disagreeable to me, mother.

MRS. CULVER. I, on the other hand, think you're inclined to be decidedly foolish.

MARTHA. Because I want to tell Constance something she ought to know?

MRS. CULVER. Ah, I *was* right then. And it's to tell her that you've broken an engagement, and left three wretched people to play cut-throat.

MARTHA. It is.

MRS. CULVER. And may I ask why you think Constance ought to know?

MARTHA. Why? Why? Why? That's one of those questions that really don't need answering.

MRS. CULVER. I've always noticed that the questions that really don't need answering are the most difficult to answer.

MARTHA. It isn't at all difficult to answer. She ought to know the truth because it's the truth.

MRS. CULVER. Of course truth is an excellent thing, but before one tells it one should be quite sure that one does so for the advantage of the person who hears it rather than for one's own self-satisfaction.

MARTHA. Mother, Constance is a very unhappy person.

MRS. CULVER. Nonsense. She eats well, sleeps well, dresses well, and she's losing weight. No woman can be unhappy in those circumstances.

MARTHA. Of course if you won't understand it's no use my trying to make you. You're a darling, but you're the most unnatural mother. Your attitude simply amazes me.

[*The door opens and* BENTLEY *ushers in* MRS. FAWCETT. MRS. FAWCETT *is a trim, business-like woman of forty.*]

BENTLEY. Mrs. Fawcett.

MRS. CULVER. Oh, Barbara, how very nice to see you.

BARBARA [*going up to her and kissing her*]. Bentley told me you were here and Constance was out. What are you doing?

MRS. CULVER. Bickering.

BARBARA. What about?

MRS. CULVER. Constance.

MARTHA. I'm glad you've come, Barbara. . . . Did you know that John was having an affair with Marie-Louise?

BARBARA. I hate giving a straight answer to a straight question.

MARTHA. I suppose everyone knows but us. How long have you known? They say it's been going on for months. I can't think how it is we've only just heard it.

MRS. CULVER [*ironically*]. It speaks very well for human nature that with the masses of dear friends we have it's only today that one of them broke the news to us.

BARBARA. Perhaps the dear friend only heard it this morning.

MARTHA. At first I refused to believe it.

MRS. CULVER. Only quite, quite at first, darling. You surrendered to the evidence with an outraged alacrity that took my breath away.

MARTHA. Of course I put two and two together. After the first shock I understood everything. I'm only astonished that it never occurred to me before.

BARBARA. Are you very much upset, Mrs. Culver?

MRS. CULVER. Not a bit. I was brought up by a very strict mother to believe that men were naturally wicked. I am seldom surprised at what they do and never upset.

MARTHA. Mother has been simply maddening. She treats it as though it didn't matter a row of pins.

MRS. CULVER. Constance and John have been married for fifteen years. John is a very agreeable man. I've sometimes wondered whether he was any more faithful to his wife than most husbands, but as it was really no concern of mine I didn't let my mind dwell on it.

MARTHA. Is Constance your daughter or is she not your daughter?

MRS. CULVER. You certainly have a passion for straight questions, my dear. The answer is yes.

MARTHA. And are you prepared to sit there quietly and let her husband grossly deceive her with her most intimate friend?

MRS. CULVER. So long as she doesn't know I can't see that she's any the worse. Marie-Louise is a nice little thing, silly of course, but that's what men like, and if John is going to deceive Constance it's much better that it should be with someone we all know.

MARTHA [*to* BARBARA]. Did you ever hear a respectable woman —and mother is respectable. . . .

MRS. CULVER [*interrupting*]. Oh, quite.

MARTHA. Talk like that?

BARBARA. You think that something ought to be done about it?

MARTHA. I am determined that something shall be done about it.

MRS. CULVER. Well, my dear, I'm determined that there's at least one thing you shan't do and that is to tell Constance.

BARBARA [*a trifle startled*]. Is that what you want to do?

MARTHA. Somebody ought to tell her. If mother won't I must.

BARBARA. I'm extremely fond of Constance. Of course I've known what was going on for a long time and I've been dreadfully worried.

MARTHA. John has put her into an odious position. No man has the right to humiliate his wife as he has humiliated Constance. He's made her perfectly ridiculous.

MRS. CULVER. If women were ridiculous because their husbands are unfaithful to them, there would surely be a great deal more merriment in the world than there is.

BARBARA [*delighted to have a good gossip*]. You know they were lunching together today?

MARTHA. We hadn't heard that. But they were dining together the night before last.

MRS. CULVER [*brightly*]. We know what they had to eat for dinner. Do you know what they had to eat for luncheon?

MARTHA. Mother.

MRS. CULVER. Well, I thought she seemed rather uppish about the lunch.

MARTHA. You have no sense of decency, mother.

MRS. CULVER. Oh, my dear, don't talk to me about decency. Decency died with dear Queen Victoria.

BARBARA [*to* MRS. CULVER]. But you can't approve of John having an open and flagrant intrigue with Constance's greatest friend.

MRS. CULVER. It may be that with advancing years my arteries have hardened. I am unable to attach any great importance to the philanderings of men. I think it's their nature. John is a very hard-working surgeon. If he likes to lunch and dine with a pretty woman now and then I don't think he's much to blame. It must be very tiresome to have three meals a day with the same woman for seven days a week. I'm a little bored myself at seeing Martha opposite me at the dinner-table. And men can't stand boredom as well as women.

MARTHA. I'm sure I'm very much obliged to you, mother.

BARBARA [*significantly*]. But they're not only lunching and dining together.

MRS. CULVER. You fear the worst, my dear?

BARBARA [*with solemnity*]. I know the worst.

MRS. CULVER. I always think that's such a comfort. With closed doors and no one listening to us, so long as a man is kind and civil to his wife do you blame him very much if he strays occasionally from the narrow path of virtue?

MARTHA. Do you mean to say that you attach no importance to husbands and wives keeping their marriage vows?

MRS. CULVER. I think wives should.

BARBARA. But that's grossly unfair. Why should *they* any more than men?

MRS. CULVER. Because on the whole they like it. We ascribe a great deal of merit to ourselves because we're faithful to our husbands. I don't believe we deserve it for a minute. We're naturally faithful creatures and we're faithful because we have no particular inclination to be anything else.

BARBARA. I wonder.

MRS. CULVER. My dear, you are a widow and perfectly free. Have you really had any great desire to do anything that the world might say you shouldn't?

BARBARA. I have my business. When you work hard eight hours a day you don't much want to be bothered with love. In the evening the tired business woman wants to go to a musical comedy or play cards. She doesn't want to be worried with adoring males.

MARTHA. By the way, how is your business?

BARBARA. Growing by leaps and bounds. As a matter of fact I came here today to ask Constance if she would like to come in with me.

MRS. CULVER. Why should she? John earns plenty of money.

BARBARA. Well, I thought if things came to a crisis she might like to know that her independence was assured.

MRS. CULVER. Oh, you want them to come to a crisis, too?

BARBARA. No, of course I don't. But, you know, they can't go on like this. It's a miracle that Constance hasn't heard yet. She's bound to find out soon.

MRS. CULVER. I suppose it's inevitable.

MARTHA. I hope she'll find out as quickly as possible. I still think it's mother's duty to tell her.

MRS. CULVER. Which I have no intention of doing.

MARTHA. And if mother won't I think I ought.

MRS. CULVER. Which I have no intention of permitting.

MARTHA. He's humiliated her beyond endurance. Her position is intolerable. I have no words to express my opinion of Marie-Louise, and the first time I see her I shall tell her exactly what I think of her. She's a horrid, ungrateful, mean and contemptible little cat.

BARBARA. Anyhow, I think it would be a comfort to Constance to know that if anything happened she has me to turn to.

MRS. CULVER. But John would make her a handsome allowance. He's a very generous man.

MARTHA [*indignantly*]. Do you think Constance would accept it?

BARBARA. Martha's quite right, Mrs. Culver. No woman in those circumstances would take a penny of his money.

MRS. CULVER. That's what she'd say. But she'd take care that her lawyer made the best arrangement he could. Few men know with what ingenuity we women can combine the disinterested gesture with a practical eye for the main chance.

BARBARA. Aren't you rather cynical, Mrs. Culver?

MRS. CULVER. I hope not. But when women are alone together I don't see why they shouldn't tell the truth now and then. It's a rest from the weary round of pretending to be something that we quite well know we're not.

MARTHA [*stiffly*]. I'm not aware that I've ever pretended to be anything I wasn't.

MRS. CULVER. I dare say not, my dear. But I've always thought you were a little stupid. You take after your poor father. Constance and I have the brains of the family.

[CONSTANCE *comes into the room. She is a handsome woman of six and thirty. She has been out and wears a hat.*]

BARBARA [*eagerly*]. Constance.

CONSTANCE. I'm so sorry I wasn't in. How nice of you all to wait. How are you, mother darling? [*She kisses them one after another.*]

MARTHA. What have you been doing all day, Constance?

CONSTANCE. Oh, I've been shopping with Marie-Louise. She's just coming up.

BARBARA [*with dismay*]. Is she here?

CONSTANCE. Yes. She's telephoning.

MARTHA [*ironically*]. You and Marie-Louise are quite inseparable.

CONSTANCE. I like her. She amuses me.

MARTHA. Were you lunching together?

CONSTANCE. No, she was lunching with a beau.

MARTHA [*with a glance at* MRS. CULVER]. Oh, really. [*Breezily*] John always comes home to luncheon, doesn't he?

CONSTANCE [*with great frankness*]. When he doesn't have to be at the hospital too early.

MARTHA. Was he lunching with you today?

CONSTANCE. No. He was engaged.

MARTHA. Where?

CONSTANCE. Good heavens, I don't know. When you've been married as long as I have you never ask your husband where he's going.

MARTHA. I don't know why not.

CONSTANCE [*smiling*]. Because he might take it into his head to ask *you*.

MRS. CULVER. And also because if you're a wise woman you have confidence in your husband.

CONSTANCE. John has never given me a moment's uneasiness yet.

MARTHA. You're lucky.

CONSTANCE [*with her tongue in her cheek*]. Or wise.

[MARIE-LOUISE *appears. She is a very pretty little thing, beautifully dressed, of the clinging, large-eyed type.*]

MARIE-LOUISE. Oh, I didn't know there was a party.

MRS. CULVER. Martha and I are just going.

CONSTANCE. You know my mother, Marie-Louise.

MARIE-LOUISE. Of course I do.

CONSTANCE. She's a very nice mother.

MRS. CULVER. With her head screwed on the right way and very active for her years.

[MARIE-LOUISE *kisses* BARBARA *and* MARTHA.]

MARIE-LOUISE. How do you do.

MARTHA [*looking at her dress*]. That's new, isn't it, Marie-Louise?

MARIE-LOUISE. Yes, I've never had it on before.

MARTHA. Oh, did you put it on because you were lunching with a beau?

MARIE-LOUISE. What makes you think I was lunching with a beau?

MARTHA. Constance told me so.

CONSTANCE. It was only a guess on my part. [*To* MARIE-LOUISE] When we met I noticed that your eyes were shining and you had that pleased, young look a woman always gets when some one has been telling her she's the most adorable thing in the world.

MARTHA. Tell us who it was, Marie-Louise.

CONSTANCE. Do nothing of the kind, Marie-Louise. Keep it a secret and give us something to gossip about.

BARBARA. How is your husband, dear?

MARIE-LOUISE. Oh, he's very well. I've just been telephoning to him.

BARBARA. I never saw anyone adore his wife so obviously as he adores you.

MARIE-LOUISE. Yes, he's sweet, isn't he?

BARBARA. But doesn't it make you a little nervous sometimes? It must be nerve-racking to be obliged to live up to such profound devotion. It would be a dreadful shock if he ever found out that you were not everything he thought you.

CONSTANCE [*charmingly*]. But Marie-Louise is everything he thinks her.

MARIE-LOUISE. And even if I weren't I think it would require more than the evidence of his eyes to persuade him.

CONSTANCE. Listen. There's John. [*She goes to the door and calls*] John! John!

JOHN [*downstairs*]. Hulloa.

CONSTANCE. Are you coming up? Marie-Louise is here.

JOHN. Yes, I'm just coming.

CONSTANCE. He's been operating all the afternoon. I expect he's tired out.

MARTHA [*with a look at* MARIE-LOUISE]. I dare say he only had a sandwich for luncheon.

[JOHN *comes in. He is a tall, spare man of about forty.*]

JOHN. Good Lord, I never saw such a lot of people. How is my mother-in-law?

MRS. CULVER. Mother-in-lawish.

JOHN [*kissing her—to* BARBARA]. You know, I only married Constance because her mother wouldn't have me.

MRS. CULVER. I was too young at the time to marry a boy twenty years younger than myself.

CONSTANCE. It hasn't prevented you from flirting outrageously with the creature ever since. It's lucky I'm not a jealous woman.

JOHN. What have you been doing all day, darling?

CONSTANCE. I've been shopping with Marie-Louise.

JOHN [*shaking hands with* MARIE-LOUISE]. Oh, how do you do? Did you lunch together?

MARTHA. No, she lunched with a beau.

JOHN. I wish it had been me. [*To* MARIE-LOUISE] What have you been doing with yourself lately? We haven't seen you for ages.

MARIE-LOUISE. You're never about. Constance and I almost live in one another's pockets.

JOHN. How's that rich husband of yours?

MARIE-LOUISE. I've just been speaking to him. Isn't it a bore, he's got to go down to Birmingham for the night.

CONSTANCE. You'd better come and dine with us.

MARIE-LOUISE. Oh, it's awfully nice of you. But I'm tired out. I shall just go to bed and have an egg.

JOHN. I was just going to tell you, Constance. I shan't be in this evening. I've got an acute appendix to do.

CONSTANCE. Oh, what a nuisance.

MARTHA. You've got a wonderful profession, John. If you ever want to do anything or go anywhere you've only got to say you've got an operation and no one can prove it's a lie.

CONSTANCE. Oh, my dear, you mustn't put suspicions into my innocent head. It would never occur to John to be so deceitful. [*To* JOHN] Would it?

JOHN. I think I'd have to go an awful long way before I managed to deceive you, darling.

CONSTANCE [*with a little smile*]. Sometimes I think you're right.

MARIE-LOUISE. I do like to see a husband and wife so devoted to one another as you and John. You've been married fifteen years, haven't you?

JOHN. Yes. And it doesn't seem a day too much.

MARIE-LOUISE. Well, I must be running along. I'm late already. Good-bye, darling. Good-bye, Mrs. Culver.

CONSTANCE. Good-bye, darling. We've had such a nice afternoon.

MARIE-LOUISE [*giving her hand to* JOHN]. Good-bye.

JOHN. Oh, I'll come downstairs with you.

MARTHA. I was just going, Marie-Louise. I'll come with you.

MARIE-LOUISE [*with presence of mind*]. John, I wonder if you'd mind looking at my knee for a minute. It's been rather painful for the last day or two.

JOHN. Of course not. Come into my consulting-room. These knee-caps are troublesome things when you once get them out of order.

MARTHA [*firmly*]. I'll wait for you. You won't be long, will you? We might share a taxi.

MARIE-LOUISE. I've got my car.

MARTHA. Oh, how nice! You can give me a lift then.

MARIE-LOUISE. Of course. I shall be delighted.

[JOHN *opens the door for* MARIE-LOUISE. *She goes out and he follows her.* CONSTANCE *has watched this little scene coolly, but with an alert mind.*]

MARTHA. What is the matter with her knee?

CONSTANCE. It slips.

MARTHA. What happens then?

CONSTANCE. She slips too.

MARTHA. Are you never jealous of these women who come and see John in his consulting-room?

CONSTANCE. He always has a nurse within call in case they should attempt to take liberties with him.

MARTHA [*amiably*]. Is the nurse there now?

CONSTANCE. And anyway I can't help thinking that the sort of woman who wants to be made love to in a consulting-room with a lively odour of antiseptics is the sort of woman who wears horrid undies. I could never bring myself to be jealous of her.

MARTHA. Marie-Louise gave me two of her chemises to copy only the other day.

CONSTANCE. Oh, did she give you the cerise one with the Irish lace insertions? I thought that sweet. I've copied that.

BARBARA. It's true that Marie-Louise is very pretty.

CONSTANCE. Marie-Louise is a darling. But she and John have known each other far too long. John likes her of course, but he says she has no brain.

MARTHA. Men don't always say what they think.

CONSTANCE. Fortunately, or we shouldn't always know what they feel.

MARTHA. Don't you think John has any secrets from you?

CONSTANCE. I'm sure of it. But of course a good wife always pretends not to know the little things her husband wishes to keep hidden from her. That is an elementary rule in matrimonial etiquette.

MARTHA. Don't forget that men were deceivers ever.

CONSTANCE. My dear, you talk like a confirmed spinster. What woman was ever deceived that didn't want to be? Do you really think that men are mysterious? They're children. Why, my dear, John at forty isn't nearly so grown up as Helen at fourteen.

BARBARA. How is your girl, Constance?

CONSTANCE. Oh, she's very well. She loves boarding-school, you know. They're like little boys, men. Sometimes of course they're rather naughty and you have to pretend to be angry with them. They attach so much importance to such entirely unimportant things that it's really touching. And they're so helpless. Have you never nursed a man when he's ill? It wrings your heart. It's just like a dog or a horse. They haven't got the sense to come in out of the rain, poor darlings. They have all the charming qualities that accompany general incompetence. They're sweet and good and silly and tiresome and selfish. You can't help liking them, they're so ingenuous and so simple. They have no complexity or finesse. I think they're sweet, but it's absurd to take them seriously. You're a wise woman, mother. What do you think?

MRS. CULVER. I think you're not in love with your husband.

CONSTANCE. What nonsense.

[JOHN *comes in.*]

JOHN. Marie-Louise is waiting for you, Martha. I've just put a little bandage round her knee.

CONSTANCE. I hope you weren't rough.

MARTHA [*to Constance*]. Good-bye, dear. Are you coming, mother?

MRS. CULVER. Not just yet.

MARTHA. Good-bye, Barbara.

[MARTHA *and* JOHN *go out.*]

BARBARA. Constance, I've got a suggestion to make to you. You know that my business has been growing by leaps and bounds and I simply cannot get along alone any more. I was wondering if you'd like to come in with me.

CONSTANCE. Oh, my dear, I'm not a business woman.

BARBARA. You've got marvellous taste and you have ideas. You could do all the decorating and I'd confine myself to buying and selling furniture.

CONSTANCE. But I've got no capital.

BARBARA. I've got all the capital I want. I must have help and I know no one more suitable than you. We'd go fifty-fifty and I think I can promise that you'd make a thousand to fifteen hundred a year.

CONSTANCE. I've been an idle woman so long. I think I'd find it dreadfully hard to work eight hours a day.

BARBARA. Won't you think it over? It's very interesting, you know. You're naturally energetic. Don't you get bored with doing nothing all the time?

CONSTANCE. I don't think John would like it. After all, it would look as though he couldn't afford to support me.

BARBARA. Oh, not nowadays, surely. There's no reason why a woman shouldn't have a career just as much as a man.

CONSTANCE. I think my career is looking after John—running a house for him, entertaining his friends and making him happy and comfortable.

BARBARA. Don't you think it rather a mistake to put all your eggs in one basket? Supposing that career failed you?

CONSTANCE. Why should it?

BARBARA. Of course I hope it won't. But men, you know, are fluctuating and various. Independence is a very good thing, and a woman who stands on her own feet financially can look upon the future with a good deal of confidence.

CONSTANCE. It's sweet of you, but so long as John and I are happy together I think I should be a fool to do anything that would vex him.

BARBARA. Of course I'm in no immediate hurry. One never knows what the future will bring forth. I want you to know that if you change your mind the job is open to you. I don't think I shall ever find any one so competent as you. You have only to say the word.

CONSTANCE. Oh, Barbara, you are kind to me. It's a splendid offer and I'm ever so grateful to you. Don't think me horrid if I say I hope I shall never need to accept it.

BARBARA. Of course not. Good-bye, darling.

CONSTANCE. Good-bye, dear.

[*They kiss, and* BARBARA *goes out.* CONSTANCE *rings the bell.*]

MRS. CULVER. Are you quite happy, dear.

CONSTANCE. Oh, quite. Don't I look it?

MRS. CULVER. I'm bound to say you do. So far as I can judge by the look of you I should say you haven't a trouble in the world.

CONSTANCE. You'd be wrong. My cook has given notice and she makes the best meringues I've ever eaten.

MRS. CULVER. I like John.

CONSTANCE. So do I. He has all the solid qualities that make a man a good husband: an agreeable temper, a sense of humour and an entire indifference to petty extravagance.

MRS. CULVER. How right you are, darling, to realize that those are the solid qualities.

CONSTANCE. It's not the seven deadly virtues that make a man a good husband: but the three hundred pleasing amiabilities.

MRS. CULVER. Of course one has to compromise in life. One has to make the best of things. One mustn't expect too much from people. If one wants to be happy in one's own way one must let others be happy in theirs. If one can't get this, that and the other the wise thing is to make up one's mind to do without it. The great thing is not to let vanity warp one's reasonable point of view.

CONSTANCE. Mother, mother, pull yourself together.

MRS. CULVER. Everybody's so clever nowadays. They see everything but the obvious. I've discovered that I only have to say it quite simply in order to be thought a most original and amusing old lady.

CONSTANCE. Spare me, darling.

MRS. CULVER [*affectionately*]. If at any time anything went wrong with you, you would tell your mother, wouldn't you?

CONSTANCE. Of course.

MRS. CULVER. I hate the thought that you might be unhappy and let a foolish pride prevent you from letting me console and advise you.

CONSTANCE [*with feeling*]. It wouldn't, mother dear.

MRS. CULVER. I had rather an odd experience the other day. A little friend of mine came to see me and told me that her husband was neglecting her. I asked her why she told me and not her own mother. She said that her mother had never wanted her to marry and it would mortify her now to have to say that she had made a mistake.

CONSTANCE. Oh, well, John never neglects me, mother.

MRS. CULVER. Of course I gave her a good talking to. She didn't get much sympathy from me.

CONSTANCE [*with a smile*]. That was very unkind, wasn't it?

MRS. CULVER. I have my own ideas about marriage. If a man neglects his wife it's her own fault, and if he's systematically unfaithful to her in nine cases out of ten she only has herself to blame.

CONSTANCE [*ringing the bell*]. Systematically is a grim word.

MRS. CULVER. No sensible woman attaches importance to an occasional slip. Time and chance are responsible for that.

CONSTANCE. And shall we say, masculine vanity?

MRS. CULVER. I told my little friend that if her husband was unfaithful to her it was because he found other women more attractive. Why should she be angry with him for that? Her business was to be more attractive than they.

CONSTANCE. You are not what they call a feminist, mother, are you?

MRS. CULVER. After all, what is fidelity?

CONSTANCE. Mother, do you mind if I open the window?

MRS. CULVER. It is open.

CONSTANCE. In that case do you mind if I shut it? I feel that when a woman of your age asks such a question I should make some sort of symbolic gesture.

MRS. CULVER. Don't be ridiculous. Of course I believe in fidelity for women. I suppose no one has ever questioned the desirability of that. But men are different. Women should remember that they have their homes and their name and position and their family, and they should learn to close their eyes when it's possible they may see something they are not meant to.

[*The* BUTLER *comes in.*]

BENTLEY. Did you ring, madam?

CONSTANCE. Yes. I am expecting Mr. Bernard Kersal. I'm not at home to anybody else.

BENTLEY. Very good, madam.

CONSTANCE. Is Mr. Middleton in?

BENTLEY. Yes, madam. He's in the consulting-room.

CONSTANCE. Very well.

[*The* BUTLER *goes out.*]

MRS. CULVER. Is that a polite way of telling me that I had better take myself off?

CONSTANCE. Of course not. On the contrary I particularly want you to stay.

MRS. CULVER. Who is this mysterious gentleman?

CONSTANCE. Mother. Bernard.

MRS. CULVER. That says nothing to me at all. Not Saint Bernard, darling?

CONSTANCE. Pull yourself together, my pet. You must remember Bernard Kersal. He proposed to me.

MRS. CULVER. Oh, my dear, you cannot expect me to remember the names of all the young men who proposed to you.

CONSTANCE. Yes, but he proposed more than any of the others.

MRS. CULVER. Why?

CONSTANCE. I suppose because I refused him. I can't think of any other reason.

MRS. CULVER. He made no impression on me.

CONSTANCE. I don't suppose he tried to.

MRS. CULVER. What did he look like?

CONSTANCE. He was tall.

MRS. CULVER. They were all tall.

CONSTANCE. He had brown hair and brown eyes.

MRS. CULVER. They all had brown hair and brown eyes.

CONSTANCE. He danced divinely.

MRS. CULVER. They all danced divinely.

CONSTANCE. I very nearly married him, you know.

MRS. CULVER. Why didn't you?

CONSTANCE. I think he was a trifle too much inclined to lie down on the floor and let me walk over him.

MRS. CULVER. In short he had no sense of humour.

CONSTANCE. I was quite certain that he loved me, and I was never absolutely sure that John did.

MRS. CULVER. Well, you're sure now, dear, aren't you?

CONSTANCE. Oh, yes. John adores me.

MRS. CULVER. And what's this young man coming for today?

CONSTANCE. He's not such a very young man any more. He was twenty-nine then and so he must be nearly forty-five now.

MRS. CULVER. He isn't still in love with you?

CONSTANCE. I shouldn't think so. Do you think it possible after fifteen years? It's surely very unlikely. Don't look at me like that, mother. I don't like it.

MRS. CULVER. Don't talk stuff and nonsense to me, child. Of course you know if he's in love with you or not.

CONSTANCE. But I haven't seen him since I married John. You see he lives in Japan. He's a merchant or something in Kobe. He was here during the war on leave. But that was when I was so dreadfully ill and I didn't see him.

MRS. CULVER. Oh! Why's he here now then? Have you been corresponding with him?

CONSTANCE. No. One can't write letters to any one one never sees for fifteen years. He always sends me flowers on my birthday.

MRS. CULVER. That's rather sweet of him.

CONSTANCE. And the other day I had a letter from him saying he was in England and would like to see me. So I asked him to come today.

MRS. CULVER. I wondered why you were so smart.

CONSTANCE. Of course he may be terribly changed. Men go off so dreadfully, don't they? He may be bald and fat now.

MRS. CULVER. He may be married.

CONSTANCE. Oh, if he were I don't think he'd want to come and see me, would he?

MRS. CULVER. I see you're under the impression that he's still in love with you.

CONSTANCE. Oh, I'm not.

MRS. CULVER. Then why are you so nervous?

CONSTANCE. It's only natural that I shouldn't want him to think me old and haggard. He adored me, mother. I suppose he still thinks of me as I was then. It wouldn't be very nice if his face fell about a yard and a half when he came into the room.

MRS. CULVER. I think I'd much better leave you to face the ordeal alone.

CONSTANCE. Oh, no, mother, you must stay. I particularly want you. You see, he may be awful and I may wish I'd never seen him again. It'll be so much easier if you're here. I may not want to be alone with him at all.

MRS. CULVER. Oh.

CONSTANCE [*with a twinkle in her eye*]. On the other hand I may.

MRS. CULVER. It seems to me you're putting me in a slightly embarrassing situation.

CONSTANCE. Now listen. If I think he's awful we'll just talk about the weather and the crops for a few minutes and then we'll have an ominous pause and stare at him. That always makes a man feel a perfect fool and the moment a man feels a fool he gets up and goes.

MRS. CULVER. Sometimes they don't know how to, poor dears, and the earth will never open and swallow them up.

CONSTANCE. On the other hand if I think he looks rather nice I shall just take out my handkerchief and carelessly place it on the piano.

MRS. CULVER. Why?

CONSTANCE. Darling, in order that you may rise to your aged feet and say, well, you really must be running along.

MRS. CULVER. Yes, I know that, but why should you carelessly place your handkerchief on the piano?

CONSTANCE. Because I am a creature of impulse. I shall have an impulse to place my handkerchief on the piano.

MRS. CULVER. Oh, very well. But I always mistrust impulses.

[BENTLEY *enters and announces* BERNARD KERSAL. *He is a tall good-looking man, sunburned and of healthy appearance. He is evidently very fit and he carries his forty-five years well.*]

BENTLEY. Mr. Kersal.

CONSTANCE. How do you do? Do you remember my mother?

BERNARD [*shaking hands with her*]. I'm sure she doesn't remember me.

[CONSTANCE *takes a small handkerchief out of her bag.*]

MRS. CULVER. That is the soft answer that turneth away wrath.

CONSTANCE. It's rather late for tea, isn't it? Would you like a drink? [*As she says this she goes towards the bell and places her handkerchief on the piano.*]

BERNARD. No, thanks. I've just this moment had one.

CONSTANCE. To brace you for seeing me?

BERNARD. I was nervous.

CONSTANCE. Have I changed as much as you expected?

BERNARD. Oh, that's not what I was nervous about.

MRS. CULVER. Is it really fifteen years since you saw Constance?

BERNARD. Yes. I didn't see her when I was last in England. When I got demobbed I had to go out to Japan again and get my business together. I haven't had a chance to come home before.

[CONSTANCE *has been giving her mother significant looks, but her mother does not notice them.* CONSTANCE *takes a second handkerchief out of her bag and when the opportunity arises places it neatly on the piano beside the first one.*]

MRS. CULVER. And are you home for long?

BERNARD. A year.

MRS. CULVER. Have you brought your wife with you?

BERNARD. I'm not married.

MRS. CULVER. Oh, Constance said you were married to a Japanese lady.

CONSTANCE. Nonsense, mother. I never said anything of the sort.

MRS. CULVER. Oh, perhaps I was thinking of Julia Linton. She married an Egyptian pasha. I believe she's very happy. At all events he hasn't killed her yet.

BERNARD. How is your husband?

CONSTANCE. He's very well. I dare say he'll be in presently.

BERNARD. Haven't you got a little sister? I suppose she's out now?[1]

MRS. CULVER. He means Martha. She's come out and gone in again.

CONSTANCE. She was not so very much younger than me, you know. She's thirty-two now. [MRS. CULVER *has taken no notice of the handkerchiefs and in desperation* CONSTANCE *takes a third from her bag and places it beside the other two.*]

MRS. CULVER. Do you like the East, Mr. Kersal?

BERNARD. One has a pretty good time there, you know.

[*Now* MRS. CULVER *catches sight of the three handkerchiefs and starts.*]

MRS. CULVER. I wonder what the time is.

CONSTANCE. It's late, mother. Are you dining out tonight? I suppose you want to have a lie-down before you dress for dinner.

MRS. CULVER. I hope I shall see you again, Mr. Kersal.

BERNARD. Thank you very much.

[CONSTANCE *accompanies her to the door.*]

MRS. CULVER. Good-bye, darling. [*In a whisper*] I couldn't remember if the handkerchiefs meant go or stay.

CONSTANCE. You had only to use your eyes. You can see at a glance that he is the kind of man one would naturally want to have a heart-to-heart talk with after fifteen years.

MRS. CULVER. You only confused me by putting more and more handkerchiefs on the piano.

---

[1] *she's out now*, she has made her debut in fashionable society.

CONSTANCE. For goodness' sake go, mother. [*Aloud*] Good-bye, my sweet. I'm sorry you've got to run away so soon.

MRS. CULVER. Good-bye. [*She goes out and* CONSTANCE *comes back into the room.*]

CONSTANCE. Did you think it very rude of us to whisper? Mother has a passion for secrets.

BERNARD. Of course not.

CONSTANCE. Now let's sit down and make ourselves comfortable. Let me look at you. You haven't changed much. You're a little thinner and perhaps a little more lined. Men are so lucky, if they have any character they grow better-looking as they grow older. Do you know I'm thirty-six now?

BERNARD. What does that matter?

CONSTANCE. Shall I tell you something? When you wrote and suggested coming here I was delighted at the thought of seeing you again and wrote at once making a date. And then I was panic-stricken. I would have given almost anything not to have sent that letter. And all today I've had such a horrible feeling at the pit of my stomach. Didn't you see my knees wobble when you came into the room?

BERNARD. In God's name, why?

CONSTANCE. Oh, my dear, I think you must be a little stupid. I should be a perfect fool if I didn't know that when I was a girl I was very pretty. It's rather a pang when you are forced to the conclusion that you're not quite so pretty as you were. People don't tell one. One tries to hide it from oneself. Anyhow I thought I'd rather know the worst. That's one of the reasons I asked you to come.

BERNARD. Whatever I thought you can hardly imagine that I should be deliberately rude.

CONSTANCE. Of course not. But I watched your face. I was afraid I'd see there: By God, how she's gone off.

BERNARD. And did you?

CONSTANCE. You were rather shy when you came in. You weren't thinking of me.

BERNARD. It's quite true, fifteen years ago you were a pretty girl. Now you're lovely. You're ten times more beautiful than you were then.

CONSTANCE. It's nice of you to say so.

BERNARD. Don't you believe it?

CONSTANCE. I think you do. And I confess that's sufficiently gratifying. Now tell me, why aren't you married? It's time you did, you know, or it'll be too late. You'll have a very lonely old age if you don't.

BERNARD. I never wanted to marry anyone but you.

CONSTANCE. Oh, come, you're not going to tell me that you've never been in love since you were in love with me?

BERNARD. No, I've been in love half a dozen times, but when it came to the point I found I still loved you best.

CONSTANCE. I like you for saying that. I shouldn't have believed it if you'd said you'd never loved anybody else and I should have been vexed with you for thinking me such a fool as to believe it.

BERNARD. You see, it was you I loved in the others. One because she had hair like yours and another because her smile reminded me of your smile.

CONSTANCE. I hate to think that I've made you unhappy.

BERNARD. But you haven't. I've had a very good time; I've enjoyed my work; I've made a bit of money and I've had a lot of fun. I don't blame you for having married John instead of me.

CONSTANCE. Do you remember John?

BERNARD. Of course I do. He was a very nice fellow. I dare say he's made you a better husband than I should have. I've had my ups and downs. I'm very irritable sometimes. John's been able to give you everything you wanted. You were much safer with him. By the way, I suppose I can still call you Constance.

CONSTANCE. Of course. Why not? Do you know, I think you have a very nice nature, Bernard.

BERNARD. Are you happy with John?

CONSTANCE. Oh, very. I don't say that he has never given me a moment's uneasiness. He did once, but I took hold of myself and saw that I mustn't be silly. I'm very glad I did. I think I can quite honestly say that ours has been a very happy and successful marriage.

BERNARD. I'm awfully glad to hear that. Do you think it's cheek to ask if John loves you?

CONSTANCE. I'm sure he loves me.

BERNARD. And do you love him?

CONSTANCE. Very much.

BERNARD. May I make you a short speech?

CONSTANCE. If I may interrupt at suitable moments.

BERNARD. I hope you're going to let me see a great deal of you during this year I've got at home.

CONSTANCE. I want to see a great deal of you.

BERNARD. There's just one thing I want to get off my chest and then I needn't refer to it again. I am just as madly in love with you as I was when I asked you to marry me fifteen years ago. I think I shall remain in love with you all my life. I'm too old a dog to learn new tricks. But I want you to know that you needn't have the smallest fear that I shall make a nuisance of myself. I should think it an awfully caddish thing to try to come between you and John. I suppose we all want to be happy, but I don't believe the best way of being that is to try to upset other people's happiness.

CONSTANCE. That's not such a very long speech after all. At a public dinner they would hardly even call it a few remarks.

BERNARD. All I ask for is your friendship and if in return I care to give you my love I don't see that it's any one's business but my own.

CONSTANCE. I don't think it is. I think I can be a very good friend, Bernard.

[*The door opens and* JOHN *comes in.*]

JOHN. Oh, I'm sorry. I didn't know you were engaged.

CONSTANCE. I'm not. Come in. This is Bernard Kersal.

JOHN. How do you do?

BERNARD. I'm afraid you don't remember me.

JOHN. If you ask me point-blank I think it's safer to confess I don't.

CONSTANCE. Don't be so silly, John. He used to come to mother's.

JOHN. Before we were married, d'you mean?

CONSTANCE. Yes. You spent several week-ends with us together.

JOHN. My dear, that was fifteen years ago. I'm awfully sorry not to remember you, but I'm delighted to see you now.

CONSTANCE. He's just come back from Japan.

JOHN. Oh, well, I hope we shall see you again. I'm just going along to the club to have a rubber before dinner, darling. [*To* BERNARD] Why don't you dine here with Constance? I've got an acute appendix and she'll be all alone, poor darling.

BERNARD. Oh, that's awfully kind of you.

CONSTANCE. It would be a friendly act. Are you free?

BERNARD. Always to do a friendly act.

CONSTANCE. Very well. I shall expect you at eight-fifteen.

act 2

The scene is the same. A fortnight has passed.

MARTHA *in walking costume and a hat is looking at an illustrated paper.*

BENTLEY *comes in.*

BENTLEY. Mr. Kersal is here, Miss.

MARTHA. Oh! Ask him if he won't come up.

BENTLEY. Very good, Miss. [*He goes out and in a moment comes in again to announce* BERNARD, *and then goes.*] Mr. Kersal.

MARTHA. Constance is dressing. She won't be very long.

BERNARD. Oh, I see. Well, there's no violent hurry.

MARTHA. You're taking her to Ranelagh,[1] aren't you?

BERNARD. That was the idea. I know some of the fellows who are playing today.

MARTHA. Are you having a good time in London?

BERNARD. Marvellous. When a man's lived in the East as long as I have, he's apt to feel rather out of it when he comes home. But Constance and John have been ripping to me.

MARTHA. Do you like John?

BERNARD. Yes. He's been awfully kind.

MARTHA. Do you know, I remember you quite well.

BERNARD. Oh, you can't. You were a kid when I used to come down and stay with your mother.

MARTHA. I was sixteen. Do you imagine I wasn't thrilled to the marrow by Constance's young men?

BERNARD. There were a good many of them. I should have thought your marrow got callous.

MARTHA. But you were one of the serious ones. I always thought you terribly romantic.

BERNARD. I was terribly romantic. I think it's becoming in the young.

MARTHA. I don't think it's unbecoming in the not quite as young.

BERNARD. Don't think I'm romantic now. I make a considerable income and I'm putting on weight. The price of silk has ousted love's young dream in my manly bosom.

[1] *Ranelagh, a fashionable sporting club, associated especially with polo, not to be confused with the famous pleasure gardens of the eighteenth century.*

MARTHA. You're an unconscionable liar.

BERNARD. To which I can only retort that you're excessively rude.

MARTHA. You were madly in love with Constance in those days, weren't you?

BERNARD. You know, it's so long ago I forget.

MARTHA. I advised her to marry you rather than John.

BERNARD. Why?

MARTHA. Well, for one thing you lived in Japan. I would have married any one who would take me there.

BERNARD. I live there still.

MARTHA. Oh, I don't want to marry you.

BERNARD. I couldn't help suspecting that.

MARTHA. I could never really quite understand what she saw in John.

BERNARD. I suppose she loved him.

MARTHA. I wonder if she ever regrets that she married John rather than you.

BERNARD. Well, don't. She's perfectly satisfied with John and wouldn't change him for anything in the world.

MARTHA. It's exasperating, isn't it?

BERNARD. I don't think so. It must make it much more comfortable for a husband and wife to be content with one another.

MARTHA. You're in love with her still, aren't you?

BERNARD. Not a bit.

MARTHA. Upon my soul, you've got a nerve. Why, you donkey, you're giving it away all the time. Do you know what you look like when she's in the room? Have you any idea how your eyes change when they rest on her? When you speak her name it sounds as though you were kissing it.

BERNARD. I thought you were an odious child when you were sixteen, Martha, and now that you're thirty-two I think you're a horrible woman.

MARTHA. I'm not really. But I'm very fond of Constance and I'm inclined to be rather fond of you.

BERNARD. Don't you think you could show your attachment by minding your own business?

MARTHA. Why does it make you angry because I've told you that no one can see you with Constance for five minutes without knowing that you adore her.

BERNARD. My dear, I'm here for one year. I want to be happy. I don't want to give trouble or cause trouble. I value my friendship with Constance and I hate the idea that anything should interfere with it.

MARTHA. Hasn't it occurred to you that she may want more than your friendship?

BERNARD. No, it has not.

MARTHA. You need not jump down my throat.

BERNARD. Constance is perfectly happy with her husband. You must think me a damned swine if you think I'm going to butt in and try to smash up a perfectly wonderful union.

MARTHA. But, you poor fool, don't you know that John has been notoriously unfaithful to Constance for ages?

BERNARD. I don't believe it.

MARTHA. Ask any one you like. Mother knows it. Barbara Fawcett knows it. Every one knows it but Constance.

BERNARD. That certainly isn't true. Mrs. Durham told me when I met her at dinner two or three days ago that John and Constance were the most devoted couple she'd ever known.

MARTHA. Did Marie-Louise tell you that?

BERNARD. She did.

[MARTHA *begins to laugh. She can hardly restrain herself.*]

MARTHA. The nerve. Marie-Louise. Oh, my poor Bernard. Marie-Louise is John's mistress.

BERNARD. Marie-Louise is Constance's greatest friend.

MARTHA. Yes.

BERNARD. If this is a pack of lies I swear I'll damned well wring your neck.

MARTHA. All right.

BERNARD. That was a silly thing to say. I'm sorry.

MARTHA. Oh, I don't mind. I like a man to be violent. I think you're just the sort of man Constance needs.

BERNARD. What the devil do you mean by that?

MARTHA. It can't go on. Constance is being made perfectly ridiculous. Her position is monstrous. I thought she ought to be told and as every one else seemed to shirk the job I was prepared to do it myself. My mother was so disagreeable about it, I've had to promise not to say a word.

BERNARD. You're not under the delusion that I'm going to tell her?

MARTHA. No, I don't really think it would come very well from you. But things can't go on. She's bound to find out. All I want you to do is to . . . well, stand by.

BERNARD. But Marie-Louise has got a husband. What about him?

MARTHA. His only ambition in life is to make a million. He's the sort of fool who thinks a woman loves him just because he loves her. Marie-Louise can turn him round her little finger.

BERNARD. Has Constance never suspected?

MARTHA. Never. You've only got to look at her. Really, her self-confidence sometimes is positively maddening.

BERNARD. I wonder if it wouldn't be better that she never did find out. She's so happy. She's entirely carefree. You've only got to look at that open brow and those frank, trustful eyes.

MARTHA. I thought you loved her.

BERNARD. Enough to want her happiness above all things.

MARTHA. You *are* forty-five, aren't you? I forgot that for a moment.

BERNARD. Dear Martha. You have such an attractive way of putting things.

[CONSTANCE's *voice on the stairs is heard calling:* "Bentley, Bentley."]

MARTHA. Oh, there's Constance. I can't imagine where mother is. I think I'll go into the brown room and write a letter.

[*Bernard takes no notice of what she says nor does he make any movement when she goes out. A moment later* CONSTANCE *comes in.*]

CONSTANCE. Have I kept you waiting?

BERNARD. It doesn't matter.

CONSTANCE. Hulloa! What's up?

BERNARD. With me? Nothing. Why?

CONSTANCE. You look all funny. Why are your eyes suddenly opaque?

BERNARD. I didn't know they were.

CONSTANCE. Are you trying to hide something from me?

BERNARD. Of course not.

CONSTANCE. Have you had bad news from Japan?

BERNARD. No. Far from it. Silk is booming.

CONSTANCE. Then you're going to tell me that you've just got engaged to a village maiden.

BERNARD. No, I'm not.

CONSTANCE. I hate people who keep secrets from me.

BERNARD. I have no secrets from you.

CONSTANCE. Do you think I don't know your face by now?

BERNARD. You'll make me vain. I would never have ventured to think that you took the trouble to look twice at my ugly face.

CONSTANCE [*with sudden suspicion*]. Wasn't Martha here when you came? She hasn't gone, has she?

BERNARD. She's waiting for her mother. She's gone into another room to write letters.

CONSTANCE. Did you see her?

BERNARD [*trying to be very casual*]. Yes. We had a little chat about the weather.

CONSTANCE [*immediately grasping what has happened*]. Oh—— Don't you think we ought to be starting?

BERNARD. There's plenty of time. It's no good getting there too early.

CONSTANCE. Then I'll take off my hat.

BERNARD. And it's jolly here, isn't it? I love your room.

CONSTANCE. Do you think it's a success? I did it myself. Barbara Fawcett wants me to go into the decorating business. She's in it, you know, and she's making quite a lot of money.

BERNARD [*smiling to hide his anxiety in asking the question*]. Aren't you happy at home?

CONSTANCE [*breezily*]. I don't think it necessarily means one's unhappy at home because one wants an occupation. One may very easily grow tired of going to parties all the time. But as a matter of fact I refused Barbara's offer.

BERNARD [*insisting*]. You are happy, aren't you?

CONSTANCE. Very.

BERNARD. You've made *me* very happy during this last fortnight. I feel as though I'd never been away. You've been awfully kind to me.

CONSTANCE. I'm very glad you think so. I don't know that I've done anything very much for you.

BERNARD. Yes, you have. You've let me see you.

CONSTANCE. I let the policeman at the corner do that, you know.

BERNARD. You mustn't think that because I take care only to talk to you of quite casual things I don't still love you with all my heart.

CONSTANCE [*quite coolly*]. We agreed when first you came back that your feelings were entirely your business.

BERNARD. Do you mind my loving you?

CONSTANCE. Oughtn't we all to love one another?

BERNARD. Don't tease me.

CONSTANCE. My dear, I can't help being pleased and flattered and rather touched. It is rather wonderful that any one should care for me. . . .

BERNARD [*interrupting*]. So much?

CONSTANCE. After so many years.

BERNARD. If any one had asked me fifteen years ago if I could love you more than I loved you then I should have said it was impossible. I love you ten times more than I ever loved you before.

CONSTANCE [*going on with her own speech*]. But I don't in the least want you to make love to me now.

BERNARD. I know. I'm not going to. I know you far too well.

CONSTANCE [*amused and a trifle taken aback*]. I don't quite know what you've been doing for the last five minutes.

BERNARD. I was merely stating a few plain facts.

CONSTANCE. Oh, I beg your pardon. I thought it was something quite different. I'm afraid you might mistake my meaning if I said I'm quite curious to see how you *do* make love.

BERNARD [*good-humouredly*]. I have a notion that you're laughing at me.

CONSTANCE. In the hope of teaching you to laugh at yourself.

BERNARD. I've been very good during the last fortnight, haven't I?

CONSTANCE. Yes, I kept on saying to myself: I wonder if a pat of butter really would melt in his mouth.

BERNARD. Well, for just a minute I'm going to let myself go.

CONSTANCE. I wouldn't if I were you.

BERNARD. Yes, but you're not. I want to tell you just once that I worship the ground you tread on. There's never been any one in the world for me but you.

CONSTANCE. Oh, nonsense. There have been half a dozen. We are seven.

BERNARD. They were all you. I love you with all my heart. I admire you more than any woman I've ever met. I respect you. I'm an awful fool when it comes to the point. I don't know how to say all I've got in my heart without feeling like a perfect ass. I love you. I want you to know that if ever you're in trouble I should look upon it as the greatest possible happiness to be allowed to help you.

CONSTANCE. That's very kind of you. I don't see why I should be in any trouble.

BERNARD. Always and in all circumstances you can count on me absolutely. I will do anything in the world for you. If ever you want me you have only to give me a sign. I should be proud and happy to give my life for you.

CONSTANCE. It's sweet of you to say so.

BERNARD. Don't you believe it?

CONSTANCE [*with a charming smile*]. Yes.

BERNARD. I should like to think that it meant—oh, not very much, but just a little to you.

CONSTANCE [*almost shaken*]. It means a great deal. I thank you.

BERNARD. Now we won't say anything more about it.

CONSTANCE [*recovering her accustomed coolness*]. But why did you think it necessary to say all this just now?

BERNARD. I wanted to get it off my chest.

CONSTANCE. Oh, really.

BERNARD. You're not angry with me?

CONSTANCE. Oh, Bernard, I'm not that kind of a fool at all. . . . It's a pity that Martha doesn't marry.

BERNARD. Don't think that I'm going to marry her.

CONSTANCE. I don't. I merely thought that a husband would be a pleasant and useful occupation for her. She's quite a nice girl, you know. A liar, of course, but otherwise all right.

BERNARD. Oh?

CONSTANCE. Yes, a terrible liar, even for a woman. . . . Shall we start now? It's no good getting there when the polo is over.

BERNARD. All right. Let's start.

CONSTANCE. I'll put my hat on again. By the way, you haven't had a taxi waiting all this time, have you?

BERNARD. No, I've got a car. I thought I'd like to drive you down myself.

CONSTANCE. Open or shut?

BERNARD. Open.

CONSTANCE. Oh, my dear, then I must get another hat. A broad brim like this is such a bore in an open car.

BERNARD. Oh, I am sorry.

CONSTANCE. It doesn't matter a bit. I shall only be a minute. And why on earth shouldn't one be comfortable if one can? [*She goes out. In a moment* BENTLEY *shows in* MARIE-LOUISE.]

MARIE-LOUISE. Oh, how do you do. [*To* BENTLEY] Will you tell Mr. Middleton at once?

BENTLEY. Yes, madam. [*Exit* BENTLEY.]

MARIE-LOUISE [*rather flustered*]. I particularly wanted to see John for a minute and there are patients waiting to see him, so I asked Bentley if he couldn't come here.

BERNARD. I'll take myself off.

MARIE-LOUISE. I'm awfully sorry, but it's rather urgent. John hates to be disturbed like this.

BERNARD. I'll go into the next room.

MARIE-LOUISE. Are you waiting for Constance?

BERNARD. Yes, I'm taking her to Ranelagh. She's changing her hat.

MARIE-LOUISE. I see. Bentley told me she was upstairs. Good-bye. I shall only be a minute. [BERNARD *goes into the adjoining room just as* JOHN *comes in.*] Oh, John, I'm sorry to drag you away from your patients.

JOHN. There's nothing urgent. They can wait for a few minutes. [BERNARD *has closed the door behind him, and* JOHN's *tone changes. They speak now in a low voice and quickly.*] Is anything the matter?

MARIE-LOUISE. Mortimer.

JOHN. What about Mortimer?

MARIE-LOUISE. I'm convinced he suspects.

JOHN. Why?

MARIE-LOUISE. He was so funny last night. He came into my room to say good-night to me. He sat on my bed. He was chatting nicely and he was asking what I'd been doing with myself all the evening. . . .

JOHN. Presumably you didn't tell him.

MARIE-LOUISE. No, I said I'd been dining here. And suddenly he got up and just said good-night and went out. His voice was so strange that I couldn't help looking at him. He was as red as a turkey cock.

JOHN. Is that all?

MARIE-LOUISE. He never came in to say good-morning to me before he went to the City.

JOHN. He may have been in a hurry.

MARIE-LOUISE. He's never in too much of a hurry for that.

JOHN. I think you're making a mountain of a mole heap.

MARIE-LOUISE. Don't be stupid, John. Can't you see I'm as nervous as a cat?

JOHN. I can. But I'm trying to persuade you there's nothing to be nervous about.

MARIE-LOUISE. What fools men are. They never will see that it's the small things that matter. I tell you I'm frightened out of my wits.

JOHN. You know there's a devil of a distance between suspicion and proof.

MARIE-LOUISE. Oh, I don't think he could prove anything. But he can make himself awfully unpleasant. Supposing he put ideas in Constance's head?

JOHN. She'd never believe him.

MARY-LOUISE. If the worst came to worst I could manage Mortimer. He's awfully in love with me. That always gives one such an advantage over a man.

JOHN. Of course you can twist Mortimer round your little finger.

MARIE-LOUISE. I should die of shame if Constance knew. After all, she's my greatest friend and I'm absolutely devoted to her.

JOHN. Constance is a peach. Of course I don't believe there's anything in this at all, but if there were, I'd be in favour of making a clean breast of it to Constance.

MARIE-LOUISE. Never!

JOHN. I expect she'd kick up a row. Any woman would. But she'd do anything in the world to help us out.

MARIE-LOUISE. A lot you know about women. She'd help you out, I dare say. But she'd stamp on me with both feet. That's only human nature.

JOHN. Not Constance's.

MARIE-LOUISE. Upon my word, it's lucky I'm fairly sure of you, John, or the way you talk of Constance would really make me jealous.

JOHN. Thank God you can smile. You're getting your nerve back.

MARIE-LOUISE. It's been a comfort to talk it over. It doesn't seem so bad now.

JOHN. I'm sure you've got nothing to be frightened about.

MARIE-LOUISE. I dare say it was only my fancy. It was a stupid risk to take all the same.

JOHN. Perhaps. Why did you look so devilish pretty?

MARIE-LOUISE. Oughtn't you to be getting back to your wretched patients?

JOHN. I suppose so. Will you stop and see Constance?

MARIE-LOUISE. I may as well. It would look rather odd if I went away without saying how d'you do to her.

JOHN [going]. I'll leave you then. And don't worry.

MARIE-LOUISE. I won't. I dare say it was only a guilty conscience. I'll go and have my hair washed.

[*As* JOHN *is about to go,* MARTHA *comes in followed by* BERNARD.]

MARTHA [*with an almost exaggerated cordiality*]. I had no idea you were here, Marie-Louise.

MARIE-LOUISE. It's not very important.

MARTHA. I was just writing letters, waiting for mother, and Bernard's only just told me.

MARIE-LOUISE. I wanted to see John about something.

MARTHA. I hope you haven't got anything the matter with you, darling.

MARIE-LOUISE. No. Mortimer's been looking rather run-down lately and I want John to persuade him to take a holiday.

MARTHA. Oh, I should have thought he'd be more likely to take a physician's advice than a surgeon's in a thing like that.

MARIE-LOUISE. He's got a tremendous belief in John, you know.

MARTHA. In which I'm sure he's justified. John is so very reliable.

JOHN. What can I do for you, Martha? If you'd like me to cut out an appendix or a few tonsils I shall be happy to oblige you.

MARTHA. My dear John, you've only left me the barest necessities of existence as it is. I don't think I could manage with anything less than I have.

JOHN. My dear, as long as a woman has a leg to stand on she need not despair of exciting her surgeon's sympathy and interest.

[CONSTANCE *comes in with* MRS. CULVER.]

MARIE-LOUISE [*kissing her*]. Darling.

CONSTANCE. How is your knee, still slipping?

MARIE-LOUISE. It always gives me more or less trouble, you know.

CONSTANCE. Yes, of course. I think you're very patient. In your place I should be furious with John. Of course I would never dream of consulting him if I had anything the matter with me.

MRS. CULVER. I'm sorry I've been so long, Martha. Have you been very impatient?

MARTHA. No, I've been passing the time very pleasantly.

MRS. CULVER. For others, darling, or only for yourself?

CONSTANCE. I met mother on the stairs and she came up with me while I changed my hat. Bernard is taking me down to Ranelagh.

JOHN. Oh, that'll be jolly.

BERNARD. We shall be dreadfully late.

CONSTANCE. Does it matter?

BERNARD. No.

[BENTLEY *comes in with a card on a small salver and takes it to* CONSTANCE. *She looks at the card and hesitates.*]

CONSTANCE. How very odd.

JOHN. What's the matter, Constance?

CONSTANCE. Nothing. [*For an instant she reflects.*] Is he downstairs?

BENTLEY. Yes, madam.

CONSTANCE. I don't know why he should send up a card. Show him up.

BENTLEY. Very good, madam. [*Exit* BENTLEY.]

JOHN. Who is it, Constance?

CONSTANCE. Come and sit down, Marie-Louise.

MARIE-LOUISE. I must go and so must you.

CONSTANCE. There's plenty of time. Do you like this hat?

MARIE-LOUISE. Yes. I think it's sweet.

CONSTANCE. What are *you* doing here, John? Haven't you got any patients today?

JOHN. Yes, there are two or three waiting. I'm just going down. As a matter of fact I thought I deserved a cigarette. [*He puts his hand to his hip pocket.*] Hang, I've mislaid my cigarette-case. You haven't seen it about, Constance?

CONSTANCE. No, I haven't.

JOHN. I looked for it everywhere this morning. I can't think where I left it. I must ring up the nursing-home and ask if I left it there.

CONSTANCE. I hope you haven't lost it.

JOHN. Oh, no. I'm sure I haven't. I've just put it somewhere.

[*The door opens and* BENTLEY *announces the visitor.*]

BENTLEY. Mr. Mortimer Durham.

MARIE-LOUISE [*startled out of her wits*]. Oh!

CONSTANCE [*quickly, seizing her wrist*]. Sit still, you fool.

[MORTIMER DURHAM *comes in. He is a stoutish biggish man of about forty, with a red face and an irascible manner. At the moment he is a prey to violent emotion.* BENTLEY *goes out.*]

CONSTANCE. Hulloa, Mortimer. What are you doing in these parts at this hour? Why on earth did you send up a card?

[*He stops and looks around.*]

MARIE-LOUISE. What is the matter, Mortimer?

MORTIMER [*to* CONSTANCE, *with difficulty restraining his fury*]. I thought you might like to know that your husband is my wife's lover.

MARIE-LOUISE. Morty!

CONSTANCE [*keeping a firm hand on* MARIE-LOUISE *and very coolly to* MORTIMER]. Oh? What makes you think that?

MORTIMER [*taking a gold cigarette-case out of his pocket*]. Do you recognize this? I found it under my wife's pillow last night.

CONSTANCE. Oh, I am relieved. I couldn't make out where I'd left it. [*Taking it from him*] Thank you so much.

MORTIMER [*angrily*]. It's not yours.

CONSTANCE. Indeed it is. I was sitting on Marie-Louise's bed and I must have slipped it under the pillow without thinking.

MORTIMER. It has John's initials on it.

CONSTANCE. I know. It was presented to him by a grateful patient and I thought it much too nice for him, so I just took it.

MORTIMER. What sort of fool do you take me for, Constance?

CONSTANCE. My dear Morty, why should I say it was my cigarette-case if it wasn't.

MORTIMER. They had dinner together.

CONSTANCE. My poor Morty, I know that. You were going to a City banquet or something, and Marie-Louise rang up and asked if she might come and take pot-luck with us.

MORTIMER. Do you mean to say she dined here?

CONSTANCE. Isn't that what she told you?

MORTIMER. Yes.

CONSTANCE. It's quite easy to prove. If you won't take my word for it we can ring for the butler, and you can ask him yourself. . . . Ring the bell, John, will you?

MORTIMER [*uneasily*]. No, don't do that. If you give me your word, of course I must take it.

CONSTANCE. That's very kind of you. I'm grateful to you for not exposing me to the humiliation of making my butler corroborate my statement.

MORTIMER. If Marie-Louise was dining here why were you sitting on her bed?

CONSTANCE. John had to go out and do an operation, and Marie-Louise wanted to show me the things she'd got from Paris, so I walked round to your house. It was a lovely night. You remember that, don't you?

MORTIMER. Damn it, I've got more important things to do than look at the night.

CONSTANCE. We tried them all on and then we were rather tired, so Marie-Louise got into bed and I sat down and we talked.

MORTIMER. If you were tired why didn't you go home and go to bed.

CONSTANCE. John had promised to come round and fetch me.

MORTIMER. And did he? At what time did he come?

JOHN. I couldn't manage it. The operation took much longer than I expected. It was one of those cases where when you once start cutting you really don't know where to stop. You know the sort of thing, don't you, Mortimer?

MORTIMER. No, I don't. How the devil should I?

CONSTANCE. All that is neither here nor there. This is a terrible accusation you've made against John and Marie-Louise and I'm very much upset. But I will remain perfectly calm till I've heard everything. Now let me have your proofs.

MORTIMER. My proofs? What d'you mean? The cigarette-case. When I found the cigarette-case I naturally put two and two together.

CONSTANCE [*with her eyes flashing*]. I quite understand, but why did you make them five?

MORTIMER [*emphatically, in order not to show that he is wavering*]. It isn't possible that I should have made a mistake.

CONSTANCE. Even the richest of us may err. I remember when Mr. Pierpont Morgan[1] died, he was found to own seven million dollars of worthless securities.

MORTIMER [*uneasily*]. You don't know what a shock it was, Constance. I had the most implicit confidence in Marie-Louise. I was knocked endways. I've been brooding over it ever since till I was afraid I should go mad.

CONSTANCE. And do you mean to say that you've come here and made a fearful scene just because you found my cigarette-case in Marie-Louise's room? I can't believe it. You're a man of the world and a business man. You're extremely intelligent. Surely you have something to go upon. You must be holding something back. Don't be afraid of hurting my feelings. You've said so much now that I must insist on your saying everything. I want the truth and the whole truth.

[*There is a pause.* MORTIMER *looks from* MARIE-LOUISE, *who is quietly weeping, to* CONSTANCE, *with the utmost bewilderment.*]

MORTIMER. I'm afraid I've made a damned fool of myself.

CONSTANCE. I'm afraid you have.

MORTIMER. I'm awfully sorry, Constance, I beg your pardon.

CONSTANCE. Oh, don't bother about me. You've exposed me to the

---

[1] *Pierpont Morgan*, J. Pierpont Morgan (1837–1913), the American financier, long a symbol of fabulous wealth.

most bitter humiliation. You've sown seeds of distrust between me and John which can never be . . . [*She looks for a word.*]

MRS. CULVER [*supplying it*]. Fertilized.

CONSTANCE [*ignoring it*]. Uprooted. But I don't matter. It's Marie-Louise's pardon you must beg.

MORTIMER [*humbly*]. Marie-Louise.

MARIE-LOUISE. Don't touch me. Don't come near me.

MORTIMER [*to* CONSTANCE, *miserably*]. You know what jealousy is.

CONSTANCE. Certainly not. I think it's a most ugly and despicable vice.

MORTIMER [*to* MARIE-LOUISE]. Marie-Louise, I'm sorry. Won't you forgive me?

MARIE-LOUISE. You've insulted me before all my friends. You know how devotedly I love Constance. You might have accused me of having an affair with anyone else—but not John.

CONSTANCE. Not her greatest friend's husband. The milkman or the dustman if you like, but not her greatest friend's husband.

MORTIMER. I've been a perfect swine. I don't know what came over me. I really wasn't responsible for my actions.

MARIE-LOUISE. I've loved you all these years. No one has ever loved you as I've loved you. Oh, it's cruel, cruel.

MORTIMER. Come away, darling. I can't say here what I want to say.

MARIE-LOUISE. No, no, no.

CONSTANCE [*putting her hand on his arm, gently*]. I think you'd better leave her here for a little while, Morty. I'll talk to her when you've gone. She's naturally upset. A sensitive little thing like that.

MORTIMER. We're dining with the Vancouvers at 8.15.

CONSTANCE. For eight-thirty. I promise I'll send her home in good time to dress.

MORTIMER. She'll give me another chance?

CONSTANCE. Yes, yes.

MORTIMER. I'd do anything in the world for her. [CONSTANCE *puts her fingers to her lips and then points significantly to the pearl chain she is wearing. For a second* MORTIMER *does not understand, but as soon as her notion dawns on him he gives a pleased nod.*] You're the cleverest woman in the world. [*As he goes out he stops and holds out his hand to* JOHN.] Will you shake hands with me, old man? I made a mistake and I'm man enough to acknowledge it.

JOHN [*very cordially*]. Not at all, old boy. I quite agree that it did look fishy, the cigarette-case. If I'd dreamt that Constance was going to leave an expensive thing like that lying about all over the place, I'm hanged if I'd have let her pinch it.

MORTIMER. You don't know what a weight it is off my mind. I felt a hundred when I came here, and now I feel like a two-year-old. [*He goes out. The moment the door is closed behind him there is a general change in every attitude. The tension disappears and there is a feeling of relief.*]

JOHN. Constance, you're a brick. I shall never forget this. Never, so long as I live. And by George, what presence of mind you showed. I went hot and cold all over, and you never batted an eye-lash.

CONSTANCE. By the way, here is your cigarette-case. You'd better have a ring made and hang it on your key-chain.

JOHN. No, no. Keep it. I'm too old to take these risks.

CONSTANCE. By the way, did anyone see you go into Morty's house last night?

JOHN. No, we let ourselves in with Marie-Louise's latch key.

CONSTANCE. That's all right then. If Mortimer asks the servants they can tell him nothing. I had to take that chance.

MARIE-LOUISE [*with a little gesture of ashamed dismay*]. Oh, Constance, what must you think of me?

CONSTANCE. I? Exactly the same as I thought before. I think you're sweet, Marie-Louise.

MARIE-LOUISE. You have every right to be angry with me.

CONSTANCE. Perhaps, but not the inclination.

MARIE-LOUISE. Oh, it's not true. I've treated you shamefully. You've made me feel such a pig. And you had your chance to get back on me and you didn't take it. I'm so ashamed.

CONSTANCE [*amused*]. Because you've been having an affair with John, or because you've been found out?

MARIE-LOUISE. Oh, Constance, don't be heartless. Say anything you like, curse me, stamp on me, but don't smile at me. I'm in a terrible position.

CONSTANCE. And you want me to make a scene. I know and I sympathize. [*Very calmly*] But the fact is that Mortimer told me nothing I didn't know before.

MARIE-LOUISE [*aghast*]. Do you mean to say that you've known all along?

CONSTANCE. All along, darling. I've been spending the last six months in a desperate effort to prevent my friends and relations from telling me your ghastly secret. It's been very difficult sometimes.

Often mother's profound understanding of life, Martha's passion for truth at any price, and Barbara's silent sympathy, have almost worn me down. But until today the t's were not definitely crossed nor the i's distinctly dotted, and I was able to ignore the facts that were staring at me—rather rudely, I must say—in the face.

MARIE-LOUISE. But why, why? It's not human. Why didn't you do anything?

CONSTANCE. That, darling, is my affair.

MARIE-LOUISE [*thinking she understands*]. Oh, I see.

CONSTANCE [*rather tartly*]. No, you don't. I have always been absolutely faithful to John. I have not winked at your intrigue in order to cover my own.

MARIE-LOUISE [*beginning to be a little put out*]. I almost think you've been laughing at me up your sleeve all the time.

CONSTANCE [*good-humouredly*]. Oh, my dear, you mustn't be offended just because I've taken away from you the satisfaction of thinking that you have been deceiving me all these months. I should hate you to think me capable of an intentional meanness.

MARIE-LOUISE. My head's going round and round.

CONSTANCE. Such a pretty head, too. Why don't you go and lie down? You want to look your best if you're dining with the Van-couvers.

MARIE-LOUISE. I wonder where Mortimer is?

CONSTANCE. You know that pearl necklace you showed me the other day and you said that Mortimer thought it cost a lot of money —well, he's gone to Cartier's to buy it for you.

MARIE-LOUISE [*excitedly*]. Oh, Constance, do you think he has?

CONSTANCE. I think all men are born with the knowledge that when they have wounded a woman's soul—and our souls are easily wounded—the only cure is a trifling, but expensive jewel.

MARIE-LOUISE. Do you think he'll have the sense to bring it home with him so that I can wear it tonight?

CONSTANCE. Oh, my dear, don't be such a fool as to accept it with alacrity. Remember that Mortimer has grievously insulted you, he's made the most shocking accusation that a man can make against his wife, he's trampled on your love and now he's destroyed your trust in him.

MARIE-LOUISE. Oh, how right you are, Constance.

CONSTANCE. Surely I need not tell you what to do. Refuse to speak to him, but never let him get a word of defense in edgeways. Cry enough to make him feel what a brute he is, but not enough to make your eyes swell. Say you'll leave him and run sobbing to the door, but take care to let him stop you before you open it. Repeat yourself. Say the same thing over and over again—it wears them down—and if he answers you take no notice, but just say it again. And at last when you've reduced him to desperation, when his head is aching as though it would split, when he's sweating at every pore, when he's harassed and miserable and haggard and broken—then consent as an unmerited favour, as a sign of your forgiving temper and the sweetness of your nature, to accept, no, don't consent, *deign* to accept the pearl necklace for which the wretch has just paid ten thousand pounds.

MARIE-LOUISE [*with peculiar satisfaction*]. Twelve, darling.

CONSTANCE. And don't thank him. That wouldn't be playing the game. Let him thank *you* for the favour you do him in allowing him to make you a paltry gift. Have you got your car here?

MARIE-LOUISE. No, I was in such a state when I came I took a taxi.

CONSTANCE. John, do take Marie-Louise down and put her in a taxi.

JOHN. All right.

MARIE-LOUISE. No, not John. I couldn't. After all, I have some delicacy.

CONSTANCE. Oh, have you? Well, let Bernard go.

BERNARD. I shall be pleased.

CONSTANCE [*to* BERNARD]. But come back, won't you?

BERNARD. Certainly.

MARIE-LOUISE [*kissing* CONSTANCE]. This has been a lesson to me, darling. I'm not a fool, Constance. I can learn.

CONSTANCE. At least prudence, I hope.

[MARIE-LOUISE *goes out followed by* BERNARD KERSAL.]

JOHN. How did you guess that Marie-Louise had said she was dining here?

CONSTANCE. She's too crafty a woman to invent a new lie when an old one will serve.

JOHN. It would have been awkward if Mortimer had insisted on asking Bentley if it was true.

CONSTANCE. I knew he wouldn't dare. It's only if a man's a gentleman that he won't hesitate to do an ungentlemanly thing. Mortimer is on the boundary line and it makes him careful.

MARTHA [*significantly*]. Don't you imagine your patients are growing a trifle restless, John?

JOHN. I like to keep them waiting. They grow more and more

nervous as the minutes pass and when I recommend an operation that will cost them two hundred and fifty pounds they are too shaken to protest.

MARTHA [*pursing her lips*]. I can't imagine you'll very much like to hear what I'm determined to say to Constance.

JOHN. It's because I shrewdly suspect that you have some very unpleasant things to say about me that I am prepared reluctantly to neglect the call of duty and listen to you with my own ears.

CONSTANCE. She's been exercising miracles of restraint for the last three months, John. I think she has a right to let herself go now.

JOHN. If she's suffering from suppressed desires she's come to the wrong establishment. She ought to go to a psycho-analyst.

MARTHA. I've only got one thing to say, John, and I'm perfectly willing that you should hear it. [*To* CONSTANCE] I don't know what your reasons were for shielding that abominable woman. I can only suppose you wanted to avoid more scandal than was necessary. . . .

MRS. CULVER [*interrupting*]. Before you go any further, my dear, you must let me put my word in. [*To* CONSTANCE] My dear child, I beg you not to decide anything in a hurry. We must all think things over. First of all you must listen to what John has to say for himself.

MARTHA. What can he have to say for himself?

CONSTANCE [*ironically*]. What indeed?

JOHN. Not the right thing anyway. I've seen too much of married life. . . .

CONSTANCE [*interrupting, with a smile*]. Let us be just. Other people's rather than your own.

JOHN [*going on*]. To imagine that even the Archangel Gabriel could say the right thing.

CONSTANCE. I've no reason, however, to suppose that the Archangel Gabriel could ever find himself in such a predicament.

JOHN. I'm for it and I'm prepared to take what's coming to me.

CONSTANCE [*to the world in general*]. No man could say handsomer than that.

JOHN. I'm expecting you to make a scene, Constance. It's your right and your privilege. I'm willing to bear it. Give me hell. I deserve it. Drag me up and down the room by the hair of the head. Kick me in the face. Stamp on me. I'll grovel. I'll eat the dust. My name is mud. Mud.

CONSTANCE. My poor John, what is there to make a scene about?

JOHN. I know how badly I've treated you. I had a wife who was good, loving and faithful, devoted to my interests, a perfect mother and an excellent housekeeper. A woman ten times too good for me. If I'd had the smallest spark of decency I couldn't have treated you like this. I haven't a word to say for myself.

MARTHA [*interrupting him*]. You've humiliated her to all her friends.

JOHN. I've behaved neither like a gentleman nor a sportsman.

MARTHA. Your conduct is inexcusable.

JOHN. I haven't a leg to stand on.

MARTHA. Even if you didn't love her, you might have treated her with respect.

JOHN. I've been as heartless as a crocodile and as unscrupulous as a typhoid bacillus.

CONSTANCE. Between you, of course, you're leaving me very little to say.

MARTHA. There *is* nothing to say. You're quite right. This is the sort of occasion when it's beneath a woman's dignity to make a scene. It just shows how little John knows women to think that you could demean yourself to vulgar abuse. [*To* JOHN] I suppose you'll have the decency to put no obstacle in the way of Constance's getting her freedom.

MRS. CULVER. Oh, Constance, you're not going to divorce him?

MARTHA. Mother, you're so weak. How can she go on living with a man for whom she has no respect? What would her life be with this creature whom she can only mistrust and despise? Besides, you have to think of their child. How can Constance allow her daughter to be contaminated by the society of a person of this character?

CONSTANCE. John has always been an excellent father. Let us give the devil his due.

MRS. CULVER. Don't be too hard, darling. I can understand that at the moment you feel bitter, but it would be very sad if you let your bitterness warp your judgment.

CONSTANCE. I don't feel in the least bitter. I wish I looked as sweet as I feel.

MRS. CULVER. You can't deceive a mother, my dear. I know the angry resentment that you feel. Under the unfortunate circumstances it's only too natural.

CONSTANCE. When I look into my heart I can't find a trace of resentment, except perhaps for John's being so stupid as to let himself be found out.

JOHN. Let me say this in justification for myself, Constance. I did my little best to prevent it. Angels could do no more.

CONSTANCE. And angels presumably have not the pernicious habit of smoking straight-cut cigarettes.

JOHN. When you once get the taste for them, you prefer them to gippies.[1]

MRS. CULVER. Don't be cynical, darling. That is the worst way to ease an aching heart. Come to your mother's arms, my dear, and let us have a good cry together. And then you'll feel better.

CONSTANCE. It's sweet of you, mother, but honestly I couldn't squeeze a tear out of my eyes if my life depended on it.

MRS. CULVER. And don't be too hard. Of course John is to blame. I admit that. He's been very, very naughty. But men are weak and women are so unscrupulous. I'm sure he's sorry for all the pain he's caused you.

MARTHA. What puzzles me is that you didn't do something the moment you discovered that John was having an affair.

CONSTANCE. To tell you the truth, I thought it no business of mine.

MARTHA [*indignantly*]. Aren't you his wife?

CONSTANCE. John and I are very lucky people. Our marriage has been ideal.

MARTHA. How can you say that?

CONSTANCE. For five years we adored each other. That's much longer than most people do. Our honeymoon lasted five years and then we had a most extraordinary stroke of luck: we ceased to be in love with one another simultaneously.

JOHN. I protest, Constance. I've never ceased to be absolutely devoted to you.

CONSTANCE. I never said you had, darling. I'm convinced of it. I've never ceased to be devoted to you. We've shared one another's interests, we've loved to be together, I've exulted in your success and you've trembled in my illness. We've laughed at the same jokes and sighed over the same worries. I don't know any couple that's been bound together by a more genuine affection. But honestly, for the last ten years have you been in love with me?

JOHN. You can't expect a man who's been married for fifteen years. . . .

---

[1] *gippies*, Egyptian blend cigarettes, as opposed to straight-cut cigarettes, made of Virginia tobacco leaves cut lengthwise.

CONSTANCE. My dear, I'm not asking for excuses. I'm only asking for a plain answer.

JOHN. In the long run I enjoy your society much more than anybody else's. There's no one I like so much as you. You're the prettiest woman I've ever known and I shall say the same when you're a hundred.

CONSTANCE. But does your heart leap into your mouth when you hear my footstep on the stairs, and when I come into the room, is your first impulse to catch me in your manly arms? I haven't noticed it.

JOHN. I don't want to make a fool of myself.

CONSTANCE. Then I think you've answered my question. You're no more in love with me than I am with you.

JOHN. You never said a word of this before.

CONSTANCE. I think most married couples tell one another far too much. There are some things that two people may know very well, but which it's much more tactful for them to pretend they don't.

JOHN. How did you find out?

CONSTANCE. I'll tell you. One night as we were dancing together, all at once I noticed that we weren't keeping such good step as we generally did. It was because my mind was wandering. I was thinking how it would suit me to do my hair like a woman who was dancing alongside of us. Then I looked at you and I saw you were thinking what pretty legs she'd got. I suddenly realized that you weren't in love with me any more and at the same moment I realized that it was a relief, because I wasn't in love with you.

JOHN. I must say it never occurred to me for a moment.

CONSTANCE. I know. A man thinks it quite natural that he should fall out of love with a woman, but it never strikes him for a moment that a woman can do anything so unnatural as to fall out of love with him. Don't be upset at that, darling, that is one of the charming limitations of your sex.

MARTHA. Do you mean mother and me to understand that since then John has been having one affair after another and you haven't turned a hair?

CONSTANCE. Since this is the first time he's been found out, let us give him the benefit of the doubt and hope that till now he has never strayed from the strict and narrow path. You're not angry with me, John?

JOHN. No, darling, not angry. But I *am* a little taken aback. I think you've been making rather a damned fool of me. It never struck me that your feelings for me had changed so much. You can't expect me to like it.

CONSTANCE. Oh, come now, you must be reasonable. You surely wouldn't wish me to have languished for all these years in a hopeless passion for you when you had nothing to give me in return but friendship and affection. Think what a bore it is to have someone in love with you whom you're not in love with.

JOHN. I can't conceive of your ever being a bore, Constance.

CONSTANCE [*kissing her hand to him*]. Don't you realize that we must thank our lucky stars? We are the favoured of the gods. I shall never forget those five years of exquisite happiness you gave me when I loved you, and I shall never cease to be grateful to you, not because you loved me, but because you inspired me with love. Our love never degenerated into weariness. Because we ceased loving one another at the very same moment we never had to put up with quarrels and reproaches, recriminations and all the other paraphernalia of a passion that has ceased on one side and is still alive and eager on the other. Our love was like a cross-word puzzle in which we both hit upon the last word at the same moment. That is why our lives since have been so happy; that is why ours is a perfect marriage.

MARTHA. Do you mean to say that it meant nothing to you when you found out that John was carrying on with Marie-Louise?

CONSTANCE. Human nature is very imperfect. I'm afraid I must admit that at the first moment I was vexed. But only at the first moment. Then I reflected that it was most unreasonable to be angry with John for giving to another something that I had no use for. That would be too much like a dog in the manger. And then I was fond enough of John to be willing that he should be happy in his own way. And if he was going to indulge in an intrigue . . . isn't that the proper phrase, John?

JOHN. I have not yet made up my mind whether it really is an indulgence.

CONSTANCE. Then it was much better that the object of his affections should be so intimate a friend of mine that I could keep a maternal eye on him.

JOHN. Really, Constance.

CONSTANCE. Marie-Louise is very pretty so that my self-esteem was not offended, and so rich that it was certain John would have no reason to squander money on her to the inconvenience of myself. She's not clever enough to acquire any ascendancy over him, and so long as I kept his heart I was quite willing that she should have his senses. If you wanted to deceive me, John, I couldn't have chosen anyone with whom I would more willingly be deceived than Marie-Louise.

JOHN. I don't gather that you have been very grossly deceived, darling. You have such penetration that when you look at me I feel as though I were shivering without a stitch of clothing on.

MRS. CULVER. I don't approve of your attitude, Constance. In my day when a young wife discovered that her husband had been deceiving her, she burst into a flood of tears and went to stay with her mother for three weeks, not returning to her husband till he had been brought to a proper state of abjection and repentance.

MARTHA. Are we to understand, then, that you are not going to divorce John?

CONSTANCE. You know, I can never see why a woman should give up a comfortable home, a considerable part of her income and the advantage of having a man about to do all the tiresome and disagreeable things for her, because he has been unfaithful to her. She's merely cutting off her nose to spite her face.

MARTHA. I am at a loss for words. I cannot conceive how a woman of any spirit can sit down and allow her husband to make a perfect damned fool of her.

CONSTANCE. You've been very stupid, my poor John. In the ordinary affairs of life stupidity is much more tiresome than wickedness. You can mend the vicious, but what in Heaven's name are you to do with the foolish?

JOHN. I've been a fool, Constance. I know it, but I'm capable of learning by experience, so I can't be a damned fool.

CONSTANCE. You mean that in the future you'll be more careful to cover your tracks?

MRS. CULVER. Oh, no, Constance, he means that this has been a lesson to him, and that in the future you'll have no cause for complaint.

CONSTANCE. I've always been given to understand that men only abandon their vices when advancing years have made them a burden rather than a pleasure. John, I'm happy to say, is still in the flower of his age. I suppose you give yourself another fifteen years, John, don't you?

JOHN. Really, Constance, I don't know what you mean. The things you say sometimes are positively embarrassing.

CONSTANCE. I think at all events we may take it that Marie-Louise will have more than one successor.

JOHN. Constance, I give you my word of honour. . . .

CONSTANCE [*interrupting*]. That is the only gift you can make for which I can find no use. You see, so long as I was able to pretend a blissful ignorance of your goings-on we could all be perfectly happy. You were enjoying yourself and I received a lot of sympathy as the outraged wife. But now I do see that the position is very difficult. You have put me in a position that is neither elegant nor dignified.

JOHN. I'm awfully sorry, Constance.

MARTHA. You're going to leave him?

CONSTANCE. No, I'm not going to leave him. John, you remember that Barbara offered to take me into her business? I refused. Well, I've changed my mind and I'm going to accept.

JOHN. But why? I don't see your point.

CONSTANCE. I'm not prepared any more to be entirely dependent upon you, John.

JOHN. But, my dear, everything I earn is at your disposal. It's a pleasure for me to provide for your wants. Heaven knows, they're not very great.

CONSTANCE. I know. Come, John, I've been very reasonable, haven't I? Don't try and thwart me when I want to do something on which I've set my heart.

[*There is an instant's pause.*]

JOHN. I don't understand. But if you put it like that, I haven't a word to say. Of course, you must do exactly as you wish.

CONSTANCE. That's a dear. Now go back to your patients or else I shall have to keep you as well as myself.

JOHN. Will you give me a kiss?

CONSTANCE. Why not?

JOHN [*kissing her*]. It's peace between us?

CONSTANCE. Peace and good-will. [JOHN *goes out.*] He is rather sweet, isn't he?

MRS. CULVER. What have you got on your mind, Constance?

CONSTANCE. I, mother? [*Teasing her*] What do you suspect?

MRS. CULVER. I don't like the look of you.

CONSTANCE. I'm sorry for that. Most people find me far from plain.

MRS. CULVER. You've got some deviltry in mind, but for the life of me I can't guess it.

MARTHA. I can't see what you expect to get out of working with Barbara.

CONSTANCE. Between a thousand and fifteen hundred a year, I believe.

MARTHA. I wasn't thinking of the money, and you know it.

CONSTANCE. I'm tired of being the modern wife.

MARTHA. What do you mean by the modern wife?

CONSTANCE. A prostitute who doesn't deliver the goods.

MRS. CULVER. My dear, what would your father say if he heard you say such things?

CONSTANCE. Darling, need we conjecture the remarks of a gentleman who's been dead for five and twenty years? Had he any gift for repartee?

MRS. CULVER. None whatever. He was good, but he was stupid. That is why the gods loved him and he died young.

[BERNARD KERSAL *opens the door and looks in.*]

BERNARD. May I come in?

CONSTANCE. Oh, there you are. I wondered what had become of you.

BERNARD. When Marie-Louise saw my car at the door she asked me to drive her. I couldn't very well refuse.

CONSTANCE. So you took her home.

BERNARD. No, she said she was in such a state she must have her hair washed. I drove her to a place in Bond Street.

CONSTANCE. And what did she say to you?

BERNARD. She said, I don't know what you must think of me.

CONSTANCE. That is what most women say to a man when his opinion doesn't matter two straws to them. And what did you answer?

BERNARD. Well, I said, I prefer not to offer an opinion on a matter which is no business of mine.

CONSTANCE. Dear Bernard, one of the things I like most in you is that you always remain so perfectly in character. If the heavens fell you would still remain the perfect English gentleman.

BERNARD. I thought it the most tactful thing to say.

CONSTANCE. Well, mother, I won't detain you any longer. I know that you and Martha have a thousand things to do.

MRS. CULVER. I'm glad you reminded me. Come, Martha. Good-bye, darling. Good-bye, Mr. Kersal.

BERNARD. Good-bye.

CONSTANCE [*to* MARTHA]. Good-bye, dear. Thank you for all your sympathy. You've been a great help in my hour of need.

MARTHA. I don't understand and it's no good saying I do.

CONSTANCE. Bless you. [MRS. CULVER *and* MARTHA *go out.* BERNARD *closes the door after them.*] Shall we be very late?

BERNARD. So late that it doesn't matter if we're a little later. I have something important to say to you.

CONSTANCE [*teasing him a little*]. Important to me or important to you?

BERNARD. I can't tell you how distressed I was at that terrible scene.

CONSTANCE. Oh, didn't you think it had its lighter moments?

BERNARD. It's only this afternoon I learned the truth, and then I never imagined for a moment that you knew it, too. I can't tell you how brave I think it of you to have borne all this torture with a smiling face. If I admired you before, I admire you ten times more now.

CONSTANCE. You're very sweet, Bernard.

BERNARD. My heart bleeds when I think of what you've gone through.

CONSTANCE. It's not a very good plan to take other people's misfortunes too much to heart.

BERNARD. Hardly an hour ago I told you that if ever you wanted me I was only too anxious to do anything in the world for you. I little thought then that the time would come so soon. There's no reason now why I shouldn't tell you of the love that consumes me. Oh, Constance, come to me. You know that if things were as I thought they were between you and John nothing would have induced me to say a word. But now he has no longer any claims on you. He doesn't love you. Why should you go on wasting your life with a man who is capable of exposing you to all this humiliation? You know how long and tenderly I've loved you. You can trust yourself to me. I'll give my whole life to making you forget the anguish you've endured. Will you marry me, Constance?

CONSTANCE. My dear, John may have behaved very badly, but he's still my husband.

BERNARD. Only in name. You've done everything in your power to save a scandal and now if you ask him to let himself be divorced he's bound to consent.

CONSTANCE. Do you really think John has behaved so very badly to me?

BERNARD [*astonished*]. You don't mean to say that you have any doubts in your mind about his relationship with Marie-Louise?

CONSTANCE. None.

BERNARD. Then what in God's name do you mean?

CONSTANCE. My dear Bernard, have you ever considered what marriage is among well-to-do people? In the working classes a woman cooks her husband's dinner, washes for him and darns his socks. She looks after the children and makes their clothes. She gives good value for the money she costs. But what is a wife in our class? Her house is managed by servants, nurses look after her children, if she has resigned herself to having any, and as soon as they are old enough she packs them off to school. Let us face it, she is no more than the mistress of a man of whose desire she has taken advantage to insist on a legal ceremony that will prevent him from discarding her when his desire has ceased.

BERNARD. She's also his companion and his helpmate.

CONSTANCE. My dear, any sensible man would sooner play bridge at his club than with his wife, and he'd always rather play golf with a man than with a woman. A paid secretary is a far better helpmate than a loving spouse. When all is said and done, the modern wife is nothing but a parasite.

BERNARD. I don't agree with you.

CONSTANCE. You see, my poor friend, you are in love and your judgment is confused.

BERNARD. I don't understand what you mean.

CONSTANCE. John gives me board and lodging, money for my clothes and my amusements, a car to drive in and a certain position in the world. He's bound to do all that because fifteen years ago he was madly in love with me, and he undertook it; though, if you'd asked him, he would certainly have acknowledged that nothing is so fleeting as that particular form of madness called love. It was either very generous of him or very imprudent. Don't you think it would be rather shabby of me to take advantage now of his generosity or his want of foresight?

BERNARD. In what way?

CONSTANCE. He paid a very high price for something that he couldn't get cheaper. He no longer wants that. Why should I resent it? I know as well as anybody else that desire is fleeting. It comes and goes and no man can understand why. The only thing that's certain is that when it's gone it's gone forever. So long as John continues to provide for me what right have I to complain that he is unfaithful to me? He bought a toy, and if he no longer wants to play with it, why should he? He paid for it.

BERNARD. That might be all right if a man had only to think about himself. What about the woman?

CONSTANCE. I don't think you need waste too much sympathy on her. Like ninety-nine girls out of a hundred, when I married I looked upon it as the only easy, honourable and lucrative calling open to me. When the average woman who has been married for fifteen years discovers her husband's infidelity it is not her heart that is wounded but her vanity. If she had any sense, she would regard it merely as one of the necessary inconveniences of an otherwise pleasant profession.

BERNARD. Then the long and short of it is that you don't love me.

CONSTANCE. You think that my principles are all moonshine?

BERNARD. I don't think they would have much influence if you were as crazy about me as I am about you. Do you still love John?

CONSTANCE. I'm very fond of him, he makes me laugh, and we get on together like a house on fire, but I'm not in love with him.

BERNARD. And is that enough for you? Isn't the future sometimes a trifle desolate? Don't you want love?

[*A pause. She gives him a long reflective look.*]

CONSTANCE [*charmingly*]. If I did I should come to you for it, Bernard.

BERNARD. Constance, what do you mean? Is it possible that you could ever care for me? Oh, my darling, I worship the ground you tread on. [*He seizes her in his arms and kisses her passionately.*]

CONSTANCE [*releasing herself*]. Oh, my dear, don't be so sudden. I should despise myself entirely if I were unfaithful to John so long as I am entirely dependent on him.

BERNARD. But if you love me?

CONSTANCE. I never said I did. But even if I did, so long as John provides me with all the necessities of existence I wouldn't be unfaithful. It all comes down to the economic situation. He has bought my fidelity and I should be worse than a harlot if I took the price he paid and did not deliver the goods.

BERNARD. Do you mean to say there's no hope for me at all?

CONSTANCE. The only hope before you at the moment is to start for Ranelagh before the game is over.

BERNARD. Do you still want to go?

CONSTANCE. Yes.

BERNARD. Very well. [*With a burst of passion*] I love you.

CONSTANCE. Then go down and start up the car, put a spot of oil in the radiator or something, and I'll join you in a minute. I want to telephone.

BERNARD. Very well. [*He goes out.* CONSTANCE *takes up the telephone.*]

CONSTANCE. Mayfair 2646 . . . Barbara? It's Constance. That offer you made me a fortnight ago—is it still open? Well, I want to accept it. . . . No, no, nothing has happened. John is very well. He's always sweet, you know. It's only that I want to earn my own living. When can I start? The sooner the better.

act 3

The scene is still the same. A year has passed. It is afternoon.

> CONSTANCE *is seated at a desk writing letters. The* BUTLER *shows in* BARBARA FAWCETT *and* MARTHA.

BENTLEY. Mrs. Fawcett and Miss Culver.

CONSTANCE. Oh! Sit down, I'm just finishing a note.

BARBARA. We met on the doorstep.

MARTHA. I thought I'd just look round and see if there was anything I could do to help you before you start.

CONSTANCE. That's very nice of you, Martha. I really don't think there is. I'm packed and ready, and for once I don't believe I've forgotten one of the things I shan't want.

BARBARA. I felt I must run in to say good-bye to you.

CONSTANCE. Now, my dear, you mustn't neglect your work the moment my back is turned.

BARBARA. Well, it's partly the work that's brought me. An order has just come in for a new house and they want an Italian room.

CONSTANCE. I don't like that look in your beady eye, Barbara.

BARBARA. Well, it struck me that as you're going to Italy you might go round the shops and buy any nice pieces that you can find.

CONSTANCE. Perish the thought. I've worked like a dog for a year and last night at six o'clock I downed tools. I stripped off my grimy overalls, wrung the sweat from my honest brow and scrubbed my horny hands. You said I could take six weeks' holiday.

BARBARA. I admit that you've thoroughly earned it.

CONSTANCE. When I closed the shop-door behind me, I ceased to be a British working-man and resumed the position of a perfect English lady.

MARTHA. I never saw you in such spirits.

CONSTANCE. Something accomplished, something done. But what I was coming to was this: for the next six weeks I refuse to give a moment's thought to bath-rooms or wall-papers, kitchen sinks, scullery floors, curtains, cushions and refrigerators.

BARBARA. I wasn't asking you to. I only wanted you to get some of that painted Italian furniture and a few mirrors.

CONSTANCE. No, I've worked hard and I've enjoyed my work, and now I'm going to enjoy a perfect holiday.

BARBARA. Oh, well, have it your own way.

MARTHA. Constance dear, I think there's something you ought to know.

CONSTANCE. I should have thought you had discovered by now that I generally know the things I ought to know.

MARTHA. You'll never guess whom I saw in Bond Street this morning.

CONSTANCE. Yes, I shall. Marie-Louise.

MARTHA. Oh!

CONSTANCE. I'm sorry to disappoint you, darling. She rang me up an hour ago.

MARTHA. But I thought she wasn't coming back for another month. She was going to stay away a year.

CONSTANCE. She arrived last night and I'm expecting her every minute.

MARTHA. Here?

CONSTANCE. Yes. She said she simply must run in and see me before I left.

MARTHA. I wonder what she wants.

CONSTANCE. Perhaps to pass the time of day. I think it's rather sweet of her, considering how busy she must be on getting back after so long.

BARBARA. She's been all over the place, hasn't she?

CONSTANCE. Yes, she's been in Malaya; Mortimer has interests there, you know, and in China, and now they've just come from India.

MARTHA. I often wondered if it was at your suggestion that they set off on that long tour immediately after that unfortunate scene.

CONSTANCE. Which, you must confess, no one enjoyed more than you, darling.

BARBARA. It was certainly the most sensible thing they could do.

MARTHA. Of course you know your own business best, darling, but don't you think it's a little unfortunate that you should be going away for six weeks just as she comes back?

CONSTANCE. We working-women have to take our holidays when we can.

BARBARA. Surely John has had his lesson. He's not going to make a fool of himself a second time.

MARTHA. Do you think he has really got over his infatuation, Constance?

CONSTANCE. I don't know at all. But here he is, you'd better ask him. [*As she says these words,* JOHN *enters.*]

JOHN. Ask him what?

MARTHA [*not at all at a loss*]. I was just wondering what you'd do with yourself during Constance's absence.

JOHN. I've got a lot of work, you know, and I shall go to the club a good deal.

MARTHA. It seems a pity that you weren't able to arrange things so that you and Constance should take your holidays together.

BARBARA. Don't blame me for that. I was quite willing to make my arrangements to suit Constance.

CONSTANCE. You see, I wanted to go to Italy and the only places John likes on the Continent are those in which it's only by an effort of the imagination that you can tell you're not in England.

MARTHA. What about Helen?

CONSTANCE. We've taken a house at Henley for August. John can play golf and go on the river, and I shall be able to come up to town every day to look after the business.

BARBARA. Well, dear, I'll leave you. I hope you'll have a wonderful holiday. You've deserved it. Do you know, I think I'm a very clever woman, John, to have persuaded Constance to work. She's been absolutely invaluable to me.

JOHN. I never liked the idea and I'm not going to say I did.

BARBARA. Haven't you forgiven me yet?

JOHN. She insisted on it and I had to make the best of a bad job.

BARBARA. Good-bye.

CONSTANCE [*kissing her*]. Good-bye, dear. Take care of your-self.

MARTHA. I'll come with you, Barbara. Mother said she'd look in for a minute to say good-bye to you.

CONSTANCE. Oh, all right. Good-bye. [*She kisses the two and accompanies them to the door. They go out.*]

JOHN. I say, Constance, I thought you had to go now because Barbara couldn't possibly get away.

CONSTANCE. Did I say that?

JOHN. Certainly.

CONSTANCE. Oh!

JOHN. If I'd dreamt that you could just as easily take your holi-day when I take mine . . .

CONSTANCE [*interrupting*]. Don't you think it's a mistake for husbands and wives to take their holidays together? The only reason one takes a holiday is for rest and change and recreation. Do you think a man really gets that when he goes away with his wife?

JOHN. It depends on the wife.

CONSTANCE. I know nothing more depressing than the sight of all those couples in a hotel dining-room, one little couple to one little table, sitting opposite to one another without a word to say.

JOHN. Oh, nonsense. You often see couples who are very jolly and cheerful.

CONSTANCE. Yes, I know, but look closely at the lady's wedding-ring and you'll see that it rests uneasily on the hand it adorns.

JOHN. We always get on like a house on fire and when I slipped a wedding-ring on your finger a bishop supervised the process. You're not going to tell me that I bore *you*.

CONSTANCE. On the contrary, you tickle me to death. It's that unhappy modesty of mine: I was afraid that you could have too much of my society. I thought it would refresh you if I left you to your own devices for a few weeks.

JOHN. If you go on pulling my leg so persistently I shall be permanently deformed.

CONSTANCE. Anyhow, it's too late now. My bags are packed, my farewells made, and nothing bores people so much as to see you tomorrow when they've made up their minds to get on without you for a month.

JOHN. H'm. Eyewash. . . . Look here, Constance, there's some-thing I want to say to you.

CONSTANCE. Yes?

JOHN. Do you know that Marie-Louise has come back?

CONSTANCE. Yes. She said she'd try and look in to say how do you do before I started. It'll be nice to see her again after so long.

JOHN. I want you to do something for me, Constance.

CONSTANCE. What is it?

JOHN. Well, you've been a perfect brick to me, and hang it all, I can't take advantage of your good nature. I must do the square thing.

CONSTANCE. I'm afraid I don't quite understand.

JOHN. I haven't seen Marie-Louise since that day when Mortimer came here and made such a fool of himself. She's been away for nearly a year and taking all things into consideration I think it would be a mistake to resume the relations that we were on then.

CONSTANCE. What makes you think she wishes to?

JOHN. The fact that she rang you up the moment she arrived looks ominous to me.

CONSTANCE. Ominous? You know some women can't see a telephone without taking the receiver off and then, when the operator says, Number, please, they have to say something. I dare say ours was the first that occurred to Marie-Louise.

JOHN. It's no good blinking the fact that Marie-Louise was madly in love with me.

CONSTANCE. Well, we can neither of us blame her for that.

JOHN. I don't want to be unkind, but after all, circumstances have forced a break upon us and I think we had better look upon it as permanent.

CONSTANCE. Of course you must please yourself.

JOHN. I'm not thinking of myself, Constance. I'm thinking partly of course of Marie-Louise's good, but, I confess, chiefly of you. I could never look you in the face again if everything between Marie-Louise and me were not definitely finished.

CONSTANCE. I should hate you to lose so harmless and inexpensive a pleasure.

JOHN. Of course it'll be painful, but if one's made up one's mind to do a thing I think it's much better to do it quickly.

CONSTANCE. I think you're quite right. I'll tell you what I'll do, as soon as Marie-Louise comes I'll make an excuse and leave you alone with her.

JOHN. That wasn't exactly my idea.

CONSTANCE. Oh?

JOHN. It's the kind of thing that a woman can do so much better than a man. It struck me that it would come better from you than from me.

CONSTANCE. Oh, did it?

JOHN. It's a little awkward for me, but it would be quite easy for you to say—well, you know the sort of thing, that you have your self-respect to think of, and to cut a long story short, she must either give me up or you'll raise hell.

CONSTANCE. But you know what a soft heart I have. If she bursts into tears and says she can't live without you I shall feel so sorry for her that I shall say, Well, damn it all, keep him.

JOHN. You wouldn't do me a dirty trick like that, Constance.

CONSTANCE. You know that your happiness is my chief interest in life.

JOHN [after a moment's hesitation]. Constance, I will be perfectly frank with you. I'm fed up with Marie-Louise.

CONSTANCE. Darling, why didn't you say that at once?

JOHN. Be a sport, Constance. You know that's not the kind of thing one can say to a woman.

CONSTANCE. I admit it's not the kind of thing she's apt to take very well.

JOHN. Women are funny. When they're tired of you they tell you so without a moment's hesitation and if you don't like it you can lump it. But if you're tired of them you're a brute and a beast and boiling oil's too good for you.

CONSTANCE. Very well, leave it to me. I'll do it.

JOHN. You're a perfect brick. But you'll let her down gently, won't you? I wouldn't hurt her feelings for the world. She's a nice little thing, Constance.

CONSTANCE. Sweet.

JOHN. And it's hard luck on her.

CONSTANCE. Rotten.

JOHN. Make her understand that I'm more sinned against than sinning. I don't want her to think too badly of me.

CONSTANCE. Of course not.

JOHN. But be quite sure it's definite.

CONSTANCE. Leave it to me.

JOHN. You're a ripper, Constance. By George, no man could want a better wife.

[The BUTLER introduces MARIE-LOUISE.]

BUTLER. Mrs. Durham.

[*The two women embrace warmly.*]

MARIE-LOUISE. Darling, how perfectly divine to see you again. It's too, too wonderful.

CONSTANCE. My dear, how well you're looking. Are those the new pearls?

MARIE-LOUISE. Aren't they sweet? But Mortimer bought me the most heavenly emeralds when we were in India. Oh, John, how are you?

JOHN. Oh, I'm all right, thanks.

MARIE-LOUISE. Aren't you a little fatter than when I saw you last?

JOHN. Certainly not.

MARIE-LOUISE. I've lost pounds. [*To* CONSTANCE] I'm so glad I caught you. I should have been so disappointed to miss you. [*To* JOHN] Where are you going?

JOHN. Nowhere. Constance is going alone.

MARIE-LOUISE. Is she? How perfectly divine. I suppose you can't get away. Are you making pots of money?

JOHN. I get along. Will you forgive me if I leave you? I've got to be off.

MARIE-LOUISE. Of course. You're always busy, aren't you?

JOHN. Good-bye.

MARIE-LOUISE. I hope we shall see something of you while Constance is away.

JOHN. Thank you very much.

MARIE-LOUISE. Mortimer's golf has improved. He'd love to play with you.

JOHN. Oh, yes, I should love it. [*He goes out.*]

MARIE-LOUISE. I did so hope to find you alone. Constance, I've got heaps and heaps to tell you. Isn't it tactful of John to leave us? First of all I want to tell you how splendidly everything has turned out. You know you were quite right. I'm so glad I took your advice and made Mortimer take me away for a year.

CONSTANCE. Mortimer is no fool.

MARIE-LOUISE. Oh, no, for a man he's really quite clever. I gave him hell, you know, for ever having suspected me, and at last he was just eating out of my hand. But I could see he wasn't quite sure of me. You know what men are—when they once get an idea in their heads it's dreadfully difficult for them to get it out again. But the journey was an inspiration; I was absolutely angelic all the time, and he made a lot of money, so everything in the garden was rosy.

CONSTANCE. I'm very glad.

MARIE-LOUISE. I owe it all to you, Constance. I made Mortimer buy you a perfectly divine star sapphire in Ceylon. I told him he owed you some sort of reparation for the insult he'd put upon you. It cost a hundred and twenty pounds, darling, and we're taking it to Cartier's to have it set.

CONSTANCE. How thrilling.

MARIE-LOUISE. You mustn't think I'm ungrateful. Now listen, Constance, I want to tell you at once that you needn't distress yourself about me and John.

CONSTANCE. I never did.

MARIE-LOUISE. I know I behaved like a little beast, but I never thought you'd find out. If I had, well, you know me well enough to be positive that nothing would have induced me to have anything to do with him.

CONSTANCE. You're very kind.

MARIE-LOUISE. I want you to do something for me, Constance. Will you?

CONSTANCE. I'm always eager to oblige a friend.

MARIE-LOUISE. Well, you know what John is. Of course he's a dear and all that kind of thing, but the thing's over and it's best that he should realize it at once.

CONSTANCE. Over?

MARIE-LOUISE. Of course I know he's head over heels in love with me still. I saw that the moment I came into the room. One can't blame him for that, can one?

CONSTANCE. Men do find you fascinating.

MARIE-LOUISE. But one has to think of oneself sometimes in this world. He must see that it could never be the same after we discovered that you knew all about it.

CONSTANCE. I kept it from you as long as I could.

MARIE-LOUISE. One couldn't help feeling then that you were rather making fools of us. It seemed to take the romance away, if you see what I mean.

CONSTANCE. Dimly.

MARIE-LOUISE. You know, I wouldn't hurt John's feelings for the world, but it's no good beating about the bush and I'm quite determined to have the thing finished and done with before you go.

CONSTANCE. This is very sudden. I'm afraid it'll be an awful shock to John.

MARIE-LOUISE. I've quite made up my mind.

CONSTANCE. There isn't much time for a very long and moving scene, but I'll see if John is in still. Could you manage it in ten minutes?

MARIE-LOUISE. Oh, but *I* can't see him. I want you to tell him.

CONSTANCE. Me!

MARIE-LOUISE. You know him so well, you know just the sort of things to say to him. It's not very nice telling a man who adores you that you don't care for him in that way any more. It's so much easier for a third party.

CONSTANCE. Do you really think so?

MARIE-LOUISE. I'm positive of it. You see, you can say that for your sake I've made up my mind that from now on we can be nothing but friends. You've been so wonderful to both of us, it would be dreadful if we didn't play the game now. Say that I shall always think of him tenderly and that he's the only man I've ever really loved, but that we must part.

CONSTANCE. But if he insists on seeing you?

MARIE-LOUISE. It's no good, Constance, I can't see him. I shall only cry and get my eyes all bunged up. You will do it for me, darling. Please.

CONSTANCE. I will.

MARIE-LOUISE. I got the most divine evening frock in pale green satin on my way through Paris, and it would look too sweet on you. Would you like me to give it to you? I've only worn it once.

CONSTANCE. Now tell me the real reason why you're so determined to get rid of John without a moment's delay.

[MARIE-LOUISE *looks at her and gives a little roguish smile.*]

MARIE-LOUISE. Swear you won't tell.

CONSTANCE. On my honour.

MARIE-LOUISE. Well, my dear, we met a perfectly divine young man in India. He was A.D.C.[1] to one of the governors and he came home on the same boat with us. He simply adores me.

CONSTANCE. And of course you adore him.

MARIE-LOUISE. My dear, I'm absolutely mad about him. I don't know what's going to happen.

CONSTANCE. I think we can both give a pretty shrewd guess.

MARIE-LOUISE. It's simply awful to have a temperament like mine. Of course you can't understand, you're cold.

CONSTANCE [*very calmly*]. You're an immoral little beast, Marie-Louise.

[1] *A.D.C., aide-de-camp.*

MARIE-LOUISE. Oh, I'm not. I have affairs—but I'm not promiscuous.

CONSTANCE. I should respect you more if you were an honest prostitute. She at least does what she does to earn her bread and butter. You take everything from your husband and give him nothing that he pays for. You are no better than a vulgar cheat.

MARIE-LOUISE [*surprised and really hurt*]. Constance, how can you say such things to me? I think it's terribly unkind of you. I thought you liked me.

CONSTANCE. I do. I think you a liar, a humbug and a parasite, but I like you.

MARIE-LOUISE. You can't if you think such dreadful things about me.

CONSTANCE. I do. You're good-tempered and generous and sometimes amusing. I even have a certain affection for you.

MARIE-LOUISE [*smiling*]. I don't believe you mean a word you say. You know how devoted I am to you.

CONSTANCE. I take people as they are and I dare say that in another twenty years you'll be the pink of propriety.

MARIE-LOUISE. Darling, I knew you didn't mean it, but you will have your little joke.

CONSTANCE. Now run along, darling, and I'll break the news to John.

MARIE-LOUISE. Well, good-bye, and be gentle with him. There is no reason why we shouldn't spare him as much as possible. [*She turns to go and at the door—stops.*] Of course I've often wondered why with your looks you don't have more success than you do. I know now.

CONSTANCE. Tell me.

MARIE-LOUISE. You see—you're a humourist and that always puts men off. [*She goes out. In a moment the door is cautiously opened and* JOHN *puts his head in.*]

JOHN. Has she gone?

CONSTANCE. Come in. A fine night and all's well.

JOHN [*entering*]. I heard the door bang. You broke it to her?

CONSTANCE. I broke it.

JOHN. Was she awfully upset?

CONSTANCE. Of course it was a shock, but she kept a stiff upper lip.

JOHN. Did she cry?

CONSTANCE. No. Not exactly. To tell you the truth I think she was stunned by the blow. But of course when she gets home and realizes the full extent of her loss, she'll cry like anything.

JOHN. I hate to see a woman cry.

CONSTANCE. It is painful, isn't it? But of course it's a relief to the nerves.

JOHN. I think you're rather cool about it, Constance. I am not feeling any too comfortable. I shouldn't like her to think I'd treated her badly.

CONSTANCE. I think she quite understands that you're doing it for my sake. She knows that you have still a very great regard for her.

JOHN. But you made it quite definite, didn't you?

CONSTANCE. Oh, quite.

JOHN. I'm really very much obliged to you, Constance.

CONSTANCE. Not at all.

JOHN. At all events I'm glad to think that you'll be able to set out on your holiday with a perfectly easy mind. By the way, do you want any money? I'll write you a cheque at once.

CONSTANCE. Oh, no, thank you. I've got plenty. I've earned fourteen hundred pounds during this year that I've been working.

JOHN. Have you, by Jove! That's a very considerable sum.

CONSTANCE. I'm taking two hundred of it for my holiday. I've spent two hundred on my clothes and on odds and ends and the remaining thousand I've paid into your account this morning for my board and lodging during the last twelve months.

JOHN. Nonsense, darling. I won't hear of such a thing. I don't want you to pay for your board and lodging.

CONSTANCE. I insist.

JOHN. Don't you love me any more?

CONSTANCE. What has that to do with it? Oh, you think a woman can only love a man if he keeps her. Isn't that rating your powers of fascination too modestly? What about your charm and good humour?

JOHN. Don't be absurd, Constance. I can perfectly well afford to support you in your proper station. To offer me a thousand pounds for your board and lodging is almost insulting.

CONSTANCE. Don't you think it's the kind of insult you could bring yourself to swallow? One can do a lot of amusing things with a thousand pounds.

JOHN. I wouldn't dream of taking it. I never liked the idea of your going into business. I thought you had quite enough to do looking after the house and so forth.

CONSTANCE. Have you been less comfortable since I began working?

JOHN. No, I can't say I have.

CONSTANCE. You can take my word for it, a lot of incompetent women talk a great deal of nonsense about housekeeping. If you know your job and have good servants it can be done in ten minutes a day.

JOHN. Anyhow, you wanted to work and I yielded. I thought in point of fact it would be a very pleasant occupation for you, but heaven knows I wasn't expecting to profit financially by it.

CONSTANCE. No, I'm sure you weren't.

JOHN. Constance, I could never help thinking that your determination had something to do with Marie-Louise.

[*There is a moment's pause and when* CONSTANCE *speaks it is not without seriousness.*]

CONSTANCE. Haven't you wondered why I never reproached you for your affair with Marie-Louise?

JOHN. Yes. I could only ascribe it to your unfathomable goodness.

CONSTANCE. You were wrong. I felt I hadn't the right to reproach you.

JOHN. What do you mean, Constance? You had every right. We behaved like a couple of swine. I may be a dirty dog, but, thank God, I know I'm a dirty dog.

CONSTANCE. You no longer desired me. How could I blame you for that? But if you didn't desire me, what use was I to you? You've seen how small a share I take in providing you with the comfort of a well-ordered home.

JOHN. You were the mother of my child.

CONSTANCE. Let us not exaggerate the importance of that, John. I performed a natural and healthy function of my sex. And all the tiresome part of looking after the child when she was born I placed in the hands of much more competent persons. Let us face it, I was only a parasite in your house. You had entered into legal obligations that prevented you from turning me adrift, but I owe you a debt of gratitude for never letting me see by word or gesture that I was no more than a costly and at times inconvenient ornament.

JOHN. I never looked upon you as an inconvenient ornament.

And I don't know what you mean by being a parasite. Have I ever in any way suggested that I grudged a penny that I spent on you?

CONSTANCE [*with mock amazement*]. Do you mean to say that I ascribed to your beautiful manners what was only due to your stupidity? Are you as great a fool as the average man who falls for the average woman's stupendous bluff that just because he's married her he must provide for her wants and her luxuries, sacrifice his pleasures and comfort and convenience, and that he must look upon it as a privilege that she allows him to be her slave and bondman? Come, come, John, pull yourself together. You're a hundred years behind the times. Now that women have broken down the walls of the harem they must take the rough-and-tumble of the street.

JOHN. You forget all sorts of things. Don't you think a man may have gratitude to a woman for the love he has had for her in the past?

CONSTANCE. I think gratitude is often very strong in men so long as it demands from them no particular sacrifices.

JOHN. Well, it's a curious way of looking at things, but obviously I have reason to be thankful for it. But after all you knew what was going on long before it came out. What happened then that made you make up your mind to go into business?

CONSTANCE. I am naturally a lazy woman. So long as appearances were saved I was prepared to take all I could get and give nothing in return. I was a parasite, but I knew it. But when we reached a situation where only your politeness or your lack of intelligence prevented you from throwing the fact in my teeth, I changed my mind. I thought that I should very much like to be in a position where, if I felt inclined to, I could tell you, with calm and courtesy, but with determination—to go to hell.

JOHN. And are you in that position now?

CONSTANCE. Precisely. I owe you nothing. I am able to keep myself. For the last year I have paid my way. There is only one freedom that is really important and that is economic freedom, for in the long run the man who pays the piper calls the tune. Well, I have that freedom, and upon my soul it's the most enjoyable sensation I can remember since I ate my first strawberry ice.

JOHN. You know, I would sooner you had made me scenes for a month on end like any ordinary woman and nagged my life out than that you should harbour this cold rancour against me.

CONSTANCE. My poor darling, what are you talking about? Have you known me for fifteen years and do you think me capable of the commonness of insincerity? I harbour no rancour. Why, my dear, I'm devoted to you.

JOHN. Do you mean to tell me that you've done all this without any intention of making me feel a perfect cad?

CONSTANCE. On my honour. If I look in my heart I can only find in it affection for you and the most kindly and charitable feelings. Don't you believe me?

[*He looks at her for a moment and then makes a little gesture of bewilderment.*]

JOHN. Yes, oddly enough, I do. You are a remarkable woman, Constance.

CONSTANCE. I know, but keep it to yourself. You don't want to give a dog a bad name.

JOHN [*with an affectionate smile*]. I wish I could get away. I don't half like the idea of your travelling by yourself.

CONSTANCE. Oh, but I'm not. Didn't I tell you?

JOHN. No.

CONSTANCE. I meant to. I'm going with Bernard.

JOHN. Oh! You never said so. Who else?

CONSTANCE. Nobody.

JOHN. Oh! [*He is rather taken aback at the news.*] Isn't that rather odd?

CONSTANCE. No. Why?

JOHN [*not knowing at all how to take it*]. Well, it's not usual for a young woman to take a six weeks' holiday with a man who can hardly be described as old enough to be her father.

CONSTANCE. Bernard's just about the same age as you.

JOHN. Don't you think it'll make people gossip a bit?

CONSTANCE. I haven't gone out of my way to spread the news. In fact, now I come to think of it, I haven't told anyone but you, and you, I am sure, will be discreet.

[JOHN *suddenly feels that his collar is a little too tight for him, and with his fingers he tries to loosen it.*]

JOHN. You're pretty certain to be seen by someone who knows you and they're bound to talk.

CONSTANCE. Oh, I don't think so. You see we're motoring all the way and we neither of us care for frequented places. One of the advantages of having really nice friends like ours is that you can always be certain of finding them at the fashionable resorts at the very moment when everybody you know is there.

JOHN. Of course I am not so silly as to think that because a man and a woman go away together it is necessary to believe the worst about them, but you can't deny that it is rather unconventional. I wouldn't for a moment suggest that there'll be anything between you, but it's inevitable that ordinary persons should think there was.

CONSTANCE [*as cool as a cucumber*]. I've always thought that ordinary persons had more sense than the clever ones are ready to credit them with.

JOHN [*deliberately*]. What on earth do you mean?

CONSTANCE. Why, of course we're going as man and wife, John.

JOHN. Don't be a fool, Constance. You don't know what you're talking about. That's not funny at all.

CONSTANCE. But, my poor John, whom do you take us for? Am I so unattractive that what I'm telling you is incredible? Why else should I go with Bernard? If I merely wanted a companion I'd go with a woman. We could have headaches together and have our hair washed at the same place and copy one another's nightdresses. A woman's a much better travelling companion than a man.

JOHN. I may be very stupid, but I don't seem to be able to understand what you're saying. Do you really mean me to believe that Bernard Kersal is your lover?

CONSTANCE. Certainly not.

JOHN. Then what *are* you talking about?

CONSTANCE. My dear, I can't put it any plainer. I'm going away for six weeks' holiday and Bernard has very kindly offered to come with me.

JOHN. And where do I come in?

CONSTANCE. You don't come in. You stay at home and look after your patients.

JOHN [*trying his best to control himself*]. I flatter myself I'm a sensible man. I'm not going to fly into a passion. Many men would stamp and rave or break the furniture. I have no intention of being melodramatic, but you must allow me to say that what you've just told me is very surprising.

CONSTANCE. Just for a moment, perhaps, but I'm sure you have only to familiarize yourself with the notion in order to become reconciled to it.

JOHN. I'm doubtful whether I shall have time to do that, for I feel uncommonly as though I were about to have an apoplectic stroke.

CONSTANCE. Undo your collar then. Now I come to look at you I confess that you are more than usually red in the face.

JOHN. What makes you think that I am going to allow you to go?

CONSTANCE [*good-humouredly*]. Chiefly the fact that you can't prevent me.

JOHN. I can't bring myself to believe that you mean what you say. I don't know what ever put such an idea into your head.

CONSTANCE [*casually*]. I thought a change might do me good.

JOHN. Nonsense.

CONSTANCE. Why? You did. Don't you remember? You were getting rather flat and stale. Then you had an affair with Marie-Louise and you were quite another man. Gay and amusing, full of life, and much more agreeable to live with. The moral effect on you was quite remarkable.

JOHN. It's different for a man than for a woman.

CONSTANCE. Are you thinking of the possible consequences? We have long passed the Victorian Era when asterisks were followed after a certain interval by a baby.

JOHN. That never occurred to me. What I meant was that if a man's unfaithful to his wife she's an object of sympathy, whereas if a woman's unfaithful to her husband he's merely an object of ridicule.

CONSTANCE. That is one of those conventional prejudices that sensible people must strive to ignore.

JOHN. Do you expect me to sit still and let this man take my wife away from under my very nose? I wonder you don't ask me to shake hands with him and wish him good luck.

CONSTANCE. That's just what I am going to do. He's coming here in a few minutes to say good-bye to you.

JOHN. I shall knock him down.

CONSTANCE. I wouldn't take any risks in your place. He's pretty hefty and I'm under the impression that he's very nippy with his left.

JOHN. I shall have great pleasure in telling him exactly what I think of him.

CONSTANCE. Why? Have you forgotten that I was charming to Marie-Louise? We were the best of friends. She never bought a hat without asking me to go and help her choose it.

JOHN. I have red blood in my veins.

CONSTANCE. I'm more concerned at the moment with the grey matter in your brain.

JOHN. Is he in love with you?

CONSTANCE. Madly. Didn't you know?

JOHN. I? How should I?

CONSTANCE. He's been here a great deal during the last year. Were you under the impression that he only came to see you?

JOHN. I never paid any attention to him. I thought him rather dull.

CONSTANCE. He is rather dull. But he's very sweet.

JOHN. What sort of a man is it who eats a fellow's food and drinks his wine and then makes love to his wife behind his back?

CONSTANCE. A man very like you, John, I should say.

JOHN. Not at all. Mortimer is the sort of man who was born to be made a fool of.

CONSTANCE. None of us know for certain the designs of Providence.

JOHN. I see you're bent on driving me to desperation. I shall break something in a minute.

CONSTANCE. There's that blue-and-white bowl that your Uncle Henry gave us as a wedding present. Break that, it's only a modern imitation.

[*He takes the bowl and hurls it on the floor so that it is shattered.*]

JOHN. There.

CONSTANCE. Do you feel better?

JOHN. Not a bit.

CONSTANCE. It's a pity you broke it then. You might have given it away as a wedding present to one of your colleagues at the hospital.

[*The* BUTLER *shows in* MRS. CULVER.]

BENTLEY. Mrs. Culver.

CONSTANCE. Oh, mother, how sweet of you to come. I was so hoping I'd see you before I left.

MRS. CULVER. Oh, you've had an accident.

CONSTANCE. No, John's in a temper and he thought it would relieve him if he broke something.

MRS. CULVER. Nonsense, John's never in a temper.

JOHN. That's what you think, Mrs. Culver. Yes, I am in a temper. I'm in a filthy temper. Are you a party to this plan of Constance's?

CONSTANCE. No, mother doesn't know.

JOHN. Can't you do something to stop it? You have some influence over her. You must see that the thing's preposterous.

MRS. CULVER. My dear boy, I haven't the ghost of an idea what you're talking about.

JOHN. She's going to Italy with Bernard Kersal. Alone.

MRS. CULVER [*with a stare*]. It's not true; how d'you know?

JOHN. She's just told me so, as bold as brass, out of a blue sky. She mentioned it in the course of conversation as if she were saying, Darling, your coat wants brushing.

MRS. CULVER. Is it true, Constance?

CONSTANCE. Quite.

MRS. CULVER. But haven't you been getting on with John? I always thought you two were as happy as the day is long.

JOHN. So did I. We've never had the shadow of a quarrel. We've always got on.

MRS. CULVER. Don't you love John any more, darling?

CONSTANCE. Yes, I'm devoted to him.

JOHN. How can you be devoted to a man when you're going to do him the greatest injury that a woman can do to a man?

CONSTANCE. Don't be idiotic, John. I'm going to do you no more injury than you did me a year ago.

JOHN [*striding up to her, thinking quite erroneously that he sees light*]. Are you doing this in order to pay me out for Marie-Louise?

CONSTANCE. Don't be such a fool, John. Nothing is further from my thoughts.

MRS. CULVER. The circumstances are entirely different. It was very naughty of John to deceive you, but he's sorry for what he did and he's been punished for it. It was all very dreadful and caused us a great deal of pain. But a man's a man and you expect that kind of thing from him. There are excuses for him. There are none for a woman. Men are naturally polygamous and sensible women have always made allowances for their occasional lapse from a condition which modern civilization has forced on them. Women are monogamous. They do not naturally desire more than one man and that is why the common sense of the world has heaped obloquy upon them when they have overstepped the natural limitations of their sex.

CONSTANCE [*smiling*]. It seems rather hard that what is sauce for the gander shouldn't also be sauce for the goose.

MRS. CULVER. We all know that unchastity has no moral effect on men. They can be perfectly promiscuous and remain upright, industrious and reliable. It's quite different with women. It ruins their character. They become untruthful and dissipated, lazy, shiftless and dishonest. That is why the experience of ten thousand years has demanded chastity in women. Because it has learnt that this virtue is the key to all others.

CONSTANCE. They were dishonest because they were giving away something that wasn't theirs to give. They had sold themselves for board, lodging and protection. They were chattels. They were dependent on their husbands and when they were unfaithful to them they were liars and thieves. I'm not dependent on John. I am economically independent and therefore I claim my sexual independence. I have this afternoon paid into John's account one thousand pounds for my year's keep.

JOHN. I refuse to take it.

CONSTANCE. Well, you'll damned well have to.

MRS. CULVER. There's no object in losing your temper.

CONSTANCE. I have mine under perfect control.

JOHN. If you think what they call free love is fun you're mistaken. Believe me, it's the most overrated amusement that was ever invented.

CONSTANCE. In that case, I wonder why people continue to indulge in it.

JOHN. I ought to know what I'm talking about, hang it all. It has all the inconveniences of marriage and none of its advantages. I assure you, my dear, the game is not worth the candle.

CONSTANCE. You may be right, but you know how hard it is to profit by anybody's experience. I think I'd like to see for myself.

MRS. CULVER. Are you in love with Bernard?

CONSTANCE. To tell you the truth I haven't quite made up my mind. How does one know if one's in love?

MRS. CULVER. My dear, I only know one test. Could you use his tooth-brush?

CONSTANCE. No.

MRS. CULVER. Then you're not in love with him.

CONSTANCE. He's adored me for fifteen years. There's something in that long devotion which gives me a funny little feeling in my heart. I should like to do something to show him that I'm not ungrateful. You see, in six weeks he goes back to Japan. There is no chance of his coming to England again for seven years. I'm thirty-six now and he adores me; in seven years I shall be forty-three. A woman of forty-three is often charming, but it's seldom that a man of fifty-five is crazy about her. I came to the conclusion that it must be now or never and so I asked him if he'd like me to spend these last six weeks with him in Italy. When I wave my handkerchief to him as the ship that takes him sails out of the harbour at Naples I hope that he will feel that all those years of unselfish love have been well worth the while.

JOHN. Six weeks. Do you intend to leave him at the end of six weeks?

CONSTANCE. Oh, yes, of course. It's because I'm putting a limit to our love that I think it may achieve the perfection of something that is beautiful and transitory. Why, John, what is it that makes a rose so lovely but that its petals fall as soon as it is full blown?

JOHN. It's all come as such a shock and a surprise that I hardly know what to say. You've got me at a complete disadvantage.

[MRS. CULVER, *who has been standing at the window, gives a little cry.*]

CONSTANCE. What is it?

MRS. CULVER. Here is Bernard. He's just driven up to the door.

JOHN. Do you expect me to receive him as if I were blissfully unconscious of your plans?

CONSTANCE. It would be more comfortable. It would be stupid to make a scene and it wouldn't prevent my going on this little jaunt with him.

JOHN. I have my dignity to think of.

CONSTANCE. One often preserves that best by putting it in one's pocket. It would be kind of you, John, to treat him just as pleasantly as I treated Marie-Louise when I knew she was your mistress.

JOHN. Does he know that I know?

CONSTANCE. Of course not. He's a little conventional, you know, and he couldn't happily deceive a friend if he thought there was no deception.

MRS. CULVER. Constance, is there nothing I can say to make you reconsider your decision?

CONSTANCE. Nothing, darling.

MRS. CULVER. Then I may just as well save my breath. I'll slip away before he comes.

CONSTANCE. Oh, all right. Good-bye, mother. I'll send you a lot of picture post-cards.

MRS. CULVER. I don't approve of you, Constance, and I can't pretend that I do. No good will come of it. Men were meant by nature to be wicked and delightful and deceive their wives, and women were meant to be virtuous and forgiving and to suffer verbosely. That was ordained from all eternity and none of your new-fangled notions can alter the decrees of Providence.

[*The* BUTLER *enters, followed by* BERNARD.]

BENTLEY. Mr. Kersal.

MRS. CULVER. How do you do, Bernard, and good-bye. I'm just going.

BERNARD. Oh, I'm sorry. Good-bye.

[*She goes out.*]

CONSTANCE [*to* BERNARD]. How d'you do? Just one moment. [*To the* BUTLER] Oh, Bentley, get my things downstairs and put them in a taxi, will you?

BENTLEY. Very good, madam.

BERNARD. Are you just starting? It's lucky I came when I did. I should have hated to miss you.

CONSTANCE. And let me know when the taxi's here.

BENTLEY. Yes, madam.

CONSTANCE. Now I can attend to you.

[*The* BUTLER *goes out.*]

BERNARD. Are you looking forward to your holiday?

CONSTANCE. Immensely. I've never gone on a jaunt like this before, and I'm really quite excited.

BERNARD. You're going alone, aren't you?

CONSTANCE. Oh, yes, quite alone.

BERNARD. It's rotten for you not to be able to get away, old man.

JOHN. Rotten.

BERNARD. I suppose these are the penalties of greatness. I can quite understand that you have to think of your patients first.

JOHN. Quite.

CONSTANCE. Of course John doesn't very much care for Italy.

BERNARD. Oh, are you going to Italy? I thought you said Spain.

JOHN. No, she always said Italy.

BERNARD. Oh, well, that's hardly your mark, is it, old boy? Though I believe there are some sporting links on the Lake of Como.

JOHN. Are there?

BERNARD. I suppose there's no chance of your being anywhere near Naples towards the end of July?

CONSTANCE. I don't really know. My plans are quite vague.

BERNARD. I was only asking because I'm sailing from Naples. It would be fun if we met there.

JOHN. Great fun.

CONSTANCE. I hope you'll see a lot of John while I'm away. I'm afraid he'll be a trifle lonely, poor darling. Why don't you dine together one day next week?

BERNARD. I'm terribly sorry, but you know I'm going away.

CONSTANCE. Oh, are you? I thought you were going to stay in London till you had to start for Japan.

BERNARD. I meant to, but my doctor has ordered me to go and do a cure.

JOHN. What sort of a cure?

BERNARD. Oh, just a cure. He says I want bucking up.

JOHN. Oh, does he? What's the name of your doctor?

BERNARD. No one you ever heard of. A man I used to know in the war.

JOHN. Oh!

BERNARD. So I'm afraid this is good-bye. Of course, it's a wrench leaving London, especially as I don't expect to be in Europe again for some years, but I always think it rather silly not to take a man's advice when you've asked for it.

JOHN. More especially when he's charged you three guineas.

CONSTANCE. I'm sorry. I was counting on you to keep John out of mischief during my absence.

BERNARD. I'm not sure if I could guarantee to do that. But we might have done a few theatres together and had a game of golf or two.

CONSTANCE. It would have been jolly, wouldn't it, John?

JOHN. Very jolly.

[*The* BUTLER *comes in.*]

BENTLEY. The taxi's waiting, madam.

CONSTANCE. Thank you.

[*The* BUTLER *goes out.*]

BERNARD. I'll take myself off. In case I don't see you again I'd like to thank you now for all your kindness to me during the year I've spent in London.

CONSTANCE. It's been very nice to see you.

BERNARD. You and John have been most awfully good to me. I never imagined I was going to have such a wonderful time.

CONSTANCE. We shall miss you terribly. It's been a great comfort to John to think that there was someone to take me out when he had to be away on one of his operations. Hasn't it, darling?

JOHN. Yes, darling.

CONSTANCE. When he knew I was with you he never worried. Did you, darling?

JOHN. No, darling.

BERNARD. I'm awfully glad if I've been able to make myself useful. Don't forget me entirely, will you?

CONSTANCE. We're not likely to do that, are we, darling?

JOHN. No, darling.

BERNARD. And if you ever have a moment to spare you will write to me, won't you? You don't know how much it means to us exiles.

CONSTANCE. Of course we will. We'll both write. Won't we, darling?

JOHN. Yes, darling.

CONSTANCE. John writes such a good letter. So chatty, you know, and amusing.

BERNARD. That's a promise. Well, good-bye, old boy. Have a good time.

JOHN. Thanks, old bean.

BERNARD. Good-bye, Constance. There's so much I want to say to you that I don't know where to begin.

JOHN. I don't want to hurry you, but the taxi is just ticking its head off.

BERNARD. John is so matter-of-fact. Well, I'll say nothing then but God bless you.

CONSTANCE. Au revoir.

BERNARD. If you do go to Naples you will let me know, won't you? If you send a line to my club, it'll be forwarded at once.

CONSTANCE. Oh, all right.

BERNARD. Good-bye.

[*He gives them both a friendly nod and goes out.* CONSTANCE *begins to giggle and soon is seized with uncontrollable laughter.*]

JOHN. Will you kindly tell me what there is to laugh at? If you think it amuses me to stand here like patience on a monument and have my leg pulled you're mistaken. What did you mean by all that balderdash about meeting you by chance in Naples?

CONSTANCE. He was throwing you off the scent.

JOHN. The man's a drivelling idiot.

CONSTANCE. D'you think so? I thought he was rather ingenious. Considering he hasn't had very much practice in this sort of thing I thought he did very well.

JOHN. Of course if you're determined to find him a pattern of perfection it's useless for me to attempt to argue. But honestly, speaking without prejudice for or against, I'm sorry to think of you throwing yourself away on a man like that.

CONSTANCE. Perhaps it's natural that a man and his wife should differ in their estimate of her prospective lover.

JOHN. You're not going to tell me he's better-looking than I am.

CONSTANCE. No. You have always been my ideal of manly beauty.

JOHN. He's no better dressed than I am.

CONSTANCE. He could hardly expect to be. He goes to the same tailor.

JOHN. I don't think you can honestly say he's more amusing than I am.

CONSTANCE. No, I honestly can't.

JOHN. Then in Heaven's name why do you want to go away with him?

CONSTANCE. Shall I tell you? Once more before it's too late I want to feel about me the arms of a man who adores the ground I walk on. I want to see his face light up when I enter the room. I want to feel the pressure of his hand when we look at the moon together and the pleasantly tickling sensation when his arm tremulously steals around my waist. I want to let my hand fall on his shoulder and feel his lips softly touch my hair.

JOHN. The operation is automatically impossible, the poor devil would get such a crick in the neck he wouldn't know what to do.

CONSTANCE. I want to walk along country lanes holding hands and I want to be called by absurd pet names. I want to talk baby-talk by the hour together.

JOHN. Oh, God.

CONSTANCE. I want to know that I'm eloquent and witty when I'm dead silent. For ten years I've been very happy in your affection, John, we've been the best and dearest friends, but now just for a little while I hanker for something else. Do you grudge it me? I want to be loved.

JOHN. But, my dear, I'll love you. I've been a brute, I've neglected you, it's not too late and you're the only woman I've ever really cared for. I'll chuck everything and we'll go away together.

CONSTANCE. The prospect does not thrill me.

JOHN. Come, darling, have a heart. I gave up Marie-Louise. Surely you can give up Bernard.

CONSTANCE. But you gave up Marie-Louise to please yourself, not to please me.

JOHN. Don't be a little beast, Constance. Come away with me. We'll have such a lark.

CONSTANCE. Oh, my poor John, I didn't work so hard to gain my economic independence in order to go on a honeymoon with my own husband.

JOHN. Do you think I can't be a lover as well as a husband?

CONSTANCE. My dear, no one can make yesterday's cold mutton into tomorrow's lamb cutlets.

JOHN. You know what you're doing. I was determined in future to be a model husband and you're driving me right into the arms of Marie-Louise. I give you my word of honour that the moment you leave this house I shall drive straight to her door.

CONSTANCE. I should hate you to have a fruitless journey. I'm afraid you won't find her at home. She has a new young man and she says he's too divine.

JOHN. What!

CONSTANCE. He's the A.D.C. of a Colonial Governor. She came here today to ask me to break the news to you that henceforth everything was over between you.

JOHN. I hope you told her first that I was firmly resolved to terminate a connection that could only cause you pain.

CONSTANCE. I couldn't. She was in such a blooming hurry to give me her message.

JOHN. Really, Constance, for your own pride I should have thought you wouldn't like her to make a perfect fool of me. Any other woman would have said, What a strange coincidence. Why it's only half an hour since John told me he had made up his mind never to see you again. But of course you don't care two straws for me any more, that's quite evident.

CONSTANCE. Oh, don't be unjust, darling. I shall always care for you. I may be unfaithful, but I am constant. I always think that's my most endearing quality.

[*The* BUTLER *opens the door.*]

JOHN [*irritably*]. What is it?

BENTLEY. I thought madam had forgotten that the taxi was at the door.

JOHN. Go to hell.

BENTLEY. Very good, sir. [*He goes out.*]

CONSTANCE. I don't see why you should be rude to him. Bernard will pay the taxi. Anyhow I must go now or he'll begin to think I'm not coming. Good-bye, darling. I hope you'll get on all right in my absence. Just give the cook her head[1] and you'll have no trouble. Won't you say good-bye to me?

JOHN. Go to the devil.

CONSTANCE. All right. I shall be back in six weeks.

JOHN. Back? Where?

CONSTANCE. Here.

JOHN. Here? Here? Do you think I'm going to take you back?

CONSTANCE. I don't see why not. When you've had time to reflect you'll realize that you have no reason to blame me. After all, I'm taking from you nothing that you want.

JOHN. Are you aware that I can divorce you for this.

CONSTANCE. Quite. But I married very prudently. I took the precaution to marry a gentleman and I know that you could never bring yourself to divorce me for doing no more than you did yourself.

JOHN. I wouldn't divorce you. I wouldn't expose my worst enemy to the risk of marrying a woman who's capable of treating her husband as you're treating me.

CONSTANCE [*at the door*]. Well, then, shall I come back?

JOHN [*after a moment's hesitation*]. You are the most maddening, wilful, capricious, wrong-headed, delightful and enchanting woman man was ever cursed with having for a wife. Yes, damn you, come back.

[*She lightly kisses her hand to him and slips out, slamming the door behind her.*]

---

[1] *give the cook her head, give her complete freedom.*

S. N. BEHRMAN (1893-   )

America's master of the comedy of manners has led a largely uneventful life, inconspicuous but for his steady stream of plays on Broadway stages during the past thirty-five years. Samuel Nathaniel Behrman was born into a middle-class Jewish family in Worcester, Massachusetts, and studied in Clark University in that city for two years. But he was stage-struck from early youth and left college to act in a vaudeville skit that he had written himself. When his parents persuaded him to go back for his degree, it was to Harvard, where he attended George Pierce Baker's "47 Workshop" in the drama.

Behrman's efforts to gain a footing in the theater were unsuccessful for many years, so that he fell back repeatedly on university life. In 1918 he took an M.A. at Columbia, studying with Brander Matthews, the drama teacher, and St. John Ervine, the famous Irish playwright. After collaborating on unsuccessful plays in 1923 and 1926, he was at last discouraged and was about to accept an instructorship in a small college when a friend persuaded him to tear up his railway ticket. A year later his career was finally launched when the Theatre Guild produced *The Second Man*. In retrospect Behrman himself is mystified by his persistence through eleven years of rejections.

Behrman's high-comedy style was developed in the carefree twenties, and his early plays—*The Second Man* (1927), *Meteor* (1929), *Brief Moment* (1931), and *Biography* (1932)—remain his purest achievements. Their sparkling dialogue and graceful wit gave the American theater its first mature comedy of manners, which could challenge

the English school of Somerset Maugham and Noel Coward
in its urbanity. Yet *Biography,* in a sense his transition
play, shows an increasing interest in character and a growing seriousness about political issues.

During the depression years Behrman's social conscience fought with his artistic talent as it came to seem
irresponsible in a comedian to ignore the grave issues of the
day. His conflicting impulses were dramatized in the character of the playwright-hero in *No Time for Comedy* (1939),
whose dilemma was stated in the title. But Behrman's
problem had already become evident in *Rain from Heaven*
(1934), *End of Summer* (1936), and *Wine of Choice* (1938),
which tried unsuccessfully to use the drawing room for
serious political discussion along with comic intrigue and
love-making. When he did return to pure comedy with
The Pirate (1942) during the war, he seemed to have lost
his early spontaneity. Thereafter he turned to collaborations,
such as *Jacobowsky and the Colonel,* with Franz Werfel
(1944), and adaptations, such as *Jane,* from Somerset
Maugham (1954), as his creative talents seemed to be dying.
Lord Pengo (1962) suddenly showed a revival of his best
manner, but his really brilliant period reached its peak in
Biography.

S. N. BEHRMAN

BIOGRAPHY[1]

CHARACTERS

Richard Kurt

Minnie
   Marion Froude's maid

Melchior Feydak
   a Viennese composer

Marion Froude

Leander Nolan

Warwick Wilson

Orrin Kinnicott

Slade Kinnicott
   his daughter

scenes

The entire action takes place in Marion Froude's studio in
New York City. The time is 1932

Act One
   About five o'clock of an afternoon in November

Act Two
   Afternoon, three weeks later

Act Three
   Late afternoon, two weeks later

The curtain is lowered during the act to denote a lapse of time

[1] Copyright, 1932, 1933 by S. N. Behrman.
   Copyright, 1936 (acting edition), by S. N. Behrman.

act 1

SCENE: *The studio apartment of* MARION FROUDE *in an old-fashioned studio building in West 57th St., New York. A great, cavernous room expressing in its polyglot furnishings the artistic patois of the various landlords who have sublet this apartment to wandering tenants like* MARION FROUDE. *The styles range from medieval Florence to contemporary Grand Rapids; on a movable raised platform in the center is a papal throne chair in red velvet and gold fringes. Not far from it is an ordinary American kitchen chair. The hanging lamp which sheds a mellow light over a French Empire sofa is filigreed copper Byzantine. Another and longer sofa across the room against the grand piano is in soft green velvet and has the gentility of a polite Park Avenue drawing room. Under the stairs, rear, which go up to* MARION's *bedroom, are stacks of her canvases. There is a quite fine wood carving of a Madonna which seems to be centuries old and in the wall spaces looking at audience are great, dim canvases— copies by some former tenant left probably in lieu of rent —of Sargent's Lord Ribblesdale and Mme. X.*

Whether it is due to the amenable spirit of the present incumbent or because they are relaxed in the democracy of art, these oddments of the creative spirit do not suggest disharmony. The room is warm, musty, with restful shadows and limpid lights. The enormous leaded window on the right, though some of its members are patched and cracked, gleams in the descending twilight with an opalescent light; even the copper cylinder of the fire extinguisher and its attendant axe, visible in the hall, seem to be not so much implements against calamity, as amusing museum-bits cherished from an earlier time. Every school is represented here except the modern. The studio has the mellowness of anachronism.

There is a door upstage left leading to the kitchen and MINNIE's *bedroom; a door, center, under the stairs leads into hallway. A door on the stair landing, center, leads to* MARION's *bedroom.*

TIME: *About five o'clock of an afternoon in November.*

AT RISE: RICHARD KURT *is finishing a nervous cigarette. He has the essential audacity which comes from having seen the worst happen, from having endured the keenest pain. He has the hardness of one who knows that he can be devastated by pity, the bitterness which comes from having seen, in early youth, justice thwarted and tears unavailing, the self-reliance which comes from having seen everything go in a disordered world save one stubborn, unyielding core of belief—at everything else he laughs, in this alone he trusts. He has the intensity of the fanatic and the carelessness of the vagabond. He goes to the door from the hall and calls.*

KURT. Say, you, hello there—what's your name?

[MINNIE, MARION FROUDE's *inseparable maid, a German woman of about fifty, comes in. She is indignant at being thus summarily summoned, and by a stranger.*]

MINNIE [*with dignity*]. My name iss Minnie, if you please.

KURT. What time did Miss Froude go out?

MINNIE. About two o'clock.

KURT. It's nearly five now. She should be home, shouldn't she?

MINNIE. She said she vas coming home to tea and that iss all I know.

KURT [*grimly*]. I know. She invited me to tea. . . . Where did she go to lunch?

MINNIE [*acidly*]. That I do not know.

KURT. Did someone call for her or did she go out alone? I have a reason for asking.

MINNIE. She went out alone. Any more questions?

KURT. No. I see there's no point in asking you questions.

MINNIE. Den vy do you ask dem? [*The doorbell rings.* MINNIE *throws up her hands in despair. She goes out muttering: "Ach Gott."* KURT *is rather amused at her. He lights another cigarette.*] . .

[*Sounds of vociferous greeting outside. "Ach mein lieber Herr Feydak . . ."* MELCHIOR FEYDAK, *the Austrian composer, comes in. He is forty-five, tall, hook-nosed, thin-faced, a humorist with a rather sad face.*]

FEYDAK. Nun, Minnie, und wo is die schlechte. . . . ?[1] [MINNIE *makes a sign to him not to disclose their free-masonry in the presence of strangers. She is cautious. . . .*] Not home yet, eh, Minnie? Where

---

[1] *Nun . . . schlechte?* Now, Minnie, where is the bad girl?

is she? Well—well. How do they say—gallivanting—I love that word
—gallivanting as usual. Well, I'll wait. It's humiliating—but I'll wait.
Chilly! Brr! I don't mind so much being cold in London or Vienna.
I expect it. But I can't stand it in New York. [*He warms himself
before fire.*] And who is this young man?

MINNIE [*shortly*]. Ich weiss nicht! . . . Er hat alle fünf Minuten
gefragt wo Sie ist—[1] [*She goes out.*]

FEYDAK. You've offended Minnie, I can see that.

KURT. That's just too bad!

FEYDAK. We all tremble before Minnie. . . . Been waiting long?

KURT. Over half an hour!

FEYDAK. Extraordinary thing—ever since I've known Marion there's
always been someone waiting for her. There are two kinds of people
in one's life—people whom one keeps waiting—and the people for
whom one waits. . . .

KURT. Is that an epigram?

FEYDAK. Do you object to epigrams?

KURT [*with some pride*]. I despise epigrams.

FEYDAK [*tolerantly sizing* KURT *up*]. Hm! Friend of Miss Froude's?

KURT. Not at all.

FEYDAK. That at least is no cause for pride.

KURT. I just don't happen to be, that's all.

FEYDAK. I commiserate you.

KURT. I despise gallantry also.

FEYDAK [*lightly*]. And I thought Americans were so sentimental. . . .

KURT. And, together with other forms of glibness, I loathe generalization. . . .

FEYDAK [*drily*]. Young man, we have a great deal in common.

KURT. Also, there is a faint flavor of condescension in the way you
say "young man" for which I don't really care. . . .

FEYDAK [*delighted and encouraging him to go on*]. What about
me do you like? There must be something.

KURT. If I were that kind your question would embarrass me.

FEYDAK [*very pleased*]. Good for Marion!

KURT. Why do you say that?

FEYDAK. She always had a knack for picking up originals!

KURT. You are under a misapprehension. Miss Froude did not pick
me up. I picked her up. [FEYDAK *stares at him. This does shock him.*]

[1] *Ich . . . ist, I don't know. He's been asking every five minutes where she is.*

I wrote Miss Froude a letter—a business-letter. She answered and gave me an appointment for four-thirty. It is now after five. She has taken a half-hour out of my life. . . .

FEYDAK. I gather that fragment of time has great value. . . .

KURT. She has shortened my life by thirty minutes. God, how I hate Bohemians!

FEYDAK [*innocently*]. Are you by any chance—an Evangelist?

KURT. I am—for the moment—a businessman. I'm not here to hold hands or drink tea. I'm here on business. My presence here is a favor to Miss Froude and likely to bring her a handsome profit. . . .

FEYDAK. Profit! Ah! That accounts for her being late. . . .

KURT [*sceptically*]. You despise profit, I suppose! Are you—by any chance—old-world?

FEYDAK. Young man, your technique is entirely wasted on me. . . .

KURT. Technique! What are you talking about?

FEYDAK. When I was a young man—before I achieved any sort of success—I was rude on principle. Deliberately rude and extravagantly bitter in order to make impression. When it is no longer necessary for you to wait around for people in order to do them favors you'll mellow down, I assure you.

KURT [*fiercely, he has been touched*]. You think so, do you! That's where you're mistaken! I'm rude now. When I'm successful I'll be murderous!

FEYDAK [*genially*]. More power to you! But I've never seen it happen yet. Success is the great muffler! Not an epigram, I hope. If it is—forgive me.

[*A moment's pause.* KURT *studies him while* FEYDAK *crosses to stove and warms his hands.*]

KURT. I know you from somewhere. It's very tantalizing.

FEYDAK. I don't think so. I have only just arrived in this country. . . .

KURT. Still I know you—I'm sure—I've seen you somewhere. . . .

FEYDAK [*understanding the familiarity*]. Maybe you know Miss Froude's portrait of me. . . .

KURT [*doubtfully*]. Yes—maybe that's it . . . may I ask . . . ?

FEYDAK. Certainly. My name is Feydak.

KURT. The composer?

FEYDAK [*drily*]. Yes. . . .

KURT. I thought he was dead. . . .

FEYDAK. That is true. But I hope you won't tell anyone—for I am his ghost. . . .

KURT [*putting this down for Continental humor and genuinely contrite*]. Forgive me. . . .

FEYDAK. But why?

KURT. If you really are Feydak the composer—I have the most enormous admiration for you. I worship music above everything.

FEYDAK [*slightly bored*]. Go on. . . .

KURT. I read in the paper—you're on your way to Hollywood. . . .

FEYDAK. Yes. I am on my way to Hollywood. . . .

KURT. In the new state men like you won't have to prostitute themselves in Hollywood. . . .

FEYDAK. Ah! A Utopian!

KURT. Yes. You use the word as a term of contempt. Why? Every artist is a Utopian. You must be very tired or you wouldn't be so contemptuous of Utopians.

FEYDAK [*with a charming smile*]. I am rather tired. Old-world, you would call it.

KURT. You can be anything you like. . . .

FEYDAK [*satirically*]. Thank you. . . .

KURT. You've written lovely music—I have a friend who plays every note of it. I didn't see your operetta when it was done here. . . . I didn't have the price . . . it was very badly done though, I heard. . . .

FEYDAK. I must explain to you—you are under a misapprehension. . . .

KURT. It was done here, wasn't it?

FEYDAK. Not about the operetta. You are under a misapprehension —about me. I am a composer—but I didn't write "Danubia." That was my brother, Victor Feydak. You are right. He is dead. You are the first person I have met in New York who even suspected it.

KURT. I'm sorry.

FEYDAK. Not at all. I am flattered. At home our identities were never confused. Is this the well-known American hospitality? It is, in some sort, compensation for his death. . . .

[KURT *is embarrassed and uncomfortable. It is part of his essential insecurity; he is only really at home in protest. He wants to get out.*]

KURT. I'm sorry—I. . . .

FEYDAK [*easily*]. But why?

KURT. I think I'll leave a note for Miss Froude—get that girl in here, will you?

FEYDAK. Let's have some tea—she's sure to be in any minute. . . .

KURT. No, thanks. And you might tell her for me that if she wants to see me about the matter I wrote her about she can come to my office. . . .

[MARION FROUDE *comes in. She is one of those women the sight of whom on Fifth Ave., where she has just been walking, causes foreigners to exclaim enthusiastically that American women are the most radiant in the world. She is tall, lithe, indomitably alive. Unlike* KURT, *the tears in things have warmed without scalding her; she floats life like a dancer's scarf in perpetual enjoyment of its colors and contours.*]

MARION [*to* KURT]. I'm *so* sorry!

FEYDAK [*coming toward her*]. I don't believe a word of it!
[*She is overjoyed at seeing* FEYDAK. *She can't believe for a second that it is he. Then she flies into his arms.*]

MARION. Feydie! Oh, Feydie, I've been trying everywhere to reach you—I can't believe it. . . . Feydie darling!

FEYDAK [*severely*]. Is this how you keep a business appointment, Miss Froude?

MARION. How long have you waited? If I'd only known. . . . [*Suddenly conscious that* KURT *had waited too*] Oh, I'm sorry, Mr.—Mr.— . . . ?

KURT. Kurt. Richard Kurt.

MARION. Oh, of course, Mr. Kurt. I say—could you possibly—would it be too much trouble—could you come back?

FEYDAK [*same tone*]. This young man is here on business. It is more important. I can wait. I'll come back.

MARION. No, no, Feydie—no, no. I can't wait for that. I'm sure Mr. Kurt will understand. Mr. Feydak is an old friend whom I haven't seen in ever so long. It isn't as if Mr. Kurt were a regular business-man.

FEYDAK [*amused*]. How do you know he isn't?

MARION [*breathless with excitement*]. I can tell. He's not a bit like his letter. When I got your letter I was sure you were jowley and, you know—[*she makes a gesture*]—convex. I'm sure, Feydie—whatever the business is—[*to* KURT]—you did say you had some, didn't you?—I'm sure it can wait. A half-hour anyway. Can't it wait a half-hour? You see, Feydie and I haven't seen each other since. . . .

KURT. Vienna!

MARION [*astonished*]. Yes. How did you know?

KURT. It's always since Vienna that Bohemians haven't seen each other, isn't it? I'll be back in thirty minutes. [*He goes.*]

MARION. What a singular young man!

FEYDAK. I've been having a very amusing talk with him. Professional rebel, I think. Well, my dear—you look marvelous!

[*They take each other in.*]

MARION. Isn't it wonderful. . . .

FEYDAK. It is nice!

[*They sit on sofa,* MARION *left of* FEYDAK.]

MARION. How long is it?

FEYDAK. Well, it's since. . . .

MARION [*firmly*]. Since Vicki died.

FEYDAK. That's right. I haven't seen you since.

MARION. Since that day—we walked behind him.

FEYDAK. Yes.

MARION. I felt I couldn't bear to stay on. I left for London that night.

FEYDAK. Yes.

MARION. It's six years, isn't it?

FEYDAK. Yes. Six years last June.

[*A pause*]

MARION. What's happened since then? Nothing. . . .

FEYDAK. How long have you been here?

MARION. Two weeks.

FEYDAK. Busy?

MARION. Not professionally, I'm afraid. People are charming—they ask me to lunch and dinner and they're—"oh, so interested"—but no commissions so far. And God, how I need it. . . .

FEYDAK. I'm surprised. I gathered you'd been very successful.

MARION. It's always sounded like it, hasn't it? The impression, I believe, is due to the extreme notoriety of some of my sitters. Oh, I've managed well enough up to now—if I'd been more provident I dare say I could have put a tidy bit by—but at the moment people don't seem in a mood to have their portraits done. Are they less vain than they used to be? Or just poorer?

FEYDAK. Both, I think. . . .

MARION. Last time I came here I was awfully busy. Had great réclame because I'd been in Russia doing leading Communists. Obeying some subtle paradox the big financiers flocked to me. Pittsburgh manufacturers wanted to be done by the same brush that had tackled Lenin. Now they seem less eager. Must be some reason, Feydie. But what about you? Let me hear about you. How's Kathie?

FEYDAK. Well. She's here with me.

MARION. And Sadye?

FEYDAK. Splendid.

MARION. She must be a big girl now.

FEYDAK. As tall as you are.

MARION. Kathie used to hate me, didn't she? Frightened to death of me. Was afraid I was after Vicki's money. . . .

FEYDAK. Yes. She was afraid you'd marry him and that we should have less from him. When we knew he was dying she was in a panic.

MARION. Poor dear—I could have spared her all that worry if she'd been halfway civil to me.

FEYDAK. Kathie is practical. And she is a good mother. Those are attributes which make women avaricious.

MARION. Did Vicki leave you very much?

FEYDAK. Not very much. Half to you.

MARION. Really? How sweet of him! How dear of him!

FEYDAK. We've spent it. . . .

MARION. Of course you should.

FEYDAK. But I'll soon be in position to repay you your share. I'm on my way to Hollywood.

MARION. Are you really? How wonderful for you, Feydie! I'm so glad.

FEYDAK. You've been there, haven't you?

MARION. Yes. Last time I was in America.

FEYDAK. Did you like it?

MARION. Well, it's the new Eldorado—art on the gold-rush.

FEYDAK [*with a kind of ironic bitterness*]. Vicki left me an inheritance subject, it appears, to perpetual renewal.

MARION. How do you mean?

FEYDAK. Things have been going from bad to worse in Vienna— you haven't been there since '25 so you don't know. The theatre's pretty well dead—even the first-rate fellows have had a hard time making their way. I managed to get several scores to do—but they were not—except that they were failures—up to my usual standard. . . .

MARION [*laughing, reproachful*]. Oh, Feydie . . . !

FEYDAK. If it weren't for the money Vicki left me—and you!—I don't know how we should have got through at all these six years. About a month ago we reached the end of our rope—we were hopelessly in debt—no means of getting out—when the miracle happened. . . .

[MARION *is excited, touches his knee with her hand.*]

MARION [*murmuring*]. I can't bear it. . . .

FEYDAK. It was my dramatic agent on the phone. A great American film magnate was in town and wanted to see me. Ausgerechnet me and no other. Even my agent couldn't keep the surprise out of his voice. Why me? I asked. God knows, says the agent. Well, we went around to the Bristol to see the magnate. And, as we talked to him, it gradually became apparent. He thought I was Vicki. He didn't know Vicki was dead! He thought I had written "Danubia."

MARION. Did he say so?

FEYDAK. No—not at all. But as we shook hands at the end he said to me: "Any man that can write a tune like this is the kind of man we want." And he whistled, so out of tune that I could hardly recognize it myself, the waltz from Danubia. Do you remember it? [*He starts to hum the waltz and* MARION *joins him. They hum together, then* FEYDAK *continues to talk as* MARION *continues to hum a few more measures.*] He was so innocent, so affable that I had an impulse to say to him: "Look here, old fellow, you don't want me, you want my brother and, in order to get him, you'll have to resurrect him!" But noble impulses are luxury impulses. You have to be well off to gratify them. I kept quiet. We shook hands and here I am. Tonight they're giving me a dinner at the Waldorf Astoria for the press to meet my brother! Irony if you like, eh, Marion?

[*There is a pause.*]

MARION. Feydie . . . [*A moment. He does not answer.*] Feydie—do you mind if I say something to you—very frankly?

FEYDAK. I doubt whether you can say anything to me more penetrating than the remarks I habitually address to myself.

MARION. You know Vicki was very fond of you. He used to say you put too high a valuation on genius.

FEYDAK. Because he had it he could afford to deprecate it.

MARION. Over and over again he used to say to me: "You know, Marion," he would say, "as a human being Feydie's far superior to me, more amiable, more witty, more talented, more patient. . . ."

FEYDAK [*shakes his head*]. Not true. I simply give the impression of these things. . . .

MARION. You underrate yourself, Feydie. . . . How this would have amused him—this incident with the Hollywood man!

FEYDAK [*smiling bitterly*]. It would rather. . . .

MARION. Why do you grudge giving him a laugh somewhere? I never had a chance to tell you in Vienna—things were so—so close and terrible—at the end—but he had the greatest tenderness for you.

He used to speak of you—I can't tell you how much. "Because of this sixth sense for making tunes which I have and he hasn't," he said to me one day—not a week before he died— "he thinks himself less than me." He used to tell me that everything he had he owed to you—to the sacrifices you made to send him to the Conservatory when he was a boy. . . . The extent to which he had outstripped you hurt him—hurt him. I felt he would have given anything to dip into the golden bowl of his genius and pour it over you. And do you know what was the terror of his life, the obsessing terror of his life? —his fear of your resenting him. . . .

FEYDAK [*moved, deeply ashamed*]. Marion. . . .

MARION. Don't resent him now, Feydie. . . . Why, it's such fun— don't you see? It's such a curious, marginal survival for him—that a badly-remembered waltz-tune, five years after his death, should be the means of helping you at a moment when you need it so badly. . . . It's delicious, Feydie. It's such fun! The only awful thing is the possibility that he is unaware of it. It would have pleased him so, Feydie. Must you grudge him it?

FEYDAK. You make me horribly ashamed. . . .

MARION [*brightly*]. Nonsense. . . .

FEYDAK. Because I did grudge him it—yes—I won't, though—I see now that it never occurred to me how . . . [*Bursts out laughing suddenly*] God, it is funny, isn't it. . . .

MARION [*joining in his laughter*]. Of course—it's delightful. . . .
[*They both laugh heartily and long.*]

MARION. And the funny thing is—you'll be much better for them out there than he would have been.

FEYDAK. Surely! They'll be able to whistle *my* tunes!

MARION. Don't you see!

FEYDAK. Oh, Lieber Schatzel,[1] come out there with me.

MARION. Can't.

FEYDAK. I wish, Marion, you would come. I never feel life so warm and good as when you are in the neighborhood.

MARION. Dear Feydie, you're very comforting.

FEYDAK. Is there someone that keeps you here?

MARION. No, there's no one. I'm quite alone.

FEYDAK. Well then . . . !

MARION. No, this isn't the moment for me, Feydie. Besides, I can't afford the journey. I'm frightfully hard up[2] at the moment.

---

[1] *Lieber Schatzel, darling.*
[2] *hard up, a plant leading to Marion's acceptance of Kurt's offer soon after.*

FEYDAK. Well, look here, I . . .

MARION. No, that's sweet of you but I couldn't.

FEYDAK. I don't see why—it's too silly. . . .

MARION. Vanity. A kind of vanity.

FEYDAK. But I owe it to you!

MARION. I suppose it is foolish in a way—but I've a kind of pride in maneuvering on my own. I always have done it—in that way at least I've been genuinely independent. I'm a little proud of my ingenuity. And do you know, Feydie, no matter how hard up I've been at different times something's always turned up for me. I have a kind of curiosity to know what it will be this time. It would spoil the fun for me to take money from my friends. Nothing so much as that would make me doubtful of my own—shall we say—marketability?

FEYDAK. Paradoxical, isn't it?

MARION. Why not? Anyway, it's a pet idée of mine, so be a darling and let me indulge it, will you, Feydie, and don't offer me money. Anyway, I've a business proposition on. . . .

FEYDAK. Have you?

MARION. That young man who was just here. Do you suppose he'll come back? Now I think of it we were a bit short with him, weren't we? I was so glad to see you I couldn't be bothered with him! [*Sound of doorbell*] Ah! You see! [*Calls outside*] Show him in, Minnie!

[MINNIE *comes in and exits hall door to admit the visitor.*]

FEYDAK. What are you doing for dinner?

MARION. There's a young man who attached himself to me on the boat.

FEYDAK. Oh, Marion!

MARION. I seem to attract youth, Feydie. What shall I do about it?

FEYDAK. Where are you dining?

MARION. I don't know. . . . Which speakeasy? Tell me which one and I'll . . .

[MINNIE *ushers in* MR. LEANDER NOLAN. *He is middle-aged, ample, handsome. Looks like the late Warren Gamaliel Harding.*[1] *Soberly dressed and wears a waistcoat with white piping on it. The façade is impeccable but in* NOLAN'S *eye you may discern, at odd moments, an uncertainty, an almost boyish anxiety to please, to be right, that is rather engaging.* MARION, *who expected the young man, is rather startled.* MR. NOLAN *regards her with satisfaction.*]

[1] *Warren Gamaliel Harding. The twenty-ninth president of the United States was a handsome middle-aged man, but otherwise undistinguished.*

NOLAN. Hello, Marion.

MARION [*doubtfully, feels she should remember him*]. How do you do? Er—will you excuse me—just a second . . . ?

NOLAN [*genially*]. Certainly. [*He moves right.* MARION *walks* FEYDIE *to the hall door.*]

FEYDAK [*under his breath to her*]. Looks like a commission. [*She makes a gesture of silent prayer.*]

MARION [*out loud*]. Telephone me in an hour, will you, Feydie, and let me know which speakeasy. . . .

FEYDAK [*once he has her in the hallway out of* NOLAN's *hearing*]. Also, du kommst ganz sicher?[1]

MARION. Vielleicht später.[2] 'Bye, Feydie dear.

[FEYDIE *goes out.* MARION *turns to face* NOLAN *who is standing with his arms behind his back rather enjoying the surprise he is about to give her.*]

NOLAN. How are you, Marion?

MARION [*delicately*]. Er—do I know you?

NOLAN. Yes. You know me.

MARION. Oh, yes—of course!

NOLAN. About time!

MARION [*brightly insecure*]. Lady Winchester's garden-party at Ascot—two summers ago. . . .

NOLAN. Guess again!

MARION. No—I know you perfectly well—it's just that—no, don't tell me. . . . [*She covers her eyes with her hand, trying to conjure him out of the past.*]

NOLAN. This is astonishing. If someone had said to me that I could walk into a room in front of Marion Froude and she not know me I'd have told 'em they were crazy . . . !

MARION [*desperate*]. I do know you. I know you perfectly well —it's just that . . .

NOLAN. You'll be awful sore at yourself—I warn you . . .

MARION. I can't forgive myself now—I know!

NOLAN. I don't believe it!

MARION. The American Embassy dinner in Rome on the Fourth of July—last year—you sat on my right.

NOLAN. I did not!

MARION [*miserably*]. Well, you sat somewhere. Where did you sit?

[1] *Also . . . sicher? So you'll come for sure?*
[2] *Vielleicht später, maybe later.*

NOLAN. I wasn't there.

MARION. Well, I think it's very unkind of you to keep me in suspense like this. I can't bear it another second!

NOLAN. I wouldn't have believed it!

MARION. Well, give me some hint, will you?

NOLAN. Think of home—think of Tennessee!

MARION. Oh . . . !

NOLAN. Little Mary Froude. . . .

MARION. [*a light breaking in on her*]. No! Oh, no!

NOLAN. Well, it's about time. . . .

MARION. But . . . ! You were . . .

NOLAN. Well, so were you!

MARION. But—Bunny—you aren't Bunny Nolan, are you? You're his brother!

NOLAN. I have no brother.

MARION. But Bunny—Bunny dear—how important you've become!

NOLAN. I haven't done badly—no.

MARION. Here, give me your coat and hat— [MARION, *taking his coat and hat, crosses upstage to piano, and leaves them there. Laughing, a little hysterical*] You should have warned me. It's not fair of you. Bunny! Of all people—I can scarcely believe it. . . . [*A moment's pause. He doesn't quite like her calling him Bunny but he doesn't know how to stop it. She sits on model stand looking up at him as she says*] You look wonderful. You look like a—like a—Senator or something monumental like that.

NOLAN [*sits on sofa below piano*]. That's a good omen. I'll have to tell Orrin.

MARION. What's a good omen? And who is Orrin?

NOLAN. Your saying I look like a Senator. Because—I don't want to be premature—but in a few months I may be one.

MARION. A Senator!

NOLAN [*smiling*]. Senator. Washington. Not Nashville.

MARION. Do you want to be a Senator or can't you help it?

NOLAN [*to whom this point of view is incomprehensible*]. What do you mean?

MARION. I'll paint you, Bunny. Toga. Ferrule. Tribune of the people.

NOLAN. Not a bad idea. Not a bad idea at all. I remember now—you were always sketching me. Sketching everything. Say, you've done pretty well yourself, haven't you?

MARION. Not as well as you have, Bunny. Imagine. Bunny Nolan

—a Senator at Washington. Well, well! And tell me—how do I seem to you? You knew me at once, didn't you?

NOLAN. Sure I did. You haven't changed so much—a little, perhaps.

MARION [*delicately*]. Ampler?

NOLAN [*inspecting her*]. No . . . not that I can notice. . . .

MARION [*with a sigh of relief*]. That's wonderful. . . .

NOLAN. You look just the same. You are just the same.

MARION. Oh, you don't know, Bunny. I'm artful. How long is it since we've seen each other? Twelve years anyway. More than that —fifteen . . .

NOLAN. Just about—hadn't even begun to practice law yet. . . .

MARION. We were just kids . . . children. . . . And now look at you! I can see how successful you are, Bunny.

NOLAN. How?

MARION. White piping on your vest. That suggests directorates to me. Multiple control. Vertical corporations. Are you vertical or horizontal, Bunny?

NOLAN. I'm both.

MARION. Good for you! Married?

NOLAN. Not yet . . .

MARION. How did you escape? You're going to be, though.

NOLAN. I'm engaged.

MARION. Who's the lucky girl?

NOLAN. Slade Kinnicott. Daughter of Orrin Kinnicott.

MARION. Orrin Kinnicott. The newspaper publisher?

NOLAN. Yes. He's backing me for the Senate.

MARION. Well, if he's backing you you ought to get in. All that circulation—not very good circulation, is it? Still, one vote's as good as another, I suppose. . . .

NOLAN [*hurt*]. In my own State the Kinnicott papers are as good as any . . .

MARION. Well, I wish you luck. I'm sure you'll have it. My! Senator Nolan!

NOLAN. If I get in I'll be the youngest Senator . . .

MARION. And the best-looking too, Bunny . . .

NOLAN [*embarrassed*]. Well . . .

MARION. You're fussed! How charming of you! [*She sits beside him.*] Oh, Bunny, I'm very proud of you, really.

NOLAN. You see, Marion, I've been pretty successful in the law. Tremendously successful, I may say. I've organized some of the biggest mergers of recent years. I've made a fortune—a sizeable fortune. Well, one day I woke up and I said to myself: Look here, Nolan, you've got to take stock. You've got to ask yourself where you're heading. I'd been so busy I'd never had a chance to ask myself these fundamental questions before. And I decided to call a halt. You've got enough, more than enough for life, I said to myself. It's time you quit piling up money for yourself and began thinking about your fellow-man. I've always been ambitious, Marion. You know that. You shared all my early dreams . . .

MARION. Of course I did. . . .

NOLAN. Remember I always told you I didn't want money and power for their own sakes—I always wanted to be a big man in a real sense—to do something for my country and my time . . .

MARION. Yes. Sometimes you sounded like Daniel Webster, darling. I'm not a bit surprised you're going in the Senate.

NOLAN. I never thought—even in my wildest dreams. . . .

MARION. Well, you see you underestimated yourself. You may go even higher—the White House—why not?

NOLAN. I never let myself think of that.

MARION. Why not? It's no more wonderful than what's happened already, is it?

NOLAN [Napoleon at Saint Helena]. Destiny!

MARION. Exactly. Destiny!

NOLAN [kind, richly human, patronizing]. And you, my dear . . . ?

MARION. As you see. Obscure. Uncertain. Alone. Nowhere at all. Not the remotest chance of my getting into the Senate—unless I marry into it. Oh, Bunny, after you get to Washington will you introduce me to some Senators?

NOLAN. Well, that's premature . . . Naturally if the people should favor me I'd do what I could. I never forget a friend. Whatever faults I may have, disloyalty, I hope, is not one of them.

MARION. Of course it isn't. You're a dear. You always were.

[A moment's pause.]

NOLAN. Who was that fellow I found you with when I came in?

MARION. An old friend of mine from Vienna—a composer.

NOLAN. You've been a lot with foreigners, haven't you?

MARION. A good deal . . .

NOLAN. Funny, I don't understand that.

MARION. Foreigners are people, you know, Bunny. Some of 'em are rather nice.

NOLAN. When I'm abroad a few weeks home begins to look pretty good to me.

MARION. I love New York but I can't say I feel an acute nostalgia for Tennessee.

> [*Another pause. He stares at her suddenly—still incredulous that he should be seeing her at all, and that, after all these years and quite without him, she should be radiant still.*]

NOLAN. Little Marion Froude! I can't believe it somehow. . . .

MARION. Oh, Bunny! You're sweet! You're so—ingenuous. That's what I always liked about you.

NOLAN. What do you mean?

MARION. The way you look at me, the incredulity, the surprise. What did you expect to see? A hulk, a remnant, a whitened sepulchre . . . what?

NOLAN [*uncomfortable at being caught*]. Not—not at all. . . .

MARION. Tell me, Bunny, what . . . ? I won't be hurt . . .

NOLAN [*miserably, stumbling*]. Well, naturally, after what I'd heard . . .

MARION. What have you heard? Oh, do tell me, Bunny.

NOLAN. Well, I mean—about your life. . . .

MARION. Racy, Bunny? Racy?

NOLAN. No use going into that. You chose your own way. Everybody has a right to live their own life, I guess.

MARION [*pats his arm*]. That's very handsome of you Bunny. I hope you take that liberal point of view when you reach the Senate.

NOLAN. I came here, Marion, in a perfectly sincere mood, to say something to you, something that's been on my mind ever since we parted, but if you're going to be flippant I suppose there's no my saying anything—I might as well go, in fact. [*But he makes no attempt to do so.*]

MARION [*seriously*]. Do forgive me, Bunny. One gets into an idiom that passes for banter but really I'm not so changed. I'm not flippant. I'm awfully glad to see you, Bunny. [*An undertone of sadness creeps into her voice.*] After all, one makes very few real friends in life—and you are part of my youth—we are part of each other's youth . . .

NOLAN. You didn't even know me!

MARION. Complete surprise! After all I've been in New York many times during these years and never once—never once have you come near me. You've dropped me all these years. [*With a sigh*] I'm afraid, Bunny, your career has been too much with you.

NOLAN [*grimly*]. So has yours!

520 S. N. *Behrman*

MARION. I detect an overtone—faint but unmistakable—of moral censure.

NOLAN [*same tone*]. Well, I suppose it's impossible to live one's life in art without being sexually promiscuous! [*He looks at her accusingly.*]

MARION. Oh, dear me, Bunny! What shall I do? Shall I blush? Shall I hang my head in shame? What shall I do? How does one react in the face of an appalling accusation of this sort? I didn't know the news had got around so widely . . .

NOLAN. Well, so many of your lovers have been famous men. . . .

MARION. Well, you were obscure . . . But you're famous now, aren't you? I seem to be stimulating if nothing else . . .

NOLAN. If I had then some of the fame I have now you probably wouldn't have walked out on me at the last minute the way you did . . .

MARION. Dear, dear Bunny, that's not quite—

NOLAN [*irritated beyond control*]. I wish you wouldn't call me Bunny. . . .

MARION. Well, I always did. What is your real name?

NOLAN. You know perfectly well . . .

MARION. I swear I don't. . . .

NOLAN. My name is Leander. . . .

MARION. Bunny, really. . . .

NOLAN. That is my name.

MARION. Really I'd forgotten that. Leander![1] Who was he—he did something in the Hellespont, didn't he? What did he do in the Hellespont?

NOLAN [*sharply*]. Beside the point.

MARION. Sorry! You say you wanted to tell me something—

NOLAN [*grimly*]. Yes!

MARION. I love to be told things.

NOLAN. That night you left me—

MARION. We'd quarrelled about something, hadn't we?

NOLAN. I realized after you left me how much I'd grown to depend on you—

MARION. Dear Bunny!

NOLAN. I plunged into work. I worked fiercely to forget you. I did forget you— [*He looks away from her.*] And yet—

[1] *Leander. According to the Greek myth the handsome youth Leander swam the Hellespont by night to see his beloved Hero on the opposite shore.*

MARION. And yet—?

NOLAN. The way we'd separated and I never heard from you—it left something bitter in my mind—something— [*He hesitates for a word.*]

MARION [*supplying it*]. Unresolved?

NOLAN [*Quickly—relieved that she understands so exactly*]. Yes. All these years I've wanted to see you, to get it off my mind—

MARION. Did you want the last word, Bunny dear?

NOLAN [*fiercely*]. I wanted to see you, to stand before you, to tell myself—"Here she is and—and what of it!"

MARION. Well, can you?

NOLAN [*heatedly, with transparent overemphasis*]. Yes! Yes!

MARION. Good for you, Bunny. I know just how you feel—like having a tooth out, isn't it? [*Sincerely*] In justice to myself—I must tell you this—that the reason I walked out on you in the summary way I did was not, as you've just suggested, because I doubted your future—it was obvious to me, even then, that you were destined for mighty things—but the reason was that I felt a disparity in our characters not conducive to matrimonial contentment. You see how right I was. I suspected in myself a—a tendency to explore, a spiritual and physical wanderlust—that I knew would horrify you once you found it out. It horrifies you now when we are no longer anything to each other. Imagine, Leander dear, if we were married how much more difficult it would be— If there is any one thing you have to be grateful to me for it is that instant's clear vision I had which made me see, which made me look ahead, which made me tear myself away from you. Why, everything you have now—your future, your prospects—even your fiancée, Leander dear—you owe to me—no, I won't say to me—to that instinct—to that premonition. . . .

NOLAN [*nostalgic*]. We might have done it together. . . .

MARION. I wouldn't have stood for a fiancée, Bunny dear—not even I am as promiscuous as that. . . .

NOLAN. Don't use that word!

MARION. But, Leander! It's your own!

NOLAN. Do you think it hasn't been on my conscience ever since, do you think it hasn't tortured me . . . !

MARION. What, dear?

NOLAN. That thought!

MARION. Which thought?

NOLAN. Every time I heard about you—all the notoriety that's attended you in the American papers . . . painting pictures of Communist statesmen, running around California with movie comedians!

MARION. I have to practice my profession, Bunny. One must live, you know. Besides, I've done Capitalist statesmen too. And at Geneva. . . .

NOLAN [*darkly*]. You know what I mean . . . !

MARION. You mean—[*she whispers through her cupped hand*]— you mean promiscuous? Has that gotten around, Bunny? Is it whispered in the sewing-circles of Nashville? Will I be burned for a witch if I go back home? Will they have a trial over me? Will you defend me?

NOLAN [*quite literally, with sincere and disarming simplicity*]. I should be forced, as an honest man, to stand before the multitude and say: In condemning this woman you are condemning me who am asking your suffrages to represent you. For it was I with whom this woman first sinned before God. As an honorable man that is what I should have to do.

MARION. And has this worried you—actually . . . !

NOLAN. It's tortured me . . . !

MARION. You're the holy man and I'm Thais![1] That gives me an idea for the portrait which I hope you will commission me to do. I'll do you in a hair-shirt. Savonarola.[2] He was a Senator too, wasn't he? Or was he?

NOLAN [*gloomily contemplating her*]. I can't forget that it was I who . . .

MARION. Did you think you were the first, Bunny? Was I so unscrupulously coquettish as to lead you to believe that I—oh, I couldn't have been. It's not like me. [*She crosses to right of model stand.*]

NOLAN [*fiercely*]. Don't lie to me!

MARION [*sitting on stand*]. Bunny, you frighten me!

NOLAN [*stands over her almost threateningly*]. You're lying to me to salve my conscience but I won't have it! I know my guilt and I'm going to bear it!

MARION. Well, I don't want to deprive you of your little pleasures but . . .

---

[1] **holy man . . . Thais.** *In the novel of Anatole France, Thais, a beautiful courtesan of Alexandria, is converted to Christianity by the young monk Paphnutius, who is at the same time tempted into an earthly love for her.*

[2] **Savonarola** *(1452-1498), the fiery religious reformer of Florence.*

NOLAN. You're evil, Marion. You haven't the face of evil but you're evil—evil!

MARION. Oh, Bunny darling, now you can't mean that surely. What's come over you? You never were like that—or were you? You know perfectly well I'm not evil. Casual—maybe—but not evil. Good Heavens, Bunny, I might as well say you're evil because you're intolerant. These are differences in temperament, that's all—charming differences in temperament.

NOLAN [*shakes his head, unconvinced*]. Sophistry!

MARION. All right, Dean Inge.[1] Sophistry. By the way I've met the Gloomy Dean and he's not gloomy at all—he's very jolly. [*Gets up from stand*] Let's have a cup of tea, shall we? Will your constituents care if you have a cup of tea with a promiscuous woman? Will they have to know?

NOLAN. I'm afraid I can't, Marion. I have to be getting on. . . .

MARION. Oh, stay and have some tea— [*Makes him sit down*] What do you have to do that can't wait for a cup of tea? . . . [*Calls off*] Minnie—Minnie. . . .

MINNIE [*appears in doorway*]. Ja, Fräulein. . . .

MARION. Bitte—Thee. . . .[2]

MINNIE. Ja, Fräulein. . . . [*She goes out.* MARION *smiles at* NOLAN *and sits beside him. He is quite uncomfortable.*]

NOLAN [*slightly embarrassed*]. About the painting, Marion. . . .

MARION. Oh, I was only joking . . . don't let yourself be bullied into it . . .

NOLAN. I've never been painted in oils. It might do for campaign purposes. And, if I should be elected, it would be very helpful to you in Washington.

MARION. You're awfully kind, Bunny. I must tell you frankly though that the dignified Senatorial style isn't exactly my forte. However, I might try. Yes—I'll try . . . [*She gives him a long look.*] I'll go the limit on you, Bunny—when I get through with you you'll be a symbol of Dignity. Solid man. No nonsense. Safe and sane. Holds the middle course—a slogan in a frock-coat. I'll make you look like Warren G. Harding—even handsomer— Get you the women's votes.

NOLAN. Well, that'll be very nice of you. . . .

[1] *Dean Inge, of St. Paul's, London, an Anglican prelate popularly known as the Gloomy Dean.*
[2] *Bitte—Thee, please, tea.*

[MARION *suddenly kisses him.*]

MARION. Thank you, darling! [*He is very uncomfortable, embarrassed and thrilled.*]

NOLAN. Marion . . . !

MARION. Just a rush of feeling, dear!

NOLAN. You understand that this—this commission . . .

MARION. Of course. Strictly business. Don't worry. I shan't kiss you again till it's finished.

NOLAN. I don't know whether I told you—I'm going to be married in a month.

MARION. I'll have the portrait ready for your wedding-day.

NOLAN. And I am devoted to Slade with ever fibre of my being. . . .

MARION. Every fibre—how thorough!

NOLAN. I'm not a Bohemian, you know, Marion.

MARION. Don't tell me! You're a gypsy! [*She continues to study him, poses him, poses his hand.* MINNIE *enters from left with tea tray containing teapot, cups and saucers, spoons, sugar and cream, and a plate of cakes. She puts tray on model stand and exits left.*] Oh, Bunny, what fun it'll be to do you. Thank you, Minnie. Tell me—how do you see yourself?

NOLAN. What do you mean?

MARION. In your heart of hearts—how do you see yourself? Napoleon, Scipio, Mussolini . . . ?

NOLAN. Nonsense! Do you think I'm an actor?

MARION. Of course. Everybody is. Everybody has some secret vision of himself. Do you know what mine is? Do you know how I see myself?

[*The doorbell rings.*]

NOLAN [*ironically*]. More visitors!

MARION [*calls to* MINNIE]. See who it is, will you, Minnie? . . . Probably the young man I met on the boat coming to take me to dinner.

NOLAN. What's his name?

MARION. I've forgotten. He's just a boy I met on the boat.

NOLAN. How can anybody live the way you live?

MARION. It's a special talent, dear. [*Doorbell rings again.*] Minnie, go to the door. [MINNIE *comes in and exits hallway.*] This is my lucky day, Bunny.

NOLAN. Would you mind, in front of strangers, not calling me Bunny?

MARION. Oh, of course, what is it?

NOLAN [*irritated*]. Leander.

MARION [*mnemonic*]. Leander—Hellespont—Leander. . . .

[MINNIE *comes downstage a few feet from the door.*]

MINNIE [*just inside the room*]. It's the Junge[1] who was here before—er sagt er ist ausgeschifft da—[2]

MARION. Oh, show him in, Minnie, and bring a cup for him too.

MINNIE [*as she goes*]. Ja.

NOLAN. And don't use these extravagant terms of endearment—
anybody who didn't know you would misunderstand it. . . .

MARION [*very happy*]. All right, darling. [MINNIE *ushers in*
RICHARD KURT, *goes out, comes back again with more tea.* MARION
comes forward to greet him.] I'm so glad to see you again, Mr.——

KURT. Kurt.

MARION. Oh. . . .

KURT. With a K.

MARION [*reassured*]. Oh—I'll try to remember. This is Senator
Nolan—Mr. Kurt. . . .

NOLAN [*glowering*]. I am not Senator Nolan.

MARION. But you will be. [*She offers him a cup of tea, he takes
it.*] Can't I just call you that—between ourselves? It gives me such
a sense of quiet power. And maybe it'll impress my visitor. Do have
a cup of tea, Mr. Kurt. [*She gives him one.*]

KURT [*puts his hat on sofa left*]. I am not impressed by politicians.
And I didn't come to drink tea. I am here on business. [*Nevertheless he takes a hearty sip.*]

MARION. Well, you can do both. They do in England. American
businessmen are so tense.

KURT. I'm not a businessman.

NOLAN. Well, whatever you are, you are very ill-mannered.

KURT [*pleased*]. That's true!

MARION [*delighted*]. Isn't it nice you agree? For a moment I
thought you weren't going to hit it off. . . .

NOLAN. In my day if a boy came in and behaved like this before a
lady he'd be horsewhipped.

KURT. Well, when you get into the Senate you can introduce a
horsewhipping bill. Probably bring you great kudos.

NOLAN. You talk like a Bolshevik.

KURT. Thank you! You talk like a Senator!

[1] *Junge, boy.*
[2] *er sagt . . . da, he says he has landed there.*

[MARION *wants to laugh but thinks better of it. She looks at* KURT *with a new eye.*]

MARION [*quickly offering him more tea.*] Another cup, Mr. Kurt. . . .

KURT [*taking it*]. Thank you.

MARION. And one of these cakes—they're very nice . . . Minnie made them—almost as good as lebkuchen. Minnie spoils me.

KURT [*taking it*]. Thank you. [*Eats cake*] Having said, from our respective points of view, the worst thing we could say about each other, having uttered the ultimate insult, there's no reason we can't be friends, Senator. Damn good cake. No lunch as a matter of fact.

MARION. That's what's the matter with him—he was hungry —hungry boy. . . .

NOLAN [*puts teacup on piano*]. He probably wants to sell you some insurance. . . .

KURT. Not at all. I'm not here to sell. I'm here to buy.

MARION. A picture!

KURT. Do I look like a picture-buyer?

MARION. As a matter of fact you don't . . . but I haven't anything to sell except pictures.

KURT [*confidently*]. I think you have!

MARION [*to* NOLAN]. This young man is very tantalizing.

NOLAN. Well, why don't you ask him to state his proposition and have done with it?

MARION [*turns to* KURT *and repeats mechanically*]. State your proposition and have done with it.

KURT [*puts his cup down on table rear of sofa left*]. What a nuisance women are!

NOLAN [*starting toward him*]. Why, you insolent young whelp— I've half a mind to . . .

KURT [*pleasantly*]. That's an impulse you'd better control. I wrote this lady a business letter asking for an appointment. She granted it to me at four o'clock. It is now six. In that interval I've climbed these five flights of stairs three times. I've lost over an hour of my life going away and coming back. An hour in which I might have read a first-class book or made love to a girl or had an idea—an irreparable hour. That's rudeness if you like. It's unbusinesslike. It's sloppy. [*To* MARION] Now will you see me alone or will you keep me here fencing with this inadequate antagonist?

MARION. You are unquestionably the most impossible young man I've ever met. Go away!

KURT. Right! [*He turns to go and means it and she knows that he means it. And she is consumed with curiosity. As he goes*] So long, Senator! Yours for the Revolution!

MARION [*as he reaches door, goes after him—pleads pitifully*]. Young man! Mr. Nolan is an old friend of mine. I should consult him in any case about whatever business you may suggest. Can't you speak in front of him? [*At the same time she shakes her head to him not to go away.*]

KURT. I cannot!

MARION. Please wait a minute. . . .

KURT. All right—one. [*He picks up a magazine and leafs through it negligently.*]

MARION [*to* LEANDER]. After all, Leander, I can't afford—it may be something. . . . [*She takes his arm and starts walking him to the door, whispering*] I'm just curious to hear what he's got to say for himself. . . .

NOLAN. I'm not sure it's safe to leave you alone with a character like that. . . .

MARION. Minnie's in her room . . . with a bow and arrow!

NOLAN [*going up to hall door*]. I have to go in any case—I'm late now.

MARION. When will I see you, Bunny? [*She is at door with him.*]

NOLAN [*taking up his hat and coat*]. I don't know. I'm very busy. I'll telephone you.

MARION. Do. Telephone me tonight. I'll tell you what he said. It'll probably be funny.

NOLAN [*out loud at* KURT]. It pains me, Marion, that you are so unprotected that any hooligan—[KURT *turns page of magazine*]— can write you and come to see you in your apartment. However, that is the way you have chosen. Good night.

MARION. Good night, dear. Are you in the book? I'll telephone you . . .

NOLAN [*hastily*]. No—no—you'd better not. I shall communicate with you. Good-bye.

KURT. Good-bye, Sir Galahad.

[NOLAN *starts to retort, changes his mind and, in a very choleric mood, he goes out. There is a pause.*]

MARION. Well, I'm afraid you didn't make a very good impression on him!

KURT [*putting magazine away*]. That's just too bad!

MARION. That's no way for a young man to get on in the world—he's a very important person.

KURT. That's what passes for importance. You're not taken in by him, are you? Stuffed shirt—flatulent and pompous—perfect legislator!

MARION. As a matter of fact he's a very nice man—simple and kindly. [*Gets cigarettes and offers one to* KURT *who takes it and lights it. She takes one too but he forgets to light hers.*]

KURT. I bet he isn't simple and he isn't kindly. I bet he's greedy and vicious. Anyway he's a hypocrite. When a man starts worrying out loud about unprotected women you may know he's a hypocritical sensualist.

MARION. You're a violent young man, aren't you? [*Not getting light from* KURT *she lights her own. Throwing match to floor*]

KURT. Yes. The world is full of things and people that make me see red. . . . Why do you keep calling me youth and young man? I'm twenty-five.

MARION. Well, you seem to have the lurid and uncorrected imagination of the adolescent.

KURT. Imagination! That's where you're wrong. I may tell you, Miss Froude, that I'm as realistic as anybody you've ever met.

MARION [*sitting on upstage arm of sofa, right*]. Anybody who'd be so unreasonable over a nice fellow like Bunny Nolan . . . if you only knew—if only you'd been present at the interview I had with him just before you came. You'd have seen how wrong you are about him. Why, he was—he was awfully funny—but he was also touching.

KURT. You're one of those tolerant people, aren't you—see the best in people?

MARION. You say that as if tolerance were a crime.

KURT. Your kind is. It's criminal because it encourages dishonesty, incompetence, weakness and all kinds of knavery. What you call tolerance I call sloppy laziness. You're like those book-reviewers who find something to praise in every mediocre book.

MARION. You are a fanatical young man.

KURT. Having said that you think you dispose of me. Well, so be it. I'm disposed of. Now, let's get down to business. [*His manner plainly says: "Well, why should I bother to convince you? What importance can it possibly have what you think of me?" It is not wasted on* MARION.]

MARION. You are also a little patronizing . . .

KURT [*pleased*]. Am I?

MARION. However, I don't mind being patronized. That's where my tolerance comes in. It even amuses me a little bit. [*Crossing to piano seat*] But as I have to change for dinner perhaps you'd better . . .

KURT. Exactly.

MARION. Please sit down . . . [*A moment . . . She sits on piano bench facing him.*]

KURT [*goes to piano and talks to her across it*]. I am the editor of a magazine called Every Week. Do you know it?

MARION. It seems to me I've seen it on newsstands. . . .

KURT. You've never read it?

MARION. I'm afraid I haven't.

KURT. That is a tribute to your discrimination. We have an immense circulation. Three millions, I believe. With a circulation of that size you may imagine that the average of our readers' intelligence cannot be very high. Yet occasionally we flatter them by printing the highbrows—in discreet doses we give them, at intervals, Shaw and Wells and Chesterton. So you'll be in good company anyway. . . .

MARION [*amazed*]. *I* will?

KURT. Yes. I want you to write your biography to run serially in Every Week. Later of course you can bring it out as a book.

MARION. My biography!

KURT. Yes. The story of your life.

MARION [*with dignity*]. I know the meaning of the word.

KURT. The money is pretty good. I am prepared to give you an advance of two thousand dollars.

MARION. Good Heavens, am I as old as that—that people want my biography?

KURT. We proceed on the theory that nothing exciting happens to people after they are forty. . . .

MARION. What a cruel idea!

KURT. Why wait till you're eighty? Your impressions will be dimmed by time. Most autobiographies are written by corpses. Why not do yours while you are still young, vital, in the thick of life?

MARION. But I'm not a writer. I shouldn't know how to begin.

KURT. You were born, weren't you? Begin with that.

MARION. I write pleasant letters, my friends tell me. . . . But look here, why should you want this story from me—why should anybody be interested?—I'm not a first-rate artist you know—not by far—I'm just clever. . . .

KURT [*bluntly*]. It's not you—it's the celebrity of your subjects. . . .

MARION [*amused*]. You're a brutal young man—I rather like you . . .

KURT. Well, you've been courageous. You've been forthright. For an American woman you've had a rather extraordinary career—you've done pretty well what you wanted. . . .

MARION. The-Woman-Who-Dared sort of thing. . . . Isn't that passé?

KURT. I think your life will make good copy. You might have stayed here and settled down and done Pictorial Review covers of mothers hovering fondly over babies. Instead you went to Europe and managed to get the most inaccessible people to sit for you. How did you do it?

MARION. You'd be surprised how accessible some of these inaccessible people are!

KURT. Well, that's just what I want to get from your story. Just that. Tell what happened to you, that's all. The impulse that made you leave home, that made you go, for instance, to Russia, before the popular emigration set in, that's made you wander ever since, that's kept you from settling down in any of the places where you had a chance to get established.

MARION [*quite seriously*]. But supposing I don't know that. . . .

KURT. Well, that's interesting. That enigma is interesting. Maybe, while writing, you can solve it. It's a form of clarification. The more I talk to you the more I feel there's a great story in you and that you'll have great fun telling it.

MARION. Young man, you make me feel like an institution!

KURT. Should do you a lot of good in your professional career too —we'll reprint the portraits you've made of Lenin, Mussolini, Shaw—anything you like. . . .

[*She begins to laugh, quietly at first, then heartily.*]

MARION. Forgive me. . . .

KURT [*unperturbed*]. What's the matter?

MARION. Something I remembered—the funniest thing—isn't it funny how the oddest things pop into your mind?

KURT. What was it?

MARION. Something that happened years ago. . . .

KURT. What?

MARION. Oh, I couldn't possibly tell you. It wouldn't be fair!

KURT. In that case it'll probably be great for the magazine. Save it!

MARION [*frightened*]. You won't do anything lurid, will you?

KURT. Just print the story—just as you write it—practically as you write it.

MARION. I'm scared! [*She puts out her cigarette in ash tray on the piano.*]

KURT. Nonsense. Here's your first check. Two thousand dollars. [*He puts the check down on the table in front of her.*]

MARION [*wretched suddenly, picks up check, rises, looks at check*]. I can't tell you how old this makes me feel!

KURT. Suppose I asked you to write a novel! That wouldn't make you feel old, would it? Well, I'm simply asking you to write a novel of your life. The only lively reading these days is biography. People are bored with fiction. It's too tame. The fiction-writers haven't the audacity to put down what actually happens to people.

MARION. You may be disappointed, you know. You probably see headlines in your mind. The Woman of a Hundred Affairs, The Last of the Great Adventuresses, The Magda[1] Who Wouldn't Go Home. I promise you—it won't be a bit like that.

KURT. We'll announce it next month—first installment the following month. O.K.?

MARION [*puts down check, paces down right*]. Oh dear! I can't promise a thing like that—I really can't. . . .

KURT. Why not?

MARION. It'll worry me too much.

KURT. Well, don't promise. Just get to work.

MARION [*faces him*]. But what'll I do first?

KURT [*getting up*]. Well, if I were you I'd sit down. [*She does so helplessly on piano bench.* KURT *then gives her paper, one of his own pencils.*] There now! You're all set!

MARION [*wailing*]. How can I go out to dinner—how can I ever do anything—with a chapter to write?

KURT. After all you don't have to make up anything. Just tell what happened to you. [*He lights a fresh cigarette.*]

MARION. Can I use names?

KURT. When they're prominent, yes. The obscure ones you can fake if you want to. Nobody'll know 'em anyway.

[1] *Magda, the famous heroine of Sudermann's play, Die Heimat, a "new woman," who returns to her father's house as the mother of an illegitimate child and encounters his implacable wrath. The play had recently been revived in New York with Bertha Kalich in the leading role.*

MARION [*looks at him*]. Oh . . . what's your name?

KURT [*looks at her*]. I told you—my name's Kurt.

MARION. I know—with a K—I can't call you Kurt! What's your *name*?

KURT [*sulkily*]. Richard.

MARION. That's better. I tell you, Dickie, when I think—when I think—of the funny men I've known . . . they're pretty nearly all brothers under the skin you know, Dickie.

KURT. Well, that, as they say in the office, is an angle.

[*Suddenly her fear vanishes and she is overcome with the marvelous possibilities.*]

MARION [*jumps up and leans toward him as if to kiss him, but quickly thinks better of it*]. Dickie, I think it'll be marvelous! It'll be a knockout. And imagine— [*picking up check*] —I'm going to be paid for it! Dickie, you're an angel!

KURT [*sardonically*]. That's me. Angel Kurt! Well, so long. I'll be seeing you. [*Starts upstage toward hall door*]

MARION [*suddenly panicky*]. Oh, don't go!

KURT. You don't think I'm going to sit here and hold your hand while you're remembering your conquests, do you?

MARION. Well, you can't go away and leave me like this—alone with my life. . . .

KURT. Perhaps it's time you got a good, straight, clear-eyed look at it—alone by yourself, without anybody around to hold your hand. . . .

MARION [*suddenly*]. No. I don't want to. [*Shrugs her shoulders as if she were cold*] I think it would worry me. Besides, I feel superstitious about it.

KURT [*following her downstage*]. Superstitious!

MARION. Yes. A kind of—ultimate act. After you've written your biography, what else could there possibly be left for you to do?

KURT. Collect material for another!

MARION. What could you do over again—that wouldn't be repetitious? [*Sits on right arm of sofa right*]

KURT. It's repetitious to eat or to make love, isn't it? You keep on doing it.

MARION. You're cynical!

KURT [*almost spits it out*]. You're sentimental.

MARION. I am—Sentimental Journey[1]—no, that's been used, hasn't it?

---

[1] Sentimental Journey, *the title of an autobiographical novel by Laurence Sterne.*

KURT. Don't worry about a title—I'll get that from the story after you've finished it.

MARION. There's something about it—I don't know—

KURT. What?

MARION. Vulgar. *Everybody* spouting memoirs. Who cares?

KURT. Well, wrong hunch! Sorry to have taken your valuable time. Good-bye.

MARION [*the finality frightens her*]. What do you mean?

KURT [*he is withering—crosses to her*]. I'm prepared to admit I was mistaken—that's all. In your desire to escape vulgarity you would probably be—thin. You might even achieve refinement. I'm not interested. Padded episodes hovering on the edge of amour—

MARION [*turns on him*]. Young man, you're insufferable!

KURT. And you're a false alarm!

MARION [*after a moment*]. I congratulate you! You've brought me to the verge of losing my temper! But I tell you this—you're quite mistaken about the character of my life—and about my relations with my friends. My story won't be thin and episodic because my life hasn't been thin and episodic. And I won't have to pad—the problem will be to select. I'm going to write the damn thing just to show you. Come in tomorrow afternoon for a cocktail.

KURT. Whose memoirs are these going to be, yours or mine?

MARION. Well, you're an editor, aren't you? [*She smiles at him.*] Come in and edit.

KURT. All right, I'll come. But if you aren't here I'll go away. I won't wait a minute. [*He goes out quickly.* MARION *stands looking after him, inclined to laugh, and yet affected. This is a new type even for her.*]

MARION [*she speaks to herself*]. What an extraordinary young man! [*In a moment* KURT *comes back in.* MARION *is very glad to see him, greets him as if there had been a long separation.*] Oh, hello!

KURT [*embarrassed*]. I forgot my hat! [*He can't see it at once.*]

MARION [*without moving nor looking away from him, she indicates the hat on the sofa left*]. There it is! Right next to mine.

KURT [*crosses for it*]. Oh yes. [*Picks up the hat*] Thanks. [*For a moment he stands uncertainly, hat in hand, looking at* MARION *who has not taken her eyes off him. He is embarrassed.*] Well, so long!

MARION. So long. [KURT *leaves again. She stands as before looking after him. She turns toward the piano—sees the check—picks it up and reads it to make sure it's true. The whole thing has a slightly fantastic quality to her. She is very happy and excited. She waves the check in her hand like a pennant and humming she crosses to the piano seat and sits and plays the waltz from "Danubia." She sees the pad and pencil on the piano and stops playing and, picking up the pencil and the pad, she crosses to the small armchair in the upstage end of the window and sits with her feet on the window seat. She repeats the first words of the first chapter aloud to herself as she writes them down*] I am born . . . [MINNIE *enters from door left to get the tea things she had left on the model stand.* MARION *taps the pencil on the pad as she repeats the words.*] I am born . . . [*The time seems remote to her.*] I am born—I meet Richard Kurt— Well, Minnie, here's the outline—I am born . . . I meet Richard Kurt —now all I have to do is to fill in. . . .

[MINNIE, *used to having irrelevancies addressed to her, takes this program rather stolidly.*]

MINNIE. Was, Marion?

MARION [*trying to get rid of her*]. Fix something light, will you, Minnie . . . I'm not going out.

MINNIE. Aber der Junge kommt![1]

MARION. What Junge?

MINNIE. Der Junge dem Sie . . . [2]

MARION. Oh, yes! The Junge I met on the boat. You'll have to send him away. I can't go out tonight. From now on, Minnie, no more frivolous engagements!

MINNIE [*astonished*]. Sie bleiben ganzen abend zu Hause?[3]

MARION. Yes, Minnie. I'm spending the evening alone with my life . . . [*She remembers* KURT'S *words and repeats them as if, after all, they have made a profound impression on her*] . . . get a good, straight, clear-eyed look at it . . .

MINNIE [*picks up the tea tray and, bustling toward the kitchen, promising delights*]. Ein Fleischbrühe und Pfannkuchen![4] . . . [MINNIE *exits door left.*]

MARION [*already brooding over her past*]. I am born. . . .
[*Slowly the curtain falls.*]

---

[1] *Aber . . . kommt!* But the boy is coming!
[2] *Der . . . Sie,* the boy that you. . . .
[3] *Sie . . . Hause?* You are spending the whole evening at home?
[4] *Ein . . . Pfannkuchen!* Consommé and pancakes.

act 2

AT RISE: MARION *is putting some touches on the full-length portrait of* LEANDER NOLAN *which stands away from the audience. She is wearing her working costume, baggy red corduroy trousers, a sash and a worn blue smock over a kind of sweater-jacket. She is very happy.... On the piano nearby are her writing things. While touching up* LEANDER *she is struck by an idea for her book. Puts down her brush and palette and goes to the piano to jot down some notes. The idea pleases her. She giggles to herself. Then she returns to her easel.* MINNIE *comes in and stands watching her a moment before* MARION *sees her.*

MARION [*sees* MINNIE *at last*]. Oh yes, Minnie—do you want anything?

MINNIE. You asked me to come right away, Marion.

MARION. Did I?

MINNIE. Ja. [*Sitting on sofa right*] Zo! You have left a note on the kitchen I should come in right away I am back from the market.

MARION [*studying the portrait*]. Of course I did. That's right, Minnie.

MINNIE. Well, what did you want, Marion?

MARION [*washing paint brush in turpentine jar*]. Did I tell you there'd be two for dinner?

MINNIE. Ja. Gewiss![1] Das ist vy I vent to the market.

MARION. Well, I've changed my plans. I'm dining out with Feydie after all.

MINNIE [*rising and looking at picture*]. Ach, Gott! [*She studies the portrait.*]

MARION [*looks humorously at* MINNIE *and puts her arm about* MINNIE's *shoulders.*] Gut?

MINNIE. Ziemlich gut—[2]

MARION. Do you know who it is?

[1] *Gewiss, certainly.*
[2] *Ziemlich gut, rather good.*

536 S. N. Behrman

MINNIE. Oh, das sieht man ja gleich. Das ist Herr Nolan![1]

MARION [*shaking her hand in gratitude*]. Thank you, Minnie. [*Doorbell rings*] See who that is, will you, Minnie?

MINNIE. Fräulein ist zu Hause?[2]

MARION. Ich erwarte Herr Feydak. Für ihn bin ich immer zu Hause.[3]

MINNIE [*agreeing heartily as she crosses to the door*]. Ja, Ja, der Herr Feydak. . . . [MINNIE *goes out.* MARION *jots down a note on the pad which is on the piano.* FEYDAK *enters.* MINNIE *closes the door and exits left.*]

MARION [*at piano*]. Hello, Feydie! Sit down!

FEYDAK. Well, my dear, which career do I interrupt?

MARION [*laughing*]. I don't know!

FEYDAK. One comes to see you with diffidence nowadays. [FEYDAK *removes coat and hat and places them on the upstage end of the sofa right, and sits on the left side of the sofa.*]

MARION. While I'm painting I think of funny things to say, funny phrases. It won't be a serious biography, thank God. I'm dedicating it to Vicki: "To Vicki—the gayest person I have ever known!" By the way, have you got any little snapshots of Vicki—all I've got are formal photographs with his orders. I'd like to get something a little more intimate.

FEYDAK. I'll hunt some up for you.

MARION. Have you heard from the Powers yet, when you are to leave?

FEYDAK. Tomorrow.

MARION [*stricken—sits right of him*]. Feydie!

FEYDAK [*fatalistically*]. Tomorrow. [*They sit.*] I shall leave you with sorrow, Marion.

MARION. I'll have no one to laugh with.

FEYDAK. For me it's an exile.

MARION. You'll have a wonderful time. I shall miss you terribly.

FEYDAK. Perhaps you'll come out.

MARION. Perhaps I will. I've always wanted to go to China. If I have enough money left from all my labors I'll stop in on you—en route to China.

FEYDAK. That would be marvelous.

[1] *Oh, das. . . . Nolan! Oh, you can see that at once. It's Mr. Nolan!*
[2] *Fräulein . . . Hause? Are you at home?*
[3] *Ich. . . . Hause, I'm expecting Mr. Feydak. I'm always at home to him.*

MARION. You know writing one's life has a sobering effect on one
—you get it together and you think: "Well! look at the damn
thing . . ."

FEYDAK. Do you want to be impressive?

MARION. Well, I don't want to be trivial . . .

FEYDAK. I think *you* escape that.

MARION. My friendships haven't been trivial. . . . [*She gives his
hand a squeeze.*]

FEYDAK. Have you seen that bombastic young man?

MARION. Oh, yes. He comes in every once in a while to see how I'm
getting on. He's quite insulting. Underneath his arrogance I suspect
he's very uncertain.

FEYDAK. Oh, now, don't tell me he has an inferiority complex!

MARION. Well, I think he has!

FEYDAK. The new psychology is very confusing. In my simple day
you said: "That young man is bumptious and insufferable" and you
dismissed him. Now you say: "He has an inferiority complex" and
you encourage him to be more bumptious and more insufferable.
It's very confusing.

MARION. There's a kind of honesty about him that I like.

FEYDAK [*instantly putting two and two together*]. Oh!

MARION. Nothing like that, Feydie! As a matter of fact—I don't
mind telling you . . . I like him very much—

FEYDAK. I think he is destined . . .

MARION. He's not interested. He's some kind of fanatic. Social, I
think: I've met that kind in Russia—quite unassailable. But I'm
optimistic. . . . [*They laugh.*] Well, one must never despair, must
one. Life is so much more resourceful and resilient than one is oneself. Three weeks ago when you came to see me I felt quite at the
end of my rope. I didn't tell you quite but I actually didn't know
which way to turn. I felt tired too—which troubled me. Well, now I
find myself, quite suddenly—[*she indicates portrait*]—doing Leander and—[*she indicates manuscript on piano*]—doing myself. New
Vista. Very exciting.

FEYDAK. All this enthusiasm for art alone?

MARION [*laughing*]. Of course!—Feydie, what did you think?

FEYDAK. I don't believe it.

MARION. Come here and have a look at Leander!

FEYDAK [*he rises—walks to the canvas on the easel*]. Hm! Formal!

MARION. It's to hang in the White House. [*She winks at him, he
laughs, puts his arm around her shoulder.*]

FEYDAK. Marion, you're adorable!

[*They walk downstage together, their arms around each other's shoulders, very affectionately.*]

MARION. Oh, Feydie, I'm having a wonderful time. Quiet too. Writing *enforces* silence and solitude on one. I've always lived in such a rush—a kind of interminable scherzo. . . .

FEYDAK. Good title! . . .

MARION. Think so? I'll put it down. . . . [*Writes on pad on piano.* FEYDAK *sits on right arm of sofa left, facing her.*] Interminable scherzo. . . . How do you spell it? A little affected. Might do for a chapter heading maybe. . . . [*Returns to him—sitting on model stand —facing him*] But I realize now I haven't in years had time to stop and think. I sit here for hours, Feydie, and nothing comes to me. Then, suddenly, the past will come in on me with such a rush—odd, remote, semi-forgotten things of the past. Are they true? How much is true? One can never be sure, can one? I remember certain griefs and fears. I remember their existence without recalling at all their intensity—their special anguish. Why? What was the matter with me? What made them so acute? It is like recalling a landscape without color, a kind of color-blindness of the memory. [*Doorbell rings. She calls out to her factotum.*] Minnie! [MINNIE *enters left and crosses rapidly to hall door.* MARION *arranges the model stand on which stands the papal armchair in red and gold.*] This is probably the Hon. Nolan. He's due for a sitting. He pretends he doesn't like to have his picture painted, but I know he does.

[MINNIE *enters from hallway. She is flustered and giggly.*]

MINNIE [*very high-pitched voice*]. Herr Varvick Vilson!

MARION. Tympi Wilson!

MINNIE [*to* FEYDAK]. Der *film star!*.

FEYDAK. So?

MINNIE [*radiant*]. Ja! Ja!

MARION. Oh, Feydie, you'll adore this. Ask him in, Minnie.

MINNIE [*as she goes out to admit* WILSON]. Gott, ist er schön!¹

MARION. Warwick's public.

FEYDAK. And mine!

MARION [*in a quick whisper*]. Whatever you do—outstay him!

[MINNIE *has opened the door and* WARWICK WILSON *enters. He is very handsome, explosively emotional, and given to cosmic generalization. He is in evening clothes, a red carnation in his buttonhole.*]

¹ *Gott . . . schön! God, is he handsome!*

WILSON [*crossing to* MARION *and kissing her hand*]. Marion!

MARION. Warwick!

WILSON. Darling! How are you?

MARION. I'm splendid. Been up all night?

WILSON. No, no! This is business.

[MINNIE *has crossed to kitchen door upper left, never taking her eyes from* WILSON.]

MARION. This is Mr. Feydak. Mr. Warwick Wilson, the famous film star.

WILSON [*crosses to sofa and shakes hands with* FEYDAK—*dramatically*]. Feydak! *The* Mr. Feydak?

FEYDAK [*again mistaken for his brother*]. Ja.

WILSON. I've heard of you indeed!

FEYDAK. Have you? Thanks.

MARION. Mr. Feydak is on his way to Hollywood. He is to write the music for . . .

WILSON [*sits on the model stand—facing front*]. Of course! I am honored, Mr. Feydak—deeply honored. That unforgettable waltz—how does it go? . . . [*He starts to hum with a swaying gesture the waltz from the "Merry Widow."*] Music's my one passion!

MARION. Once you said it was me.

WILSON. A lot of good it did me!

MARION [*to* WILSON]. Well, tell me . . . [*She sees* MINNIE, *who is still staring at* WILSON.] Look at Minnie. The mere sight of you has upset her so that she's speechless.

MINNIE. Aber, Fräulein![1]

[WILSON *rises graciously and gives* MINNIE *a friendly wave of the hand. He's no snob.* MINNIE, *speechless with delight, exits left.* WILSON *returns to his position on the model stand.*]

MARION. All right, Minnie! Warwick, Warwick! You mustn't do things like that to Minnie, at her age!

WILSON [*tragically*]. There you are! This face! This cursed face! I should go masked really. One has no private life!

MARION [*sits in throne chair on model stand*]. What would you do with it if you had it, eh, Tympi?

WILSON [*delighted*]. That nickname!

MARION. It just rolled off my tongue. Did I call you that?

WILSON. You did! You invented it. No one's called me that since you left Hollywood. And you promised to explain the significance to me, but you never did.

[1] *Aber, Fräulein! But, Miss!*

MARION. Did it have a significance?

FEYDAK. Marion has a knack for nicknames.

MARION. I love 'em. I'd like to do a chapter on nicknames.

WILSON [*highly pleased*]. Tympi! Tympi! [*Very patronizing to* FEYDAK] You are an intuitive person, Mr. Feydak. I can see that. [FEYDAK *ad libs: "Danke schön."*] Can you imagine what she meant?

FEYDAK. Her vagaries are beyond me, Mr. Wilson.

WILSON [*leaning back toward* MARION]. Speak, Oracle! No! Don't tell me now. Put it into that book you're writing.

MARION [MARION *and* FEYDAK *exchange glances*]. How things get around.

WILSON. It's been in the back of my mind for years, Marion . . . to have you paint me. Now that we're both in town together . . .

MARION. Well, I'd *love* to . . .

WILSON. In the costume of the Dane. [MARION *and* FEYDAK *exchange a look. Strikes a pose*] I'd like to be done in *his* costume. I hope, Mr. Feydak, that they won't break your spirit in Hollywood as they've almost broken mine!

FEYDAK [*with a smile*]. My spirit is indestructible!

WILSON [*rises and crosses to rear of sofa and pats* FEYDAK *on the back*]. I'm glad to hear it. [*Returns to left of model stand and stands with his right foot on it*] You know, for years I've been begging them to do Shakespeare. [*Gesticulates*]

MARION [*interrupting him*]. Sit down and be comfortable.

WILSON. They simply won't listen. But I'm going to give up acting and produce!

MARION. Oh, good God! Don't do that!

WILSON. Why not?

MARION. What would Minnie do with her night off?

WILSON [*smiles*]. My public, eh?

MARION. Yes!

WILSON. Quite so! [*Patronizingly*] You artists who work in media like painting or literature—[*to* FEYDAK]—or music, that too is a beautiful art, Mr. Feydak—transcends speech—transcends everything; by saying nothing it says all.

FEYDAK. Ja!

[*The doorbell rings.*]

WILSON. You are certainly lucky compared to us poor actors. We— [MINNIE *enters and crosses to hall door upper center.*] Wouldn't it be ironic if all that remained of me after I am gone were your painting of me? That is why I want it, perhaps—my poor grasp on immortality.

FEYDAK. You see, Marion, you confer immortality!

MARION. I think immortality is an overrated commodity. But tell me, Tympi, what are you doing away from Hollywood?

MINNIE [*comes in announcing*]. Der Herr Nolan! [MINNIE *then looks at* WILSON. WILSON *stands—looks at* MINNIE.]

MARION. Show him in. Show him in. [*With a lingering look at* WILSON, MINNIE *goes back. To others, after watching* MINNIE *exit*] You see!

FEYDAK. The effect is instantaneous—like music . . .

[NOLAN *enters.* MINNIE *follows* NOLAN *in and exits into kitchen, murmuring ecstatically, "Gottl Ist er schön!", looking at* WIL-SON.]

MARION. Hello, Bunny. [*Introducing* NOLAN] You know Mr. Fey-dak. Mr. Nolan, this is Warwick Wilson, you've heard of him.

[FEYDAK *bows to* NOLAN, *who returns the bow.*]

WILSON. It's a pleasure, Mr. Nolan. I've heard of you indeed!

[*They shake hands.*]

MARION. You're late for your sitting, Bunny. Will the presence of these gentlemen embarrass you? I don't mind if you don't.

NOLAN [*has entered rather worried and angry. He has a magazine rolled in his hand. He now speaks very irritatedly*]. As a matter of fact, Marion . . .

MARION [*putting him in throne chair on model stand*]. Oh, sit down, like a good fellow. The light is getting bad. [NOLAN *sits.* WILSON *sits on the right arm of the sofa left on which* FEYDAK *is sitting.* MARION *gets to work on* BUNNY.] How did you find me, Tympi?

WILSON. I read in a magazine that you were barging into litera-ture . . .

NOLAN [*half rising, showing magazine*]. This is true then!

MARION. Don't get up, Bunny . . . [*Nevertheless she takes the magazine and looks at it.*] Well, Dickie has gone and spread himself, hasn't he? [*She sits on sofa left between* WILSON *and* FEYDAK.] Look here, Feydie! [*Shows him the full-page announcement of her book in magazine.*]

FEYDAK [*looking*]. Do you think you can live up to this?

MARION. Why will they write this sort of thing? [*Rises and goes back*] Makes me out a kind of female Casanova. [*She drops the magazine on the stand at* NOLAN's *feet.*] Well, they'll be disappointed.

NOLAN [*bitterly*]. Will they?

MARION. Bunny! [*But she thinks nothing of it—merely pushes him into a better light.*]

FEYDAK [*tactfully—he senses danger*]. May I ask, Mr. Wilson—are you making a picture at the moment?

WILSON. No, I'm in New York making some personal appearances.

MARION. Personal appearances. I love that phrase. Has such an air of magnanimity about it. [*Crosses to painting*]

WILSON. Pretty boring, I can tell you! I've got writer's cramp signing autograph books. It's a perfect martyrdom I assure you. It's no fun at all. [WILSON *crosses to stand—puts his right foot on it, leans on his knee with his right arm and studies* NOLAN, *his face not six inches away from* NOLAN's. NOLAN *fidgets.*]

MARION. I can imagine! What's the matter, Bunny? You seem under a strain today . . . not relaxed.

NOLAN [*bursting out and glaring at all of them*]. It's like being watched while you're taking a bath!

MARION. Oh, I'm so sorry, Bunny!

FEYDAK [*rising*]. I quite sympathize with Mr. Nolan.

WILSON [*moves away*]. Supposing I were so shy, eh, Mr. Nolan?

FEYDAK [*crosses to* MARION *who is above her easel, right*]. I'm off, Marion. [*Kisses her hand*] Auf Wiedersehen!

MARION [*meaningfully*]. You'll have to go—[WILSON *sits again on arm of sofa left*]—both of you . . .

WILSON [*rises*]. I was just going myself. My next appearance is at 6:45. [*Speaks to others*]

FEYDAK [*to help her*]. Perhaps I can drop you, Mr. Wilson.

WILSON [*faces* FEYDAK]. No, I'll drop you . . . [*Turns to* MARION] I say, Marion . . .

[FEYDAK, *helpless, goes upstage putting on coat.*]

MARION. Yes, Tympi?

WILSON. If you started my portrait right away and it turns out—I am sure it will turn out—you might put it in your book, mightn't you? I'm frankly sick of just appearing in fan magazines.

MARION. We'll see. Why not?

WILSON. Splendid! *Don't fail to come tonight.* Good-bye, dearest

Marion. Good-bye again, Mr. Nolan. [*He starts to shake* NOLAN's *hand but is interrupted by* MARION, *almost screaming.*]

MARION. No, no, no! Don't do *that*—don't touch him.

WILSON. Most happy! See you later. . . . [*He waves himself off at last*—MARION *returns to her easel.*]

MARION [*to* FEYDAK]. Don't forget—I'm dining with you.

FEYDAK [*like the player in "Hamlet" who burlesques Polonius*]. Most happy—see you later. [FEYDAK *leaves.*]

MARION [*with relief*]. Now then . . .

NOLAN [*muttering to himself*]. Silly ass!

MARION [*working on painting*]. That young man is one of the most famous people in the world, do you realize that, Bunny? His profile follows you all over Europe—*and* Asia. Ubiquitous profile. Have you ever seen him?

NOLAN [*unswerved*]. He's a silly ass!

MARION. I admit he's somewhat on that side—but that other one—that Feydie—he's the darling of the world!

NOLAN [*very short—bitterly*]. Evidently!

MARION [*surprised*]. Bunny!

NOLAN [*savage now*]. Who isn't a darling? Everyone's a darling as far as I can see! The world's full of darlings. Your world at any rate.

MARION. But, darling . . . [*She suddenly stops—sits at right end of sofa right.*] Oh, Bunny, I remember now!

NOLAN. You remember what?

MARION. Tympi! Why I nicknamed him Tympi. Don't you see?

NOLAN. No, I don't see . . .

MARION. For tympanum—a large instrument in the orchestra producing a hollow sound. [*She beats an imaginary drum with her paint brush.*] Boom! [*Suddenly* NOLAN *quits the pose.*] What is it?

NOLAN. I can't sit today. I'm not in the mood.

MARION. I could tell there was something worrying you.

NOLAN. There is something worrying me!

MARION. Well, what is it?

NOLAN. This confounded story! Are you really writing it?

MARION. Well, yes—I am.

NOLAN. What do you intend to tell?

MARION. Well, that's a rather difficult question to answer—it's like asking me what I've been doing all my life.

NOLAN. When does this biography start?

MARION [*beginning to wonder about this questioning*]. With my birth—coincidence, isn't it?

NOLAN. All the time back home—when you were a girl in Knox-ville?

MARION. Yes, of course. I've had a wonderful time going back over it all.

NOLAN. Everything?

MARION. Everything I can remember.

NOLAN. Do I come into it?

MARION [*smiling to herself*]. You do! You certainly do!

NOLAN. You must leave me out of that story!

MARION. But Bunny, how can I possibly leave you out?

NOLAN. You must, that's all!

MARION. But how can I? You were too important—think of the rôle you played in my life. By your own confession, Bunny darling, you—you started me. That's a good idea for a chapter heading, isn't it? "Bunny Starts Me." I must put that down.

NOLAN. This is no joke, Marion. [*With menace*] I warn you . . .

MARION. Warn me! Let me understand you. Are you seriously asking me to give up an opportunity like this just because . . .

NOLAN [*rises and gets down from the model stand. Speaks with brutal command*]. Opportunity! Cheap exhibitionism! A chance to flaunt your affairs in a rag like this. [*Indicating magazine on piano*] I won't be drawn into it. I can tell you that! [*He is in a towering rage.*]

MARION [*after a pause*]. I know that by your standards, Bunny, I'm a loose character. But there are other standards, there just are.

NOLAN [*crosses to center—drops magazine on model stand*]. Not in Tennessee!

MARION [*rises*]. I'm afraid you're provincial, Bunny.

NOLAN. I'm sorry.

MARION [*takes off her smock, crosses to small table down right, gets her notes, then crosses to desk upper right*]. I don't care what the advertisements say about my story—I know what I'm writing . . .

NOLAN. I'm sorry.

MARION. That's all right. [*But this has gone pretty deep.*]

NOLAN [*after a pause*]. If you're doing this for money—[*She turns and watches him.*] I know you've been pretty hard up—I promise you I'll get you commissions enough to more than make up for this story. I was talking about you only the other day to my prospective father-in-law. He's a big man, you know. I am sure I can get him to sit for you . . .

MARION. The tip isn't big enough.

NOLAN [*scared now that he sees the extent to which he has hurt her*]. Marion! . . .

MARION. It amuses me to write my life. I am pleasure-loving—you know that—I will therefore pass up the opportunity of painting your big father-in-law. I will even give up the pleasure of painting you. And we can part friends, then, can't we? [*She reaches out her hand to him.*] Good-bye, Bunny.

NOLAN [*devastated*]. Marion—you can't do this to me—you can't send me away like this . . .

MARION. I don't think I've ever in my life had a vulgar quarrel with anyone. This is the nearest I've come to it. I'm a little annoyed with you for that. I think it's better we part now while we can still do so with some—dignity. Shall we?

NOLAN. You don't realize what's involved—or you wouldn't talk like that . . .

MARION. What *is* involved?

NOLAN. My entire career. That's what's involved.

MARION. Oh!

NOLAN. This is the most critical moment of my life. My fiancée's father is the most powerful leader of opinion in my state. Frankly, I depend on him for support. To have this kind of thing bandied about now might cause a permanent rift between him and me—might seriously interfere, not only with my candidacy for the Senate, but with my marriage.

MARION. They are interlocking—I quite understand.

NOLAN. A revelation of this kind—coming at this moment—might be fatal . . .

MARION. Revelation! You make me feel like—I can't tell you what you make me feel like . . . [*She laughs—semihysterically.*]

NOLAN [*sepulchral*]. You must give this up, Marion.

MARION. I've met distinguished men abroad—politicians, statesmen—a Prime Minister even—and this kind of "revelation"—as you so luridly call it—is no more to them than a theme for after-dinner banter. They take it in their stride. My God, Bunny, you take it so big!

NOLAN. These people I'm depending on to elect me aren't sophisticated like you or me. [MARION *looks at* NOLAN *with some surprise.*] What I mean is—they're country people essentially—my future father-in-law is sympathetic to their point of view.

MARION. Tell me—your father-in-law, is he the man with the chest expansion?

NOLAN. He's a fine sturdy man—as you perhaps know, he makes a fetish of exercise.

MARION [*bubbling again*]. You see his pictures in shorts in health magazines.

NOLAN. There's no disgrace in that.

MARION [*sits on right arm of sofa left*]. It doesn't shock me, Bunny. I was just identifying him, that's all.

NOLAN. I owe everything to Kinnicott—I wouldn't be running for the Senate right now if not for him. I can't risk offending him.

MARION. What the devil's happened to you anyway? You used to be quite a nice boy—even fun occasionally . . .

NOLAN [*wistful—turns away*]. Maybe—if you had stuck to me . . .

MARION. Ts! Ts! Ts! Poor Bunny. I'm sorry for you. Really I am. [*She strokes his arm.*]

NOLAN [*suddenly passionate—faces her*]. Don't touch me!

MARION [*amazed*]. Bunny!

NOLAN. Do you think I'm not human!

MARION. Well, if you aren't the most contradictory . . .

NOLAN. I realized the moment I came in here the other day—the moment I saw you . . .

MARION [*interrupting*]. But Bunny! You're engaged and you're going to be a Senator.

NOLAN [*walks away from her*]. Forget it! Forget I ever said it. . . .

MARION. You bewilder me . . .

NOLAN [*bitterly*]. I'm not surprised I bewilder you. You've spent your life among a lot of foreign counts. It's well known that foreigners are more immoral than we are.

MARION. I'm very touched. I am really. [*She kisses him in a friendly way.*]

NOLAN. Don't do that! I forbid you!

MARION. All right. I'll never attack you again, I promise.

NOLAN. I wish I had never come back into your life—it was a terrible mistake—you'd forgotten me.

MARION [*seriously*]. Oh, you're wrong. First love—one doesn't forget that.

NOLAN [*passionately*]. But you did! You forgot me! And if you got the chance again, you'd humiliate me again.

MARION. Humiliate! What queer notions you have— Is it a question of pride or vanity between us? We're old friends—friends.

NOLAN [*moves a step right*]. Please forget this—I don't know what came over me—I . . .

MARION. Of course. There's nothing to forget. [*Moves a step toward him*] It's quite all right, dear . . . [*She pats him on his hand.*] . . . Oh, excuse me . . .

NOLAN. I warn you, Marion—I solemnly warn you—if you persist in this—

MARION. Never in my life have I seen a man vacillate so between passion and threat . . .

NOLAN. I shall find ways to stop you. Mr. Kinnicott, my future father-in-law, is a powerful man.

MARION. I know. Extraordinary biceps.

NOLAN. I warn you, Marion. This matter is beyond flippancy.

MARION [*sits*]. There'll be some very distinguished people in my biography. You needn't be ashamed.

NOLAN. That movie-actor!

MARION. Tympi in Hamlet costume—you in a toga. I'll print your portraits on opposite pages—my two men!

NOLAN. You are malicious!

MARION. I must admit, Bunny, that you provoke in me all my malicious impulses. You come here suddenly and you convey to me what I've missed in not marrying you. [*The back-door bell rings.* MINNIE *crosses to answer it during* MARION's *speech.*] You dangle before me the inventory of your felicities—a career, a fortune, a fabulous bride—and then, because I get a chance to chronicle my own adventures—you object—you tell me I mustn't! I have a nice nature, Bunny, or I should be angry—I should be indignant.

[KURT *enters.*]

NOLAN [*sharply and with threat*]. Now, Marion, I've warned you . . . You'll regret this.

MARION. Hello, Dickie, do talk to Bunny for a minute, will you? [*Crosses to the stairs and starts up them to her bedroom*] I've simply got to change. [MINNIE *enters up center and exits left.*] Feydie's coming to take me out to dinner.

NOLAN. But, Marion . . .

MARION. I couldn't do anything about this in any case, Bunny dear, because I've promised Dickie. In fact, I signed something, didn't I,

Dickie? Don't go away, either of you. . . . [MARION *blows them a kiss and exits into her bedroom. A pause between the two men.* KURT *crosses downstage to above the model stand. Suddenly,* NOLAN *goes to* KURT *and reaches out his hand to him.*]

NOLAN. How do you do, young man?

KURT [*very much surprised*]. How do *you* do? [*He looks at him narrowly, his head a little on one side, a terrier appraising a mastiff.*]

NOLAN. I am very glad to see you.

KURT. Isn't that nice . . . ?

NOLAN. You may be surprised to learn that on the one occasion when we met you made quite an impression on me.

KURT. Did I?

NOLAN [*sits on sofa right*]. You did. Sit down. In fact—I hope you don't mind—if you will allow me as a prerogative of seniority—to ask you a few questions. I have a purpose in mind and not—I trust—an idle purpose.

KURT. Shoot! [*Sits*] Anything to enlighten the professor! [*He knows he is going to be pumped and has decided to be casual, naive and even respectful.*]

NOLAN [*clearing his throat*]. Now then—your present position on the magazine you represent—have you been on it long?

KURT. About two years.

NOLAN. And before that?

KURT. Newspaper work.

NOLAN. And before that?

KURT. Tramping around the world. Odd jobs. Quite a variety.

NOLAN. College?

KURT. Believe it or not—Yale—two years . . . worked my way through—washed dishes.

NOLAN. Very interesting preparation . . . very interesting . . . Tell me now—your present work—do you find it interesting? Is the remuneration satisfactory?

KURT. Two hundred smackers a week. That's twice what I've ever earned in my life before.

NOLAN. Now then—to come to the point—no doubt you've heard of my prospective father-in-law, Mr. Orrin Kinnicott?

KURT. Heard of him! We pay him the compliment of imitation. He is our model, our criterion, our guiding star!

NOLAN. As you know, Mr. Kinnicott's interests are varied. He owns some powerful newspapers in my state. The other day I heard him say that he wanted a new man in Washington.

KURT [*playing naively excited*]. Now that's something to give one's eye-teeth for!

NOLAN [*pleased at the result*]. I think it might be possible to swing it—very possible.

KURT. God, what a break!

NOLAN. As it happens, Mr. Kinnicott is at present in town. I shall arrange an appointment for you in the next few days. Naturally, I expect you to keep the matter entirely confidential.

KURT. Naturally! You needn't worry on that score, Senator, I assure you.

NOLAN. Thank you, Mr. Kurt. That is all I ask.

[*A pause*]

KURT. Mr. Nolan—do you mind if I ask *you* something?

NOLAN. Certainly not . . .

KURT. You won't consider me impertinent?

NOLAN [*with a smile*]. I don't object to impertinence, Mr. Kurt. I was often considered impertinent myself when I was your age.

KURT. Why are you making me this offer?

NOLAN. I am not making you an offer. I shall merely attempt to expedite . . .

KURT. Why? The first time we met we didn't exactly hit it off, now, did we? Why then are you going to all this trouble?

NOLAN. I have discussed you with Miss Froude, who is an old friend of mine and whose opinion I greatly respect. She thinks very highly of you, Mr. Kurt. My own impression . . .

KURT [*inexorably*]. Why? What, as they say, is the pay-off?

NOLAN. I'll tell you. I'll tell you quite frankly. I don't want Miss Froude's autobiography, which you have persuaded her to write, to appear in your magazine. I want it killed!

KURT. Oh! You want it killed?

NOLAN. Exactly.

KURT. Why?

NOLAN. Marion knows why. We needn't go into that.

KURT [*wounded by a sudden and devastating jealousy*]. Good God! You! You too!

[MARION *enters from balcony. She is wearing a dove-colored evening dress—the gamine transformed into lady-of-the-world.*]

MARION. Well! How have you two boys been getting on? What do you think?

KURT [*seething. Crosses to foot of stairs*]. I'll tell you what I think. . . .

MARION. About the dress I mean . . . [*She does a turn for them.*]

NOLAN [*without looking up at her or the dress. He is watching* KURT]. It's charming.

MARION. Thank you, Bunny. With all his faults Bunny is much more satisfactory than you are, Dickie.

KURT [*at boiling point*]. He's chivalrous, he is! His chivalry is so exquisite that he has just been attempting to bribe me to keep your story from being published. His gallantry is so delicate that he's terrified about being mentioned in it.

MARION [*comes down stairs during* KURT's *speech*]. Don't be so worked up about it, Dickie. You're another one who takes it big. It's catching!

KURT [*flaring at her*]. You're not very sensitive. . . .

MARION. Why should I be? You misapprehend Bunny. If he doesn't want to be in the same story with me that's his business. And it's nothing to do with chivalry or gallantry or nonsense like that.

NOLAN. Marion—this young man . . .

KURT [*taunting him*]. What about Washington, Mr. Nolan? Mr. Nolan, a prospective Senator, offers to bribe me with a post in Washington controlled by his prospective father-in-law. . . .

MARION. If it's a good job take it, Dickie, by all means. . . .

KURT. I am afraid, Marion, that your code is more relaxed than mine . . .

MARION. Code, nonsense! I gave up codes long ago. I'm a big laissez-faire girl!

NOLAN. If this young man is an example of the distinguished company you've come to associate with, Marion . . .

MARION. Don't quarrel, children—please. It distresses me.

NOLAN. He's extremely objectionable.

KURT. What about Washington, now, *Senator*? Are you still willing to expedite . . . ! [KURT *and* NOLAN *stand glaring at each other.* MARION *tries to calm the troubled waters. Crosses to* NOLAN]

MARION. Really, Dickie, you're very naughty. Don't mind him, Bunny. He's very young.

KURT. And incorruptible!

NOLAN. Marion, I claim the privilege of a friendship that antedates Mr. Kurt's by some years, to beg you, very solemnly, not to prostitute your talents to his contemptible, sensation-mongering rag.

KURT [*faces them*]. There's a Senatorial sentence!

MARION. Hush, Dickie, hush! Bunny darling, it's true that Dickie's magazine isn't the Edinburgh Review. On the other hand your assumption that my story will be vulgar and sensational is a little gratuitous, isn't it?

NOLAN. You *refuse* then?

MARION [*gently but with a serious overtone*]. Yes. This—censorship before publication seems to me, shall we say, unfair. It is—even in an old friend—dictatorial.

NOLAN [*with an air of finality*]. You leave me then no alternative. I am very sorry.

KURT. Don't let him frighten you, Marion, he can't do anything.

NOLAN. I can forgive you anything, Marion, but the fact that you value my wishes below those of this insolent young man.

MARION. But this insolent young man hasn't anything to do with it! Can't you see, Bunny—it's my own wish that is involved.

NOLAN. I have explained to you the special circumstances. If you would consent to delay publication till after election. . . .

[*She turns to* KURT *to ask him to make this concession but can't get a word in. She is wedged between both of them.*]

KURT. She has nothing to do with the publication date. That's my province. Gosh, what a chance for the circulation manager in Tennessee! [*He rubs his palms together in mock anticipation of profits.*]

NOLAN [*losing his temper at last*]. You are tampering with more than you bargain for Mr.— Mr.— . . .

KURT. Kurt.

MARION. With a "K."

NOLAN. There are ways of dealing with a young man like this and you'll soon find out what they are!

KURT. Them's harsh words, Senator!

NOLAN. You wait and see.

MARION. Bunny!

NOLAN. Don't speak to me! I never want to see you again! [*He goes out.*]

MARION [*really distressed*]. This is awful!

KURT [*highly elated*]. It's wonderful!

MARION. But I'm very fond of Bunny. Oh dear! I'll telephone him tonight . . .

KURT [*grimly*]. Over my dead body!

MARION. Can it be, Dickie, that I control the election of Senators from Tennessee? [*Sits at right end of sofa left*]

KURT [*after a moment*]. How could you ever have loved a stuffed shirt like that?

MARION. He wasn't a stuffed shirt. That's the funny part. He was charming. He was a charming boy. Rather thin. Rather reticent. He was much nicer than you, as a matter of fact. . . .

KURT. I'm sure he was!

MARION. He was much less violent!

KURT [*sits*]. Hypocritical old buccaneer!

MARION. He used to work hard all day and at night he studied law. We used to walk the country lanes and dream about the future. He was scared—he was wistful. How did he emerge into this successful, ambitious, overcautious—mediocrity? How do we all emerge into what we are? How did I emerge into what I am? I've dug up some of my old diaries. I was a tremulous young girl. I was eager. I believe I was naive. Look at me now! Time, Dickie . . . What will you be at forty? A bondholder and a commuter . . . Oh, Dickie!

KURT [*tensely*]. I'll never be forty!

MARION [*laughing*]. How will you avoid it?

KURT [*same tone*]. I'll use myself up before I'm forty.

MARION. Do you think so? I don't think so. [*Rises*] I sometimes wake up on certain mornings feeling absolutely — immortal! Indestructible! One is perpetually reborn, I think, Dickie. Everyone should write one's life, I think—but not for publication. For oneself. A kind of spiritual Spring-cleaning!

KURT. The Ego preening . . . !

MARION [*sitting on right arm of sofa left*]. Well, why not? After all, one's ego is all one really has.

KURT. Reminiscence is easy. So is anticipation. It's the *present* that's difficult and most people are too lazy or too indifferent to cope with it.

MARION. It's natural for you to say that—at your age one has no past and no future either, because the intimation of the future comes only with the sense of the past . . .

KURT [*with sudden bitterness*]. *I* see the past as an *evil thing*—to be extirpated.

MARION. How awful! [*Pause*] Why?

KURT. That's not important.

MARION [*rises*]. You freeze up so whenever I try to find out anything about you. I'm not used to that. Usually people open up to me —I'm a born confidante. But not you. . . . I'm interested too, because in an odd way I've become very fond of you.

KURT. My life's very dull, I assure you. *My* past lacks completely what you would call *glamour*.

MARION. No, Dickie. I don't believe that. I don't believe that's true of anybody's life.

KURT. Well, it's true. Moreover it's true of most people's lives. It's easy for anyone who's lived as you have to make romantic generalizations. It's very pleasant for you to believe them. Well, I shan't disillusion you. [*Turns away from her*] Why should I? It's not important. [*She is sitting down, smoking a cigarette in a holder, watching him. He becomes conscious that she is studying him.*]

MARION. I had no idea you felt this way about me—you despise me, don't you? [*He doesn't answer.*] Don't you?

KURT. Yes.

MARION. Why?

KURT [*rises. Walks away*]. Why did we start this?

MARION. You're annoyed at having even momentarily revealed yourself, aren't you? I'll have your secret, Dickie—I'll pluck out the heart of your mystery.

KURT. Secret! Mystery! More romantic nonsense. I have no secret. Nobody has a secret. There are different kinds of greed, different kinds of ambition—that's all!

MARION. Oh, you simplify too much—really I'm afraid you do. Tell me—why do you disapprove of me? Is it—as Bunny does—on moral grounds?

KURT [*right end of sofa left—angrily*]. You're superficial and casual and irresponsible. You take life, which is a tragic thing, as though it were a trivial bedroom farce. You're a second-rate artist who's acquired a reputation through vamping celebrities to sit for you.

MARION [*quietly, she continues smoking*]. Go on . . .

KURT. As an unglamorous upstart who has been forced to make my way I resent parasitism, that's all!

MARION. Isn't there in biology something about benevolent parasites, Dickie? Many great men, I believe, owe a debt of gratitude to their parasites, as many plants do . . . there are varieties. Again, Dickie, you simplify unduly. It is a defect of the radical and the young.

KURT. To return to the Honorable Nolan . . .

MARION. I return to him with relief . . .

KURT. He may exert pressure on us, you know . . .

MARION. How? I'm very interested. . . .

KURT. Well, for one thing, his future father-in-law might get me fired.

MARION. Could he do that?

KURT. He might. He might easily. [MARION *sits upright and looks at him.*] Some form of bribery. He might go to my chief and offer him a bigger job—anything.

MARION. All on account of my poor little biography— It seems incredible that anyone would take all this trouble. . . .

KURT. I'd just like to see them try—I'd just like to, that's all . . .

MARION. What would you do?

KURT. Do? I'd make the Honorable Nolan the laughing stock of the country, and his athletic father-in-law too. I'd just plaster them, that's what I'd do.

MARION. You sound vindictive.

KURT. Baby, I am vindictive!

MARION. Funny, I'm just amused. . . .

KURT. Well, everything's a spectacle to you! [*Turns away from her*] God, how I hate detachment!

MARION. Your desire to break up Bunny is quite impersonal then.

KURT. Surgical. Just as impersonal as that.

MARION. You're a funny boy, Dickie.

KURT [*turns away from her*]. I'm not funny and I'm not a boy. You've been around with dilettantes so long you don't recognize seriousness when you see it.

MARION. But it's the serious people who are funny, Dickie! Look at Bunny.

KURT [*faces her*]. Yes, look at him! An epitome of the brainless muddle of contemporary life, of all the self-seeking second-raters who rise to power and wield power. That's why I'm going to do him in. [*The phone rings—for a moment they pay no attention to it.*] It's the most beautiful chance anybody ever had and I'd just like to see them try and stop me.

[*Phone keeps ringing.* MARION *answers it.*]

MARION. Yes . . . yes . . . certainly. [*To* KURT—*a bit surprised*] It's for you . . . [*She hands him hand-receiver.*]

KURT [*takes phone and talks from rear of sofa*]. Yes. Hello . . . sure. Well, what about it? . . . Oh, you want to talk to me about it, do you? . . . I thought you would . . . I'll be around . . . sure . . . so long. [*He hangs up.*] They've begun! [*He is almost gay with the heady scent of battle.*]

MARION. What do you mean?

KURT. That was my chief. He wants to talk to me about your

story. Kinnicott's begun to put the screws on him. He's going to ask
me to kill it. All right—I'll kill it!

MARION [*faintly*]. I can't believe it. . . .

KURT. Neff's had a call from the father-in-law . . .

MARION. Did he say so?

KURT. No, but you can bet he has!

MARION. I must say this puts my back up . . .

KURT. I'll make a fight for it to keep my job. But if he's stubborn
I'll tell him to go to hell—and go to a publisher with your manu-
script. And if I don't get quick action that way I'll publish it myself
—I'll put every penny I've saved into it . . .

MARION. But why should you? Why does it mean so much to you?

KURT. Do you think I'd miss a chance like this?— It'll test the
calibre of our magazines, of our press, our Senators, our morality . . .

MARION. All on account of my poor little story—how Vicki would
have laughed.

KURT [*a spasm of jealousy again*]. Who's Vicki?

MARION [*aware of it*]. An old friend to whom I'm dedicating the
biography.

KURT. Yeah! [*Sits beside her, then speaks*] Where is he now?

MARION. He's dead. [*A pause. She gets up and crosses to center.*]
I've always rather despised these contemporary women who publi-
cize their emotions. [*Another moment. She walks upstage. She is
thinking aloud.*] And here I am doing it myself. Too much self-
revelation these days. Loud speakers in the confessional. Why should
I add to the noise? I think, as far as this story is concerned, I'll call
it a day, Dickie.

KURT. What!

MARION. Let's forget all about it, shall we?

KURT. If you let me down now, I'll hate you.

MARION. Will you? Why won't you take me into your confidence
then? Why won't you tell me about yourself? What are you after?

KURT [*after a moment of inhibition decides to reveal his secret
dream*]. My ambition is to be critic-at-large of things-as-they-are. I
want to find out everything there is to know about the intimate
structure of things. I want to reduce the whole system to absurdity.
I want to laugh the powers-that-be out of existence in a great winnow-
ing gale of laughter.

MARION. That's an interesting research. Of course it strikes me
it's vitiated by one thing—you have a preconceived idea of what you

will find. In a research biased like that from the start you are apt to overlook much that is noble and generous and gentle.

KURT [*challenging and bitter*]. Have you found generosity and gentleness and nobility?

MARION. A good deal—yes.

KURT. Well, I haven't!

MARION. I'm sorry for you.

KURT. You needn't be. Reserve your pity for weaklings. I don't need it!

MARION. Are you so strong? [*A pause.* KURT *doesn't answer.*] How old are you, Dickie?

KURT [*turns away*]. What difference does that make?

MARION. Who do you live with?

KURT. I live alone.

MARION. Are you in love with anybody?

KURT. No.

MARION. Where are your parents?

KURT. They're dead.

MARION. Long?

KURT. My mother is. I hardly remember her. Just barely remember her.

MARION. Your father? [*He doesn't answer.*] Do you remember your father?

KURT [*in a strange voice*]. Yes. I remember him all right.

MARION. What did your father do?

KURT. He was a coal miner.

MARION. Oh! Won't you tell me about him? I'd like to know.

KURT. I was a kid of fourteen. There was a strike. One day my father took me out for a walk. Sunny spring morning. We stopped to listen to an organizer. My father was a mild little man with kind of faded, tired blue eyes. We stood on the outskirts of the crowd. My father was holding me by the hand. Suddenly somebody shouted: "The militia!" There was a shot. Everybody scattered. My father was bewildered—he didn't know which way to turn. A second later he crumpled down beside me. He was bleeding. He was still holding my hand. He died like that. . . . [*A moment. He concludes harshly—coldly—like steel*] Are there any other glamorous facts of my existence you would like to know?

MARION [*stirred to her heart*]. You poor boy . . . I knew there was something . . . I knew . . . !

KURT [*hard and ironic*]. It's trivial really. People exaggerate the importance of human life. One has to die. [*Turns to her*] The point is to have fun while you're alive, isn't it? Well, you've managed. I congratulate you!

MARION [*her heart full*]. Dickie darling—why are you so bitter against me? Why against me . . . ?

KURT. Do you want to know that too? Well, it's because . . . [*His voice rises. She suddenly doesn't want him to speak.*].

MARION. Hush, dearest—hush—don't say any more—I understand —not any more . . .

[*His defenses vanish suddenly. He sinks to his knees beside her, his arms around her.*]

KURT. Marion, my angel!

MARION [*infinitely compassionate, stroking his hair*]. Dickie— Dickie—Dickie . . . Why have you been afraid to love me?

CURTAIN

act 3

SCENE: *The same.*

TIME: *Late afternoon. Two weeks later.*

The telephone is ringing as the curtain rises. There is a moment and MINNIE *enters and crosses to rear of the table, rear of the sofa left. She picks up the receiver.*

MINNIE [*speaking into the phone*]. Hello.—No, Mr. Kurt, she's not yet back. Vot? You're not coming home to dinner?!—But I've made the Pfannkuchen you like— Vot?— You're tired of my damn Pfannkuchen—[*She shouts angrily.*] Every night I make dinner and you and Marion go out!—I'm *not* yelling— Vot? Vot shall I tell Marion?— Vot?— [*Doorbell rings.*] Vait—vait a minute.— Someone's ringing. [*She puts the receiver on the table and goes to the door.* MINNIE *shows in* LEANDER NOLAN, *who is followed by* ORRIN KINNICOTT, *who is a big, well-developed Southerner, about fifty-five, with a high-pitched voice. He is a superbly-built man with a magnificent chest development. He is aware that he is a fine figure of a man, impeccably dressed in formal afternoon clothes.*]

NOLAN [to MINNIE, *who has preceded him into the room*]. Did Miss Froude say she was expecting us for tea, Minnie?

MINNIE. No, Mr. Nolan. She didn't say nothing to me.

NOLAN. Not even when she'd be back?

MINNIE [*hangs up coats*]. No. She just went out.

NOLAN. All right, Minnie. We'll wait.

MINNIE. Yes, Mr. Nolan. [*She is about to go out into kitchen when she remembers that* KURT *is on the telephone. She picks up the receiver and says*] Hello—Mr. Kurt—you dere?— Good-bye! [*She then hangs up the receiver and exits left.*]

KINNICOTT [*querulously. Sits on sofa right*]. Did you tell her four o'clock?

NOLAN. Yes. I told her. [NOLAN's *manner with his father-in-law-to-be in this scene conveys the beginnings of a secret irritation, an inner rebellion.*]

KINNICOTT. Does she know I'm a busy man?

NOLAN [*gloomily*]. She's not impressed much by busy men.

KINNICOTT. I know these fly-by-night characters. I've dealt with 'em before . . . Bad— [*he sniffs the air of the room*] —bad air. [*Rises—tries to open window, fails, sits on window seat*] Bet she's underexercised.

NOLAN. On the contrary—she's radiantly healthy!

KINNICOTT. Cosmetics, I bet! These fly-by-night characters. . . .

NOLAN [*very irritated*]. Why do you keep calling her a fly-by-night character? She's nothing of the sort!

KINNICOTT [*crosses to* NOLAN]. Look here, Leander. . . .

NOLAN. Well?

KINNICOTT. Have you been entirely frank with me, in this matter?

NOLAN. Of course I have. . . .

KINNICOTT [*cryptic*]. About the past—yes. But I refer to the present.

NOLAN. I don't know what you mean.

KINNICOTT. I think you do know what I mean. Sometimes the way you talk I suspect—I suspect, Leander—that you are still in love with this woman.

NOLAN. Nonsense! I simply tell you that she's not a fly-by-night character. That doesn't mean I'm in love with her!

KINNICOTT. My daughter feels the same thing.

NOLAN. Slade! You've discussed this with Slade!

KINNICOTT. She's discussed it with me. She's no fool, that girl. She's noticed things lately.

NOLAN. What things?

KINNICOTT. She says she talks to you and that you're off somewhere else—dreaming. I tried to put her on another scent—but she was positive. She said: "Come on now, dad—don't stall me—come clean!" So I told her!

NOLAN. You did!

KINNICOTT. Yes.

NOLAN. When?

KINNICOTT. Yesterday. Told her it happened fifteen years ago, that you were a naive young feller, didn't know anything about women, were just naturally taken in . . .

NOLAN. That's not true though. I was not taken in.

KINNICOTT. There you go again—defending the woman that's endangering your entire career and using up my energies and yours when you ought to be home right now getting together with folks and thinking how to cinch this here election. Not going to be a walk-over, you know. [*Again trying the window*] How do you open this thing to get some air? [*Sits on window seat*]

NOLAN. I don't know. What did Slade say when you told her?

KINNICOTT. Nothin'. You know Slade's not the talkin' kind.

NOLAN. Funny she didn't mention it to me last night.

KINNICOTT. Didn't want to worry yer probably . . . all wool and a yard wide that girl is. I warn you, Leander, don't tamper with the most precious and rare thing. . . .

NOLAN [*impatient of oratory*]. I know—I know. The point is—what are we going to do?

KINNICOTT. 'Course I can get that young fellow—what's his name?

NOLAN. Kurt.

KINNICOTT. I can get him fired all right. From what you've told me, Leander, he's got something else up his sleeve. . . .

NOLAN. I'm afraid so.

KINNICOTT. That's what I want to find out from your lady friend. And I've got a pretty sure idea right now what it is.

NOLAN. What do you mean?

KINNICOTT. Money!

NOLAN [*still not understanding*]. Money . . .?

KINNICOTT. Blackmail!

NOLAN. You're crazy!

KINNICOTT. You don't know much about women, Leander; when you know the sex as well as I do you'll know that every woman has blackmail up her sleeve.

NOLAN. Look here, Orrin . . . !

KINNICOTT [*rises, confronts* NOLAN]. Now, you listen to me for a moment, son. . . . This situation's gone about far enough right now. You'd better make up your mind whether you want this blackmailing female or whether you want my daughter . . . and you'd better make it up right quick.

NOLAN [*flaring up*]. I resent your tone, Orrin, and I won't be ordered around as if I were a high-grade servant!

KINNICOTT. Now son, when you get control of your temper, and cool down a little bit, you'll see that my ordering hasn't been so bad for you. I'll acknowledge you were mighty successful as a lawyer, but in politics, you're nothing but a novice.

NOLAN [*resentful*]. Am I?

[*Doorbell*]

KINNICOTT. Just look back a bit, that's all—I've had to push and bolster you to get you where you are.

NOLAN [*desperately*]. I know—I have every reason to be grateful to you—that's the worst of it.

[MINNIE *enters and crosses to hall door. Both men turn and watch to see who it is that is calling.*]

MINNIE [*speaking to someone at the door*]. Ja, Fräulein?

SLADE [*off stage*]. Is Miss Froude in?

MINNIE. Nein, Fräulein.

SLADE [*entering*]. Well, I'll just wait. [SLADE KINNICOTT *is a good-looking, dark, high-spirited girl, a rather inspiriting and healthy example of the generation growing up on D. H. Lawrence.*[1] *To her father and* NOLAN *as she crosses downstage between them*] Hello.

NOLAN. Slade!

KINNICOTT [*severely*]. Daughter! What are you doing here?

SLADE. Came to have my picture painted. What are you?

KINNICOTT. Your coming here at this time is most inopportune, daughter. We are here on business.

SLADE [*mischievously*]. I can imagine!

NOLAN. I'm very glad you came, Slade. I want you to meet the woman whom your father has just been accusing of the most reprehensible crimes!

SLADE. I'm pretty anxious to get a load of her myself. [*Looks about the room taking it in and then sits on the left end of the sofa*

---

[1] *D. H. Lawrence, British author whose writings took a liberal attitude toward free love.*

below the piano] Nice lay-out. Gee, I wish I were artistic. What a lucky gal she is! A paint-brush and an easel and she can set up shop anywhere in the world. That's independence for you! Gosh! [*She looks about, admiring and envious.*]

KINNICOTT. Why must you come here to get your picture painted? We have tolerable good artists in Knoxville.

SLADE. Well, if you *must* know I'm very keen to have a heart-to-heart talk with my fiancé's old girl. Natural, isn't it?

KINNICOTT. No, it isn't natural!

NOLAN [*crosses angrily to window and back toward* KINNICOTT *and sits down on stool right near sofa on which* SLADE *and her father are sitting*]. This is what you get for telling her, Orrin.

SLADE. If you think I didn't suspect something was up ever since Froude arrived here, you don't know your little bride. Maybe I haven't been watching the clouds gather on that classic brow! Where is my rival? Don't tell me she's holding up two big shots like you two boys.

KINNICOTT. Slade, this is no time . . . please leave us before she comes.

SLADE. Not I! Just my luck; when a story is going to come out which has something in it *I* want to read, you two killjoys are going to suppress it!

NOLAN. This isn't exactly a joke, you know, Slade. . . .

SLADE. I mean it. . . .

KINNICOTT [*sadly*]. I've spoiled you, Slade—I've been too easy with you. . . .

SLADE. At least I hope you'll buy the *manuscript*. My God, father, I'm curious. Can't you understand that? I want to find out what Leander was like before he became ambitious. I've a right to know! This story might hurt you with the voters in Tennessee, Leander, but it's given me a kick out of you I didn't know was there! How did she make you, Leander—that's what I'd like to know. You've been pretty unapproachable to me but I sort of took it for granted National Figures were like that. Also I'd gotten to the point when I was going to suggest that we break our engagement, but this little incident revives my interest.

NOLAN [*furious*]. Indeed!

SLADE. Yes indeed. Where is this woman? What is that secret? How to Make National Figures . . . there's a title for you!

KINNICOTT. Slade, you're talking too much! Shut up!

NOLAN [*rises and moves stool toward them a bit*]. No, she isn't at all. . . . [*To* SLADE] If your interest in me requires the artificial stimulus of an episode that happened twenty years ago . . .

SLADE [*leaning toward him*]. It requires something. . . .

NOLAN [*leaning closer toward her. The three heads are now close together,* KINNICOTT's *in the center*]. Does it?

SLADE. It does. We were getting so that conversation, when we were alone, was rather difficult.

[NOLAN *starts to argue.*]

KINNICOTT [*pushes them apart*]. Children! Children!

NOLAN. We're not children! [*To* SLADE] If our relationship is so—

SLADE. Tenuous . . . ?

NOLAN. . . . That it requires artificial . . .

SLADE. Respiration . . . ?

NOLAN. If it's as bad as that then I think perhaps we'd both better . . .

SLADE. Call it a day? . . . You'll need me in the Senate, Leander, to fill in the gaps when you get hung up in a speech. Consider carefully what you are discarding. . . .

NOLAN. If that is the case I tell you solemnly we'd better separate now.

SLADE [*mock tragedy*]. Father, Leander is giving your daughter the air. Do something!

KINNICOTT. I don't blame him for being irritated. You should not be here. Please go home.

SLADE [*lights cigarette*]. Don't worry, dad. I'll get him back.

KINNICOTT. This is a bad mess, Leander. And I must tell you frankly that I don't altogether approve of your attitude . . .

NOLAN. And I must tell you frankly that I don't approve of *yours.* . . .

KINNICOTT. Is that so!

NOLAN. I don't like your tone in speaking of a woman with whom at one time I had a relation of the tenderest emotion—for whom I still have a high regard. . . .

KINNICOTT. That's evident anyway!

NOLAN. When you apply to such a woman the terms you used before Slade came in, when you impute to her motives so base, you cast an equal reflection on my judgment and my character. . . .

SLADE. And that, pop, is lèse-majesté.

NOLAN. And it may be perfectly true, Slade, that knowing Miss Froude has spoiled me for the flippant modernisms with which you study. . . .

SLADE. I'm dying to ask her one thing: when you made love to her in the old days did it always sound like a prepared speech on tariff schedules?

KINNICOTT. This is getting us nowhere. . . .

SLADE. Well, dad, what do you expect? Leander and I have broken our engagement since I came into this room. That's progress, isn't it?

KINNICOTT. Your coming here at this time was most unfortunate.

SLADE. Leander doesn't think so. [*Ironically*] He's free now to pursue the lady for whom he still has a high regard. [*Rises*] Are we no longer engaged, Leander?

NOLAN. That's not for me to say.

SLADE [*rises and shakes hands with* NOLAN]. Gentleman to the last! And at the very moment—

KINNICOTT [*in despair—speaks as* SLADE *starts to speak*]. Slade, if you would only go home!

SLADE [*crosses left*]. Just at the very moment when I was saying to myself: Well, if a brilliant and beautiful woman who has played footie with royalty in the capitals of the world loved him, maybe there's a secret charm in him that I've overlooked—just when I was saying that and preparing to probe and discover—[*lightly*]—he gives me the air. [*Sits on sofa left*] By God, Orrin, there's life for you. [*Bell rings.*] Ah, that must be my rival!

[NOLAN *gets up and fixes his tie, expecting* MARION. *But it is* KURT *who comes in. He faces them. He is in a white heat of anger.*]

KURT. Well, gentlemen, I'm not surprised to find you here! [*Drops hat on model stand and comes downstage left*]

NOLAN [*about to introduce* KINNICOTT]. How do you do, Mr. Kurt . . . this is. . . .

KURT. I can guess who it is. I can guess why you're here. Having failed to intimidate *me* you are here to intimidate Miss Froude. [SLADE *rises, excited by this tempest.*] Well, I can advise you that you will fail with her too.

NOLAN. This is his usual style, Orrin. Don't mind him.

KURT. I have just come from my office where I have been informed by Mr. Neff— [SLADE *stands below* KURT—*just behind him—watching him*]—whom *you* doubtless know, Mr. Kinnicott—that I could decide between publishing Miss Froude's story or giving up my job. I invited him to go to hell. That invitation I now cordially extend to you two gentlemen.

SLADE. Why doesn't somebody introduce me to this interesting young man? [*She comes toward him.* KURT *is embarrassed, but covers it in a gruff manner. He has actually not been aware of her in the room.*]

KURT. I'm sorry—I—I didn't know.

SLADE. Why are you sorry? I'm Slade Kinnicott. [*She gives him her hand. He takes it, limply.*]

KURT. All right—all right. [*He is disarmed and feels, suddenly, rather foolish.*]

SLADE. Leander, why have you kept me apart from this young man?

KURT. I'm sorry—I . . .

SLADE. Nonsense. What's your name?

KURT. Richard Kurt.

SLADE. Go to it— [*Turns him toward others*]

KINNICOTT [*impressively—interposing between them*]. You're being very foolish, young man.

KURT [*crosses toward them—to right of model stand*]. Possibly.

NOLAN. You can't argue with him. I've tried it. He's a fanatic.

KURT. But if you ask me I think *you're* being very foolish.

KINNICOTT [*who wants to find out what's in* KURT's *mind*]. Are we? How do you figure that, young man?

SLADE [*parroting—crosses and sits on model stand. She is having a wonderful time*]. Yes, how!

KINNICOTT. Oh, hush your mouth.

KURT. Because I'm going to publish Miss Froude's book myself. And I promise you that it'll be the best-advertised first book that's come out in a long time.

SLADE. Thank God! Will you send me the advance sheets? I'll make it worth your while, Mr. Kurt.

KINNICOTT. I can see you are an extremely impulsive young man. Have you ever inquired, may I ask . . . ?

SLADE [*edges a bit closer to* KURT]. This is going to be dangerous! Look out, Richard. . . .

[NOLAN *sits on stool, disgusted with* SLADE.]

KINNICOTT [*smoothly*]. Have you inquired into the penalties for libel, Mr. Kurt?

KURT. Libel! You're going to sue me for libel, are you?

KINNICOTT [*same voice*]. Yes. You and Miss Froude both . . . yes. . . .

KURT. Well, you just go ahead and try it, that's all I can tell you.

Go ahead and sue. [*Crosses to above* NOLAN] It'll put Mr. Nolan in a charming position before those *moral* constituents of his, won't it? [*Includes both* NOLAN *and* KINNICOTT] Go ahead and sue, both of you—sue your heads off . . . ! I promise the two of you I'll give you the fight of your lives!

SLADE [*delighted*]. Good for you, Richard!

[MARION *comes in. She wears a long red velvet coat, and a little red cap stuck on the side of her golden head—she looks a little like Portia.*[1] *She is at the top of her form.*]

MARION [*beaming with hospitality*]. Well! How nice! Minnie!

KURT [*goes upstage to right of* MARION]. This chivalrous gentleman has just been proposing to sue you for libel—he considers . . .

SLADE [*who rises and stands just below the model stand*]. I'm Slade Kinnicott.

MARION [*crosses downstage to her and they shake hands over the model stand*]. How very nice of you to come! [*Turns and faces* KINNICOTT] Is this Mr. Kinnicott? [*He bows.*] I'm so glad to see you. [*They shake hands.*] I'm so sorry to be late. [*Waves hello to* NOLAN] Hello, Bunny.

SLADE [*this is too much for her*]. Oh, my God—BUNNY! [*She sits, overcome.*]

MARION [*to* NOLAN]. I'm so sorry . . .

NOLAN [*glaring at* SLADE]. It's all right, Marion!

MARION. Has Minnie given you tea? I'll just . . . Minnie! [MINNIE *enters.*] Tea, Minnie, please. . . . [*To the men*] Or cocktails—highballs . . . ?

KINNICOTT. I never drink alcoholic mixtures.

NOLAN [*asserting his independence*]. I'll have a highball!

KINNICOTT. I must tell you, Leander, that I do not approve—

NOLAN. I'll have *two* whiskies straight!

MARION. Good! Highball for you, Miss Kinnicott?

SLADE. Thanks.

MARION. I'll fix them myself, Minnie. Just bring us some tea, Minnie.

KINNICOTT. Nor do I wish any tea.

KURT [*crosses down left*]. Nor do I.

MARION. Do you mind if I have a cup? Do sit down, Miss Kinnicott. A tiring day. . . . [SLADE *sits on model stand.* MARION *goes up to rear of piano.*] Minnie, please bring me a cup of tea—

---

[1] *Portia, the heroine of* The Merchant of Venice, *dressed for her role as lawyer.*

MINNIE. Ja, Fräulein. [*Remembering*] A telegram for you, Fräulein.

MARION. Oh, thank you, Minnie. Just put it there on the table. [MINNIE *leaves the telegram on the table rear of the sofa left and then exits left.* MARION *removes her coat and hat and crosses to rear of piano and starts to mix the highballs.*] Now then! What is all this nice cheerful talk about a libel suit? That's what they're always having in England, isn't it, on the least provocation. It's when you've circulated a lie about someone—defamed someone—maliciously—isn't it? Bunny! [*She gives* NOLAN *his two drinks. He takes them and returns to his position.* MARION *picks up the other glass and crosses with it to* SLADE.] Now then—whom have I defamed?

KURT. You've defamed the Honorable Mr. Nolan!

MARION [*hands drink to* SLADE]. Have I? Oh, I am tired. . . . [*She sits on sofa.*] Sit by me, won't you, Miss Kinnicott?

SLADE [*sauntering over*]. Thanks. [*She sits by* MARION *on the sofa.*]

MARION. You're very pretty. . . .

SLADE [*more warmly*]. Thanks!

MARION. Bunny, I congratulate you. I've heard so much about you, Miss Kinnicott. And I think it's very gracious of you to come and see me. If Bunny lets me I'd like to paint you—[MINNIE *enters*]—and give you the portrait for a wedding-present. [*She rises and crosses to above model stand to get cup of tea from* MINNIE. MINNIE *exits left.*] Thank you, Minnie.

SLADE. You're very lovely.

MARION. Thank you, my dear.

SLADE. I can't tell you how curious I've been about you—I—

KINNICOTT. This is all very well—but I'm a busy man . . .

MARION [*looks at* KINNICOTT *as she crosses and sits right of* SLADE. *A moment, then* MARION *speaks*]. It seems so strange to see you with all your clothes on. It seems a pity—as an artist I must say it seems a pity—to conceal that wonderful chest development that I've admired so often in The Body Beautiful.

KINNICOTT. That's neither here nor there.

MARION [*this is almost an aside to* SLADE]. It seems to me that it's decidedly *there*. [MARION *and* SLADE *laugh quietly together.*]

KINNICOTT. Slade, you've upset everything by coming here. . . .

[KURT *comes forward. He has been eaten up with irritation that the superb indignation he felt should have been so dissipated by this cascade of small talk. He can stand it no longer.*]

KURT [*crosses to right of model stand*]. If you understood better what these gentlemen mean to do . . . !

NOLAN [*protests*]. It wasn't my idea!

KURT. You wouldn't be quite so friendly, Marion. . . .

MARION. I couldn't possibly be unfriendly to anyone so frank— and—and gladiatorial—as Mr. Kinnicott.

KURT [*furious at her for not letting him launch into it*]. A libel suit . . . !

MARION. Oh, yes! A libel suit! It sounds so cozy. Sit down, won't you? [KINNICOTT *sits on stool*.] A libel suit. Now then—what shall it be about?

KURT. The Honorable Nolan is going to sue you for libel. . . .

NOLAN. I'll punch your head if you say that again. . . .

KURT. On the assumption that when you say in your story that you and he were lovers you are lying and defaming his character!

MARION. Dear Bunny, you must want to be a Senator very very badly!

NOLAN [*in despair*]. I never said it, I tell you!

MARION. As a matter of fact, how could I prove it? Come to think of it, are there any letters? Did you ever write to me, Bunny?

NOLAN. I don't remember.

MARION. I don't think you ever did. You see—we were always— during that dim brief period of your youth—we were always so close —letters were hardly necessary, were they? Did I ever send you any letters, Bunny?

NOLAN. I don't remember, I tell you.

MARION. Neither do I. You might look around in old trunks and places and see if you can find some old letters of an affectionate nature —I'd love to read them—they'd probably make wonderful reading now. Why is it that the things one writes when one's young always sound so foolish afterwards? Has that ever occurred to you, Mr. Kinnicott?

KINNICOTT. I don't admit the fact.

MARION. No.

KINNICOTT. No. I was looking over some old editorials of mine written in the depression of 1907 and they're just as apropos today. I haven't changed my ideas in twenty-five years.

MARION. Haven't you really? How very steadfast. Now if the world were equally changeless, how consistent that would make you. [*To* KURT] Well, there isn't any documentary evidence.

KURT. It doesn't matter. . . .

KINNICOTT. As I said before, this is getting us nowhere. Don't you think, Miss Froude, that the only way we can settle this is by ourselves? [*She smiles at him.*] I can see you're a sensible woman.

MARION. I am very sensible.

KINNICOTT. And you and I can settle this matter in short order.

KURT. You don't have to talk to him at all if you don't want to.

MARION [*smiling at* KINNICOTT]. But I'd love to. I've always wanted to meet Mr. Kinnicott. There are some questions I want very much to ask him. [*To the others*] You can all wait in my bedroom. It's fairly tidy, I think.

SLADE [*to* KURT— *Rises, crosses to him*]. Why don't you take me for a walk, Richard?

MARION [*as* KURT *hesitates*]. Do that, Dickie. A walk'll do you good.

NOLAN. What'll I do?

MARION [*as if it were another dilemma*]. You wait in my bedroom. [*Aware suddenly of the proprieties*] No—in Minnie's bedroom. It's just next to the kitchen.

NOLAN [*defiantly*]. I will! [*He exits into bedroom.*]

KURT [*sulky—he doesn't quite like the turn affairs have taken*]. We'll be back in ten minutes.

SLADE [*as they go out*]. You can't tell, Richard. [SLADE *and* KURT *exit.*]

[MARION *draws a deep breath. She assumes at once with* KIN-NICOTT *the air of two equals, mature people talking freely to each other after they've gotten rid of the children.*]

MARION [*they cross to sofa left*]. Now we can talk! It's funny— I feel we've put the children to bed and can have a quiet talk after a lot of chatter.

KINNICOTT. Same here!

MARION. Please sit down. [*They do.*]

KINNICOTT. I feel sure you and I can come to an understanding.

MARION. I'm sure we can.

KINNICOTT. Now then, about this little matter of the story— You won't mind if I speak very frankly to you . . . ?

MARION. Not at all.

KINNICOTT. You see, Miss Froude . . .

MARION. Oh, call me Marion. Everybody does.

KINNICOTT. Thanks. Call me Orrin.

MARION. All right, I'll try. Not a very usual name. Orrin. Fits you. Strong. Rugged strength.

KINNICOTT. Thank you.

MARION. You're welcome. What were you going to say when I interrupted you? You were going to say something. . . .

KINNICOTT. I was going to say—you're not at all what I expected to meet.

MARION. No? What did you think I'd be like? Tell me—I'd love to know.

KINNICOTT. Well, you're kind of homey—you know—folksy . . .

MARION. Folksy. [*Smiles*] After all, there's no reason I shouldn't be, is there? I'm just a small-town girl from Tennessee. I sometimes wonder at myself—how I ever got so far away. . . .

KINNICOTT [*positively*]. Metabolism!

MARION. I beg your pardon. . . .

KINNICOTT. I always say—take most of the bad men and most of the loose women and correct their metabolism and you'll correct them.

MARION. Really?

KINNICOTT [*seriously*]. Absolutely. Trouble with our penology experts—so-called—is that they're psychologists—so-called—when they should be physiologists.

MARION. That is very interesting indeed. Have you ever written anything about that?

KINNICOTT. Off and on.

MARION. Any definitive work I mean?

KINNICOTT. I'm considering doing that right now.

MARION. Oh, I do wish you would! It's extraordinary how little one knows about one's own body, isn't it? I get so impatient of myself sometimes—of my physical limitations. My mind is seething with ideas but I haven't the physical energy to go on working. I tire so quickly—and often for no apparent reason. Why is that, Mr. Kinnicott?

KINNICOTT. Defective—

[*She says at same time with him*]

MARION—KINNICOTT. Metabolism!

KINNICOTT. Tell me—

MARION. What?

KINNICOTT. Do you eat enough roughage?

MARION. I don't know, offhand.

KINNICOTT [*firmly*]. Well, you should know!

MARION. As I say, Orrin—one is so ignorant of these fundamental things.

KINNICOTT [*definitely aware now of* MARION *as a personal possibility*]. I can see this, Marion—if you'd met me—instead of Leander —when you were a young girl—you'd have been a different woman.

MARION. I'm sure I would. Imagine—with one's metabolism disciplined early in life—how far one could go.

KINNICOTT [*confidentially offering her hope*]. It's not too late!

MARION. Isn't it?

KINNICOTT. Er. . . . [*He drops his voice still lower.*] What are you doing tomorrow evenin'?

MARION. I—I'm free.

KINNICOTT [*same voice*]. Will you have dinner with me?

MARION. I'd be delighted.

KINNICOTT. Fine! Then we can go over this little matter of the story and Leander quietly. Leander isn't strong on tact. . . .

MARION. You know, some men aren't.

KINNICOTT. You and I can make a friendly adjustment.

MARION. What fun! [*They chuckle.*]

KINNICOTT. What time shall we meet? Say seven-thirty?

MARION. Let's say eight . . . do you mind?

KINNICOTT. My apartment?

MARION. If you like.

KINNICOTT. Here's my card with the address. It's a roof apartment. I'm a widower.

MARION. Irresistible combination!

KINNICOTT. By the way—

MARION. What?

KINNICOTT. Don't mention our little date for tomorrow evenin' to Leander.

MARION [*rising*]. No, I agree with you. I don't think that would be wise.

KINNICOTT [*nodding trustingly—rises*]. Fine! At seven-thirty?

MARION. No—no. Eight.

KINNICOTT. Oh yes . . . eight. [*A moment's pause. He visibly preens before her, buttoning his beautifully-fitting frock coat across his heroic chest.*]

MARION [*approving*]. Wonderful! Wonderful!

KINNICOTT [*going toward bedroom. To her*]. Do you mind if I . . . Leander . . .

MARION. Not at all.

KINNICOTT. I'll take the load off his mind.

[*He goes out. She can't believe it. The whole situation is so fantastic. She flings off her little red cap and shaking with laughter collapses on the couch.* MINNIE *comes in to clear up the tea-things.*]

MARION [*as* MINNIE *enters*]. It's too good to be true, Minnie. . . .

MINNIE. Vat is too good to be true?

MARION. I must write some of it down before I forget it . . . [*The bell again.* MARION *gets up to make notes on her script.*] —A widower's penthouse— [*With an irritated sigh* MINNIE *goes out to answer bell.* MARION *sits at desk jotting notes very fast.* SLADE *and* KURT *come in.* KURT *is morose.* MARION *gets up to greet them.*] Well, children?

SLADE. That walk was a total loss.

MARION [*laughing*]. What did you expect?

SLADE. Well, a little encouragement—just a soupçon . . .

MARION. Dickie's very serious.

SLADE. How did you come out with dad?

MARION. Wonderful! I'm crazy about him!

SLADE. But he got you to renege on the story . . .

MARION. Well, he thinks so. However, we're going to discuss it tomorrow evenin'.

SLADE. Thought he'd date you up—could tell by the way he eyed you. . . .

MARION. He's going to teach me how to live in a state of virtuous metabolism.

SLADE. Oh! Don't you believe it! Dad's an awful old chaser.

MARION [*rather shocked*]. Slade!

SLADE [*amused*]. Are you shocked?

MARION. You make me feel a little old-fashioned.

[KURT *is intensely irritated by this conversation.*]

KURT. Where are they?

MARION. They're in there sitting on Minnie's bed. Orrin is probably telling Bunny that everything'll be all right.

SLADE [*sits left of* MARION]. Marion. . . .

MARION. Yes. . . .

SLADE. What is there about Bunny you can't help liking?

[*Utterly disgusted,* KURT *goes to sofa down left and sits staring moodily into a gloomily-tinted future.*]

MARION. He's a dear—there's something very touching about Bunny —sweet . . .

SLADE. Were you in love with him once?

MARION. Yes.

SLADE. Are you in love with him now?

MARION. No.

SLADE [*in a whisper*]. Are you in love with—someone else?

MARION [*a moment's pause*]. Yes.

SLADE. I thought you were. He's mad about you.— I envy you, Marion.

MARION. Do you? Why?

SLADE. You're independent. You're—yourself. You can do anything you like.

MARION. Yes, I know. But it's possible one can pay too much for independence. I'm adrift. Sometimes—you know what seems to me the most heavenly thing—the only thing—for a woman? Marriage, children—the dear boundaries of routine . . .

SLADE. If you had married Bunny he would've given 'em to you. He's still in love with you, but he doesn't quite know it. Shall I tell him?

MARION [*parrying*]. What are you talking about?

SLADE. I wish we could change places, Marion. You can with me but I can't with you.

[KINNICOTT *and* NOLAN *come in from the bedroom.* KINNICOTT *is at his most oleaginous.*]

KINNICOTT [*to* KURT]. Well, young man! Over your little temper?

KURT. No, I'm not over it! What makes you think I'm over it?

KINNICOTT. Well, well, well! As far as I'm concerned there are no hard feelings. I'm going to call up your employer myself when I get home and tell him, that as far as you are concerned, to let bygones be bygones. Can't do more than that, can I?

KURT. To what do I owe this generosity?

KINNICOTT. To the fact that in Miss Froude you have a most gracious friend and intercepter. [*He gives* MARION *a gallant, old-South bow.*] Miss Froude—this has been a very great pleasure.

MARION [*rises—with an answering bow*]. Thank you!

[SLADE *also rises.*]

KINNICOTT [*giving her his hand*]. Auf wiedersehen.

MARION. Auf Wiedersehen. Ich kann es kaum erwarten![1]

KINNICOTT [*pretending to understand*]. Yes, oh, yes, yes, of course! [*To* SLADE] Come, Slade. [*He goes to hall door.*]

SLADE. All right, dad. [*To* NOLAN] Coming—Bunny?

NOLAN. Well, yes—I'm coming.

SLADE [*to* NOLAN]. You want to stay. Why don't you?

[1] *Ich . . . erwarten! I can hardly wait!*

KINNICOTT [*quickly marshaling his little following with a military precision*]. I think Leander had better come with us—

SLADE [*to* MARION]. Good-bye, Marion.

MARION [*to* SLADE]. Good-bye, Slade. [*They shake hands.*] Come to see me.

SLADE. Thanks, I will.

KINNICOTT [*smiles at* MARION]. Miss Froude! [*Bows to* MARION *who returns his bow*] Come, daughter. Come, Leander. [*To* KURT] Good-bye, young man. No hard feelings. [KURT *glares at him.* KINNICOTT *again bows to* MARION.] Miss Froude! [MARION *is startled into still a third bow. He calls without looking back*] Come, Slade! Leander!!

SLADE [*as she exits*]. Bunny!

NOLAN [*lingers an instant then crosses to* MARION]. I'll be back.

MARION. When?

NOLAN. In a few minutes. All right?

MARION. I'll be in. [*He goes out quickly.* MARION *is in wonderful spirits. She runs to* KURT *and throws her arms around him.*] Oh, Dickie. That Orrin! That Orrin!

KURT. What did you say to him that put him in such good spirits?

MARION. Everything I said put him in good spirits. I can't wait for tomorrow evenin'. I can't wait for that dinner. It'll probably consist entirely of roughage—just imagine! He's the quaintest man I ever met in my life. He's too good to be true. [*Sits right of* KURT]

KURT. Well, he may be quaint to you but to me he's a putrescent old hypocrite and I don't see how you can bear to have him come near you, say less go to dinner with him!

MARION [*sobered by his intensity*]. You're so merciless in your judgments, Dickie. You quite frighten me sometimes—you do really.

KURT. And so do you me.

MARION. I do? That's absurd!

KURT. You do. It's like thinking a person fastidious and exacting and finding her suddenly . . .

MARION. Gross—indiscriminating?

KURT [*bluntly*]. Yes!

MARION. You know, Dickie, I adore you and I'm touched by you and I love you but I'd hate to live in a country where you were Dictator. It would be all right while you loved me but when you stopped. . . .

KURT. It wouldn't make any difference if I stopped—I shouldn't be that kind of a Dictator . . .

MARION [*glances at him. Almost sadly*]. I see you've thought of it. . . .

KURT [*inexorably*]. What did you say to Kinnicott?

MARION. Your manner is so—inquisitorial. I haven't been able to get used to it.

KURT [*angry and jealous*]. I heard you tell Nolan to come back too . . . How do you think I feel?

MARION. Dickie!

KURT. When Nolan sat there and told me he had been your lover, I felt like socking him. Even when we're alone together, I can't forget that . . . yet you encourage him, and Kinnicott— My God, Marion, you seem to like these people!

MARION. I certainly like Slade.

KURT. Well I don't. She's conceited and overbearing. Thinks she can have anything she likes because she's Orrin Kinnicott's daughter.

MARION. That's where you're wrong. She's a nice girl—and she's unhappy.

KURT [*bitterly*]. Maladjusted, I suppose!

MARION. Dickie, Dickie, Dickie! Studying you, I can see why so many movements against injustice become such absolute—tyrannies.

KURT. That beautiful detachment again. . . . [*He is white with fury. He hates her at this moment.*]

MARION [*with a little laugh*]. You hate me, don't you . . . ?

KURT. Yes! Temporizing with these . . . ! Yes . . . ! I hate you. [*She says nothing, sits there looking at him.*] These people flout you, they insult you in the most flagrant way. God knows I'm not a gentleman, but it horrifies me to think of the insufferable arrogance of their attitude toward you . . . as if the final insult to their pride and their honor could only come from the discovery that this stuffed shirt Nolan had once been your lover! The blot on the immaculate Tennessee scutcheon! Why, it's the God-damndest insolence I ever heard of. And yet you flirt and curry favor and bandy with them. And you're amused—always amused!

MARION. Yes. I am amused.

KURT. I can't understand such . . . !

MARION. Of course you can't. That's the difference—one of the differences—between 25 and 35!

KURT. If the time ever comes when I'm amused by what I should hate, I hope somebody shoots me. What did you tell Kinnicott?

MARION. Nothing. Simply nothing. I saw no point in having a scene with him so I inquired into his favorite subject. He gave me health hints. He thinks tomorrow night he will cajole me—through the exercise of his great personal charm—into giving up my plan to publish.

KURT. Well, why didn't you tell him right out that you wouldn't?

MARION. Because I wanted to avoid a scene.

KURT. You can't always avoid scenes. That's the trouble with you —you expect to go through life as if it were a beautifully-lit drawing room with modulated voices making polite chatter. Life isn't a drawing room . . . !

MARION. I have—once or twice—suspected it.

KURT [*rises*]. What the devil are you afraid of, anyway? I had a scene today in the office and I was prepared for one here—until you let me down—

MARION [*lightly*]. Prepared? I think you were eager. . . .

KURT. What if I was! It's in your behalf, isn't it?

MARION. Is it? But you forget, Dickie. You're a born martyr. I'm not. I think the most uncomfortable thing about martyrs is that they look down on people who aren't. [*Thinks—looks at him*] As a matter of fact, Dickie, I don't really understand. Why do you insist so on this story? Why is it so important—now wouldn't it be better to give it up?

KURT. Give it up!

MARION. Yes.

KURT. You'd give it up!

MARION. Why not?

KURT [*obeying a sudden manic impulse*]. After all this—after all I've—! Oh, yes, of course! Then you could marry Nolan and live happily forever after. And be amused. Good-bye! [*He rushes up center, grabs his hat from the stand as he passes it, and continues on out the door.*]

MARION [*rises and runs after him*]. Dickie!

KURT [*going out the door*]. Good-bye!

MARION. Dickie! Dickie! [*The door slams.* MARION *walks back into the room. A pause. She stands still for a moment; she shakes her head. . . . She is very distressed and saddened and a deep unhappiness is gnawing in her heart, an awareness of the vast, uncrossable deserts between the souls of human beings. She makes a little helpless gesture with her hands, murmuring to herself*] Poor Dickie! Poor boy! [*In its Italian folder the manuscript of her book is lying on the piano before her. She picks it up—she gives the effect of weighing the script in her hand. Slowly, as if in a trance, she walks with the script to the Franklin stove downstage left and sits before it on a little stool. She opens the manuscript and then the isinglass door of the stove. The light from behind it glows on her face. She looks again down on her manuscript, at this morsel of her recorded past. She tears out a page or two and puts them into the fire. A moment and she has put the entire script into the stove and she sits there watching its cremation. The doorbell rings. As* MINNIE *comes in to answer it, she shuts the door of the stove quickly.*]

MARION. It's probably Mr. Nolan.

[MINNIE *goes out.* MARION *makes a visible effort to shake herself out of her mood.* NOLAN *comes in followed by* MINNIE *who crosses stage and goes in the bedroom left.* NOLAN *is excited and distrait.*]

NOLAN. Hello, Marion. . . .

MARION. Hello, Bunny dear.

NOLAN [*sparring for time*]. Excuse me for rushing in on you like this . . . I . . .

MARION. I've been expecting you.

NOLAN. That's right! I told you I was coming back, didn't I? . . .

MARION. You did—yes.

NOLAN. I must have known—I must have felt it—what would happen. . . . Marion . . .

MARION. Bunny dear, you're all worked up. Won't you have a highball?

NOLAN. No, thanks. Marion. . . .

MARION. Yes, Bunny . . .

NOLAN. I've done it!

MARION. You've done what?

NOLAN. I've broken with Slade. I've broken with Kinnicott. I've broken with all of them.

MARION. You haven't!

NOLAN. Yes! I have!

MARION. Oh—oh, Bunny!

NOLAN [*sits*]. When Orrin told me what you'd done—that you were going to give up the story. . . .

MARION. But I—

NOLAN. He said he was sure he could get you to do it. It all came over me—your generosity—your wonderful generosity.

MARION [*beyond words*]. Oh, Bunny! [*Sits. She is in a sort of laughing despair. He hardly notices her attitude. He rushes on.*]

NOLAN. I realized in that moment that in all this time—since I'd been seeing you—I'd been hoping you wouldn't give up the story, that you would go through with it, that my career would go to smash. . . .

MARION [*faintly*]. Bunny. . . .

NOLAN. I saw then that all this—which I'd been telling myself I wanted—Slade, a career, Washington, public life—all of it—that I didn't want it, that I was sick at the prospect of it—that I wasn't up to it, that I was scared to death of it. I saw all that—and I told her—I told Slade. . . .

MARION. You did!

NOLAN. Yes.

MARION. What did she say?

NOLAN. She said she knew it. She's clever, that girl. She's cleverer than I am. She's cleverer than you are. I'm afraid of her cleverness. I'm uncomfortable with it. Marion, I know I seem stupid and ridiculous to you—just a Babbitt—clumsy—but I love you, Marion. I always have—never anyone else. Let me go with you wherever you go— [*lest she think it a "proposition"*] —I mean—I want to marry you.

MARION. I'm terribly touched by this, Bunny darling, but I can't marry you.

NOLAN. Why not?

MARION. If I married you it would be for the wrong reasons. And it wouldn't be in character really—neither for me—nor for you. Besides that, I think you're wrong about Slade. She's very nice, you know. I like her very much.

NOLAN. I don't understand her. I never will.

MARION. If you did you'd like her. You better have another try. Really, Bunny, I wish you would.

NOLAN. Letting me down easy, aren't you?

MARION. It's Slade's manner that shocks you—her modern—gestures. If you really understood me—as you think you do—I'd really shock you very much, Bunny.

NOLAN. I'll risk it. Marion, my dearest Marion, won't you give me some hope? . . .

MARION [*sees she must tell him*]. Besides,—I'm in love.

NOLAN [*stunned*]. Really! With whom?

MARION. Dickie . . . You see, Bunny . . . [*He can't get over this. There is a considerable pause.*] You see, Bunny . . .

NOLAN [*slowly*]. Do you mean that you and he—you don't mean that . . . ?

MARION. Yes, Bunny.

NOLAN [*dazed*]. Are you going to marry him?

MARION. No.

NOLAN [*he passes his hand over his forehead*]. This is a shock to me, Marion.

MARION [*gently*]. I thought it only fair to tell you.

NOLAN [*in a sudden passion*]. You—you. . . . [*He feels like striking her, controls himself with difficulty.*] Anybody else but him . . . !

MARION. You see, Bunny.

NOLAN [*after a moment—rises*]. Sorry! Funny, isn't it? Joke, isn't it?

MARION. I'm terribly fond of you, Bunny. [*Takes his hand*] I always will be. That kind of tenderness outlasts many things.

NOLAN [*blindly*]. I'll go on, I suppose.

MARION. Of course you will! [NOLAN *crosses to model stand and gets his hat.* KURT *comes in. There is a silence.* NOLAN *forces himself to look at him.* KURT *does not meet his glance.* KURT *is white and shaken—not in the least truculent.*] Good-bye, Bunny dear. Bunny!

NOLAN. Yes, Marion.

MARION. Will you do me a favor?

NOLAN. Yes.

MARION. Will you please tell Mr. Kinnicott for me—that as I've been called out of town suddenly—I can't dine with him tomorrow night. You *will* see him, won't you, and you'll tell him?

NOLAN. Yes. [NOLAN *leaves. A silence again.* . . . *Suddenly* KURT *goes to her, embraces her with a kind of hopeless intensity.*]

KURT [*in a whisper, like a child*]. Please forgive me. . . .

MARION. Yes.

KURT. These moods come over me—I can't control myself—afterwards I hate myself—it's because I love you so much—I can't bear to. . . .

MARION. I know, dear—I know. . . .

KURT. I'm torn up all the time—torn to bits.

MARION. I know, dear . . .

KURT. When this is all blown over—could we—do you think . . .

MARION. What, dear?

KURT. If we could only go away together, the two of us—somewhere away from people, by ourselves?

MARION. Why not, Dickie? We can go now, if you want to. . . .

KURT. Now? But you're crazy. How can we possibly leave now—with the book. . . .

MARION. Dickie—I must tell you. . . .

KURT. You must tell me what?

MARION. You must be patient—you must hear me out for once—you must try to understand my point of view. [*She leads him to sofa left and sits beside him.*]

KURT. What do you mean?

MARION. You know, Dickie, I've been very troubled about you. I've been sad. I've been sad.

KURT. I was angry . . . I didn't mean . . . It was just that . . .

MARION. No, you don't understand—it wasn't your anger that troubled me. It was ourselves—the difference between us—not the years alone but the immutable difference in temperament. Your hates frighten me, Dickie. These people—poor Bunny, that ridiculous fellow Kinnicott—to you these rather ineffectual, blundering people symbolize the forces that have hurt you and you hate them. But I don't hate them. I can't hate them. Without feeling it, I can understand your hate but I can't bring myself to foster it. To you, this book has become a crusade. It couldn't be to me. Do you know, Dickie dear—and this has made me laugh so to myself—that there was nothing in the book about Bunny that would ever have been recognized by anybody. It was an idyllic chapter of first love—that's all—and there was nothing in it that could remotely have been connected with the Bunny that is now. . . .

KURT. So much the better—! Think of the spectacle they'll make of themselves—destroyed by laughter. . . .

MARION. I don't believe in destructive campaigns, Dickie . . . outside of the shocking vulgarity of it all—I couldn't do it—for the distress it would cause. . . .

KURT. You've decided not to publish then. . . .

MARION. I've destroyed the book, Dickie.

KURT. You've destroyed it!

MARION. Yes. I'm sorry.

KURT. You traitor!

MARION. It seemed the simple thing to do—the inevitable thing.

KURT. What about *me?* You might have consulted me—after what I've . . .

MARION. I'm terribly sorry—but I couldn't possibly have published that book.

KURT [*in a queer voice*]. I see now why everything is this way. . . .

MARION. I couldn't . . . !

KURT. Why the injustice and the cruelty go on—year after year—century after century—without change—because—as they grow older—people become—*tolerant!* Things amuse them. I hate you and I hate your tolerance. I always did.

MARION. I know you do. You hate my essential quality—the thing that is me. That's what I was thinking just now and that's what made me sad.

KURT. Nothing to be said, is there? [*Rises*] Good-bye.

MARION [*rises*]. All right! [KURT *starts to go. She calls after him, pitifully*] Won't you kiss me good-bye?

KURT. All right.

[MARION *goes up after him. They kiss each other passionately.*]

MARION [*whispering to him*]. I would try to change you. I know I would. And if I changed you I should destroy what makes me love you. Good-bye, my darling. Good-bye, my dearest. Go quickly. [KURT *goes upstage and exits without a word. He is blinded by pain.*] Dickie . . . !

[MARION *is left alone. She is trembling a little. She feels cold. She goes to the stove and sits in front of it, her back to it, trying to get warm. She becomes aware that her eyes are full of tears. As* MINNIE *comes in, she brushes them away.*]

MINNIE. Are you worried from anything, Marion?

MARION. No, Minnie. I'm all right.

MINNIE. I tink maybe dot telegram bring you bad news.

MARION. Telegram? What telegram?

MINNIE. Dot telegram I bring you.

MARION. Of course—I haven't even—where is it?

MINNIE [*gets telegram from table rear of sofa left and hands it to* MARION]. There it is!

MARION. Thank you, Minnie. [*Opens telegram and reads it*] This is from heaven! Minnie, I want you to pack right away. We're leaving! [*She springs up.*]

MINNIE. Leaving? Ven?

MARION. Right away. Tonight! This is from Feydie! Listen! [*Reads telegram aloud to* MINNIE] "Can get you commission to paint prize winners Motion Picture Academy—wire answer at once. Feydie." [*Hysterically grateful for the mercy of having something to do at once, of being busy, of not having time to think*] Something always turns up for me! Pack everything, Minnie. I want to get out right away. [*She rushes upstage right, picks up her hat and coat and then runs to the stairs left.*]

MINNIE. Don't you tink you better vait till tomorrow?

MARION. No, Minnie. Once the temptation to a journey comes into my head I can't bear it till I'm on my way! This time, Minnie, we'll have a real trip. From Hollywood we'll go to Honolulu and from Honolulu to China. How would you like that, Minnie? [*She starts up the stairs.*]

MINNIE [*for her, enthusiastic*]. Fine, Marion! [*Calls after her as she runs upstairs*] Dot crazy Kurt he goes vit us?

MARION [*as she disappears into her bedroom*]. No, Minnie— no one—we travel alone!

[*Quick curtain*]

TENNESSEE WILLIAMS (1914-   )

The international reputation of Tennessee Williams as the most considerable American playwright of the war generation may at first seem surprising, since his best-known works present characters and problems rooted in the highly provincial locale of the American South. We may well wonder what the personal defeats of frail Southern belles out of step with the harsh realities of twentieth-century life can mean to audiences in London, Paris, and Buenos Aires. Yet once more we are reminded that if the greatest of our realistic writers have usually chosen to write of a limited area that they know intimately, it is only to see in this small segment of the world problems common to all humanity. In the frustrations and despair of the heroines of *The Glass Menagerie* and *A Streetcar Named Desire* theater audiences the world over may well discern the general bewilderment and weariness of the Western world in the past decade.

Williams is a Southerner who was uprooted from his boyhood home in Mississippi during his school years and came to see his provincial background half romantically, half critically from the border point of St. Louis. Christened Thomas Lanier, he adopted the name of Tennessee, perhaps as a tribute to his pioneering ancestors in that state. His grandfather, a cultured Episcopalian minister, encouraged his early interest in literature, and his mother provided a model for his later portrait of the delicate and charming Southern aristocrat, Amanda Wingfield. But his father was a salesman who had his difficulties, and Williams' study at the University of Missouri was interrupted by the decline of the family's fortunes during the depression years. After taking his degree at the University of Iowa, he worked at a variety of odd jobs around the country before eventually reaching New York for a career in the theater.

Although he experimented industriously with several kinds of writing, he made his first stir with his one-act plays, which are still considered among the best of his works. Winning a prize from the Group Theatre for a series of these, he was brought to the attention of the Theatre Guild, which produced his full-length play, *Battle of the Angels,* in Boston in 1940. After the failure of this tryout he waited nearly five years for his second production and first success, *The Glass Menagerie.* With the aging star, Laurette Taylor, making a remarkable comeback as Amanda (the rôle which proved to be her swan song), this subtle, pathetic play achieved a surprising popularity as well as great critical acclaim.

Williams' record on Broadway has been "every other one." His greatest success is without a doubt *A Streetcar Named Desire* (1947), which is also his most harrowing play —a morbid tragedy about the complete collapse of a well-born Southern girl into prostitution and insanity under the pressure of economic and sexual problems with which her gentle training has not prepared her to cope. When a similar heroine appeared in Williams' next play, *Summer and Smoke,* a year later, even the friendliest of his critics began to fear that he was limited to a single formula. But in 1951 he broke away from it with *The Rose Tattoo,* the lightest of his full-length plays, which set forth the tempestuous love life of an Italian woman living in an American Gulf Coast village. This near-comedy may reflect William's enthusiasm for Italy, where he has spent a great deal of his life. But he is no literary expatriate: his art remains fixed in the American scene and the aspects of it that he knows best.

With *Camino Real* (1953), his most eccentric play, he made a belated and ill-fated excursion into the expressionism of the twenties. But he came back the next year with one of the most powerful and morbid of his dramas of family life, *Cat on a Hot Tin Roof. Sweet Bird of Youth* (1959) and *The Night of the Iguana* (1962), two more dramas of tormented, abnormal people caught up in agonizing sex-relationships, showed his continuing power as a playwright. Whether one likes his subject matter or not, there is no denying his mastery of dramatic dialogue and style and his unerring sense of the stage.

TENNESSEE WILLIAMS

THE GLASS MENAGERIE

Nobody, not even the rain, has such small hands.

CHARACTERS

Amanda Wingfield (the mother)
> A little woman of great but confused vitality clinging frantically
> to another time and place. Her characterization must be care-
> fully created, not copied from type. She is not paranoiac, but her
> life is paranoia. There is much to admire in Amanda, and as
> much to love and pity as there is to laugh at. Certainly she has
> endurance and a kind of heroism, and though her foolishness
> makes her unwittingly cruel at times, there is tenderness in her
> slight person.

Laura Wingfield (her daughter)
> Amanda, having failed to establish contact with reality, continues
> to live vitally in her illusions, but Laura's situation is even graver.
> A childhood illness has left her crippled, one leg slightly shorter
> than the other, and held in a brace. This defect need not be more
> than suggested on the stage. Steming from this, Laura's separa-
> tion increases till she is like a piece of her own glass collection,
> too exquisitely fragile to move from the shelf.

Tom Wingfield (her son)
  And the narrator of the play. A poet with a job in a warehouse.
  His nature is not remorseless, but to escape from a trap he has
  to act without pity.

Jim O'Connor (the gentleman caller)
  A nice, ordinary, young man.

Scene

AN ALLEY IN ST. LOUIS
  PART I. *Preparation for a Gentleman Caller*
  PART II. *The Gentleman calls*

Time: Now and the Past

PRODUCTION NOTES

Being a "memory play," The Glass Menagerie *can be presented with unusual freedom of convention. Because of its
considerably delicate or tenuous material, atmospheric
touches and subtleties of direction play a particularly important part. Expressionism and all other unconventional
techniques in drama have only one valid aim, and that is a
closer approach to truth. When a play employs unconventional techniques, it is not, or certainly shouldn't be, trying
to escape its responsibility of dealing with reality, or inter-
preting experience, but is actually or should be attempting
to find a closer approach, a more penetrating and vivid expression of things as they are. The straight realistic play with
its genuine frigidaire and authentic ice-cubes, its characters*

that speak exactly as its audience speaks, corresponds to the academic landscape and has the same virtue of a photographic likeness. Everyone should know nowadays the unimportance of the photographic in art: that truth, life, or reality is an organic thing which the poetic imagination can represent or suggest, in essence, only through transformation, through changing into other forms than those which were merely present in appearance.

These remarks are not meant as a preface only to this particular play. They have to do with a conception of a new, plastic theatre which must take the place of the exhausted theatre of realistic conventions if the theatre is to resume vitality as a part of our culture.

the screen device

There is only one important difference between the original and acting version of the play *and that is the* omission *in the latter of the device which I tentatively included in my* original *script. This device was the use of a screen on which were projected magic-lantern slides bearing images or titles. I do not regret the omission of this device from the present Broadway production. The extraordinary power of Miss Taylor's performance made it suitable to have the utmost simplicity in the physical production. But I think it may be interesting to some readers to see how this device was conceived. So I am putting it into the published manuscript. These images and legends, projected from behind, were cast on a section of wall between the front-room and dining-room areas, which should be indistinguishable from the rest when not in use.*

The purpose of this will probably be apparent. It is to give accent to certain values in each scene. Each scene contains a particular point (or several) which is structurally the most important. In an episodic play, such as this, the basic structure or narrative line may be obscured from the audience; the effect may seem fragmentary rather than architectural. This may not be the fault of the play so much as a lack of

*attention in the audience. The legend or image upon the
screen will strengthen the effect of what is merely allusion
in the writing and allow the primary point to be made more
simply and lightly than if the entire responsibility were on
the spoken lines. Aside from this structural value, I think the
screen will have a definite emotional appeal, less definable
but just as important. An imaginative producer or director
may invent many other uses for this device than those indicated in the present script. In fact the possibilities of the
device seem much larger to me than the instance of this play
can possibly utilize.*

the music

*Another extra-literary accent in this play is provided by the
use of music. A single recurring tune, "The Glass Menagerie," is used to give emotional emphasis to suitable passages.
This tune is like circus music, not when you are on the
grounds or in the immediate vicinity of the parade, but when
you are at some distance and very likely thinking of something else. It seems under those circumstances to continue
almost interminably and it weaves in and out of your preoccupied consciousness; then it is the lightest, most delicate
music in the world and perhaps the saddest. It expresses the
surface vivacity of life with the underlying strain of immutable and inexpressible sorrow. When you look at a piece of
delicately spun glass you think of two things: how beautiful
it is and how easily it can be broken. Both of those ideas
should be woven into the recurring tune, which dips in and
out of the play as if it were carried on a wind that changes.
It serves as a thread of connection and allusion between the
narrator with his separate point in time and space and the
subject of his story. Between each episode it returns as
reference to the emotion, nostalgia, which is the first condition of the play. It is primarily Laura's music and therefore comes out most clearly when the play focuses upon her
and the lovely fragility of glass which is her image.*

the lighting

The lighting in the play is not realistic. In keeping with the atmosphere of memory, the stage is dim. Shafts of light are focused on selected areas or actors, sometimes in contradistinction to what is the apparent center. For instance, in the quarrel scene between Tom and Amanda, in which Laura has no active part, the clearest pool of light is on her figure. This is also true of the supper scene, when her silent figure on the sofa should remain the visual center. The light upon Laura should be distinct from the others, having a peculiar pristine clarity such as light used in early religious portraits of female saints or madonnas. A certain correspondence to light in religious paintings, such as El Greco's, where the figures are radiant in atmosphere that is relatively dusky, could be effectively used throughout the play. (It will also permit a more effective use of the screen.) A free, imaginative use of light can be of enormous value in giving a mobile, plastic quality to plays of a more or less static nature.

T. W.

scene 1

The Wingfield apartment is in the rear of the building, one of those vast hive-like conglomerations of cellular living-units that flower as warty growths in overcrowded urban centers of lower middle-class population and are symptomatic of the impulse of this largest and fundamentally enslaved section of American society to avoid fluidity and differentiation and to exist and function as one interfused mass of automatism.

The apartment faces an alley and is entered by a fire-escape, a structure whose name is a touch of accidental poetic truth, for all of these huge buildings are always burning with the slow and implacable fires of human desperation. The fire-escape is included in the set—that is, the landing of it and steps descending from it.

The scene is memory and is therefore nonrealistic. Memory takes a lot of poetic license. It omits some details; others are exaggerated, according to the emotional value of the articles it touches, for memory is seated predominantly in the heart. The interior is therefore rather dim and poetic.

At the rise of the curtain, the audience is faced with the dark, grim rear wall of the Wingfield tenement. This building, which runs parallel to the footlights, is flanked on both sides by dark, narrow alleys which run into murky canyons of tangled clotheslines, garbage cans and the sinister latticework of neighboring fire-escapes. It is up and down these side alleys that exterior entrances and exits are made, during the play. At the end of TOM's opening commentary, the dark tenement wall slowly reveals (by means of a transparency) the interior of the ground floor Wingfield apartment.

Downstage is the living room, which also serves as a sleeping room for LAURA, the sofa unfolding to make her bed. Upstage, center, and divided by a wide arch or second proscenium with transparent faded portieres (or second curtain), is the dining room. In an old-fashioned what-not in the living room are seen scores of transparent glass animals. A blown-up photograph of the father hangs on the wall of the living room, facing the audience, to the left of the archway. It is the face of a very handsome young man in a doughboy's First World War cap. He is gallantly smiling, ineluctably smiling, as if to say, "I will be smiling forever."

The audience hears and sees the opening scene in the dining room through both the transparent fourth wall of the building and the transparent gauze portieres of the dining-room arch. It is during this revealing scene that the fourth wall slowly ascends, out of sight. This transparent exterior wall is not brought down again until the very end of the play, during TOM's final speech.

The narrator is an undisguised convention of the play. He takes whatever license with dramatic convention as is convenient to his purposes.

TOM enters dressed as a merchant sailor from alley, stage left, and strolls across the front of the stage to the fire-escape. There he stops and lights a cigarette. He addresses the audience.

TOM. Yes, I have tricks in my pocket, I have things up my sleeve. But I am the opposite of a stage magician. He gives you illusion that has the appearance of truth. I give you truth in the pleasant disguise of illusion.

To begin with, I turn back time. I reverse it to that quaint period, the thirties, when the huge middle class of America was matriculating in a school for the blind. Their eyes had failed them, or they had failed their eyes, and so they were having their fingers pressed forcibly down on the fiery Braille alphabet of a dissolving economy.

In Spain there was revolution. Here there was only shouting and confusion.

In Spain there was Guernica.[1] Here there were disturbances of labor, sometimes pretty violent, in otherwise peaceful cities such as Chicago, Cleveland, Saint Louis . . .

This is the social background of the play.

[MUSIC]

The play is memory.

Being a memory play, it is dimly lighted, it is sentimental, it is not realistic.

In memory everything seems to happen to music. That explains the fiddle in the wings.

I am the narrator of the play, and also a character in it.

The other characters are my mother, Amanda, my sister, Laura, and a gentleman caller who appears in the final scenes.

He is the most realistic character in the play, being an emissary from a world of reality that we were somehow set apart from.

But since I have a poet's weakness for symbols,[2] I am using this character also as a symbol; he is the long delayed but always expected something that we live for.

There is a fifth character in the play who doesn't appear except in this larger-than-life-size photograph over the mantel.

This is our father who left us a long time ago.

---

[1] *Guernica*, the Basque town in northern Spain which was singled out by General Franco's forces for terroristic bombing from the air early in the Spanish revolution. An autonomous Basque government had been established there briefly. Especially because of a famous painting by the Spanish artist Picasso, Guernica became for liberals and radicals a symbol of the fascist attack upon democracy.

[2] *poet's . . . symbols.* Williams' fondness for symbols sometimes leads him to pretentious extremes. The invitation to interpret the gentleman caller in allegorical terms overreaches the touching realism of the scenes in which he appears.

He was a telephone man who fell in love with long distances; he gave up his job with the telephone company and skipped the light fantastic out of town . . .

The last we heard of him was a picture post-card from Mazatlan, on the Pacific coast of Mexico, containing a message of two words—

"Hello— Good-bye!" and no address.

I think the rest of the play will explain itself. . . .

    [AMANDA's *voice becomes audible through the portieres.*]

        [LEGEND ON SCREEN: "OU SONT LES NEIGES"]

    [*He divides the portieres and enters the upstage area.*]

    [AMANDA *and* LAURA *are seated at a drop-leaf table. Eating is indicated by gestures without food or utensils.* AMANDA *faces the audience.* TOM *and* LAURA *are seated in profile.*]

    [*The interior has lit up softly and through the scrim we see* AMANDA *and* LAURA *seated at the table in the upstage area.*]

AMANDA [*calling*]. Tom?

TOM. Yes, Mother.

AMANDA. We can't say grace until you come to the table!

TOM. Coming, Mother. [*He bows slightly and withdraws, reappearing a few moments later in his place at the table.*]

AMANDA [*to her son*]. Honey, don't *push* with your *fingers.* If you have to push with something, the thing to push with is a crust of bread. And chew—chew! Animals have sections in their stomachs which enable them to digest food without mastication, but human beings are supposed to chew their food before they swallow it down. Eat food leisurely, son, and really enjoy it. A well-cooked meal has lots of delicate flavors that have to be held in the mouth for appreciation. So chew your food and give your salivary glands a chance to function!

    [TOM *deliberately lays his imaginary fork down and pushes his chair back from the table.*]

TOM. I haven't enjoyed one bite of this dinner because of your constant directions on how to eat it. It's you that make me rush through meals' with your hawk-like attention to every bite I take. Sickening—spoils my appetite—all this discussion of—animal's secretion—salivary glands—mastication!

AMANDA [*lightly*]. Temperament like a Metropolitan star! [*He rises and crosses downstage.*] You're not excused from the table.

TOM. I'm getting a cigarette.

AMANDA. You smoke too much.

[LAURA *rises.*]

LAURA. I'll bring in the blanc mange.

[*He remains standing with his cigarette by the portieres during the following.*]

AMANDA [*rising*]. No, sister, no, sister—you be the lady this time and I'll be the darky.

LAURA. I'm already up.

AMANDA. Resume your seat, little sister—I want you to stay fresh and pretty—for gentlemen callers!

LAURA. I'm not expecting any gentlemen callers.

AMANDA [*crossing out to kitchenette. Airily*]. Sometimes they come when they are least expected! Why, I remember one Sunday afternoon in Blue Mountain— [*Enters kitchenette*]

TOM. I know what's coming!

LAURA. Yes. But let her tell it.

TOM. Again?

LAURA. She loves to tell it.

[AMANDA *returns with bowl of dessert.*]

AMANDA. One Sunday afternoon in Blue Mountain—your mother received—*seventeen!*—gentlemen callers! Why, sometimes there weren't chairs enough to accommodate them all. We had to send the nigger over to bring in folding chairs from the parish house.

TOM [*remaining at portieres*]. How did you entertain those gentlemen callers?

AMANDA. I understood the art of conversation!

TOM. I bet you could talk.

AMANDA. Girls in those days *knew* how to talk, I can tell you.

TOM. Yes?

[IMAGE: AMANDA AS A GIRL ON A PORCH, GREETING CALLERS]

AMANDA. They knew how to entertain their gentlemen callers. It wasn't enough for a girl to be possessed of a pretty face and a graceful figure—although I wasn't slighted in either respect. She also needed to have a nimble wit and a tongue to meet all occasions.

TOM. What did you talk about?

AMANDA. Things of importance going on in the world! Never anything coarse or common or vulgar. [*She addresses* TOM *as though he were seated in the vacant chair at the table though he remains by portieres. He plays this scene as though he held the book.*] My callers were gentlemen—all! Among my callers were some of the most prominent young planters of the Mississippi Delta —planters and sons of planters!

[TOM *motions for music and a spot of light on* AMANDA.]
[*Her eyes lift, her face glows, her voice becomes rich and elegiac.*]

[SCREEN LEGEND: "OU SONT LES NEIGES"]

There was young Champ Laughlin who later became vice-president of the Delta Planters Bank.

Hadley Stevenson who was drowned in Moon Lake and left his widow one hundred and fifty thousand in Government bonds.

There were the Cutrere brothers, Wesley and Bates. Bates was one of my bright particular beaux! He got in a quarrel with that wild Wainwright boy. They shot it out on the floor of Moon Lake Casino. Bates was shot through the stomach. Died in the ambulance on his way to Memphis. His widow was also well-provided for, came into eight or ten thousand acres, that's all. She married him on the rebound—never loved her—carried my picture on him the night he died!

And there was that boy that every girl in the Delta had set her cap for! That beautiful, brilliant young Fitzhugh boy from Greene County!

TOM. What did he leave his widow?

AMANDA. He never married! Gracious, you talk as though all of my old admirers had turned up their toes to the daisies!

TOM. Isn't this the first you've mentioned that still survives?

AMANDA. That Fitzhugh boy went North and made a fortune —came to be known as the Wolf of Wall Street! He had the Midas touch, whatever he touched turned to gold! And I could have been Mrs. Duncan J. Fitzhugh, mind you! But—I picked your *father!*

LAURA [*rising*]. Mother, let me clear the table.

AMANDA. No, dear, you go in front and study your typewriter chart. Or practice your shorthand a little. Stay fresh and pretty!— It's almost time for our gentlemen callers to start arriving. [*She flounces girlishly toward the kitchenette.*] How many do you suppose we're going to entertain this afternoon?

[TOM *throws down the paper and jumps up with a groan.*]

LAURA [*alone in the dining room*]. I don't believe we're going to receive any, Mother.

AMANDA [*reappearing, airily*]. What? No one—not one? You must be joking! [LAURA *nervously echoes her laugh. She slips in a fugitive manner through the half-open portieres and draws them gently behind her. A shaft of very clear light is thrown on her face against the faded tapestry of the curtains.* MUSIC: "THE GLASS MENAGERIE" UNDER FAINTLY. *Lightly*] Not one gentleman caller? It can't be true! There must be a flood, there must have been a tornado!

LAURA. It isn't a flood, it's not a tornado, Mother. I'm just not popular like you were in Blue Mountain. . . . [TOM *utters another groan.* LAURA *glances at him with a faint, apologetic smile. Her voice catching a little*] Mother's afraid I'm going to be an old maid.

THE SCENE DIMS OUT WITH "GLASS MENAGERIE" MUSIC

scene 2

"Laura, Haven't You Ever Liked Some Boy?"

On the dark stage the screen is lighted with the image of blue roses.

Gradually LAURA's figure becomes apparent and the screen goes out.

The music subsides.

LAURA *is seated in the delicate ivory chair at the small claw-foot table.*

She wears a dress of soft violet material for a kimono— her hair tied back from her forehead with a ribbon.

She is washing and polishing her collection of glass.

AMANDA *appears on the fire-escape steps. At the sound of her ascent,* LAURA *catches her breath, thrusts the bowl of ornaments away and seats herself stiffly before the diagram of the typewriter keyboard as though it held her spellbound.*

Something has happened to AMANDA. *It is written in her face as she climbs to the landing: a look that is grim and hopeless and a little absurd.*

She has on one of those cheap or imitation velvety-looking cloth coats with imitation fur collar. Her hat is five or six years old, one of those dreadful cloche hats that were worn in the late twenties and she is clasping an enormous black patent-leather pocketbook with nickel clasps and initials. This is her full-dress outfit, the one she usually wears to the D.A.R.

Before entering she looks through the door.

She purses her lips, opens her eyes very wide, rolls them upward and shakes her head.

Then she slowly lets herself in the door. Seeing her mother's expression LAURA *touches her lips with a nervous gesture.*

LAURA. Hello, Mother, I was— [*She makes a nervous gesture toward the chart on the wall.* AMANDA *leans against the shut door and stares at* LAURA *with a martyred look.*]

AMANDA. Deception? Deception? [*She slowly removes her hat and gloves, continuing the sweet suffering stare. She lets the hat and gloves fall on the floor—a bit of acting.*]

LAURA [*shakily*]. How was the D.A.R. meeting? [AMANDA *slowly opens her purse and removes a dainty white handkerchief which she shakes out delicately and delicately touches to her lips and nostrils.*] Didn't you go to the D.A.R. meeting, Mother?

AMANDA [*faintly, almost inaudibly*]. —No.—No. [*Then more forcibly*] I did not have the strength—to go to the D.A.R. In fact, I did not have the courage! I wanted to find a hole in the ground and hide myself in it forever! [*She crosses slowly to the wall and removes the diagram of the typewriter keyboard. She holds it in front of her for a second, staring at it sweetly and sorrowfully— then bites her lips and tears it in two pieces.*]

LAURA [*faintly*]. Why did you do that, Mother? [AMANDA *repeats the same procedure with the chart of the Gregg Alphabet.*] Why are you—

AMANDA. Why? Why? How old are you, Laura?

LAURA. Mother, you know my age.

AMANDA. I thought that you were an adult; it seems that I was mistaken. [*She crosses slowly to the sofa and sinks down and stares at* LAURA.]

LAURA. Please don't stare at me, Mother.

[AMANDA *closes her eyes and lowers her head. Count ten*]

AMANDA. What are we going to do, what is going to become of us, what is the future?

[*Count ten*]

LAURA. Has something happened, Mother? [AMANDA *draws a long breath and takes out the handkerchief again. Dabbing process*] Mother, has—something happened?

AMANDA. I'll be all right in a minute, I'm just bewildered— [*count five*]—by life. . . .

LAURA. Mother, I wish that you would tell me what's happened!

AMANDA. As you know, I was supposed to be inducted into my office at the D.A.R. this afternoon. [IMAGE: A SWARM OF TYPE-WRITERS] But I stopped off at Rubicam's business college to speak to your teachers about your having a cold and ask them what progress they thought you were making down there.

LAURA. Oh. . . .

AMANDA. I went to the typing instructor and introduced myself as your mother. She didn't know who you were. Wingfield, she said. We don't have any such student enrolled at the school!

I assured her she did, that you had been going to classes since early in January.

"I wonder," she said, "if you could be talking about that terribly shy little girl who dropped out of school after only a few days' attendance?"

"No," I said, "Laura, my daughter, has been going to school every day for the past six weeks!"

"Excuse me," she said. She took the attendance book out and there was your name, unmistakably printed, and all the dates you were absent until they decided that you had dropped out of school.

I still said, "No, there must have been some mistake! There must have been some mix-up in the records!"

And she said, "No—I remember her perfectly now. Her hands shook so that she couldn't hit the right keys! The first time we gave a speed-test, she broke down completely—was sick at the stomach and almost had to be carried into the wash-room! After that morning she never showed up any more. We phoned the house but never got any answer"—while I was working at Famous and Barr, I suppose, demonstrating those— Oh!

I felt so weak I could barely keep on my feet!

I had to sit down while they got me a glass of water!

Fifty dollars' tuition, all of our plans—my hopes and ambitions for you—just gone up the spout, just gone up the spout like that.

[LAURA *draws a long breath and gets awkwardly to her feet. She crosses to the victrola and winds it up.*]

What are you doing?

LAURA. Oh! [*She releases the handle and returns to her seat.*]

AMANDA. Laura, where have you been going when you've gone out pretending that you were going to business college?

LAURA. I've just been going out walking.

AMANDA. That's not true.

LAURA. It is. I just went walking.

AMANDA. Walking? Walking? In winter? Deliberately courting pneumonia in that light coat? Where did you walk to, Laura?

LAURA. All sorts of places—mostly in the park.

AMANDA. Even after you'd started catching that cold?

LAURA. It was the lesser of two evils, Mother. [IMAGE: WINTER SCENE IN PARK] I couldn't go back up. I—threw up—on the floor!

AMANDA. From half past seven till after five every day you mean to tell me you walked around in the park, because you wanted to make me think that you were still going to Rubicam's Business College?

LAURA. It wasn't as bad as it sounds. I went inside places to get warmed up.

AMANDA. Inside where?

LAURA. I went in the art museum and the bird-houses at the Zoo. I visited the penguins every day! Sometimes I did without lunch and went to the movies. Lately I've been spending most of my afternoons in the Jewel-box, that big glass house[1] where they raise the tropical flowers.

AMANDA. You did all this to deceive me, just for deception? [LAURA *looks down.*] Why?

LAURA. Mother, when you're disappointed, you get that awful suffering look on your face, like the picture of Jesus' mother in the museum!

AMANDA. Hush!

LAURA. I couldn't face it.

[*Pause. A whisper of strings*]
[LEGEND: "THE CRUST OF HUMILITY"]

AMANDA [*hopelessly fingering the huge pocketbook*]. So what are we going to do the rest of our lives? Stay home and watch the parades go by? Amuse ourselves with the glass menagerie, darling? Eternally play those worn-out phonograph records your father left as a painful reminder of him?

We won't have a business career—we've given that up because it

---

[1] *big glass house.* Note the recurrent identification of Laura with the fragility of glass objects.

gave us nervous indigestion! [*Laughs wearily*] What is there left but dependency all our lives? I know so well what becomes of unmarried women who aren't prepared to occupy a position. I've seen such pitiful cases in the South—barely tolerated spinsters living upon the grudging patronage of sister's husband or brother's wife!—stuck away in some little mouse-trap of a room—encouraged by one in-law to visit another—little birdlike women without any nest—eating the crust of humility all their life!

Is that the future that we've mapped out for ourselves?

I swear it's the only alternative I can think of!

It isn't a very pleasant alternative, is it?

Of course—some girls *do marry*.

[LAURA *twists her hands nervously.*]

Haven't you ever liked some boy?

LAURA. Yes. I liked one once. [*Rises*] I came across his picture a while ago.

AMANDA [*with some interest*]. He gave you his picture?

LAURA. No, it's in the year-book.

AMANDA [*disappointed*]. Oh—a high-school boy.

[SCREEN IMAGE: JIM AS HIGH-SCHOOL HERO BEARING A SILVER CUP]

LAURA. Yes. His name was Jim. [LAURA *lifts the heavy annual from the claw-foot table.*] Here he is in *The Pirates of Penzance*.

AMANDA [*absently*]. The what?

LAURA. The operetta the senior class put on. He had a wonderful voice and we sat across the aisle from each other Mondays, Wednesdays and Fridays in the Aud. Here he is with the silver cup for debating! See his grin?

AMANDA [*absently*]. He must have had a jolly disposition.

LAURA. He used to call me—Blue Roses.

[IMAGE: BLUE ROSES]

AMANDA. Why did he call you such a name as that?

LAURA. When I had that attack of pleurosis—he asked me what was the matter when I came back. I said pleurosis—he thought that I said Blue Roses! So that's what he always called me after that. Whenever he saw me, he'd holler, "Hello, Blue Roses!" I didn't care for the girl that he went out with. Emily Meisenbach. Emily was the best-dressed girl at Soldan. She never struck me, though, as being sincere . . . It says in the Personal Section—they're engaged. That's—six years ago! They must be married by now.

AMANDA. Girls that aren't cut out for business careers usually wind up married to some nice man. [*Gets up with a spark of revival*] Sister, that's what you'll do!

[LAURA *utters a startled, doubtful laugh. She reaches quickly for a piece of glass.*]

LAURA. But, Mother—

AMANDA. Yes? [*Crossing to photograph*]

LAURA [*in a tone of frightened apology*]. I'm—crippled!

[IMAGE: SCREEN]

AMANDA. Nonsense! Laura, I've told you never, never to use that word. Why, you're not crippled, you just have a little defect —hardly noticeable, even! When people have some slight disadvantage like that, they cultivate other things to make up for it— develop charm—and vivacity—and—*charm!* That's all you have to do! [*She turns again to the photograph.*] One thing your father had *plenty of*—was *charm!*

[TOM *motions to the fiddle in the wings.*]

THE SCENE FADES OUT WITH MUSIC

scene 3

LEGEND ON SCREEN: "AFTER THE FIASCO—"
TOM *speaks from the fire-escape landing.*

TOM. After the fiasco at Rubicam's Business College, the idea of getting a gentleman caller for Laura began to play a more and more important part in Mother's calculations.

It became an obsession. Like some archetype of the universal unconscious, the image of the gentleman caller haunted our small apartment. . . .

[IMAGE: YOUNG MAN AT DOOR WITH FLOWERS]

An evening at home rarely passed without some allusion to this image, this spectre, this hope. . . .

Even when he wasn't mentioned, his presence hung in Mother's preoccupied look and in my sister's frightened, apologetic manner —hung like a sentence passed upon the Wingfields!

Mother was a woman of action as well as words.

She began to take logical steps in the planned direction.

Late that winter and in the early spring—realizing that extra money would be needed to properly feather the nest and plume the bird—she conducted a vigorous campaign on the telephone, roping in subscribers to one of those magazines for matrons called *The Home-maker's Companion,* the type of journal that features the serialized sublimations of ladies of letters who think in terms of delicate cup-like breasts, slim, tapering waists, rich, creamy thighs, eyes like wood-smoke in autumn, fingers that soothe and caress like strains of music, bodies as powerful as Etruscan sculpture.

[SCREEN IMAGE: GLAMOR MAGAZINE COVER]

[AMANDA *enters with phone on long extension cord. She is spotted in the dim stage.*]

AMANDA. Ida Scott? This is Amanda Wingfield!

We *missed* you at the D.A.R. last Monday!

I said to myself: She's probably suffering with that sinus condition! How is that sinus condition?

Horrors! Heaven have mercy!—You're a Christian martyr, yes, that's what you are, a Christian martyr!

Well, I just now happened to notice that your subscription to the *Companion's* about to expire! Yes, it expires with the next issue, honey!—just when that wonderful new serial by Bessie Mae Hopper is getting off to such an exciting start. Oh, honey, it's something that you can't miss! You remember how *Gone With the Wind* took everybody by storm? You simply couldn't go out if you hadn't read it. All everybody *talked* was Scarlett O'Hara. Well, this is a book that critics already compare to *Gone With the Wind.* It's the *Gone With the Wind* of the post-World War generation!— What?—Burning?—Oh, honey, don't let them burn, go take a look in the oven and I'll hold the wire! Heavens—I think she's hung up!

DIM OUT

[LEGEND ON SCREEN: "YOU THINK I'M IN LOVE WITH CONTINENTAL SHOEMAKERS?"]

[*Before the stage is lighted, the violent voices of* TOM *and* AMANDA *are heard.*]

[*They are quarreling behind the portieres. In front of them stands* LAURA *with clenched hands and panicky expression.*]

[*A clear pool of light on her figure throughout this scene*]

TOM. What in Christ's name am I—

AMANDA [*shrilly*]. Don't you use that—

TOM. Supposed to do!

AMANDA. Expression! Not in my—

TOM. Ohhh!

AMANDA. Presence! Have you gone out of your senses?

TOM. I have, that's true, *driven* out!

AMANDA. What is the matter with you, you—big—big—IDIOT!

TOM. Look!—I've got *no thing,* no single thing—

AMANDA. Lower your voice!

TOM. In my life here that I can call my OWN! Everything is—

AMANDA. Stop that shouting!

TOM. Yesterday you confiscated my books! You had the nerve to—

AMANDA. I took that horrible novel back to the library—yes! That hideous book by that insane Mr. Lawrence. [TOM *laughs wildly.*] I cannot control the output of diseased minds or people who cater to them— [TOM *laughs still more wildly.*] BUT I WON'T ALLOW SUCH FILTH BROUGHT INTO MY HOUSE! No, no, no, no, no!

TOM. House, house! Who pays rent on it, who makes a slave of himself to—

AMANDA [*fairly screeching*]. Don't you DARE to—

TOM. No, no, *I* mustn't say things! *I've* got to just—

AMANDA. Let me tell you—

TOM. I don't want to hear any more! [*He tears the portieres open. The upstage area is lit with a turgid smoky red glow.*]

[AMANDA's *hair is in metal curlers and she wears a very old bathrobe, much too large for her slight figure, a relic of the faithless Mr. Wingfield.*]

[*An upright typewriter and a wild disarray of manuscripts is on the drop-leaf table. The quarrel was probably precipitated by* AMANDA's *interruption of his creative labor. A chair lying overthrown on the floor*]

[*Their gesticulating shadows are cast on the ceiling by the fiery glow.*]

AMANDA. You *will* hear more, you—

TOM. No, I won't hear more, I'm going out!

AMANDA. You come right back in—

TOM. Out, out, out! Because I'm—

AMANDA. Come back here, Tom Wingfield! I'm not through talking to you!

TOM. Oh, go—

LAURA [*desperately*]. —Tom!

AMANDA. You're going to listen, and no more insolence from you! I'm at the end of my patience!

[*He comes back toward her.*]

TOM. What do you think I'm at? Aren't I supposed to have any patience to reach the end of, Mother? I know, I know. It seems unimportant to you, what I'm *doing*—what I *want* to do—having a little *difference* between them! You don't think that—

AMANDA. I think you've been doing things that you're ashamed of. That's why you act like this. I don't believe that you go every night to the movies. Nobody goes to the movies night after night. Nobody in their right minds goes to the movies as often as you pretend to. People don't go to the movies at nearly midnight, and movies don't let out at two A.M. Come in stumbling. Muttering to yourself like a maniac! You get three hours' sleep and then go to work. Oh, I can picture the way you're doing down there. Moping, doping, because you're in no condition.

TOM [*wildly*]. No, I'm in no condition!

AMANDA. What right have you got to jeopardize your job? Jeopardize the security of us all? How do you think we'd manage if you were—

TOM. Listen! You think I'm crazy *about* the *warehouse?* [*He bends fiercely toward her slight figure.*] You think I'm in love with the Continental Shoemakers? You think I want to spend fifty-five *years* down there in that—*celotex interior!* with—*fluorescent—tubes!* Look! I'd rather somebody picked up a crowbar and battered out my brains—than go back mornings! I *go!* Every time you come in yelling that God damn *"Rise and Shine!" "Rise and Shine!"* I say to myself, "How *lucky dead* people are!" But I get up. I *go!* For sixty-five dollars a month I give up all that I dream of doing and being *ever!* And you say self—*self's* all I ever think of. Why, listen, if self is what I thought of, Mother, I'd be where he is—GONE! [*Pointing to father's picture*] As far as the system of transportation reaches! [*He starts past her. She grabs his arm.*] Don't grab at me, Mother!

AMANDA. Where are you going?

TOM. I'm going to the *movies!*

AMANDA. I don't believe that lie!

TOM [*crouching toward her, overtowering her tiny figure. She backs away, gasping*]. I'm going to opium dens! Yes, opium dens, dens of vice and criminals' hang-outs, Mother. I've joined the Hogan gang, I'm a hired assassin, I carry a tommy-gun in a violin case! I run a string of cat-houses in the Valley! They call me Killer, Killer Wingfield, I'm leading a double-life, a simple, honest warehouse worker by day, by night a dynamic *czar* of the *underworld,*

Mother. I go to gambling casinos, I spin away fortunes on the roulette table! I wear a patch over one eye and a false mustache, sometimes I put on green whiskers. On those occasions they call me —*El Diablo!* Oh, I could tell you things to make you sleepless! My enemies plan to dynamite this place. They're going to blow us all sky-high some night! I'll be glad, very happy, and so will you! You'll go up, up on a broomstick, over Blue Mountain with seventeen gentlemen callers! You ugly—babbling old—*witch.* . . . [*He goes through a series of violent, clumsy movements, seizing his overcoat, lunging to the door, pulling it fiercely open. The women watch him, aghast. His arm catches in the sleeve of the coat as he struggles to pull it on. For a moment he is pinioned by the bulky garment. With an outraged groan he tears the coat off again, splitting the shoulder of it, and hurls it across the room. It strikes against the shelf of* LAURA'S *glass collection, there is a tinkle of shattering glass.* LAURA *cries out as if wounded.*]

[MUSIC. LEGEND: "THE GLASS MENAGERIE"]

LAURA [*shrilly*]. My glass!—menagerie. . . . [*She covers her face and turns away.*]

[*But* AMANDA *is still stunned and stupefied by the "ugly witch" so that she barely notices this occurrence. Now she recovers her speech.*]

AMANDA [*in an awful voice*]. I won't speak to you—until you apologize! [*She crosses through portieres and draws them together behind her.* TOM *is left with* LAURA. LAURA *clings weakly to the mantel with her face averted.* TOM *stares at her stupidly for a moment. Then he crosses to shelf. Drops awkwardly on his knees to collect the fallen glass, glancing at* LAURA *as if he would speak but couldn't*]

"The Glass Menagerie" steals in as
THE SCENE DIMS OUT

scene 4

The interior is dark. Faint light in the alley.

A deep-voiced bell in a church is tolling the hour of five as the scene commences.

TOM *appears at the top of the alley. After each solemn boom of the bell in the tower, he shakes a little noise-maker*

*or rattle as if to express the tiny spasm of man in contrast
to the sustained power and dignity of the Almighty. This
and the unsteadiness of his advance make it evident that he
has been drinking.*

*As he climbs the few steps to the fire-escape landing light
steals up inside.* LAURA *appears in night-dress, observing*
TOM's *empty bed in the front room.*

TOM *fishes in his pockets for door-key, removing a motley
assortment of articles in the search, including a perfect
shower of movie-ticket stubs and an empty bottle. At last
he finds the key, but just as he is about to insert it, it slips
from his fingers. He strikes a match and crouches below the
door.*

TOM [*bitterly*]. One crack—and it falls through!
                [LAURA *opens the door.*]
LAURA. Tom! Tom, what are you doing?
TOM. Looking for a door-key.
LAURA. Where have you been all this time?
TOM. I have been to the movies.
LAURA. All this time at the movies?
TOM. There was a very long program. There was a Garbo pic-
ture and a Mickey Mouse and a travelogue and a newsreel and a
preview of coming attractions. And there was an organ solo and
a collection for the milk-fund—simultaneously—which ended up
in a terrible fight between a fat lady and an usher!
LAURA [*innocently*]. Did you have to stay through everything?
TOM. Of course! And, oh, I forgot! There was a big stage show!
The headliner on this stage show was Malvolio the Magician. He
performed wonderful tricks, many of them, such as pouring water
back and forth between pitchers. First it turned to wine and then
it turned to beer and then it turned to whiskey. I know it was
whiskey it finally turned into because he needed somebody to come
up out of the audience to help him, and I came up—both shows!
It was Kentucky Straight Bourbon. A very generous fellow, he
gave souvenirs. [*He pulls from his back pocket a shimmering
rainbow-colored scarf.*] He gave me this. This is his magic scarf.
You can have it, Laura. You wave it over a canary cage and you
get a bowl of gold-fish. You wave it over the gold-fish bowl and
they fly away canaries. . . . But the wonderfullest trick of all was
the coffin trick. We nailed him into a coffin and he got out of the

coffin without removing one nail. [*He has come inside.*] There is a trick that would come in handy for me—get me out of this 2 by 4 situation! [*Flops onto bed and starts removing shoes*]

LAURA. Tom—Shhh!

TOM. What're you shushing me for?

LAURA. You'll wake up Mother.

TOM. Goody, goody! Pay 'er back for all those "Rise an' Shines." [*Lies down, groaning*] You know it don't take much intelligence to get yourself into a nailed-up coffin, Laura. But who in hell ever got himself out of one without removing one nail?

[*As if in answer, the father's grinning photograph lights up.*]

SCENE DIMS OUT

[*Immediately following: The church bell is heard striking six. At the sixth stroke the alarm clock goes off in* AMANDA's *room, and after a few moments we hear her calling: "Rise and Shine! Rise and Shine! Laura, go tell your brother to rise and shine!"*]

TOM [*sitting up slowly*]. I'll rise—but I won't shine.

[*The light increases.*]

AMANDA. Laura, tell your brother his coffee is ready.

[LAURA *slips into front room.*]

LAURA. Tom!—It's nearly seven. Don't make Mother nervous. [*He stares at her stupidly. Beseechingly*] Tom, speak to Mother this morning. Make up with her, apologize, speak to her!

TOM. She won't to me. It's her that started not speaking.

LAURA. If you just say you're sorry she'll start speaking.

TOM. Her not speaking—is that such a tragedy?

LAURA. Please—please!

AMANDA [*calling from kitchenette*]. Laura, are you going to do what I asked you to do, or do I have to get dressed and go out myself?

LAURA. Going, going—soon as I get on my coat! [*She pulls on a shapeless felt hat with nervous, jerky movement, pleadingly glancing at* TOM. *Rushes awkwardly for coat. The coat is one of* AMANDA's, *inaccurately made-over, the sleeves too short for* LAURA.] Butter and what else?

AMANDA [*entering upstage*]. Just butter. Tell them to charge it.

LAURA. Mother, they make such faces when I do that.

AMANDA. Sticks and stones can break our bones, but the expression on Mr. Garfinkel's face won't harm us! Tell your brother his coffee is getting cold.

LAURA [*at door*]. Do what I asked you, will you, will you, Tom?

[*He looks sullenly away.*]

AMANDA. Laura, go now or just don't go at all!

LAURA [*rushing out*]. Going—going! [*A second later she cries out.* TOM *springs up and crosses to door.* AMANDA *rushes anxiously in.* TOM *opens the door.*]

TOM. Laura?

LAURA. I'm all right. I slipped, but I'm all right.

AMANDA [*peering anxiously after her*]. If anyone breaks a leg on those fire-escape steps, the landlord ought to be sued for every cent he possesses! [*She shuts door. Remembers she isn't speaking and returns to other room.*]

[*As* TOM *enters listlessly for his coffee, she turns her back to him and stands rigidly facing the window on the gloomy gray vault of the areaway. Its light on her face with its aged but childish features is cruelly sharp, satirical as a Daumier print.*]

[MUSIC UNDER: "AVE MARIA"]

[TOM *glances sheepishly but sullenly at her averted figure and slumps at the table. The coffee is scalding hot; he sips it and gasps and spits it back in the cup. At his gasp,* AMANDA *catches her breath and half turns. Then catches herself and turns back to window*]

[TOM *blows on his coffee, glancing sidewise at his mother. She clears her throat.* TOM *clears his. He starts to rise. Sinks back down again, scratches his head, clears his throat again.* AMANDA *coughs.* TOM *raises his cup in both hands to blow on it, his eyes staring over the rim of it at his mother for several moments. Then he slowly sets the cup down and awkwardly and hesitantly rises from the chair.*]

TOM [*hoarsely*]. Mother. I—I apologize, Mother. [AMANDA *draws a quick, shuddering breath. Her face works grotesquely. She breaks into childlike tears.*] I'm sorry for what I said, for everything that I said, I didn't mean it.

AMANDA [*sobbingly*]. My devotion has made me a witch and so I make myself hateful to my children!

TOM. *No*, you *don't*.

AMANDA. I worry so much, don't sleep, it makes me nervous!

TOM [*gently*]. I understand that.

AMANDA. I've had to put up a solitary battle all these years. But you're my right-hand bower! Don't fall down, don't fail!

TOM [*gently*]. I try, Mother.

AMANDA [*with great enthusiasm*]. Try and you will SUCCEED! [*The notion makes her breathless.*] Why, you—you're just *full* of natural endowments! Both of my children—they're *unusual* children! Don't you think I know it? I'm so—*proud!* Happy and—feel I've—so much to be thankful for but— Promise me one thing, Son!

TOM. What, Mother?

AMANDA. Promise, son, you'll—never be a drunkard!

TOM [*turns to her grinning*]. I will never be a drunkard, Mother.

AMANDA. That's what frightened me so, that you'd be drinking! Eat a bowl of Purina!

TOM. Just coffee, Mother.

AMANDA. Shredded wheat biscuit?

TOM. No. No, Mother, just coffee.

AMANDA. You can't put in a day's work on an empty stomach. You've got ten minutes—don't gulp! Drinking too-hot liquids makes cancer of the stomach. . . . Put cream in.

TOM. No, thank you.

AMANDA. To cool it.

TOM. No! No, thank you, I want it black.

AMANDA. I know, but it's not good for you. We have to do all that we can to build ourselves up. In these trying times we live in, all that we have to cling to is—each other. . . . That's why it's so important to— Tom, I— I sent out your sister so I could discuss something with you. If you hadn't spoken I would have spoken to you. [*Sits down*]

TOM [*gently*]. What is it, Mother, that you want to discuss?

AMANDA. *Laura!*

[TOM *puts his cup down slowly.*]
[LEGEND ON SCREEN: "LAURA"]
[MUSIC: "THE GLASS MENAGERIE"]

TOM. —Oh.—Laura . . .

AMANDA [*touching his sleeve*]. You know how Laura is. So quiet but—still water runs deep! She notices things and I think she—broods about them. [TOM *looks up.*] A few days ago I came in and she was crying.

TOM. What about?

AMANDA. You.

TOM. Me?

AMANDA. She has an idea that you're not happy here.

TOM. What gave her that idea?

AMANDA. What gives her any idea? However, you do act strangely. I—I'm not criticizing, understand *that!* I know your ambitions do not lie in the warehouse, that like everybody in the whole wide world—you've had to—make sacrifices, but—Tom— Tom—life's not easy, it calls for—Spartan endurance! There's so many things in my heart that I cannot describe to you! I've never told you but I—*loved* your father. . . .

TOM [*gently*]. I know that, Mother.

AMANDA. And you—when I see you taking after his ways! Staying out late—and—well, you *had* been drinking the night you were in that—terrifying condition! Laura says that you hate the apartment and that you go out nights to get away from it! Is that true, Tom?

TOM. No. You say there's so much in your heart that you can't describe to me. That's true of me, too. There's so much in my heart that I can't describe to *you!* So let's respect each other's—

AMANDA. But, why—*why,* Tom—are you always so *restless?* Where do you *go* to, nights?

TOM. I—go to the movies.

AMANDA. Why do you go to the movies so much, Tom?

TOM. I go to the movies because—I like adventure. Adventure is something I don't have much of at work, so I go to the movies.

AMANDA. But, Tom, you go to the movies *entirely* too *much!*

TOM. I like a lot of adventure.

[AMANDA *looks baffled, then hurt. As the familiar inquisition resumes he becomes hard and impatient again.* AMANDA *slips back into her querulous attitude toward him.*]

[IMAGE ON SCREEN: SAILING VESSEL WITH JOLLY ROGER]

AMANDA. Most young men find adventure in their careers.

TOM. Then most young men are not employed in a warehouse.

AMANDA. The world is full of young men employed in warehouses and offices and factories.

TOM. Do all of them find adventure in their careers?

AMANDA. They do or they do without it! Not everybody has a craze for adventure.

TOM. Man is by instinct a lover, a hunter, a fighter, and none of those instincts are given much play at the warehouse!

AMANDA. Man is by instinct! Don't quote instinct to me! Instinct is something that people have got away from! It belongs to animals! Christian adults don't want it!

TOM. What do Christian adults want, then, Mother?

AMANDA. Superior things! Things of the mind and the spirit! Only animals have to satisfy instincts! Surely your aims are somewhat higher than theirs! Than monkeys—pigs—

TOM. I reckon they're not.

AMANDA. You're joking. However, that isn't what I wanted to discuss.

TOM [*rising*]. I haven't much time.

AMANDA [*pushing his shoulders*]. Sit down.

TOM. You want me to punch in red at the warehouse, Mother?

AMANDA. You have five minutes. I want to talk about Laura.

[LEGEND: "PLANS AND PROVISIONS"]

TOM. All right! What about Laura?

AMANDA. We have to be making some plans and provisions for her. She's older than you, two years, and nothing has happened. She just drifts along doing nothing. It frightens me terribly how she just drifts along.

TOM. I guess she's the type that people call home girls.

AMANDA. There's no such type, and if there is, it's a pity! That is unless the home is hers, with a husband!

TOM. What?

AMANDA. Oh, I can see the handwriting on the wall as plain as I see the nose in front of my face! It's terrifying!

More and more you remind me of your father! He was out all hours without explanation!—then *left! Good-bye!*

And me with the bag to hold. I saw that letter you got from the Merchant Marine. I know what you're dreaming of. I'm not standing here blindfolded.

Very well, then. Then *do* it!

But not till there's somebody to take your place.

TOM. What do you mean?

AMANDA. I mean that as soon as Laura has got somebody to take care of her, married, a home of her own, independent—why, then you'll be free to go wherever you please, on land, on sea, whichever way the wind blows you!

But until that time you've got to look out for your sister. I don't say me because I'm old and don't matter! I say for your sister because she's young and dependent.

I put her in business college—a dismal failure! Frightened her so it made her sick at the stomach.

I took her over to the Young People's League at the church. Another fiasco. She spoke to nobody, nobody spoke to her. Now all she does is fool with those pieces of glass and play those worn-out records. What kind of a life is that for a girl to lead?

TOM. What can I do about it?

AMANDA. Overcome selfishness!

Self, self, self is all that you ever think of!

[TOM *springs up and crosses to get his coat. It is ugly and bulky. He pulls on a cap with earmuffs.*]

Where is your muffler? Put your wool muffler on!

[*He snatches it angrily from the closet and tosses it around his neck and pulls both ends tight.*]

Tom! I haven't said what I had in mind to ask you.

TOM. I'm too late to—

AMANDA [*catching his arm—very importunately. Then shyly*]. Down at the warehouse, aren't there some—nice young men?

TOM. No!

AMANDA. There *must* be—*some* . . .

TOM. Mother—

[*Gesture*]

AMANDA. Find out one that's clean-living—doesn't drink and—ask him out for sister!

TOM. What?

AMANDA. For *sister!* To *meet!* Get *acquainted!*

TOM [*stamping to door*]. Oh, my *go-osh!*

AMANDA. Will you? [*He opens door. Imploringly*] Will you? [*He starts down.*] Will you? *Will* you, dear?

TOM [*calling back*]. Yes!

[AMANDA *closes the door hesitantly and with a troubled but faintly hopeful expression.*]

[SCREEN IMAGE: GLAMOR MAGAZINE COVER]

[*Spot* AMANDA *at phone*]

AMANDA. Ella Cartwright? This is Amanda Wingfield!

How are you, honey?

How is that kidney condition?

[*Count five*]

Horrors!

[*Count five*]

You're a Christian martyr, yes, honey, that's what you are, a Christian martyr!

Well, I just now happened to notice in my little red book that your subscription to the *Companion* has just run out! I knew that you wouldn't want to miss out on the wonderful serial starting in this new issue. It's by Bessie Mae Hopper, the first thing she's written since *Honeymoon for Three*.

Wasn't that a strange and interesting story? Well, this one is even lovelier, I believe. It has a sophisticated, society background. It's all about the horsey set on Long Island!

FADE OUT

scene 5

LEGEND ON SCREEN: "ANNUNCIATION." *Fade with music.*

It is early dusk of a spring evening. Supper has just been finished in the Wingfield apartment. AMANDA *and* LAURA *in light-colored dresses are removing dishes from the table, in the upstage area, which is shadowy, their movements formalized almost as a dance or ritual, their moving forms as pale and silent as moths.*

TOM, *in white shirt and trousers, rises from the table and crosses toward the fire-escape.*

AMANDA [*as he passes her*]. Son, will you do me a favor?

TOM. What?

AMANDA. Comb your hair! You look so pretty when your hair is combed! [TOM *slouches on sofa with evening paper. Enormous caption "Franco Triumphs"*] There is only one respect in which I would like you to emulate your father.

TOM. What respect is that?

AMANDA. The care he always took of his appearance. He never allowed himself to look untidy. [*He throws down the paper and crosses to fire-escape.*] Where are you going?

TOM. I'm going out to smoke.

AMANDA. You smoke too much. A pack a day at fifteen cents a pack. How much would that amount to in a month? Thirty times fifteen is how much, Tom? Figure it out and you will be astounded at what you could save. Enough to give you a night-school course in accounting at Washington U! Just think what a wonderful thing that would be for you, Son!

[TOM *is unmoved by the thought.*]

TOM. I'd rather smoke. [*He steps out on landing, letting the screen door slam.*]

AMANDA [*sharply*]. I know! That's the tragedy of it. . . . [*Alone, she turns to look at her husband's picture.*]

[DANCE MUSIC: "ALL THE WORLD IS WAITING FOR THE SUN-RISE!"]

TOM [*to the audience*]. Across the alley from us was the Para-dise Dance Hall. On evenings in spring the windows and doors were open and the music came outdoors. Sometimes the lights were turned out except for a large glass sphere that hung from the ceiling. It would turn slowly about and filter the dusk with deli-cate rainbow colors. Then the orchestra played a waltz or a tango, something that had a slow and sensuous rhythm. Couples would come outside, to the relative privacy of the alley. You could see them kissing behind ash-pits and telephone poles.

This was the compensation for lives that passed like mine, with-out any change or adventure.

Adventure and change were imminent in this year. They were waiting around the corner for all these kids.

Suspended in the mist over Berchtesgaden,[1] caught in the folds of Chamberlain's umbrella—[2]

In Spain there was Guernica!

But here there was only hot swing music and liquor, dance halls, bars, and movies, and sex that hung in the gloom like a chandelier and flooded the world with brief, deceptive rainbows. . . .

All the world was waiting for bombardments!

[AMANDA *turns from the picture and comes outside.*]

AMANDA [*sighing*]. A fire-escape landing's a poor excuse for a porch. [*She spreads a newspaper on a step and sits down, grace-fully and demurely as if she were settling into a swing on a Mis-sissippi veranda.*] What are you looking at?

[1] *Berchtesgaden, the mountain retreat of Adolf Hitler, who held the key to Europe's fate at the time.*
[2] *Chamberlain's umbrella. Arthur Neville Chamberlain, the 70-year-old Con-servative prime minister of England in the years leading to the Second World War, habitually carried an umbrella, which became a symbol of his timid and ineffectual policies.*

TOM. The moon.

AMANDA. Is there a moon this evening?

TOM. It's rising over Garfinkel's Delicatessen.

AMANDA. So it is! A little silver slipper of a moon. Have you made a wish on it yet?

TOM. Um-hum.

AMANDA. What did you wish for?

TOM. That's a secret.

AMANDA. A secret, huh? Well, I won't tell mine either. I will be just as mysterious as you.

TOM. I bet I can guess what yours is.

AMANDA. Is my head so transparent?

TOM. You're not a sphinx.

AMANDA. No, I don't have secrets. I'll tell you what I wished for on the moon. Success and happiness for my precious children! I wish for that whenever there's a moon, and when there isn't a moon, I wish for it, too.

TOM. I thought perhaps you wished for a gentleman caller.

AMANDA. Why do you say that?

TOM. Don't you remember asking me to fetch one?

AMANDA. I remember suggesting that it would be nice for your sister if you brought home some nice young man from the warehouse. I think that I've made that suggestion more than once.

TOM. Yes, you have made it repeatedly.

AMANDA. Well?

TOM. We are going to have one.

AMANDA. *What?*

TOM. A gentleman caller!

[THE ANNUNCIATION IS CELEBRATED WITH MUSIC.]

[AMANDA *rises.*]

[IMAGE ON SCREEN: CALLER WITH BOUQUET]

AMANDA. You mean you have asked some nice young man to come over?

TOM. Yep. I've asked him to dinner.

AMANDA. You really did?

TOM. I did!

AMANDA. You did, and did he—*accept?*

TOM. He did!

AMANDA. Well, well—well, well! That's—lovely!

TOM. I thought that you would be pleased.

AMANDA. It's definite, then?

TOM. Very definite.

AMANDA. Soon?

TOM. Very soon.

AMANDA. For heaven's sake, stop putting on and tell me some things, will you?

TOM. What things do you want me to tell you?

AMANDA. *Naturally* I would like to know when he's *coming!*

TOM. He's coming tomorrow.

AMANDA. *Tomorrow?*

TOM. Yep. Tomorrow.

AMANDA. But, Tom!

TOM. Yes, Mother?

AMANDA. Tomorrow gives me no time!

TOM. Time for what?

AMANDA. Preparations! Why didn't you phone me at once, as soon as you asked him, the minute that he accepted? Then, don't you see, I could have been getting ready!

TOM. You don't have to make any fuss.

AMANDA. Oh, Tom, Tom, Tom, of course I have to make a fuss! I want things nice, not sloppy! Not thrown together. I'll certainly have to do some fast thinking, won't I?

TOM. I don't see why you have to think at all.

AMANDA. You just don't know. We can't have a gentleman caller in a pig-sty! All my wedding silver has to be polished, the monogrammed table linen ought to be laundered! The windows have to be washed and fresh curtains put up. And how about clothes? We have to *wear* something, don't we?

TOM. Mother, this boy is no one to make a fuss over!

AMANDA. Do you realize he's the first young man we've introduced to your sister?

It's terrible, dreadful, disgraceful that poor little sister has never received a single gentleman caller! Tom, come inside! [*She opens the screen door.*]

TOM. What for?

AMANDA. I want to ask you some things.

TOM. If you're going to make such a fuss, I'll call it off, I'll tell him not to come!

AMANDA. You certainly won't do anything of the kind. Nothing offends people worse than broken engagements. It simply means I'll have to work like a Turk! We won't be brilliant, but we will pass inspection. Come on inside. [TOM *follows, groaning.*] Sit down.

TOM. Any particular place you would like me to sit?

AMANDA. Thank heavens I've got that new sofa! I'm also making payments on a floor lamp I'll have sent out! And put the chintz covers on, they'll brighten things up! Of course I'd hoped to have these walls re-papered. . . . What is the young man's name?

TOM. His name is O'Connor.

AMANDA. That, of course, means fish—tomorrow is Friday! I'll have that salmon loaf—with Durkee's dressing! What does he do? He works at the warehouse?

TOM. Of course! How else would I—

AMANDA. Tom, he—doesn't drink?

TOM. Why do you ask me that?

AMANDA. Your father *did!*

TOM. Don't get started on that!

AMANDA. He *does* drink, then?

TOM. Not that I know of!

AMANDA. Make sure, be certain! The last thing I want for my daughter's a boy who drinks!

TOM. Aren't you being a little bit premature? Mr. O'Connor has not yet appeared on the scene!

AMANDA. But will tomorrow. To meet your sister, and what do I know about his character? Nothing! Old maids are better off than wives of drunkards!

TOM. Oh, my God!

AMANDA. Be still!

TOM [*leaning forward to whisper*]. Lots of fellows meet girls whom they don't marry!

AMANDA. Oh, talk sensibly, Tom—and don't be sarcastic! [*She has gotten a hairbrush.*]

TOM. What are you doing?

AMANDA. I'm brushing that cow-lick down!

What is this young man's position at the warehouse?

TOM [*submitting grimly to the brush and the interrogation*]. This young man's position is that of a shipping clerk, Mother.

AMANDA. Sounds to me like a fairly responsible job, the sort of a job *you* would be in if you just had more *get-up.*

What is his salary? Have you any idea?

TOM. I would judge it to be approximately eighty-five dollars a month.

AMANDA. Well—not princely, but—

TOM. Twenty more than I make.

AMANDA. Yes, how well I know! But for a family man, eighty-five dollars a month is not much more than you can just get by on. . . .

TOM. Yes, but Mr. O'Connor is not a family man.

AMANDA. He might be, mightn't he? Some time in the future?

TOM. I see. Plans and provisions.

AMANDA. You are the only young man that I know of who ignores the fact that the future becomes the present, the present the past, and the past turns into everlasting regret if you don't plan for it!

TOM. I will think that over and see what I can make of it.

AMANDA. Don't be supercilious with your mother! Tell me some more about this—what do you call him?

TOM. James D. O'Connor. The D. is for Delaney.

AMANDA. Irish on *both* sides! *Gracious!* And doesn't drink?

TOM. Shall I call him up and ask him right this minute?

AMANDA. The only way to find out about those things is to make discreet inquiries at the proper moment. When I was a girl in Blue Mountain and it was suspected that a young man drank, the girl whose attentions he had been receiving, if any girl *was,* would sometimes speak to the minister of his church, or rather her father would if her father was living, and sort of feel him out on the young man's character. That is the way such things are discreetly handled to keep a young woman from making a tragic mistake!

TOM. Then how did you happen to make a tragic mistake?

AMANDA. That innocent look of your father's had everyone fooled!

He *smiled*—the world was *enchanted!*

No girl can do worse than put herself at the mercy of a handsome appearance!

I hope that Mr. O'Connor is not too good-looking.

TOM. No, he's not too good-looking. He's covered with freckles and hasn't too much of a nose.

AMANDA. He's not right-down homely, though?

TOM. Not right-down homely. Just medium homely, I'd say.

AMANDA. Character's what to look for in a man.

TOM. That's what I've always said, Mother.

AMANDA. You've never said anything of the kind and I suspect you would never give it a thought.

TOM. Don't be so suspicious of me.

AMANDA. At least I hope he's the type that's up and coming.

TOM. I think he really goes in for self-improvement.

AMANDA. What reason have you to think so?

TOM. He goes to night school.

AMANDA [*beaming*]. Splendid! What does he do, I mean study?

TOM. Radio engineering and public speaking!

AMANDA. Then he has visions of being advanced in the world! Any young man who studies public speaking is aiming to have an executive job some day!

And radio engineering? A thing for the future!

Both of these facts are very illuminating. Those are the sort of things that a mother should know concerning any young man who comes to call on her daughter. Seriously or—not.

TOM. One little warning. He doesn't know about Laura. I didn't let on that we had dark ulterior motives. I just said, why don't you come and have dinner with us? He said okay and that was the whole conversation.

AMANDA. I bet it was! You're eloquent as an oyster.

However, he'll know about Laura when he gets here. When he sees how lovely and sweet and pretty she is, he'll thank his lucky stars he was asked to dinner.

TOM. Mother, you mustn't expect too much of Laura.

AMANDA. What do you mean?

TOM. Laura seems all those things to you and me because she's ours and we love her. We don't even notice she's crippled any more.

AMANDA. Don't say crippled! You know that I never allow that word to be used!

TOM. But face facts, Mother. She is and—that's not all—

AMANDA. What do you mean "not all"?

TOM. Laura is very different from other girls.

AMANDA. I think the difference is all to her advantage.

TOM. Not quite all—in the eyes of others—strangers—she's terribly shy and lives in a world of her own and those things make her seem a little peculiar to people outside the house.

AMANDA. Don't say peculiar.

TOM. Face the facts. She is.

[THE DANCE-HALL MUSIC CHANGES TO A TANGO THAT HAS A MINOR AND SOMEWHAT OMINOUS TONE.]

AMANDA. In what way is she peculiar—may I ask?

TOM [*gently*]. She lives in a world of her own—a world of— little glass ornaments, Mother. . . . [*Gets up.* AMANDA *remains holding brush, looking at him, troubled.*] She plays old phonograph records and—that's about all— [*He glances at himself in the mirror and crosses to door.*]

AMANDA [*sharply*]. Where are you going?

TOM. I'm going to the movies. [*Out screen door*]

AMANDA. Not to the movies, every night to the movies! [*Follows quickly to screen door*] I don't believe you always go to the movies! [*He is gone.* AMANDA *looks worriedly after him for a moment. Then vitality and optimism return and she turns from the door. Crossing to portieres*] Laura! Laura! [LAURA *answers from kitchenette.*]

LAURA. Yes, Mother.

AMANDA. Let those dishes go and come in front! [LAURA *appears with dish towel. Gaily*] Laura, come here and make a wish on the moon!

[SCREEN IMAGE: MOON]

LAURA [*entering*]. Moon—moon?

AMANDA. A little silver slipper of a moon.

Look over your left shoulder, Laura, and make a wish!

[LAURA *looks faintly puzzled as if called out of sleep.* AMANDA *seizes her shoulders and turns her at an angle by the door.*]

Now!

Now, darling, *wish!*

LAURA. What shall I wish for, Mother?

AMANDA [*her voice trembling and her eyes suddenly filling with tears*]. Happiness! Good fortune!

[*The violin rises and the stage dims out.*]

CURTAIN

scene 6

IMAGE: HIGH SCHOOL HERO.

And so the following evening I brought Jim home to dinner. I had known Jim slightly in high school. In high school Jim was a hero. He had tremendous Irish good nature and vitality with the scrubbed and polished look of white chinaware. He seemed to move in a continual spotlight. He was a star in basketball, captain of the debating club, president of the senior class and the glee club and he sang the male lead in the annual light operas. He was always running or bounding, never just walking. He seemed always at the point of defeating the law of gravity. He was shooting with such velocity through his adolescence that you would logically expect him to arrive at nothing short of the White House by the time he was thirty. But Jim apparently ran into more interference after his graduation from Soldan. His speed had definitely slowed. Six years after he left high school he was holding a job that wasn't much better than mine.

[IMAGE: CLERK]

He was the only one at the warehouse with whom I was on friendly terms. I was valuable to him as someone who could remember his former glory, who had seen him win basketball games and the silver cup in debating. He knew of my secret practice of retiring to a cabinet of the wash-room to work on poems when business was slack in the warehouse. He called me Shakespeare. And while the other boys in the warehouse regarded me with suspicious hostility, Jim took a humorous attitude toward me. Gradually his attitude affected the others, their hostility wore off and they also began to smile at me as people smile at an oddly fashioned dog who trots across their path at some distance.

I knew that Jim and Laura had known each other at Soldan, and I had heard Laura speak admiringly of his voice. I didn't know if Jim remembered her or not. In high school Laura had been as unobtrusive as Jim had been astonishing. If he did remember Laura, it was not as my sister, for when I asked him to dinner, he grinned and said, "You know, Shakespeare, I never thought of you as having folks!"

He was about to discover that I did. . . .

[LIGHT UP STAGE]

[LEGEND ON SCREEN: "THE ACCENT OF A COMING FOOT"]

[*Friday evening. It is about five o'clock of a late spring evening which comes "scattering poems in the sky."*]

[*A delicate lemony light is in the Wingfield apartment.*]

[AMANDA *has worked like a Turk in preparation for the gentleman caller. The results are astonishing. The new floor lamp with its rose-silk shade is in place, a colored paper lantern conceals the broken light fixture in the ceiling, new billowing white curtains are at the windows, chintz covers are on chairs and sofa, a pair of new sofa pillows make their initial appearance.*]

[*Open boxes and tissue paper are scattered on the floor.*]
[LAURA *stands in the middle with lifted arms while* AMANDA *crouches before her, adjusting the hem of the new dress, devout and ritualistic. The dress is colored and designed by memory. The arrangement of* LAURA'S *hair is changed; it is softer and more becoming. A fragile, unearthly prettiness has come out in* LAURA: *she is like a piece of translucent glass touched by light, given a momentary radiance, not actual, not lasting.*]

AMANDA [*impatiently*]. Why are you trembling?

LAURA. Mother, you've made me so nervous!

AMANDA. How have I made you nervous?

LAURA. By all this fuss! You make it seem so important!

AMANDA. I don't understand you, Laura. You couldn't be satisfied with just sitting home, and yet whenever I try to arrange something for you, you seem to resist it.

[*She gets up.*]

Now take a look at yourself.

No, wait! Wait just a moment—I have an idea!

LAURA. What is it now?

[AMANDA *produces two powder puffs which she wraps in handkerchiefs and stuffs in* LAURA'S *bosom.*]

LAURA. Mother, what are you doing?

AMANDA. They call them "Gay Deceivers"!

LAURA. I won't wear them!

AMANDA. You will!

LAURA. Why should I?

AMANDA. Because, to be painfully honest, your chest is flat.

LAURA. You make it seem like we were setting a trap.

AMANDA. All pretty girls are a trap, a pretty trap, and men expect them to be.

[LEGEND: "A PRETTY TRAP"]

Now look at yourself, young lady. This is the prettiest you will ever be!

I've got to fix myself now! You're going to be surprised by your mother's appearance! [*She crosses through portieres, humming gaily.*]

[LAURA *moves slowly to the long mirror and stares solemnly at herself.*]

[*A wind blows the white curtains inward in a slow, graceful motion and with a faint, sorrowful sighing.*]

AMANDA [*off stage*]. It isn't dark enough yet. [*She turns slowly before the mirror with a troubled look.*]

[LEGEND ON SCREEN: "THIS IS MY SISTER: CELEBRATE HER WITH STRINGS!" MUSIC]

AMANDA [*laughing, off*]. I'm going to show you something. I'm going to make a spectacular appearance!

LAURA. What is it, Mother?

AMANDA. Possess your soul in patience—you will see!

Something I've resurrected from that old trunk! Styles haven't changed so terribly much after all. . . .

[*She parts the portieres.*]

Now just look at your mother!

[*She wears a girlish frock of yellowed voile with a blue silk sash. She carries a bunch of jonquils—the legend of her youth is nearly revived. Feverishly*]

This is the dress in which I led the cotillion. Won the cakewalk twice at Sunset Hill, wore one spring to the Governor's ball in Jackson!

See how I sashayed around the ballroom, Laura?

[*She raises her skirt and does a mincing step around the room.*]

I wore it on Sundays for my gentlemen callers! I had it on the day I met your father—

I had malaria fever all that spring. The change of climate from East Tennessee to the Delta—weakened resistance—I had a little temperature all the time—not enough to be serious—just enough to make me restless and giddy!—Invitations poured in—parties all over the Delta!—"Stay in bed," said Mother, "you have fever!"—but I just wouldn't.—I took quinine but kept on going, going!—Evenings, dances!—Afternoons, long, long rides! Picnics—lovely!—So lovely, that country in May.—All lacy with dogwood, literally flooded with jonquils!—That was the spring I had the craze for jonquils. Jonquils became an absolute obsession. Mother said, "Honey, there's no more room for jonquils." And still I kept on bringing in more jonquils. Whenever, wherever I saw them, I'd say, "Stop! Stop! I see jonquils!" I made the young men help me gather the jonquils! It was a joke, Amanda and her jonquils! Finally there were no more vases to hold them, every available space was filled with jonquils. No vases to hold them? All right, I'll hold them myself! And then I—[*She stops in front of the picture. MUSIC*] met your father!

Malaria fever and jonquils and then—this—boy. . . .

[*She switches on the rose-colored lamp.*]

I hope they get here before it starts to rain.

[*She crosses upstage and places the jonquils in bowl on table.*]

I gave your brother a little extra change so he and Mr. O'Connor could take the service car home.

LAURA [*with altered look*]. What did you say his name was?

AMANDA. O'Connor.

LAURA. What is his first name?

AMANDA. I don't remember. Oh, yes, I do. It was—Jim!

[LAURA *sways slightly and catches hold of a chair.*]

[LEGEND ON SCREEN: "NOT JIM!"]

LAURA [*faintly*]. Not—Jim!

AMANDA. Yes, that was it, it was Jim! I've never known a Jim that wasn't nice!

[MUSIC: OMINOUS]

LAURA. Are you sure his name is Jim O'Connor?

AMANDA. Yes. Why?

LAURA. Is he the one that Tom used to know in high school?

AMANDA. He didn't say so. I think he just got to know him at the warehouse.

LAURA. There was a Jim O'Connor we both knew in high school —[*Then, with effort*] If that is the one that Tom is bringing to dinner—you'll have to excuse me, I won't come to the table.

AMANDA. What sort of nonsense is this?

LAURA. You asked me once if I'd ever liked a boy. Don't you remember I showed you this boy's picture?

AMANDA. You mean the boy you showed me in the year book?

LAURA. Yes, that boy.

AMANDA. Laura, Laura, were you in love with that boy?

LAURA. I don't know, Mother. All I know is I couldn't sit at the table if it was him!

AMANDA. It won't be him! It isn't the least bit likely. But whether it is or not, you will come to the table. You will not be excused.

LAURA. I'll have to be, Mother.

AMANDA. I don't intend to humor your silliness, Laura. I've had too much from you and your brother, both!

So just sit down and compose yourself till they come. Tom has forgotten his key so you'll have to let them in, when they arrive.

LAURA [*panicky*]. Oh, Mother—*you* answer the door!

AMANDA [*lightly*]. I'll be in the kitchen—busy!

LAURA. Oh, Mother, please answer the door, don't make me do it!

AMANDA [*crossing into kitchenette*]. I've got to fix the dressing for the salmon. Fuss, fuss—silliness!—over a gentleman caller!

[*Door swings shut. LAURA is left alone.*]

[LEGEND: "TERROR!"]

[*She utters a low moan and turns off the lamp, sits stiffly on the edge of the sofa, knotting her fingers together.*]

[LEGEND ON SCREEN: "THE OPENING OF A DOOR!"]

[*TOM and JIM appear on the fire-escape steps and climb to landing. Hearing their approach, LAURA rises with a panicky gesture. She retreats to the portieres.*]

[*The doorbell. LAURA catches her breath and touches her throat. Low drums*]

AMANDA [*calling*]. Laura, sweetheart! The door!

[*LAURA stares at it without moving.*]

JIM. I think we just beat the rain.

TOM. Uh-huh. [*He rings again, nervously. JIM whistles and fishes for a cigarette.*]

AMANDA [*very, very gaily*]. Laura, that is your brother and Mr. O'Connor! Will you let them in, darling?

[*LAURA crosses toward kitchenette door.*]

LAURA [*breathlessly*]. Mother—you go to the door!

[*AMANDA steps out of kitchenette and stares furiously at LAURA. She points imperiously at the door.*]

LAURA. Please, please!

AMANDA [*in a fierce whisper*]. What is the matter with you, you silly thing?

LAURA [*desperately*]. Please, you answer it, *please!*

AMANDA. I told you I wasn't going to humor you, Laura. Why have you chosen this moment to lose your mind?

LAURA. Please, please, please, you go!

AMANDA. You'll have to go to the door because I can't!

LAURA [*despairingly*]. I can't either!

AMANDA. *Why?*

LAURA. I'm *sick!*

AMANDA. I'm sick, too—of your nonsense! Why can't you and your brother be normal people? Fantastic whims and behavior!

[*TOM gives a long ring.*]

Preposterous goings on! Can you give me one reason—[*Calls*

out lyrically] COMING! JUST ONE SECOND!—why you should be afraid to open a door? Now you answer it, Laura!

LAURA. Oh, oh, oh . . . [*She returns through the portieres. Darts to the victrola and winds it frantically and turns it on*]

AMANDA. Laura Wingfield, you march right to that door!

LAURA. Yes—yes, Mother!

[*A faraway, scratchy rendition of "Dardanella" softens the air and gives her strength to move through it. She slips to the door and draws it cautiously open.*]

[TOM *enters with the caller,* JIM O'CONNOR.]

TOM. Laura, this is Jim. Jim, this is my sister, Laura.

JIM [*stepping inside*]. I didn't know that Shakespeare had a sister!

LAURA [*retreating stiff and trembling from the door*]. How— how do you do?

JIM [*heartily extending his hand*]. Okay!

[LAURA *touches it hesitantly with hers.*]

JIM. Your hand's *cold,* Laura!

LAURA. Yes, well—I've been playing the victrola. . . .

JIM. Must have been playing classical music on it! You ought to play a little hot swing music to warm you up!

LAURA. Excuse me—I haven't finished playing the victrola. . . . [*She turns awkwardly and hurries into the front room. She pauses a second by the victrola. Then catches her breath and darts through the portieres like a frightened deer*]

JIM [*grinning*]. What was the matter?

TOM. Oh—with Laura? Laura is—terribly shy.

JIM. Shy, huh? It's unusual to meet a shy girl nowadays. I don't believe you ever mentioned you had a sister.

TOM. Well, now you know. I have one. Here is the *Post Dispatch*. You want a piece of it?

JIM. Uh-huh.

TOM. What piece? The comics?

JIM. Sports! [*Glances at it*] Ole Dizzy Dean[1] is on his bad behavior.

TOM [*disinterest*]. Yeah? [*Lights cigarette and crosses back to fire-escape door*]

[1] *Ole Dizzy Dean, Jerome Hanna "Dizzy" Dean, whose brilliant career as a baseball pitcher for the St. Louis Cardinals was disrupted by a shoulder injury in 1937.*

JIM. Where are *you* going?

TOM. I'm going out on the terrace.

JIM [*goes after him*]. You know, Shakespeare—I'm going to sell you a bill of goods!

TOM. What goods?

JIM. A course I'm taking.

TOM. Huh?

JIM. In public speaking! You and me, we're not the warehouse type.

TOM. Thanks—that's good news.

But what has public speaking got to do with it?

JIM. It fits you for—executive positions!

TOM. Awww.

JIM. I tell you it's done a helluva lot for me.

[IMAGE: EXECUTIVE AT DESK]

TOM. In what respect?

JIM. In every! Ask yourself what is the difference between you an' me and men in the office down front? Brains?—No!—Ability? —No! Then what? Just one little thing—

TOM. What is that one little thing?

JIM. Primarily it amounts to—social poise! Being able to square up to people and hold your own on any social level!

AMANDA [*off stage*]. Tom?

TOM. Yes, Mother?

AMANDA. Is that you and Mr. O'Connor?

TOM. Yes, Mother.

AMANDA. Well, you just make yourselves comfortable in there.

TOM. Yes, Mother.

AMANDA. Ask Mr. O'Connor if he would like to wash his hands.

JIM. Aw, no—no—thank you—I took care of that at the warehouse. Tom—

TOM. Yes?

JIM. Mr. Mendoza was speaking to me about you.

TOM. Favorably?

JIM. What do you think?

TOM. Well—

JIM. You're going to be out of a job if you don't wake up.

TOM. I am waking up—

JIM. You show no signs.

TOM. The signs are interior.

[IMAGE ON SCREEN: THE SAILING VESSEL WITH JOLLY ROGER AGAIN]

TOM. I'm planning to change. [*He leans over the rail speaking with quiet exhilaration. The incandescent marquees and signs of the first-run movie houses light his face from across the alley. He looks like a voyager.*] I'm right at the point of committing myself to a future that doesn't include the warehouse and Mr. Mendoza or even a night-school course in public speaking.

JIM. What are you gassing about?

TOM. I'm tired of the movies.

JIM. Movies!

TOM. Yes, movies! Look at them— [*A wave toward the marvels of Grand Avenue*] All of those glamorous people—having adventures—hogging it all, gobbling the whole thing up! You know what happens? People go to the *movies* instead of *moving!* Hollywood characters are supposed to have all the adventures for everybody in America, while everybody in America sits in a dark room and watches them have them! Yes, until there's a war. That's when adventure becomes available to the masses! *Everyone's* dish, not only Gable's! Then the people in the dark room come out of the dark room to have some adventures themselves—Goody, goody! —It's our turn now, to go to the South Sea Island—to make a safari—to be exotic, far-off!—But I'm not patient. I don't want to wait till then. I'm tired of the *movies* and I am *about* to *move!*

JIM [*incredulously*]. Move?

TOM. Yes.

JIM. When?

TOM. Soon!

JIM. Where? Where?

[THEME THREE MUSIC SEEMS TO ANSWER THE QUESTION, WHILE TOM THINKS IT OVER. HE SEARCHES AMONG HIS POCKETS.]

TOM. I'm starting to boil inside. I know I seem dreamy, but inside—well, I'm boiling!—Whenever I pick up a shoe, I shudder a little thinking how short life is and what I am doing!—Whatever that means, I know it doesn't mean shoes—except as something to wear on a traveler's feet! [*Finds paper*] Look—

JIM. What?

TOM. I'm a member.

JIM [*reading*]. The Union of Merchant Seamen.

TOM. I paid my dues this month, instead of the light bill.

JIM. You will regret it when they turn the lights off.

TOM. I won't be here.

JIM. How about your mother?

TOM. I'm like my father. The bastard son of a bastard! See how he grins? And he's been absent going on sixteen years!

JIM. You're just talking, you drip. How does your mother feel about it?

TOM. Shhh!—Here comes Mother! Mother is not acquainted with my plans!

AMANDA [*enters portieres*]. Where are you all?

TOM. On the terrace, Mother.

[*They start inside. She advances to them.* TOM *is distinctly shocked at her appearance. Even* JIM *blinks a little. He is making his first contact with girlish Southern vivacity and in spite of the night-school course in public speaking is some-what thrown off the beam by the unexpected outlay of social charm.*]

[*Certain responses are attempted by* JIM *but are swept aside by* AMANDA's *gay laughter and chatter.* TOM *is embarrassed but after the first shock* JIM *reacts very warmly. Grins and chuckles, is altogether won over*]

[IMAGE: AMANDA AS A GIRL]

AMANDA [*coyly smiling, shaking her girlish ringlets*]. Well, well, well, so this is Mr. O'Connor. Introductions entirely un-necessary. I've heard so much about you from my boy. I finally said to him, Tom—good gracious!—why don't you bring this para-gon to supper? I'd like to meet this nice young man at the ware-house!—Instead of just hearing him sing your praises so much!

I don't know why my son is so stand-offish—that's not Southern behavior!

Let's sit down and—I think we could stand a little more air in here! Tom, leave the door open. I felt a nice fresh breeze a mo-ment ago. Where has it gone to?

Mmm, so warm already! And not quite summer, even. We're going to burn up when summer really gets started.

However, we're having—we're having a very light supper. I think light things are better fo' this time of year. The same as light clothes are. Light clothes an' light food are what warm weather calls fo'. You know our blood gets so thick during th' winter—it takes a while fo' us to *adjust* ou'selves!—when the season changes . . .

It's come so quick this year. I wasn't prepared. All of a sudden—

heavens! Already summer!—I ran to the trunk an' pulled out this light dress— Terribly old! Historical almost! But feels so good —so good an' co-ol, y' know. . . .

TOM. Mother—

AMANDA. Yes, honey?

TOM. How about—supper?

AMANDA. Honey, you go ask Sister if supper is ready! You know that Sister is in full charge of supper!

Tell her you hungry boys are waiting for it.

[*To* JIM]

Have you met Laura?

JIM. She—

AMANDA. Let you in? Oh, good, you've met already! It's rare for a girl as sweet an' pretty as Laura to be domestic! But Laura is, thank heavens, not only pretty but also very domestic. I'm not at all. I never was a bit. I never could make a thing but angel-food cake. Well, in the South we had so many servants. Gone, gone, gone. All vestige of gracious living! Gone completely! I wasn't prepared for what the future brought me. All of my gentlemen callers were sons of planters and so of course I assumed that I would be married to one and raise my family on a large piece of land with plenty of servants. But man proposes—and woman accepts the proposal!—To vary that old, old saying a little bit—I married no planter! I married a man who worked for the telephone company!—That gallantly smiling gentleman over there! [*Points to the picture*] A telephone man who—fell in love with long-distance!—Now he travels and I don't even know where!—But what am I going on for about my—tribulations?

Tell me yours—I hope you don't have any!

Tom?

TOM [*returning*]. Yes, Mother?

AMANDA. Is supper nearly ready?

TOM. It looks to me like supper is on the table.

AMANDA. Let me look— [*She rises prettily and looks through portieres.*] Oh, lovely!—But where is Sister?

TOM. Laura is not feeling well and she says that she thinks she'd better not come to the table.

AMANDA. What?—Nonsense!—Laura? Oh, Laura!

LAURA [*off stage, faintly*]. Yes, Mother.

AMANDA. You really must come to the table. We won't be seated until you come to the table!

Come in, Mr. O'Connor. You sit over there, and I'll—
Laura? Laura Wingfield!

You're keeping us waiting, honey! We can't say grace until you
come to the table!

[*The back door is pushed weakly open and* LAURA *comes in.
She is obviously quite faint, her lips trembling, her eyes wide
and staring. She moves unsteadily toward the table.*]

[LEGEND: "TERROR!"]

[*Outside a summer storm is coming abruptly. The white curtains billow inward at the windows and there is a sorrowful
murmur and deep blue dusk.*]

[LAURA *suddenly stumbles—she catches at a chair with a faint
moan.*]

TOM. Laura!

AMANDA. Laura!

[*There is a clap of thunder.*]

[LEGEND: "AH!"]

[*Despairingly*]

Why, Laura, you *are* sick, darling! Tom, help your sister into
the living room, dear!

Sit in the living room, Laura—rest on the sofa.

Well!

[*To the gentleman caller*]

Standing over the hot stove made her ill!—I told her that it
was just too warm this evening, but—

[TOM *comes back in.* LAURA *is on the sofa.*]

Is Laura all right now?

TOM. Yes.

AMANDA. What *is* that? Rain? A nice cool rain has come up!

[*She gives the gentleman caller a frightened look.*]

I think we may—have grace—now . . .

[TOM *looks at her stupidly.*]

Tom, honey—you say grace!

TOM. Oh . . .

"For these and all thy mercies—"

[*They bow their heads,* AMANDA *stealing a nervous glance at*
JIM. *In the living room* LAURA, *stretched on the sofa, clenches
her hands to her lips, to hold back a shuddering sob.*]

God's Holy Name be praised—

THE SCENE DIMS OUT

scene 7

A Souvenir.

Half an hour later. Dinner is just being finished in the upstage area which is concealed by the drawn portieres.

As the curtain rises LAURA *is still huddled upon the sofa, her feet drawn under her, her head resting on a pale blue pillow, her eyes wide and mysteriously watchful. The new floor lamp with its shade of rose-colored silk gives a soft, becoming light to her face, bringing out the fragile, unearthly prettiness which usually escapes attention. There is a steady murmur of rain, but it is slackening and stops soon after the scene begins; the air outside becomes pale and luminous as the moon breaks out.*

A moment after the curtain rises, the lights in both rooms flicker and go out.

JIM. Hey, there, Mr. Light Bulb!

[AMANDA *laughs nervously.*]

[LEGEND: "SUSPENSION OF A PUBLIC SERVICE"]

AMANDA. Where was Moses when the lights went out? Ha-ha. Do you know the answer to that one, Mr. O'Connor?

JIM. No, Ma'am, what's the answer?

AMANDA. In the dark!

[JIM *laughs appreciatively.*]

Everybody sit still. I'll light the candles. Isn't it lucky we have them on the table? Where's a match? Which of you gentlemen can provide a match?

JIM. Here.

AMANDA. Thank you, sir.

JIM. Not at all, Ma'am!

AMANDA. I guess the fuse has burnt out. Mr. O'Connor, can you tell a burnt-out fuse? I know I can't and Tom is a total loss when it comes to mechanics.

[SOUND: GETTING UP: VOICES RECEDE A LITTLE TO KITCHENETTE]

Oh, be careful you don't bump into something. We don't want our gentleman caller to break his neck. Now wouldn't that be a fine howdy-do?

JIM. Ha-ha!

Where is the fuse-box?

AMANDA. Right here next to the stove. Can you see anything?

JIM. Just a minute.

AMANDA. Isn't electricity a mysterious thing? Wasn't it Benjamin Franklin who tied a key to a kite? We live in such a mysterious universe, don't we? Some people say that science clears up all the mysteries for us. In my opinion it only creates more! Have you found it yet?

JIM. No, Ma'am. All these fuses look okay to me.

AMANDA. Tom!

TOM. Yes, Mother?

AMANDA. That light bill I gave you several days ago. The one I told you we got the notices about?

[LEGEND: "HA!"]

TOM. Oh.—Yeah.

AMANDA. You didn't neglect to pay it by any chance?

TOM. Why, I—

AMANDA. Didn't! I might have known it!

JIM. Shakespeare probably wrote a poem on that light bill, Mrs. Wingfield.

AMANDA. I might have known better than to trust him with it! There's such a high price for negligence in this world!

JIM. Maybe the poem will win a ten-dollar prize.

AMANDA. We'll just have to spend the remainder of the evening in the nineteenth century, before Mr. Edison made the Mazda lamp!

JIM. Candlelight is my favorite kind of light.

AMANDA. That shows you're romantic! But that's no excuse for Tom. Well, we got through dinner. Very considerate of them to let us get through dinner before they plunged us into everlasting darkness, wasn't it, Mr. O'Connor?

JIM. Ha-ha!

AMANDA. Tom, as a penalty for your carelessness you can help me with the dishes.

JIM. Let me give you a hand.

AMANDA. Indeed you will not!

JIM. I ought to be good for something.

AMANDA. Good for something? [*Her tone is rhapsodic.*]

You? Why, Mr. O'Connor, nobody, *nobody's* given me this much entertainment in years—as you have!

JIM. Aw, now, Mrs. Wingfield!

AMANDA. I'm not exaggerating, not one bit! But Sister is all by her lonesome. You go keep her company in the parlor!

I'll give you this lovely old candelabrum that used to be on the altar at the church of the Heavenly Rest. It was melted a little out of shape when the church burnt down. Lightning struck it one spring. Gypsy Jones was holding a revival at the time and he intimated that the church was destroyed because the Episcopalians gave card parties.

JIM. Ha-ha.

AMANDA. And how about you coaxing Sister to drink a little wine? I think it would be good for her! Can you carry both at once?

JIM. Sure. I'm Superman!

AMANDA. Now, Thomas, get into this apron!

[*The door of kitchenette swings closed on* AMANDA's *gay laughter; the flickering light approaches the portieres.*]

[LAURA *sits up nervously as he enters. Her speech at first is low and breathless from the almost intolerable strain of being alone with a stranger.*]

[THE LEGEND: "I DON'T SUPPOSE YOU REMEMBER ME AT ALL!"]

[*In her first speeches in this scene, before* JIM's *warmth overcomes her paralyzing shyness,* LAURA's *voice is thin and breathless as though she has just run up a steep flight of stairs.*]

[JIM's *attitude is gently humorous. In playing this scene it should be stressed that while the incident is apparently unimportant, it is to* LAURA *the climax of her secret life.*]

JIM. Hello, there, Laura.

LAURA [*faintly*]. Hello. [*She clears her throat.*]

JIM. How are you feeling now? Better?

LAURA. Yes. Yes, thank you.

JIM. This is for you. A little dandelion wine. [*He extends it toward her with extravagant gallantry.*]

LAURA. Thank you.

JIM. Drink it—but don't get drunk!

[*He laughs heartily.* LAURA *takes the glass uncertainly; laughs shyly.*]

Where shall I set the candles?

LAURA. Oh—oh, anywhere . . .

JIM. How about here on the floor? Any objections?

LAURA. No.

JIM. I'll spread a newspaper under to catch the drippings. I like to sit on the floor. Mind if I do?

LAURA. Oh, no.

JIM. Give me a pillow?

LAURA. What?

JIM. A pillow!

LAURA. Oh . . . [*Hands him one quickly*]

JIM. How about you? Don't you like to sit on the floor?

LAURA. Oh—yes.

JIM. Why don't you, then?

LAURA. I—will.

JIM. Take a pillow! [LAURA *does. Sits on the other side of the candelabrum.* JIM *crosses his legs and smiles engagingly at her.*] I can't hardly see you sitting way over there.

LAURA. I can—see you.

JIM. I know, but that's not fair, I'm in the limelight. [LAURA *moves her pillow closer.*] Good! Now I can see you! Comfortable?

LAURA. Yes.

JIM. So am I. Comfortable as a cow! Will you have some gum?

LAURA. No, thank you.

JIM. I think that I will indulge, with your permission. [*Musingly unwraps it and holds it up*] Think of the fortune made by the guy that invented the first piece of chewing gum. Amazing, huh? The Wrigley Building is one of the sights of Chicago. I saw it summer before last when I went up to the Century of Progress.[1] Did you take in the Century of Progress?

LAURA. No, I didn't.

JIM. Well, it was quite a wonderful exposition. What impressed me most was the Hall of Science. Gives you an idea of what the future will be in America, even more wonderful than the present time is! [*Pause. Smiling at her*] Your brother tells me you're shy. Is that right, Laura?

LAURA. I—don't know.

JIM. I judge you to be an old-fashioned type of girl. Well, I

---

[1] *Century of Progress, the world's fair held in Chicago in 1933-1934.*

think that's a pretty good type to be. Hope you don't think I'm being too personal—do you?

LAURA [*hastily, out of embarrassment*]. I believe I *will* take a piece of gum, if you—don't mind. [*Clearing her throat*] Mr. O'Connor, have you—kept up with your singing?

JIM. Singing? Me?

LAURA. Yes. I remember what a beautiful voice you had.

JIM. When did you hear me sing?

[VOICE OFF STAGE IN THE PAUSE]

VOICE [*off stage*].

O blow, ye winds, heigh-ho,
A-roving I will go!
I'm off to my love
With a boxing glove—
Ten thousand miles away!

JIM. You say you've heard me sing?

LAURA. Oh, yes! Yes, very often . . . I—don't suppose—you remember me—at all?

JIM [*smiling doubtfully*]. You know I have an idea I've seen you before. I had that idea soon as you opened the door. It seemed almost like I was about to remember your name. But the name that I started to call you—wasn't a name! And so I stopped myself before I said it.

LAURA. Wasn't it—Blue Roses?

JIM [*springs up. Grinning*]. Blue Roses!—My gosh, yes—Blue Roses!

That's what I had on my tongue when you opened the door!

Isn't it funny what tricks your memory plays? I didn't connect you with high school somehow or other.

But that's where it was; it was high school. I didn't even know you were Shakespeare's sister!

Gosh, I'm sorry.

LAURA. I didn't expect you to. You—barely knew me!

JIM. But we did have a speaking acquaintance, huh?

LAURA. Yes, we—spoke to each other.

JIM. When did you recognize me?

LAURA. Oh, right away!

JIM. Soon as I came in the door?

LAURA. When I heard your name I thought it was probably you. I knew that Tom used to know you a little in high school. So when you came in the door—

Well, then I was—sure.

JIM. Why didn't you *say* something, then?

LAURA [*breathlessly*]. I didn't know what to say, I was—too surprised!

JIM. For goodness' sakes! You know, this sure is funny!

LAURA. Yes! Yes, isn't it, though . . .

JIM. Didn't we have a class in something together?

LAURA. Yes, we did.

JIM. What class was that?

LAURA. It was—singing—Chorus!

JIM. Aw!

LAURA. I sat across the aisle from you in the Aud.

JIM. Aw.

LAURA. Mondays, Wednesdays and Fridays.

JIM. Now I remember—you always came in late.

LAURA. Yes, it was so hard for me, getting upstairs. I had that brace on my leg—it clumped so loud!

JIM. I never heard any clumping.

LAURA [*wincing at the recollection*]. To me it sounded like—thunder!

JIM. Well, well, well, I never even noticed.

LAURA. And everybody was seated before I came in. I had to walk in front of all those people. My seat was in the back row. I had to go clumping all the way up the aisle with everyone watching!

JIM. You shouldn't have been self-conscious.

LAURA. I know, but I was. It was always such a relief when the singing started.

JIM. Aw, yes, I've placed *you* now! I used to call you Blue Roses. How was it that I got started calling you that?

LAURA. I was out of school a little while with pleurosis. When I came back you asked me what was the matter. I said I had pleurosis—you thought I said Blue Roses. That's what you always called me after that!

JIM. I hope you didn't mind.

LAURA. Oh, no—I liked it. You see, I wasn't acquainted with many—people. . . .

JIM. As I remember you sort of stuck by yourself.

LAURA. I—I—never have had much luck at—making friends.

JIM. I don't see why you wouldn't.

LAURA. Well, I—started out badly.

JIM. You mean being—

LAURA. Yes, it sort of—stood between me—

JIM. You shouldn't have let it!

LAURA. I know, but it did, and—

JIM. You were shy with people!

LAURA. I tried not to be but never could—

JIM. Overcome it?

LAURA. No, I—I never could!

JIM. I guess being shy is something you have to work out of kind of gradually.

LAURA [*sorrowfully*]. Yes—I guess it—

JIM. Takes time!

LAURA. Yes—

JIM. People are not so dreadful when you know them. That's what you have to remember! And everybody has problems, not just you, but practically everybody has got some problems.

You think of yourself as having the only problems, as being the only one who is disappointed. But just look around you and you will see lots of people as disappointed as you are. For instance, I hoped when I was going to high school that I would be further along at this time, six years later, than I am now— You remember that wonderful write-up I had in *The Torch?*

LAURA. Yes! [*She rises and crosses to table.*]

JIM. It said I was bound to succeed in anything I went into! [LAURA *returns with the annual.*] Holy Jeez! *The Torch!* [*He accepts it reverently. They smile across it with mutual wonder.* LAURA *crouches beside him and they begin to turn through it.* LAURA's *shyness is dissolving in his warmth.*]

LAURA. Here you are in *The Pirates of Penzance!*

JIM [*wistfully*]. I sang the baritone lead in that operetta.

LAURA [*raptly*]. So—beautifully!

JIM [*protesting*]. Aw—

LAURA. Yes, yes—beautifully—beautifully!

JIM. You heard me?

LAURA. All three times!

JIM. No!

LAURA. Yes!

JIM. All three performances?

LAURA [*looking down*]. Yes.

JIM. Why?

LAURA. I—wanted to ask you to—autograph my program.

JIM. Why didn't you ask me to?

LAURA. You were always surrounded by your own friends so much that I never had a chance to.

JIM. You should have just—

LAURA. Well, I—thought you might think I was—

JIM. Thought I might think you was—what?

LAURA. Oh—

JIM [*with reflective relish*]. I was beleaguered by females in those days.

LAURA. You were terribly popular!

JIM. Yeah—

LAURA. You had such a—friendly way—

JIM. I was spoiled in high school.

LAURA. Everybody—liked you!

JIM. Including you?

LAURA. I—yes, I—I did, too— [*She gently closes the book in her lap.*]

JIM. Well, well, well!—Give me that program, Laura. [*She hands it to him. He signs it with a flourish.*] There you are—better late than never!

LAURA. Oh, I—what a—surprise!

JIM. My signature isn't worth very much right now.

But some day—maybe—it will increase in value!

Being disappointed is one thing and being discouraged is something else. I am disappointed but I am not discouraged.

I'm twenty-three years old.

How old are you?

LAURA. I'll be twenty-four in June.

JIM. That's not old age!

LAURA. No, but—

JIM. You finished high school?

LAURA [*with difficulty*]. I didn't go back.

JIM. You mean you dropped out?

LAURA. I made bad grades in my final examinations. [*She rises and replaces the book and the program. Her voice strained.*] How is—Emily Meisenbach getting along?

JIM. Oh, that kraut-head!

LAURA. Why do you call her that?

JIM. That's what she was.

LAURA. You're not still—going with her?

JIM. I never see her.

LAURA. It said in the Personal Section that you were—engaged!

JIM. I know, but I wasn't impressed by that—propaganda!

LAURA. It wasn't—the truth?

JIM. Only in Emily's optimistic opinion!

LAURA. Oh—

[LEGEND: "WHAT HAVE YOU DONE SINCE HIGH SCHOOL?"]

[JIM *lights a cigarette and leans indolently back on his elbows smiling at* LAURA *with a warmth and charm which lights her inwardly with altar candles. She remains by the table and turns in her hands a piece of glass to cover her tumult.*]

JIM [*after several reflective puffs on a cigarette*]. What have you done since high school? [*She seems not to hear him.*] Huh? [LAURA *looks up.*] I said what have you done since high school, Laura?

LAURA. Nothing much.

JIM. You must have been doing something these six long years.

LAURA. Yes.

JIM. Well, then, such as what?

LAURA. I took a business course at business college—

JIM. How did that work out?

LAURA. Well, not very—well—I had to drop out, it gave me—indigestion—

[JIM *laughs gently.*]

JIM. What are you doing now?

LAURA. I don't do anything—much. Oh, please don't think I sit around doing nothing! My glass collection takes up a good deal of time. Glass is something you have to take good care of.

JIM. What did you say—about glass?

LAURA. Collection I said—I have one— [*She clears her throat and turns away again, acutely shy.*]

JIM [*abruptly*]. You know what I judge to be the trouble with you?

Inferiority complex! Know what that is? That's what they call it when someone low-rates himself!

I understand it because I had it, too. Although my case was not so aggravated as yours seems to be. I had it until I took up public speaking, developed my voice, and learned that I had an aptitude for science. Before that time I never thought of myself as being outstanding in any way whatsoever!

Now I've never made a regular study of it, but I have a friend

who says I can analyze people better than doctors that make a profession of it. I don't claim that to be necessarily true, but I can sure guess a person's psychology, Laura! [*Takes out his gum*] Excuse me, Laura. I always take it out when the flavor is gone. I'll use this scrap of paper to wrap it in. I know how it is to get it stuck on a shoe.

Yep—that's what I judge to be your principal trouble. A lack of confidence in yourself as a person. You don't have the proper amount of faith in yourself. I'm basing that fact on a number of your remarks and also on certain observations I've made. For instance that clumping you thought was so awful in high school. You say that you even dreaded to walk into class. You see what you did? You dropped out of school, you gave up an education because of a clump, which as far as I know was practically non-existent! A little physical defect is what you have. Hardly noticeable even! Magnified thousands of times by imagination!

You know what my strong advice to you is? Think of yourself as *superior* in some way!

LAURA. In what way would I think?

JIM. Why, man alive, Laura! Just look about you a little. What do you see? A world full of common people! All of 'em born and all of 'em going to die!

Which of them has one-tenth of your good points! Or mine! Or anyone else's, as far as that goes—Gosh!

Everybody excels in some one thing. Some in many!

[*Unconsciously glances at himself in the mirror*]

All you've got to do is discover in *what!*

Take me, for instance.

[*He adjusts his tie at the mirror.*]

My interest happens to lie in electro-dynamics. I'm taking a course in radio engineering at night school, Laura, on top of a fairly responsible job at the warehouse. I'm taking that course and studying public speaking.

LAURA. Ohhhh.

JIM. Because I believe in the future of television!

[*Turning back to her*]

I wish to be ready to go up right along with it. Therefore I'm planning to get in on the ground floor. In fact I've already made the right connections and all that remains is for the industry itself to get under way! Full steam—

[*His eyes are starry.*]

Knowledge—Zzzzzp! *Money*—Zzzzzzp!—*Power!*
That's the cycle democracy is built on!

[*His attitude is convincingly dynamic.* LAURA *stares at him, even her shyness eclipsed in her absolute wonder. He suddenly grins.*]

I guess you think I think a lot of myself!

LAURA. No—o-o-o, I—

JIM. Now how about you? Isn't there something you take more interest in than anything else?

LAURA. Well, I do—as I said—have my—glass collection—

[*A peal of girlish laughter from the kitchen*]

JIM. I'm not right sure I know what you're talking about. What kind of glass is it?

LAURA. Little articles of it, they're ornaments mostly!
Most of them are little animals made out of glass, the tiniest little animals in the world. Mother calls them a glass menagerie! Here's an example of one, if you'd like to see it!
This one is one of the oldest. It's nearly thirteen.

[MUSIC: "THE GLASS MENAGERIE"]
[*He stretches out his hand.*]

Oh, be careful—if you breathe, it breaks!

JIM. I'd better not take it. I'm pretty clumsy with things.

LAURA. Go on, I trust you with him!

[*Places it in his palm*]

There now—you're holding him gently!
Hold him over the light, he loves the light! You see how the light shines through him?

JIM. It sure does shine!

LAURA. I shouldn't be partial, but he is my favorite one.

JIM. What kind of a thing is this one supposed to be?

LAURA. Haven't you noticed the single horn on his forehead?

JIM. A unicorn, huh?

LAURA. Mmm-hmmm!

JIM. Unicorns, aren't they extinct in the modern world?

LAURA. I know!

JIM. Poor little fellow, he must feel sort of lonesome.

LAURA [*smiling*]. Well, if he does he doesn't complain about it. He stays on a shelf with some horses that don't have horns and all of them seem to get along nicely together.

JIM. How do you know?

LAURA [*lightly*]. I haven't heard any arguments among them!

JIM [*grinning*]. No arguments, huh? Well, that's a pretty good sign!

Where shall I set him?

LAURA. Put him on the table. They all like a change of scenery once in a while!

JIM [*stretching*]. Well, well, well, well—

Look how big my shadow is when I stretch!

LAURA. Oh, oh, yes—it stretches across the ceiling!

JIM [*crossing to door*]. I think it's stopped raining. [*Opens fire-escape door*] Where does the music come from?

LAURA. From the Paradise Dance Hall across the alley.

JIM. How about cutting the rug a little, Miss Wingfield?

LAURA. Oh, I—

JIM. Or is your program filled up? Let me have a look at it. [*Grasps imaginary card*] Why, every dance is taken! I'll just have to scratch some out. [WALTZ MUSIC: "LA GOLONDRINA"] Ahhh, a waltz! [*He executes some sweeping turns by himself then holds his arms toward LAURA.*]

LAURA [*breathlessly*]. I—can't dance!

JIM. There you go, that inferiority stuff!

LAURA. I've never danced in my life!

JIM. Come on, try!

LAURA. Oh, but I'd step on you!

JIM. I'm not made out of glass.

LAURA. How—how—how do we start?

JIM. Just leave it to me. You hold your arms out a little.

LAURA. Like this?

JIM. A little bit higher. Right. Now don't tighten up, that's the main thing about it—relax.

LAURA [*laughing breathlessly*]. It's hard not to.

JIM. Okay.

LAURA. I'm afraid you can't budge me.

JIM. What do you bet I can't? [*He swings her into motion.*]

LAURA. Goodness, yes, you can!

JIM. Let yourself go, now, Laura, just let yourself go.

LAURA. I'm—

JIM. Come on!

LAURA. Trying!

JIM. Not so stiff— Easy does it!

LAURA. I know but I'm—

JIM. Loosen th' backbone! There now, that's a lot better.

LAURA. Am I?

JIM. Lots, lots better! [*He moves her about the room in a clumsy waltz.*]

LAURA. Oh, my!

JIM. Ha-ha!

LAURA. Oh, my goodness!

JIM. Ha-ha-ha! [*They suddenly bump into the table.* JIM *stops.*] What did we hit on?

LAURA. Table.

JIM. Did something fall off it? I think—

LAURA. Yes.

JIM. I hope that it wasn't the little glass horse with the horn!

LAURA. Yes.

JIM. Aw, aw, aw. Is it broken?

LAURA. Now it is just like all the other horses.

JIM. It's lost its—

LAURA. Horn![1]

It doesn't matter. Maybe it's a blessing in disguise.

JIM. You'll never forgive me. I bet that that was your favorite piece of glass.

LAURA. I don't have favorites much. It's no tragedy, Freckles. Glass breaks so easily. No matter how careful you are. The traffic jars the shelves and things fall off them.

JIM. Still I'm awfully sorry that I was the cause.

LAURA [*smiling*]. I'll just imagine he had an operation. The horn was removed to make him feel less—freakish!

[*They both laugh.*]

Now he will feel more at home with the other horses, the ones that don't have horns . . .

JIM. Ha-ha, that's very funny!

[*Suddenly serious*]

I'm glad to see that you have a sense of humor.

You know—you're—well—very different!

Surprisingly different from anyone else I know!

[*His voice becomes soft and hesitant with a genuine feeling.*]

Do you mind me telling you that?

[LAURA *is abashed beyond speech.*]

I mean it in a nice way . . .

[LAURA *nods shyly, looking away.*]

You make me feel sort of—I don't know how to put it!

[1] *Horn!* The symbolism is almost too clear.

I'm usually pretty good at expressing things, but—
This is something that I don't know how to say!

[LAURA *touches her throat and clears it—turns the broken unicorn in her hands.*]

[*Even softer*]

Has anyone ever told you that you were pretty?

[PAUSE: MUSIC]

[LAURA *looks up slowly, with wonder, and shakes her head.*]

Well, you are! In a very different way from anyone else.
And all the nicer because of the difference, too.

[*His voice becomes low and husky.* LAURA *turns away, nearly faint with the novelty of her emotions.*]

I wish that you were my sister. I'd teach you to have some confidence in yourself. The different people are not like other people, but being different is nothing to be ashamed of. Because other people are not such wonderful people. They're one hundred times one thousand. You're one times one! They walk all over the earth. You just stay here. They're common as—weeds, but—you—well, you're—*Blue Roses!*

[IMAGE ON SCREEN: BLUE ROSES]

[MUSIC CHANGES]

LAURA. But blue is wrong for—roses . . .

JIM. It's right for you!—You're—pretty!

LAURA. In what respect am I pretty?

JIM. In all respects—believe me! Your eyes—your hair—are pretty! Your hands are pretty!

[*He catches hold of her hand.*]

You think I'm making this up because I'm invited to dinner and have to be nice. Oh, I could do that! I could put on an act for you, Laura, and say lots of things without being very sincere. But this time I am. I'm talking to you sincerely. I happened to notice you had this inferiority complex that keeps you from feeling comfortable with people. Somebody needs to build your confidence up and make you proud instead of shy and turning away and—blushing—
Somebody—ought to—
Ought to—*kiss* you, Laura!

[*His hand slips slowly up her arm to her shoulder.*]

[MUSIC SWELLS TUMULTUOUSLY.]

[*He suddenly turns her about and kisses her on the lips.*]

[*When he releases her,* LAURA *sinks on the sofa with a bright, dazed look.*]

[JIM *backs away and fishes in his pocket for a cigarette.*]

[LEGEND ON SCREEN: "SOUVENIR"]

Stumble-john!

[*He lights the cigarette, avoiding her look.*]

[*There is a peal of girlish laughter from* AMANDA *in the kitchen.*]

[LAURA *slowly raises and opens her hand. It still contains the little broken glass animal. She looks at it with a tender, bewildered expression.*]

Stumble-john!

I shouldn't have done that— That was way off the beam.

You don't smoke, do you?

[*She looks up, smiling, not hearing the question.*]

[*He sits beside her a little gingerly. She looks at him speechlessly—waiting.*]

[*He coughs decorously and moves a little farther aside as he considers the situation and senses her feelings, dimly, with perturbation.*]

[*Gently*]

Would you—care for a—mint?

[*She doesn't seem to hear him but her look grows brighter even.*]

Peppermint—Life-Saver?

My pocket's a regular drug store—wherever I go . . .

[*He pops a mint in his mouth. Then gulps and decides to make a clean breast of it. He speaks slowly and gingerly.*]

Laura, you know, if I had a sister like you, I'd do the same thing as Tom. I'd bring out fellows and—introduce her to them. The right type of boys of a type to—appreciate her.

Only—well—he made a mistake about me.

Maybe I've got no call to be saying this. That may not have been the idea in having me over. But what if it was?

There's nothing wrong about that. The only trouble is that in my case—I'm not in a situation to—do the right thing.

I can't take down your number and say I'll phone.

I can't call up next week and—ask for a date.

I thought I had better explain the situation in case you—misunderstood it and—hurt your feelings. . . .

[*Pause*]

[*Slowly, very slowly,* LAURA's *look changes, her eyes returning slowly from his to the ornament in her palm.*]

[AMANDA *utters another gay laugh in the kitchen.*]

LAURA [*faintly*]. You—won't—call again?

JIM. No, Laura, I can't.

[*He rises from the sofa.*]

As I was just explaining, I've—got strings on me.

Laura, I've—been going steady!

I go out all of the time with a girl named Betty. She's a home-girl like you, and Catholic, and Irish, and in a great many ways we —get along fine.

I met her last summer on a moonlight boat trip up the river to Alton, on the *Majestic*.

Well—right away from the start it was—love!

[LEGEND: LOVE!]

[LAURA *sways slightly forward and grips the arm of the sofa. He fails to notice, now enrapt in his own comfortable being.*]

Being in love has made a new man of me!

[*Leaning stiffly forward, clutching the arm of the sofa,* LAURA *struggles visibly with her storm. But* JIM *is oblivious, she is a long way off.*]

The power of love is really pretty tremendous!

Love is something that—changes the whole world, Laura!

[*The storm abates a little and* LAURA *leans back. He notices her again.*]

It happened that Betty's aunt took sick, she got a wire and had to go to Centralia. So Tom—when he asked me to dinner—I naturally just accepted the invitation, not knowing that you—that he—that I—

[*He stops awkwardly.*]

Huh—I'm a stumble-john!

[*He flops back on the sofa.*]

[*The holy candles in the altar of* LAURA's *face have been snuffed out. There is a look of almost infinite desolation.*]

[JIM *glances at her uneasily.*]

I wish that you would—say something. [*She bites her lip which was trembling and then bravely smiles. She opens her hand again on the broken glass ornament. Then she gently takes his hand and raises it level with her own. She carefully places the unicorn in the palm of his hand, then pushes his fingers closed upon it.*] What are

you—doing that for? You want me to have him?—Laura? [*She nods.*] What for?

LAURA. A—souvenir . . .

[*She rises unsteadily and crouches beside the victrola to wind it up.*]

[LEGEND ON SCREEN: "THINGS HAVE A WAY OF TURNING OUT SO BADLY!"]

[OR IMAGE: "GENTLEMAN CALLER WAVING GOOD-BYE!—GAILY"]

[*At this moment* AMANDA *rushes brightly back in the front room. She bears a pitcher of fruit punch in an old-fashioned cut-glass pitcher and a plate of macaroons. The plate has a gold border and poppies painted on it.*]

AMANDA. Well, well, well! Isn't the air delightful after the shower?

I've made you children a little liquid refreshment.

[*Turns gaily to the gentleman caller*]

Jim, do you know that song about lemonade?

"Lemonade, lemonade
Made in the shade and stirred with a spade—
Good enough for any old maid!"

JIM [*uneasily*]. Ha-ha! No—I never heard it.

AMANDA. Why, Laura! You look so serious!

JIM. We were having a serious conversation.

AMANDA. Good! Now you're better acquainted!

JIM [*uncertainly*]. Ha-ha! Yes.

AMANDA. You modern young people are much more serious-minded than my generation. I was so gay as a girl!

JIM. You haven't changed, Mrs. Wingfield.

AMANDA. Tonight I'm rejuvenated! The gaiety of the occasion, Mr. O'Connor!

[*She tosses her head with a peal of laughter. Spills lemonade*]

Oooo! I'm baptizing myself!

JIM. Here—let me—

AMANDA [*setting the pitcher down*]. There now. I discovered we had some maraschino cherries. I dumped them in, juice and all!

JIM. You shouldn't have gone to that trouble, Mrs. Wingfield.

AMANDA. Trouble, trouble? Why, it was loads of fun!

Didn't you hear me cutting up in the kitchen? I bet your ears were burning! I told Tom how outdone with him I was for keeping

you to himself so long a time! He should have brought you over much, much sooner! Well, now that you've found your way, I want you to be a very frequent caller! Not just occasional but all the time.

Oh, we're going to have a lot of gay times together! I see them coming!

Mmm, just breathe that air! So fresh, and the moon's so pretty!

I'll skip back out—I know where my place is when young folks are having a—serious conversation!

JIM. Oh, don't go out, Mrs. Wingfield. The fact of the matter is I've got to be going.

AMANDA. Going, now? You're joking! Why, it's only the shank of the evening, Mr. O'Connor!

JIM. Well, you know how it is.

AMANDA. You mean you're a young workingman and have to keep workingmen's hours. We'll let you off early tonight. But only on the condition that next time you stay later.

What's the best night for you? Isn't Saturday night the best night for you workingmen?

JIM. I have a couple of time-clocks to punch, Mrs. Wingfield. One at morning, another one at night!

AMANDA. My, but you *are* ambitious! You work at night, too?

JIM. No, Ma'am, not work but—Betty! [*He crosses deliberately to pick up his hat. The band at the Paradise Dance Hall goes into a tender waltz.*]

AMANDA. Betty? Betty? Who's—Betty!

[*There is an ominous cracking sound in the sky.*]

JIM. Oh, just a girl. The girl I go steady with! [*He smiles charmingly. The sky falls.*]

[LEGEND: "THE SKY FALLS."]

AMANDA [*a long-drawn exhalation*]. Ohhhh . . . Is it a serious romance, Mr. O'Connor?

JIM. We're going to be married the second Sunday in June.

AMANDA. Ohhhh—how nice!

Tom didn't mention that you were engaged to be married.

JIM. The cat's not out of the bag at the warehouse yet.

You know how they are. They call you Romeo and stuff like that.

[*He stops at the oval mirror to put on his hat. He carefully shapes the brim and the crown to give a discreetly dashing effect.*]

It's been a wonderful evening, Mrs. Wingfield. I guess this is what they mean by Southern hospitality.

AMANDA. It really wasn't anything at all.

JIM. I hope it don't seem like I'm rushing off. But I promised Betty I'd pick her up at the Wabash depot, an' by the time I get my jalopy down there her train'll be in. Some women are pretty upset if you keep 'em waiting.

AMANDA. Yes, I know— The tyranny of women!

[*Extends her hand*]

Good-bye, Mr. O'Connor.

I wish you luck—and happiness—and success! All three of them, and so does Laura!—Don't you, Laura?

LAURA. Yes!

JIM [*taking her hand*]. Good-bye, Laura. I'm certainly going to treasure that souvenir. And don't you forget the good advice I gave you.

[*Raises his voice to a cheery shout*]

So long, Shakespeare!

Thanks again, ladies— Good night!

[*He grins and ducks jauntily out.*]

[*Still bravely grimacing,* AMANDA *closes the door on the gentleman caller. Then she turns back to the room with a puzzled expression. She and* LAURA *don't dare to face each other.* LAURA *crouches beside the victrola to wind it.*]

AMANDA [*faintly*]. Things have a way of turning out so badly. I don't believe that I would play the victrola.

Well, well—well—

Our gentleman caller was engaged to be married!

Tom!

TOM [*from back*]. Yes, Mother?

AMANDA. Come in here a minute. I want to tell you something awfully funny.

TOM [*enters with macaroon and a glass of the lemonade*]. Has the gentleman caller gotten away already?

AMANDA. The gentleman caller has made an early departure. What a wonderful joke you played on us!

TOM. How do you mean?

AMANDA. You didn't mention that he was engaged to be married.

TOM. Jim? Engaged?

AMANDA. That's what he just informed us.

TOM. I'll be jiggered! I didn't know about that.

AMANDA. That seems very peculiar.

TOM. What's peculiar about it?

AMANDA. Didn't you call him your best friend down at the warehouse?

TOM. He is, but how did I know?

AMANDA. It seems extremely peculiar that you wouldn't know your best friend was going to be married!

TOM. The warehouse is where I work, not where I know things about people!

AMANDA. You don't know things anywhere! You live in a dream; you manufacture illusions!

[*He crosses to door.*]

Where are you going?

TOM. I'm going to the movies.

AMANDA. That's right, now that you've had us make such fools of ourselves. The effort, the preparations, all the expense! The new floor lamp, the rug, the clothes for Laura! All for what? To entertain some other girl's fiancé!

Go to the movies, go! Don't think about us, a mother deserted, an unmarried sister who's crippled and has no job! Don't let anything interfere with your selfish pleasure!

Just go, go, go—to the movies!

TOM. All right, I will! The more you shout about my selfishness to me the quicker I'll go, and I won't go to the movies!

AMANDA. Go, then! Then go to the moon—you selfish dreamer!

[TOM *smashes his glass on the floor. He plunges out on the fire-escape, slamming the door.* LAURA *screams—cut by door.*]

[*Dance-hall music up.* TOM *goes to the rail and grips it desperately, lifting his face in the chill white moonlight penetrating the narrow abyss of the alley.*]

[LEGEND ON SCREEN: "AND SO GOOD-BYE . . ."]

[TOM's *closing speech is timed with the interior pantomime. The interior scene is played as though viewed through soundproof glass.* AMANDA *appears to be making a comforting speech to* LAURA *who is huddled upon the sofa. Now that we cannot hear the mother's speech, her silliness is gone and she has dignity and tragic beauty.* LAURA's *dark hair hides her face until at the end of the speech she lifts it to smile at her mother.* AMANDA's *gestures are slow and graceful, almost dance-like, as she comforts the daughter. At the end of her*

speech she glances a moment at the father's picture—then withdraws through the portieres. At close of TOM's *speech,* LAURA *blows out the candles, ending the play.*].

TOM. I didn't go to the moon, I went much further—for time is the longest distance between two places—

Not long after that I was fired for writing a poem on the lid of a shoe-box.

I left Saint Louis. I descended the steps of this fire-escape for a last time and followed, from then on, in my father's footsteps, attempting to find in motion what was lost in space—

I traveled around a great deal. The cities swept about me like dead leaves, leaves that were brightly colored but torn away from the branches.

I would have stopped, but I was pursued by something.

It always came upon me unawares, taking me altogether by surprise. Perhaps it was a familiar bit of music. Perhaps it was only a piece of transparent glass—

Perhaps I am walking along a street at night, in some strange city, before I have found companions. I pass the lighted window of a shop where perfume is sold. The window is filled with pieces of colored glass,[1] tiny transparent bottles in delicate colors, like bits of a shattered rainbow.

Then all at once my sister touches my shoulder. I turn around and look into her eyes . . .

Oh, Laura, Laura, I tried to leave you behind me, but I am more faithful than I intended to be!

I reach for a cigarette, I cross the street, I run into the movies or a bar, I buy a drink, I speak to the nearest stranger—anything that can blow your candles out!

[LAURA *bends over the candles.*]

—for nowadays the world is lit by lightning! Blow out your candles, Laura—and so good-bye. . . .

[*She blows the candles out.*]

THE SCENE DISSOLVES

---

[1] *pieces of colored glass. The reminiscent spirit of Proust is embodied in this passage.*

CHRISTOPHER FRY (1907-   )

The liveliest phenomenon in the postwar British theater was Christopher Fry, whose plays in the late forties displayed a rare combination of graces and arts to please. Actually he has been associated with the stage as an actor since the twenties, as a director since 1934, and as a writer since 1935. His first published play, *The Boy with a Cart,* appeared in 1939, but it was not until the production of *The Lady's Not for Burning* in 1948 that he won any general attention. By 1950 he had four plays running in London simultaneously and was acclaimed as the new wonder of the theater. When we consider that his medium is the verse play, which has not been a popular form in our century, the suddenness of his rise to fame is remarkable indeed.

Fry (whose real name is Harris) is a native of Bristol, the seat of the oldest theater building in England, which now houses a company of Old Vic Players, an offshoot of the famous Old Vic Theatre in London. His father, an architect, was also a lay preacher in the Church of England, but Christopher adopted his mother's Quaker faith and his grandmother's maiden name (as "a matter of euphony"). The family was tightly pinched after his father's death, but his mother managed to send him to a private school until he was eighteen, when he left it to become a teacher.

Fry had been stage-struck from an early age, and he had ambitiously attempted a verse drama at fourteen. So when teaching began to pall after three years, he turned actor and director in various repertory companies in the provinces, an experience that gave him his grasp of stage techniques. For ten years after leaving school he wrote not

a line, but in 1935 he composed a musical revue that was presented in London, and then, under the prodding of a poet-friend Robert Gittings, he began to experiment with verse plays.

The first of these were semiprofessionally produced at religious and charitable festivals, but with the arrival of the war he had completed his apprenticeship. Being a Quaker, he served between 1940 and 1944 in a noncombat unit whose duty it was to clear up air-raid damage in various parts of England. The end of the war found Fry ready to launch his theater career in earnest. *A Phoenix Too Frequent* was successfully produced in 1946, and with *The Lady's Not for Burning* (1948) his reputation was established. A third comedy, *Venus Observed* (1950), seemed to confirm the impression created by the other two that Fry is essentially a comic spirit in the theater.

However, in 1946 he had published a biblical tragedy, *The Firstborn,* and in 1951 he produced a highly serious play of contemporary spiritual issues, *Sleep of Prisoners,* which was staged in churches on both sides of the Atlantic. Clearly, Fry does not want to be classified as a poetic humorist, though this is the rôle that he has played most successfully so far. English critics hailed *Sleep of Prisoners* as his finest work, but it found less favor in America. After *The Dark Is Light Enough* (1954) Fry unaccountably stopped writing original plays and took to translating French comedies by Anouilh and Giraudoux. One can only hope that his remarkable talents as a comedian in verse have not burnt themselves out so soon. He has recently shown renewed activity.

CHRISTOPHER FRY

A PHOENIX TOO FREQUENT

'To whom conferr'd a peacock's undecent,
A squirrel's harsh, a phoenix too frequent.'
                    Robert Burton quoting Martial

CHARACTERS

Dynamene
> young widow of Virilius, lately deceased, at whose tomb she
> has elected to die of grief.

Doto
> maid to Dynamene, who has vowed to share her mistress' fate.

Tegeus-Chromis
> a corporal ordered to guard the corpses of six men who have
> been publicly hanged.

Scene

The tomb of Virilius, near Ephesus; night.

Note

The story was got from Jeremy Taylor who had it from Petronius.[1]

> *An underground tomb, in darkness except for the very low light of an oil-lamp. Above ground the starlight shows a line of trees on which hang the bodies of several men. It also penetrates a gate and falls on to the first of the steps which descend into the darkness of the tomb.* DOTO *talks to herself in the dark.*

DOTO. Nothing but the harmless day gone into black
Is all the dark is. And so what's my trouble?
Demons is so much wind. Are so much wind.
I've plenty to fill my thoughts. All that I ask
Is don't keep turning men over in my mind,
Venerable Aphrodite.[2] I've had my last one
And thank you. I thank thee. He smelt of sour grass
And was likeable. He collected ebony quoits.
                              [*An owl hoots near at hand.*]
O Zeus! O some god or other, where is the oil?
Fire's from Prometheus.[3] I thank thee. If I
Mean to die I'd better see what I'm doing.
      [*She fills the lamp with oil. The flame burns up brightly and
         shows* DYNAMENE, *beautiful and young, leaning asleep beside a
                                                                    bier.*]

Honestly, I would rather have to sleep
With a bald bee-keeper who was wearing his boots
Than spend more days fasting and thirsting and crying
In a tomb. I shouldn't have said that. Pretend
I didn't hear myself. But life and death
Is cat and dog in this double-bed of a world.
My master, my poor master, was a man
Whose nose was as straight as a little buttress,

---

[1] *The play retells the famous tale of the Widow of Ephesus from the* Satyricon *of Petronius, the ancient Roman novelist.*
[2] *Aphrodite, Greek goddess of love.*
[3] *Prometheus, the Titan who gave man the gift of fire.*

And now he has taken it into Elysium[1]
Where it won't be noticed among all the other straightness.

                 [*The owl cries again and wakens* DYNAMENE.]
Oh, them owls. Those owls. It's woken her.

DYNAMENE. Ah! I'm breathless. I caught up with the ship
But it spread its wings, creaking a cry of *Dew,*
Dew! and flew figurehead foremost into the sun.

DOTO. How crazy, madam.

DYNAMENE.   Doto, draw back the curtains.
I'll take my barley-water.

DOTO.   We're not at home
Now, madam. It's the master's tomb.

DYNAMENE.   Of course!
Oh, I'm wretched. Already I have disfigured
My vigil. My cynical eyelids have soon dropped me
In a dream.

DOTO.   But then it's possible, madam, you might
Find yourself in bed with him again
In a dream, madam. Was he on the ship?

DYNAMENE. He was the ship.

DOTO.   Oh. That makes it different.

DYNAMENE. He was the ship. He had such a deck, Doto,
Such a white, scrubbed deck. Such a stern prow,
Such a proud stern, so slim from port to starboard.
If ever you meet a man with such fine masts
Give your life to him, Doto. The figurehead
Bore his own features, so serene in the brow
And hung with a little seaweed. O Virilius,
My husband, you have left a wake in my soul.
You cut the glassy water with a diamond keel.
I must cry again.

DOTO.   What, when you mean to join him?
Don't you believe he will be glad to see you, madam?
Thankful to see you, I should imagine, among
Them shapes and shades; all shapes of shapes and all
Shades of shades, from what I've heard. I know
I shall feel odd at first with Cerberus,
Sop or no sop.[2] Still, I know how you feel, madam.

[1] *Elysium, the abode of the happy in Hades.*
[2] *Cerberus, sop or no sop. Cerberus, the three-headed dog that guarded the*
entrance to Hades, could be placated with a honey-cake.

You think he may find a temptation in Hades.
I shouldn't worry. It would help him to settle down.

[DYNAMENE *weeps.*]

It would only be *fun,* madam. He couldn't go far
with a shade.

DYNAMENE.   He was one of the coming men.
He was certain to have become the most well-organized provost
The town has known, once they had made him provost.
He was so punctual, you could regulate
The sun by him. He made the world succumb
To his daily revolution of habit. But who,
In the world he has gone to, will appreciate that?
O poor Virilius! To be a coming man
Already gone—it must be distraction.
Why did you leave me walking about our ambitions
Like a cat in the ruins of a house? Promising husband,
Why did you insult me by dying? Virilius,
Now I keep no flower, except in the vase
Of the tomb.

DOTO.   O poor madam! O poor master!
I presume so far as to cry somewhat for myself
As well. I know you won't mind, madam. It's two
Days not eating makes me think of my uncle's
Shop in the country, where he has a hardware business,
Basins, pots, ewers, and alabaster birds.
He makes you die of laughing. O madam,
Isn't it sad?   [*They both weep.*]

DYNAMENE.   How could I have allowed you
To come and die of my grief? Doto, it puts
A terrible responsibility on me. Have you
No grief of your own you could die of?

DOTO.   Not really, madam.

DYNAMENE. Nothing?

DOTO.   Not really. They was all one to me.
Well, all but two was all one to me. And they,
Strange enough, was two who kept recurring.
I could never be sure if they had gone for good
Or not; and so that kept things cheerful, madam.
One always gave a wink before he deserted me,
The other slapped me as it were behind, madam;
Then they would be away for some months.

DYNAMENE. Oh Doto,
What an unhappy life you were having to lead.

DOTO. Yes, I'm sure. But never mind, madam,
It seemed quite lively then. And now I know
It's what you say; life is more big than a bed
And full of miracles and mysteries like
One man made for one woman, etcetera, etcetera.
Lovely. I feel sung, madam, by a baritone
In mixed company with everyone pleased.
And so I had to come with you here, madam,
For the last sad chorus of me. It's all
Fresh to me. Death's a new interest in life,
If it doesn't disturb you, madam, to have me crying.
It's because of us not having breakfast again.
And the master, of course. And the beautiful world.
And you crying too, madam. Oh—Oh!

DYNAMENE. I can't forbid your crying; but you must cry
On the other side of the tomb. I'm becoming confused.
This is my personal grief and my sacrifice
Of self, solus.[1] Right over there, darling girl.

DOTO. What here?

DYNAMENE. Now, if you wish, you may cry, Doto.
But our tears are very different. For me
The world is all with Charon,[2] all, all,
Even the metal and plume of the rose garden,
And the forest where the sea fumes overhead
In vegetable tides, and particularly
The entrance to the warm baths in Arcite Street
Where we first met;—all!—the sun itself
Trails an evening hand in the sultry river
Far away down by Acheron. I am lonely,
Virilius. Where is the punctual eye
And where is the cautious voice which made
Balance-sheets sound like Homer and Homer sound
Like balance-sheets? The precision of limbs, the amiable
Laugh, the exact festivity? Gone from the world.
You were the peroration of nature, Virilius.
You explained everything to me, even the extremely

[1] *solus, alone.*
[2] *Charon, the boatman who ferried the spirits of the dead across the River Acheron (or Styx).*

Complicated gods. You wrote them down
In seventy columns. Dear curling calligraphy!
Gone from the world, once and for all. And I taught you
In your perceptive moments to appreciate me.
You said I was harmonious, Virilius,
Moulded and harmonious, little matronal
Ox-eye, your package. And then I would walk
Up and down largely, as it were making my own
Sunlight. What a mad blacksmith creation is
Who blows his furnaces until the stars fly upward
And iron Time is hot and politicians glow
And bulbs and roots sizzle into hyacinth
And orchis, and the sand puts out the lion,
Roaring yellow, and oceans bud with porpoises,
Blenny, tunny and the almost unexisting
Blindfish; throats are cut, the masterpiece
Looms out of labour; nations and rebellions
Are spat out to hang on the wind—and all is gone
In one Virilius, wearing his office tunic,
Checking the pence column as he went.
Where's animation now? What is there that stays
To dance? The eye of the one-eyed world is out.   [*She weeps.*]
     DOTO. I shall try to grieve a little, too.
It would take lessons, I imagine, to do it out loud
For long. If I could only remember
Any one of those fellows without wanting to laugh.
Hopeless, I am. Now those good pair of shoes
I gave away without thinking, that's a different—
Well, I've cried enough about *them,* I suppose.
Poor madam, poor master.
     [TEGEUS *comes through the gate to the top of the steps.*]
     TEGEUS.   What's your trouble?
     DOTO.   Oh!
Oh! Oh, a man. I thought for a moment it was something
With harm in it. Trust a man to be where it's dark.
What is it? Can't you sleep?
     TEGEUS.   Now, listen—
     DOTO.   Hush!
Remember you're in the grave. You must go away.
Madam is occupied.

TEGEUS.   What, here?

DOTO.   Becoming
Dead. We both are.

TEGEUS.   What's going on here?

DOTO.   Grief.
Are you satisfied now?

TEGEUS.   Less and less. Do you know
What the time is?

DOTO.   I'm not interested.
We've done with all that. Go away. Be a gentleman.
If we can't be free of men in a grave
Death's a dead loss.

TEGEUS.   It's two in the morning. All
I ask is what are women doing down here
At two in the morning?

DOTO.   Can't you see she's crying?
Or is she sleeping again? Either way
She's making arrangements to join her husband.

TEGEUS.   Where?

DOTO. Good god, in the Underworld, dear man. Haven't you
    learnt
About life and death?

TEGEUS.   In a manner, yes; in a manner;
The rudiments. So the lady means to die?

DOTO. For love; beautiful, curious madam.

TEGEUS.   Not curious;
I've had thoughts like it. Death is a kind of love.
Not anything I can explain.

DOTO.   You'd better come in
And sit down.

TEGEUS.   I'd be grateful.

DOTO.   Do. It will be my last
Chance to have company, in the flesh.

TEGEUS.   Do you mean
You're going too?

DOTO.   Oh, certainly I am.
Not anything I can explain.
It all started with madam saying a man
Was two men really, and I'd only noticed one,
One each, I mean. It seems he has a soul

As well as his other troubles. And I like to know
What I'm getting with a man. I'm inquisitive,
I suppose you'd call me.

    TEGEUS.   It takes some courage.

    DOTO.   Well, yes
And no. I'm fond of change.

    TEGEUS.   Would you object
To have me eating my supper here?

    DOTO.   Be careful
Of the crumbs. We don't want a lot of squeaking mice
Just when we're dying.

    TEGEUS.   What a sigh she gave then.
Down the air like a slow comet.
And now she's all dark again. Mother of me.
How long has this been going on?

    DOTO.   Two days.
It should have been three by now, but at first
Madam had difficulty with the Town Council. They said
They couldn't have a tomb used as a private residence.
But madam told them she wouldn't be eating here,
Only suffering, and they thought that would be all right.

    TEGEUS. Two of you. Marvellous. Who would have said
I should ever have stumbled on anything like this?
Do you have to cry? Yes, I suppose so. It's all
Quite reasonable.

    DOTO.   Your supper and your knees.
That's what's making me cry. I can't bear sympathy
And they're sympathetic.

    TEGEUS.   Please eat a bit of something.
I've no appetite left.

    DOTO.   And see her go ahead of me?
Wrap it up; put it away. You sex of wicked beards!
It's no wonder you have to shave off your black souls
Every day as they push through your chins.
I'll turn my back on you. It means utter
Contempt. Eat? Utter contempt. Oh, little new rolls!

    TEGEUS. Forget it, forget it; please forget it. Remember
I've had no experience of this kind of thing before.
Indeed I'm as sorry as I know how to be. Ssh,
We'll disturb her. She sighed again. O Zeus,
It's terrible! Asleep, and still sighing.

Mourning has made a warren in her spirit,
All that way below. Ponos![1] the heart
Is the devil of a medicine.

DOTO.   And I don't intend
To turn round.

TEGEUS.   I understand how you must feel.
Would it be—have you any objection
To my having a drink? I have a little wine here.
And, you probably see how it is: grief's in order,
And death's in order, and women—I can usually
Manage that too; but not all three together
At this hour of the morning. So you'll excuse me.
How about you? It would make me more comfortable
If you'd take a smell of it.

DOTO.   One for the road?

TEGEUS. One for the road.

DOTO.   It's the dust in my throat. The tomb
Is so dusty. Thanks, I will. There's no point in dying
Of everything, simultaneous.

TEGEUS.   It's lucky
I brought two bowls. I was expecting to keep
A drain for my relief when he comes in the morning.

DOTO. Are you on duty?

TEGEUS.   Yes.

DOTO.   It looks like it.

TEGEUS.   Well,
Here's your good health.

DOTO.   What good is that going to do me?
Here's to an easy crossing and not too much waiting
About on the bank. Do you have to tremble like that?

TEGEUS. The idea—I can't get used to it.

DOTO.   For a member
Of the forces, you're peculiarly queasy. I wish
Those owls were in Hades—oh no; let them stay where they are.
Have you never had nothing to do with corpses before?

TEGEUS. I've got six of them outside.

DOTO.   Morpheus,[2] that's plenty.
What are they doing there?

---

[1] *Ponos, pain, personified as the son of Eris, the goddess of discord.*
[2] *Morpheus, god of dreams.*

TEGEUS.   Hanging.

DOTO.   Hanging?

TEGEUS.   On trees.

Five plane trees and a holly. The holly-berries
Are just reddening. Another drink?

DOTO.   Why not?

TEGEUS. It's from Samos.[1] Here's—

DOTO.   All right. Let's just drink it.

—How did they get in that predicament?

TEGEUS. The sandy-haired fellow said we should collaborate
With everybody; the little man said he wouldn't
Collaborate with anybody; the old one
Said that the Pleiades[2] weren't sisters but cousins
And anyway were manufactured in Lacedaemon.[3]
The fourth said that we hanged men for nothing
The other two said nothing. Now they hang
About at the corner of the night, they're present
And absent, horribly obsequious to every
Move in the air, and yet they keep me standing
For five hours at a stretch.

DOTO.   The wine has gone
Down to my knees.

TEGEUS.   And up to your cheeks. You're looking
Fresher. If only—

DOTO.   Madam? She never would.
Shall I ask her?

TEGEUS.   No; no, don't dare, don't breathe it.
This is privilege, to come so near
To what is undeceiving and uncorrupt
And undivided; this is the clear fashion
For all souls, a ribbon to bind the unruly
Curls of living, a faith, a hope, Zeus
Yes, a fine thing. I am human, and this
Is human fidelity, and we can be proud
And unphilosophical.

---

[1] *Samos, the Greek island in the Aegean Sea, famous for its wine.*
[2] *Pleiades, the constellation of seven stars, thought by the Greeks to be the seven daughters of Atlas.*
[3] *Lacedaemon, Sparta.*

DOTO.   I need to dance
But I haven't the use of my legs.

TEGEUS.   No, no, don't dance,
Or, at least, only inwards; don't dance; cry
Again. We'll put a moat of tears
Round her bastion of love, and save
The world. It's something, it's more than something,
It's regeneration, to see how a human cheek
Can become as pale as a pool.

DOTO.   Do you love me, handsome?

TEGEUS. To have found life, after all, unambiguous!

DOTO. Did you say Yes?

TEGEUS.   Certainly; just now I love all men.

DOTO. So do I.

TEGEUS.   And the world is a good creature again.
I'd begun to see it as mildew, verdigris,
Rust, woodrot, or as though the sky had uttered
An oval twirling blasphemy with occasional vistas
In country districts. I was within an ace
Of volunteering for overseas service. Despair
Abroad can always nurse pleasant thoughts of home.
Integrity, by god!

DOTO.   I love all the world
And the movement of the apple in your throat.
So shall you kiss me? It would be better, I should think,
To go moistly to Hades.

TEGEUS.   Her's is the way,
Luminous with sorrow.

DOTO.   Then I'll take
Another little swiggy. I love all men,
Everybody, even you, and I'll pick you
Some outrageous honeysuckle for your helmet,
If only it lived here. Pardon.

DYNAMENE.   Doto. Who is it?

DOTO. Honeysuckle, madam. Because of the bees.
Go back to sleep, madam.

DYNAMENE.   What person is it?

DOTO. Yes, I see what you mean, madam. It's a kind of
Corporal talking to his soul, on a five-hour shift,
Madam, with six bodies. He's been having his supper.

TEGEUS. I'm going. It's terrible that we should have disturbed her.

DOTO. He was delighted to see you so sad, madam.
It has stopped him going abroad.

DYNAMENE.   One with six bodies?
A messenger, a guide to where we go.
It is possible he has come to show us the way
Out of these squalid suburbs of life, a shade,
A gorgon,[1] who has come swimming up, against
The falls of my tears (for which in truth he would need
Many limbs) to guide me to Virilius.
I shall go quietly.

TEGEUS.   I do assure you—
Such clumsiness, such a vile and unforgivable
Intrusion. I shall obliterate myself
Immediately.

DOTO.   Oblit—oh, what a pity
To oblit. Pardon. Don't let him, the nice fellow.

DYNAMENE. Sir: your other five bodies: where are they?

TEGEUS.   Madam—
Outside; I have them outside. On trees.

DYNAMENE.   Quack!

TEGEUS. What do I reply?

DYNAMENE.   Quack, charlatan!
You've never known the gods. You came to mock me.
Doto, this never was a gorgon, never.
Nor a gentleman either. He's completely spurious.
Admit it, you creature. Have you even a feather
Of the supernatural in your system? Have you?

TEGEUS. Some of my relations—

DYNAMENE.   Well?

TEGEUS.   Are dead, I think;
That is to say I have connexions—

DYNAMENE.   Connexions
With pickpockets. It's a shameless imposition.
Does the army provide you with no amusements?
If I were still of the world, and not cloistered
In a colourless landscape of winter thought
Where the approaching Spring is desired oblivion,
I should write sharply to your commanding officer.

---

[1] *gorgon, a winged female monster with hair of snakes.*

It should be done, it should be done. If my fingers
Weren't so cold I would do it now. But they are,
Horribly cold. And why should insolence matter
When my colour of life is unreal, a blush on death,
A partial mere diaphane? I don't know
Why it should matter. Oafish, non-commissioned
Young man! The boots of your conscience will pinch for ever
If life's dignity has any self-protection.
Oh, I have to sit down. The tomb's going round.

DOTO. Oh, madam, don't give over. I can't remember
When things were so lively. He looks marvellously
Marvellously uncomfortable. Go on, madam.
Can't you, madam? Oh, madam, don't you feel up to it?
There, do you see her, you acorn-chewing infantryman?
You've made her cry, you square-bashing barbarian.

TEGEUS. O history, my private history, why
Was I led here? What stigmatism has got
Into my stars? Why wasn't it my brother?
He has a tacit misunderstanding with everybody
And washes in it. Why wasn't it my mother?
She makes a collection of other people's tears
And dries them all. Let them forget I came;
And lie in the terrible black crystal of grief
Which held them, before I broke it. Outside, Tegeus.

DOTO. Hey, I don't think so, I shouldn't say so. Come
Down again, uniform. Do you think you're going
To half kill an unprotected lady and then
Back out upwards? Do you think you can leave her like this?

TEGEUS. Yes, yes, I'll leave her. O directorate of gods,
How can I? Beauty's bit is between my teeth.
She has added another torture to me. Bottom
Of Hades' bottom.

DOTO.   Madam. Madam, the corporal
Has some wine here. It will revive you, madam.
And then you can go at him again, madam.

TEGEUS. It's the opposite of everything you've said,
I swear. I swear by Horkos[1] and the Styx,
I swear by the nine acres of Tityos,[2]

[1] *Horkos, god of the oath and punisher of perjurers.*
[2] *Tityos, a villain, punished in Hades by having his liver perpetually gnawed at by two vultures. His body covered nine acres.*

I swear the Hypnotic oath,[1] by all the Titans—
By Koeos, Krios, Iapetos, Krónos,[2] and so on—
By the three Hekatoncheires,[3] by the insomnia
Of Tisiphone,[4] by Jove, by jove, and the dew
On the feet of my boyhood, I am innocent
Of mocking you. Am I a Salmoneus[5]
That, seeing such a flame of sorrow—

DYNAMENE.   You needn't
Labour to prove your secondary education.
Perhaps I jumped to a wrong conclusion, perhaps
I was hasty.

DOTO.   How easy to swear if you're properly educated.
Wasn't it pretty, madam? Pardon.

DYNAMENE.   If I misjudged you
I apologize, I apologize. Will you please leave us?
You were wrong to come here. In a place of mourning
Light itself is a trespasser; nothing can have
The right of entrance except those natural symbols
Of mortality, the jabbing, funeral, sleek-
With-omen raven, the death-watch beetle which mocks
Time: particularly, I'm afraid, the spider
Weaving his home with swift self-generated
Threads of slaughter; and, of course, the worm.
I wish it could be otherwise. Oh dear,
They aren't easy to live with.

DOTO.   Not even a *little* wine, madam?

DYNAMENE. Here, Doto?

DOTO.   Well, on the steps perhaps,
Except it's so draughty.

DYNAMENE.   Doto! Here?

DOTO.   No, madam;
I quite see.

---

[1] *Hypnotic oath,* to Hypnos, god of sleep.
[2] *Koeos, Krios, Iapetos, Kronos,* Titans who ruled the universe until they were deposed by Zeus and the gods.
[3] *Hekatoncheires, the three giants, each with a hundred arms and fifty hands, who guarded the imprisoned Titans.
[4] *Tisiphone, the avenger of murder, one of the Erinyes, or Furies.
[5] *Salmoneus, whose boast of equality with Zeus led the king of the gods to destroy him with a thunderbolt.

DYNAMENE. I might be wise to strengthen myself
In order to fast again; it would make me abler
For grief. I will breathe a little of it, Doto.

DOTO. Thank god. Where's the bottle?

DYNAMENE.   What an exquisite bowl.

TEGEUS. Now that it's peacetime we have pottery classes.

DYNAMENE. You made it yourself?

TEGEUS.   Yes. Do you see the design?
The corded god, tied also by the rays
Of the sun, and the astonished ship erupting
Into vines and vine-leaves, inverted pyramids
Of grapes, the uplifted hands of the men (the raiders),
And here the headlong sea, itself almost
Venturing into leaves and tendrils, and Proteus[1]
With his beard braiding the wind, and this
Held by other hands is a drowned sailor—

DYNAMENE. Always, always.

DOTO.   Hold the bowl steady, madam.
Pardon.[2]

DYNAMENE. Doto, have you been drinking?

DOTO.   Here, madam?
I coaxed some a little way towards my mouth, madam,
But I scarcely swallowed except because I had to. The hiccup
Is from no breakfast, madam, and not meant to be funny.

DYNAMENE. You may drink this too. Oh, how the inveterate body,
Even when cut from the heart, insists on leaf,
Puts out, with a separate meaningless will,
Fronds to intercept the thankless sun.
How it does, oh, how it does. And how it confuses
The nature of the mind.

TEGEUS.   Yes, yes, the confusion;
That's something I understand better than anything.

DYNAMENE. When the thoughts would die, the instincts will set
        sail
For life. And when the thoughts are alert for life
The instincts will rage to be destroyed on the rocks.
To Virilius it was not so; his brain was an ironing-board

----

[1] *Proteus, the prophetic old man of the sea.*
[2] *Pardon. Doto has hiccuped.*

For all crumpled indecision: and I follow him,
The hawser of my world. You don't belong here,
You see; you don't belong here at all.

TEGEUS.   If only
I did. If only you knew the effort it costs me
To mount those steps again into an untrustworthy,
Unpredictable, unenlightened night,
And turn my back on—on a state of affairs,
I can only call it a vision, a hope, a promise,
A— By that I mean loyalty, enduring passion,
Unrecking bravery and beauty all in one.

DOTO. He means you, or you and me; or me, madam.

TEGEUS. It only remains for me to thank you, and to say
That whatever awaits me and for however long
I may be played by this poor musician, existence,
Your person and sacrifice will leave their trace
As clear upon me as the shape of the hills
Around my birthplace. Now I must leave you to your husband.

DOTO. Oh! You, madam.

DYNAMENE.   I'll tell you what I will do.
I will drink with you to the memory of my husband,
Because I have been curt, because you are kind,
And because I'm extremely thirsty. And then we will say
Good-bye and part to go to our opposite corruptions,
The world and the grave.

TEGEUS.   The climax to the vision.

DYNAMENE [*drinking*]. My husband, and all he stood for.

TEGEUS.   Stands for.

DYNAMENE.   Stands for.

TEGEUS. Your husband.

DOTO.   The master.

DYNAMENE.   How good it is,
How it sings to the throat, purling with summer.

TEGEUS. It has a twin nature, winter and warmth in one,
Moon and meadow. Do you agree?

DYNAMENE.   Perfectly;
A cold bell sounding in a golden month.

TEGEUS. Crystal in harvest.

DYNAMENE.   Perhaps a nightingale
Sobbing among the pears.

TEGEUS.   In an old autumnal midnight.

DOTO. Grapes.—Pardon. There's some more here.

TEGEUS.   Plenty.
I drink to the memory of your husband.

DYNAMENE.   My husband.

DOTO.   The master.

DYNAMENE. He was careless in his choice of wines.

TEGEUS.   And yet
Rendering to living its rightful poise is not
Unimportant.

DYNAMENE.   A mystery's in the world
Where a little liquid, with flavour, quality, and fume
Can be as no other, can hint and flute our senses
As though a music played in harvest hollows
And a movement was in the swathes of our memory.
Why should scent, why should flavour come
With such wings upon us? Parsley, for instance.

TEGEUS. Seaweed.

DYNAMENE.   Lime trees.

DOTO.   Horses.

TEGEUS.   Fruit in the fire.

DYNAMENE. Do I know your name?

TEGEUS.   Tegeus.

DYNAMENE.   That's very thin for you,[1]
It hardly covers your bones. Something quite different,
Altogether other. I shall think of it presently.

TEGEUS. Darker vowels, perhaps.

DYNAMENE.   Yes, certainly darker vowels.
And your consonants should have a slight angle,
And a certain temperature. Do you know what I mean?
It will come to me.

TEGEUS.   Now *your* name—

DYNAMENE.   It is nothing
To any purpose. I'll be to you the She
In the tomb. You have the air of a natural-historian
As though you were accustomed to handling birds' eggs,
Or tadpoles, or putting labels on moths. You see?
The genius of dumb things, that they are nameless.
Have I found the seat of the weevil in human brains?

---

[1] *That's very thin for you. This is a pun on the Latin* teges, *a thin covering (from* tegere, *to cover).*

Our names. They make us broody; we sit and sit
To hatch them into reputation and dignity.
And then they set upon us and become despair,
Guilt and remorse. We go where they lead. We dance
Attendance on something wished upon us by the wife
Of our mother's physician. But insects meet and part
And put the woods about them, fill the dusk
And freckle the light and go and come without
A name among them, without the wish of a name
And very pleasant too. Did I interrupt you?

TEGEUS. I forget. We'll have no names then.

DYNAMENE.   I should like
You to have a name, I don't know why; a small one
To fill out the conversation.

TEGEUS.   I should like
You to have a name too, if only for something
To remember. Have you still some wine in your bowl?

DYNAMENE. Not altogether.

TEGEUS.   We haven't come to the end
By several inches.[1] Did I splash you?

DYNAMENE.   It doesn't matter.
Well, here's to my husband's name.

TEGEUS.   Your husband's name.

DOTO. The master.

DYNAMENE.   It was kind of you to come.

TEGEUS. It was more than coming. I followed my future here,
As we all do if we're sufficiently inattentive
And don't vex ourselves with questions; or do I mean
Attentive? If so, attentive to what? Do I sound
Incoherent?

DYNAMENE.   You're wrong. There isn't a future here,
Not here, not for you.

TEGEUS.   Your name's Dynamene.

DYNAMENE. Who—Have I been utterly irreverent? Are you—
Who made you say that? Forgive me the question,
But are you dark or light? I mean which shade
Of the supernatural? Or if neither, what prompted you?

TEGEUS. Dynamene——

DYNAMENE.   No, but I'm sure you're the friend of nature,

[1] *By several inches. He then fills her bowl.*

It must be so, I think I see little Phoebuses[1]
Rising and setting in your eyes.

DOTO.   They're not little Phoebuses,
They're hoodwinks, madam. Your name is on your brooch.
No little Phoebuses to-night.

DYNAMENE.   That's twice
You've played me a trick. Oh, I know practical jokes
Are common on Olympus, but haven't we at all
Developed since the gods were born? Are gods
And men both to remain immortal adolescents?
How tiresome it all is.

TEGEUS.   It was you, each time,
Who said I was supernatural. When did I say so?
You're making me into whatever you imagine
And then you blame me because I can't live up to it.

DYNAMENE. I shall call you Chromis. It has a breadlike sound.
I think of you as a crisp loaf.

TEGEUS.   And now
You'll insult me because I'm not sliceable.

DYNAMENE. I think drinking is harmful to our tempers.

TEGEUS. If I seem to be frowning, that is only because
I'm looking directly into your light: I must look
Angrily, or shut my eyes.

DYNAMENE.   Shut them.—Oh,
You have eyelashes! A new perspective of you.
Is that how you look when you sleep?

TEGEUS.   My jaw drops down.

DYNAMENE. Show me how.

TEGEUS.   Like this.

DYNAMENE.   It makes an irresistible
Moron of you. Will you waken now?
It's morning; I see a thin dust of daylight
Blowing on to the steps.

TEGEUS.   Already? Dynamene,
You're tricked again. This time by the moon.

DYNAMENE.   Oh well,
Moon's daylight, then. Doto is asleep.

TEGEUS.   Doto
Is asleep . . .

---

[1] *little Phoebuses. Phoebus Apollo was the god of light (and the sun).*

DYNAMENE.   Chromis, what made you walk about
In the night? What, I wonder, made you not stay
Sleeping wherever you slept? Was it the friction
Of the world on your mind? Those two are difficult
To make agree. Chromis—now try to learn
To answer your name. I won't say Tegeus.

TEGEUS.   And I
Won't say Dynamene.

DYNAMENE.   Not?

TEGEUS.   It makes you real.
Forgive me, a terrible thing has happened. Shall I
Say it and perhaps destroy myself for you?
Forgive me first, or, more than that, forgive
Nature who winds her furtive stream all through
Our reason. Do you forgive me?

DYNAMENE.   I'll forgive
Anything, if it's the only way I can know
What you have to tell me.

TEGEUS.   I felt us to be alone;
Here in a grave, separate from any life,
I and the only one of beauty, the only
Persuasive key to all my senses,
In spite of my having lain day after day
And pored upon the sepals, corolla, stamen, and bracts
Of the yellow bog-iris. Then my body ventured
A step towards interrupting your perfection of purpose
And my own renewed faith in human nature.
Would you have believed that possible?

DYNAMENE.   I have never
Been greatly moved by the yellow bog-iris. Alas,
It's as I said. This place is for none but the spider,
Raven and worms, not for a living man.

TEGEUS. It has been a place of blessing to me. It will always
Play in me, a fountain of confidence
When the world is arid. But I know it is true
I have to leave it, and though it withers my soul
I must let you make your journey.

DYNAMENE.   No.

TEGEUS.   Not true?

DYNAMENE. We can talk of something quite different.

TEGEUS.   Yes, we can!

Oh yes, we will! Is it your opinion
That no one believes who hasn't learned to doubt?
Or, another thing, if we persuade ourselves
To one particular Persuasion, become Sophist,
Stoic, Platonist, anything whatever,
Would you say that there must be areas of soul
Lying unproductive therefore, or dishonoured
Or blind?

DYNAMENE.   No, I don't know.

TEGEUS.   No. It's impossible
To tell. Dynamene, if only I had
Two cakes of pearl-barley and hydromel
I could see you to Hades, leave you with your husband
And come back to the world.

DYNAMENE.   Ambition, I suppose,
Is an appetite particular to man.
What is your definition?

TEGEUS.   The desire to find
A reason for living.

DYNAMENE.   But then, suppose it leads,
As often, one way or another, it does, to death.

TEGEUS. Then that may be life's reason. Oh, but how
Could I bear to return, Dynamene? The earth's
Daylight would be my grave if I had left you
In that unearthly night.

DYNAMENE.   O Chromis——

TEGEUS.   Tell me,
What is your opinion of Progress? Does it, for example,
Exist? Is there ever progression without retrogression?
Therefore is it not true that mankind
Can more justly be said increasingly to Gress?
As the material improves, the craftsmanship deteriorates
And honour and virtue remain the same. I love you,
Dynamene.

DYNAMENE. Would you consider we go round and round?

TEGEUS. We concertina, I think; taking each time
A larger breath, so that the farther we go out
The farther we have to go in.

DYNAMENE.   There'll come a time
When it will be unbearable to continue.

TEGEUS. Unbearable.

DYNAMENE. Perhaps we had better have something
To eat. The wine has made your eyes so quick
I am breathless beside them. It *is*
Your eyes, I think; or your intelligence
Holding my intelligence up above you
Between its hands. Or the cut of your uniform.

TEGEUS. Here's a new roll with honey. In the gods' names
Let's sober ourselves.

DYNAMENE. As soon as possible.

TEGEUS. Have you
Any notion of algebra?

DYNAMENE. We'll discuss you, Chromis.
We will discuss you, till you're nothing but words.

TEGEUS. I? There is nothing, of course, I would rather discuss,
Except—if it would be no intrusion—you, Dynamene.

DYNAMENE. No, you couldn't want to. But your birthplace,
    Chromis,
With the hills that placed themselves in you for ever
As you say, where was it?

TEGEUS. My father's farm at Pyxa.

DYNAMENE. There? Could it be there?

TEGEUS. I was born in the hills
Between showers, a quarter of an hour before milking time.
Do you know Pyxa? It stretches to the crossing of two
Troublesome roads, and buries its back in beechwood,
From which come the white owls of our nights
And the mulling and cradling of doves in the day.
I attribute my character to those shadows
And heavy roots; and my interest in music
To the sudden melodious escape of the young river
Where it breaks from nosing through the cresses and kingcups.
That's honestly so.

DYNAMENE. You used to climb about
Among the windfallen tower of Phrasidemus
Looking for bees' nests.

TEGEUS. What? When have I
Said so?

DYNAMENE. Why, all the children did.

TEGEUS. Yes: but, in the name of light, how do you *know* that?

DYNAMENE. I played there once, on holiday.

TEGEUS.   O Klotho,
Lachesis and Atropos![1]

DYNAMENE.   It's the strangest chance:
I may have seen, for a moment, your boyhood.

TEGEUS.   I may
Have seen something like an early flower
Something like a girl. If I only could remember how I must
Have seen you. Were you after the short white violets?
Maybe I blundered past you, taking your look,
And scarcely acknowledged how a star
Ran through me, to live in the brooks of my blood for ever.
Or I saw you playing at hiding in the cave
Where the ferns are and the water drips.

DYNAMENE. I was quite plain and fat and I was usually
Hitting someone. I wish I could remember you.
I'm envious of the days and children who saw you
Then. It is curiously a little painful
Not to share your past.

TEGEUS.   How did it come
Our stars could mingle for an afternoon
So long ago, and then forget us or tease us
Or helplessly look on the dark high seas
Of our separation, while time drank
The golden hours? What hesitant fate is that?

DYNAMENE. Time? Time? Why—how old are we?

TEGEUS.   Young,
Thank both our mothers, but still we're older than to-night
And so older than we should be. Wasn't I born
In love with what, only now, I have grown to meet?
I'll tell you something else. I was born entirely
For this reason. I was born to fill a gap
In the world's experience, which had never known
Chromis loving Dynamene.

DYNAMENE.   You are so
Excited, poor Chromis. What is it? Here you sit
With a woman who has wept away all claims
To appearance, unbecoming in her oldest clothes,
With not a trace of liveliness, a drab

---

[1] *Klotho, Lachesis, and Atropos, the three Fates.*

Of melancholy, entirely shadow without
A smear of sun. Forgive me if I tell you
That you fall easily into superlatives.

 TEGEUS. Very well. I'll say nothing, then. I'll fume
With feeling.

 DYNAMENE.   Now you go to the extreme. Certainly
You must speak. You may have more to say. Besides
You might let your silence run away with you
And not say something that you should. And how
Should I answer you then? Chromis, you boy,
I can't look away from you. You use
The lamplight and the moon so skilfully,
So arrestingly, in and around your furrows.
A humorous ploughman goes whistling to a team
Of sad sorrow, to and fro in your brow
And over your arable cheek. Laugh for me. Have you
Cried for women, ever?

 TEGEUS.   In looking about for you.
But I have recognized them for what they were.

 DYNAMENE. What were they?

 TEGEUS.   Never you: never, although
They could walk with bright distinction into all men's
Longest memories, never you, by a hint
Or a faint quality, or at least not more
Than reflectively, stars lost and uncertain
In the sea, compared with the shining salt, the shiners,
The galaxies, the clusters, the bright grain whirling
Over the black threshing-floor of space.
Will you make some effort to believe that?

 DYNAMENE.   No, no effort.
It lifts me and carries me. It may be wild
But it comes to me with a charm, like trust indeed,
And eats out of my heart, dear Chromis,
Absurd, disconcerting Chromis. You make me
Feel I wish I could look my best for you.
I wish, at least, that I could believe myself
To be showing some beauty for you, to put in the scales
Between us. But they dip to you, they sink
With masculine victory.

 TEGEUS.   Eros,[1] no! No!

[1] *Eros, that is, by Cupid!*

If this is less than your best, then never, in my presence,
Be more than your less: never! If you should bring
More to your mouth or to your eyes, a moisture
Or a flake of light, anything, anything fatally
More, perfection would fetch her unsparing rod
Out of pickle to flay me, and what would have been love
Will be the end of me. O Dynamene,
Let me unload something of my lips' longing
On to yours receiving. Oh, when I cross
Like this the hurt of the little space between us
I come a journey from the wrenching ice
To walk in the sun. That is the feeling.

    DYNAMENE.   Chromis,
Where am I going? No, don't answer. It's death
I desire, not you.

    TEGEUS.   Where is the difference? Call me
Death instead of Chromis. I'll answer to anything.
It's desire all the same, of death in me, or me
In death, but Chromis either way. Is it so?
Do you not love me, Dynamene?

    DYNAMENE.   How could it happen?
I'm going to my husband. I'm too far on the way
To admit myself to life again. Love's in Hades.

    TEGEUS. Also here. And here are we, not there
In Hades. Is your husband expecting you?

    DYNAMENE. Surely, surely?

    TEGEUS.   Not necessarily. I,
If I had been your husband, would never dream
Of expecting you. I should remember your body
Descending stairs in the floating light, but not
Descending in Hades. I should say 'I have left
My wealth warm on the earth, and, hell, earth needs it.'
'Was all I taught her of love,' I should say, 'so poor
That she will leave her flesh and become shadow?'
'Wasn't our love for each other' (I should continue)
'Infused with life, and life infused with our love?
Very well; repeat me in love, repeat me in life,
And let me sing in your blood for ever.'

    DYNAMENE. Stop, stop, I shall be dragged apart!
Why should the fates do everything to keep me
From dying honourably? They must have got

Tired of honour in Elysium. Chromis, it's terrible
To be susceptible to two conflicting norths.[1]
I have the constitution of a whirlpool.
Am I actually twirling, or is it just sensation?

TEGEUS. You're still; still as the darkness.

DYNAMENE.   What appears
Is so unlike what is. And what is madness
To those who only observe, is often wisdom
To those to whom it happens.

TEGEUS.   Are we compelled
To go into all this?

DYNAMENE.   Why, how could I return
To my friends? Am I to be an entertainment?

TEGEUS. That's for to-morrow. To-night I need to kiss you,
Dynamene. Let's see what the whirlpool does
Between my arms; let it whirl on my breast. O love,
Come in.

DYNAMENE. I am there before I reach you; my body
Only follows to join my longing which
Is holding you already.—Now I am
All one again.

TEGEUS.   I feel as the gods feel:
This is their sensation of life, not a man's:
Their suspension of immortality, to enrich
Themselves with time. O life, O death, O body,
O spirit, O Dynamene.

DYNAMENE.   O all
In myself; it so covets all in you,
My care, my Chromis. Then I shall be
Creation.

TEGEUS.   You have the skies already;
Out of them you are buffeting me with your gales
Of beauty. Can we be made of dust, as they tell us?
What! dust with dust releasing such a light
And such an apparition of the world
Within one body? A thread of your hair has stung me.
Why do you push me away?

---

[1] *two conflicting norths, as if the needle of a compass were attracted simultaneously to two points as north.*

DYNAMENE.   There's so much metal
About you. Do I have to be imprisoned
In an armoury?

TEGEUS.   Give your hand to the buckles and then
To me.

DYNAMENE. Don't help; I'll do them all myself.

TEGEUS. O time and patience! I want you back again.

DYNAMENE. We have a lifetime. O Chromis, think, think
Of that. And even unfastening a buckle
Is loving. And not easy. Very well,
You can help me. Chromis, what zone of miracle
Did you step into to direct you in the dark
To where I waited, not knowing I waited?

TEGEUS.   I saw
The lamplight. That was only the appearance
Of some great gesture in the bed of fortune.
I saw the lamplight.

DYNAMENE.   But here? So far from life?
What brought you near enough to see lamplight?

TEGEUS.   Zeus,
That reminds me.

DYNAMENE.   What is it, Chromis?

TEGEUS.   I'm on duty.

DYNAMENE. Is it warm enough to do without your greaves?[1]

TEGEUS. Darling loom of magic, I must go back
To take a look at those boys. The whole business
Of guard had gone out of my mind.

DYNAMENE.   What boys, my heart?

TEGEUS. My six bodies.

DYNAMENE.   Chromis, not that joke
Again.

TEGEUS. No joke, sweet. To-day our city
Held a sextuple hanging. I'm minding the bodies
Until five o'clock. Already I've been away
For half an hour.

DYNAMENE.   What can they do, poor bodies,
In half an hour, or half a century?
You don't really mean to go?

---

[1] *greaves, armor for the leg below the knee.*

TEGEUS.   Only to make
My conscience easy. Then, Dynamene,
No cloud can rise on love, no hovering thought
Fidget, and the night will be only to *us.*

DYNAMENE. But if every half-hour——

TEGEUS.   Hush, smile of my soul,
My sprig, my sovereign: this is to hold your eyes,
I sign my lips on them both: this is to keep
Your forehead—do you feel the claim of my kiss
Falling into your thought? And now your throat
Is a white branch and my lips two singing birds—
They are coming to rest. Throat, remember me
Until I come back in five minutes. Over all
Here is my parole: I give it to your mouth
To give me again before it's dry. I promise:
Before it's dry, or not long after.

DYNAMENE.   Run,
Run all the way. You needn't be afraid of stumbling.
There's plenty of moon. The fields are blue. Oh, wait,
Wait! My darling. No, not now: it will keep
Until I see you; I'll have it here at my lips.
Hurry.

TEGEUS. So long, my haven.

DYNAMENE.   Hurry, hurry!   [*Exit* TEGEUS.]

DOTO. Yes, madam, hurry; of course. Are we there
Already? How nice. Death doesn't take
Any doing at all. We were gulped into Hades
As easy as an oyster.

DYNAMENE.   Doto!

DOTO.   Hurry, hurry,
Yes, madam.—But they've taken out all my bones.
I haven't a bone left. I'm a Shadow: wonderfully shady
In the legs. We shall have to sit out eternity, madam,
If they've done the same to you.

DYNAMENE.   You'd better wake up.
If you can't go to sleep again, you'd better wake up.
Oh dear.—We're still alive, Doto, do you hear me?

DOTO. You must speak for yourself, madam. I'm quite dead.
I'll tell you how I know. I feel
Invisible. I'm a wraith, madam; I'm only
Waiting to be wafted.

DYNAMENE. If only you *would* be.
Do you see where you are? Look. Do you see?

DOTO. Yes. You're right, madam. We're still alive.
Isn't it enough to make you swear?
Here we are, dying to be dead,
And where does it get us?

DYNAMENE. Perhaps you should try to die
In some other place. Yes! Perhaps the air here
Suits you too well. You were sleeping very heavily.

DOTO. And all the time you alone and dying.
I shouldn't have. Has the corporal been long gone,
Madam?

DYNAMENE. He came and went, came and went,
You know the way.

DOTO. Very well I do. And went
He should have, come he should never. Oh dear, he must
Have disturbed you, madam.

DYNAMENE. He could be said
To've disturbed me. Listen; I have something to say to you.

DOTO. I expect so, madam. Maybe I *could* have kept him out
But men are in before I wish they wasn't.
I think quickly enough, but I get behindhand
With what I ought to be saying. It's a kind of stammer
In my way of life, madam.

DYNAMENE. I have been unkind,
I have sinfully wronged you, Doto.

DOTO. Never, madam.

DYNAMENE. Oh yes. I was letting you die with me, Doto, without
Any fair reason. I was drowning you
In grief that wasn't yours. That was wrong, Doto.

DOTO. But I haven't got anything against dying, madam.
I may *like* the situation, as far as I like
Any situation, madam. Now if you'd said mangling,
A lot of mangling, I might have thought twice about staying.
We all have our dislikes, madam.

DYNAMENE. I'm asking you
To leave me, Doto, at once, as quickly as possible,
Now, before—now, Doto, and let me forget
My bad mind which confidently expected you
To companion me to Hades. Now good-bye,
Good-bye.

DOTO.   No, it's not good-bye at all.
I shouldn't know another night of sleep, wondering
How you got on, or what I was missing, come to that.
I should be anxious about you, too. When you belong
To an upper class, the netherworld might come strange.
Now I was born nether, madam, though not
As nether as some. No, it's not good-bye, madam.

DYNAMENE. Oh Doto, go; you must, you must! And if I seem
Without gratitude, forgive me. It isn't so,
It is far, far from so. But I can only
Regain my peace of mind if I know you're gone.

DOTO. Besides, look at the time, madam. Where should I go
At three in the morning? Even if I was to think
Of going; and think of it I never shall.

DYNAMENE. Think of the unmatchable world, Doto.

DOTO.   I do
Think of it, madam. And when I think of it, what
Have I thought? Well, it depends, madam.

DYNAMENE.   I insist,
Obey me! At once! Doto!

DOTO.   Here I sit.

DYNAMENE. What shall I do with you?

DOTO.   Ignore me, madam.
I know my place. I shall die quite unobtrusive.
Oh look, the corporal's forgotten to take his equipment.

DYNAMENE. Could he be so careless?

DOTO.   I shouldn't hardly have thought so.
Poor fellow. They'll go and deduct it off his credits.
I suppose, madam, I suppose he couldn't be thinking
Of coming back?

DYNAMENE.   He'll think of these. He will notice
He isn't wearing them. He'll come; he is sure to come.

DOTO. Oh.

DYNAMENE. I know he will.

DOTO.   Oh, oh.
Is that all for to-night, madam? May I go now, madam?

DYNAMENE. Doto! Will you?

DOTO.   Just you try to stop me, madam.
Sometimes going is a kind of instinct with me.
I'll leave death to some other occasion.

DYNAMENE.   Do,

Doto. Any other time. Now you must hurry.
I won't delay you from life another moment.
Oh, Doto, good-bye.

DOTO. Good-bye. Life is unusual,
Isn't it, madam? Remember me to Cerberus.

[*Re-enter* TEGEUS. DOTO *passes him on the steps.*]

DOTO [*as she goes*]. You left something behind. Ye gods, what a
   moon!

DYNAMENE. Chromis, it's true; my lips are hardly dry.
Time runs again; the void is space again;
Space has life again; Dynamene has Chromis.

TEGEUS. It's over.

DYNAMENE. Chromis, you're sick. As white as wool.
Come, you covered the distance too quickly.
Rest in my arms; get your breath again.

TEGEUS. I've breathed one night too many. Why did I see you,
Why in the name of life did I see you?

DYNAMENE. Why?
Weren't we gifted with each other? O heart,
What do you mean?

TEGEUS. I mean that joy is nothing
But the parent of doom. Why should I have found
Your constancy such balm to the world and yet
Find, by the same vision, its destruction
A necessity? We're set upon by love
To make us incompetent to steer ourselves,
To make us docile to fate. I should have known:
Indulgences, not fulfilment, is what the world
Permits us.

DYNAMENE. Chromis, is this intelligible?
Help me to follow you. What did you meet in the fields
To bring about all this talk? Do you still love me?

TEGEUS. What good will it do us? I've lost a body.

DYNAMENE. A body?
One of the six? Well, it isn't with them you propose
To love me; and you couldn't keep it for ever.
Are we going to allow a body that isn't there
To come between us?

TEGEUS. But I'm responsible for it.
I have to account for it in the morning. Surely
You see, Dynamene, the horror we're faced with?

The relatives have had time to cut him down
And take him away for burial. It means
A court martial. No doubt about the sentence.
I shall take the place of the missing man.
To be hanged, Dynamene! Hanged, Dynamene!

DYNAMENE. No; it's monstrous! Your life is yours, Chromis.

TEGEUS. Anything but. That's why I have to take it.
At the best we live our lives on loan,
At the worst in chains. And I was never born
To have life. Then for what? To be had by it,
And so are we all. But I'll make it what it is,
By making it nothing.

DYNAMENE.   Chromis, you're frightening me.
What are you meaning to do?

TEGEUS.   I have to die,
Dance of my heart, I have to die, to die,
To part us, to go to my sword and let it part us.
I'll have my free will even if I'm compelled to it.
I'll kill myself.

DYNAMENE.   Oh, no! No, Chromis!
It's all unreasonable—no such horror
Can come of a pure accident. Have you hanged?
How can they hang you for simply not being somewhere?
How can they hang you for losing a dead man?
They must have wanted to lose him, or they wouldn't
Have hanged him. No, you're scaring yourself for nothing
And making me frantic.

TEGEUS.   It's section six, paragraph
Three in the Regulations. That's my doom.
I've read it for myself. And, by my doom,
Since I have to die, let me die here, in love,
Promoted by your kiss to tower, in dying,
High above my birth. For god's sake let me die
On a wave of life, Dynamene, with an action
I can take some pride in. How could I settle to death
Knowing that you last saw me stripped and strangled
On a holly tree? Demoted first and then hanged!

DYNAMENE. Am I supposed to love the corporal
Or you? It's you I love, from head to foot
And out to the ends of your spirit. What shall I do

If you die? How could I follow you? I should find you
Discussing me with my husband, comparing your feelings,
Exchanging reactions. Where should I put myself?
Or am I to live on alone, or find in life
Another source of love, in memory
Of Virilius and of you?

TEGEUS.   Dynamene,
Not that! Since everything in the lives of men
Is brief to indifference, let our love at least
Echo and perpetuate itself uniquely
As long as time allows you. Though you go
To the limit of age, it won't be far to contain me.

DYNAMENE. It will seem like eternity ground into days and days.

TEGEUS. Can I be certain of you, for ever?

DYNAMENE.   But, Chromis,
Surely you said——

TEGEUS.   Surely we have sensed
Our passion to be greater than mortal? Must I
Die believing it is dying with me?

DYNAMENE.   Chromis,
You must never die, never! It would be
An offence against truth.

TEGEUS.   I cannot live to be hanged.
It would be an offence against life. Give me my sword,
Dynamene. O Hades, when you look pale
You take the heart out of me. I could die
Without a sword by seeing you suffer. Quickly!
Give me my heart back again with your lips
And I'll live the rest of my ambitions
In a last kiss.

DYNAMENE.   Oh, no, no, no!
Give my blessing to your desertion of me?
Never, Chromis, never. Kiss you and then
Let you go? Love you, for death to have you?
Am I to be made the fool of courts martial?
Who are they who think they can discipline souls
Right off the earth? What discipline is that?
Chromis, love is the only discipline
And we're the disciples of love. I hold you to that:
Hold you, hold you.

TEGEUS.   We have no chance. It's determined
In section six, paragraph three, of the Regulations.
That has more power than love. It can snuff the great
Candles of creation. It makes me able
To do the impossible, to leave you, to go from the light
That keeps you.

DYNAMENE.   No!

TEGEUS.   O dark, it does. Good-bye,
My memory of earth, my dear most dear
Beyond every expectation. I was wrong
To want you to keep our vows existent
In the vacuum that's coming. It would make you
A heaviness to the world, when you should be,
As you are, a form of light. Dynamene, turn
Your head away. I'm going to let my sword
Solve all the riddles.

DYNAMENE.   Chromis, I have it! I know!
Virilius will help you.

TEGEUS.   Virilius?

DYNAMENE. My husband. He can be the other body.

TEGEUS. Your husband can?

DYNAMENE.   He has no further use
For what he left of himself to lie with us here.
Is there any reason why he shouldn't hang
On your holly tree? Better, far better, he,
Than you who are still alive, and surely better
Than *idling* into corruption?

TEGEUS.   Hang your husband?
Dynamene, it's terrible, horrible.

DYNAMENE. How little you can understand. I loved
His life not his death. And now we can give his death
The power of life. Not horrible: wonderful!
Isn't it so? That I should be able to feel
He moves again in the world, accomplishing
Our welfare? It's more than my grief could do.

TEGEUS. What can I say?

DYNAMENE.   That you love me; as I love him
And you. Let's celebrate your safety then.
Where's the bottle? There's some wine unfinished in this bowl.
I'll share it with you. Now forget the fear

We were in; look at me, Chromis. Come away
From the pit you nearly dropped us in. My darling,
I give you Virilius.

    TEGEUS.   Virilius.

And all that follows.

    DOTO [*on the steps, with the bottle*]. The master. Both the masters.

CURTAIN

PLAYS BY THE AUTHORS
IN THIS BOOK

The following are the dates of composition when those dates are known. In the case of Synge, the dates are of the first productions.

HENRIK IBSEN

AUGUST STRINDBERG

ANTON CHEKHOV

BERNARD SHAW

JOHN MILLINGTON SYNGE

SEAN O'CASEY

EUGENE O'NEILL

1943   *A Moon for the Misbegotten.* Produced in 1947
1943   *Hughie.* Produced in 1958

W. SOMERSET MAUGHAM

1903   *Marriages Are Made in Heaven*
1903   *A Man of Honour*
1904   *Mlle. Zampa*
1904   *Mrs. Dot*
1907   *Lady Frederick*
1908   *Jack Straw*
1908   *The Explorer*
1908   *Penelope* or *Man and Wife*
1909   *The Noble Spaniard.* From Grenet-Dancourt's *Les Gaîtés du Veuvage*
1909   *Smith*
1910   *The Tenth Man*
1910   *The Landed Gentry*
1911   *Loaves and Fishes*
1913   *The Perfect Gentleman.* From Molière's *Le Bourgeois Gentilhomme*
1913   *The Land of Promise*
1916   *Caroline* or *The Unattainable*
1917   *The Keys to Heaven*
1917   *Our Betters*
1917   *Mrs. Beamish*
1918   *Love in a Cottage*
1919   *Caesar's Wife*
1919   *Home and Beauty,* or *Too Many Husbands,* or *Not Tonight, Josephine*
1920   *The Unknown*
1921   *The Circle*
1922   *East of Suez*
1924   *The Camel's Back*
1924   *The Mask and the Face.* From the Italian of Luigi Chiarelli
1926   *The Constant Wife*
1927   *The Letter*
1928   *The Sacred Flame*
1928   *The Force of Nature*
1930   *The Breadwinner*

1932   *For Services Rendered*
1933   *Sheppey*
       With Guy Bolton:
1941   *Theatre*

S. N. BEHRMAN

1927   *The Second Man*
1928   *Serena Blandish*
1929   *Meteor*
1931   *Brief Moment*
1932   *Biography*
1934   *Love Story*
1935   *Rain from Heaven*
1936   *End of Summer*
1937   *Amphitryon 38.* From the French of Jean Giraudoux
1938   *Wine of Choice*
1939   *No Time for Comedy*
1941   *The Talley Method*
1942   *The Pirate*
1945   *Dunnigan's Daughter*
1946   *Jane.* From a story by Somerset Maugham
1949   *I Know My Love.* From the French of Marcel Archard
1958   *The Cold Wind and the Warm*
1962   *Lord Pengo*
       With Kenyon Nicholson:
1924   *Bedside Manners*
1927   *Love Is Like That*
       With Owen Davis:
1927   *The Man Who Forgot*
       With Franz Werfel:
1944   *Jacobowsky and the Colonel*
       With Joshua Logan:
1949   *Fanny.* Based on the trilogy of Marcel Pagnol

TENNESSEE WILLIAMS

1940   *Battle of Angels*
1945   *The Glass Menagerie*

CHRISTOPHER FRY

1 2 3 4 5 6 7 8 9 10 11 12 13 14 15 16 17 18 19 20 21 22 23 24 25 K 72 71 70 69 68 67 66 65 64